The Postmodernism Reader

'The great virtue of *The Postmodernism Reader* is its purposely narrow, delightfully relentless focus on the specific philosophical underpinnings of postmodernism. Drolet's lengthy, exceptionally clear introduction will be warmly appreciated by students.'

Peter Brunette, George Mason University

'This Reader will be useful to philosophers and literary theorists not only for its selection of seminal texts but also for its comprehensive and judicious introduction.'

Christina Howells, Wadham College, Oxford

Postmodernism too often seems to be an evasive body of ideas rather than a clear-cut concept, mainly characterized by all-embracing assertions. Yet it can be referred to as an intellectual project with specific roots and a historical development. *The Postmodernism Reader* traces the origins, evolution and politics of postmodernism through the key writings of postmodernist thinkers. This collection of foundational essays restores the poignancy that has been lost – or even emphatically rejected – in the debate about postmodernism by focusing on central formative texts and the predominant thinkers we have come to associate with postmodernist theory.

Michael Drolet's authoritative introductory essay and his careful selection of texts provide a solid basis for the study of postmodernism by uncovering the philosophical origins of present theories and focusing on their major aspects, guiding the reader through the maze of knowledge that we call postmodernism. Arranged in three parts, the essays cover the origins of the term postmodernism, its evolution and its political ramifications. Included are writings by Foucault, Derrida, Deleuze, Baudrillard, Lyotard, Bauman, Jameson, Berman and Irigaray.

Michael Drolet teaches History of Political Thought at Royal Holloway, University of London.

The
Postmodernism
Reader

Foundational texts

Edited by

Michael Drolet

Routledge
Taylor & Francis Group

LONDON AND NEW YORK

First published 2004
by Routledge
New Fetter Lane, London EC4P 4EE

Simultaneously published in the US
by Routledge
29 West 35th Street, New York, NY 10001

Routledge is an imprint of the Taylor & Francis Group

Typeset in Perpetua and Bell Gothic by
HWA Text and Data Management, Tunbridge Wells
Printed and bound in Great Britain by
TJ International Ltd, Padstow, Cornwall

British Library Cataloguing in Publication Data
A catalogue record for this book is available from the British Library

Library of Congress Cataloging in Publication Data
The postmodernism reader : foundational texts / edited by Michael Drolet.
    p. cm.
Includes bibliographical references and index.
1. Postmodernism. I. Drolet, Michael

B831.1.2.P682 2003
149'.97–dc21   200311019

ISBN 0–415–16083–9 (hbk)
ISBN 0–415–16084–7 (pbk)

For Rosalind

Contents

Acknowledgements   xi

Introduction   1
Michael Drolet

PART ONE
**The crisis of modernity and the birth of the concept
of postmodernism**   37

1 Michel Foucault
   WHAT IS ENLIGHTENMENT?   41

2 Marshall Berman
   from INTRODUCTION — MODERNITY: YESTERDAY, TODAY AND
   TOMORROW in *ALL THAT IS SOLID MELTS INTO AIR: THE
   EXPERIENCE OF MODERNITY*   53

3 Michel Foucault
   THE ORDER OF THINGS   67

4 Michel Foucault
   NIETZSCHE, GENEALOGY, HISTORY   72

5 Jacques Derrida
   COGITO AND THE HISTORY OF MADNESS in *WRITING
   AND DIFFERENCE*   86

  6 Gilles Deleuze
     DIONYSUS AND ZARATHUSTRA and CONCLUSION in *NIETZSCHE
     AND PHILOSOPHY*   112

PART TWO
The postmodern condition: a concept in emergence   119

  7 Jean-François Lyotard
     from *THE POSTMODERN CONDITION: A REPORT ON KNOWLEDGE*   123

  8 Jacques Derrida
     OUTWORK, PREFACING in *DISSEMINATION*   147

  9 Gilles Deleuze
     from INTRODUCTION IN *DIFFERENCE AND REPETITION*   154

 10 Michel Foucault
     from THEATRUM PHILOSOPHICUM   161

 11 Jacques Derrida
     THE TIME OF A THESIS: PUNCTUATIONS   167

 12 Gilles Deleuze
     IMMANENCE: A LIFE in *PURE IMMANENCE: ESSAYS ON A LIFE*   178

 13 Jean-François Lyotard
     THE INTIMACY OF TERROR in *POSTMODERN FABLES*   181

 14 Fredric Jameson
     from *POSTMODERNISM, OR, THE CULTURAL LOGIC OF LATE
     CAPITALISM*   189

PART THREE
Difference, aesthetics, politics and history:
postmodern reflections   203

 15 Jean-François Lyotard
     from *THE DIFFEREND: PHRASES IN DISPUTE*   207

 16 Luce Irigaray
     from *AN ETHICS OF SEXUAL DIFFERENCE*   222

17 Jean-François Lyotard
from ANSWER TO THE QUESTION: WHAT IS THE POSTMODERN? in
THE POSTMODERN EXPLAINED TO CHILDREN: CORRESPONDENCE
1982–1985   230

18 Zygmunt Bauman
A SOCIOLOGICAL THEORY OF POSTMODERNITY in *INTIMATIONS OF*
POSTMODERNITY   238

19 Jean-François Lyotard
PSYCHOANALYSIS, AESTHETICS AND THE POLITICS OF
DIFFERENCE AN INTERVIEW WITH JEAN-FRANÇOIS LYOTARD   250

20 Jean Baudrillard
from *THE ILLUSION OF THE END*   272

21 Jacques Derrida
from INJUNCTIONS OF MARX in *SPECTERS OF MARX:*
THE STATE OF THE DEBT, THE WORK OF MOURNING, AND THE
NEW INTERNATIONAL   279

Notes   288
Glossary of names   312
Select bibliography   321
Index   326

Acknowledgements

I wish to thank the many friends and institutions for helping me to write this book. My first debt is to David McLellan. His inspiration, guidance and generosity of spirit I can never adequately repay. I owe special thanks to Koula Mellos for introducing me to structuralist and poststructuralist thought and for her encouragement of my studies of Jean-François Lyotard. Gregory Claeys helped me a great deal in the early stages of this project and his encouragement was invaluable. For comments on the introduction I owe special thanks to Justin Champion, Mary Hickman and Dan Stone. Their exacting questions and constructive comments helped me improve it considerably. I am grateful to Chris Mounsey for enlightening me on numerous points.

The staff of the British Library assisted me in my researches. They have been wonderful in every respect.

Many thanks to Ariela Atzmon, Oren Ben Dor, Marie-Hélène Baneth-Jakob, Pierre Boyer, Kayvon Boyhan, Alison Brown, Richard Cockett, Janet Coleman, Pene Corefield, Vince Geoghegan, Patrick Hill, François Houle, Margaret Humphrey, Joel Isaac, Richard Jay, Fionnula Jay-O'Boyle, Gerd Jakob, Jeanne Laux, Scott Lewis, Bob Mayo, Douglas Moggach, Debby Murphy, Alan Neil, Francis Robinson, Stef Slater, Tony Stockwell, Claire Touraine-Sjolander, André Vachet and José Luis Valdés-Ugalde for advice and encouragement.

Many thanks to Heather McCallum who commissioned this project and to Victoria Peters for seeing it through. She has been a superb and very patient editor. Sünje Redies has been a sharp and brilliant editorial assistant. I thank her, my copy-editor Carolyn Newton and John Hodgson for shepherding this book through production.

My greatest debts are to my family, Monique as always, and to Rosalind to whom I dedicate this book.

The author and publishers wish to thank the following for their permission to reproduce copyright material:

Part one

Michel Foucault, 'What is Enlightenment?', translated by C. Porter, from *The Foucault Reader*, edited by P. Rabinow, published by Penguin Books, 1984. Reproduced by permission of Penguin Group UK.

Marshall Berman, *All That Is Solid Melts Into Air: The Experience of Modernity*, published by Verso, 1983. Reproduced by permission of Verso, London.

Michel Foucault, 'The Order of Things', translated by J. Johnston, from *The Essential Works of Michel Foucault, 1954–1984: Volume II, Aesthetics, Method, and Epistemology*, edited by J.D. Faubion, published by Allen Lane, 1998. Reproduced by permission of Penguin Group UK and Editions Gallimard.

Michel Foucault, 'Nietzsche, Genealogy, History', from *The Essential Works of Michel Foucault, 1954–1984, Volume II: Aesthetics, Method, and Epistemology*, edited by J.D. Faubion, published by Allen Lane, 1998. Reproduced by permission of Penguin Group UK and Editions Gallimard.

Jacques Derrida, 'Cogito and the History of Madness', from *Writing and Difference*, translated by A. Bass, first published by Routledge & Kegan Paul Ltd, 1978, first published in Routledge Classics, 2001. Reproduced by permission of Taylor & Francis Books Ltd and the University of Chicago Press.

Gilles Deleuze, *Nietzsche and Philosophy*, translated by H. Tomlinson, first published in Great Britain by The Athlone Press, 1983. Reproduced by permission of The Continuum International Publishing Group Ltd.

Part two

Jean-François Lyotard, *The Postmodern Condition: A Report on Knowledge*, translated by G. Bennington and B. Massumi, Manchester University Press, 1984. English translation and Foreword copyright © 1984 by the University of Minnesota. Original French-Language edition copyright © 1979 by Les Editions de Minuit. Reproduced by permission of Manchester University Press and the University of Minnesota Press.

Jacques Derrida, *Dissemination*, translated by B. Johnson, first published in Great Britain by The Athlone Press, 1981. Reproduced by permission of The Continuum International Publishing Group Ltd.

Gilles Deleuze, *Difference and Repetition*, translated by P. Patton, first published in Great Britain by The Athlone Press, 1994. Reproduced by permission of The Continuum International Publishing Group Ltd.

Michel Foucault, 'Theatrum Philosophicum', from *The Essential Works of Michel Foucault, 1954–1984, Volume II: Aesthetics, Method, and Epistemology*, edited by J.D. Faubion, published by Allen Lane, 1998. Reproduced by permission of Penguin Group UK and Editions Gallimard.

Jacques Derrida, 'The Time of a Thesis: Punctuations', from *Philosophy in France Today*, translated by K. McLaughlin, edited by A. Montefiore, published 1983 copyright © Cambridge University Press, 1983. Reproduced by permission of Cambridge University Press.

Gilles Deleuze, *Pure Immanence: Essays On A Life*, translated by A. Boyman, published by Zone Books, New York, 2001. Reproduced by permission of Zone Books.

Jean-François Lyotard, 'The Intimacy of Terror', from *Postmodern Fables*, translated by G. van den Abbeele, published by University of Minnesota Press, 1997. Copyright © 1997 by the Regents of the University of Minnesota. Originally published as *Moralités postmodernes*, copyright © 1993 by Editions Galilée, Paris.

Fredric Jameson, *Postmodernism, or, The Cultural Logic of Late Capitalism*, published by Verso, 1991. Reproduced by permission of Verso, London.

Part three

Jean-François Lyotard, *The Differend: Phrases in Dispute*, translated by G. van den Abbeele, published by University of Minnesota Press, 1998. Originally published in France as *Le Différend*, copyright © 1983 by Les Editions de Minuit. English translation copyright © 1988 by the University of Minnesota.

Luce Irigaray, *An Ethics of Sexual Difference*, translated by C. Burke and G.C. Gill, translation copyright © 1993 by Cornell University. Used by permission of the publisher, Cornell University Press, and by permission of The Continuum International Publishing Group Ltd.

Zygmunt Bauman, *Intimations of Postmodernity*, first published in 1992 by Routledge. Reproduced by permission of Taylor & Francis Books Ltd.

Willem Van Reijen and Dick Veerman, 'Psychoanalysis, Aesthetics and the Politics of Difference: An Interview with Jean-François Lyotard', from *Theory, Culture and Society*, 5, 1988. Reprinted by permission of Sage Publications Ltd.

Jean Baudrillard, *The Illusion of the End*, translated by C. Turner, published by Polity Press, 1994. Reproduced by permission of Blackwell Publishing and Stanford University Press, www.sup.org.

Jacques Derrida, *Specters of Marx*, translated by P. Kamuf, published by Routledge, 1994. Reproduced by permission of Routledge, Inc, part of the Taylor & Francis Group.

Every effort has been made to obtain permission to reproduce copyright material. If any proper acknowledgement has not been made, we would invite copyright holders to inform us of the oversight.

I mistrust all systematizers and avoid them. The will to a system is a lack of integrity.

Friedrich Nietzsche, *Twilight of the Idols*

Introduction

■ Michael Drolet

WHAT IS POSTMODERNISM? How does it differ from postmodernity? And how do these concepts relate to the postmodern? Finding clear and comprehensible definitions to these concepts is not easy. Postmodernism, postmodernity and the postmodern have been ascribed a bewildering array of meanings which vary frequently from discipline to discipline. The terms are often associated with philosophical writings and social and political theories that are complex, dense, esoterically sophisticated and all too often replete with jargon and incomprehensible prose, which intimidate even the most sophisticated readers. The terms often provoke strong reactions including deep suspicion and or even outright hostility.[1] These reactions are common. They attest to an understandable response to what is perceived as fuzzy thinking or a fashionable but muddled recourse to the use of these terms to describe just about any phenomenon, which is odd and new.

But postmodernism, postmodernity and the postmodern need not cause bewilderment or provoke such hostility. The terms can be defined clearly. And the introduction to this *Reader* will endeavour to do so. Its principal objective is to show what these terms mean, why they are important, and how they have evolved within, and emerged from, different artistic communities and the academic pursuits of the humanities and social sciences. In this respect this *Reader* is meant as an introduction to postmodernism, postmodernity and the postmodern. Its purpose, in bringing together a number of foundational works, is to show the relevance and importance of these concepts to the student who is inclined to give up on trying to understand what they mean or dismiss their relevance. Yet the introduction to this *Reader* is not written with the intention of praising postmodernism, celebrating postmodernity or embracing the postmodern. It seeks to analyse these terms critically and make a disinterested assessment of their social, political, artistic, literary and, above all, philosophical impact. In order to achieve these objectives the introduction will examine how the terms were first employed, how they were used in different disciplines and at different times, and how their different usages retain a shared meaning and common impulse. This history of the concepts of postmodernism, postmodernity and the postmodern will focus on theology, literary criticism, history and, most importantly, architecture.

The second objective of this introduction is to unearth the philosophical roots of postmodernism, postmodernity and the postmodern, and to place them within the broader context of the opposition between romanticism and classicism. Within this context postmodernism can be seen as contiguous with romantic sensibility and its critique of rationalism and system building. Postmodernism therefore challenges the fundamental assumptions of the Enlightenment, while – as the philosopher and historian Michel Foucault (1926–84) pointed out in a 1978 address to the Société française de philosophie entitled 'What is critique' and then again in his 1984 essay, reprinted here, 'What is Enlightenment?' (Chapter 1) – retaining the Enlightenment's impulse toward individual and social liberation. Postmodernity and the postmodern are the sociological or historical expressions of postmodernism, much like 'romantic' or the 'romantic age' are similar expressions of romanticism. By examining postmodernism in this way it will be possible to answer clearly the questions set at the opening of this introduction.

Finally, we will explore in detail the thoughts of the philosophers and social theorists whose works are foundational to postmodernism. This will provide the reader with the background necessary to make effective use of the selections included here. Our exploration of the thoughts of these seminal thinkers will also reveal how postmodernism is not some form of trendy thinking which is here today and will be gone tomorrow, but rather a serious intellectual engagement which is part of a deep and enduring questioning of humanity's engagement with itself and the world.

Disciplines and definitions: or how postmodernism, postmodernity and the postmodern were first defined

Why postmodernism, postmodernity and the postmodern should lack clear definitions can be attributed, in part, to confusion over how these concepts were employed by different disciplines. When, for example, the term postmodernism was referred to with any regularity in the late 1950s it applied to the work of artists like Robert Rauschenberg and poets such as Charles Olson, who sought to challenge received wisdom and established norms in their respective disciplines. At that time the term was employed prescriptively, and was associated with movements that judged modernism to have become entrenched and conventional and therefore no longer capable of spawning new forms of artistic or poetic expression.

By the 1960s and 1970s the term became popular among artists, writers, poets and some literary critics. It was at this time too that it was adopted by a number of prominent architects such as Robert Venturi and Charles Jencks who, in understanding that the intention of good architecture was to express meaning or convey a message, were receptive to new developments in linguistics – particularly the renewed interest in the writings of the late nineteenth-century Swiss linguistic philosopher Ferdinand de Saussure (1857–1913) – literature, art and the latest works by sociologists of mass media, such as the Canadian Marshall McLuhan (1911–80) and the Frenchman Roland Barthes (1915–80). In this way clear affinities emerged between the way the term was understood in art and literature and the way it was used in architecture. These different disciplines saw postmodernism as a movement whose conscious purpose was to overturn ideas integral to modernism, in particular those of narrative and representation. But the way architectural postmodernism went about this was somewhat different from the way it was done in the arts. The term was bound to different contexts that altered the ways it was employed. This contributed to confusion about the term's meaning.

Though architects, artists and writers understood postmodernism as a movement for change, the term was also employed in the 1970s by sociologists such as Daniel Bell (b. 1919) who used the concept descriptively, much like the expression 'the postmodern' is now used. In *The Coming of Post-Industrial Society* (1973) Bell equated postmodernism with a 'new sensibility' which 'breaks down all genres and denies that there is any distinction between art and life'.[2] Three years later in *The Cultural Contradictions of Capitalism* (1976) he attacked postmodernism as 'the psychedelic effort to expand consciousness without boundaries'.[3] This new 'cultural mode', he believed, was 'simply the decomposition of the self in an effort to erase individual ego'.[4] Its intellectual inspiration lay in structuralism, which rejected the idea that the human subject is autonomous, coherent, can discern an overall pattern to human history, and thereby improve on the past. This conception of the human subject, emphatically expressed in the writings of René Descartes (1596–1650), became an established dogma within Western thought. The human subject had become, according to the French structuralist anthropologist Claude Lévi-Strauss (b. 1908) 'the spoilt brat of philosophy'. Structuralism therefore sought not to constitute the subject, but to dissolve it. And this was what Bell reacted so strongly against.

Structuralism's attempts to dissolve the human subject were part of a deeper disenchantment with a general and stultifying complacency within academic disciplines and political movements. The failure of liberal democracies to achieve genuine equality and promote social justice, and the collapse of political ideologies, such as Marxism, motivated by grand designs to liberate individuals and transform society, seemed to confirm the reflections of intellectuals who emphasised the limits to human reason and the folly of schemes that sought to rationally engineer individual and social liberation. These modern-day considerations stressed that the collapse of grand ideologies was the manifestation of a deeper tendency, the breakdown of rationality and of the Western philosophical tradition itself. Within this extensive body of writing some works were prescriptive, such as those by Michel Foucault or the French feminist philosopher Luce Irigaray. These asserted that forms of human liberation were possible, but that liberation could be conceived only within a new philosophical context, one that explicitly repudiated the central tenets of the Western philosophical tradition. Other, descriptive writings, which referred to postmodernity or the postmodern, such as those by the sociologist Jean Baudrillard and the political philosopher Jean-François Lyotard, adhered to similar philosophical premises but claimed that the profound changes experienced by Western industrial societies in the last four decades of the twentieth century were the consequence of the way Western thought shaped individuals' and societies' orientation toward themselves and the transformation of their natural and social worlds. These descriptive works arrived at a deeply pessimistic conclusion, contending that Western societies now functioned and were organised in such a way as to make individual and human liberation impossible. But contrary to this pessimistic diagnosis there was a group of descriptive works that was optimistic about the possibilities of human liberation. These writings pointed to developments specific to contemporary society that were novel and without historical precedent, contending these changes were characteristic of a postmodern age. Some, like those of the Marxist political theorist Fredric Jameson, argued that a postmodern age offered new possibilities for a revolutionary left. Others, like those of the sociologist Zygmunt Bauman, contended that in the postmodern age traditional ideologies became meaningless and failed to have any moral or persuasive power over individuals. A new series of circumstances and social conventions required a total rethinking of political practices and of the nature of politics itself, and this could become part of a new form of individual and human liberation.

To better grasp these different understandings of postmodernism we must first look at the context from which the term first emerged. In order to achieve this it will be indispensable to examine the first instances where the terms postmodern and postmodernism appeared, for those early uses embody many of the core values that define the terms today.

The origins of the concept of postmodernism

Postmodernism is generally understood to have emerged from a politics of the left. The names of intellectuals commonly associated with it, such as Jean Baudrillard, Zygmunt Bauman, Michel Foucault, Fredric Jameson and Jean-François Lyotard, all had solid leftist credentials. But when the concept was first used it had very different connotations. Postmodernism had a conservative meaning. It was a reaction to political, cultural and artistic movements whose perceived excesses were understood to be symptomatic of the cultural decline of the West.

The first reference to postmodernism can be found in the 1926 work of the Catholic theologian Bernard Iddings Bell entitled *Postmodernism and Other Essays*.[5] Bell's postmodernism embodied ideas he believed to be superior to those associated with the modern era, such as the modern faith in the power of reason to free the human spirit from bondage arising out of ignorance and prejudice. Postmodern ideas would supersede modern ones. And they characterised the era that would follow on from the modern age; they defined the *post*-modern age. When Bell spoke of postmodernism he referred to something that was both ideological and historical. It was a body of ideas and a new epoch.

Bell considered postmodernism to be an intelligent alternative to the two rival ideologies that dominated Western societies in the 1920s: ideologies that, despite their fundamental differences, shared values that he believed made them quint-essentially modern. These were, according to Bell, liberalism and totalitarianism. Bell believed liberalism and totalitarianism shared a faith in mankind's ability to discover the underlying principles that govern nature and societies through the right use of reason. The discovery of these principles or laws empowered individuals, liberating them from the obscure and uncontrollable forces of nature. It bestowed upon them a knowledge that served to promote wealth creation and increase national power. But Bell believed that liberalism's and totalitarianism's faith in reason brought about the impoverishment of the human condition rather than its improvement. He assailed liberalism because he believed that it stressed the values of economic and material prosperity and intellectual tolerance, which spawned societies that were intellectually and culturally mediocre and politically complacent. And he attacked totalitarianism as an alternative to liberalism because it deprived individuals of free thought, left them spiritually impoverished, and subordinated them to the state. In criticising both liberalism and totalitarianism, Bell also attacked values he believed to be rooted in what he called 'the pseudo-moralities of science'. The faith in scientific objectivity and progress, he thought left individuals spiritually weak, and emptied life of metaphysical wonder.

Bell's critique of the modern age shared the sceptical and stoical outlook at the heart of the work of the fifth-century Christian philosopher St Augustine. Just as Augustine thought that the ancient philosophers, Plato and Aristotle, were mistaken to believe that we could obtain objective knowledge of ourselves and fashion communities that were true to our natures, so Bell thought the same of modern philosophers. Their faith in reason and human progress rested on a mistaken estimation of man's ability to change the world around him, and this was symptomatic of arrogance toward God and his infinite and fathomless wisdom. Just as Augustine judged the ancient philosophies to have led man to ignorance and spiritual isolation, Bell believed that modern ideas emptied man's experience of the world of awe and wonder. And whereas Augustine believed that only through faith could individuals be returned to the path of salvation, Bell considered that the core characteristic of the postmodern individual was to be 'intellectually humble and spiritually hungry'. The postmodern man drew his strength and solace 'not from within his own ego but from Heaven'; he was an individual who 'longs to fall upon his knees and worship a comprehending Absolute'.[6]

This first use of the term postmodernism was rooted in an ancient scepticism about humans' ability to fathom the workings of the universe and somehow change their place within it. The term's meaning was theological and conservative. Postmodernism stressed the mysterious and unknowable nature of the universe. And it emphasised humanity's feebleness and its need to turn toward God for strength, solace and salvation. Though its theological meaning made Bell's use of postmodernism singular, his usage did encompass a number of values that it would come to share with later definitions of the term, such as, for example, a sceptical disposition toward reason and science, and a belief in the mysterious, wondrous and ultimately unknowable nature of man and the universe.

Eight years after the publication of Bell's *Postmodernism and Other Essays* the concept was used again by the Mexican literary critic Federico de Onis. In his 1934 *Antología de la Poesía Española e Hispanoamericana (1882–1932)* (*Anthology of*

Spanish and Latin American Poetry),[7] Onis used the concept to denote both an historical epoch and a literary movement. The postmodern epoch covered the period between 1905 and 1914. It lay between the modernist era, which Onis believed lasted only nine years, from 1896 to 1905, and the ultramodernist period that comprised the years 1914 to 1932.

Onis's postmodernism corresponded to a genre of Spanish and Latin American poetry that reacted to the excesses of modernism, a conservative inclination within modernism rather than a traditional or romantic rejection of it. Postmodernism sought to rein in modernism's excesses. Though it shared twentieth-century modernism's characteristics − the rejection of the traditional narrative framework in favour of stream-of-consciousness presentation and the propensity toward experimentation − it checked modernism's drift toward dehumanisation by stressing the human elements that had been predominant in romantic and naturalistic poetry. Postmodernism was characterised by a commitment to detail, a refined tone, simplicity of prose and ironic humour. It was also highly contemplative, directed toward introspection. While it remained wedded to twentieth-century European modernism, it was also infused by native and feminine themes and rhythms. These gave it an energy and identity that was both new and distinctly Latin American. According to Onis the postmodern movement was short-lived. It was superseded by ultramodernism which returned to modernist ambitions but intensified the search for poetic innovation and symbolic and formal representation. Ultramodernism deepened modernism's radical impulses and intensified its avant-gardist tendencies.

In the same year that Onis's book was published, the English historian Arnold Toynbee began work on what was to be his monumental *A Study of History*. The central thesis of this work was that the history of the West had been shaped by two powerful forces: Industrialism and Nationalism. Before the last quarter of the nineteenth century, these forces had a positive effect in shaping Western civilisation, but after that time they entered into a destructive contradiction with each other. Whereas industry expanded outwards, becoming international and bursting the bounds of the nation state, nationalism extended inwards, affecting progressively smaller and less viable ethnic communities. Toynbee concluded that the First World War was the outcome of the clash between industrialism and nationalism. He believed this was the definitive sign that a new and *post*-modern age had come into being, one that rendered otiose the category of the nation state. The task of the historian, according to Toynbee, was to think on this new age, discern its contours and establish its fundamental characteristics. This was the task he set himself.

With the advent of the Second World War in 1939 Toynbee's most pessimistic sentiments about human nature and the forces of historical change in the contemporary age were confirmed. Yet it was not until 1954, at the height of the Cold War, and in the eighth volume of *A Study of History*, that Toynbee finally used the term 'post-modern' to designate the period that began 'at the turn of the nineteenth and twentieth centuries'.[8]

Toynbee's definition of the 'post-modern age' was negative. It was an era that, in supplanting the modern age, was the prelude to the decline of civilisation itself. According to Toynbee the modern era had been characterised by the ideas and achievements of a bourgeoisie whose intellectual competence, commercial and industrial acumen and majority status made it a progressive and innovating class. His definition of the bourgeoisie was very similar to Marx's: it was a revolutionary class. But by the end of the nineteenth century this previously revolutionary class had become self-centred, complacent and hubristic. Toynbee contended that

> ... an unprecedently prosperous and comfortable Western middle class was taking it as a matter of course that the end of one age of one civilization's history was the end of History itself – at least as far as they and their kind were concerned. They were imagining that, for their benefit, a sane, safe, satisfactory Modern Life had miraculously come to stay as a timeless present.[9]

But this 'timeless present' was symptomatic of the decline of the modern era and the rise of the 'post-modern age'. Because the bourgeoisie, the class that was synonymous with modernity itself, had become complacent to the point of becoming decadent, its role as a revolutionary class was now challenged by a rising industrial urban working class and by nationalist intellectuals outside the West. Here, industrialism and nationalism combined to threaten the modernity from within and without. The industrial working class challenged the bourgeoisie from inside the West. From outside it nationalist intellectuals appropriated the revolutionary ideas of modernity and turned them against the West. But the modern age also succumbed to other revolutionary forces within it. What Toynbee had in mind were the technological advances that outpaced individuals' ability to adapt to them. He believed the rate of change exceeded the adaptational capacity of a single life. This, he concluded, precipitated an unprecedented crisis in human affairs.

According to Toynbee this crisis began with the First World War where the scale of destruction and loss of life had surpassed any previous conflict in human history. But even though this was the case, the world was plunged into a second devastating conflict. By the end of the Second World War technology had so far outpaced and exceeded individuals' abilities to adapt that the threat of a third, and nuclear, conflict caused Toynbee to judge the concept of civilisation itself irrelevant. Western civilisation, in becoming universal, was on the brink of its own annihilation.[10]

Toynbee's use of 'post-modern' to denote a specific historical period was also used by the American poet Charles Olson (1910–70) who saw it as the period which followed the industrial and imperial eras. Though he used the term descriptively,[11] he was much more concerned with assigning it a prescriptive meaning. Olson understood postmodernism to be a reaction against modernism and its defining attributes: the formal and symbolic representation of reality and experience as means to both deepen humanity's self-knowledge and strengthen its ability to master the universe. Finding inspiration both in the work of the German philosopher Martin Heidegger (1889–1976) and in psychoanalysis, Olson believed Western civilisation had closed itself off from what was fundamental or authentic to the human experience. The fully authentic experience of life was no longer possible in Western civilisation because its intellectual and spiritual orientation was overly rationalised. Western civilisation was obsessive and relentless in intellectualising all human experience.[12] Like Heidegger before him,

Olson traced this intellectualisation of human experience back to Ancient Greek Socratic philosophy. And also like Heidegger he thought that art and aesthetic experience had an important function in developing 'an alternative to the whole Greek system'.[13] He believed, along with Heidegger, that art and aesthetic experience could direct civilisation away from 'that peculiar presumption by which western man has interposed himself between what he is as a creature of nature (with certain instructions to carry out) and those other creations of nature which we may, with no derogation, call objects'.[14] Art was crucial to returning humanity to what was truly authentic. To this end he sought to develop a new form of poetic expression, one he defined as postmodern.

Olson's first attempt at creating a new postmodern aesthetic began with the publication of his aesthetic manifesto, *Projective Verse* (1950). This essay advocated a form of poetic expression which surpassed the Imagism of Ezra Pound and William Carlos Williams, in which formal abstraction and symbolic representation were rejected in favour of a clear and precise presentation of image. The contours of Olson's postmodern aesthetic became more sharply defined throughout the 1950s when as Rector of Black Mountain College in the country highlands near Asheville North Carolina he helped organise a famous anti-modernist workshop-performance involving the composer John Cage, the painter Robert Rauschenberg, the dancer Merce Cunningham, and a number of lesser known artists. This event experimented with chance and improvisation as a means to establish a new aesthetic that would precipitate the recovery of the senses in their pristineness. This aesthetic repudiated the rational conceptualisation of sense experience as a prelude to formal representation, narration and interpretation. What it strived for was pure, untranslated sensuous immediacy. Only in this way could art lead individuals to regain an authentic experience of life. As he later made clear in his Beloit lectures, postmodern art was 'that emergence of image from an enormous condition of creation which we only poke at'.[15] Olson believed this new postmodern aesthetic would liberate human potentialities that hitherto had been stifled and suppressed by the intellectualisation of human experience. These potentialities coupled to collective action would lead to a new form of human self-determination that would restore an impoverished world to a vitality, wonderment and richness not experienced since the time of the pre-Socratics.

Olson's work proved very compelling to a group of literary critics who, led and inspired by William Spanos, founded in 1972 *boundary 2: a journal of postmodern literature and culture*. The journal stressed the role aesthetics could play in recovering humanity's authenticity. To this end Spanos and his group employed an 'aesthetic of de-composition'. This aesthetic — which bore striking parallels to Heidegger's idea of *Destruktion* and the method of 'deconstruction' employed by the French philosopher Jacques Derrida in his 1967 *Of Grammatology* (discussed below) — sought to provoke an experience of deracination in the reader or beholder which, Spanos and his group believed, could be associated with the experiences of dread and despair first discussed by the Danish existentialist philosopher Søren Kierkegaard (1813–55).

According to Kierkegaard, dread and despair were integral to our encounters with death. At the same time, however, we gain true self-awareness or become conscious of our selfhood when we face death, and therefore dread and despair were indicative of a fundamental fear of conscious selfhood. Kierkegaard thought that individuals' lifestyles, goals and ideals of fulfilment all revealed this fundamental fear. People led lives that distanced them as far as possible from their encounter with death; they thereby became less self-aware and increasingly remote from conscious selfhood. Individuals' lives became unreflective and superficial: impoverished to the extent of becoming pointless. Spanos and the founders of *boundary 2* saw in these ideas a penetrating critique of American consumer culture. But its force was greatly enhanced when Spanos and the founders of *boundary 2* tied it to Martin Heidegger's critique of knowledge in the modern world.

Spanos and the contributors to *boundary 2* were captivated by Heidegger's belief that within the Western philosophical tradition 'knowing' is construed essentially as 'representing'. They concurred with Heidegger's belief that within the Western philosophical tradition we 'understand ourselves as "picturing" the world, and the world as whatever can be successfully pictured by us'.[16] But according to Heidegger this represented a transformation of both humanity and the world into objects. Therefore, he concluded, the Western philosophical tradition culminates in the objectification of reality, and that this is at the heart of man's alienation from himself and the world.

Spanos and the contributors to *boundary 2* argued that the rational principles associated with the Western philosophical tradition, the principles conjoined to modernity itself, which governed the way individuals thought and made sense of their surroundings, alienated them from it. These principles, concepts and categories erected barriers against conscious selfhood and therefore were obstacles to individuals' self-awareness. According to Spanos, postmodernism's aesthetic of 'de-composition', the provoking of a state of rootlessness, rendered powerless the concepts and categories of Western rationality and, in a manner akin to restoring our encounter with death, restored conscious selfhood. Spanos and the contributors to *boundary 2* understood the postmodern aesthetic as an aesthetic of direct or unmediated experience. It was an aesthetic of freedom, hope and infinite possibility.[17]

Like Olson, Spanos and his followers believed that a postmodern aesthetic should be firmly rooted in philosophic writings that contested the veracity and legitimacy of principles, concepts and categories that were broadly accepted as part of the Western philosophic tradition. But as we shall see later, writers who did not describe or conceive of their works as postmodern, but were equally critical of the Western philosophic tradition, were engaged in their own assaults on the philosophical canons of modernity. Their works would become central to a prescriptive postmodernism. But before we pursue that discussion it will be necessary to explore briefly the way postmodernism was used in a discipline tightly wedded to aesthetic considerations and theories of poetic expression: architecture. For just as postmodernism's role in literary criticism was to have profound implications for and repercussions on other academic and artistic pursuits, the role it came to play in architecture had foundational repercussions for other disciplines.

Architectural postmodernism

At roughly the same time as Toynbee and Olson were writing, the American architect Joseph Hudnut introduced postmodernism into architecture. In 1945 Hudnut wrote an article for the *Architectural Record* entitled 'The postmodern house'.[18] In it he defined 'postmodern' as both a new historical category, referring to the atomic and computer era, and an aesthetic ideal, harnessing scientific and technical advances so that they could foster the flourishing of unmediated authentic human experiences. Hudnut's characterisation of the postmodern ideal was diametrically opposed to the modern ideal which he believed had mechanised and standardised contemporary life. Yet his insightful critique of architectural modernism and his vision for postmodern architecture failed to attract a wide following, and it would take two decades before that ideal gained any adherents.

Hudnut's belief that modern science and technology created a mechanically perfected world of social uniformity and 'outward control' became central to the attack on architectural modernism begun in 1961 with Jane Jacobs' *The Death and Life of Great American Cities*.[19] But it was not until 1966 that a radical vision for postmodern architecture was enunciated with the publication of Robert Venturi's *Complexity and Contradiction in Architecture*. Like Hudnut before him, Venturi (b. 1925) believed that modern architecture reinforced the mechanisation and standardisation of contemporary life.

While Venturi admired modernism's achievements, he was critical of modern architecture's claim that its aesthetic principles were universal, ahistorical and timeless. Modernism's purist International Style resulted in uniform and oppressive buildings and cities. It created a built environment that suppressed individual expression and enforced social uniformity. In *Complexity and Contradiction* Venturi argued that modern architecture could not accommodate modern life's richness and complexity. Only a new form of architecture could take account of the diversity of the human experience and facilitate its expression through new ideas about design and planning. This postmodern architecture Venturi called 'complex and contradictory'.[20]

Venturi's attack on architectural modernism culminated with *Learning from Las Vegas* (1972). Here, Venturi and his co-authors Denise Scott Brown and Steven Izenour repeated the claim that modern architecture suppressed individuality and enforced social conformity. He explored in greater depth ideas advanced in *Complexity and Contradiction*, in particular, architecture's communicative attributes, stressing terms such as 'symbolic meaning', 'rhetoric', and 'architectural language'. Venturi claimed that modern architecture had lost its ability to communicate with a general populace because it used a language that was self-assured, intimidating and elitist. Its language reinforced its tendency toward hermeticism, formalisation and unidimensionality. The result was that modern architecture looked to itself alone for inspiration and thereby lost all vitality.

Venturi's diagnosis on the ills of modern architecture revealed the extent to which the beliefs he held were similar to Olson's and Spanos's in literature and the arts. But where Venturi differed from them was in what he believed could be learned from the past. Whereas Olson followed Heidegger in returning to the pre-Socratics for inspiration, Venturi turned to pre-modern forms of architecture, such as the Baroque, which drew on other traditions and disciplines for inspiration. These pre-modern architectures were exciting and expressed a natural vitality because they employed a tradition of iconology in which painting, sculpture and graphics were combined with architecture. Postmodern architecture returned to this pre-modern tradition of iconology. It looked to other disciplines for inspiration, integrated into its own medium different art forms, and mixed diverse pre-modern architectural traditions.[21] Encompassing this multiplicity of artistic and architectural languages made postmodern architecture polyvalent.

The mixing of traditions and appropriation of ideas from different art forms and disciplines was a return to an era when the boundaries that existed between disciplines were vague and porous, allowing ideas to move easily between them. This idea resonated with Heidegger's and Olson's nostalgia for a pre-Socratic way of thinking about and experiencing the world in which spheres of knowledge were both vaguely defined and open, allowing ideas to move readily between them.

Venturi's critique of, and postmodern alternative to, modern architecture were commendable. But the examples he cited of postmodern architecture and urban planning such as the urban commercial sprawl of Las Vegas shocked many. His postmodern alternative to architectural modernism also provoked outrage because it failed to engage architecture in a wider social critique by not questioning 'the morality of commercial advertising, gambling interests' or criticising 'the competitive instinct'. Rather, postmodern architecture was all about awakening architects to the possibilities offered by the 'the commercial strip'.[22] Though this provoked a barrage of criticisms, Venturi's critique of architectural modernism remained profoundly influential, laying the foundations for a more rigorous theorisation of postmodern architecture in the work of Charles Jencks, 'the acknowledged guru of Post-Modernism'.[23]

In 1975 Jencks (b. 1939) endorsed Venturi's critique of modern architecture in a short article in *Architecture Association Quarterly* entitled 'The Rise of Post-Modern Architecture'.[24] In this essay he argued that postmodern architecture looked to different disciplines for inspiration, and mixed other architectural traditions and styles. He also stressed commercial capitalism's positive effect in giving urban living a vibrancy and diversity, and concluded that postmodern architecture, 'ersatz architecture', was consumer-orientated. This first attempt at defining postmodern architecture differed little from Venturi's description of it. Later, in his famous *The Language of Post-Modern Architecture* (1977), he again employed a definition of postmodern architecture that was very similar to Venturi's. But as he continued to write on postmodern architecture, important differences between the two authors emerged.

These first appeared in the second edition of Jencks's *The Language of Post-Modern Architecture* (1978). Jencks substantially re-worked his ideas on postmodern architecture and gave a new definition of it that incorporated an elitist element repudiated in the earlier edition. Jencks's elitism – a response to critics' assertions that postmodern architecture was nothing more than 'dumbed down' architecture – stemmed from the idea that postmodern architecture should communicate to two groups of individuals: an international architectural elite which determined standards of beauty through a shared aesthetic sensibility and 'the man in the street' whose aesthetic sensibility was informed by a local culture, traditions and issues.[25] Postmodern architecture used forms and symbols that were meaningful to an international elite and had relevance to a local population. This was a defining attribute of postmodern architecture, and it was what Jencks termed 'double-coding'. 'Double-coding' ensured that postmodern architecture communicated both with 'architects and a concerned minority who care about specifically architectural meanings and [with] the public at large, or the local inhabitants, who care about other issues concerned with comfort, traditional building and a way of life'.[26] In the third edition of *The Language of Post-Modern Architecture* (1981), this definition was further refined so that double-coding meant 'an eclectic mix of traditional or local codes with Modern ones'.[27]

Jencks's ideas on postmodern architecture matured throughout the 1980s. He came to periodise postmodernism into three distinct stages – pluralist, eclectic and 'classical' – and concluded that it had now culminated into what he called 'Free-Style Classicism', a kind of 'world consensus' in art and architecture. The emergence of this consensus was proof of postmodern architecture's success in exposing the shortcomings of modern architecture and presenting itself as a better alternative. Postmodern architecture's ability to fulfil the 'need for a universal language, a public language',[28] enabled it to supplant modernism as the universal idiom of architecture and art. Yet this triumph seemed hollow as postmodern architecture now accommodated virtually all idioms except purist modernism.[29] What had originally been critical and innovative had now become commonplace and conventional.

Venturi and Jencks's failure to theorise a postmodern architecture that itself did not succumb to their own critique of architectural modernism was testimony to the depth and acuity of ideas, drawn from the same sources in Kierkegaard, Nietzsche and Heidegger, which nourished Olson's and Spanos's critique of modernism and their belief that postmodernism would restore an impoverished humanity to vitality. These ideas challenged the fundamental beliefs of modernity. Their incorporation in the works of philosophers like Michel Foucault, Jacques Derrida, Gilles Deleuze and Félix Guattari was to have explosive consequences for the humanities, overturning conventional wisdom and established practices, changing forever the face of the human sciences. Let us now explore in greater depth those foundational ideas of postmodernism.

Postmodernism and the humanities

Though Venturi and Jencks furnished a powerful critique of architectural modernism, their postmodern alternative was criticised as a failure of imagination because it was nothing more than an eclectic mixture of pre-modern forms. It was also attacked for a failure of nerve because it was unable to free itself from commercial imperatives and glossed over this shortcoming by redefining the social issues that lay at the heart of contemporary architecture as 'questions of style'.[30] Among Venturi and Jencks's most severe critics was the German philosopher Jürgen Habermas who identified their work, and postmodernism in other disciplines, with what he perceived to be a wider phenomenon of anti-progressive thinking that had become fashionable in philosophy, politics and sociology from the mid-1970s onward. Habermas associated postmodernism with neoconservatism. But for all of the force of his argument, he found the works of philosophers such as Foucault and Derrida more difficult to dismiss as neoconservative. Not only were the causes to which they were committed as public intellectuals identified with the left, but the revolutionary implications of their writings was universally acknowledged as breathtaking.

In order to better understand just how radical these implications were an examination of postmodernism's philosophical origins is indispensable.

Postmodernism's philosophical origins

The philosophical origins of postmodernism can be traced back to the eighteenth century and the intellectuals who spawned the counter-enlightenment. Johann Georg Hamann (1730–88) and his disciple Johann Gottfried Herder (1744–1803) were the true founders of anti-rationalism and romanticism. They influenced many of the most outstanding philosophers of the nineteenth century including Søren Kierkegaard, Arthur Schopenhauer and Friedrich Nietzsche who, like them, did not see reality as dead matter obeying fixed laws but rather as a process of organic growth, 'a thrusting forward of a living will'.[31]

Hamann and Herder shared a keen awareness of the profundity of human life, of its vitality, sheer diversity and total wonderment. They believed it to be palpable, sensuous and passionate. They revered its organic reality. And they denounced theories, generalisations and abstractions of it as arbitrary intellectual constructions that alienated men from the world and themselves. They raged against the fundamental kernel of rationality, which is that all principles of explanation everywhere must be the same. And they rejected utterly the corollary that language corresponded approximately to some objective or higher reality than that experienced and created by individuals. They understood language as what we think with, not translate into. It was a creative energy, a force through which, as Hamann said, 'are *all things* made'.[32] They believed the champions of the Enlightenment, French philosophers such as Etienne Condillac (1715–80) and Jean d'Alembert (1717–83) or the German philosopher Immanuel Kant (1724–1804), committed the gravest of errors when they confused '*words* with *concepts* and *concepts* with *real things*'.[33] Real things were not the approximations of words which, in turn, roughly corresponded to pure concepts. Rather, words were 'the living carriers of feeling', the 'stamp of life'. Their connection to our senses, thoughts and emotions was organic, singular and indissoluble.

These convictions spawned a new aesthetics of art as 'the sensual expression of individual or collective personality'.[34] They were the core of Hamann's religious mysticism and historical relativism and the foundation to Herder's social psychology and belief that men are 'deeply rooted in a texture of beliefs, institutions, forms of life, in terms of which alone they can be accounted for and their thought and action explained'.[35] These ideas became the deep roots to postmodern theories on language, history, aesthetics and culture, from Olson's postmodern poetry to Lyotard's postmodern sublime. But it was Hamann and Herder's stress on the sensuous and passionate vitality of human life, of its unplumbed depths, that was to prove most attractive to thinkers who, like them, believed the Enlightenment transformed life into dead matter. This, the German philosopher Arthur Schopenhauer (1788–1860) explored in *The World as Will and Representation* (1818) – a work that proved to be the classic formulation of the belief that the human mind could reach beyond the mere appearance of reality and attain knowledge of something more real, something more profound.[36]

In *The World as Will and Representation* Schopenhauer presented the world as having two facets to it. There was the physical aspect of appearance, what he called 'the surface', and there was the interior, 'which is not merely superficies but possesses cubic content'. Schopenhauer believed that philosophy had become dominated by phenomenology which reached its apogee in the work of his archenemy G. W. F. Hegel (1770–1831). According to Schopenhauer phenomenology was concerned merely with the surface of reality. It considered phenomena and explored the causal connections between them. But this kind of philosophical outlook, he thought, ignored the substratum of reality, its 'cubic content', the domain of metaphysics, and thus failed to consider the deeper issues of being and existence – issues at the very heart of the writings of Foucault, Derrida and Deleuze.

Being and existence was what interested Schopenhauer. His whole approach to exploring it was directed by his belief that the human mind comprised both the capacity for rational thought, which governed our consciousness and ability to represent the world and understand our place within it, and, at a deeper level, an uncontrolled, irrational process of striving which governed, nourished, but also conflicted with the higher, conscious or rational part of our character.[37]

Schopenhauer's conclusions on human experience were fundamentally pessimistic. He believed that life could be understood as a two-part task. First, it was about survival, and in this humans were no different than animals. This was the raw expression of the irrational process of striving, what he called 'will'. Once this first task was accomplished the will strived for more. At this point life became subject to a second and 'burdensome' task: busying itself 'so as to ward off boredom', 'the sensation of the emptiness of existence'. To keep boredom at bay individuals filled up their lives with various activities and pursuits, but in doing so failed to reflect upon their situation. Most people went through life unthinkingly, leading lives that were monotonous and common as if they were 'factory-made'.[38]

Schopenhauer's concern was to expose the deeper psychic and philosophic reasons for people's mundane and unthinking existence. He explained that individuals' higher faculty became subject to the immediate desires of the will, and knowledge became restricted to what served the fulfilment of those desires. Individuals became prisoners of their will. And they remained captive because the way they reflected upon the world, which was both phenomenological and utilitarian, prevented them from thinking beyond the immediate desires of the will and reaching a level of thinking in which thought is 'an end in itself',[39] the true '*aim* of the whole of life'.[40]

Schopenhauer's pessimistic ideas reflect his diagnosis on the state of his age. They deepened romantic criticisms of nineteenth-century bourgeois culture and gave expression to a growing disillusionment with Enlightenment values. Like Immanuel

Kant (1724–1804), whose philosophy he revered, Schopenhauer placed individual liberty at the centre of his philosophical enterprise. He pursued Kant's principal claim made in his famous 1784 essay 'An Answer to the Question: "What is Enlightenment?"' that 'Enlightenment is man's emergence from his self-incurred immaturity'.[41] He believed, like Kant, that the problem confronting the modern age was that individuals were either too lazy or too cowardly to free themselves of the opinions of others: they lacked the courage to think independently. And it was this that guaranteed that they ultimately remained ignorant and in bondage. Whereas Kant was optimistic about the prospects of 'each separate individual' being able to 'work his way out of [...] immaturity',[42] Schopenhauer remained pessimistic. It was a sentiment shared by his greatest follower, Friedrich Nietzsche.

Nietzsche wasted no time in diagnosing the predicament of modernity: it was what he called 'nihilism' or 'the radical repudiation of value, meaning, and desirability'.[43] In his very first work, *The Birth of Tragedy,* he unearthed the origins of this condition. He argued that Western philosophy was characterised by a duality between what is apparent and what is real. This was hardly an original thesis. But the way he examined this duality was stunningly unique. By focusing on aesthetic experience, something not normally considered by philosophers at the time, Nietzsche believed he could analyse the nature of metaphysics and show where the origins of the crisis of Western philosophy lay.

Nietzsche believed that the duality that existed within Western thought could be traced back to 'the *Apollonian* and *Dionysian* duality' which characterised Greek art. He argued these two different tendencies, named after the Greek gods Apollo and Dionysis, ran parallel but were in opposition to each other. Their parallel movement but open variance caused them to 'continually incite each other to new and more powerful births'.[44] The Apollonian was the art of appearance, sculpture, painting and above all the epic, with the proudest manifestation of the latter being Homer's the *Iliad.* It embodied the qualities associated with the plastic arts: beauty, hard edges and clarity. And it included those virtues associated with epic drama too, particularly heroism. Yet it was also the art of appearance and not that of what at bottom was real. It was, as Nietzsche characterised it, the 'art world' of dreams which, when experienced at its 'most intense', led to 'the sensation' that there was some deeper reality that lay beneath it. This was a 'world of intoxication'. A formless swirling of intense pleasure and pain, at once sublime but also destructive and cruel. It was the world of Dionysis and it was expressed in art, music and tragedy. Dionysian art was aligned with intoxication, lack of clarity and the merging of individualities through the shared experience of ecstasy. As Nietzsche described it: 'the most immediate effect of the Dionysian tragedy [... is] that the state and society and, quite generally, the gulfs between man and man give way to an overwhelming feeling of unity leading back to the very heart of nature'.[45] This description of the submerging of individuality into a collective experience of nature, inspired by Schopenhauer's belief that through suffering and self-renunciation one's own inner being became united with all things, resonated with Hamann's and Herder's conviction that the spirit of community was generated by its members being united in a common experience, and the aesthetic ideas of German romantic thinkers such as J. J. Winckelmann (1717–68), G. E. Lessing

(1729–81) and Friedrich Schiller (1759–1805).[46] As we shall see later, the same idea came to occupy a central position in the writings of Michel Foucault and Gilles Deleuze.

Though Nietzsche stressed that the Dionysian led to the submerging of individuality into a collective experience of nature, he was careful to show that the special quality of Greek tragedy depended on the balance between Dionysian and Apollonian. The Apollonian, associated with poise, individuality and consciousness, allowed the Greeks to face the raw, chaotic and terrifying impulses of nature called up by the Dionysian. The balance between these two elements allowed the Greeks to comfort themselves after 'having looked boldly right into the terrible destructiveness of so-called world history as well as the cruelty of nature'.[47]

Nietzsche believed this special quality of Greek tragedy afforded the Greeks both 'an interpretation of life' and a way to 'train' themselves for it.[48] Yet this was lost with the advent of Plato's philosophy which, because of a secret loathing of randomness, chance, contingency and the brute particularity of nature, emphasised a timeless, never changing world of order, symmetry and perfect form. Platonic philosophy became complicit with the Apollonian. And the latter soon dominated the Dionysian. The result was that form and beauty suppressed formlessness, ecstasy and terror. Plato's philosophy justified the illusion that form and beauty were the true reality. This, according to Nietzsche, was part of a strategy of human self-empowerment. It was a way of turning the blind and capricious forces of nature into something comprehensible and therefore less terrifying, a way of making the world manageable, as well as technically manipulable by humans. This was what Nietzsche called man's 'revenge against time'. With philosophy dominating art, the raw emotional energy that gave vitality to Greek culture soon dissipated.[49] The forces of life were, as Nietzsche lamented, ground down by 'the enormous driving-wheel of logical Socratism'.[50] This was the death of tragedy and the birth of a life-denying philosophy which, when allied with Christianity, would dominate the West for two millennia. Postmodern thinkers, especially Michel Foucault (Chapter 4) and Gilles Deleuze (Chapter 6), were deeply inspired by Nietzsche's critique: so profoundly moved that in the case of Foucault he experimented with ways of experiencing ecstasy and terror.[51]

Nietzsche pursued the central theme of *The Birth of Tragedy* in all his major works including *Attempt at a Self-Criticism, On the Genealogy of Morals* and *Twilight of the Idols*.[52] But his alternative to the life-denying philosophy spawned by Platonism and 'the most prodigal elaboration of the moral theme to which humanity has ever been subjected', Christianity, appeared with a work that challenges our inviolable beliefs. *Thus Spoke Zarathustra* affirmed the relativity and transitoriness of our values, and through the affirmation of the will to power it suggested the absence of any truth about the nature of everything.[53] It elevated the idea of the noble spirit 'who has to be a creator in good and evil, truly, has first to be a destroyer and break values'. And it presented the heroism of the superman who breaks those values and rises above morality, beyond the concern with the good, 'and manages in spite of suffering and disorder and the absence of all justice to respond to something like the beauty of it all'.[54] The heroic figure of the superman is 'an advocate' of life in all its beauty, ugliness and terror and craves for nothing more than to experience life in all its fullness (Chapters 2 and 6).

These reflections were pursued by the German philosopher and Rector of the University of Freiburg under the Nazis, Martin Heidegger. Heidegger's famous lectures on Nietzsche given in the 1930s and 1940s explored many of Nietzsche's claims about Western philosophy but radicalised their conclusions. Heidegger contended Nietzsche was right to focus on the central role of 'value' in Western metaphysics and to judge the act of valuing as part of a strategy of human self-empowerment, a way of rendering chance, contingency and the brute particularity of existence comprehensible, psychologically manageable and less frightful. Heidegger went on to argue that within the modern age 'knowing' is construed as 'representing'. He contended that we understand ourselves in 'picturing' the world, and understand the world as whatever can be pictured by us successfully. Being, or existence – and this was Heidegger's principal concern – he asserted was the result of representing reality according to a method or by laws that are agreed upon by common consent. But Heidegger believed that that way of thinking about Being was fundamentally flawed, with its utter failure fully exposed in the modern age, 'the age of consummate meaninglessness', as he called it.[55] This judgement on modernity differed little from Nietzsche's account of nihilism as the crisis of modern thought. But where Heidegger departed from Nietzsche was in his assessment of what needed to be done, preparing the way for a whole new way of thinking.[56]

Heidegger contended that within the Western philosophical tradition all attempts at asking about the nature of the world were flawed because our fundamental outlook on the world constrained us from asking the important question about our nature and the nature of Being. His contention was that individuals are *already determined* and that Being reveals itself through our individual existences. This is what Heidegger called 'the Being of beings'.

Heidegger went on to argue that Western thinking was dominated by a subjectivism or humanism in which individuals defined and manipulated reality according to their needs. In this way subjects defined themselves and moulded a world that was just 'there'. He believed humanism to be an historically motivated and psychologically consoling strategy, and he devoted much thought and energy to attacking its principal aspects associated with the modern age – science and technology – which he believed to be the worst and most alienating aspects of Western thought because they objectified reality and constrained thought to instrumental reasoning.

Heidegger's critique of humanism and his belief that individual existences were the expression of Being were easily incorporated in the structuralist enterprise of dissolving the subject. His assault on science and technology was reinforced by the work of French philosophers of science such as Gaston Bachelard (1884–1962) and Georges Canguilhem (1904–95), whose influence on the structuro-marxist Louis Althusser (1918–90) and Michel Foucault was crucial.[57] And his endeavour to destroy traditional metaphysics and replace it with a new way of thinking gave a leading role to artists, poets and thinkers such as Hamann or Nietzsche, whose works brought about the 'unconcealing' of Being, and proved profoundly influential to poets like Olson and thinkers classified as deconstructionist or postmodernist such as Jacques Derrida (Chapter 11).

The crisis of humanism and the rise of postmodernism

Heidegger's assault on humanism was the most impressive example of what was to become a sustained attack from the 1940s onward on the idea that an autonomous and coherent human subject could discern an overall pattern to human history and thereby improve on the past. This campaign gained ground in the 1950s under the guidance of the anthropologist Claude Lévi-Strauss, and the philosopher Maurice Merleau-Ponty who introduced into philosophical discussions Saussure's structural linguistics and Lévi-Strauss's structural anthropology. The effects of this structuralist revolution were profound. In political philosophy Louis Althusser revolutionised interpretations of Marx and ideas on ideology. In psychoanalysis orthodox beliefs and practices established since the time of Freud were overturned by Jacques Lacan (1901–81). And the fields of linguistics, literary criticism and cultural studies were radically altered by Roland Barthes. It seemed as though ideas that had gone unchallenged for so long were now being swept aside by a new revolutionary way of thinking. Within this context a new generation of intellectuals such as Michel Foucault and Jacques Derrida began their own assault on what Foucault called 'totalising systems'. But their own critique of the human sciences was strikingly different from the structuralist critique and was called 'poststructuralist'. One of clearest definitions of poststructuralism is given by Gary Gutting who shows that it

> combines the structuralist *style* of objective, technical, and even formal discourse about the human world with a rejection of the structuralist *claim* that there is any deep or final truth that such discourse can uncover. The poststructuralist project need not be self-contradictory, but it is inevitably ironic, since it sees its methods of analysis as both necessary and, given traditional goals, doomed to failure.[58]

The poststructuralist project was the beginnings of the postmodern revolution in the human sciences, and it is to the thought and works of the thinkers who led it that we will now turn.

Michel Foucault

During his thirty years as a philosopher, historian, public intellectual and political activist, Foucault produced books on the treatment of mental illness, the birth of clinical medicine, the development of the human sciences, the methodology of the history of ideas, the origins of the prison and the history of sexuality. His works were widely read and extremely influential. In 1970 they earned him a sufficient reputation to be awarded a personal chair in the History of Systems of Thought at France's most prestigious academic institution, the Collège de France. The title of this chair, chosen by Foucault himself, encapsulated his primary unit of analysis at the time, the *epistémè* or structure of thought. Foucault described the *epistémè* in his magisterial study on the history of the human sciences *Les Mots et les choses: une archéologie des sciences humaines* (1966) (translated as *The Order of Things: An Archaeology of the Human Sciences*). The *epistémè* was an 'historical *a priori*' which

> in a given period, delimits in the totality of experience a field of knowledge, defines the mode of being of the objects that appear in that field, provides man's everyday perception with theoretical powers, and defines the conditions in which he can sustain a discourse about things that is recognized to be true.[59]

It was the 'conceptual strata underpinning various fields of knowledge' in a given epoch, with the *epistémès* of one historical epoch being not only incompatible but also entirely incommensurable with those of another.[60] Though *epistémès* provided the necessary preconditions for interpreting reality and making statements about it, they remained obscured from view and were not consciously adopted nor consciously understood.

The deployment of *epistémè* allowed Foucault to argue that traditional approaches to the human sciences were historically contingent and needed to be abandoned. Like Nietzsche before him, he believed that humans' natural and social universes were neither ordered nor fundamentally intelligible. Instead they were characterised by randomness and discontinuity. Whatever order was established was fundamentally without foundation, historically contingent, and always caused terrible wrongs – the latter point having been made both in his 1961 doctoral thesis on the history of mental illness, *Folie et déraison: Histoire de la folie à l'âge classique* (*Madness and Civilization: A History of Insanity in the Age of Reason*) and his path-breaking study on the history of psychiatry, *Naissance de la clinique: Une archéologie du regard médical* (*Birth of the Clinic: An Archaeology of Medical Perception*) of 1963.[61]

The use of *epistémè* emerged from Foucault's conviction that those engaged in intellectual enquiry confined themselves to the study of mere appearances or 'knowledge of things' and failed to explore the foundations to human knowledge. These reflections were similar to those made a century earlier by Schopenhauer and Nietzsche. And like these philosophers Foucault saw the need for a new and critical orientation of thought. What was needed was a deep form of analysis which could elucidate the predicament of the present. This critical approach involved investigating the fundamental structures of thought. Foucault described this approach as archaeological, a sifting through the layers of surface reality in order to penetrate to the deeper and hidden rules that govern the way individuals know and understand themselves (Chapter 3). The archaeological method demonstrated the futility of the traditional human sciences, which maintained the core conviction in an autonomous and coherent human subject capable of discerning an overall pattern to human history and thereby show how the past informed the present. And it revealed how historical epochs were incommensurable. Yet by 1969, when he had refined his ideas further in *The Archaeology of Knowledge*, Foucault was keen to stress an important timeless element.[62] This was that all epochs, despite their incommensurabilities, had embedded within them power relations which structured people's outlooks on reality and relations between themselves.

This was a significant shift in thinking from *The Order of Things* whose unit of analysis, the *epistémè*, was both too abstract and restricted. In *The Archaeology of Knowledge* Foucault adopted instead the concept of discourse. This new concept bore a family resemblance to *epistémè* but, rather than referring uniquely to a system of thought, it designated encompassed *practices* ordered according to certain underlying or hidden rules. Foucault believed the concept to be far more robust than *epistémè*, because it took account of non-discursive elements such as social and political events and institutions, or economic processes or practices.[63] It could account for how non-discursive elements altered theoretical outlooks or systems of thought. Yet in *The Archaeology of Knowledge* Foucault maintained his deep conviction that the past was characterised by randomness and discontinuity, that historical epochs were incommensurable. The concept of discourse was bound up with his understanding of the past through the idea of *archive*. This he defined as 'the law of what can be said, the system that governs the appearance of statements as unique events'. It corresponded to the 'play of rules which determines within a culture the appearance and disappearance of statements' and was '*the general system of formation and transformation of statements*'.[64] The introduction of discourse and archive was Foucault's response to his critics who contended that his work was confined exclusively to the domain of theory and was unable to address the relation between knowledge and human practice.[65]

The introduction of discourse and archive reflected Foucault's deepening engagement with politics and the study of power. The focus of his writings soon moved away from the methodological considerations to more political and 'tactical' concerns that were to be firmly tied to the Nietzschean idea of genealogy (Chapter 4). The shift was clearly discerned in his 1970 inaugural lecture at the Collège de France entitled *L'Ordre du discours*.[66] The lecture reflected his long acknowledged debt to Nietzsche as his intellectual and spiritual inspiration, but also highlighted his preoccupation with the power/knowledge matrix that he believed dominated modern societies (Chapter 1). Just as Nietzsche revealed in *The Genealogy of Morals*[67] how morality was oppressive and life denying in the way it limited the scope for human creativity, Foucault saw discourses in a complex relation with power whereby certain forms of knowledge or human practices were marginalised or repressed. Foucault was most interested in directing his genealogical method against what he called the 'totalising discourses', those great systems, syntheses or ideologies that dominate the modern thought and practices. By genealogy he understood the 'painstaking rediscovery of struggles', the rediscovery of 'fragmented, subjugated, local and specific knowledge', the knowledge of marginalised individuals or groups. The aim of genealogy was to expose the workings of power, to illuminate a society's 'will to truth': repressive and permissive procedures that determine how knowledge is valued, applied, distributed and rejected.[68] Genealogical history would tell the story of a constant struggle between different powers which try to impose their own 'will to truth'. This was the object of *Discipline and Punish: the Birth of the Prison* (1975), a history of prisons and punishment, and the monumental three volume *The History of Sexuality* (1976, 1984). Along with his early works on mental illness and psychiatry, *Madness and Civilization* and *The Birth of the Clinic*, these works revolutionised disciplines such as clinical psychiatry, psychology, philosophy, criminology, sociology and political theory.[69] They were a fillip to new and developing areas of research such as gender studies, and they opened up whole new areas of research for historians, such as the history of medicine or the history of sexuality, and altered fundamentally historians' ideas on and approaches to the past. Foucault's archaeological method and genealogical approach made a significant contribution to the shattering of barriers between established academic disciplines. This was particularly true of a new generation of historians such as Frank Ankersmit, Hans Kellner and Hayden White who turned to philosophy and literary criticism in theorising a postmodernist history.

These transformations to academic disciplines were the natural outcome of a political engagement that rested on genealogy. Genealogy served as the foundation to the elaboration of a strategy of resistance, particularly for those groups who suffered from institutionalised subjugation and social marginalisation: the clinically insane, prison inmates, sexual deviants, social misfits. Yet genealogy was never intended as a means by which one 'totalising discourse' or grand ideology might overturn another. It was really about showing that where order seemed obvious there was in fact conflict; where there was consensus there was in fact incessant dissent. It was a way of releasing and bringing 'into play' 'local discursivities' and 'subjected knowledges'.[70] It was about giving voice to marginalised individuals or groups in their struggles to resist domination and transgress the boundaries of social propriety. It gave impetus to an anarchic impulse but did not guarantee liberation, 'as the exercise of power over others is built on the premise that the tables can always be turned, dissolved or reconstituted'.[71] This was not a politics of ideological struggle, it was a micropolitics of resistance that would be identified with the postmodern politics of Gilles Deleuze, Jean-François Lyotard and Jacques Derrida.[72]

Jacques Derrida

Despite the appeal and influence of Foucault's archaeological method and genealogy, they were fiercely criticised. One of the most important attacks to come from a more traditional quarter of academe – and a direct assault on *Madness and Civilization* – was *La pratique de l'esprit humain: l'institution asilaire et la révolution démocratique* (1980) by the historian and political theorist Marcel Gauchet and the psychoanalyst Gladys Swain.[73] Among poststructuralists, the most penetrating critique was Jacques Derrida's essay 'Cogito and the History of Madness' (Chapter 5), a brilliant early example of deconstruction, the approach that has become synonymous with Derrida's name.

While Derrida (b. 1930) agreed with Foucault that the traditional approach to the human sciences was dead and not worth reviving, he believed Foucault's archaeology and genealogy still adhered to the assumption underpinning Western philosophical tradition that there was an objective body of knowledge or ultimate truth that could be discovered. He concluded that Foucault was unable to accomplish the post-structuralist project and therefore failed to go far enough in his efforts to break free from humanism. Derrida aimed for a definitive rupture and the ultimate success of poststucturalism. The way he set out to achieve this was alien to conventional philosophy, belonging, as Derrida insisted, neither 'to the "philosophical" register nor to the "literary" register'.[74] Derrida's style of writing was, and remains, contorted and opaque. He uses strange terminology and his narrative thread is broken by numerous long digressions which are all designed to push language beyond the boundaries of convention or, as he says himself, 'to make the limits of language tremble'. The coalescence of these elements makes his works frustratingly difficult to comprehend.

Derrida was interested in the works of Hegel, Husserl and Heidegger from the time he began studying philosophy at the École Normale Supérieure in 1952 (Chapter 11). In 1960 he began teaching general philosophy and logic at the Sorbonne as an assistant to Suzanne Bachelard (Gaston Bachelard's daughter), Georges Canguilhem, Paul Ricœur and Jean Wahl. He first became known as a Husserl scholar with his introduction to and translation of Husserl's *Origin of Geometry* (1962).[75] His introduction was widely admired within the French academic establishment and won the Jean-Cavaillès prize in modern epistemology. But this admiration was short-lived, for as Heidegger's influence on Derrida grew the esteem he gained within the French academy diminished to the point where he was consistently denied employment within the French university system despite obtaining numerous prizes and being fêted with invitations to teach and honorary doctorates from American and European universities.[76] Heidegger was the inspiration behind the composition of Derrida's doctoral thesis *De la grammatologie* (*Of Grammatology*) (1967).[77] This work set out a new approach to philosophy known as deconstruction (Chapter 8). And deconstruction threatened the established canons of the discipline.

Like Heidegger before him, Derrida believed that the picturing of the world which dominated the Western philosophical tradition – what Derrida referred to as logo-centrism (the logic of identity and non-contradiction) – was firmly rooted in the Platonic metaphysics of sameness or 'presence'. This kind of metaphysics – called humanism by Heidegger – was misleading because it was anthropomorphic, equating man and being as the same; it was also flawed and ultimately destructive. It led humans to be divorced both from nature and from each other. This led Heidegger and later Derrida to judge humanism to be fundamentally inhumane. Derrida believed that it was necessary to abandon the anthropomorphic conception of being and to look upon Being as something more than man. His early endorsement of structuralism paved the way to his acceptance of Heidegger's philosophy. But it was not long before he concluded that Heidegger had not gone far enough in his break from humanism. He believed Heidegger's nostalgia for pre-Socratic unveilings of Being was a lapse back into the metaphysics of 'presence', the metaphysics at the heart of humanism. Derrida set out to give his own deeper and more penetrating analysis of humanism, and thereby achieve a final separation from it.

In *Of Grammatology* Derrida contrasted the metaphysics of *sameness* and *presence* with the ideas of *otherness* and *absence*. Both otherness and absence lie at the heart of his belief 'that reality is to be understood both in terms of difference, rather than self-identity, and in terms of perpetual deferment, rather than eternal presence'.[78] Central to this is the concept of *différance* which means both difference and to defer, where meaning itself is forever postponed. *Différance* is central to his mode of philosophical questioning and his attack on humanism. Derrida believes philosophers have traditionally assessed arguments and statements by determining whether or not they are contradictory, logically coherent and correspond to an independently verifiable reality. They approach works of philosophy by showing how they work, how arguments fit together and how meaning is coherently conveyed. Derrida, however, proceeds differently. He is not interested in focusing on core ideas or arguments, nor is he interested in offering a complete or definitive account of a work or philosopher's thought. Rather, he is concerned with modes of presentation, with the ordering of terms, the use of metaphors, the employment of rhetorical devices. He focuses on everything that is glossed over by traditional philosophers: subterranean influences, the unconscious elements that creep into even the most sober philosophical writing. And his intention is to show how a text fails to succeed in communicating its message or representing reality.

Derrida works on the assumption that traditional philosophy, in delivering a coherent, comprehensive and definitive portrayal or account of a given work or philosopher's thought, is a kind of conjuring trick. Deconstruction, however, 'shows the failure of a work's attempt at representation and, by implication, the possibility of comparable failure by any such work, or by any text whatsoever'.[79] It exposes traditional philosophy as illusory.

This kind of philosophical approach is understood as hermeneutics or the philosophical enquiry into understanding or interpretation.[80] Like other philosophers engaged in hermeneutics, Derrida contends that we make sense of the world through language and that there is no way of stepping outside of language to determine whether the world represented by it is consistent with it; language *is* the world – a belief advocated by Hamann, Herder and their romantic followers. But what distinguishes Derrida from other hermeneutic philosophers is that he goes well beyond their claim that there is no writing or reading that is not already an interpretation to assert that 'any apparently coherent system of thought can be shown to have underlying irresolvable antinomies, such that there are multiple and conflicting readings that must be held simultaneously'.[81] This is precisely what Derrida is engaged in when employing the interpretative practice of dissemination (Chapter 8), which, by exploring associative possibilities and multiple contexts, allows for an infinite number of interpretations. The implication of this is not that there is no such thing as truth, but that there is a plethora of truths.

This is not merely a text-based conclusion; it has profound implications for language and ethics. Derrida believes the emphasis on difference strains language to its limits and thereby reveals what cannot be said.[82] Insight into Being is what the limit-experience of language can achieve. Derrida, like Foucault, turned to avant-garde writers such as Maurice Blanchot and Georges Bataille for examples of the kind of writing that made the 'limits of our language tremble'. The kind of experience of Being that Derrida sought to provoke through language was the kind of experience Charles Olson sought to achieve through poetry and artistic experimentation.

Derrida's approach blurs the distinction between philosophy and other forms of writing such as literature. For this reason his work has been attacked by philosophers but embraced by literary theorists, such as William Spanos, who see in it both a new way of reading but also writing texts. The approach has also attracted followers in other disciplines such as law and history that work to accumulate evidence and interpret it. By undermining the traditional boundaries between disciplines and by offering a rigorous critique of the modern conviction in progressive history governed by self-reflexive individuals who act according to an objectively discoverable set of universal ethical rules – something Derrida has done to great effect in *Specters of Marx* (Chapter 21) by deconstructing the idea of 'the end of history' – Derrida's whole approach to philosophy makes it not only poststructuralist but also quintessentially postmodern. And it is to Derrida's contemporary, who introduced the term to a large audience, that we must now turn.

Jean-François Lyotard

Like Derrida, Jean-François Lyotard (1924–98) had a keen interest in the works of Nietzsche and Heidegger. But unlike him Lyotard's principal preoccupation was not so much philosophical as political. From 1956 when he became devoted to the reworking of Marxism by joining *Socialisme ou Barbarie* to his participation in the anarchist group *Le mouvement du 22 mars* in 1968, Lyotard had a deep commitment to politics which in turn influenced his writings. In early works such as *Discours, figure* (1971), *Dérive à partir de Marx et Freud* (1973) and *L'économie libidinale* (1974)[83] Lyotard borrowed ideas from Marxism and psychoanalysis in order to explore the creative role of psychic drives and unarticulated physical experiences. In 1979 he published his Québec government-commissioned 'report on knowledge' *La condition postmoderne* (Chapter 7). It is his best-known work.

The Postmodern Condition was Lyotard's account of 'the condition of knowledge in the most highly developed societies'. Much of what he had to say on information technology and the legitimation of scientific knowledge was unoriginal. But his study was original in the way it extended to society the poststructuralist critique of philosophy. Lyotard believed poststructualism had triumphed over humanism and that this altered the nature of knowledge, requiring it to adopt a new role in a postmodern world.

Lyotard began his work by drawing a distinction between scientific knowledge and other forms of knowledge which he called 'narrative' knowledge. Scientific knowledge, he believed, was in a state of competition and conflict with narrative knowledge and that it was successful in supplanting narrative knowledge, thereby encroaching upon and colonising all areas of life. The apparent triumph of scientific knowledge over narrative knowledge had to do with its ability to appeal to a more encompassing narrative, or 'meta-narrative' as he called it, which embodied the values that comprised the transcendent and universal truths which legitimated modern society, such as universal reason, the progressive course of history, and the universal capacity for individuals to act freely: the values of humanism. This 'triumph' of scientific knowledge, however, was only apparent because Western societies had undergone important changes which, because of the spread of secularism and the breakdown of political authority, gave rise to an 'incredulity towards metanarratives'. It was this that defined the postmodern condition.[84]

Just as Derrida believed that all human activity was reducible to language, so too did Lyotard. Yet whereas Derrida used deconstruction and dissemination as a method and strategy of analysis, Lyotard drew on a different set of concepts. Chief among these was 'language game', a concept he adopted from the later work of the Cambridge-based philosopher Ludwig Wittgenstein (1889–1951) who believed that in using the term and pursuing the line of philosophical enquiry that went with it, he could debunk the metaphysical pursuit of essences (that there is something in common to all entities, which we commonly subsume under a general term) that had dominated philosophy since Plato. According to Wittgenstein this search for essences became ever more firmly rooted within philosophy because of philosophers' preoccupation with the method of science. The scientific method involved 'reducing the explanation of natural phenomena to the smallest possible number of primitive natural laws'. This led to a 'contemptuous attitude towards the particular case', and was 'the real source of metaphysics, [which] leads the philosopher into complete darkness'.[85] The idea of language game revealed that words obtained their meaning in the course of particular activities in which humans were engaged. By examining the role a word 'really plays in our usage of language', by 'looking at the *whole language game*', Wittgenstein believed he could help philosophers out of muddles into which they had unwittingly ventured.[86] This was no longer philosophy on a grand or metaphysical scale, rather it was a form of philosophical therapy.

There were important reasons why Lyotard was drawn to the idea of language game. First, its purpose was to dispel from philosophy the method of science that had for so long dominated philosophers' thinking. Second, it was introduced to undermine the use of generalisation and the unifying treatment of different topics that had led to a 'contemptuous attitude' towards particulars. Third, its introduction showed that philosophers' quest to find metaphysical essences was the result of muddled thinking. Most importantly, however, it stressed a political dimension in which language was characterised in terms of combat: 'to speak is to fight, in the sense of playing, and speech acts fall within the domain of general agonistics'.[87] This was the first principle underlying Lyotard's method as a whole and it was intended to expose the hidden power relations that fashioned and dominated modern thought – the objective of Foucault's archaeology – and to show how seemingly coherent narratives split into a multitude of divergent and incommensurable meanings – the aim of deconstruction.

Lyotard believed that the *grand narratives* which had dominated Western thought had been exposed as powerful ideological forces which organised and fettered individual and social behaviour. He contended too that the seeming coherency of these narratives was illusory. The postmodern condition therefore was characterised by a general scepticism toward grand narratives. Yet within the economically advanced societies of the West Lyotard believed that science retained a privileged and wholly unmerited status. Scientific knowledge was marked by a contradiction in which it 'cannot know and make known that it is the true knowledge without resorting to the other, narrative, kind of knowledge, which from its point of view is no knowledge at all'.[88] Yet this is precisely what it did by having recourse to a higher narrative of legitimation. This higher narrative existed in two forms. The first was philosophical and inherited from German idealism.[89] The second was political and derived from the French

Enlightenment which gave 'the empirical subject the means to emancipate itself from alienation and repression'.[90] By emphasising this contradiction inherent in scientific knowledge, Lyotard showed that science was like all other human activity and therefore part of a web of intertextuality.

Because science was ultimately legitimated by a higher narrative that itself had lost credibility, Lyotard was able to show that there was a general erosion of the legitimacy principle of knowledge itself which led to a 'loosening [of] the weave of the encyclopaedic net in which each science was to find its place'. The result, he concluded, was that the 'classical dividing lines between the various fields of science are thus called into question – disciplines disappear, overlappings occur at the borders between sciences, and from these new territories are born'.[91]

This breaking down of barriers between disciplines was a central characteristic of the kind of postmodernism that featured in the writings of literary critics like Olson and Spanos, and architects such as Venturi and Jencks. But what was different about Lyotard's description of it was that it had now become an objective condition of a postmodern world. Despite this conclusion Lyotard was aware that the disintegration of barriers between disciplines was not total, but evolving. This process had developed sufficiently to become identifiable, but it was hampered in its natural progression by economic, institutional and political interests that combined with modern science to maintain the legitimacy of stable, timeless representations of the world (Chapter 13). These retarding forces, however, were inherently unstable and ineffectual. Modern science would ultimately become supplanted by postmodern science.

> Postmodern science – by concerning itself with such things as undecidables, the limits of precise control, conflicts characterized by incomplete information, 'fracta', catastrophes, and pragmatic paradoxes – is theorizing its own evolution as discontinuous, catastrophic, nonrectifiable, and paradoxical. It is changing the meaning of the word *knowledge*, while expressing how such a change can take place. It is producing not the known, but the unknown. And it suggests a model of legitimation that has nothing to do with maximized performance, but has as its basis difference understood as paralogy.[92]

Lyotard's definition of postmodern science and the terms in which it is legitimated is both striking and, at first glance, mystifying. Upon closer inspection, however, its intention becomes clear. Lyotard believed that the crisis of modern-day knowledge was the result of an outlook that limited human creativity and confined the human spirit. His stress on paralogy indicated the importance he attached to understanding knowledge as springing from psychic drives or aesthetic experiences such as the sublime. His early writings such as *Dérive à partir de Marx et Freud* (1973) and *Economie libidinale* (*Libidinal Economy*) (1974) explored the psychic dimension to human knowledge and conduct. His later works, particularly *Leçons sur l'analytique du sublime* (*Lessons on the Analytic of the Sublime*) examined the role of the sublime in the creation of spontaneous and inexpressible knowledge (Chapters 17 and 19).[93] This shift of emphasis was indicative of a more general shift within postmodern thinking, and the organisation of the chapters and selections that make up this *Reader* reflect this.

Lyotard's definition of postmodern science, however, was not without shortcomings. In particular it justified a host of conceptual abuses documented in Alan Sokal and Jean Bricmont's *Intellectual Impostures*.[94] By contending that the breakdown of barriers between disciplines was a central characteristic of the postmodern condition, Lyotard and other poststructuralists and postmodernists believed they were entitled to employ theorems, symbols and formulae artistically, rhetorically and playfully. But these usages bore no relation to any recognisable science and ultimately were meaningless. The indiscriminate use of mathematical symbols, such as Lacan's use of $\sqrt{-1}$ to denote the erectile organ,[95] was part of a political or intellectual strategy designed to break science's stranglehold on the modern intellect and thereby free the human spirit. But one might justly ask whether such uses suggest that poststructuralists and postmodernists employed these symbols in order to lend credibility to fuzzy thinking. If this is the case, then Lyotard's assertion that scientific knowledge is undergoing a crisis of legitimation seems hollow indeed.

Lyotard's description of postmodern science, with its stress on undecidables, the limits of control, conflict, paradoxes, discontinuity and the production of the unknown, bears striking similarities to Derrida's concept of dissemination, the method of revealing that texts have no decidable meaning. But it was Lyotard's emphasis on the idea of the differend, evoked in *The Postmodern Condition* but only fully theorised in *Le Différend* (1983) (Chapter 15) that the greatest affinities with Derrida exist. Here he adopted Derrida's own idea of *différance*, with its stress on difference, otherness, incommensurability and defferal. Like Derrida, he employed the term to denote 'the unsurpassable boundary of thought and, therefore, the inadequacy of traditional philosophizing'.[96] But whereas Derrida employed it in a purely philosophic context, Lyotard saw its relevance in other areas, most notably politics. Différend acquired a central place in Lyotard's thoughts on the nature of postmodern politics. His description of it bore striking affinities to certain forms of anarchism and avant-gardism.[97] These found their philosophical expression in the work of an avowed follower of Nietzsche: Derrida and Lyotard's contemporary, Gilles Deleuze.

Gilles Deleuze

Gilles Deleuze explored many of the same issues and themes examined by Lyotard and Derrida. But Deleuze's early works were far more traditional in their approach to philosophy than either Lyotard's or Derrida's. Deleuze was not concerned with endorsing declarations about the death of philosophy, and he went so far as to endorse traditional metaphysics. But from his earliest works he was clearly inspired by Nietzsche, and like other poststructuralists and postmodernists he sought to explore ways to free individuals from the constraints of traditional ideas on knowledge. As he and his collaborator, the psychoanalyst and political theorist Félix Guattari (1930–92), declared in their critique of traditional philosophising in *What is Philosophy?*, '(...) thought as such produces something *interesting* when it accedes to the infinite movement that frees it from truth as supposed paradigm and reconquers an immanent power of creation'.[98]

Like Nietzsche and Heidegger before him, Deleuze believed traditional philosophy to be flawed because it was governed by logic and 'the constraints of a recognition of truth in the proposition'.[99] Traditional philosophy functioned like a closed system by assimilating experiences and knowledge through pre-established categories into a fundamental structure, thereby restricting knowledge. In this way philosophy, as an essential life experience, was diminishing rather than enriching. Philosophy needed to be restored to an 'immanent power of creation'. This could be achieved by understanding thought as corresponding to diversity rather than unity, and correspondingly, by thinking upon Being as radically diverse rather than uniquely singular. Deleuze attempted to bring about this change by deploying concepts such as 'multiplicity', 'difference' and 'event'. He drew on the spiritualist philosophy of Henri Bergson (1859–1941), and the ethical writings of Benedict de Spinoza (1632–77), Nietzsche and Heidegger in formulating an ontology, ethics, and politics of multiplicity.[100] But it was with his works *Différance et répétition* (*Difference and Repetition*) (1968) (Chapter 9) and *Logique du sens* (*The Logic of Sense*) (1969) that the concepts of difference and event acquired their full significance.[101] In these works Deleuze contended that Being was not unity, as in traditional metaphysics, but diversity: 'at root to be is not to be one but to be diverse'.[102] The concept of diversity became central to both Deleuze's ethics and his politics, which was worked out in his two principal collaborative works with Guattari, *L'anti-oedipe* (*Anti-Oedipus*) (1972) and *Mille plateaux* (*A Thousand Plateaus*) (1980).[103] These works were fundamental questionings of both traditional philosophic thinking and Freudian and Lacanian psychoanalysis. They were part of a project entitled '*Capitalisme et schizophrénie*' ('Capitalism and schizophrenia'), and they defied, and continue to defy, categorisation. Described as 'consciously dadaist and carnivalesque' in style,[104] they explored a kind of Nietzschean will to power, a radical affirmation of difference or otherness through the evocation of the idea of desire and the creative power of 'schizophrenia'.[105] While 'Capitalism and schizophrenia' employed ideas that were strikingly similar to those employed by Lyotard and Derrida, the emphasis on intensity and unmediated experience associated with Lacan's account of schizophrenia and used in the avant-gardist writings of Philippe Soler and those associated with his journal *Tel quel*, such as the Lacanian analyst and literary theorist Julia Kristeva (b. 1941), acquired a prominent place within postmodern literary theory, architectural postmodernism and postmodern redefinitions of time and space so central to sociology and geography[106] – issues that feature prominently in Fredric Jameson's essay included here (Chapter 14). Deleuze's emphasis on the diversity of Being and his philosophy of difference had important implications for ideas on sexual difference and the reshaping of feminism.

Luce Irigaray

Deleuze and Guattari's philosophy of difference had obvious appeal to feminist writers such as Luce Irigaray (b. 1932) who considers sexual difference as 'one of the major philosophical issues, if not the issue, of our age'.[107] Irigaray has been particularly influential. She has sought to go beyond the focus of traditional feminism which traced sexism to economic, social and political practices. Instead she contends that sexism is at the core of language and philosophical outlooks on the world. Her approach to the issue is psychoanalytic, linguistic and philosophical, reflecting her own intellectual trajectory which began with a degree in psychopathology (1962), a doctorate in linguistics (1968), and a *doctorat d'État* in philosophy (1974). Her interests in psycho-analysis and linguistics are combined in her main focus which is philosophy. In her 1977 *This Sex Which Is Not One* (*Ce sexe qui n'est pas un*) she set out to explore philosophy as the 'discourse [that] sets forth the law for all others, inasmuch as it constitutes the discourse on discourse'.[108] According to Irigaray traditional philosophy reduces all experience to a fixed set of fundamental categories. This judgement was similar to that passed by other poststructuralists and postmodernists. But her work is different in the role it assigns to psychoanalysis in resolving this philosophical problem. Irigaray uses psychoanalysis to expose the deep-rooted and implicit sexism within traditional philosophy which is the root cause to logocentrism and the Platonic metaphysics of sameness or 'presence'.

Though Irigaray is extremely critical of Freudian psychoanalysis and wrote a probing and insightful critique of it in *Speculum of the Other Woman* (1974)[109] she sees in his writings the foundations to a new way of theorising sexual difference based on a distinctive feminine identity which would emerge from the construction of a feminine 'imaginary'. This 'imaginary' is understood much like Barthes' exploding of mythologies, or Derrida's deconstruction, or Lyotard's postmodern science with its potential to 'destabilise', or Deleuze and Guattari's radical politics of difference with its associative power of creation. Its objective is 'jamming the theoretical machinery itself' through 'disruptive *excess*'.[110] This has important implications for language and identity. Irigaray follows Lacan in asserting that language is primary, or as Eric Matthews has said, 'that the construction of an identity is the construction of a language of one's own'.[111] Within a patriarchal society women are denied an identity because society's language excludes them. By deconstructing patriarchal language and philosophy we embark on a total rethinking of the categories that orientate our thought. This enterprise encompasses all branches of philosophy and results in a 'change in our perception and conception of *space-time,* the *inhabiting of places,* and of *containers* or *envelopes of identity'*.[112]

The articulation of feminine 'imaginary' is the essential precursor of a viable ethics. Irigaray sees sexism not only as an epistemological and ontological problem but as an ethical problem too and one whose answer lies not simply in the creation of a separate feminine identity, as some radical feminists would contend, but in the fundamental transformation of male identity too (Chapter 16). This is precisely what is involved in the 'transcendence' of a male world view that has dominated Western philosophy through categories of knowledge and understanding which reduce difference to sameness.

Irigaray's feminist philosophy of difference is exemplary of the radical 'trans-valuation of all values' that postmodern thinkers brought to philosophical reflection. This revolution was to have profound social and political consequences. Not only did it transform outlooks on society and politics, but it altered fundamentally the nature of society and politics. These profound changes were discussed by theorists of post-modernity and the postmodern.

Theorists of postmodernity and the postmodern

At the time Irigaray was rethinking the fundamental concepts of the Western philosophical tradition, and embarking on her critical engagement with its preoccupation with discovering essences and effacing difference, there was a re-evaluation of the fundamental precepts and categories of analysis of sociology and political theory. Much of this work was undertaken by sociologists and political theorists of the left who had come to the conclusion that traditional theoretical models of capital accumulation were no longer adequate to explain changes to systems of production, consumption and accumulation. A total re-thinking of society and culture was needed and this was undertaken. While Roland Barthes had gone some way to achieving this in the domain of culture, and Althusser in politics, their structuralist approaches were subject to serious limitations. A more radical orientation was needed, and this was what was attempted by Jean Baudrillard (b. 1929).

Jean Baudrillard

Jean Baudrillard's 1968 *Le système des objets* was an adaptation of Saussure's structuro-linguistics and Barthes' semiotics to a neo-Marxist analysis of consumer culture.[113] In this work he explored, in the words of Mark Poster, 'the possibility that consumption ha[d] become the chief basis of the social order and of its internal classifications'.[114] Baudrillard's semiotic approach revealed that sign function was the primary function of consumer products. Products' sign function was promoted by a vast advertising network whose sole purpose was to persuade consumers to buy into the lifestyles embodied in the products. He argued that 'what we buy is not so much the product as its sign value, which then differentiates us from others'.[115] This analysis, remarkably prescient of contemporary views on branding,[116] was widened in his 1970 *La société de consommation*.[117] Here he argued that the sign system that governed individual consumption now defined society as a whole. Baudrillard refined this analysis in *Pour une critique de l'économie politique du signe* (1972) which was a radical re-evaluation of Marxist political economy and semiotics.[118] The work's principal thesis was profoundly pessimistic, for what he contended was that within advanced consumer societies the Marxist distinction between use value and exchange value was effaced just as the semiotic distinction between referent and signified had been. The result was that everything was reduced to an effect of sign: 'the process of signification is, at bottom, nothing but a gigantic *simulation model of meaning*'.[119] In this way everything served a vast, infinitely adaptable and omnipotent 'totalitarian economy' or system. Baudrillard's *De la Séduction* (1979), *Simulacres et simulation* (*Simulacra and Simulation*) (1981) and *Les Stratégies fatales* (1983)[120] explored the operations of this system and showed how the utopian impulses that drove the great ideologies of the modern world had failed, being integrated into the system of signs itself. From this nightmare vision of contemporary consumer society there was only one escape and that was the evocation of that which lies outside the sign: the symbolic. Baudrillard's 'symbolic' was that which was inexpressible, something akin to Lyotard's sublime and therefore beyond categorisation. It was the kernel to a political strategy that involved emphasising extremes in order to destabilise the system. But even here Baudrillard held out little hope that the symbolic itself could escape sign control.[121] And he concluded that in this age of information and the Internet we have all become 'victims of a technological determinism that through its unassailable code serves the interest of a hyperreal, meaningless capitalist order'.[122]

Baudrillard's extreme pessimism is not widely endorsed. His critics, and they are legion, have accused him of false reasoning, of moving 'straight on from a descriptive account of certain prevalent conditions in the late twentieth-century lifeworld to a wholesale anti-realist stance which takes those conditions as a pretext for dismantling every last claim to validity or truth'.[123] He himself seemed to give credence to these criticisms with the publication in 1991 of his controversial *The Gulf War Did Not Take Place*[124] and a collection of essays on the state of contemporary society assembled under the title *L'illusion de la fin ou la grève des événements* (*The Illusion of the End*) (1992) (Chapter 20). Nevertheless, his theorisation of simulacrum, simulations, hyper-reality and extreme phenomena had a significant impact on sociological and cultural accounts of postmodernism and would feature in his analyses of the end of the last millennium and the events of September 11, 2001.[125] Baudrillard's early work, particularly his *The System of Objects* and *For a Critique of the Political Economy of the Sign*[126] inspired social and cultural theorists on the left, such as Scott Lash, Mike Featherstone and David Harvey.[127] His writings were extremely important to the Polish-born sociologist and philosopher Zygmunt Bauman (Chapter 18) and to the Marxist cultural critic Fredric Jameson. Because Jameson has so ingeniously integrated many of the ideas we have explored in this introduction, we will conclude it with an analysis of his work.

Fredric Jameson

Jameson's early works, such as *Marxism and Form* (1971), a panoramic and highly original study of the intellectual canon of Western Marxism, *The Prison-House of Language* (1972), his study of linguistic theories, French structuralism and semiotics, and his Marxist literary critical work *The Political Unconscious: Narrative as Socially Symbolic Act* (1981), demonstrated his serious commitment to analysing language and literary works within a social and political context.[128] It is therefore not surprising that his interest in postmodernism should be cultural. Jameson first addressed the issue of postmodernism in a lecture to the Whitney Museum of Contemporary Arts in 1982. The following year he published 'Postmodernism and Consumer Society'. Both lecture and article formed the basis to his now famous 1984 article for the *New Left Review* entitled 'Postmodernism, or, the Cultural Logic of Late Capitalism'.[129] This article equated late capitalism, a concept Jameson explicitly drew from the work of Marxist political economist Ernest Mandel, with postmodernism, a term he borrowed from the architectural writings of Robert Venturi and Charles Jencks.

Jameson set out to show that postmodernism was not some kind of artistic or architectural style that could be used instead of some other style, but was a particular historical era: his definition was historical.[130] His principal thesis was that developments within capitalism, principally the shift within advanced Western economies away from industrial production toward information production, led to the collapse of an independent and critical sphere of culture. Within late capitalism aesthetic production had 'become integrated into commodity production generally'.[131] According to Jameson the age of high modernism (roughly the end of the nineteenth century and the first decades of the twentieth century) saw aesthetic production as a critique of commodity production. Within this period there was a strict distinction between high culture and popular culture. But with the transition from an industrial to a post-industrial or consumer society (1940s and 1950s America and late 1950s Europe) that distinction began to disappear. The postmodern age was that period in which the distinction between high and low culture was effaced. Whereas in high modernism aesthetic production was considered a distinct form and elevated above commodity production, in the postmodern age aesthetic production had become integrated into commodity production. Jameson contended that in post-industrial capitalism, rates of accumulation increased. It appeared that a kind of 'frantic economic urgency of producing fresh waves of ever more novel-seeming goods (from clothing to airplanes), at ever greater rates of turnover, now assigns an increasingly essential structural function and position to aesthetic innovation and experimentation'.[132] He devoted much space to postmodern architecture because it was 'the closest constitutively to the economic'. He evaluated it critically, explaining that it was 'not surprising to find the extraordinary flowering of the new postmodern architecture grounded in the patronage of multinational business, whose expansion and development is strictly contemporaneous with it'.[133] Though his account of postmodern architecture was critical, it was crucial to his discussion on postmodernism generally, not only because it played such an important role in the geographical makeup of cities and the lived environment by shaping individuals' and groups' behaviour,[134] but because it was, as a cultural expression, subject to the exigencies of capitalism, driven to the same outcome as other forms of art.

Jameson contended that commodification of art resulted in its rapid and accelerated reproduction. Combined with the effacement of the distinction between high and low culture the result was that, in the postmodern era, art and other cultural expressions became increasingly superficial, they acquired what he called a 'new depthlessness'. But this depthlessness or flatness was extended to the compression of object or subject and image, of, in semiotic terms, the referent and sign. The result was simulacrum, where image and reality are the same. Postmodern art and culture have no critical edge and are nothing more than a replication of copies. Art and culture in the postmodern world are, just as Baudrillard contends, a vast collection of images.

> Appropriately enough, the cultural of the simulacrum comes to life in a society where exchange value has been generalized to the point at which the very memory of use value is effaced, [such that] the image has become the final form of commodity reification.[135]

The consequence of this is that forms of cultural production such as architecture 'randomly and without principle but with gusto cannibalize all the architectural styles of the past and combine them in overstimulating ensembles'.[136] In cinema 'nostalgia films restructure the whole issue of pastiche and project it into a collective and social level, where the desperate attempt to appropriate a missing past is not refracted through the iron law of fashion change and the emergent ideology of the generation'.[137]

Jameson extended his analysis of postmodern art as simulacrum to 'historical time'. He asserted that the 'past is thereby itself modified'. The consequence is that 'the retrospective dimension indispensable to any vital reorientation of our collective future – has meanwhile itself become a vast collection of images, a multitudinous photographic simulacrum'.[138] The superficiality and randomness of the past ends in the absence of a dominant cultural impulse. The consequence is that postmodern culture and the postmodern world itself is marked by heterogeneity and random difference. In the postmodern era we are unable to offer a coherent account of reality because reality itself is heterogeneous. This description of postmodern reality bore striking resemblances to Deleuze's understanding of thought as corresponding to diversity rather than unity and his conception of Being as radically diverse. But it also had strong affinities to Baudrillard's own gloomy diagnosis on the condition of postmodernity, which was that we are unable to offer a coherent account of reality, because reality itself is heterogeneous. For Jameson, as with Baudrillard, we experience reality not as a coherent whole, or in aesthetic terms, as something marked by symmetry and order, but rather we experience it as something that is overwhelming, constantly changing and always outside our grasp. This is what Lyotard discussed when he equated the postmodern with the sublime. Just as with the sublime experience where our mind is striving, through our faculties of imagination and understanding, to grasp what is unfolding before us, but always fails to do so because of the event's sheer magnitude or energy, so too we experience the postmodern. The result is that 'we are condemned to live in a perpetual, discontinuous, present'. This is a kind of schizophrenia described by Lacan and celebrated as creative by Deleuze and Guattari, which is 'an experience of isolated, disconnected, discontinuous material signifiers which fail to link up into a coherent sequence'.[139] Both within the sublime and the postmodern we experience reality as 'intensity'. The postmodern era is, above all, one of feeling.

As an avowed Marxist Jameson was fascinated by the problems the postmodern condition raised for a politics of agency and emancipation. His essay should be read as an attempt to surmount the crisis of contemporary Marxism. To this end he employed the concept of cognitive mapping which he equated with the more traditional Marxist notion of class-consciousness. This concept, which he borrowed from Kevin Lynch's *The Image of the City*,[140] was seen in relation to alienation within the city 'a space in which people are unable to map (in their minds) either their own positions or the urban totality in which they find themselves'. It was seen as a cure to alienation:

> Disalienation in the traditional city, then, involves the practical reconquest of a sense of place and the construction or reconstruction of an articulated ensemble which can be retained in memory and which the individual subject can map and remap along the moments of mobile, alternative trajectories.[141]

Jameson believed this idea was highly suggestive. When combined with the 'Althusserian (and Lacanian) redefinition of ideology as "the representation of the subject's *Imaginary* relationship to his or her *Real* conditions of existence"',[142] cognitive mapping would 'enable a situational representation on the part of the individual subject to that vaster and properly unrepresentable totality which is the ensemble of society's structures as a whole'.[143] In this idea Jameson sees the kernel of a political postmodernism which 'will have as its vocation the invention and projection of a global cognitive mapping, on a social as well as a spatial scale'.[144] There are serious difficulties with this kind of political postmodernism. Most serious is that it accepts that it is possible to give a scientific account of an objective economic reality (Jameson's endorsement of Mandel's analysis of late capitalism) when such accounts are apparently impossible because they are part of an intellectual and cultural superstructure that cannot be represented because it is always changing and just out of reach of our faculties of imagination and understanding.

Whereas Jameson accepts that the cultural logic of late capitalism is postmodernism, and appropriates many of the core ideas of postmodernists like Baudrillard, Lyotard and Deleuze, he endeavours to integrate these ideas into a new project of class emancipation. It is a thoroughly modern enterprise.

Conclusion

In a curious way Jameson's postmodern politics brings us full circle because it reveals that what postmodernism and modernism share is the deep impulse to liberate the human spirit from intellectual and cultural constraints. Both Michel Foucault, with whom we began our discussion on the crisis of the modern human sciences, and Immanuel Kant, the champion of the Enlightenment, were united in their use of Kant's own motto for the Enlightenment: '*Sapere aude!* Have courage to use your *own* understanding!' This maxim expressed the revolutionary impulse that was to free the human spirit from the shackles of ignorance and prejudice that had fettered it for so long. It spawned a new and feverishly creative era which we associate with modernity. But as the modern age soon exhausted its inventive impulse, modern thought and the modernist movement in the arts reached an impasse. As we have seen throughout this introduction, postmodernism is a serious response to that crisis. It has given birth to a flourishing of new and creative approaches in architecture, as we have already seen, and in areas like the visual arts of painting, photography, cinema and video. But its impact within more formally academic disciplines is no less profound. Within philosophy, as we have seen, postmodernism has overturned the traditional idea of the self-conscious human subject, the Cartesian subject of 'I think therefore I am'. This has had important consequences for literature and literary criticism where the traditional understanding of an author has come in for questioning by, for instance, Julia Kristeva. In history the idea of objectivity or the value of narration have been severely tested by Hayden White and Frank Ankersmit. Conceptions of identity, so central to sociology, psychology, gender studies and post-colonial studies, are undergoing radical changes as has been made clear by Baudrillard and others. Jameson has shown that notions of time and space have been totally altered. According to Edward Soja the implications of this are revolutionary for geography.[145] And in political theory and law, conceptions of power or ideas on justice have been totally thought anew by the followers of Foucault, Irigaray and Lyotard.

Despite these accomplishments postmodern writings continue to provoke deep suspicion. The publication of Alan Sokal and Jean Bricmont's *Intellectual Impostures* in 1997[146] confirmed the prejudices of many who were bewildered by postmodernism and dismissed it as fraudulent and intellectually dishonest. At first sight this opinion seemed to be justified. This was confirmed by the publication in the leading cultural studies journal *Social Text* in 1996 of a hoax article by Sokal entitled 'Transgressing the Boundaries: Towards a Transformative Hermeneutics of Quantum Gravity'. Similarly, the titles of books or essays such as *Double Death, Double Ethics: On Language and the Community of Finitude* or *Counter-Actualization and Body Memories* give rise to dumbfounded responses in uninitiated readers.[147] But as I have tried to show in this introduction, postmodernism's most prominent representative thinkers have probed seriously issues that lie at the heart of the Western philosophical tradition. The selection of essays included in this *Reader* are not only foundational in that they establish the bases to and define the contours of postmodernism, but they are fundamental because they probe issues and seek answers to problems that have bedevilled the greatest minds for centuries. For this reason postmodernism will continue to define our intellectual landscape.

PART ONE

The crisis of modernity and the birth of the concept of postmodernism

THE SELECTIONS THAT MAKE UP this first Part are exemplary of the various interpretations of and responses to the crisis of modernity. The selections by Michel Foucault stress elements of his method and emphasise the importance of genealogy as a way of deracinating deeply rooted power structures that arbitrarily restrict human outlooks and conduct. The theme of transcending restrictive practices and perspectives runs through the remaining selections of this Part with each one representing an example of possible responses.

Michel Foucault's essay 'What is Enlightenment?' (Chapter 1) returns to the eighteenth-century practice of periodical editors who questioned the 'public on problems that did not yet have solutions'. The issue examined in this essay is just such a problem: the crisis of modernity and the impasse of modern thought. Foucault begins his essay by exploring the work of Immanuel Kant, the most famous respondent to the question 'What is Enlightenment?', which appeared in the November 1784 issue of the *Berlinische Monatschrift*. Kant is commonly considered the intellectual champion of the Enlightenment, and so the way he approached the question and his answer to it were of considerable interest to Foucault. Foucault would use Kant's essay as a prelude to his own reflections on the state of contemporary thought.

Kant believed Enlightenment was the antithesis of intellectual immaturity in which individuals obediently accepted the authority of others. Enlightenment was, as Foucault contends, 'defined by a modification of the preexisting relation linking will, authority, and the use of reason'. It represented a revolution, a complete overturning, of the passive condition of individuals' and humanity's stationary predicament. And its motto was, according to Kant, '*Sapere Aude*! Have courage to use your *own* understanding!'[1] Foucault's thesis is that the revolution in thinking brought about by Enlightenment was itself to result in a new form of intellectual dogmatism or immaturity which is what lies at the heart of the current crisis of the human sciences. This was because Enlightenment, as 'a process in which men participate collectively' and 'an act of courage to be accomplished personally', became the attitude of modernity. It was both a 'form of relationship to the present' but also 'a mode of relationship that has to be established with oneself'. The result, as Foucault tells us, was the elaboration of 'a discipline more despotic than the most terrible religions'. Foucault sets out to try and free us from this discipline. His essay, through the use of the archaeological method, seeks to unearth the origins of discipline. He endeavours to undermine it through the use of genealogy. He does this by arguing for a new philosophical ethos of 'limit attitude'. This is not, as he contends, the renewal of the critique so central to humanism, but rather 'a practical critique that takes the form of a possible transgression'. In this way Foucault would pave the way to the elaboration of a new orientation in thought and attitude toward existence: a new and postmodern enlightenment.

As with Foucault's 'What is Enlightenment?', the experience of modernity is the central theme of Marshall Berman's historical and sociological work *All that is Solid Melts into Air: The Experience of Modernity* (the introduction to which, 'Modernity: Yesterday, Today and Tomorrow', is extracted in Chapter 2). Berman argues that modernity incorporates both *modernisation* and *modernism*. Modernisation involves the great discoveries of the physical sciences, industrialisation, demographic upheavals and all the things that contribute to the dramatic social changes of the last two hundred years. Modernism grows out of modernisation. It encompasses visions, values and ideas 'that aim to make men and women the subjects as well as the objects of modernisation'. Berman explores these visions, values and ideas through their artistic, literary and philosophical expressions. This enables him to delineate three phases of modernity. The first begins around the sixteenth century and ends at the end of the eighteenth. This phase is marked by a modernisation whose corresponding visions, values and ideas are barely consciously recognised. Individuals, he contends, 'grope, desperately but half blindly, for an adequate vocabulary' to express the changes that are taking place before them and of which they are a part. The second period begins with the French Revolution in 1789 and ends in the twentieth century. This stage is marked by a public that 'shares the feeling of living in a revolutionary age' but can also 'remember what it is like to live materially and spiritually' in a pre-modern age. The final stage encompasses our own age. Here, the process of modernisation is so rapid and the achievements of modernism so spectacular, that they surpass individuals' psychological and intellectual abilities to make sense of what is taking place around them. The result is that the 'idea of modernity ... loses its capacity to organize and give meaning to people's lives' – a theme that will be reiterated in Part Two by Lyotard in *The Postmodern Condition* and Jameson in *Postmodernism, or, the Cultural Logic of Late Capitalism*.

Berman explores the various reactions to this situation. Unlike Foucault and many of the other thinkers whose works are included in this *Reader*, he rejects structuralist, post-structuralist and postmodernist responses, describing them as 'closed' or isolated from the past and their roots. Because they seek a total rupture with modern thought they become separated from its roots. The result is that they fail to comprehend the crisis of modernity and thereby furnish a way out of it. Instead, Berman contends that we need to reflect on our age in a way that allows us, like the individuals of the second stage of the modern world, to regain knowledge of our own roots. Only in this way may we overcome our current crisis.

While Berman offers a considered and thoroughly modern response to the crisis of modernity by appealing to the kind of grand emancipatory politics of nineteenth-century thinkers like Marx, Foucault explicitly rejects this kind of solution to our current predicament. His 1966 interview with Raymound Bellours entitled 'The Order of Things' is a brilliant, concise and lucid exposition of his archaeological method. As its title suggests, this interview followed the publication of Foucault's *The Order of Things*. It deals with the relation between this work and his earlier publications *Madness and Civilization* (1961) and *The Birth of the Clinic* (1963).[2] Foucault shows that through the archaeological method he was able to pinpoint the origins to the crisis of modern thought, which, he believes, lies with the emergence at the end of the seventeenth century of man, or the subject, which displaced 'the power special to discourse, the verbal order, to represent the order of things'. Foucault's contention is that once 'discourse ceased to play the organizing role that it had in Classical knowledge' the transparency that existed between the order of things 'and the representations that one could have of them', ceased. Authenticity and unmediated experience were lost, and life and experience were now mediated through the concept of the 'subject' or 'man'. This anthropomorphism or humanism spawned a new disciplinary order, which, as we have already seen in our discussion on 'What is Enlightenment?', was internalised within the individual and social psyche. The result, as Foucault had demonstrated in *Madness and Civilization* and *The Birth of the Clinic*, was the incarceration of the insane. But this injustice was perpetrated on the whole of humanity in many different forms. The archaeological method exposes these, but more importantly it reveals instances of resistance to this imposition of discipline. And here Foucault shows that it was Nietzsche who rediscovered that the 'dimension proper to language is incompatible to man'. In Nietzsche's philosophy lies the means by which the yoke of humanism might be broken and authenticity restored. This is explored in the next essay by Foucault, 'Nietzsche, Genealogy, History'.

This text reveals Foucault's profound debt to Nietzsche. It stresses that Nietzsche is the inspiration to Foucault's own conception of genealogy. And it examines genealogy and history. Foucault's principal contention is that traditional history seeks to impose upon the past an order and coherence it does not have. This is but another manifestation of the disciplinary order emerging from humanism. Instead of mapping out the destiny of a people, genealogy reveals the disjunctures in history. It emphasises history's heterogeneity or randomness. This approach to the past Foucault calls 'effective history'. Its ultimate objective in exploring 'the most unpromising places, in what we tend to feel is without history' is, as he states, 'not to discover the roots of our identity, but to commit itself to its dissipation'. For only through the dissipation of our identity, as we saw in the previous essay, can man or the subject be effaced and 'the power special to discourse, the verbal order, to represent the order of things' be restored.

This undertaking was not without its pitfalls. These were exposed by Jacques Derrida in his famous 1967 critique of Foucault's *Madness and Civilization* entitled

'Cogito and the History of Madness'. This essay, reprinted here in full, was a brilliant early example of deconstruction. It was a complex and difficult work, which was to prove especially damaging to Foucault who responded first by suppressing his own preface to the first edition of *Madness and Civilization* and then by writing a blistering attack on Derrida and deconstruction in an essay '*Mon corps, ce papier, ce feu*' ('My Body, This Paper, this Fire') (1971) which later appeared as an appendix to the second (1972) edition of *Madness and Civilization*.[3]

Derrida begins his analysis by focusing on a seemingly insignificant aspect of Foucault's work: a certain passage from the first of Descartes's *Meditations*. This was highly characteristic of Derrida's method of deconstruction. For in focusing on a tiny passage he then proceeds to unravel the whole of Foucault's enterprise by exposing its internal contradictions and weaknesses. He begins by questioning whether Foucault's reading of Descartes's famous '*Cogito, ergo sum*' ('I think, therefore I am') is in fact correct. Foucault understood this expression of hyperbolic doubt as, to quote Christopher Norris, 'an allegory of modern thought in its relation to madness as the feared and excluded "other" of rational discourse'.[4] Derrida offers his own reading of Descartes which leads to a re-evaluation of Foucault. He contends, rightly, that Foucault's intention was to write a history of madness from its own perspective and not from the prespective of philosophic reason. But Derrida shows that this enterprise is doomed to failure. His contention, the essay's principal thesis, is that it is impossible to achieve a perspective outside the discourse of philosophic reason. This thesis had the most profound implications for the whole of Foucault's archaeological method and genealogy. Yet Foucault marshalled a blistering response by meeting Derrida on his own ground and by showing how a close reading of Descartes actually undermined Derrida's own ideas on interpretation. He dismissed Derrida and deconstruction as 'a little pedagogy historically well determined which, in a very visible way, we are dealing with. A pedagogy which teaches the student that there is nothing outside the text (...); that it is therefore not necessary to search elsewhere. Pedagogy which inversely gives to the master's voice that sovereignty without limit which permits it to restate the text indefinitely.'[5] Foucault rejected deconstruction because it was incapable of an active engagement with the politics of knowledge.

It was exactly this kind of engagement that motivated Gilles Deleuze's return to Nietzsche as the the speculative teacher of 'becoming', 'multiplicity' and 'chance'. For according to Deleuze, Nietzsche's philosophy is pure affirmation because it is the philosophy of difference. Deleuze's reading of Nietzsche represents not only an endorsement of Foucault's 'effective history' and genealogy, but also of Derrida's deconstruction. This attempt to unite elements of both approaches would prove fundamental to the intellectual engagements of a prescriptive postmodernism; the object of Part Two.

Chapter 1

Michel Foucault

■ **WHAT IS ENLIGHTENMENT?** in Paul Rabinow (ed.), *The Foucault Reader,* Catherine Porter trans., London: Penguin Books, 1984

I

TODAY WHEN A PERIODICAL asks its readers a question, it does so in order to collect opinions on some subject about which everyone has an opinion already; there is not much likelihood of learning anything new. In the eighteenth century, editors preferred to question the public on problems that did not yet have solutions. I don't know whether or not that practice was more effective; it was unquestionably more entertaining.

In any event, in line with this custom, in November 1784 a German periodical, *Berlinische Monatschrift*, published a response to the question: *Was ist Aufklärung?* (What is Enlightenment?) And the respondent was Kant.

A minor text, perhaps. But it seems to me that it marks the discreet entrance into the history of thought of a question that modern philosophy has not been capable of answering, but that it has never managed to get rid of, either. And one that has been repeated in various forms for two centuries now. From Hegel through Nietzsche or Max Weber to Horkheimer or Habermas, hardly any philosophy has failed to confront this same question, directly or indirectly. What, then, is this event that is called the *Aufklärung* and that has determined, at least in part, what we are, what we think, and what we do today? Let us imagine that the *Berlinische Monatschrift* still exists and that it is asking its readers the question: What is modern philosophy? Perhaps we could respond with an echo: modern philosophy is the philosophy that is attempting to answer the question raised so imprudently two centuries ago: *Was ist Aufklärung?*

Let us linger a few moments over Kant's text. It merits attention for several reasons.

1 To this same question, Moses Mendelssohn had also replied in the same journal, just two months earlier. But Kant had not seen Mendelssohn's text when he wrote his. To be sure, the encounter of the German philosophical movement with the new develop-

ment of Jewish culture does not date from this precise moment. Mendelssohn had been at that crossroads for thirty years or so, in company with Lessing. But up to this point it had been a matter of making a place for Jewish culture within German thought – which Lessing had tried to do in *Die Juden* – or else of identifying problems common to Jewish thought and to German philosophy; this is what Mendelssohn had done in his *Phädon; oder, Über die Unsterblichkeit der Seele*. With the two texts published in the *Berlinische Monatschrift*, the German Aufklärung and the Jewish Haskala recognize that they belong to the same history; they are seeking to identify the common processes from which they stem. And it is perhaps a way of announcing the acceptance of a common destiny – we now know to what drama that was to lead.

2   But there is more. In itself and within the Christian tradition, Kant's text poses a new problem.

It was certainly not the first time that philosophical thought had sought to reflect on its own present. But, speaking schematically, we may say that this reflection had until then taken three main forms.

- The present may be represented as belonging to a certain era of the world, distinct from the others through some inherent characteristics, or separated from the others by some dramatic event. Thus, in Plato's *The Statesman* the interlocutors recognize that they belong to one of those revolutions of the world in which the world is turning backwards, with all the negative consequences that may ensue.
- The present may be interrogated in an attempt to decipher in it the heralding signs of a forthcoming event. Here we have the principle of a kind of historical hermeneutics of which Augustine might provide an example.
- The present may also be analyzed as a point of transition toward the dawning of a new world. That is what Vico describes in the last chapter of *La Scienza Nuova*; what he sees "today" is "a complete humanity … spread abroad through all nations, for a few great monarchs rule over this world of peoples"; it is also "Europe … radiant with such humanity that it abounds in all the good things that make for the happiness of human life."[1]

Now the way Kant poses the question of *Aufklärung* is entirely different: it is neither a world era to which one belongs, nor an event whose signs are perceived, nor the dawning of an accomplishment. Kant defines *Aufklärung* in an almost entirely negative way, as an *Ausgang*, an "exit," a "way out." In his other texts on history, Kant occasionally raises questions of origin or defines the internal teleology of a historical process. In the text on *Aufklärung*, he deals with the question of contemporary reality alone. He is not seeking to understand the present on the basis of a totality or of a future achievement. He is looking for a difference: What difference does today introduce with respect to yesterday?

3   I shall not go into detail here concerning this text, which is not always very clear despite its brevity. I should simply like to point out three or four features that seem to me important if we are to understand how Kant raised the philosophical question of the present day.

Kant indicates right away that the "way out" that characterizes Enlightenment is a process that releases us from the status of "immaturity." And by "immaturity," he means a certain state of our will that makes us accept someone else's authority to lead us in areas where the use of reason is called for. Kant gives three examples: we are in a state of "immaturity" when a book takes the place of our understanding, when a spiritual director takes the place of our conscience, when a doctor decides for us what our diet is to be. (Let us note in passing that the register of these three critiques is easy to recognize, even though the text does not make it explicit.) In any case, Enlightenment is defined by a modification of the preexisting relation linking will, authority, and the use of reason.

We must also note that this way out is presented by Kant in a rather ambiguous manner. He characterizes it as a phenomenon, an ongoing process; but he also presents it as a task and an obligation. From the very first paragraph, he notes that man himself is responsible for his immature status. Thus it has to be supposed that he will be able to escape from it only by a change that he himself will bring about in himself. Significantly, Kant says that this Enlightenment has a *Wahlspruch*: now a *Wahlspruch* is a heraldic device, that is, a distinctive feature by which one can be recognized, and it is also a motto, an instruction that one gives oneself and proposes to others. What, then, is this instruction? *Aude sapere*: "dare to know," "have the courage, the audacity, to know."[2] Thus Enlightenment must be considered both as a process in which men participate collectively and as an act of courage to be accomplished personally. Men are at once elements and agents of a single process. They may be actors in the process to the extent that they participate in it; and the process occurs to the extent that men decide to be its voluntary actors.

A third difficulty appears here in Kant's text, in his use of the word "mankind," *Menschheit*. The importance of this word in the Kantian conception of history is well known. Are we to understand that the entire human race is caught up in the process of Enlightenment? In that case, we must imagine Enlightenment as a historical change that affects the political and social existence of all people on the face of the earth. Or are we to understand that it involves a change affecting what constitutes the humanity of human beings? But the question then arises of knowing what this change is. Here again, Kant's answer is not without a certain ambiguity. In any case, beneath its appearance of simplicity, it is rather complex.

Kant defines two essential conditions under which mankind can escape from its immaturity. And these two conditions are at once spiritual and institutional, ethical and political.

The first of these conditions is that the realm of obedience and the realm of the use of reason be clearly distinguished. Briefly characterizing the immature status, Kant invokes the familiar expression: "Don't think, just follow orders"; such is, according to him, the form in which military discipline, political power, and religious authority are usually exercised. Humanity will reach maturity when it is no longer required to obey, but when men are told: "Obey, and you will be able to reason as much as you like." We must note that the German word used here is *räsonieren*; this word, which is also used in the *Critiques*, does not refer to just any use of reason, but to a use of reason in which reason has no other end but itself: *räsonieren* is to reason for reasoning's sake. And Kant gives examples, these too being perfectly trivial in appearance: paying one's taxes, while being able to argue as much as one likes about the system of taxation, would be characteristic of the mature state; or again, taking responsibility for parish service, if one is a pastor, while reasoning freely about religious dogmas.

We might think that there is nothing very different here from what has been meant, since the sixteenth century, by freedom of conscience: the right to think as one pleases so long as one obeys as one must. Yet it is here that Kant brings into play another distinction, and in a rather surprising way. The distinction he introduces is between the private and public uses of reason. But he adds at once that reason must be free in its public use, and must be submissive in its private use. Which is, term for term, the opposite of what is ordinarily called freedom of conscience.

But we must be somewhat more precise. What constitutes, for Kant, this private use of reason? In what area is it exercised? Man, Kant says, makes a private use of reason when he is "a cog in a machine"; that is, when he has a role to play in society and jobs to do: to be a soldier, to have taxes to pay, to be in charge of a parish, to be a civil servant, all this makes the human being a particular segment of society; he finds himself thereby placed in a circumscribed position, where he has to apply particular rules and pursue particular ends. Kant does not ask that people practice a blind and foolish obedience, but that they adapt the use they make of their reason to these determined circumstances; and reason must then be subjected to the particular ends in view. Thus there cannot be, here, any free use of reason.

On the other hand, when one is reasoning only in order to use one's reason, when one is reasoning as a reasonable being (and not as a cog in a machine), when one is reasoning as a member of reasonable humanity, then the use of reason must be free and public. Enlightenment is thus not merely the process by which individuals would see their own personal freedom of thought guaranteed. There is Enlightenment when the universal, the free, and the public uses of reason are superimposed on one another.

Now this leads us to a fourth question that must be put to Kant's text. We can readily see how the universal use of reason (apart from any private end) is the business of the subject himself as an individual; we can readily see, too, how the freedom of this use may be assured in a purely negative manner through the absence of any challenge to it; but how is a public use of that reason to be assured? Enlightenment, as we see, must not be conceived simply as a general process affecting all humanity; it must not be conceived only as an obligation prescribed to individuals: it now appears as a political problem. The question, in any event, is that of knowing how the use of reason can take the public form that it requires, how the audacity to know can be exercised in broad daylight, while individuals are obeying as scrupulously as possible. And Kant, in conclusion, proposes to Frederick II, in scarcely veiled terms, a sort of contract – what might be called the contract of rational despotism with free reason: the public and free use of autonomous reason will be the best guarantee of obedience, on condition, however, that the political principle that must be obeyed itself be in conformity with universal reason.

Let us leave Kant's text here. I do not by any means propose to consider it as capable of constituting an adequate description of Enlightenment; and no historian, I think, could be satisfied with it for an analysis of the social, political, and cultural transformations that occurred at the end of the eighteenth century.

Nevertheless, notwithstanding its circumstantial nature, and without intending to give it an exaggerated place in Kant's work, I believe that it is necessary to stress the connection that exists between this brief article and the three *Critiques*. Kant in fact describes Enlightenment as the moment when humanity is going to put its own reason to use, without subjecting itself to any authority; now it is precisely at this moment that the critique is necessary, since its role is that of defining the conditions under which the use of reason is legitimate in order to determine what can be known, what must be done, and what may be hoped. Illegitimate uses of reason are what give rise to dogmatism and heteronomy, along with illusion; on the other hand, it is when the legitimate use of reason has been clearly defined in its principles that its autonomy can be assured. The critique is, in a sense, the handbook of reason that has grown up in Enlightenment; and, conversely, the Enlightenment is the age of the critique.

It is also necessary, I think, to underline the relation between this text of Kant's and the other texts he devoted to history. These latter, for the most part, seek to define the internal teleology of time and the point toward which history of humanity is moving. Now the analysis of Enlightenment, defining this history as humanity's passage to its adult status, situates contemporary reality with respect to the overall movement and its basic directions. But at the same time, it shows how, at this very moment, each individual is responsible in a certain way for that overall process.

The hypothesis I should like to propose is that this little text is located in a sense at the crossroads of critical reflection and reflection on history. It is a reflection by Kant on the contemporary status of his own enterprise. No doubt it is not the first time that a philosopher has given his reasons for undertaking his work at a particular moment. But it seems to me that it is the first time that a philosopher has connected in this way, closely and from the inside, the significance of his work with respect to knowledge, a reflection on history and a particular analysis of the specific moment at which he is writing and because of which he is writing. It is in the reflection on "today" as difference in history and as motive for a particular philosophical task that the novelty of this text appears to me to lie.

And, by looking at it in this way, it seems to me we may recognize a point of departure: the outline of what one might call the attitude of modernity.

II

I know that modernity is often spoken of as an epoch, or at least as a set of features characteristic of an epoch; situated on a calendar, it would be preceded by a more or less naive or archaic premodernity, and followed by an enigmatic and troubling "postmodernity." And then we find ourselves asking whether modernity constitutes the sequel to the Enlightenment and its development, or whether we are to see it as a rupture or a deviation with respect to the basic principles of the eighteenth century.

Thinking back on Kant's text, I wonder whether we may not envisage modernity rather as an attitude than as a period of history. And by "attitude," I mean a mode of relating to contemporary reality; a voluntary choice made by certain people; in the end, a way of thinking and feeling; a way, too, of acting and behaving that at one and the same time marks a relation of belonging and presents itself as a task. A bit, no doubt, like what the Greeks called an ethos. And consequently, rather than seeking to distinguish the "modern era" from the "premodern" or "postmodern," I think it would be more useful to try to find out how the attitude of modernity, ever since its formation, has found itself struggling with attitudes of "countermodernity."

To characterize briefly this attitude of modernity, I shall take an almost indispensable example, namely, Baudelaire; for his consciousness of modernity is widely recognized as one of the most acute in the nineteenth century.

1   Modernity is often characterized in terms of consciousness of the discontinuity of time: a break with tradition, a feeling of novelty, of vertigo in the face of the passing moment. And this is indeed what Baudelaire seems to be saying when he defines modernity as "the ephemeral, the fleeting, the contingent."[3] But, for him, being modern does not lie in recognizing and accepting this perpetual movement; on the contrary, it lies in adopting a certain attitude with respect to this movement; and this deliberate, difficult attitude consists in recapturing something eternal that is not beyond the present instant, nor behind it, but within it. Modernity is distinct from fashion, which does no more than call into question the course of time; modernity is the attitude that makes it possible to grasp the "heroic" aspect of the present moment. Modernity is not a phenomenon of sensitivity to the fleeting present; it is the will to "heroize" the present.

I shall restrict myself to what Baudelaire says about the painting of his contemporaries. Baudelaire makes fun of those painters who, finding nineteenth-century dress excessively ugly, want to depict nothing but ancient togas. But modernity in painting does not consist, for Baudelaire, in introducing black clothing onto the canvas. The modern painter is the one who can show the dark frock-coat as "the necessary costume of our time," the one who knows how to make manifest, in the fashion of the day, the essential, permanent, obsessive relation that our age entertains with death. "The dress-coat and frock-coat not only possess their political beauty, which is an expression of universal equality, but also their poetic beauty, which is an expression of the public soul — an immense cortège of undertaker's mutes (mutes in love, political mutes, bourgeois mutes ...). We are each of us celebrating some funeral."[4] To designate this attitude of modernity, Baudelaire sometimes employs a litotes that is highly significant because it is presented in the form of a precept: "You have no right to despise the present."

2   This heroization is ironical, needless to say. The attitude of modernity does not treat the passing moment as sacred in order to try to maintain or perpetuate it. It certainly does not involve harvesting it as a fleeting and interesting curiosity. That would be what Baudelaire would call the spectator's posture. The *flâneur*, the idle, strolling spectator, is satisfied to keep his eyes open, to pay attention and to build up a storehouse of memories. In opposition to the *flâneur*, Baudelaire describes the man of modernity: "Away he goes, hurrying, searching. ... Be very sure that this man ... — this solitary, gifted with an active imagination, ceaselessly journeying across the great human desert — has an aim loftier than that of a mere *flâneur*, an aim more general, something other than the fugitive pleasure of circumstance. He is looking for that quality which you must allow me to call 'modernity.' ... He makes it his business to extract from fashion whatever element it may contain of poetry within history." As an example of modernity, Baudelaire cites the artist Constantin Guys. In appearance a spectator, a collector of curiosities, he remains "the last to linger wherever there can be a glow of light, an echo of poetry, a quiver of life or a chord of music; wherever a passion can pose before him, wherever natural man and conventional man display themselves in a strange beauty, wherever the sun lights up the swift joys of the *depraved animal*."[5]

But let us make no mistake. Constantin Guys is not a *flâneur*; what makes him the modern painter *par excellence* in Baudelaire's eyes is that, just when the whole world is falling asleep, he begins to work, and he transfigures that world. His transfiguration does not entail an annulling of reality, but a difficult interplay between the truth of what is real and the exercise of freedom; "natural" things become "more than natural," "beautiful" things become "more than beautiful," and individual objects appear "endowed with an impulsive life like the soul of [their] creator."[6] For the attitude of modernity, the high value of the present is indissociable from a desperate eagerness to imagine it, to imagine it otherwise than it is, and to transform it not by destroying it but by grasping it in what it is. Baudelairean modernity is an exercise in which extreme attention to what is real is confronted with the practice of a liberty that simultaneously respects this reality and violates it.

3 However, modernity for Baudelaire is not simply a form of relationship to the present; it is also a mode of relationship that has to be established with oneself. The deliberate attitude of modernity is tied to an indispensable asceticism. To be modern is not to accept oneself as one is in the flux of the passing moments; it is to take oneself as object of a complex and difficult elaboration: what Baudelaire, in the vocabulary of his day, calls *dandysme*. Here I shall not recall in detail the well-known passages on "vulgar, earthy, vile nature"; on man's indispensable revolt against himself; on the "doctrine of elegance" which imposes "upon its ambitious and humble disciples" a discipline more despotic than the most terrible religions; the pages, finally, on the asceticism of the dandy who makes of his body, his behavior, his feelings and passions, his very existence, a work of art. Modern man, for Baudelaire, is not the man who goes off to discover himself, his secrets and his hidden truth; he is the man who tries to invent himself. This modernity does not "liberate man in his own being"; it compels him to face the task of producing himself.

4 Let me add just one final word. This ironic heroization of the present, this transfiguring play of freedom with reality, this ascetic elaboration of the self – Baudelaire does not imagine that these have any place in society itself, or in the body politic. They can only be produced in another, a different place, which Baudelaire calls art.

I do not pretend to be summarizing in these few lines either the complex historical event that was the Enlightenment, at the end of the eighteenth century, or the attitude of modernity in the various guises it may have taken on during the last two centuries.

I have been seeking, on the one hand, to emphasize the extent to which a type of philosophical interrogation – one that simultaneously problematizes man's relation to the present, man's historical mode of being, and the constitution of the self as an autonomous subject – is rooted in the Enlightenment. On the other hand, I have been seeking to stress that the thread that may connect us with the Enlightenment is not faithfulness to doctrinal elements, but rather the permanent reactivation of an attitude – that is, of a philosophical ethos that could be described as a permanent critique of our historical era. I should like to characterize this ethos very briefly.

A *Negatively*

1 This ethos implies, first, the refusal of what I like to call the "blackmail" of the Enlightenment. I think that the Enlightenment, as a set of political, economic, social, institutional, and cultural events on which we still depend in large part, constitutes a privileged domain for analysis. I also think that as an enterprise for linking the progress of truth and the history of liberty in a bond of direct relation, it formulated a philosophical question that remains for us to consider. I think, finally, as I have tried to show with reference to Kant's text, that it defined a certain manner of philosophizing.

But that does not mean that one has to be "for" or "against" the Enlightenment. It even means precisely that one has to refuse everything that might present itself in the form of a simplistic and authoritarian alternative: you either accept the Enlightenment and remain within the tradition of its rationalism (this is considered a positive term by some and used by others, on the contrary, as a reproach); or else you criticize the Enlightenment and then try to escape from its principles of rationality (which may be seen once again as good or bad). And we do not break free of this blackmail by introducing "dialectical" nuances while seeking to determine what good and bad elements there may have been in the Enlightenment.

We must try to proceed with the analysis of ourselves as beings who are historically determined, to a certain extent, by the Enlightenment. Such an analysis implies a series of historical inquiries that are as precise as possible; and these inquiries will not be oriented retrospectively toward the "essential kernel of rationality" that can be found in the Enlightenment and that would have to be preserved in any event; they will be oriented toward the "contemporary limits of the necessary," that is, toward what is not or is no longer indispensable for the constitution of ourselves as autonomous subjects.

2 This permanent critique of ourselves has to avoid the always too facile confusions between humanism and Enlightenment.

We must never forget that the Enlightenment is an event, or a set of events and complex historical processes, that is located at a certain point in the development of European societies. As such, it includes elements of social transformation, types of political institution, forms of knowledge, projects of rationalization of knowledge and practices, technological mutations that are very difficult to sum up in a word, even if many of these phenomena remain important today. The one I have pointed out and that seems to me to have been at the basis of an entire form of philosophical reflection concerns only the mode of reflective relation to the present.

Humanism is something entirely different. It is a theme or, rather, a set of themes that have reappeared on several occasions, over time, in European societies; these themes, always tied to value judgments, have obviously varied greatly in their content, as well as in the values they have preserved. Furthermore, they have served as a critical principle of differentiation. In the seventeenth century, there was a humanism that presented itself as a critique of Christianity or of religion in general; there was a Christian humanism opposed to an ascetic and much more theocentric humanism. In the nineteenth century, there was a suspicious humanism, hostile and critical toward science, and another that, to the contrary, placed its hope in that same science. Marxism has been a humanism; so have existentialism and personalism; there was a time when people supported the humanistic values represented by National Socialism, and when the Stalinists themselves said they were humanists.

From this, we must not conclude that everything that has ever been linked with humanism is to be rejected, but that the humanistic thematic is in itself too supple, too diverse, too inconsistent to serve as an axis for reflection. And it is a fact that, at least since the seventeenth century, what is called humanism has always been obliged to lean on certain conceptions of man borrowed from religion, science, or politics. Humanism serves to color and to justify the conceptions of man to which it is, after all, obliged to take recourse.

Now, in this connection, I believe that this thematic, which so often recurs and which always depends on humanism, can be opposed by the principle of a critique and a permanent creation of ourselves in our autonomy: that is, a principle that is at the heart of the historical consciousness that the Enlightenment has of itself. From this standpoint, I am inclined to see Enlightenment and humanism in a state of tension rather than identity.

In any case, it seems to me dangerous to confuse them; and further, it seems historically inaccurate. If the question of man, of the human species, of the humanist, was important throughout the eighteenth century, this is very rarely, I believe, because the Enlightenment considered itself a humanism. It is worthwhile, too, to note that throughout the nineteenth century, the historiography of sixteenth-century humanism, which was so important for people like Saint-Beuve or Burckhardt, was always distinct from and sometimes explicitly opposed to the Enlightenment and the eighteenth century. The nineteenth century had a tendency to oppose the two, at least as much as to confuse them.

In any case, I think that, just as we must free ourselves from the intellectual blackmail of "being for or against the Enlightenment," we must escape from the historical and moral confusionism that mixes the theme of humanism with the question of the Enlightenment. An analysis of their complex relations in the course of the last two centuries would be a worthwhile project, an important one if we are to bring some measure of clarity to the consciousness that we have of ourselves and of our past.

B   Positively

Yet while taking these precautions into account, we must obviously give a more positive content to what may be a philosophical ethos consisting in a critique of what we are saying, thinking, and doing, through a historical ontology of ourselves.

1   This philosophical ethos may be characterized as a *limit attitude*. We are not talking about a gesture of rejection. We have to move beyond the outside-inside alternative; we have to be at the frontiers. Criticism indeed consists of analyzing and reflecting upon limits. But if the Kantian question was that of knowing what limits knowledge has to renounce transgressing, it seems to me that the critical question today has to be turned back into a positive one: in what is given to us as universal, necessary, obligatory, what place is occupied by whatever is singular, contingent, and the product of arbitrary constraints? The point, in brief, is to transform the critique conducted in the form of necessary limitation into a practical critique that takes the form of a possible transgression.

This entails an obvious consequence: that criticism is no longer going to be practiced in the search for formal structures with universal value, but rather as a historical investigation into the events that have led us to constitute ourselves and to recognize ourselves as subjects of what we are doing, thinking, saying. In that sense, this criticism is not transcendental, and its goal is not that of making a metaphysics possible: it is genealogical in its design and archaeological in its method. Archaeological – and not transcendental – in the sense that it will not seek to identify the universal structures of all knowledge or of all possible moral action, but will seek to treat the instances of discourse that articulate what we think, say, and do as so many historical events. And this critique will be genealogical in the sense that it will not deduce from the form of what we are what it is impossible for us to do and to know; but it will separate out, from the contingency that has made us what we are, the possibility of no longer being, doing, or thinking what we are, do, or think. It is not seeking to make possible a metaphysics that has finally become a science; it is seeking to give new impetus, as far and wide as possible, to the undefined work of freedom.

2   But if we are not to settle for the affirmation or the empty dream of freedom, it seems to me that this historico-critical attitude must also be an experimental one. I mean that this work done at the limits of ourselves must, on the one hand, open up a realm of historical inquiry and, on the other, put itself to the test of reality, of contemporary reality, both to grasp the points where change is possible and desirable, and to determine the precise form this change should take. This means that the historical ontology of ourselves must turn away from all projects that claim to be global or radical. In fact we know from experience that the claim to escape from the system of contemporary reality so as to produce the overall programs of another society, of another way of thinking, another culture, another vision of the world, has led only to the return of the most dangerous traditions.

I prefer the very specific transformations that have proved to be possible in the last twenty years in a certain number of areas that concern our ways of being and thinking, relations to authority, relations between the sexes, the way in which we perceive insanity or illness; I prefer even these partial transformations that have been made in the correlation of historical analysis and the practical attitude, to the programs for a new man that the worst political systems have repeated throughout the twentieth century.

I shall thus characterize the philosophical ethos appropriate to the critical ontology of ourselves as a historico-practical test of the limits that we may go beyond, and thus as work carried out by ourselves upon ourselves as free beings.

3   Still, the following objection would no doubt be entirely legitimate: if we limit ourselves to this type of always partial and local inquiry or test, do we not run the risk of letting ourselves be determined by more general structures of which we may well not be conscious, and over which we may have no control?

To this, two responses. It is true that we have to give up hope of ever acceding to a point of view that could give us access to any complete and definitive knowledge of what may constitute our historical limits. And from this point of view the theoretical and practical experience that we have of our limits and of the possibility of moving beyond them is always limited and determined; thus we are always in the position of beginning again.

But that does not mean that no work can be done except in disorder and contingency. The work in question has its generality, its systematicity, its homogeneity, and its stakes.

(a) *Its Stakes*

These are indicated by what might be called "the paradox of the relations of capacity and power." We know that the great promise or the great hope of the eighteenth century, or a part of the eighteenth century, lay in the simultaneous and proportional growth of individuals with respect to one another. And, moreover, we can see that throughout the entire history of Western societies (it is perhaps here that the root of their singular historical destiny is located – such a peculiar destiny, so different from the others in its trajectory and so universalizing, so dominant with respect to the others), the acquisition of capabilities and the struggle for freedom have constituted permanent elements. Now the relations between the growth of capabilities and the growth of autonomy are not as simple as the eighteenth century may have believed. And we have been able to see what forms of power relation were conveyed by various technologies (whether we are speaking of productions with economic aims, or institutions whose goal is social regulation, or of techniques of communication): disciplines, both collective and individual, procedures of normalization exercised in the name of the power of the state, demands of society or of population zones, are examples. What is at stake, then, is this: How can the growth of capabilities be disconnected from the intensification of power relations?

(b) *Homogeneity*

This leads to the study of what could be called "practical systems." Here we are taking as a homogeneous domain of reference not the representations that men give of themselves, not the conditions that determine them without their knowledge, but rather what they do and the way they do it. That is, the forms of rationality that organize their ways of doing things (this might be called the technological aspect) and the freedom with which they act within these practical systems, reacting to what others do, modifying the rules of the game, up to a certain point (this might be called the strategic side of these practices). The homogeneity of these historico-critical analyses is thus ensured by this realm of practices, with their technological side and their strategic side.

(c) *Systematicity*

These practical systems stem from three broad areas: relations of control over things, relations of action upon others, relations with oneself. This does not mean that each of these three areas is completely foreign to the others. It is well known that control over things is mediated by relations with others; and relations with others in turn always entail relations with oneself, and vice versa. But we have three axes whose specificity and whose interconnections have to be analyzed: the axis of knowledge, the axis of power, the axis of ethics. In other terms, the historical ontology of ourselves has to answer an open series of questions; it has to make an indefinite number of inquiries which may be multiplied and specified as much as we like, but which will all address the questions systematized as follows: How are we constituted as subjects of our own knowledge? How are we constituted as subjects who exercise or submit to power relations? How are we constituted as moral subjects of our own actions?

(d)   Generality

Finally, these historico-critical investigations are quite specific in the sense that they always bear upon a material, an epoch, a body of determined practices and discourses. And yet, at least at the level of the Western societies from which we derive, they have their generality, in the sense that they have continued to recur up to our time: for example, the problem of the relationship between sanity and insanity, or sickness and health, or crime and the law; the problem of the role of sexual relations; and so on.

But by evoking this generality, I do not mean to suggest that it has to be retraced in its metahistorical continuity over time, nor that its variations have to be pursued. What must be grasped is the extent to which what we know of it, the forms of power that are exercised in it, and the experience that we have in it of ourselves constitute nothing but determined historical figures, through a certain form of problematization that defines objects, rules of action, modes of relation to oneself. The study of [modes of] problematization (that is, of what is neither an anthropological constant nor a chronological variation) is thus the way to analyze questions of general import in their historically unique form.

A brief summary, to conclude and to come back to Kant.

I do not know whether we will ever reach mature adulthood. Many things in our experience convince us that the historical event of the Enlightenment did not make us mature adults, and we have not reached that stage yet. However, it seems to me that a meaning can be attributed to that critical interrogation on the present and on ourselves which Kant formulated by reflecting on the Enlightenment. It seems to me that Kant's reflection is even a way of philosophizing that has not been without its importance or effectiveness during the last two centuries. The critical ontology of ourselves has to be considered not, certainly, as a theory, a doctrine, nor even as a permanent body of knowledge that is accumulating; it has to be conceived as an attitude, an ethos, a philosophical life in which the critique of what we are is at one and the same time the historical analysis of the limits that are imposed on us and an experiment with the possibility of going beyond them.

This philosophical attitude has to be translated into the labor of diverse inquiries. These inquiries have their methodological coherence in the at once archaeological and genealogical study of practices envisaged simultaneously as a technological type of rationality and as strategic games of liberties; they have their theoretical coherence in the definition of the historically unique forms in which the generalities of our relations to things, to others, to ourselves, have been problematized. They have their practical coherence in the care brought to the process of putting historico-critical reflection to the test of concrete practices. I do not know whether it must be said today that the critical task still entails faith in Enlightenment; I continue to think that this task requires work on our limits, that is, a patient labor giving form to our impatience for liberty.

Chapter 2

Marshall Berman

■ from INTRODUCTION – MODERNITY: YESTERDAY,
TODAY AND TOMORROW in *All That is Solid Melts into Air:
The Experience of Modernity,* London: Verso, 1983

THERE IS A MODE OF VITAL EXPERIENCE – experience of space and time, of the self and others, of life's possibilities and perils – that is shared by men and women all over the world today. I will call this body of experience "modernity." To be modern is to find ourselves in an environment that promises us adventure, power, joy, growth, transformation of ourselves and the world – and, at the same time, that threatens to destroy everything we have, everything we know, everything we are. Modern environments and experiences cut across all boundaries of geography and ethnicity, of class and nationality, of religion and ideology: in this sense, modernity can be said to unite all mankind. But it is a paradoxical unity, a unity of disunity: it pours us all into a maelstrom of perpetual disintegration and renewal, of struggle and contradiction, of ambiguity and anguish. To be modern is to be part of a universe in which, as Marx said, "all that is solid melts into air."

People who find themselves in the midst of this maelstrom are apt to feel that they are the first ones, and maybe the only ones, to be going through it; this feeling has engendered numerous nostalgic myths of pre-modern Paradise Lost. In fact, however, great and ever-increasing numbers of people have been going through it for close to five hundred years. Although most of these people have probably experienced modernity as a radical threat to all their history and traditions, it has, in the course of five centuries, developed a rich history and a plenitude of traditions of its own. I want to explore and chart these traditions, to understand the ways in which they can nourish and enrich our own modernity, and the ways in which they may obscure or impoverish our sense of what modernity is and what it can be.

The maelstrom of modern life has been fed from many sources: great discoveries in the physical sciences, changing our images of the universe and our place in it; the industrialization of production, which transforms scientific knowledge into technology, creates new human environments and destroys old ones, speeds up the whole tempo of life, generates new forms of corporate power and class struggle; immense demographic upheavals, severing millions of people from their ancestral habitats, hurtling them halfway across the world into new lives; rapid and often cataclysmic urban growth; systems of mass communication, dynamic in their development, enveloping and binding together the most diverse people and societies; increasingly powerful national states, bureaucratically structured and operated, constantly striving to expand their powers; mass social movements of people, and peoples, challenging their political and economic rulers, striving to gain some control over their lives; finally, bearing and driving all these people and institutions along, an ever-expanding, drastically fluctuating capitalist world market. In the twentieth century, the social processes that bring this maelstrom into being, and keep it in a state of perpetual becoming, have come to be called "modernization." These world-historical processes have nourished an amazing variety of visions and ideas that aim to make men and women the subjects as well as the objects of modernization, to give them the power to change the world that is changing them, to make their way through the maelstrom and make it their own. Over the past century, these visions and values have come to be loosely grouped together under the name of "modernism." This [...] is a study in the dialectics of modernization and modernism.

In the hope of getting a grip on something as vast as the history of modernity, I have divided it into three phases. In the first phase, which goes roughly from the start of the sixteenth century to the end of the eighteenth, people are just beginning to experience modern life; they hardly know what has hit them. They grope, desperately but half blindly, for an adequate vocabulary; they have little or no sense of a modern public or community within which their trials and hopes can be shared. Our second phase begins with the great revolutionary wave of the 1790s. With the French Revolution and its reverberations, a great modern public abruptly and dramatically comes to life. This public shares the feeling of living in a revolutionary age, an age that generates explosive upheavals in every dimension of personal, social and political life. At the same time, the nineteenth-century modern public can remember what it is like to live, materially and spiritually, in worlds that are not modern at all. From this inner dichotomy, this sense of living in two worlds simultaneously, the ideas of modernization and modernism emerge and unfold. In the twentieth century, our third and final phase, the process of modernization expands to take in virtually the whole world, and the developing world culture of modernism achieves spectacular triumphs in art and thought. On the other hand, as the modern public expands, it shatters into a multitude of fragments, speaking incommensurable private languages; the idea of modernity, conceived in numerous fragmentary ways, loses much of its vividness, resonance and depth, and loses its capacity to organize and give meaning to people's lives. As a result of all this, we find ourselves today in the midst of a modern age that has lost touch with the roots of its own modernity.

If there is one archetypal modern voice in the early phase of modernity, before the American and French revolutions, it is the voice of Jean-Jacques Rousseau. Rousseau is the first to use the word *moderniste* in the ways in which the nineteenth and twentieth centuries will use it; and he is the source of some of our most vital modern traditions, from nostalgic reverie to psychoanalytic self-scrutiny to participatory democracy. Rousseau was, as everyone knows, a deeply troubled man. Much of his anguish springs from sources peculiar to his own strained life; but some of it derives from his acute responsiveness to social conditions that were coming to shape millions of people's lives. Rousseau astounded his contemporaries by proclaiming that European society was "at the edge of the abyss," on the verge of the most explosive revolutionary upheavals. He experienced everyday life in that society – especially in Paris, its capital – as a whirlwind, *le tourbillon social*.[1] How was the self to move and live in the whirlwind?

In Rousseau's romantic novel *The New Eloïse*, his young hero, Saint-Preux, makes an exploratory move – an archetypal move for millions of young people in the centuries to come – from the country to the city. He writes to his love, Julie, from the depths of *le tourbillon social*, and tries to convey his wonder and dread. Saint-Preux experiences metropolitan life as "a perpetual clash of groups and cabals, a continual flux and reflux of prejudices and conflicting opinions ... Everyone constantly places himself in contradiction with himself," and "everything is absurd, but nothing is shocking, because everyone is accustomed to everything." This is a world in which "the good, the bad, the beautiful, the ugly, truth, virtue, have only a local and limited existence." A multitude of new experiences offer themselves; but anyone who wants to enjoy them "must be more pliable than Alcibiades, ready to change his principles with his audience, to adjust his spirit with every step." After a few months in this environment,

> I'm beginning to feel the drunkenness that this agitated, tumultuous life plunges you into. With such a multitude of objects passing before my eyes, I'm getting dizzy. Of all the things that strike me, there is none that holds my heart, yet all of them together disturb my feelings, so that I forget what I am and who I belong to.

He reaffirms his commitment to his first love; yet even as he says it, he fears that "I don't know one day what I'm going to love the next." He longs desperately for something solid to cling to, yet "I see only phantoms that strike my eye, but disappear as soon as I try to grasp them."[2] This atmosphere – of agitation and turbulence, psychic dizziness and drunkenness, expansion of experiential possibilities and destruction of moral boundaries and personal bonds, self-enlargement and self-derangement, phantoms in the street and in the soul – is the atmosphere in which modern sensibility is born.

If we move forward a hundred years or so and try to identify the distinctive rhythms and timbres of nineteenth-century modernity, the first thing we will notice is the highly developed, differentiated and dynamic new landscape in which modern experience takes place. This is a landscape of steam engines, automatic factories, railroads, vast new industrial zones; of teeming cities that have grown overnight, often with dreadful human consequences; of daily newspapers, telegraphs, telephones and other mass media, communicating on an ever wider scale; of increasingly strong national states and multinational aggregations of capital; of mass social movements fighting these modernizations from above with their own modes of modernization from below; of an ever-expanding world market embracing all, capable of the most spectacular growth, capable of appalling waste and devastation, capable of everything except solidity and stability. The great modernists of the nineteenth century all attack this environment passionately, and strive to tear it down or explode it from within; yet all find themselves remarkably at home in it, alive to its possibilities, affirmative even in their radical negations, playful and ironic even in their moments of gravest seriousness and depth.

We can get a feeling for the complexity and richness of nineteenth-century modernism, and for the unities that infuse its diversity, if we listen briefly to two of its most distinctive voices: Nietzsche, who is generally perceived as a primary source of many of the modernisms of our time, and Marx, who is not ordinarily associated with any sort of modernism at all.

Here is Marx, speaking in awkward but powerful English in London in 1856.[3] "The so-called revolutions of 1848 were but poor incidents," he begins, "small fractures and fissures in the dry crust of European society. But they denounced the abyss. Beneath the apparently solid surface, they betrayed oceans of liquid matter, only needing expansion to rend into fragments continents of hard rock." The ruling classes of the reactionary 1850s tell the world that all is solid again; but it is not clear if even they themselves believe it. In fact, Marx says, "the atmosphere in which we live weighs upon everyone with a 20,000-pound force, but do you feel it?" One of Marx's most urgent aims is to make people "feel it"; this is why his ideas are expressed in such intense and extravagant images – abysses, earthquakes, volcanic eruptions, crushing gravitational force – images that will continue to resonate in our own century's modernist art and thought. Marx goes on: "There is one great fact, characteristic of this our nineteenth century, a fact which no party dares deny." The basic fact of modern life, as Marx experiences it, is that this life is radically contradictory at its base:

> On the one hand, there have started into life industrial and scientific forces which no epoch of human history had ever suspected. On the other hand, there exist symptoms of decay, far surpassing the horrors of the latter times of the Roman Empire. In our days everything seems pregnant with its contrary. Machinery, gifted with the wonderful power of shortening and fructifying human labor, we behold starving and overworking it. The new-fangled sources of wealth, by some weird spell, are turned into sources of want. The victories of art seem bought by the loss of character. At the same pace that mankind masters nature, man seems to become enslaved to other men or to his own infamy. Even the pure light of science seems unable to shine but on the dark background of ignorance. All our invention and progress seem to result in endowing material forces with intellectual life, and stultifying human life into a material force.

These miseries and mysteries fill many moderns with despair. Some would "get rid of modern arts, in order to get rid of modern conflicts"; others will try to balance progress in industry with a neofeudal or neoabsolutist regression in politics. Marx, however, proclaims a paradigmatically modernist faith:

> On our part, we do not mistake the shrewd spirit that continues to mark all these contradictions. We know that to work well ... the new-fangled forces of society want only to be mastered by new-fangled men – and such are the working men. They are as much the invention of modern time as machinery itself.

Thus a class of "new men," men who are thoroughly modern, will be able to resolve the contradictions of modernity, to overcome the crushing pressures, earthquakes, weird spells, personal and social abysses, in whose midst all modern men and women are forced to live. Having said this, Marx turns abruptly playful and connects his vision of the future with the past – with English folklore, with Shakespeare: "In the signs that bewilder the middle class, the aristocracy and the poor prophets of regression, we recognize our brave friend Robin Goodfellow, the old mole that can work in the earth so fast, that worthy pioneer – the Revolution."

Marx's writing is famous for its endings. But if we see him as a modernist, we will notice the dialectical motion that underlies and animates his thought, a motion that is open-ended, and that flows against the current of his own concepts and desires. Thus, in the *Communist Manifesto*, we see that the revolutionary dynamism that will overthrow the modern bourgeoisie springs from that bourgeoisie's own deepest impulses and needs:

> The bourgeoisie cannot exist without constantly revolutionizing the instruments of production, and with them the relations of production, and with them all the relations of society. … Constant revolutionizing of production, uninterrupted disturbance of all social relations, everlasting uncertainty and agitation, distinguish the bourgeois epoch from all earlier ones.

This is probably the definitive vision of the modern environment, that environment which has brought forth an amazing plenitude of modernist movements, from Marx's time to our own. The vision unfolds:

> All fixed, fast-frozen relations, with their train of ancient and venerable prejudices and opinions, are swept away, all new-formed ones become antiquated before they can ossify. All that is solid melts into air, all that is holy is profaned, and men at last are forced to face … the real conditions of their lives and their relations with their fellow men.[4]

Thus the dialectical motion of modernity turns ironically against its prime movers, the bourgeoisie. But it may not stop turning there: after all, all modern movements are caught up in this ambience — including Marx's own. Suppose, as Marx supposes, that bourgeois forms decompose, and that a communist movement surges into power: what is to keep this new social form from sharing its predecessor's fate and melting down in the modern air? Marx understood this question and suggested some answers, which we will explore later on. But one of the distinctive virtues of modernism is that it leaves its questions echoing in the air long after the questioners themselves, and their answers, have left the scene.

If we move a quarter century ahead, to Nietzsche in the 1880s, we will find very different prejudices, allegiances and hopes, yet a surprisingly similar voice and feeling for modern life. For Nietzsche, as for Marx, the currents of modern history were ironic and dialectical: thus Christian ideals of the soul's integrity and the will to truth had come to explode Christianity itself. The results were the traumatic events that Nietzsche called "the death of God" and "the advent of nihilism." Modern mankind found itself in the midst of a great absence and emptiness of values and yet, at the same time, a remarkable abundance of possibilities. Here, in Nietzsche's *Beyond Good and Evil* (1882), we find, just as we found in Marx, a world where everything is pregnant with its contrary:[5]

> At these turning points in history there shows itself, juxtaposed and often entangled with one another, a magnificent, manifold, jungle-like growing and striving, a sort of tropical tempo in rivalry of development, and an enormous destruction and self-destruction, thanks to egoisms violently opposed to one another, exploding, battling each other for sun and light, unable to find any limitation, any check, any considerateness within the morality at their disposal. … Nothing but new "wherefores," no longer any communal formulas; a new

allegiance of misunderstanding and mutual disrespect; decay, vice, and the most superior desires gruesomely bound up with one another, the genius of the race welling up over the cornucopias of good and ill; a fateful simultaneity of spring and autumn. ... Again there is danger, the mother of morality –great danger – but this time displaced onto the individual, onto the nearest and dearest, onto the street, onto one's own child, one's own heart, one's own innermost secret recesses of wish and will.

At times like these, "the individual dares to individuate himself." On the other hand, this daring individual desperately "needs a set of laws of his own, needs his own skills and wiles for self-preservation, self-heightening, self-awakening, self-liberation." The possibilities are at once glorious and ominous. "Our instincts can now run back in all sorts of directions; we ourselves are a kind of chaos." Modern man's sense of himself and his history "really amounts to an instinct for everything, a taste and tongue for everything." So many roads open up from this point. How are modern men and women to find the resources to cope with their "everything"? Nietzsche notes that there are plenty of "Little Jack Horners" around whose solution to the chaos of modern life is to try not to live at all: for them, "'Become mediocre' is the only morality that makes sense."

Another type of modern throws himself into parodies of the past: he "needs history because it is the storage closet where all the costumes are kept. He notices that none really fits him" – not primitive, not classical, not medieval, not Oriental – "so he keeps trying on more and more," unable to accept the fact that a modern man "can never really look well-dressed," because no social role in modern times can ever be a perfect fit. Nietzsche's own stance toward the perils of modernity is to embrace them all with joy: "We moderns, we half-barbarians. We are in the midst of our bliss only when we are most in danger. The only stimulus that tickles us is the infinite, the immeasurable." And yet Nietzsche is not willing to live in the midst of this danger forever. As ardently as Marx, he asserts his faith in a new kind of man – "the man of tomorrow and the day after tomorrow" – who, "standing in opposition to his today," will have the courage and imagination to "create new values" that modern men and women need to steer their way through the perilous infinities in which they live.

What is distinctive and remarkable about the voice that Marx and Nietzsche share is not only its breathless pace, its vibrant energy, its imaginative richness, but also its fast and drastic shifts in tone and inflection, its readiness to turn on itself, to question and negate all it has said, to transform itself into a great range of harmonic or dissonant voices, and to stretch itself beyond its capacities into an endlessly wider range, to express and grasp a world where everything is pregnant with its contrary and "all that is solid melts into air." This voice resonates at once with self-discovery and self-mockery, with self-delight and self-doubt. It is a voice that knows pain and dread, but believes in its power to come through. Grave danger is everywhere, and may strike at any moment, but not even the deepest wounds can stop the flow and overflow of its energy. It is ironic and contradictory, polyphonic and dialectical, denouncing modern life in the name of values that modernity itself has created, hoping – often against hope – that the modernities of tomorrow and the day after tomorrow will heal the wounds that wreck the modern men and women of today. All the great modernists of the nineteenth century – spirits as diverse as Marx and Kierkegaard, Whitman and Ibsen, Baudelaire, Melville, Carlyle, Stirner, Rimbaud, Strindberg, Dostoevsky, and many more – speak in these rhythms and in this range.

What has become of nineteenth-century modernism in the twentieth century? In some ways it has thrived and grown beyond its own wildest hopes. In painting and sculpture, in poetry and the novel, in theater and dance, in architecture and design, in a whole array of electronic media and a wide range of scientific disciplines that didn't even exist a century ago, our century has produced an amazing plenitude of works and ideas of the highest quality. The twentieth century may well be the most brilliantly creative in the history of the world, not least because its creative energies have burst out in every part of the world. The brilliance and depth of living modernism – living in the work of Grass, Garcia Márquez, Fuentes, Cunningham, Nevelson, di Suvero, Kenzo Tange, Fassbinder, Herzog, Sembene, Robert Wilson, Philip Glass, Richard Foreman, Twyla Tharp, Maxine Hong Kingston, and so many more who surround us – give us a great deal to be proud of, in a world where there is so much to be ashamed and afraid of. And yet, it seems to me, we don't know how to use our modernism; we have missed or broken the connection between our culture and our lives. Jackson Pollock imagined his drip paintings as forests in which spectators might lose (and, of course, find) themselves; but we have mostly lost the art of putting ourselves in the picture, of recognizing ourselves as participants and protagonists in the art and thought of our time. Our century has nourished a spectacular modern art; but we seem to have forgotten how to grasp the modern life from which this art springs. In many ways, modern thought since Marx and Nietzsche has grown and developed; yet our thinking about modernity seems to have stagnated and regressed.

If we listen closely to twentieth-century writers and thinkers about modernity and compare them to those of a century ago, we will find a radical flattening of perspective and shrinkage of imaginative range. Our nineteenth-century thinkers were simultaneously enthusiasts and enemies of modern life, wrestling inexhaustibly with its ambiguities and contradictions; their self-ironies and inner tensions were a primary source of their creative power. Their twentieth-century successors have lurched far more toward rigid polarities and flat totalizations. Modernity is either embraced with a blind and uncritical enthusiasm, or else condemned with a neo-Olympian remoteness and contempt; in either case, it is conceived as a closed monolith, incapable of being shaped or changed by modern men. Open visions of modern life have been supplanted by closed ones, Both/And by Either/Or.

The basic polarizations take place at the very start of our century. Here are the Italian futurists, passionate partisans of modernity in the years before the First World War: "Comrades, we tell you now that the triumphant progress of science makes changes in humanity inevitable, changes that are hacking an abyss between those docile slaves of tradition and us free moderns who are confident in the radiant splendor of our future."[6] There are no ambiguities here: "tradition" – all the world's traditions thrown together – simply equals docile slavery, and modernity equals freedom; there are no loose ends.

> Take up your pickaxes, your axes and hammers, and wreck, wreck the venerable cities, pitilessly! Come on! set fire to the library shelves! Turn aside the canals to flood the museums! … So let them come, the gay incendiaries with charred fingers! Here they are! Here they are!

Now, Marx and Nietzsche could also rejoice in the modern destruction of traditional structures; but they knew the human costs of this progress, and knew that modernity would have a long way to go before its wounds could be healed.

We will sing of great crowds excited by work, by pleasure and by riot; we will sing of the multicolored, polyphonic tides of revolution in the modern capitals; we will sing of the nightly fervor of arsenals and shipyards blazing with violent electric moons; greedy railway stations that devour smoke-plumed serpents; factories hung on clouds by the crooked lines of their smoke; bridges that stride the rivers like giant gymnasts, flashing in the sun with a glitter of knives; adventurous steamers ... deep-chested locomotives ... and the sleek light of planes [etc., etc.].[7]

Seventy years later, we can still feel stirred by the futurists' youthful verve and enthusiasm, by their desire to merge their energies with modern technology and create the world anew. But so much is left out of this new world! We can see it even in that marvelous metaphor "the multicolored, polyphonic tides of revolution." It is a real expansion of human sensibility to be able to experience political upheaval in an aesthetic (musical, painterly) way. On the other hand, what happens to all the people who get swept away in those tides? Their experience is nowhere in the futurist picture. It appears that some very important kinds of human feeling are dying, even as machines are coming to life. Indeed, in later futurist writing, "we look for the creation of a nonhuman type in whom moral suffering, goodness of heart, affection, and love, those corrosive poisons of vital energy, interrupters of our powerful bodily electricity, will be abolished."[8] On this note, the young futurists ardently threw themselves into what they called "war, the world's only hygiene," in 1914. Within two years, their two most creative spirits – the painter-sculptor Umberto Boccioni, the architect Antonio Sant'Elia – would be killed by the machines they loved. The rest survived to become cultural hacks in Mussolini's mills, pulverized by the dead hand of the future.

The futurists carried the celebration of modern technology to a grotesque and self-destructive extreme, which ensured that their extravagances would never be repeated. But their uncritical romance of machines, fused with their utter remoteness from people, would be reincarnated in modes that would be less bizarre and longer-lived. We find this mode of modernism after World War One in the refined forms of the "machine aesthetic," the technocratic pastorals of the Bauhaus, Gropius and Mies van der Rohe, Le Corbusier and Léger, the *Ballet Mécanique*. We find it again, after another World War, in the spaced-out high-tech rhapsodies of Buckminster Fuller and Marshall McLuhan and in Alvin Toffler's *Future Shock*. Here, in McLuhan's *Understanding Media*, published in 1964,

The computer, in short, promises by technology a Pentecostal condition of universal understanding and unity. The next logical step would seem to be ... to bypass languages in favor of a general cosmic consciousness ... The condition of "weightlessness," that biologists say promises a physical immortality, may be paralleled by the condition of speechlessness that could confer a perpetuity of collective harmony and peace.[9]

This modernism underlay the models of modernization which post-war American social scientists, often working under lavish government and foundation subsidies, developed for export to the Third World. Here, for instance, is a hymn to the modern factory by the social psychologist Alex Inkeles:

A factory guided by modern management and personnel policies will set its workers an example of rational behavior, emotional balance, open communication, and respect for the opinions, the feelings, and the dignity of the worker, which can be a powerful example of the principles and practices of modern living.[10]

The futurists might deplore the low intensity of this prose, but they would surely be delighted with the vision of the factory as an exemplary human being which men and women should take as a model for their lives. Inkeles' essay is entitled "The Modernization of Man," and is meant to show the importance of human desire and initiative in modern life. But its problem, and the problem of all modernisms in the futurist tradition, is that, with brilliant machines and mechanical systems playing all the leading roles — just as the factory is the subject in the quotation above — there is precious little for modern man to do except to plug in.

If we move to the opposite pole of twentieth-century thought, which says a decisive "No!" to modern life, we find a surprisingly similar vision of what that life is like. At the climax of Max Weber's *The Protestant Ethic and the Spirit of Capitalism*, written in 1904, the whole "mighty cosmos of the modern economic order" is seen as, "an iron cage." This inexorable order, capitalistic, legalistic and bureaucratic, "determines the lives of all individuals who are born into this mechanism ... with irresistible force." It is bound to "determine man's fate until the last ton of fossilized coal is burnt out." Now, Marx and Nietzsche — and Tocqueville and Carlyle and Mill and Kierkegaard and all the other great nineteenth-century critics — also understood the ways in which modern technology and social organization determined man's fate. But they all believed that modern individuals had the capacity both to understand this fate and, once they understood it, to fight it. Hence, even in the midst of a wretched present, they could imagine an open future. Twentieth-century critics of modernity almost entirely lack this empathy with, and faith in, their fellow modern men and women. To Weber, his contemporaries are nothing but "specialists without spirit, sensualists without heart; and this nullity is caught in the delusion that it has achieved a level of development never before attained by mankind."[11] Thus, not only is modern society a cage, but all the people in it are shaped by its bars; we are beings without spirit, without heart, without sexual or personal identity ("this nullity ... caught in the delusion that it has achieved ...") — we might almost say without being. Here, just as in futurist and techno-pastoral forms of modernism, modern man as a subject — as a living being capable of response, judgment and action in and on the world — has disappeared. Ironically, twentieth-century critics of "the iron cage" adopt the perspective of the cage's keepers: since those inside are devoid of inner freedom or dignity, the cage is not a prison; it merely furnishes a race of nullities with the emptiness they crave and need.

Weber had little faith in the people, but even less in their ruling classes, whether aristocratic or bourgeois, bureaucratic or revolutionary. Hence his political stance, at least in the last years of his life, was a perpetually embattled liberalism. But when the Weberian remoteness and contempt for modern men and women were split off from Weberian skepticism and critical insight, the result was a politics far to the right of Weber's own. Many twentieth-century thinkers have seen things this way: the swarming masses who press upon us in the street and in the state have no sensitivity, spirituality or dignity like our own; isn't it absurd, then, that these "mass men" (or "hollow men") should have not only the right to govern themselves but also, through their mass majorities, the power to govern us? In the ideas and intellectual gestures of Ortega, Spengler, Maurras, T.S. Eliot and Allen Tate, we see Weber's neo-Olympian perspective appropriated, distorted and magnified by the modern mandarins and would-be aristocrats of the twentieth-century right.

What is more surprising, and more disturbing, is the extent to which this perspective thrived among some of the participatory democrats of the recent New Left. But this is what happened, at least for a time, at the very end of the 1960s, when Herbert Marcuse's "One-Dimensional Man" became the dominant paradigm in critical thought. According to this paradigm, both Marx and Freud are obsolete: not only class and social struggles but also psychological conflicts and contradictions have been abolished by the state of "total administration." The masses have no egos, no ids, their souls are devoid of inner tension or dynamism: their ideas, their needs, even their dreams, are "not their own"; their inner lives are "totally administered," programmed to produce exactly those desires that the social system can satisfy, and no more. "The people recognize themselves in their commodities; they find their soul in their automobiles, hi-fi sets, split-level homes, kitchen equipment."[12]

Now this is a familiar twentieth-century refrain, shared by those who love the modern world and those who hate it: modernity is constituted by its machines, of which modern men and women are merely mechanical reproductions. But it is a travesty of the nineteenth-century modern tradition in whose orbit Marcuse claimed to move, the critical tradition of Hegel and Marx. To invoke those thinkers while rejecting their vision of history as restless activity, dynamic contradiction, dialectical struggle and progress, is to retain little but their names. Meanwhile, even as the young radicals of the 1960s fought for changes that would enable the people around them to control their lives, the "one-dimensional" paradigm proclaimed that no change was possible and that, indeed, these people weren't even really alive. Two roads opened up from this point. One was the search for a vanguard that was wholly "outside" modern society: "the substratum of outcasts and outsiders, the exploited and persecuted of other races and other colors, the unemployed and the unemployable."[13] These groups, whether in America's ghettos and prisons or in the Third World, could qualify as a revolutionary vanguard because they were supposedly untouched by modernity's kiss of death. Of course, such a search is doomed to futility; no one in the contemporary world is or can be "outside." For radicals who understood this, yet took the one-dimensional paradigm to heart, it seemed that the only thing left was futility and despair.

The volatile atmosphere of the 1960s generated a large and vital body of thought and controversy over the ultimate meaning of modernity. Much of the most interesting of this thought revolved around the nature of modernism. Modernism in the 1960s can be roughly divided into three tendencies, based on attitudes toward modern life as a whole: affirmative, negative and withdrawn. This division may sound crude, but recent attitudes toward modernity have in fact tended to be cruder and simpler, less subtle and dialectical than those of a century ago.

The first of these modernisms, the one that strives to withdraw from modern life, was proclaimed most forcefully by Roland Barthes in literature and Clement Greenberg in tile visual arts. Greenberg argued that the only legitimate concern of modernist art was art itself; furthermore, the only rightful focus for an artist in any given form or genre was the nature and limits of that genre: the medium is the message. Thus, for instance, the only permissible subject for a modernist painter was the flatness of the surface (canvas, etc.) on which the painting takes place, because "flatness alone is unique and exclusive to the art."[14] Modernism, then, was the quest for the pure, self-referential art object. And that was all it was: the proper relationship of modern art to modern social life was no relationship at all. Barthes put this absence in a positive, even a heroic light: the modern writer "turns his back on society and confronts the world of objects without going through any of the forms of History or social life."[15] Modernism thus appeared as a great attempt to free modern artists from the impurities, vulgarities of modern life. Many artists and writers – and, even more, art and literary critics – have been grateful to this modernism for establishing the autonomy and dignity of their vocations. But very few modern artists or writers have stayed with this modernism for long: an art without personal feelings or social relationships is bound to seem arid and lifeless after a little while. The freedom it confers is the freedom of a beautifully formed, perfectly sealed tomb.

Then there was the vision of modernism as an unending permanent revolution against the totality of modern existence: it was "a tradition of overthrowing tradition" (Harold Rosenberg),[16] an "adversary culture" (Lionel Trilling),[17] a "culture of negation" (Renato Poggioli).[18] The modern work of art was said to "molest us with an aggressive absurdity" (Leo Steinberg).[19] It seeks the violent overthrow of all our values, and cares little about reconstructing the worlds it destroys. This image gained force and credence as the 1960s progressed and the political climate heated up: in some circles, "modernism" became a code word for all the forces in revolt.[20] This obviously tells part of the truth, but it leaves far too much out. It leaves out the great romance of construction, a crucial force in modernism from Carlyle and Marx to Tatlin and Calder, Le Corbusier and Frank Lloyd Wright, Mark di Suvero and Robert Smithson. It leaves out all the affirmative and life sustaining force that in the greatest modernists is always interwoven with assault and revolt: the erotic joy, natural beauty and human tenderness in D.H. Lawrence, always locked in mortal embrace with his nihilistic rage and despair; the figures in Picasso's *Guernica*, struggling to keep life itself alive even as they shriek their death; the triumphant last choruses of Coltrane's *A Love Supreme*; Alyosha Karamazov, in the midst of chaos and anguish, kissing and embracing the earth; Molly Bloom bringing the archetypal modernist book to an end with "yes I said yes I will Yes."

There is a further problem with the idea of modernism as nothing but trouble: it tends to posit a model of modern society as one that is in itself devoid of trouble. It leaves out all the "uninterrupted disturbances of all social relations, everlasting uncertainty and agitation" that have for two hundred years been basic facts of modern life. When students at Columbia University rebelled in 1968, some of their conservative professors described their action as "modernism in the streets." Presumably those streets would have been calm and orderly – in the middle of Manhattan, yet! – if only modern culture could somehow have been kept off them, and confined to university classrooms and libraries and Museums of Modern Art.[21] Had the professors learned their own lessons, they would have remembered how much of modernism – Baudelaire, Boccioni, Joyce, Mayakovsky, Léger, et al. – has nourished itself on the real trouble in the modern streets, and transformed their noise and dissonance into beauty and truth. Ironically, the radical image of modernism as pure subversion helped to nourish the neoconservative fantasy of a world purified of modernist subversion. "Modernism has been the seducer," Daniel Bell wrote in *The Cultural Contradictions of Capitalism*. "The modern movement disrupts the unity of culture," "shatters the 'rational cosmology' that underlay the bourgeois world view of an ordered relation between space and time," etc., etc.[22] If only the modernist snake could be expelled from the modern garden, space, time and the cosmos would straighten themselves out. Then, presumably, a techno-pastoral golden age would return, and men and machines could lie down together happily forevermore.

The affirmative vision of modernism was developed in the 1960s by a heterogeneous group of writers, including John Cage, Lawrence Alloway, Marshall McLuhan, Leslie Fiedler, Susan Sontag, Richard Poirier, Robert Venturi. It coincided loosely with the emergence of pop art in the early 1960s. Its dominant themes were that we must "wake up to the very life we're living" (Cage), and "cross the border, close the gap" (Fiedler).[23] This meant, for one thing, breaking down the barriers between "art" and other human activities, such as commercial entertainment, industrial technology, fashion and design, politics. It also encouraged writers, painters, dancers, composers and filmmakers to break down the boundaries of their specializations and work together on mixed-media productions and performances that would create richer and more multivalent arts.

For modernists of this variety, who sometimes called themselves "postmodernists," the modernism of pure form and the modernism of pure revolt were both too narrow, too self-righteous, too constricting to the modern spirit. Their ideal was to open oneself to the immense variety and richness of things, materials and ideas that the modern world inexhaustibly brought forth. They breathed fresh air and playfulness into a cultural ambience which in the 1950s had become unbearably solemn, rigid and closed. Pop modernism recreated the openness to the world, the generosity of vision, of some of the great modernists of the past – Baudelaire, Whitman, Apollinaire, Mayakovsky, William Carlos Williams. But if this modernism matched their imaginative sympathy, it never learned to recapture their critical bite. When a creative spirit like John Cage accepted the support of the Shah of Iran, and performed modernist spectacles a few miles from where political prisoners shrieked and died, the failure of moral imagination was not his alone. The trouble was that pop modernism never developed a critical perspective which might have clarified the point where openness to the modern world has got to stop, and the point where the modern artist needs to see and to say that some of the powers of this world have got to go.

All the modernisms and anti-modernisms of the 1960s, then, were seriously flawed. But their sheer plenitude, along with their intensity and liveliness of expression, generated a common language, a vibrant ambience, a shared horizon of experience and desire. All these visions and revisions of modernity were active orientations toward history, attempts to connect the turbulent present with a past and a future, to help men and women all over the contemporary world to make themselves at home in this world. These initiatives all failed, but they sprang from a largeness of vision and imagination, and from an ardent desire to seize the day. It was the absence of these generous visions and initiatives that made the 1970s such a bleak decade. Virtually no one today seems to want to make the large human connections that the idea of modernity entails. Hence discourse and controversy over the meaning of modernity, so lively a decade ago, have virtually ceased to exist today.

Many artistic and literary intellectuals have immersed themselves in the world of structuralism, a world that simply wipes the question of modernity – along with all other questions about the self and history – off the map. Others have embraced a mystique of postmodernism, which strives to cultivate ignorance of modern history and culture, and speaks as if all human feeling, expressiveness, play, sexuality and community have only just been invented – by the postmodernists – and were unknown, even inconceivable, before last week.[24] Meanwhile, social scientists, embarrassed by critical attacks on their techno-pastoral models, have fled from the task of building a model that might be truer to modern life. Instead, they have split modernity into a series of separate components – industrializa-tion, state-building, urbanization, development of markets, elite formation – and resisted any attempt to integrate them into a whole. This has freed them from extravagant generalizations and vague totalities – but also from thought that might engage their own lives and works and their place in history.[25] The eclipse of the problem of modernity in the 1970s has meant the destruction of a vital form of public space. It has hastened the disintegration of our world into an aggregation of private material and spiritual interest groups, living in windowless monads, far more isolated than we need to be.

Just about the only writer of the past decade who has had anything substantial to say about modernity is Michel Foucault. And what he has to say is an endless, excruciating series of variations on the Weberian themes of the iron cage and the human nullities whose souls are shaped to fit the bars. Foucault is obsessed with prisons, hospitals, asylums, with what Erving Goffman has called "total institutions." Unlike Goffman, however, Foucault denies the possibility of any sort of freedom, either outside these institutions or within their interstices. Foucault's totalities swallow up every facet of modern life. He develops these themes with obsessive relentlessness and, indeed, with sadistic flourishes, clamping his ideas down on his readers like iron bars, twisting each dialectic into our flesh like a new turn of the screw.

Foucault reserves his most savage contempt for people who imagine that it is possible for modern mankind to be free. Do we think we feel a spontaneous rush of sexual desire? We are merely being moved by "the modern technologies of power that take life as their object," driven by "the deployment of sexuality by power in its grip on bodies and their materiality, their forces, their energies, sensations and pleasures." Do we act politically, overthrow tyrannies, make revolutions, create constitutions to establish and protect human rights? Mere "juridical regression" from the feudal ages, because constitutions and bills of rights are merely "the forms that [make] an essentially normalizing power acceptable.[26] Do we use our minds to unmask oppression – as Foucault appears to be trying to do? Forget it, because all forms of inquiry into the human condition "merely refer individuals from one disciplinary authority to another," and hence only add to the triumphant "discourse of power." Any criticism rings hollow, because the critic himself or herself is "in the panoptic machine, invested by its effects of power, which we bring to ourselves, since we are part of its mechanism."[27]

After being subjected to this for a while, we realize that there is no freedom in Foucault's world, because his language forms a seamless web, a cage far more airtight than anything Weber ever dreamed of, into which no life can break. The mystery is why so many of today's intellectuals seem to want to choke in there with him. The answer, I suspect, is that Foucault offers a generation of refugees from the 1960s a world-historical alibi for the sense of passivity and helplessness that gripped so many of us in the 1970s. There is no point in trying to resist the oppressions and injustices of modern life, since even our dreams of freedom only add more links to our chains; however, once we grasp the total futility of it all, at least we can relax.

In this bleak context, I want to bring the dynamic and dialectical modernism of the nineteenth century to life again. A great modernist, the Mexican poet and critic Octavio Paz, has lamented that modernity is "cut off from the past and continually hurtling forward at such a dizzy pace that it cannot take root, that it merely survives from one day to the next: it is unable to return to its beginnings and thus recover its powers of renewal."[28] [My argument] is that, in fact, the modernisms of the past can give us back a sense of our own modern roots, roots that go back two hundred years. They can help us connect our lives with the lives of millions of people who are living through the trauma of modernization thousands of miles away, in societies radically different from our own – and with millions of people who lived through it a century or more ago. They can illuminate the contradictory forces and needs that inspire and torment us: our desire to be rooted in a stable and coherent personal and social past, and our insatiable desire for growth – not merely for economic growth but for growth in experience, in pleasure, in knowledge, in sensibility – growth that destroys both the physical and social landscapes of our past, and our emotional links with those lost worlds; our desperate allegiances to ethnic, national, class and sexual groups which we hope will give us a firm "identity," and the internationalization of everyday life – of our clothes and household goods, our books and music, our ideas and fantasies – that spreads all our identities all over the map; our desire for clear and solid values to live by, and our desire to embrace the limitless possibilities of modern life and experience that obliterate all values; the social and political forces that propel us into explosive conflicts with other people and other peoples, even as we develop a deeper sensitivity and empathy toward our ordained enemies and come to realize, sometimes too late, that they are not so different from us after all. Experiences like these unite us with the nineteenth-century modern world: a world where, as Marx said, "everything is pregnant with its contrary" and "all that is solid melts into air"; a world where, as Nietzsche said, "there is danger, the mother of morality – great danger ... displaced onto the individual, onto the nearest and dearest, onto the street, onto one's own child, one's own heart, one's own innermost secret recesses of wish and will." Modern machines have changed a great deal in the years between the nineteenth-century modernists and ourselves; but modern men and women, as Marx and Nietzsche and Baudelaire and Dostoevsky saw them then, may only now be coming fully into their own.

Chapter 3

Michel Foucault

■ **THE ORDER OF THINGS** (Interview with Raymond Bellours) in James D. Faubion (ed.), *Essential Works of Michel Foucault, 1954–84. Volume II: Aesthetics, Method, and Epistemology*, Robert Hurley et al. trans., London: Penguin Books, 1998

R.B.[1] How is *The Order of Things* related to *Madness and Civilization?*[2]

M.F. *Madness and Civilization*, roughly speaking, was the history of a division, the history above all of a certain break that every society finds itself obliged to make. On the other hand, in this book I wanted to write a history of order, to state how a society reflects upon resemblances among things and how differences between things can be mastered, organized into networks, sketched out according to rational schemes. *Madness and Civilization* is the history of difference, *The Order of Things* the history of resemblance, sameness, and identity

R.B. The book's subtitle once again includes this word "archaeology." It appeared in the subtitle of *The Birth of the Clinic* and again in the preface to *Madness and Civilization*.[3]

M.F. By "archaeology" I would like to designate not exactly a discipline but a domain of research, which would be the following: in a society, different bodies of learning, philosophical ideas, everyday opinions, but also institutions, commercial practices and police activities, mores – all refer to a certain implicit knowledge [*savoir*] special to this society. This knowledge is profoundly different from the bodies of learning [*des connaissances*] that one can find in scientific books, philosophical theories and religious justifications, but it is what makes possible at a given moment the appearance of a theory, an opinion, a practice. Thus, in order for the big centers of internment to be opened at the end of the seventeenth century, it was necessary that a certain knowledge of madness be opposed to non-madness, of order to disorder, and it's this knowledge that I wanted to investigate, as the condition of possibility of knowledge [*connaissance*], of institutions, of practices.

This style of research has for me the following interests: it allows me to avoid every problem concerning the anteriority of theory in relation to practice, and the reverse. In fact, I deal with practices, institutions and theories on the same plane and according to the same isomorphisms, and I look for the underlying knowledge [*savoir*] that makes them possible, the stratum of knowledge that constitutes them historically.

Rather than try to explain this knowledge from the point of view of the practico-inert, I try to formulate an analysis from the position of what one could call the 'theoretico-active.'[4]

R.B.   You find yourself therefore confronting a double problem – of history and formalization.

M.F.   All these practices, then, these institutions and theories, I take at the level of traces, that is, almost always at the level of verbal traces. The ensemble of these traces constitutes a sort of domain considered to be homogeneous: one doesn't establish any differences a priori. The problem is to find common traits between these traces of orders different enough to constitute what logicians call "classes," aestheticians call "forms," social scientists call "structures," which are the invariants common to a certain number of traces.

R.B.   How have you raised the problem of choice and nonchoice?

M.F.   I will say that, in fact, there should not be any privileged choice. One should be able to read everything, to know all the institutions and all the practices. None of the values traditionally recognized in the history of ideas and philosophy should be accepted as such. One is dealing with a field that will ignore the differences and traditionally important things. Which means that one will take up *Don Quixote*, Descartes, and a decree by Pomponne de Bellièvre about houses of internment in the same stroke. One will perceive that the grammarians of the eighteenth century have as much importance as the recognized philosophers of the same period.

R.B.   It is in this sense that you say, for example, that Cuvier and Ricardo have taught you as much or more than Kant and Hegel. But then the question of information becomes the pressing one: how do you read everything?

M.F.   One can read all the grammarians, and all the economists. For T*he Birth of the Clinic* I read every medical work of importance for the methodology of the period 1780–1820. The choices that one could make are inadmissible and shouldn't exist. One ought to read everything, study everything. In other words, one must have at one's disposal the general archive of a period at a given moment. And archaeology is, in a strict sense, the science of this archive.

R.B.   What determines the choice of historic period (here, as in *Madness and Civilization*, you go from the Renaissance to the present), and its relationship with the "archaeological" perspective that you adopt?

M.F.   This kind of research is only possible as the analysis of our own subsoil. It's not a defect of these retrospective disciplines to find their point of departure in our own actuality. There can be no doubt that the problem of the division between reason and unreason became possible only with Nietzsche and Artaud. And it's the subsoil of our modern consciousness of madness that I have wanted to investigate. If there were not something like a fault line in this soil, archaeology would not have been possible or necessary. In the same way, if the question of meaning and of the relation between meaning and the sign had not appeared in European culture with Freud, Saussure, and Husserl, it is obvious that it would not have been necessary to investigate the subsoil of our consciousness of meaning. In the two cases these are the critical analysis of our own condition.

R.B.   What has brought you to adopt the three axes that orient your whole analysis?

M.F.   Roughly this. The human sciences that have appeared since the end of the nineteenth century are caught, as it were, in a double obligation, a double and simultaneous postulation: that of hermeneutics, interpretation, or exegesis – one must understand a hidden meaning. And the other: one must formalize, discover the system, the structural invariant, the network of simultaneities. Yet these two questions seemed to comfort each other in a privileged fashion in the human sciences, to the point that one has the impression that it is necessary that they be one or the other, interpretation or formalization. What I undertook was precisely the archaeological research of what had made this ambiguity possible. I wanted to find the branch that bore this fork. Thus I had to respond to a double question concerning the Classical period – that of the theory of signs, and that of the empirical order, of the constitution of empirical orders.

It appeared to me that, in fact, the Classical age, usually considered as the age of the radical mechanization of nature, of the mathematization of the living, was in reality something entirely different – that there existed a very important domain that included general grammar, natural history and the analysis of wealth; and that this empirical domain is based on the project of an ordering of things, and this thanks not to mathematics and geometry but to a systematics of signs, a sort of general and systematic taxonomy of things.

R.B.   It's thus a return to the Classical age that has determined the three axes. How, then, is the passage in these three domains from the Classical age to the nineteenth century effected?

M.F.   It revealed one thing that came to me as a complete surprise – that man didn't exist within Classical knowledge [*savoir*]. What existed in the place where we now discover man was the power special to discourse, to the verbal order, to represent the order of things. In order to study grammar or the system of wealth, there was no need to pass through a human science, just through discourse.

R.B.   Yet, apparently, if ever a literature seemed to speak of man, it was our literature of the seventeenth century.

M.F.   Insofar as what existed in Classical knowledge were representations ordered in a discourse, all the notions that are fundamental for our conception of man – such as those of life, work, and language – had no basis in that period, and no place.

At the end of the seventeenth century, discourse ceased to play the organizing role that it had in Classical knowledge. There was no longer any transparency between the order of things and the representations that one could have of them; things were folded somehow onto their own thickness and onto a demand exterior to representation. It's for this reason that languages with their history, life with its organization and its autonomy, and work with its own capacity for production appeared. In the face of that, in the lacuna left by discourse, man constituted himself, a man who is as much one who lives, who speaks and who works, as one who experiences [*connaît*] life, language and work, as one finally who can be known to the extent that he lives, speaks and works.

R.B.   Against this background, how does our situation today present itself?

M.F.   At the moment we find ourselves in a very ambiguous situation. Man has existed since the beginning of the nineteenth century only because discourse ceased to have the force of law over the empirical world. Man has existed where discourse was silenced. Yet with Saussure, Freud, and Hegel, at the heart of what is most fundamental in the knowledge of man, the problem of meaning and the sign reappeared. Now, one can wonder if this return of the great problem of the sign and meaning, of the order of signs, constitutes a kind of superimposition in our culture over what had constituted the Classical age and modernity – or, rather, if it's a question of omens announcing that man is disappearing – since, until the present, the order of man and that of signs have in our culture been incompatible with each other. Man would die from the signs that were born in him – that's what Nietzsche, the first one to see this, meant.

R.B.   It seems to me that this idea of an incompatibility between the order of signs and the order of man must have a certain number of consequences.

M.F.   Yes. For example:

1   It makes an idle fancy of the idea of a science of man that would be at the same time an analysis of signs.
2   It announces the first deterioration in European history of the anthropological and humanist episode that we experienced in the nineteenth century, when one thought that the sciences of man would be at the same time the liberation of man, of the human being in his plenitude. Experience has shown that the human sciences, in their development, led to the disappearance of man rather than to his apotheosis.
3   Literature, whose status changed in the nineteenth century when it ceased to belong to the order of discourse and became the manifestation of language in its thickness, must no doubt now assume another status, is assuming another status; and the hesitation that it manifests between the vague humanisms and the pure formalism of language is, no doubt, only one of the manifestations of this phenomenon, which is fundamental for us and makes us oscillate between interpretation and formalizations, man and signs.

R.B.   Thus one sees clearly the great determination of French literature since the Classical age take form – in particular, the scheme that leads from a first humanism, that of Romanticism, to Flaubert, then to this literature of the subject embodied in the generation of the *Nouvelle revue française*, to the new humanism, of before and after the war, and today to the formation of the *nouveau roman*. Yet German literature holds this kind of evolutionary scheme in check, however one envisages it.

M.F.   Perhaps insofar as German classicism was contemporary with this age of history and interpretation, German literature found itself from its origins in this confrontation we are experiencing today. That would explain why Nietzsche didn't do anything but become aware of this situation; and now he's the one who serves as a light for us.

R.B.   That would explain why he can appear throughout your book as the exemplary figure, the nonarchaeologizable subject (or not yet); since it is starting from what he opened that the question is raised in all its violence.

M.F.   Yes, he is the one who through German culture understood that the rediscovery of the dimension proper to language is incompatible with man. From that point, Nietzsche has taken on a prophetic value for us. And then, on the other hand, it is necessary to condemn with the most complete severity all the attempts to dull the problem. For example, the use of the most familiar notions of the eighteenth century, the schemes of resemblance and contiguity, all of that which is used to build the human sciences, to found them, all that appears to me to be a form of intellectual cowardice that serves to confirm what Nietzsche signified to us for almost a century – that where there is a sign, there man cannot be, and that where one makes signs speak, there man must fall silent.

What appears to me to be deceiving and naive in reflections on and analyses of signs is that one supposes them to be always already there, deposited on the figure of the world, or constituted by men, and that one never investigates their being. What does it mean, the fact that there are signs and marks of language? One must pose the problem of the being of language as a task, in order not to fall back to a level of reflection that would be that of the eighteenth century, to the level of empiricism.

R.B.   One thing in your book struck me very sharply — the perfect singularity of its position toward philosophy, the philosophical tradition and history, on the one hand, and, on the other, toward the history of ideas, methods, and concepts.

M.F.   I was shocked by the fact that there existed on one side a history of philosophy which gave itself as a privileged object, the philosophical edifices that the tradition signaled as important (at the very most it meant accepting, since it was a little trendy, that it had to do with the birth of industrial capitalism); and, on the other side, a history of ideas, that is to say subphilosophies, which took for their privileged object the texts of Montesquieu, Diderot or, Fontenelle.

If one adds to that the histories of the sciences, one cannot fail to be struck by the impossibility of our culture of raising the problem of the history of its own thought. It's why I have tried to make, obviously in a rather particular style, the history not of thought in general but of all that "contains thought" in a culture, of all in which there is thought. For there is thought in philosophy, but also in a novel, in jurisprudence, in law, in an administrative system, in a prison.

Chapter 4

Michel Foucault

■   **NIETZSCHE, GENEALOGY, HISTORY**[1] in James D.
Faubion (ed.), *Essential Works of Michel Foucault, 1954–84.
Volume II: Aesthetics, Method, and Epistemology*, Robert
Hurley et al. trans., London: Penguin Books, 1998

1

GENEALOGY IS GRAY, METICULOUS, and patiently documentary.
It operates on a field of entangled and confused parchments, on documents that
have been scratched over and recopied many times.

On this basis, it is obvious that Paul Ree was wrong to follow the English tendency in
describing the history of morality in terms of a linear development – in reducing its entire
history and genesis to an exclusive concern for utility. He assumed that words had kept
their meaning, that desires still pointed in a single direction, and that ideas retained their
logic; and he ignored the fact that the world of speech and desires has known invasions,
struggles, plundering, disguises, ploys. From these elements, however, genealogy retrieves
an indispensable restraint: it must record the singularity of events outside of any monotonous
finality; it must seek them in the most unpromising places, in what we tend to feel is
without history – in sentiments, love, conscience, instincts; it must be sensitive to their
recurrence, not in order to trace the gradual curve of their evolution but to isolate the
different scenes where they engaged in different roles. Finally, genealogy must define even
those instances when they are absent, the moment when they remained unrealized (Plato,
at Syracuse, did not become Muhammed).

Genealogy, consequently, requires patience and a knowledge of details, and it depends
on a vast accumulation of source material. Its "cyclopean monuments"[2] are constructed
from "discreet and apparently insignificant truths and according to a rigorous method";
they cannot be the product of "large and well-meaning errors."[3] In short, genealogy
demands relentless erudition. Genealogy does not oppose itself to history as the lofty and
profound gaze of the philosopher might compare to the molelike perspective of the scholar;
on the contrary, it rejects the metahistorical deployment of ideal significations and indefinite
teleologies. It opposes itself to the search for "origins."

2

In Nietzsche, we find two uses of the word *Ursprung*. The first is unstressed, and it is found alternately with other terms such as *Entstehung, Herkunft, Abkunft, Geburt*. In *The Genealogy of Morals*, for example, *Entstehung* or *Ursprung* serves equally well to denote the origin of duty or guilty conscience;[4] and in the discussion of logic and knowledge in *The Gay Science*, their origin is indiscriminately referred to as *Ursprung, Entstehung*, or *Herkunft*.[5]

The other use of the word is stressed. On occasion, Nietzsche places the term in opposition to another: in the first paragraph of *Human, All Too Human* the miraculous origin [*Wunderursprung*] sought by metaphysics is set against the analyses of historical philosophy, which poses questions *über Herkunft und Anfang. Ursprung* is also used in an ironic and deceptive manner. In what, for instance, do we find the original basis [*Ursprung*] of morality, a foundation sought after since Plato? "In detestable, narrow-minded conclusions. *Pudenda origo*."[6] Or again, Where should we seek the origin of religion [*Ursprung*], which Schopenhauer located in a particular metaphysical sentiment of the hereafter? It belongs, very simply, to an invention [*Erfindung*], a sleight-of-hand, an artifice [*Kunststück*], a secret formula, in the rituals of black magic, in the work of the *Schwarzkünstler*.[7]

One of the most significant texts with respect to the use of all these terms and to the variations in the use of *Ursprung* is the preface to *The Genealogy*. At the beginning of the text its objective is defined as an examination of the origin of moral preconceptions and the term used is *Herkunft*. Then Nietzsche proceeds by retracing his personal involvement with this question: he recalls the period when he "calligraphied" philosophy, when he questioned if God must be held responsible for the origin of evil. He now finds this question amusing and properly characterizes it as a search for *Ursprung* (he will shortly use the same term to summarize Paul Ree's activity).[8] Farther on he evokes the analyses that are characteristically Nietzschean and that begin with *Human, All Too Human*. Here he speaks of *Herkunft-hypothesen*. This use of the word *Herkunft* cannot be arbitrary, since it serves to designate a number of texts, beginning with *Human, All Too Human*, which deal with the origin of morality, asceticism, justice, and punishment. And yet the word used in all these works had been *Ursprung*.[9] It would seem that at this point in *The Genealogy* Nietzsche wished to validate an opposition between *Herkunft* and *Ursprung* that he had not put into play ten years earlier. But immediately following the use of the two terms in a specific sense, Nietzsche reverts, in the final paragraphs of the preface, to a usage that is neutral and equivalent.[10]

Why did Nietzsche challenge the pursuit of the origin [*Ursprung*], at least on those occasions when he is truly a genealogist? First, because it is an attempt to capture the exact essence of things, their purest possibilities, and their carefully protected identities; because this search assumes the existence of immobile forms that precede the external world of accident and succession. This search is directed to "that which was already there," the "very same" of an image of a primordial truth fully adequate to its nature, and it necessitates the removal of every mask to ultimately disclose an original identity. However, if the genealogist refuses to extend his faith in metaphysics, if he listens to history, he finds that there is "something altogether different" behind things: not a timeless and essential secret but the secret that they have no essence, or that their essence was fabricated in a piecemeal fashion from alien forms. Examining the history of reason, he learns that it was born in an altogether "reasonable" fashion – from chance;[11] devotion to truth and the precision of scientific methods arose from the passion of scholars, their reciprocal hatred, their fanatical and unending discussions, and their spirit of competition – the personal conflicts that slowly forged the weapons of reason.[12] Further, genealogical analysis shows that the concept of liberty is an "invention of the ruling classes"[13] and not fundamental to man's nature or at the root of his attachment to being and truth. What is found at the historical beginning of things is not the inviolable identity of their origin; it is the dissension of other things. It is disparity.

History also teaches us how to laugh at the solemnities of the origin. The lofty origin is no more than "a metaphysical extension which arises from the belief that things are most precious and essential at the moment of birth."[14] We tend to think that this is the moment of their greatest perfection, when they emerged dazzling from the hands of a creator or in the shadowless light of a first morning. The origin always precedes the Fall. It comes before the body, before the world and time; it is associated with the gods, and its story is always sung as a theogony. But historical beginnings are lowly: not in the sense of modest or discreet, like the steps of a dove, but derisive and ironic, capable of undoing every infatuation. "We wished to awaken the feeling of man's sovereignty by showing his divine birth: this path is now forbidden, since a monkey stands at the entrance."[15] Man began with a grimace at what he would become; and Zarathustra himself is plagued by a monkey who jumps along behind him, pulling on his coattails.

The final postulate of the origin is linked to the first two: it would be the site of truth. From the vantage point of an absolute distance, free from the restraints of positive knowledge [*connaissance*], the origin makes possible a field of knowledge [*savoir*] whose function is to recover it, but always in a false recognition due to the excesses of its own speech. The origin lies at a place of inevitable loss, the point where the truth of things is knotted to a truthful discourse, the site of a fleeting articulation that discourse has obscured and finally lost. It is a new cruelty of history that compels a reversal of this relationship and the abandonment of "adolescent" quests: behind the always recent, avaricious, and measured truth, it posits the ancient proliferation of errors. It is now impossible to believe that "in the rending of the veil, truth remains truthful; we have lived long enough not to be taken in."[16] Truth is undoubtedly the sort of error that cannot be refuted because it was hardened into an unalterable form in the long baking process of history.[17] Moreover, the very question of truth, the right it appropriates to refute error and oppose itself to appearance, the manner in which by turns it was initially made available to the wise, then was withdrawn by men of piety to an unattainable world where it was given the double role of consolation and imperative, finally rejected as a useless notion, superfluous and contradicted on all sides – does this not form a history, the history of an error we call truth? Truth, and its original reign, has had a history within history from which we are barely emerging "in the time of the shortest shadow," when light no longer seems to flow from the depths of the sky or to arise from the first moments of the day.[18]

A genealogy of values, morality, asceticism, and knowledge will never confuse itself with a quest for their "origins," will never neglect as inaccessible all the episodes of history. On the contrary, it will cultivate the details and accidents that accompany every beginning; it will be scrupulously attentive to their petty malice; it will await their emergence, once unmasked, as the face of the other. Wherever it is made to go, it will not be reticent – in "excavating the depths," in allowing time for these elements to escape from a labyrinth where no truth had ever detained them. The genealogist needs history to dispel the chimeras of the origin, somewhat in the manner of the pious philosopher who needs a doctor to exorcise the shadow of his soul. He must be able to recognize the events of history, its jolts, its surprises, its unsteady victories and unpalatable defeats – the basis of all beginnings, atavisms, and heredities. Similarly, he must be able to diagnose the illnesses of the body, its conditions of weakness and strength, its breakdowns and resistances, to be in a position to judge philosophical discourse. History is the concrete body of becoming; with its moments of intensity, its lapses, its extended periods of feverish agitation, its fainting spells; and only a metaphysician would seek its soul in the distant ideality of the origin.

3

Entstehung and *Herkunft* are more exact than *Ursprung* in recording the true object of genealogy; and, though they are ordinarily translated as "origin," we must attempt to re-establish their proper use.

Herkunft is the equivalent of stock or *descent*; it is the ancient affiliation to a group, sustained by the bonds of blood, tradition, or social status. The analysis of *Herkunft* often involves a consideration of race or social type.[19] But the traits it attempts to identify are not the exclusive generic characteristics of an individual, a sentiment, or an idea, which permit us to qualify them as "Greek" or "English"; rather, it seeks the subtle, singular, and sub-individual marks that might possibly intersect in them to form a network that is difficult to unravel. Far from being a category of resemblance, this origin allows the setting apart, the sorting out of different traits: the Germans imagined they had finally accounted for their complexity by saying they possessed a double soul; they were fooled by a simple computation, or rather, they were simply trying to master the racial disorder from which they had formed themselves.[20] Where the soul pretends unification or the Me fabricates a coherent identity, the genealogist sets out to study the beginning – numberless beginnings, whose faint traces and hints of color are readily seen by a historical eye. The analysis of descent permits the dissociation of the Me, its recognition and displacement as an empty synthesis, in liberating a profusion of lost events.

An examination of descent also permits the discovery, under the unique aspect of a trait or a concept, of the myriad events through which – thanks to which, against which – they were formed. Genealogy does not pretend to go back in time to restore an unbroken continuity that operates beyond the dispersion of oblivion; its task is not to demonstrate that the past actively exists in the present, that it continues secretly to animate the present, having imposed a predetermined form on all its vicissitudes. Genealogy does not resemble the evolution of a species and does not map the destiny of a people. On the contrary, to follow the complex course of descent is to maintain passing events in their proper dispersion; it is to identify the accidents, the minute deviations – or conversely, the complete reversals – the errors, the false appraisals, and the faulty calculations that gave birth to those things which continue to exist and have value for us; it is to discover that truth or being lies not at the root of what we know and what we are but the exteriority of accidents.[21] This is undoubtedly why every origin of morality from the moment it stops being pious – and *Herkunft* can never be – has value as a critique.[22]

Deriving from such a source is a dangerous legacy. In numerous instances, Nietzsche associates the terms *Herkunft* and *Erbschaft*. Nevertheless, we should not be deceived into thinking that this heritage is an acquisition, a possession that grows and solidifies; rather, it is an unstable assemblage of faults, fissures, and heterogeneous layers that threaten the fragile inheritor from within or from underneath: "injustice or instability in the minds of certain men, their disorder and lack of decorum, are the final consequences of their ancestors' numberless logical inaccuracies, hasty conclusions, and superficiality."[23] The search for descent is not the erecting of foundations: on the contrary, it disturbs what was previously considered immobile; it fragments what was thought unified; it shows the heterogeneity of what was imagined consistent with itself. What convictions and, far more decisively, what knowledge can resist it? If a genealogical analysis of a scholar were made — of one who collects facts and carefully accounts for them — his *Herkunft* would quickly divulge the official papers of the scribe and the pleadings of the lawyer — their father[24] — in their apparently disinterested attention, in their "pure" devotion to objectivity.

Finally, descent attaches itself to the body.[25] It inscribes itself in the nervous system, in temperament, in the digestive apparatus; it appears in faulty respiration, in improper diets, in the debilitated and prostrate bodies of those whose ancestors committed errors. Fathers have only to mistake effects for causes, believe in the reality of an "afterlife" or maintain the value of eternal truths, and the bodies of their children will suffer. Cowardice and hypocrisy, for their part, are the simple offshoots of error: not in a Socratic sense, not that evil is the result of a mistake, not because of a turning away from an original truth, but because the body maintains, in life as in death, through its strength or weakness, the sanction of every truth and error, as it sustains, in an inverse manner, the origin — descent. Why did men invent the contemplative life? Why give a supreme value to this form of existence? Why maintain the absolute truth of those fictions which sustain it? "During barbarous ages ... if the strength of an individual declined, if he felt himself tired or sick, melancholy or satiated and, as a consequence, without desire or appetite for a short time, he became relatively a better man, that is, less dangerous. His pessimistic ideas only take form as words or reflections. In this frame of mind, he either became a thinker and prophet or used his imagination to feed his superstitions."[26] The body — and everything that touches it: diet, climate, and soil — is the domain of the *Herkunft*. The body manifests the stigmata of past experience and also gives rise to desires, failings, and errors. These elements may join in a body where they achieve a sudden expression, but just as often, their encounter is an engagement in which they efface each other, and pursue their insurmountable conflict.

The body is the surface of the inscription of events (traced by language and dissolved by ideas), the locus of the dissociation of the Me (to which it tries to impart the chimera of a substantial unity), and a volume in perpetual disintegration. Genealogy, as an analysis of descent, is thus situated within the articulation of the body and history. Its task is to expose a body totally imprinted by history and the process of history's destruction of the body.

4

Entstehung designates emergence, the moment of arising. It stands as the principle and the singular law of an apparition. As it is wrong to search for descent in an uninterrupted continuity, we should avoid accounting for emergence by appeal to its final term; the eye was not always intended for contemplation, and punishment has had other purposes than setting an example. These developments may appear as a culmination, but they are merely the current episodes in a series of subjugations: the eye initially responded to the requirements of hunting and warfare; and punishment has been subjected by turns to a variety of needs – revenge, excluding an aggressor, compensating a victim, creating fear. In placing present needs at the origin, the metaphysician would convince us of an obscure purpose that seeks its realization at the moment it arises. Genealogy, however, seeks to reestablish the various systems of subjection: not the anticipatory power of meaning, but the hazardous play of dominations.

Emergence is always produced in a particular state of forces. The analysis of the *Entstehung* must delineate this interaction, the manner of the struggle that these forces wage against each other or against adverse circumstances, and the attempt to avoid degeneration and regain strength by dividing these forces against themselves. It is in this sense that the emergence of a species (animal or human) and its solidification are secured "in an extended battle against conditions which are essentially and constantly unfavorable." In fact, "the species must realize itself as a species, as something – characterized by the durability, uniformity, and simplicity of its form – which can prevail in the perpetual struggle against outsiders or the uprising of those it oppresses from within." On the other hand, individual differences emerge in another state of the relationship of forces, when the species has become victorious and when it is no longer threatened from outside. In this condition, we find a struggle "of egoisms turned against each other, each bursting forth in a splintering of forces and a general striving for the sun and for the light."[27] There are also times when force contends against itself, and not only in the intoxication of an abundance, which allows it to divide itself, but at the moment when it weakens. Force reacts against its growing lassitude and gains strength; it imposes limits, inflicts torments and mortifications; it masks these actions as a higher morality and, in exchange, regains its strength. In this manner, the ascetic ideal was born, "in the instinct of a decadent life which ... struggles for its own existence."[28] This also describes the movement in which the Reformation arose, precisely where the Church was least corrupt;[29] German Catholicism, in the sixteenth century, retained enough strength to turn against itself, to mortify its own body and history, and to spiritualize itself into a pure religion of conscience.

Emergence is thus the entry of forces; it is their eruption, the leap from the wings to center stage, each in its youthful strength. What Nietzsche calls the *Entstehungsherd* of the concept of goodness is not specifically the energy of the strong or the reaction of the weak, but precisely this scene where they are displayed superimposed or face to face.[30] It is nothing but the space that divides them, the void through which they exchange their threatening gestures and speeches. As descent qualifies the strength or weakness of an instinct and its inscription on a body, emergence designates a place of confrontation, but not as a closed field offering the spectacle of a struggle among equals. Rather, as Nietzsche demonstrates in his analysis of good and evil, it is a "nonplace," a pure distance, which indicates that the adversaries do not belong to a common space. Consequently, no one is responsible for an emergence; no one can glory in it, since it always occurs in the interstice.

In a sense, only a single drama is ever staged in this "nonplace," the endlessly repeated play of dominations. The domination of certain men over others leads to the differentiation of values;[31] class domination generates the idea of liberty;[32] and the forceful appropriation of things necessary to survival and the imposition of a duration not intrinsic to them account for the origin of logic.[33] This relationship of domination is no more a "relationship" than the place where it occurs is a place; and, precisely for this reason, it is fixed, throughout its history, in rituals, in meticulous procedures that impose rights and obligations. It establishes marks of its power and engraves memories on things and even within bodies. It makes itself accountable for debts and gives rise to the universe of rules, which is by no means designed to temper violence, but rather to satisfy it. It would be wrong to follow traditional beliefs in thinking that total war exhausts itself in its own contradictions and ends by renouncing violence and submitting to civil laws. On the contrary, the law is the calculated pleasure of relentlessness. It is the promised blood, which permits the perpetual instigation of new dominations and the staging of meticulously repeated scenes of violence. The desire for peace, the serenity of compromise, and the tacit acceptance of the law, far from representing a major moral conversion or a utilitarian calculation that gave rise to the law, are but its result and, in point of fact, its perversion: "guilt, conscience, and duty had their threshold of emergence in the right to secure obligations; and their inception, like that of any major event on earth, was saturated in blood."[34] Humanity does not gradually progress from combat to combat until it arrives at universal reciprocity, where the rule of law finally replaces warfare; humanity installs each of its violences in a system of rules and thus proceeds from domination to domination.

And it is these rules which allow violence to be inflicted on violence and the resurgence of new forces that are sufficiently strong to dominate those in power. Rules are empty in themselves, violent and unfinalized; they are made to serve this or that, and can be bent to any purpose. The successes of history belong to those who are capable of seizing these rules, to replace those who had used them, to disguise themselves so as to pervert them, invert their meaning, and redirect them against those who had initially imposed them; introducing themselves into this complex mechanism, they will make it function in such a way that the dominators find themselves dominated by their own rules. The isolation of different points of emergence does not conform to the successive configurations of an identical meaning; rather, they result from substitutions, displacements, disguised conquests, and systematic reversals. If interpretation were the slow exposure of the meaning hidden in an origin, then only metaphysics could interpret the development of humanity. But if interpretation is the violent or surreptitious appropriation of a system of rules, which in itself has no essential meaning, in order to impose a direction, to bend it to a new will, to force its participation in a different game, and to subject it to secondary rules, then the development of humanity is a series of interpretations. The role of genealogy is to record its history: the history of morals, ideals, and metaphysical concepts, the history of the concept of liberty or of the ascetic life; as they stand for the emergence of different interpretations, they must be made to appear as events in the theater of procedures.

5

What is the relationship between genealogy, seen as the examination of *Herkunft* and *Entstehung*, and history in the traditional sense? We could, of course, examine Nietzsche's celebrated apostrophes against history, but we will put these aside for the moment and consider those instances when he conceives of genealogy as *wirkliche Historie*, or its more frequent characterization as historical "spirit" or "sense."[35] In fact, Nietzsche's criticism, beginning with the second of the *Untimely Meditations*, always questioned the form of history that reintroduces (and always assumes) a suprahistorical perspective: a history whose function is to compose the finally reduced diversity of time into a totality fully closed upon itself; a history that always encourages subjective recognitions and attributes a form of reconciliation to all the displacements of the past; a history whose perspective on all that precedes it implies the end of time, a completed development. The historian's history finds its support outside of time and claims to base its judgments on an apocalyptic objectivity. This is only possible, however, because of its belief in eternal truth, the immortality of the soul, and the nature of consciousness as always identical to itself. Once the historical sense is mastered by a suprahistorical perspective, metaphysics can bend it to its own purpose, and, by aligning it to the demands of objective science, it can impose its own "Egyptianism." On the other hand, the historical sense can evade metaphysics and become a privileged instrument of genealogy if it refuses the certainty of absolutes. Given this, it corresponds to the acuity of a glance that distinguishes, separates, and disperses; that is capable of liberating divergence and marginal elements – the kind of dissociating view that is capable of decomposing itself, capable of shattering the unity of man's being through which it was thought that he could extend his sovereignty to the events of his past.

Historical sense reintroduces into the realm of becoming everything considered immortal in man, and just so does it practice *wirkliche Historie*. We believe that feelings are immutable, but every sentiment, particularly the noblest and most disinterested, has a history. We believe in the dull constancy of instinctual life and imagine that it continues to exert its force indiscriminately in the present as it did in the past. But historical knowledge easily disintegrates this unity, points out its avatars, depicts its wavering course, locates its moments of strength and weakness, and defines its oscillating reign. It easily seizes the slow elaboration of instincts and those movements where, in turning upon themselves, they relentlessly set about their self-destruction.[36] We believe, in any event, that the body obeys the exclusive laws of physiology, and that it escapes the influence of history, but this too is false. The body is molded by a great many distinct regimes; it is broken down by the rhythms of work, rest, and holidays; it is poisoned by food or values, through eating habits or moral laws; it constructs resistances.[37] "Effective" history differs from the history of historians in being without constants. Nothing in man – not even his body – is sufficiently stable to serve as the basis for self-recognition or for understanding other men. The traditional devices for constructing a comprehensive view of history and for retracing the past as a patient and continuous development must be systematically dismantled. Necessarily, we must dismiss those tendencies which encourage the consoling play of recognitions. Knowledge [*savoir*], even under the banner of history, does not depend on "rediscovery," and it emphatically excludes the "rediscovery of ourselves." History becomes "effective" to the degree that it introduces discontinuity into our very being – as it divides our emotions, dramatizes our instincts, multiplies our body and sets it against itself. "Effective" history leaves nothing around the self, deprives the self of the reassuring stability of life and nature, and it will not permit itself to be transported by a voiceless obstinacy toward a millennial ending. It will uproot its traditional foundations and relentlessly disrupt its pretended continuity. This is because knowledge is not made for understanding; it is made for cutting.

From these observations, we can grasp the particular traits of the historical sense as Nietzsche understood it – the sense which opposes *wirkliche Historie* to traditional history. The former inverts the relationship ordinarily established between the eruption of an event and necessary continuity. An entire historical tradition (theological or rationalistic) aims at dissolving the singular event into an ideal continuity – as a theological movement or a natural process. "Effective" history, however, deals with events in terms of their most unique characteristics, their most acute manifestations. An event, consequently, is not a decision, a treaty, a reign, or a battle, but the reversal of a relationship of forces, the usurpation of power, the appropriation of a vocabulary turned against those who had once used it, a domination that grows feeble, poisons itself, grows slack, the entry of a masked "other." The forces operating in history do not obey destiny or regulative mechanisms, but the luck of the battle.[38] They do not manifest the successive forms of a primordial intention and their attention is not that of a conclusion, for they always appear through the singular randomness of events. The inverse of the Christian world, spun entirely by a divine spider, and different from the world of the Greeks, divided between the realm of will and the great cosmic folly, the world of effective history knows only one kingdom, without providence or final cause, where there is only "the iron hand of necessity shaking the dice-box of chance."[39] Chance is not simply the drawing of lots but raising the stakes in every attempt to master chance through the will to power, and giving rise to the risk of an even greater chance.[40] The world such as we are acquainted with it is not this ultimately simple configuration where events are reduced to accentuate their essential traits, their final meaning, or their initial and final value. On the contrary, it is a profusion of entangled events. If it appears as a "marvelous motley, profound and totally meaningful," this is because it began and continues its secret existence through a "host of errors and phantasms."[41] We want historians to confirm our belief that the present rests upon profound intentions and immutable necessities. But the true historical sense confirms our existence among countless lost events, without a landmark or a point of reference.

The historical sense can also invert the relationship that traditional history, in its dependence on metaphysics, establishes between proximity and distance. The latter is given to a contemplation of distances and heights: the noblest periods, the highest forms, the most abstract ideas, the purest individualities. It accomplishes this by getting as near as possible, placing itself at the foot of its mountain peaks, at the risk of adopting the famous perspective of frogs. Effective history, on the other hand, shortens its vision to those things nearest to it – the body, the nervous system, nutrition, digestion, and energies; it unearths decadence, and if it chances upon lofty epochs, it is with the suspicion – not vindictive but joyous – of finding a barbarous and shameful confusion. It has no fear of looking down, but it looks from above and descends to seize the various perspectives, to disclose dispersions and differences, to leave things undisturbed in their own dimension and intensity. It reverses the surreptitious practice of historians, their pretension to examine things farthest from themselves, the groveling manner in which they approach this promising distance (like the metaphysicians who proclaim the existence of an afterlife, situated at a distance from this world, as a promise of their reward). Effective history studies what is closest, but in an abrupt dispossession, so as to seize it at a distance (an approach similar to that of a doctor who looks closely, who plunges to make a diagnosis and to state its difference). Historical sense has more in common with medicine than philosophy; and it should not surprise us that Nietzsche occasionally employs the phrase "historically and physiologically,"[42] since among the philosopher's idiosyncrasies is a complete denial of the body. This includes, as well, "the absence of historical sense, a hatred for the idea of development, Egyptianism," the obstinate "placing of conclusions at the beginning," of "making last things first."[43] History has a more important task than to be a handmaiden to philosophy, to recount the necessary birth of truth and values; it should become a differential knowledge [*connaissance*] of energies and failings, heights and degenerations, poisons and antidotes. Its task is to become a curative science.[44]

The final trait of effective history is its affirmation of a perspectival knowledge [*savoir*]. Historians take unusual pains to erase the elements in their work which reveal their grounding in a particular time and place, their preferences in a controversy – the unavoidable obstacles of their passion. Nietzsche's version of historical sense is explicit in its perspective and acknowledges its system of injustice. Its perception is slanted, being a deliberate appraisal, affirmation, or negation; it follows the lingering and poisonous traces, prescribes the best antidote. It is not given to a discreet effacement before the objects it observes and does not submit itself to their processes; nor does it seek laws, since it gives equal weight to its own sight and to its objects. Through this historical sense, knowledge is allowed to create its own genealogy in the act of cognition; and *wirkliche Historie* composes a genealogy of history as the vertical projection of its position.

6

In that genealogy of history he sketches in several versions, Nietzsche links historical sense to the historian's history. They share a beginning that is similarly impure and confused, share the same sign in which the symptoms of sickness can be recognized as well as the seed of an exquisite flower.[45] They arose simultaneously to follow their separate ways, but our task is to trace their common genealogy.

The descent [*Herkunft*] of the historian is unequivocal: he is of humble birth. A characteristic of history is to be without choice: it is prepared to acquaint itself with everything, without any hierarchy of importance; to understand everything, without regard to eminence; to accept everything, without making any distinctions. Nothing must escape it and, more important, nothing must be excluded. Historians argue that this proves their tact and discretion. After all, what right have they to impose their tastes and preferences when they seek to determine what actually occurred in the past? What they in fact exhibit is a total lack of taste, a certain crudity that tries to take liberties with what is most exalted, a satisfaction in meeting up with what is base. The historian is insensitive to all disgusting things; or rather, he especially enjoys those things which should be repugnant to him. His apparent serenity follows from his concerted avoidance of the exceptional and his reduction of all things to the lowest common denominator. Nothing is allowed to stand above him; and underlying his desire for total knowledge is his search for the secrets that belittle everything: "base curiosity." What is the source of history? It comes from the plebs. To whom is it addressed? To the plebs. And its discourse strongly resembles the demagogue's refrain: "No one is greater than you and anyone who presumes to get the better of you — you who are good — is evil." The historian, who functions as his double, can be heard to echo: "No past is greater than your present, and, through my meticulous erudition, I will rid you of your infatuations and transform the grandeur of history into pettiness, evil, and misfortune." The historian's ancestry goes back to Socrates.

This demagoguery, of course, must be masked. It must hide its singular malice under the cloak of universals. As the demagogue is obliged to invoke truth, laws of essences, and eternal necessity, the historian must invoke objectivity, the accuracy of facts, and the permanence of the past. The demagogue denies the body to secure the sovereignty of a timeless idea, and the historian effaces his proper individuality so that others may enter the stage and reclaim their own speech. He is divided against himself, forced to silence his preferences and overcome his distaste, to blur his own perspective and replace it with the fiction of a universal geometry, to mimic death in order to enter the kingdom of the dead, to adopt a faceless anonymity. In this world where he has conquered his individual will, he becomes a guide to the inevitable law of a superior will. Having curbed the demands of his individual will in his knowledge, he will disclose the form of an eternal will in his object of study. The objectivity of historians inverts the relationships of will and knowledge, and it is, in the same stroke, a necessary belief in providence, in final causes and teleology. The historian belongs to the family of ascetics. "I can't stand these lustful eunuchs of history, all the seductions of an ascetic ideal; I can't stand these blanched tombs producing life or those tired and indifferent beings who dress up in the part of wisdom and adopt an objective point of view."[46]

The *Entstehung* of history is found in nineteenth-century Europe: the land of interminglings and bastardy, the period of the "man-of-mixture." We have become barbarians with respect to those rare moments of high civilization: cities in ruin and enigmatic monuments are spread out before us; we stop before gaping walls; we ask what gods inhabited these empty temples. Great epochs lacked this curiosity, lacked our excessive deference; they ignored their predecessors: the Classical period ignored Shakespeare. The decadence of Europe presents an immense spectacle (while stronger periods refrained from such exhibitions), and the nature of this scene is to represent a theater; lacking monuments of our own making, which properly belong to us, we live among a crowd of scenery. But there is more. Europeans no longer know themselves; they ignore their mixed ancestries and seek a proper role. They lack individuality. We can begin to understand the spontaneous historical bent of the nineteenth century: the anemia of its forces and those mixtures that effaced all its individual traits produced the same results as the mortifications of asceticism; its inability to create, its absence of artistic works, and its need to rely on past achievements forced it to adopt the base curiosity of plebs.

If this fully represents the genealogy of history, how could it become, in its own right, a genealogical analysis? Why did it not continue as a form of demogogic or religious knowledge? How could it change roles on the same stage? Only by being seized, dominated, and turned against its birth. And it is this movement which properly describes the specific nature of the *Entstehung*: it is not the unavoidable conclusion of a long preparation but a scene where forces are risked and confront one another where they emerge triumphant, where they can also be confiscated. The locus of emergence for metaphysics was surely Athenian demogoguery, the vulgar spite of Socrates and his belief in immortality, and Plato could have seized this Socratic philosophy to turn it against itself. Undoubtedly, he was often tempted to do so, but his defeat lies in its consecration. The problem was similar in the nineteenth century – to avoid doing for the popular asceticism of historians what Plato did for Socrates. This historical trait should not be founded on a philosophy of history, but dismantled, beginning with the things it produced. It is necessary to master history so as to turn it to genealogical uses, that is, strictly anti-Platonic purposes. Only then will the historical sense free itself from the demands of a suprahistorical history.

7

The historical sense gives rise to three uses that oppose and correspond to the three Platonic modalities of history. The first is parodic, directed against reality, and opposes the theme of history as reminiscence or recognition; the second is dissociative, directed against identity, and opposes history given as continuity or representative of a tradition; the third is sacrificial, directed against truth, and opposes history as knowledge [*connaissance*]. They imply a use of history that severs its connection to memory, its metaphysical and anthropological model, and constructs a countermemory — a transformation of history into a totally different form of time.

First, the parodic and farcical use. The historian offers this confused and anonymous European, who no longer knows himself or what name he should adopt, the possibility of alternative identities, more individualized and real than his own. But the man with historical sense will see that this substitution is simply a disguise. Historians supplied the Revolution with Roman prototypes, Romanticism with knight's armor, and the Wagnerian era was given the sword of a German hero — ephemeral props whose unreality points to our own. No one kept them from venerating these religions, from going to Bayreuth to commemorate a new afterlife; they were free, as well, to be transformed into street vendors of empty identities. The good historian, the genealogist, will know what to make of this masquerade.

He will not be too serious to enjoy it; on the contrary, he will push the masquerade to its limit and prepare the great carnival of time where masks are constantly reappearing. No longer the identification of our faint individuality with the solid identities of the past, but our "unrealization" through the excessive choice of identities — Frederick of Hohenstaufen, Caesar, Jesus, Dionysus, and possibly Zarathustra. Taking up these masks, revitalizing the buffoonery of history, we adopt an identity whose unreality surpasses that of God, who started the charade. "Perhaps, we can discover a realm where originality is again possible as parodists of history and buffoons of God."[47] In this, we recognize the parodic double of what the second of the *Untimely Meditations* called "monumental history": a history given to reestablishing the high points of historical development and their maintenance in a perpetual presence, given to the recovery of works, actions, and creations through the monogram of their personal essence. But in 1874 Nietzsche accused this history, one totally devoted to veneration, of barring access to the actual intensities and creations of life. The parody of his last texts serves to emphasize that "monumental history" is itself a parody. Genealogy is history in the form of a concerted carnival.

The second use of history is the systematic dissociation of our identity. For this rather weak identity, which we attempt to support and to unify under a mask, is in itself only a parody: it is plural; countless souls dispute its possession; numerous systems intersect and dominate one another. The study of history makes one "happy, unlike the metaphysicians, to possess in oneself not an immortal soul but many mortal ones."[48] And in each of these souls, history will discover not a forgotten identity, eager to be reborn, but a complex system of distinct and multiple elements, unable to be mastered by the powers of synthesis: "It is a sign of superior culture to maintain, in a fully conscious way, certain phases of its evolution which lesser men pass through without thought. The initial result is that we can understand those who resemble us as a completely determined system and as representative of diverse cultures, that is to say, as necessary and capable of modification. And, in return, we are able to separate the phases of our own evolution and consider them individually."[49] The purpose of history, guided by genealogy, is not to discover the roots of our identity, but to commit itself to its dissipation. It does not seek to define our unique threshold of emergence, the homeland to which metaphysicians promise a return; it seeks to make visible all of those discontinuities that cross us. "Antiquarian history," according to the *Untimely Meditations*, pursues opposite goals. It seeks the continuities of soil, language, and urban life in which our present is rooted, and, "by cultivating in a delicate manner that which existed for all time, it tries to conserve for posterity the conditions under which we were born."[50] This type of history was objected to in the *Meditations* because it tended to block creativity in support of the laws of fidelity. Somewhat later — and already in *Human,*

All Too Human — Nietzsche reconsiders the task of the antiquarian, but with an altogether different emphasis. If genealogy in its own right gives rise to questions concerning our native land, native language, or the laws that govern us, its intention is to reveal the heterogeneous systems that, masked by the self, inhibit the formation of any form of identity.

The third use of history is the sacrifice of the subject of knowledge [*connaissance*]. In appearance or, rather, according to the mask it bears, historical consciousness is neutral, devoid of passions, and committed solely to truth. But if it examines itself and if, more generally, it interrogates the various forms of scientific consciousness in its history, it finds that all these forms and transformations are aspects of the will to knowledge [*savoir*]: instinct, passion, the inquisitor's devotion, cruel subtlety, and malice. It discovers the violence of a position that sides against those who are happy in their ignorance, against the effective illusions by which humanity protects itself, a position that encourages the dangers of research and delights in disturbing discoveries.[51] The historical analysis of this rancorous will to knowledge[52] [*vouloir-savoir*] reveals that all knowledge [*connaissance*] rests upon injustice (that there is no right, not even in the act of knowing, to truth or a foundation for truth), and that the instinct for knowledge is malicious (something murderous, opposed to the happiness of mankind). Even in the greatly expanded form it assumes today, the will to knowledge does not achieve a universal truth; man is not given an exact and serene mastery of nature. On the contrary, it ceaselessly multiplies the risks, creates dangers in every area; it breaks down illusory defences; it dissolves the unity of the subject; it releases those elements of itself that are devoted to its subversion and destruction. Knowledge [*savoir*] does not slowly detach itself from its empirical roots, the initial needs from which it arose, to become pure speculation subject only to the demands of reason; its development is not tied to the constitution and affirmation of a free subject; rather, it creates a progressive enslavement to its instinctive violence. Where religions once demanded the sacrifice of bodies, knowledge now calls for experimentation on ourselves,[53] calls us to the sacrifice of the subject of knowledge [*connaissance*]. "Knowledge [*connaissance*] has been transformed among us into a passion which fears no sacrifice, which fears nothing but its own extinction. It may be that mankind will eventually perish from this passion for knowledge. If not through passion, then through weakness. We must be prepared to state our choice: do we wish humanity to end in fire and light or to end on the sands?"[54] We should now replace the two great problems of nineteenth-century philosophy, passed on by Fichte and Hegel (the reciprocal basis of truth and liberty and the possibility of absolute knowledge [*savoir*]), with the theme that "to perish through absolute knowledge [*connaissance*] may well form a part of the basis of being."[55] This does not mean, in terms of a critical procedure, that the will to truth is limited by the intrinsic finitude of cognition [*connaissance*], but that it loses all sense of limitations and all claim to truth in its unavoidable sacrifice of the subject of knowledge [*connaissance*]. "It may be that there remains one prodigious idea which might be made to prevail over every other aspiration, which might overcome the most victorious: the idea of humanity sacrificing itself. It seems indisputable that if this new constellation appeared on the horizon, only the desire to know truth, with its enormous prerogatives, could direct and sustain such a sacrifice. For to knowledge [*connaissance*], no sacrifice is too great. Of course, this problem has never been posed."[56]

The *Untimely Meditations* discussed the critical use of history: its just treatment of the past, its decisive cutting of the roots, its rejection of traditional attitudes of reverence, its liberation of man by presenting him with other origins than those in which he prefers to see himself. Nietzsche, however, reproached critical history for detaching us from every real source and for sacrificing the very movement of life to the exclusive concern for truth. Somewhat later, as we have seen, Nietzsche reconsiders this line of thought he had at first refused, but he directs it to altogether different ends. It is no longer a question of judging the past in the name of a truth that only we can possess in the present, but of risking the destruction of the subject who seeks knowledge [*connaissance*], in the endless deployment of the will to knowledge [*savoir*].

In a sense, genealogy returns to the three modalities of history that Nietzsche recognized in 1874. It returns to them in spite of the objections that Nietzsche raised in the name of the affirmative and creative powers of life. But they are metamorphosed: the veneration of monuments becomes parody; the respect for ancient continuities becomes systematic dissociation; the critique of the injustices of the past by a truth held by men in the present becomes the destruction of the man who maintains knowledge [*connaissance*] by the injustice proper to the will to knowledge.

Chapter 5

Jacques Derrida

■ COGITO AND THE HISTORY OF MADNESS in *Writing and Difference,* Alan Bass trans., London and New York: Routledge, 2002

The Instant of Decision is Madness.

(Kierkegaard)

In any event this book was terribly daring. A transparent sheet separates it from madness.

(Joyce, speaking of *Ulysses*)

THESE REFLECTIONS HAVE as their point of departure, as the title of this lecture[1] clearly indicates, Michel Foucault's book *Folie et déraison: Histoire de la folie à l'âge classique.*[2]

This book, admirable in so many respects, powerful in its breadth and style, is even more intimidating for me in that, having formerly had the good fortune to study under Michel Foucault, I retain the consciousness of an admiring and grateful disciple. Now, the disciple's consciousness, when he starts, I would not say to dispute, but to engage in dialogue with the master or, better, to articulate the interminable and silent dialogue which made him into a disciple – this disciple's consciousness is an unhappy consciousness. Starting to enter into dialogue in the world, that is, starting to answer back, he always feels "caught in the act," like the "infant" who, by definition and as his name indicates, cannot speak and above all must not answer back. And when, as is the case here, the dialogue is in danger of being taken – incorrectly – as a challenge, the disciple knows that he alone finds himself already challenged by the master's voice within him that precedes his own. He feels himself indefinitely challenged, or rejected or accused; as a disciple, he is challenged by the master who speaks within him and before him, to reproach him for making this challenge and to reject it in advance, having elaborated it before him; and having interiorized the master, he is also challenged by the disciple that he himself is. This interminable unhappiness of the disciple perhaps stems from the fact that he does not yet know – or is still concealing from himself – that the master, like real life, may always be absent. The disciple must break the glass, or better the mirror, the reflection, his infinite speculation on the master. And start to speak.

As the route that these considerations will follow is neither direct nor unilinear – far from it – I will sacrifice any further preamble and go straight to the most general questions that will serve as the focal points of these reflections. General questions that will have to be determined and specified along the way, many of which, most, will remain open.

My point of departure might appear slight and artificial. In this 673-page book, Michel Foucault devotes three pages – and, moreover, in a kind of prologue to his second chapter – to a certain passage from the first of Descartes's *Meditations*. In this passage madness, folly, dementia, insanity seem, I emphasize *seem*, dismissed, excluded, and ostracized from the circle of philosophical dignity, denied entry to the philosopher's city, denied the right to philosophical consideration, ordered away from the bench as soon as summoned to it by Descartes – this last tribunal of a Cogito that, by its essence, *could not possibly* be mad.

In alleging – correctly or incorrectly, as will be determined – that the sense of Foucault's entire project can be pinpointed in these few allusive and somewhat enigmatic pages, and that the reading of Descartes and the Cartesian Cogito proposed to us engages in its problematic the totality of this *History of Madness* as regards both its intention and its feasibility, I shall therefore be asking myself, in two series of questions, the following:

1. First, and in some ways this is a prejudicial question: is the *interpretation* of Descartes's intention that is proposed to us justifiable? What I here call interpretation is a certain passage, a certain semantic relationship proposed by Foucault between, *on the one hand*, what Descartes said – or what he is believed to have said or meant – and *on the other hand*, let us say, with intentional vagueness for the moment, a certain "historical structure," as it is called, a certain meaningful historical totality, a total historical project through which we think what Descartes said – or what he is believed to have said or meant – can *particularly* be demonstrated. In asking if the interpretation is justifiable, I am therefore asking about two things, putting two preliminary questions into one: (a) Have we fully understood the *sign* itself, in itself? In other words, has what Descartes said and meant been clearly perceived? This comprehension of the sign in and of itself, in its immediate materiality as a sign, if I may so call it, is only the first moment but also the indispensable condition of all hermeneutics and of any claim to transition from the sign to the signified. When one attempts, in a general way, to pass from an obvious to a latent language, one must first be rigorously sure of the obvious meaning.[3] The analyst, for example, must first speak the same language as the patient. (b) Second implication of the first question: once understood as a sign, does Descartes's stated intention have with the total historical structure to which it is to be related the relationship assigned to it? *Does it have the historical meaning assigned to it?* "Does it have the historical meaning assigned to it?" That is, again, two questions in one: Does it have *the* historical meaning assigned to it? Does it have *this* meaning, a *given* meaning Foucault assigns to it? Or, second, does it have the *historical* meaning assigned to it? Is this meaning exhausted by its historicity? In other words, is it fully, in each and every one of its aspects, historical, in the classical sense of the word?

2. Second series of questions (and here we shall go somewhat beyond the case of Descartes, beyond the case of the Cartesian Cogito, which will be examined no longer in and of itself but as the index of a more general problematic): in the light of the rereading of the Cartesian Cogito that we shall be led to propose (or rather to recall, for, let it be said

at the outset, this will in some ways be the most classical, banal reading, even if not the easiest one), will it not be possible to interrogate *certain* philosophical and methodological presuppositions of this history of madness? *Certain ones* only, for Foucault's enterprise is too rich, branches out in too many directions to be preceded by a method or even by a *philosophy*, in the traditional sense of the word. And if it is true, as Foucault says, as he admits by citing Pascal, that one cannot speak of madness except in relation to that "other form of madness" that allows men "not to be mad," that is, except in relation to reason,[4] it will perhaps be possible not to add anything whatsoever to what Foucault has said, but perhaps only to *repeat* once more, on the site of this *division* between reason and madness of which Foucault speaks so well, the meaning, a meaning of the Cogito or (plural) Cogitos (for the Cogito of the Cartesian variety is neither the first nor the last form of Cogito), and also to determine that what is in question here is an experience which, at its furthest reaches, is perhaps no less adventurous, perilous, nocturnal, and pathetic than the experience of madness, and is, I believe, much less adverse to and accusatory of madness, that is, accusative and objectifying of it, than Foucault seems to think.

As a first stage, we will attempt a commentary, and will accompany or follow as faithfully as possible Foucault's intentions in reinscribing an interpretation of the Cartesian Cogito within the total framework of the *History of Madness*. What should then become apparent in the course of this first stage is the meaning of the Cartesian Cogito as read by Foucault. To this end, it is necessary to recall the general plan of the book and to open several marginal questions, destined to remain open and marginal.

In writing a history of madness, Foucault has attempted – and this is the greatest merit, but also the very infeasibility of his book – to write a history of madness *itself*. *Itself*. Of madness itself. That is, by letting madness speak for itself. Foucault wanted madness to be the *subject* of his book in every sense of the word: its theme and its first-person narrator, its author, madness speaking about itself. Foucault wanted to write a history of madness *itself*, that is madness speaking on the basis of its own experience and under its own authority, and not a history of madness described from within the language of reason, the language of psychiatry *on* madness – the agonistic and rhetorical dimensions of the preposition *on* overlapping here – on madness already crushed beneath psychiatry, dominated, beaten to the ground, interned, that is to say, madness made into an object and exiled as the other of a language and a historical meaning which have been confused with logos itself. "A history not of psychiatry," Foucault says, "but of madness itself, in its most vibrant state, before being captured by knowledge."

It is a question, therefore, of escaping the trap or objectivist naiveté that would consist in writing a history of untamed madness, of madness as it carries itself and breathes before being caught and paralyzed in the nets of classical reason, from within the very language of classical reason itself, utilizing the concepts that were the historical instruments of the capture of madness – the restrained and restraining language of reason. Foucault's determination to avoid this trap is constant. It is the most audacious and seductive aspect of his venture, producing its admirable tension. But it is also, with all seriousness, the *maddest* aspect of his project. And it is remarkable that this obstinate determination to avoid the trap – that is, the trap set by classical reason to catch madness and which can now catch Foucault as he attempts to write a history of madness itself without repeating the aggression of rationalism – this determination to bypass reason is expressed in two ways difficult to reconcile at first glance. Which is to say that it is expressed uneasily.

Sometimes Foucault globally rejects the language of reason, which itself is the language of order (that is to say, simultaneously the language of the system of objectivity, of the universal rationality of which psychiatry wishes to be the expression, and the language of the body politic — the right to citizenship in the philosopher's city overlapping here with the right to citizenship anywhere, the philosophical realm functioning, within the unity of a certain structure, as the metaphor or the metaphysics of the political realm). At these moments he writes sentences of this type (he has just evoked the broken dialogue between reason and madness at the end of the eighteenth century, a break that was finalized by the annexation of the totality of language — and of the right to language — by psychiatric reason as the delegate of societal and governmental reason; madness has been stifled): "The language of psychiatry, which is a monologue of reason *on* madness, could be established only on the basis of such a silence. I have not tried to write the history of that language but, rather, the archaeology of that silence."[5] And throughout the book runs the theme linking madness to silence, to "words without language" or "without the voice of a subject," "obstinate murmur of a language that speaks by itself, without speaker or interlocutor, piled up upon itself, strangulated, collapsing before reaching the stage of formulation, quietly returning to the silence from which it never departed. The calcinated root of meaning." The history of madness itself is therefore the archaeology of a silence.

But, first of all, is there a history of silence? Further, is not an archaeology, even of silence, a logic, that is, an organized language, a project, an order, a sentence, a syntax, a work?[6] Would not the archaeology of silence be the most efficacious and subtle restoration, the *repetition*, in the most irreducibly ambiguous meaning of the word, of the act perpetrated against madness — and be so at the very moment when this act is denounced? Without taking into account that all the signs which allegedly serve as indices of the origin of this silence and of this stifled speech, and as indices of everything that has made madness an interrupted and forbidden, that is, arrested, discourse — all these signs and documents are borrowed without exception, from the juridical province of interdiction.

Hence, one can inquire — as Foucault does also, at moments other than those when he contrives to speak of silence (although in too lateral and implicit a fashion from my point of view) — about the source and the status of the language of this archaeology, of this language which is to be understood by a reason that is not classical reason. What is the historical responsibility of this logic of archaeology? Where should it be situated? Does it suffice to stack the tools of psychiatry neatly, inside a tightly shut workshop, in order to return to innocence and to end all complicity with the rational or political order which keeps madness captive? The psychiatrist is but the delegate of this order, one delegate among others. Perhaps it does not suffice to imprison or to exile the delegate, or to stifle him; and perhaps it does not suffice to deny oneself the conceptual material of psychiatry in order to exculpate one's own language. All our European languages, the language of everything that has participated, from near or far, in the adventure of Western reason — all this is the immense delegation of the project defined by Foucault under the rubric of the capture or objectification of madness. *Nothing* within this language, and *no one* among those who speak it, can escape the historical guilt — if there is one, and if it is historical in a classical sense — which Foucault apparently wishes to put on trial. But such a trial may be impossible, for by the simple fact of their articulation the proceedings and the verdict unceasingly reiterate the crime. If the *Order* of which we are speaking is so powerful, if its power is unique of its kind, this is so precisely by virtue of the universal, structural, universal, and infinite complicity in which it compromises all those who understand it in its own language, even when this language provides them with the form of their own denunciation. Order is then denounced within order.

Total disengagement from the *totality* of the historical language responsible for the exile of madness, liberation from this language in order to write the archaeology of silence, would be possible in only two ways.

Either do not mention a certain silence (a *certain* silence which, again, can be determined only within a *language* and an *order* that will preserve this silence from contamination by any given muteness), *or* follow the madman down the road of his exile. The misfortune of the mad, the interminable misfortune of their silence, is that their best spokesmen are those who betray them best; which is to say that when one attempts to convey their silence *itself*, one has already passed over to the side of the enemy, the side of order, even if one fights against order from within it, putting its origin into question. There is no Trojan horse unconquerable by Reason (in general). The unsurpassable, unique, and imperial grandeur of the order of reason, that which makes it not just another actual order or structure (a determined historical structure, one structure among other possible ones), is that one cannot speak out against it except by being for it, that one can protest it only from within it; and within its domain, Reason leaves us only the recourse to strategems and strategies. The revolution against reason, in the historical form of classical reason (but the latter is only a determined example of Reason in general. And because of this oneness of Reason the expression "history of reason" is difficult to conceptualize, as is also, consequently, a "history of madness"), the revolution against reason can be made only within it, in accordance with a Hegelian law to which I myself was very sensitive in Foucault's book, despite the absence of any precise reference to Hegel. Since the revolution against reason, from the moment it is articulated, can operate only *within* reason, it always has the limited scope of what is called, precisely in the language of a department of *internal* affairs, a disturbance. A history, that is, an archaeology against reason doubtless cannot be written, for, despite all appearances to the contrary, the concept of history has always been a rational one. It is the meaning of "history" or *archia* that should have been questioned first, perhaps. A writing that exceeds, by questioning them, the values "origin," "reason," and "history" could not be contained within the metaphysical closure of an archaeology.

As Foucault is the first to be conscious – and acutely so – of this daring, of the necessity of speaking and of drawing his language from the wellspring of a reason more profound than the reason which issued forth during the classical age, and as he experiences a necessity of speaking which must escape the objectivist project of classical reason – a necessity of speaking even at the price of a war declared by the language of reason against itself, a war in which language would recapture itself, destroy itself, or unceasingly revive the act of its own destruction – the allegation of an archaeology of silence, a purist, intransigent, nonviolent, nondialectical allegation, is often counterbalanced, equilibrated, I should even say contradicted by a discourse in Foucault's book that is not only the admission of a difficulty, but the formulation of *another* project, a project that is not an expediency, but a different and more ambitious one, a project more effectively ambitious than the first one.

The admission of the difficulty can be found in sentences such as these, among others, which I simply cite, in order not to deprive you of their dense beauty: "The perception that seeks to grasp them [in question are the miseries and murmurings of madness] in their wild state, necessarily belongs to a world that has already captured them. The liberty of madness can be understood only from high in the fortress that holds madness prisoner.

And there madness possesses only the morose sum of its prison experiences, its mute experience of persecution, and we — we possess only its description as a man wanted." And, later, Foucault speaks of a madness "whose wild state can never be restored in and of itself" and of an "inaccessible primitive purity."

Because this difficulty, or this impossibility, must reverberate within the language used to describe this history of madness, Foucault, in effect, acknowledges the necessity of maintaining his discourse within what he calls a "relativity without recourse," that is, without support from an absolute reason or logos. The simultaneous necessity and impossibility of what Foucault elsewhere calls "a language without support," that is to say, a language declining, in principle if not in fact, to articulate itself along the lines of the syntax of reason. In principle if not in fact, but here the fact cannot easily be put between parentheses. The fact of language is probably the only fact ultimately to resist all parenthization. "There, in the simple problem of articulation," Foucault says later, "was hidden and expressed the major difficulty of the enterprise."

One could perhaps say that the resolution of this difficulty is *practiced* rather than *formulated*. By necessity. I mean that the silence of madness is not *said*, cannot be said in the logos of this book, but is indirectly, metaphorically, made present by its pathos — taking this word in its best sense. A new and radical praise of folly whose intentions cannot be admitted because the *praise* [*éloge*] of silence always takes place within *logos*,[7] the language of objectification. "To speak well of madness" would be to annex it once more, especially when, as is the case here, "speaking well of" is also the wisdom and happiness of eloquent speech.

Now, to state the difficulty, to state the difficulty of stating, is not yet to surmount it — quite the contrary. First, it is not to say in which language, through the agency of what speech, the difficulty is stated. Who perceives, who enunciates the difficulty? These efforts can be made neither in the wild and inaccessible silence of madness, nor simply in the language of the jailer, that is, in the language of classical reason, but only in the language of someone *for whom* is meaningful and *before whom* appears the dialogue or war or misunderstanding or confrontation or double monologue that opposes reason and madness during the classical age. And thereby we can envision the historic liberation of a logos in which the two monologues, or the broken dialogue, or especially the breaking point of the dialogue between a *determined* reason and a *determined* madness, could be produced and can today be understood and enunciated. (Supposing that they can be; but here we are assuming Foucault's hypothesis.)

Therefore, if Foucault's book, despite all the acknowledged impossibilities and difficulties, was capable of being written, we have the right to ask what, in the last resort, supports this language without recourse or support: who enunciates the possibility of nonrecourse? Who wrote and who is to understand, in what language and from what historical situation of logos, who wrote and who is to understand this history of madness? For it is not by chance that such a project could take shape today. Without forgetting, *quite to the contrary*, the audacity of Foucault's act in the *History of Madness*, we must assume that a certain liberation of madness has gotten underway, that psychiatry has opened itself up, however minimally, and that the concept of madness as unreason, if it ever had a unity, has been dislocated. And that a project such as Foucault's can find its historical origin and passageway in the opening produced by this dislocation.

If Foucault, more than anyone else, is attentive and sensitive to these kinds of questions, it nevertheless appears that he does not acknowledge their quality of being prerequisite methodological or philosophical considerations. And it is true that once the question and the privileged difficulty are understood, to devote a preliminary work to them would have entailed the sterilization or paralysis of all further inquiry. Inquiry can prove through its very act that the movement of a discourse on madness is possible. But is not the foundation of this possibility still too classical?

Foucault's book is not one of those that abandons itself to the prospective lighthearted-ness of inquiry. That is why, behind the admission of the difficulty concerning the archaeology of silence, a *different* project must be discerned, one which perhaps contradicts the projected archaeology of silence.

Because the silence whose archaeology is to be undertaken is not an original muteness or nondiscourse, but a subsequent silence, a discourse arrested by *command*, the issue is therefore to reach the origin of the protectionism imposed by a reason that insists upon being sheltered, and that also insists upon providing itself with protective barriers against madness, thereby making itself into a barrier against madness; and to reach this origin from within a logos of free trade, that is, from within a logos that preceded the split of reason and madness, a logos which within itself permitted dialogue between what were later called reason and madness (unreason), permitted their free circulation and exchange, just as the medieval city permitted the free circulation of the mad within itself. The issue is therefore to reach the point at which the dialogue was broken off, dividing itself into two soliloquies — what Foucault calls, using a very strong word, the *Decision*. The Decision, through a single act, links and separates reason and madness, and it must be understood at once both as the original act of an order, a fiat, a decree, and as a schism, a caesura, a separation, a dissection. I would prefer *dissension*, to underline that in question is a self-dividing action, a cleavage and torment interior to meaning *in general*, interior to logos in general, a divison within the very act of *sentire*. As always, the dissension is internal. The exterior (is) the interior, is the fission that produces and divides it along the lines of the Hegelian *Entzweiung*.

It thus seems that the project of convoking the first dissension of logos against itself is quite another project than the archaeology of silence, and raises different questions. This time it would be necessary to exhume the virgin and unitary ground upon which the decisive act linking and separating madness and reason obscurely took root. The reason and madness of the classical age had a common root. But this common root, which is a logos, this unitary foundation is much more ancient than the medieval period, brilliantly but briefly evoked by Foucault in his very fine opening chapter. There must be a founding unity that already carries within it the "free trade" of the Middle Ages, and this unity is already the unity of a logos, that is, of a reason; an already historical reason certainly, but a reason much less determined than it will be in its so-called classical form, having not yet received the determinations of the "classical age." It is within the element of this archaic reason that the dissection, the dissension, will present itself as a modification or, if you will, as an overturning, that is, a revolution but an internal revolution, a revolution affecting the self, occurring within the self. For this logos which is in the beginning, is not only the common ground of all dissension, but also — and no less importantly — the very atmosphere in which Foucault's language moves, the atmosphere in which a history of madness during the classical age not only appears *in fact* but is also *by all rights* stipulated and specified in terms of its limits. In order to account simultaneously for the origin (or the possibility) of the decision and for the origin (or the possibility) of its narration, it might have been necessary to start by reflecting this original logos in which the violence of the classical era played itself out. This history of logos before the Middle Ages and before the classical age is not, if this need be said at all, a nocturnal and mute prehistory. Whatever the momentary break, if there is one, of the Middle Ages with the Greek tradition, this break and this alteration are late and secondary developments as concerns the fundamental permanence of the logico-philosophical heritage.

That the embedding of the decision in its true historical grounds has been left in the shadows by Foucault is bothersome, and for at least two reasons:

1. It is bothersome because at the outset Foucault makes a somewhat enigmatic allusion to the Greek logos, saying that, unlike classical reason, it "had no contrary." To cite Foucault: "The Greeks had a relation to something that they called *hybris*. This relation was not merely one of condemnation; the existence of Thrasymacus or of Callicles suffices to prove it, even if their language has reached us already enveloped in the reassuring dialectic of Socrates. But the Greek Logos had no contrary."[8]

[One would have to assume, then, that the Greek logos had no contrary, which is to say, briefly, that the Greeks were in the greatest proximity to the elementary, primordial, and undivided Logos with respect to which contradiction in general, all wars or polemics, could only be ulterior developments. This hypothesis forces us to admit, as Foucault above all does *not*, that the history and lineage of the "reassuring dialectic of Socrates" in their *totality* had already fallen outside and been exiled from this Greek logos that had no contrary. For if the Socratic dialectic is reassuring, in the sense understood by Foucault, it is so only in that it has already expulsed, excluded, objectified or (curiously amounting to the same thing) assimilated and mastered as one of its moments, "enveloped" the contrary of reason; and also only in that it has tranquilized and reassured itself into a pre-Cartesian certainty, a *sophrosyne*, a wisdom, a reasonable good sense and prudence.

Consequently, it must be *either* (a) that the Socratic moment and its entire posterity immediately partake in the Greek logos that has no contrary; and that consequently, the Socratic dialectic could not be reassuring (we may soon have occasion to show that it is no more reassuring than the Cartesian Cogito). In this case, in this hypothesis, the fascination with the pre-Socratics to which we have been provoked by Nietzsche, then by Heidegger and several others, would carry with it a share of mystification whose historico-philosophical motivations remain to be examined. *Or* (b) that the Socratic moment and the victory over the Calliciesian hybris already are the marks of a deportation and an exile of logos from itself, the wounds left in it by a decision, a difference; and then the structure of exclusion which Foucault wishes to describe in his book could not have been born with classical reason. It would have to have been consummated and reassured and smoothed over throughout all the centuries of philosophy. It would be essential to the entirety of the history of philosophy and of reason. In this regard, the classical age could have neither specificity nor privilege. And all the signs assembled by Foucault under the chapter heading *Stultifera navis* would play themselves out only on the surface of a chronic dissension. The free circulation of the mad, besides the fact that it is not as simply free as all that, would only be a socioeconomic epiphenomenon on the surface of a reason divided against itself since the dawn of its Greek origin. What seems to me sure in any case, regardless of the hypothesis one chooses concerning what is doubtless only a false problem and a false alternative, is that Foucault cannot *simultaneously* save the affirmation of a reassuring dialectic of Socrates and his postulation of a specificity of the classical age whose reason would reassure itself by excluding its contrary, that is, by *constituting* its contrary as an object in order to be protected from it and be rid of it. In order to lock it up.

The attempt to write the history of the decision, division, difference runs the risk of construing the division as an event or a structure subsequent to the unity of an original presence, thereby confirming metaphysics in its fundamental operation.

Truthfully, for one or the other of these hypotheses to be true and for there to be a real choice between them, it must be assumed in *general* that reason can have a contrary, that there can be an other of reason, that reason itself can construct or discover, and that the opposition of reason to its other is *symmetrical*. This is the heart of the matter. Permit me to hold off on this question.

However one interprets the situation of classical reason, notably as regards the Greek logos (and whether or not this latter experienced dissension), *in all cases* a doctrine of *tradition*, of the tradition of logos (is there any other?) seems to be the prerequisite implied by Foucault's enterprise. No matter what the relationship of the Greeks to *hybris*, a relationship that was certainly not simple ... (Here, I wish to open a parenthesis and a question: in the name of what invariable meaning of "madness" does Foucault associate, whatever the meaning of this association, Madness and *Hybris*? A problem of translation, a philosophical problem of translation is posed – and it is serious – even if *Hybris* is not *Madness* for Foucault. The determination of their difference supposes a hazardous linguistic transition. The frequent imprudence of translators in this respect should make us very wary. I am thinking in particular, and in passing, of what is translated by madness and fury in the *Philebus* (45e).[9] Further, if madness has an invariable meaning, what is the relation of this meaning to the a posteriori *events* which govern Foucault's analysis? For, despite everything, even his method is not empiricist, Foucault proceeds by inquiry and inquest. What he is writing is a history, and the recourse to events, in the last resort, is indispensable and determining, at least in principle. Now, is not the concept of madness – never submitted to a thematic scrutiny by Foucault – today a false and disintegrated concept, outside current and popular language which always lags longer than it should behind its subversion by science and philosophy? Foucault, in rejecting the psychiatric or philosophical material that has always emprisoned the mad, winds up employing – inevitably – a popular and equivocal notion of madness, taken from an unverifiable source. This would not be serious if Foucault used the word only in quotation marks, as if it were the language of others, of those who, during the period under study, used it as a historical instrument. But everything transpires as if Foucault knew what "madness" means. Everything transpires as if, in a continuous and underlying way, an assured and rigorous precomprehension of the concept of madness, or at least of its nominal definition, were possible and acquired. In fact, however, it could be demonstrated that as Foucault intends it, if not as intended by the historical current he is studying, the concept of madness overlaps everything that can be put under the rubric of *negativity*. One can imagine the kind of problems posed by such a usage of the notion of madness. The same kind of questions could be posed concerning the notion of truth that runs throughout the book ... I close this long parenthesis.) Thus, whatever the relation of the Greeks to *hybris*, and of Socrates to the original logos, it is in any event certain that classical reason, and medieval reason before it, bore a relation to Greek reason, and that it is within the milieu of this more or less immediately perceived heritage, which itself is more or less crossed with other traditional lines, that the adventure or misadventure of classical reason developed; if dissension dates from Socrates, then the situation of the madman in the Socratic and post-Socratic worlds – assuming that there is, then, something that can be called mad – perhaps deserves to be examined first. Without this examination, and as Foucault does not proceed in a simply aprioristic fashion, his historical description poses the banal but inevitable problems of periodization and of geographical, political, ethnological limitation, etc. If, on the contrary, the unopposed and unexcluding unity of logos were maintained until the classical "crisis," then this latter is, if I may say so, secondary and derivative. It does not engage the entirety of reason. And in this case, even if stated in passing, Socratic discourse would be nothing less than reassuring. It can be proposed that the classical crisis developed from and within the elementary tradition of a logos that has no opposite but carries within itself and *says* all determined contradictions. This doctrine of the tradition of meaning and of reason would be even further necessitated by the fact that it alone can give meaning and rationality in *general* to Foucault's discourse and to any discourse on the war between reason and unreason. For these discourses intend above all to be understood.]

2. I stated above that leaving the history of the preclassical logos in the shadows is bothersome for *two* reasons. The second reason, which I will adduce briefly before going on to Descartes, has to do with the profound link established by Foucault between the division, the dissension, and the possibility of history itself. "*The necessity of madness*, throughout the history of the West, is linked to the deciding gesture which detaches from the background noise, and from its continuous monotony, a meaningful language that is transmitted and consummated in time; briefly, it is linked to the *possibility of history*."

Consequently, if the decision through which reason constitutes itself by excluding and objectifying the free subjectivity of madness is indeed the origin of history, if it is historicity itself, the condition of meaning and of language, the condition of the tradition of meaning, the condition of the work in general, if the structure of exclusion is the fundamental structure of historicity, then the "classical" moment of this exclusion described by Foucault has neither absolute privilege nor archetypal exemplarity. It is an example as sample and not as model. In any event, in order to evoke the singularity of the classical moment, which is profound, perhaps it would be necessary to underline, not the aspects in which it is a structure of exclusion, but those aspects in which, and especially for what end, its own structure of exclusion is historically distinguished from the others, from all others. And to pose the problem of its exemplarity: are we concerned with an example among others or with a "good example," an example that is revelatory by privilege? Formidable and infinitely difficult problems that haunt Foucault's book, more present in his intentions than his words.

Finally, a *last question*: if this great division is the possibility of history itself, the historicity of history, what does it mean, here, "to write the history of this division"? To write the history of historicity? To write the history of the origin of history? The *hysteron proteron* would not here be a simple "logical fallacy," a fallacy within logic, within an established rationality. And its denunciation is not an act of ratiocination. If there is a historicity proper to reason in general, the history of reason cannot be the history of its origin (which, for a start, demands the historicity of reason in general), but must be that of one of its determined figures.

This second project, which would devote all its efforts to discovering the common root of meaning and nonmeaning and to unearthing the original logos in which *a* language and *a* silence are divided from one another is not at all an expediency as concerns everything that could come under the heading "archaeology of silence," the archaeology which simultaneously claims to say madness itself and renounces this claim. The expression "to say madness itself" is self-contradictory. To say madness without expelling it into objectivity is to let it say itself. But madness is what by essence cannot be said: it is the "absence of the work," as Foucault profoundly says.

Thus, not an expediency, but a different and more ambitious design, one that should lead to a praise of reason (there is no praise [*éloge*], by essence, except of reason),[10] but this time of a reason more profound than that which opposes and determines itself in a historically determined conflict. Hegel again, always ... Not an expediency, but a more ambitious ambition, even if Foucault writes this: "*Lacking* this inaccessible primitive purity [of madness itself], a structural study must go back toward the decision that simultaneously links and separates reason and madness; it must aim to uncover the perpetual exchange, the obscure common root, the original confrontation that gives meaning to the unity, as well as to the opposition, of sense and non-sense" [J.D.'s italics].

Before describing the moment when the reason of the classical age will reduce madness to silence by what he calls a "strange act of force," Foucault shows how the exclusion and internment of madness found a sort of structural niche prepared for it by the history of another exclusion: the exclusion of leprosy. Unfortunately, we cannot be detained by the brilliant passages of the chapter entitled "*Stultifera navis.*" They would also pose numerous questions.

We thus come to the "act of force," to the great internment which, with the creation of the houses of internment for the mad and others in the middle of the seventeenth century, marks the advent and first stage of a classical process described by Foucault throughout his book. Without establishing, moreover, whether an event such as the creation of a house of internment is a sign among others, whether it is a fundamental symptom or a cause. This kind of question could appear exterior to a method that presents itself precisely as structuralist, that is, a method for which everything within the structural totality is interdependent and circular in such a way that the classical problems of causality themselves would appear to stem from a misunderstanding. Perhaps. But I wonder whether, when one is concerned with history (and Foucault wants to write a history), a strict structuralism is possible, and, especially, whether, if only for the sake of order and within the order of its own descriptions, such a study can avoid all etiological questions, all questions bearing, shall we say, on the center of gravity of the structure. The legitimate renunciation of a certain style of causality perhaps does not give one the right to renounce all etiological demands.

The passage devoted to Descartes opens the crucial chapter on "the great internment." It thus opens the book itself, and its location at the beginning of the chapter is fairly unexpected. More than anywhere else, the question I have just asked seems to me unavoidable here. We are not told whether or not this passage of the first *Meditation*, interpreted by Foucault as a *philosophical* internment of madness, is destined, as a prelude to the historical and sociopolitical drama, to set the tone for the *entire* drama to be played. Is this "act of force," described in the dimension of theoretical knowledge and metaphysics, a symptom, a cause, a language? What must be assumed or elucidated so that the meaning of this question or dissociation can be neutralized? And if this act of force has a structural affinity with the totality of the drama, what is the status of this affinity? Finally, whatever the place reserved for philosophy in this total historical structure may be, why the sole choice of the Cartesian example? What is the exemplarity of Descartes, while so many other philosophers of the same era were interested or – no less significantly – not interested in madness in various ways?

Foucault does not respond directly to any of these more than methodological questions, summarily, but inevitably, invoked. A single sentence, in his preface, settles the question. To cite Foucault: "To write the history of madness thus will mean the execution of a structural study of an historical ensemble — notions, institutions, juridical and police measures, scientific concepts — which holds captive a madness whose wild state can never in itself be restored." How are these elements organized in the "historical ensemble"? What is a "notion"? Do philosophical notions have a privilege? How are they related to scientific concepts? A quantity of questions that besiege this enterprise.

I do not know to what extent Foucault would agree that the prerequisite for a response to such questions is first of all the internal and autonomous analysis of the philosophical content of philosophical discourse. Only when the totality of this content will have become manifest in its meaning for me (but this is impossible) will I rigorously be able to situate it in its total historical form. It is only then that its reinsertion will not do it violence, that there will be a legitimate reinsertion of *this* philosophical meaning *itself*. As to Descartes in particular, no historical question about him — about the latent historical meaning of his discourse, about its place in a total structure — can be answered before a rigorous and exhaustive internal analysis of his manifest intentions, of the manifest meaning of his philosophical discourse has been made.

We will now turn to this manifest meaning, this properly philosophical intention that is not legible in the immediacy of a first encounter. But first by reading over Foucault's shoulder.

There had to be folly so that wisdom might overcome it.

(Herder)

Descartes, then, is alleged to have executed the act of force in the first of the *Meditations*, and it would very summarily consist in a summary expulsion of the possibility of madness from thought itself.

I shall first cite the decisive passage from Descartes, the one cited by Foucault. Then we shall follow Foucault's reading of the text. Finally, we shall establish a dialogue between Descartes and Foucault.

Descartes writes the following (at the moment when he undertakes to rid himself of all the opinions in which he had hitherto believed, and to start all over again from the foundations: *a primis fundamentis*. To do so, it will suffice to ruin the ancient foundations without being obliged to submit all his opinions to doubt one by one, for the ruin of the foundations brings down the entire edifice. One of these fragile foundations of knowledge, the most naturally apparent, is sensation. The senses deceive me sometimes; they can thus deceive me all the time, and I will therefore submit to doubt all knowledge whose origin is in sensation): "All that up to the present time I have accepted as most true and certain I have learned either from the senses or through the senses; but it is sometimes proved to me that these senses are deceptive, and it is wiser not to trust entirely to any thing by which we have once been deceived."

Descartes starts a new paragraph.

"But. ..." (*sed forte* ... I insist upon the *forte* which the Duc de Luynes left untranslated, an omission that Descartes did not deem necessary to correct when he went over the translation. It is better, as Baillet says, to compare "the French with the Latin" when reading the *Meditations*. It is only in the second French edition by Clerselier that the *sed forte* is given its full weight and is translated by "but yet perhaps …" The importance of this point will soon be demonstrated.) Pursuing my citation: "But it may be that although the senses sometimes deceive us concerning things which are *hardly perceptible, or very far away*, there are yet many others to be met with as to which we cannot reasonably have any doubt …" [J.D.'s italics]. There would be, *there would perhaps be* data of sensory origin which cannot reasonably be doubted. "And how could I deny that these hands and this body are mine, were it not perhaps that I compare myself to certain persons, devoid of sense, whose cerebella are so troubled and clouded by the violent vapours of black bile, that they constantly assure us that they think they are kings when they are really quite poor, or that they are clothed in purple when they are really without covering, or who imagine that they have an earthenware head or are nothing but pumpkins or are made of glass …"

And now the most significant sentence in Foucault's eyes: "But they are mad, *sed amentes sunt isti*, and I should not be any the less insane (*demens*) were I to follow examples so extravagant."[11]

I interrupt my citation not at the end of this paragraph, but on the first words of the following paragraph, which reinscribe the lines I have just read in a rhetorical and pedagogical movement with highly compressed articulations. These first words are *Praeclare sane* … Also translated as *toutefois* [but at the same time (trans.)]. And this is the beginning of a paragraph in which Descartes imagines that he can always dream, and that the world might be no more real than his dreams. And he generalizes by hyperbole the hypothesis of sleep and dream ("Now let us assume that we are asleep . . ."); this hypothesis and this hyperbole will serve in the elaboration of doubt founded on natural reasons (for there is also a hyperbolical moment of this doubt), beyond whose reach will be only the truths of nonsensory origin, mathematical truths notably, which are true "whether I am awake or asleep" and which will capitulate only to the artificial and metaphysical assault of the evil genius.

How does Foucault read this text?

According to Foucault, Descartes, encountering madness alongside (the expression *alongside* is Foucault's) dreams and all forms of sensory error, refuses to accord them all the same treatment, so to speak. "In the economy of doubt," says Foucault, "there is a fundamental imbalance between madness, on the one hand, and error, on the other …" (I note in passing that elsewhere Foucault often denounces the classical reduction of madness to error.) He pursues: "Descartes does not avoid the peril of madness in the same way he circumvents the eventuality of dream and error."

Foucault establishes a parallelism between the following two procedures:

1. The one by which Descartes wishes to demonstrate that the senses can deceive us only regarding things which are "hardly perceptible," or "very far away." These would be the limits of the error of sensory origin. And in the passage I just read, Descartes did say: "But it may be that although the senses sometimes deceive us concerning things which are hardly perceptible, or very far away, there are yet many others to be met with as to which we cannot reasonably have any doubt …" Unless one is mad, a hypothesis seemingly excluded in principle by Descartes in the same passage.

2. The procedure by which Descartes shows that imagination and dreams cannot themselves create the simple and universal elements which enter into their creations, as, for example, "corporeal nature in general, and its extension, the figure of extended things,

their quantity or magnitude and number,"[12] that is, everything which precisely is not of sensory origin, thereby constituting the objects of mathematics and geometry, which themselves are invulnerable to natural doubt. It is thus tempting to believe, along with Foucault, that Descartes wishes to find in the analysis (taking this word in its strict sense) of dreams and sensation a nucleus, an element of proximity and simplicity irreducible to doubt. It is *in* dreams and *in* sensory perception that I surmount or, as Foucault says, that I "circumvent" doubt and reconquer a basis of certainty.

Foucault writes thus: "Descartes does not avoid the *peril* of madness in the same way he circumvents the *eventuality* of dreams or of error... Neither image-peopled sleep, nor the clear consciousness that the senses can be deceived is able to take doubt to the extreme point of its universality; let us admit that our eyes deceive us, 'let us assume that we are asleep' – truth will not entirely slip out into the night. For madness, it is otherwise." Later: "In the economy of doubt, there is an imbalance between madness, on the one hand, and dream and error, on the other. Their situation in relation to the truth and to him who seeks it is different; dreams or illusions are surmounted within the structure of truth; but madness is inadmissible for the doubting subject."

It indeed appears, then, that Descartes does not delve into the experience of madness as he delves into the experience of dreams, that is, to the point of reaching an irreducible nucleus which nonetheless would be interior to madness itself. Descartes is not interested in madness, he does not welcome it as a hypothesis, he does not consider it. He excludes it by decree. I would be insane if I thought that I had a body made of glass. But this is excluded, since I am thinking. Anticipating the moment of the Cogito, which will have to await the completion of numerous stages, highly rigorous in their succession, Foucault writes: "impossibility of being mad that is essential not to the object of thought, but to the thinking subject." Madness is expelled, rejected, denounced in its very impossibility from the very interiority of thought itself.

Foucault is the first, to my knowledge, to have isolated delirium and madness from sensation and dreams in this first *Meditation*. The first to have isolated them in their philosophical sense and their methodological function. Such is the originality of his reading. But if the classical interpreters did not deem this dissociation auspicious, is it because of their inattentiveness? Before answering this question, or rather before continuing to ask it, let us recall along with Foucault that this decree of inadmissibility which is a forerunner of the political decree of the great internment, or corresponds to it, translates it, or accompanies it, or in any case is in solidarity with it – this decree would have been impossible for a Montaigne, who was, as we know, haunted by the possibility of being mad, or of becoming completely mad in the very action of thought itself. The Cartesian decree therefore marks, says Foucault, "the advent of a *ratio*." But as the advent of a *ratio* is not "exhausted" by "the progress of rationalism," Foucault leaves Descartes there, to go on to the historical (politico-social) structure of which the Cartesian act is only a sign. For "more than one sign," Foucault says, "betrays the classical event."

We have attempted to read Foucault. Let us now naïvely attempt to reread Descartes and, before repeating the question of the relationship between the "sign" and the "structure," let us attempt to see, as I had earlier mentioned, what the *sense of the sign itself* may be. (Since the sign here already has the autonomy of a philosophical discourse, is already a relationship of signifier to signified.)

In rereading Descartes, I notice two things:

1. That in the passage to which we have referred and which corresponds to the phase of *doubt* founded on *natural* reasons, Descartes *does not* circumvent the eventuality of

sensory error or of dreams, and does not "surmount" them "within the structure of truth;" and *all* this for the simple reason that he apparently does not ever, nor in any way, surmount them or circumvent them, and does not ever set aside the possibility of total error for *all* knowledge gained from the senses or from imaginary constructions. It must be understood that the hypothesis of dreams is the radicalization or, if you will, the hyperbolical exaggeration of the hypothesis according to which the senses could *sometimes* deceive me. In dreams, the *totality* of sensory images is illusory. It follows that a certainty invulnerable to dreams would be *a fortiori* invulnerable to *perceptual* illusions of the sensory kind. It therefore suffices to examine the case of dreams in order to deal with, on the level which is ours for the moment, the case of natural doubt, of sensory error in general. Now, which are the certainties and truths that escape perception, and therefore also escape sensory error or imaginative and oneiric composition? They are certainties and truths of a nonsensory and nonimaginative origin. They are *simple* and *intelligible* things.

In effect, if I am asleep, everything I perceive while dreaming may be, as Descartes says, "false and illusory," particularly the existence of my hands and my body and the actions of opening my eyes, moving my head, etc. In other words, what was previously excluded, according to Foucault, as insanity, is admissible within dreams. And we will see why in a moment. But, says Descartes, let us suppose that all my oneirical representations are illusory. Even in this case, there must be some representations of things as naturally certain as the body, hands, etc., however illusory this representation may be, and however false its relation to that which it represents. Now, within these representations, these images, these ideas in the Cartesian sense, everything may be fictitious and false, as in the representations of those painters whose imaginations, as Descartes expressly says, are "extravagant" enough to invent something so new that its like has never been seen before. But in the case of painting, at least, there is a final element which cannot be analyzed as illusion, an element that painters cannot counterfeit: color. This is only an *analogy*, for Descartes does not posit the necessary existence of color in general: color is an object of the senses among others. But, *just as* there always remains in a painting, however inventive and imaginative it may be, an irreducibly simple and real element – color – *similarly*, there is in dreams an element of noncounterfeit simplicity presupposed by all fantastical compositions and irreducible to all analysis. But this time – and this is why the example of the painter and of color was only an analogy – this element is neither sensory nor imaginative: it is intelligible.

Foucault does not concern himself with this point. Let me cite the passage from Descartes that concerns us here:

> For, as a matter of fact, painters, even when they study with the greatest skill to represent sirens and satyrs by forms the most strange and extraordinary, cannot give them natures which are entirely new, but merely make a certain medley of the members of different animals; or if their imagination is extravagant enough to invent something so novel that nothing similar has ever before been seen, and that then their work represents a thing purely fictitious and absolutely false, it is certain all the same that the colours of which this is composed are necessarily real. And for the same reason, although these general things, to wit, a body, eyes, a head, hands, and such like, may be imaginary, we are bound at the same time to confess that there are at least some other objects yet more simple and more universal, which are real and true; and of these just in the same way as with

certain real colours, all these images of things which dwell in our thoughts, whether true and real or false and fantastic, are formed.

To such a class of things pertains corporeal nature in general, and its extension, the figure of extended things, their quantity or magnitude and number, as also the place in which they are, the time which measures their duration, and so on.

That is possibly why our reasoning is not unjust when we conclude from this that Physics, Astronomy, Medicine and all other sciences which have as their end the consideration of composite things, are very dubious and uncertain; but that Arithmetic, Geometry and other sciences of that kind which only treat of things that are very simple and very general, without taking great trouble to ascertain whether they are actually existent or not, contain some measure of certainty and an element of the indubitable. For whether I am awake or asleep, two and three together always form five, and the square can never have more than four sides, and it does not seem possible that truths so clear and apparent can be suspected of any falsity.[13]

And I remark that the following paragraph also starts with a "nevertheless" (*verumtamen*) which will soon be brought to our attention.

Thus the certainty of this simplicity of *intelligible* generalization – which is soon after submitted to metaphysical, artificial, and hyperbolical doubt through the fiction of the evil genius – is in no way obtained by a continuous reduction which finally lays bare the resistance of a nucleus of sensory or imaginative certainty. There is discontinuity and a transition to another order of reasoning. The nucleus is purely intelligible, and the still natural and provisional certainty which has been attained supposes a radical break with the senses. At this moment of the analysis, no imaginative or sensory signification, as such, has been saved, *no invulnerability of the senses to doubt has been experienced. All* significations or "ideas" of sensory origin are *excluded* from the realm of truth, *for the same reason as madness* is excluded from it. And there is nothing astonishing about this: madness is only a particular case, and, moreover, not the most serious one, of the sensory illusion which interests Descartes at this point. It can thus be stated that:

2. The hypothesis of insanity – at this moment of the Cartesian order – seems neither to receive any privileged treatment nor to be submitted to any particular exclusion. Let us reread, in effect, the passage cited by Foucault in which insanity appears. Let us resituate it. Descartes has just remarked that since the senses sometimes deceive us, "It is wiser not to trust entirely to any thing by which we have once been deceived."[14] He then starts a new paragraph with the *sed forte* which I brought to your attention a few moments ago. Now, the entire paragraph which follows does not express Descartes's final, definitive conclusions, but rather the astonishment and objections of the non-philosopher, of the novice in philosophy who is frightened by this doubt and protests, saying: I am willing to let you doubt certain sensory perceptions concerning "things which are hardly perceptible, or very far away," but the others! that you are in this place, sitting by the fire, speaking thus, this paper in your hands and other seeming certainties! Descartes then assumes the astonishment of this reader or naïve interlocutor, pretends to take him into account when he writes: "And how could I deny that these hands and this body are mine, were it not perhaps that I compare myself to certain persons, devoid of sense, whose ..., etc." "And I should not be any the less insane were I to follow examples so extravagant."

The pedagogical and rhetorical sense of the *sed forte* which governs this paragraph is clear. It is the "but perhaps" of the feigned objection. Descartes has just said that all knowledge of sensory origin could deceive him. He pretends to put to himself the astonished objection of an imaginary nonphilosopher who is frightened by such audacity and says: no, not all sensory knowledge, for then you would be mad and it would be unreasonable to follow the example of madmen, to put forth the ideas of madmen. Descartes *echoes* this objection: since I am here, writing, and you understand me, I am not mad, nor are you, and we are all sane. The example of madness is therefore not indicative of the fragility of the sensory idea. So be it. Descartes acquiesces to this natural point of view, or rather he feigns to rest in this natural comfort in order better, more radically and more definitively, to unsettle himself from it and to discomfort his interlocutor. So be it, he says, you think that I would be mad to doubt that I am sitting near the fire, etc., that I would be insane to follow the example of madmen. I will therefore propose a hypothesis which will seem much more natural to you, will not disorient you, because it concerns a more common, and more universal experience than that of madness: the experience of sleep and dreams. Descartes then elaborates the hypothesis that will ruin *all* the *sensory* foundations of knowledge and will lay bare only the *intellectual* foundations of certainty. This hypothesis above all will not run from the possibility of an insanity – an epistemological one – much more serious than madness.

The reference to dreams is therefore not put off to one side – quite the contrary – in relation to a madness potentially respected or even excluded by Descartes. It constitutes, in the methodical order which here is ours, the hyperbolical exasperation of the hypothesis of madness. This latter affected only certain areas of sensory perception, and in a contingent and partial way. Moreover, Descartes is concerned here not with determining the concept of madness but with utilizing the popular notion of insanity for juridical and methodological ends, in order to ask questions of principle regarding only the *truth* of ideas.[15] What must be grasped here is that *from this point of view* the sleeper, or the dreamer, is madder than the madman. Or, at least, the dreamer, insofar as concerns the problem of knowledge which interests Descartes here, is further from true perception than the madman. It is in the case of sleep, and not in that of insanity, that the *absolute totality* of ideas of sensory origin becomes suspect, is stripped of "objective value" as M. Guéroult puts it. The hypothesis of insanity is therefore not a good example, a revelatory example, a good instrument of doubt – and for at least two reasons. (a) It does not cover the *totality* of the field of sensory perception. The madman is not always wrong about everything; he is not wrong often enough, is never mad enough. (b) It is not a useful or happy example pedagogically, because it meets the resistance of the nonphilosopher who does not have the audacity to follow the philosopher when the latter agrees that he might indeed be mad at the very moment when he speaks.

Let us turn to Foucault once more. Confronted with the situation of the Cartesian text whose principles I have just indicated, Foucault could – and this time I am only extending the logic of his book without basing what I say on any particular text – Foucault could recall *two truths* that on a second reading would justify his interpretations, which would then only apparently differ from the interpretation I have just proposed.

1. It appears, on this second reading, that, for Descartes, madness is thought of only as a single case – and not the most serious one – among all cases of sensory error. (Foucault would then assume the perspective of the factual determination of the concept of madness by Descartes, and not his juridical usage of it.) Madness is only a sensory and corporeal

fault, a bit more serious than the fault which threatens all waking but normal men, and much less serious, within the epistemological order, than the fault to which we succumb in dreams. Foucault would then doubtless ask whether this reduction of madness to an example, to a case of sensory error, does not constitute an exclusion, an internment of madness, and whether it is not above all a sheltering of the Cogito and everything relative to the intellect and reason from madness. If madness is only a perversion of the senses – or of the imagination – it is corporeal, in alliance with the body. The real distinction of substances expels madness to the outer shadows of the Cogito. Madness, to use an expression proposed elsewhere by Foucault, is confined to the interior of the exterior and to the exterior of the interior. It is the other of the Cogito. I cannot be mad when I think and when I have clear and distinct ideas.

2. Or, while assuming our hypothesis, Foucault could also recall the following: Descartes, by inscribing his reference to madness within the problematic of knowledge, by making madness not only a thing of the body but an *error* of the body, by concerning himself with madness only as the modification of ideas, or the faculties of representation or judgment, intends to neutralize the originality of madness. He would even, in the long run, be condemned to construe it, like all errors, not only as an epistemological deficiency but also as a moral failure linked to a precipitation of the will; for will alone can consecrate the intellectual finitude of perception as error. It is only one step from here to making madness a sin, a step that was soon after cheerfully taken, as Foucault convincingly demonstrates in other chapters.

Foucault would be perfectly correct in recalling these two truths to us if we were to remain at the naïve, natural, and premetaphysical stage of Descartes's itinerary, the stage marked by natural doubt as it intervenes in the passage that Foucault cites. However, it seems that these two truths become vulnerable in turn, as soon as we come to the properly philosophical, metaphysical, and critical phase of doubt.[16]

1. Let us first notice how, in the rhetoric of the first *Meditation*, the first *toutefois* [at the same time] which announced the "natural" hyperbole of dreams (just after Descartes says, "But they are mad, and I should not be any the less insane," etc.) is succeeded by a second *toutefois* [nevertheless] at the beginning of the next paragraph.[17] To "at the same time," marking the *hyperbolical moment within natural doubt*, will correspond a "nevertheless," marking the *absolutely hyperbolical moment* which gets us out of natural doubt and leads to the hypothesis of the evil genius. Descartes has just admitted that arithmetic, geometry, and simple notions escape the first doubt, and he writes, "Nevertheless I have long had fixed in my mind the belief that an all-powerful God existed by whom I have been created such as I am."[18] This is the onset of the well-known movement leading to the fiction of the evil genius.

Now, the recourse to the fiction of the evil genius will evoke, conjure up, the possibility of a *total madness*, a total derangement over which I could have no control because it is inflicted upon me – hypothetically – leaving me no responsibility for it. Total derangement is the possibility of a madness that is no longer a disorder of the body, of the object, the body-object outside the boundaries of the *res cognitans*, outside the boundaries of the policed city, secure in its existence as thinking subjectivity, but is a madness that will bring subversion to pure thought and to its purely intelligible objects, to the field of its clear and distinct ideas, to the realm of the mathematical truths which escape natural doubt.

This time madness, insanity, will spare nothing, neither bodily nor purely intellectual perceptions. And Descartes successively judges admissible: (a) That which he pretended not to admit while conversing with the nonphilosopher. To cite Descartes (he has just evoked "some evil genius not less powerful than deceitful"): "I shall consider that the heavens, the earth, colours, figures, sound, and all other external things are nought but the illusions and dreams of which this genius has availed himself in order to lay traps for my credulity; I shall consider myself as having no hands, no eyes, no flesh, no blood, nor any senses, yet falsely believing myself to possess all these things."[19] These ideas will be taken up again in the second *Meditation*. We are thus quite far from the dismissal of insanity made above. (b) That which escapes natural doubt: "But how do I know that Hell (i.e., the deceiving God, before the recourse to the evil genius) has not brought it to pass that … I am not deceived every time that I add two and three, or count the sides of a square …?"[20]

Thus, ideas of neither sensory nor intellectual origin will be sheltered from this new phase of doubt, and everything that was previously set aside as insanity is now welcomed into the most essential interiority of thought.

In question is a philosophical and juridical operation (but the first phase of doubt was already such) which no longer names madness and reveals all principled possibilities. *In principle* nothing is opposed to the subversion named insanity, although *in fact* and from a natural point of view, for Descartes, for his reader, and for us, no natural anxiety is possible regarding this actual subversion. (Truthfully speaking, to go to the heart of the matter, one would have to confront directly, in and of itself, the question of what is *de facto* and what *de jure* in the relations of the Cogito and madness.) Beneath this natural comfort, beneath this apparently prephilosophical confidence is hidden the recognition of an essential and principled truth: to wit, if discourse and philosophical communication (that is, language itself) are to have an intelligible meaning, that is to say, if they are to conform to their essence and vocation as discourse, they must simultaneously in fact and in principle escape madness. They must carry normality within themselves. And this is not a specifically Cartesian weakness (although Descartes never confronts the question of his own language),[21] is not a defect or mystification linked to a determined historical structure, but rather is an essential and universal necessity from which no discourse can escape, for it belongs to the meaning of meaning. It is an essential necessity from which no discourse can escape, even the discourse which denounces a mystification or an act of force. And, paradoxically, what I am saying here is strictly Foucauldian. For we can now appreciate the profundity of the following affirmation of Foucault's that curiously also saves Descartes from the accusations made against him: "Madness is the absence of a work." This is a fundamental motif of Foucault's book. Now, the work starts with the most elementary discourse, with the first articulation of a meaning, with the first syntactical usage of an "as such,"[22] for to make a sentence is to *manifest* a possible meaning. By its essence, the sentence is normal. It carries normality within it, that is, *sense*, in every sense of the word – Descartes's in particular. It carries me, in every sense of the word normality and sense within it, and does so whatever the state, whatever the health or madness of him who propounds it, or whom it passes through, on whom, in whom it is articulated. In its most impoverished syntax, logos is reason and, indeed, a historical reason. And if madness in general, beyond any factitious and determined historical structure, is the absence of a work, then madness is indeed, essentially and generally, silence, stifled speech, within a caesura and a wound that *open up* life as *historicity in general*. Not a determined silence, imposed at one given moment rather than at any other, but a silence essentially linked to an act of force and a prohibition which open history and speech. *In general*. Within the dimension of historicity in general, which is to be confused neither with some ahistorical eternity, nor with an empirically determined moment of the history of facts, silence plays the irreducible role of that which bears and haunts language, outside and *against* which alone language can emerge – "against" here simultaneously designating the content from which form takes off by force, and the adversary against whom I assure and reassure myself by force. Although the silence of madness is the absence of a work, this silence is not simply the work's epigraph, nor is it, as concerns language and meaning, outside the work. Like nonmeaning, silence is the work's limit and profound resource. Of course, in essentializing madness this way one runs the risk of disintegrating the factual findings of psychiatric efforts. This is a permanent danger, but it should not discourage the demanding and patient psychiatrist.

So that, to come back to Descartes, any philosopher or speaking subject (and the philosopher is but the speaking subject par excellence) who must evoke madness from the *interior* of thought (and not only from within the body or some other extrinsic agency), can do so only in the realm of the *possible* and in the language of fiction or the fiction of language. Thereby, through his own language, he reassures himself against any actual madness – which may sometimes appear quite talkative, another problem – and can keep his distance, the distance indispensable for continuing to speak and to live. But this is not a weakness or a search for security proper to a given historical language (for example, the search for certainty in the Cartesian style), but is rather inherent in the essence and very project of all language in general; and even in the language of those who are apparently the maddest; and even and above all in the language of those who, by their praise of madness, by their complicity with it, measure their own strength against the greatest possible proximity to madness. Language being the break with madness, it adheres more thoroughly to its essence and vocation, makes a cleaner break with madness, if it pits itself against madness more freely and gets closer and closer to it: to the point of being separated from it only by the "transparent sheet" of which Joyce speaks, that is, by itself – for this diaphaneity is nothing other than the language, meaning, possibility, and elementary discretion of a nothing that neutralizes everything. In this sense, I would be tempted to consider Foucault's book a powerful gesture of protection and internment. A Cartesian gesture for the twentieth century. A reappropriation of negativity. To all appearances, it is reason that he interns, but, like Descartes, he chooses the reason of yesterday as his target and not the possibility of meaning in general.

2. As for the second truth Foucault could have countered with, it too seems valid only during the natural phase of doubt. Descartes not only ceases to reject madness during the phase of radical doubt, he not only installs its possible menace at the very heart of the intelligible, he also in principle refuses to let any determined knowledge escape from madness. A menace to all knowledge, insanity – the hypothesis of insanity – is not an internal modification of knowledge. At no point will knowledge alone be able to dominate madness, to master it in order to objectify it – at least for as long as doubt remains unresolved. For the end of doubt poses a problem to which we shall return in a moment.

The act of the Cogito and the certainty of existing indeed escape madness the first time; but aside from the fact that for the first time, it is no longer a question of objective, representative knowledge, it can no longer literally be said that the Cogito would escape madness because it keeps itself beyond the grasp of madness, or because, as Foucault says, "I who think, I cannot be mad"; the Cogito escapes madness only because at its own moment, under its own authority, it is valid *even if I am mad*, even if my thoughts are completely mad. There is a value and a meaning of the Cogito, as of existence, which escape the alternative of a determined madness or a determined reason. Confronted with the critical experience of the Cogito, insanity, as stated in the *Discourse on Method*, is irremediably on a plane with scepticism. Thought no longer fears madness: "... remarking that this truth '*I think, therefore I am*' was so certain and so assured that all the most extravagant suppositions brought forward by the sceptics were incapable of shaking it."[23] The certainty thus attained need not be sheltered from an emprisoned madness, for it is attained and ascertained within madness itself. It is valid *even if I am mad* – a supreme self-confidence that seems to require neither the exclusion nor the circumventing of madness. Descartes never interns madness, neither at the stage of natural doubt nor at the stage of metaphysical doubt. *He only claims to exclude it during the first phase of the first stage, during the non-hyperbolical moment of natural doubt.*

The hyperbolical audacity of the Cartesian Cogito, its mad audacity, which we perhaps no longer perceive as such because, unlike Descartes's contemporary, we are too well assured of ourselves and too well accustomed to the framework of the Cogito, rather than to the critical experience of it – its mad audacity would consist in the return to an original point which no longer belongs to either a *determined* reason or a *determined* unreason, no longer belongs to them as opposition or alternative. Whether I am mad or not, *Cogito, sum*. Madness is therefore, in every sense of the word, only one *case* of thought (*within* thought), it is therefore a question of drawing back toward a point at which all determined contradictions, in the form of given, factual historical structures, can appear, and appear as relative to this zero point at which determined meaning and nonmeaning come together in their common origin. From the point of view which here is ours, one could perhaps say the following about this zero point, determined by Descartes as Cogito.

Invulnerable to all determined opposition between reason and unreason, it is the point starting from which the history of the determined forms of this opposition, this opened or broken-off dialogue, can appear as such and be stated. It is the impenetrable point of certainty in which the possibility of Foucault's narration, as well as of the narration of the totality, or rather of *all* the determined forms of the exchanges between reason and madness are embedded. It is the point[24] at which the project of thinking this totality by escaping it is embedded. By escaping it: that is to say, by exceeding the totality, which – within existence – is possible only in the direction of infinity or nothingness; for even if the totality of what I think is imbued with falsehood or madness, even if the totality of the world does not exist, even if nonmeaning has invaded the totality of the world, up to and including the very contents of my thought, I still think, I am *while* I think. Even if I do not *in fact* grasp the totality, if I neither understand nor embrace it, I still formulate the project of doing so, and this project is meaningful in such a way that it can be defined only in relation to a precomprehension of the infinite and undetermined totality. This is why, by virtue of this margin of the possible, the principled, and the meaningful, which exceeds all that is real, factual, and existent, this project is mad, and acknowledges madness as its liberty and its very possibility. This is why it is not human, in the sense of anthropological factuality, but is rather metaphysical and demonic: it first awakens to itself in its war with the demon, the evil genius of nonmeaning, by pitting itself against the strength of the evil genius, and by resisting him through reduction of the natural man within itself. In this sense, nothing is less reassuring than the Cogito at its proper and inaugural moment. The project of exceeding the totality of the world, as the totality of what I can think in general, is no more reassuring than the dialectic of Socrates when it, too, overflows the totality of beings, planting us in the light of a hidden sun which is *epekeina tes ousias*. And Glaucon was not mistaken when he cried out: "Lord! what demonic hyperbole? *daimonias hyperboles*," which is perhaps banally translated as "marvelous transcendence."[25] This demonic hyperbole goes further than the passion of hybris, at least if this latter is seen only as the pathological modification of the being called man. Such a hybris keeps itself within the world. Assuming that it is deranged and excessive, it implies the fundamental derangement and excessiveness of the hyperbole which opens and founds the world as such by exceeding it. Hybris is excessive and exceeds only *within* the space opened by the demonic hyperbole.

The extent to which doubt and the Cartesian Cogito are *punctuated* by this project of a singular and unprecedented excess — an excess in the direction of the nondetermined, Nothingness or Infinity, an excess which overflows the totality of that which can be thought, the totality of beings and determined meanings, the totality of factual history — is also the extent to which any effort to reduce this project, to enclose it within a determined historical structure, however comprehensive, risks missing the essential, risks dulling the *point* itself. Such an effort risks doing violence to this project in turn (for there is also a violence applicable to rationalists and to sense, to *good* sense; and this, perhaps, is what Foucault's book definitely demonstrates, for the victims of whom he speaks are always the bearers of sense, the *true* bearers of the *true* and *good* sense hidden and oppressed by the *determined* "good sense" of the "division" — the "good sense" that never divides itself enough and is always determined too quickly) — risks doing it violence in turn, and a violence of a totalitarian and historicist style which eludes meaning and the origin of meaning.[26] I use "totalitarian" in the structuralist sense of the word, but I am not sure that the two meanings do not beckon each other historically. Structuralist totalitarianism here would be responsible for an internment of the Cogito similar to the violences of the classical age. I am not saying that Foucault's book is totalitarian, for at least at its outset it poses the question of the origin of historicity *in general*, thereby freeing itself of historicism; I am saying, however, that by virtue of the construction of his project he sometimes runs the risk of being totalitarian. Let me clarify: when I refer to the forced entry into the world of that which is not there and is supposed by the world, or when I state that the *compelle intrare* (epigraph of the chapter on "the great internment") becomes *violence itself* when it turns toward the hyperbole in order to make hyperbole reenter the world, or when I say that this reduction to intraworldliness is the origin and very meaning of what is called violence, making possible all straitjackets, I am not invoking an *other world*, an alibi or an evasive transcendence. That would be yet another possibility of violence, a possibility that is, moreover, often the accomplice of the first one.

I think, therefore, that (in Descartes) everything can be reduced to a determined historical totality except the hyperbolical project. Now, this project belongs to the narration narrating itself and not to the narration narrated by Foucault. It cannot be recounted, cannot be objectified as an event in a determined history.

I am sure that within the movement which is called the *Cartesian Cogito* this hyperbolical extremity is not the only element that should be, like pure madness in general, silent. As soon as Descartes has reached this extremity, he seeks to reassure himself, to certify the Cogito through God, to identify the act of the Cogito with a reasonable reason. And he does so as soon as he *proffers* and *reflects* the Cogito. That is to say, he must temporalize the Cogito, which itself is valid only during the instant of intuition, the instant of thought being attentive to itself, at the point, the sharpest point, of the instant. And here one should be attentive to this link between the Cogito and the movement of temporalization. For if the Cogito is valid even for the maddest madman, one must, in fact, not be mad if one is to reflect it and retain it, if one is to communicate it and its meaning. And here, with the reference to God *and* to a certain memory,[27] would begin the hurried repatriation of all mad and hyperbolical wanderings which now take shelter and are given reassurance within the order of reasons, in order once more to take possession of the truths they had left behind. Within Descartes's text, at least, the internment takes place at this point. It is here that hyperbolical and mad wanderings once more become itinerary and method, "assured" and "resolute" progression through our existing world, which is given to us by God as terra firma. For, finally, it is God alone who, by permitting me to extirpate myself from a Cogito that at its proper moment can always remain a silent madness, also insures my representations and my cognitive determinations, that is, my discourse against madness. It is without doubt that, for Descartes, God alone[28] protects me against the madness to which the Cogito, left to its own authority, could only open itself up in the most hospitable way. And Foucault's reading seems to me powerful and illuminating not at the stage of the text which he cites, which is anterior and secondary to the Cogito, but from the moment which immediately succeeds the instantaneous experience of the Cogito at its most intense, when reason and madness have not yet been separated, when to take the part of the Cogito is neither to take the part of reason as reasonable order, nor the part of disorder and madness, but is rather to grasp, once more, the source which permits reason *and* madness to be determined and stated. Foucault's interpretation seems to me illuminating from the moment when the Cogito must reflect and proffer itself in an organized philosophical discourse. That is, *almost always.* For if the Cogito is valid even for the madman, to be mad – if, once more, this expression has a singular philosophical meaning, which I do not believe: it simply says the other of each determined form of the logos – is not to be able to reflect and to say the Cogito, that is, not to be able to make the Cogito appear as such for an other; an other who may be myself. From the moment when Descartes pronounces the Cogito, he inscribes it in a system of deductions and protections that betray its wellspring and constrain the wandering that is proper to it so that error may be circumvented. At bottom, leaving in silence the problem of speech posed by the Cogito, Descartes seems to imply that thinking *and* saying what is clear and distinct are the same thing. One can say *what* one thinks and *that* one thinks without betraying one or the other. Analogously – analogously only – Saint Anselm saw in the *insipiens*, the insane man, someone who could not think because he could not think what he said. Madness was for him too, a silence, the voluble silence of a thought that did not think its own words. This also is a point which must be developed further. In any event, the Cogito is a work as soon as it is assured of what it says. But before it is a work, it is madness. If the madman could rebuff the evil genius, he could not tell himself so. He therefore cannot say so. And in any event, Foucault is right in the extent to which the project of constraining any wandering already animated a doubt which was always proposed as methodical. This identification of the Cogito with reasonable – normal – reason need not even await – in fact, if not in principle – the proofs of the existence of a veracious God as the supreme protective barrier against madness. This identification intervenes from the moment when Descartes *determines natural light* (which in its undetermined source should be valid even for the mad), from the moment when he pulls himself out of madness by determining natural light through a series of principles and axioms (axiom of causality according to which there must be at least as much reality in the cause as in the effect; then, after this axiom permits the proof of the existence of God, the axioms that "the light of nature teaches us that fraud and deception necessarily proceed from some defect").[29] These dogmatically determined axioms escape doubt, are never even submitted to its scrutiny, are established only reciprocally, on the basis of the existence and truthfulness of God. Due to this fact, they fall within the province of the history of knowledge and the determined structures of philosophy. This is why the act of the Cogito, at the hyperbolical moment when it pits itself against madness, or rather lets itself be pitted against madness, must be repeated and distinguished from the language or the deductive system in which Descartes must inscribe it as soon as he proposes it for apprehension and communication, that is, as soon as he reflects the Cogito for the other, which means for oneself. It is through this relationship to the other as an other self that meaning reassures itself against madness and nonmeaning. And philosophy is perhaps the reassurance given against the anguish of being mad at the point of greatest proximity to madness. This silent and specific moment could be called *pathetic*. As for the functioning of the hyperbole in the structure of Descartes's discourse and in the order of reasons, our reading is therefore, despite all appearances to the contrary, profoundly aligned with Foucault's. It is indeed Descartes – and everything for which this name serves as an index – it is indeed the system of certainty that first of all functions in order to inspect, master, and limit hyperbole, and does so both by determining it in the ether of a natural light whose axioms are from the outset exempt from hyperbolical doubt, and by making of hyperbolical doubt a point of transition firmly maintained within the chain of reasons. But it is our belief that this movement can be described within its own time and place only if one has previously disengaged the extremity of hyperbole, which Foucault seemingly has not done. In the fugitive and, by its essence, ungraspable moment when it still escapes the linear order of reasons, the order of reason in general and the determinations of natural light, does not the Cartesian Cogito lend itself to repetition, up to a certain point, by the Husserlian Cogito and by the critique of Descartes implied in it?

This would be an example only, for some day the dogmatic and historically determined grounds – ours – will be discovered, which the critique of Cartesian deductivism, the impetus and madness of the Husserlian reduction of the totality of the world, first had to rest on, and then had to fall onto in order to be stated. One could do for Husserl what Foucault has done for Descartes: demonstrate how the neturalization of the factual world is a neutralization (in the sense in which to neutralize is also to master, to reduce, to leave free in a straitjacket) of nonmeaning, the most subtle form of an act of force. And in truth, Husserl increasingly associated the theme of normality with the theme of the transcendental reduction. The embedding of transcendental phenomenology in the metaphysics of presence, the entire Husserlian thematic of the living present is the profound *reassurance* of the certainty of *meaning*.

By separating, within the Cogito, *on the one hand*, hyperbole (which I maintain cannot be enclosed in a factual and determined historical structure, for it is the project of exceeding every finite and determined totality), and, *on the other hand*, that in Descartes's philosophy (or in the philosophy supporting the Augustinian Cogito or the Husserlian Cogito as well) which belongs to a factual historical structure, I am not proposing the separation of the wheat from the tares in every philosophy in the name of some *philosophia perennis*. Indeed, it is exactly the contrary that I am proposing. In question is a way of accounting for the very historicity of philosophy. I believe that historicity in general would be impossible without a history of philosophy, and I believe that the latter would be impossible if we possessed only hyperbole, on the one hand, or, on the other, only determined historical structures, finite *Weltanschauungen*. The historicity proper to philosophy is located and constituted in the transition, the dialogue between hyperbole and the finite structure, between that which exceeds the totality and the closed totality, in the difference between history and historicity; that is, in the place where, or rather at the moment when, the Cogito and all that it symbolizes here (madness, derangement, hyperbole, etc.) pronounce and reassure themselves then to fall, necessarily forgetting themselves until their reactivation, their reawakening in another statement of the excess which also later will become another decline and another crisis. From its very first breath, speech, confined to this temporal rhythm of crisis and reawakening, is able to open the space for discourse only by emprisoning madness. This rhythm, moreover, is not an alternation that additionally would be temporal. It is rather the movement of temporalization itself as concerns that which unites it to the movement of logos. But this violent liberation of speech is possible and can be pursued only in the extent to which it keeps itself resolutely and consciously at the greatest possible proximity to the abuse that is the usage of speech – just close enough to *say* violence, to dialogue with itself as irreducible violence, and just far enough to *live* and live as speech. Due to this, crisis or oblivion perhaps is not an accident, but rather the destiny of speaking philosophy – the philosophy which lives only by emprisoning madness, but which would die as thought, and by a still worse violence, if a new speech did not at every instant liberate previous madness while enclosing within itself, in its present existence, the madman of the day. It is only by virtue of this oppression of madness that finite-thought, that is to say, history, can reign. Extending this truth to historicity in general, without keeping to a determined historical moment, one could say that the reign of finite thought can be established only on the basis of the more or less disguised internment, humiliation, fettering and mockery of the madman within us, of the madman who can only be the fool of a logos which is father, master, and king. But that is another discourse and another story. I will conclude by citing Foucault once more. Long after the passage on Descartes, some three hundred pages later, introducing *Rameau's Nephew* Foucault writes, with a sigh of remorse: "In doubt's confrontation with its major dangers, Descartes realized that he could not be mad – though he was to acknowledge for a long time to come that all the powers of unreason kept vigil around his thought."[30] What we have attempted to do here [...] is to situate ourselves within the interval of this remorse, Foucault's remorse, Descartes's remorse according to Foucault; and within the space of stating that, "though he was to acknowledge for a long time to come," we have attempted not to extinguish the *other* light, a black and hardly natural light, the vigil of "powers of unreason" around the Cogito. We have attempted to *requite* ourselves toward the gesture which Descartes uses to requite himself as concerns the menacing powers of madness which are the adverse origin of philosophy.

Among all Foucault's claims to my gratitude, there is thus also that of having made me better anticipate, more so by his monumental book than by the naïve reading of the *Meditations*, to what degree the philosophical act can no longer be in memory of Cartesianism, if to be Cartesian, as Descartes himself doubtless understood it, is to attempt to be Cartesian. That is to say, as I have at least tried to demonstrate, to-attempt-to-say-the-demonic-hyperbole from whose heights thought is announced to itself, *frightens* itself, and *reassures* itself against being annihilated or wrecked in madness or in death. *At its height* hyperbole, the absolute opening, the uneconomic expenditure, is always reembraced by an *economy* and is overcome by economy. The relationship between reason, madness, and death is an economy, a structure of deferral whose irreducible originality must be respected. This attempt-to-say-the-demonic-hyperbole is not an attempt among others; it is not an attempt which would occasionally and eventually be completed by the saying of it, or by its object, the direct object of a willful subjectivity. This attempt to say, which is not, moreover, the antagonist of silence, but rather the condition for it, is the original profundity of will in general. Nothing, further, would be more incapable of regrasping this will than voluntarism, for, as finitude and as history, this attempt is also a first passion. It keeps within itself the trace of a violence. It is more written than said, it is *economized*. The economy of this writing is a regulated relationship between that which exceeds and the exceeded totality: the *différence* of the absolute excess.

To define philosophy as the attempt-to-say-the-hyperbole is to confess — and philosophy is perhaps this gigantic confession — that by virtue of the historical enunciation through which philosophy tranquilizes itself and excludes madness, philosophy also betrays itself (or betrays itself as thought), enters into a crisis and a forgetting of itself that are an essential and necessary period of its movement. I philosophize only in *terror*, but in the *confessed* terror of going mad. The confession is simultaneously, at its *present* moment, oblivion and unveiling, protection and exposure: economy.

But this crisis in which reason is madder than madness — for reason is nonmeaning and oblivion — and in which madness is more rational than reason, for it is closer to the wellspring of sense, however silent or murmuring — this crisis has always begun and is interminable, it suffices to say that, if it is classic, it is not so in the sense of the *classical age* but in the sense of eternal and essential classicism, and is also historical in an unexpected sense.

And nowhere else and never before has the concept of *crisis* been able to enrich and reassemble all its potentialities, all the energy of its meaning, as much, perhaps, as in Michel Foucault's book. Here, the crisis is on the one hand, in Husserl's sense, the danger menacing reason and meaning under the rubric of objectivism, of the forgetting of origins, of the blanketing of origins by the rationalist and transcendental unveiling itself. Danger as the movement of reason menaced by its own security, etc.

But the crisis is also decision, the caesura of which Foucault speaks, in the sense of *krinein*, the choice and division between the two ways separated by Parmenides in his poem, the way of logos and the nonway, the labyrinth, the *palintrope* in which logos is lost; the way of meaning and the way of nonmeaning; of Being and of non-Being. A division on whose basis, after which, logos, in the necessary violence of its irruption, is separated from itself as madness, is exiled from itself, forgetting its origin and its own possibility. Is not what is called finitude possibility as crisis? A certain identity between the consciousness of crisis and the forgetting of it? Of the thinking of negativity and the reduction of negativity?

Crisis of reason, finally, access to reason and attack of reason. For what Michel Foucault teaches us to think is that there are crises of reason in strange complicity with what the world calls crises of madness.

Chapter 6

Gilles Deleuze

■ DIONYSUS AND ZARATHUSTRA and CONCLUSION in *Nietzsche and Philosophy*, Hugh Tomlinson trans., London: Continuum, 1983

THE LESSON OF THE ETERNAL RETURN is that there is no return of the negative. The eternal return means that being is selection. Only that which affirms or is affirmed returns. The eternal return is the reproduction of becoming but the reproduction of becoming is also the production of becoming active: child of Dionysus and Ariadne. In the eternal return being ought to belong to becoming, but the being of becoming ought to belong to a single becoming-active. Nietzsche's speculative teaching is as follows: becoming, multiplicity and chance do not contain any negation; difference is pure affirmation; return is the being of difference excluding the whole of the negative. And this teaching would perhaps remain obscure without the practical clarity in which it is steeped. Nietzsche exposes all the mystifications which disfigure philosophy: the apparatus of bad conscience, the false marvels of the negative which turn multiplicity, becoming, chance and difference itself into so many misfortunes of consciousness itself and turn misfortunes of consciousness into so many moments of formation, reflection or development. Nietzsche's practical teaching is that difference is happy; that multiplicity, becoming and chance are adequate objects of joy by themselves and that only joy returns. Multiplicity, becoming and chance are the properly philosophical joy in which unity rejoices in itself and also in being and necessity. Not since Lucretius has the critical enterprise which characterises philosophy been taken so far (with the exception of Spinoza). Lucretius exposes the trouble of the soul and those who need it to establish their power – Spinoza exposes sorrow, all the causes of sorrow and all those who found their power at the heart of this sorrow – Nietzsche exposes *ressentiment*, bad conscience and the power of the negative which serves as their principle: the "untimeliness" of a philosophy which has liberation as its object. There is no unhappy consciousness which is not also man's enslavement, a trap for the will and an opportunity for all basenesses of thought. The reign of the negative is the reign of powerful beasts, Churches and States, which fetter us to their own ends. The murderer of God committed a sad crime because his motivation was sad: he wanted to take God's place, he killed in order to "steal", he remained in the negative whilst taking on the attributes of divinity. The death of God needs time finally to find its essence and become a joyful event. Time to expel the negative, to exorcise the reactive – the time of a becoming-active. This time is the cycle of the eternal return.

The negative expires at the gates of being. Opposition ceases its labour and difference begins its play. But is there any being which does not belong to another world and how is the selection made? Nietzsche calls the point of conversion of the negative *transmutation*. The negative loses its power and quality. Negation ceases to be an autonomous power, that is to say a quality of the will to power. Transmutation relates the negative to affirmation in the will to power, it is turned into a simple mode of being of the powers of affirming. Instead of the labour of opposition or the suffering of the negative we have the warlike play of difference, affirmation and the joy of destruction. The no stripped of its power, transformed into the opposite quality, turned affirmative and creative: such is transmutation. This transmutation of values is what essentially defines Zarathustra. If Zarathustra passes through the negative as his disgusts and temptations show, it is not in order to make use of it as a motor, nor to take on its burden or product, but to reach the point where the motor is changed, the product surmounted and the whole of the negative vanquished or transmuted.

Zarathustra's whole story is contained in his relationship with nihilism, that is to say with the demon. The demon is the spirit of the negative, the power of denying which plays several, apparently opposed roles. Sometimes *he gets man to carry him*, suggesting to him that the weight he is burdened with is positivity itself. Sometimes, on the contrary, *he jumps over man*, taking all forces and will from him.[1] The contradiction is only apparent: in the first case man is the reactive being who wants to seize power, to substitute his own strength for the power which dominates him. But in fact the demon finds the opportunity here to get himself carried, to get himself taken on, to pursue his task, disguised by a false positivity. In the second case, man is the last man: still a reactive being, he no longer has the strength to take possession of willing, the demon takes all man's strength and leaves him without strength or will. In both cases the demon appears as the spirit of the negative which, through all the avatars of man, *preserves his power and keeps his quality*. He stands for the will to nothingness which makes use of man as a reactive being which gets itself carried by him but which, at the same time, does not fuse with him and "jumps over". From all these points of view transmutation differs from the will to nothingness, just as Zarathustra differs from his demon. With Zarathustra negation loses its power and quality: beyond the reactive man, there is *the destroyer of known values*; beyond the last man there is *the man who wants to perish or to be overcome*. Zarathustra stands for affirmation, the spirit of affirmation as the power which turns the negative into a mode and man into an active being who wants to be overcome (not "jumped-over"). Zarathustra's sign is the sign of the lion: the first book of Zarathustra opens with the lion and the last closes with it. But the lion is precisely the "holy no" become creative and affirmative, this no which only affirmation knows how to say, in which the whole of the negative is converted, transmuted in power and quality. With transmutation, the will to power ceases to be fettered to the negative as the *ratio* by which it is known to us, it reveals its unknown face, the unknown *raison d'être* which makes the negative a simple mode of being.

Zarathustra has, moreover, a complex relation to Dionysus, as transmutation does to the eternal return. In a certain way Zarathustra is cause of the eternal return and father of the Overman. The man who wants to perish, the man who wants to be overcome, is the ancestor and father of the Overman. The destroyer of all known values, the lion of the holy no prepares its final metamorphosis: it becomes a child. And, with his hands thrust into the lion's fleece, Zarathustra feels that his children are near or that the Overman is approaching. But in what sense is Zarathustra father of the Overman and cause of the eternal return? In the sense of a precondition. In another way the eternal return has an unconditioned principle to which Zarathustra himself is subject. From the perspective of the principle which conditions it, the eternal return depends on transmutation but, from the perspective of its unconditioned principle, transmutation depends more profoundly on the eternal return. Zarathustra is subject to Dionysus: "Who am I? I await one who is more worthy; I am not worthy even to break myself against him" (Z II "The Stillest Hour", p. 167). In the trinity of the Antichrist – Dionysus, Ariadne and Zarathustra – Zarathustra is Ariadne's conditional fiancé, but Ariadne is Dionysus' unconditioned fiancée. This is why Zarathustra is always in an inferior position in relation to the eternal return and the Overman. He is the cause of the eternal return, but a cause which delays producing its effect. A prophet who hesitates to deliver his message, who knows the vertigo and the temptation of the negative, who must be encouraged by his animals. Father of the Overman, but a father whose products are ripe before he is ripe for his products, a lion who still lacks a final metamorphosis.[2] In fact the eternal return and the Overman are at the crossing of two genealogies, of two unequal genetic lines.

On the one hand they relate to Zarathustra as to the conditioning principle which "posits" them in a merely hypothetical manner. On the other hand, they relate to Dionysus as the unconditioned principle which is the basis of their apodictic and absolute character. Thus in Zarathustra's exposition it is always the entanglement of causes or the connection of moments, the synthetic relation of moments to each other, which determines the hypothesis of the return of the same moment. But, from Dionysus' perspective by contrast, it is the synthetic relation of the moment to itself, as past, present and to come, which absolutely determines its relations with all other moments. The return is not the passion of one moment pushed by others, but the activity of the moment which determined the others in being itself determined through what it affirms. Zarathustra's constellation is the constellation of the lion, but that of Dionysus is the constellation of being: the yes of the child-player is more profound than the holy no of the lion. The whole of Zarathustra is affirmative: even when he who knows how to say no, says no. But Zarathustra is not the whole of affirmation, nor what is most profound in it.

Zarathustra relates the negative to affirmation in the will to power. It is still necessary for the will to power to be related to affirmation as its *raison d'être*, and for affirmation to be related to the will to power as the element which produces, reflects and develops its own *ratio*. This is the task of Dionysus. All affirmation finds its condition in Zarathustra but its unconditioned principle in Dionysus. Zarathustra determines the eternal return, moreover he determines it to produce its effect, the Overman. But this determination is the same as the series of conditions which finds its final term in the lion, in the man who wants to be overcome, in the destroyer of all known values. Dionysus' determination is of another kind, identical to the absolute principle without which the conditions would themselves remain powerless. And this is Dionysus' supreme disguise – to subject his products to conditions which are themselves subject to him, conditions that these products themselves surpass. The lion becomes a child, the destruction of known values makes possible a creation of new values. But the creation of values, the yes of the child-player, would not be formed under these conditions if they were not, at the same time, subject to a deeper genealogy. It is no surprise, therefore, to find that every Nietzschean concept lies at the crossing of two unequal genetic lines. Not only the eternal return and the Overman, but laughter, play and dance. In relation to Zarathustra laughter, play and dance are affirmative powers of transmutation: dance transmutes heavy into light, laughter transmutes suffering into joy and the play of throwing (the dice) transmutes low into high. But in relation to Dionysus dance, laughter and play are affirmative powers of reflection and development. Dance affirms becoming and the being of becoming; laughter, roars of laughter, affirm multiplicity and the unity of multiplicity; play affirms chance and the necessity of chance.

Conclusion

Modern philosophy presents us with amalgams which testify to its vigour and vitality, but which also have their dangers for the spirit. A strange mixture of ontology and anthropology, of atheism and theology. A little Christian spiritualism, a little Hegelian dialectic, a little phenomenology (our modern scholasticism) and a little Nietzschean fulguration oddly combined in varying proportions. We see Marx and the Pre-Socratics, Hegel and Nietzsche, dancing hand in hand in a round in celebration of the surpassing of metaphysics and even the death of philosophy properly speaking. And it is true that Nietzsche *did* intend to "go beyond" metaphysics. But so did Jarry in what, invoking etymology, he called "pataphysics". We have imagined Nietzsche withdrawing his stake from a game which is not his own. Nietzsche called the philosophers and philosophy of his time "the portrayal of all that has ever been believed". He might say the same of today's philosophy where Nietzscheanism, Hegelianism and Husserlianism are the scraps of the new gaudily painted canvas of modern thought.

There is no possible compromise between Hegel and Nietzsche. Nietzsche's philosophy has a great polemical range; it forms an absolute anti-dialectics and sets out to expose all the mystifications that find a final refuge in the dialectic. What Schopenhauer dreamed of but did not carry out, caught as he was in the net of Kantianism and pessimism, Nietzsche carries out at the price of his break with Schopenhauer, setting up a new image of thought, freeing thought from the burdens which are crushing it. Three ideas define the dialectic: the idea of a power of the negative as a theoretical principle manifested in opposition and contradiction; the idea that suffering and sadness have value, the valorisation of the "sad passions", as a practical principle manifested in splitting and tearing apart; the idea of positivity as a theoretical and practical product of negation itself. It is no exaggeration to say that the whole of Nietzsche's philosophy, in its polemical sense, is the attack on these three ideas.

If the speculative element of the dialectic is found in opposition and contradiction this is primarily because it reflects a false image of difference. Like the eye of the ox it reflects an inverted image of difference. The Hegelian dialectic is indeed a reflection on difference, but it inverts its image. For the affirmation of difference as such it substitutes the negation of that which differs; for the affirmation of self it substitutes the negation of the other, and for the affirmation of affirmation it substitutes the famous negation of the negation. – But this inversion would be meaningless if it were not in fact animated by forces with an "interest" in doing so. The dialectic expresses every combination of reactive forces and nihilism, the history or evolution of their relations. Opposition substituted for difference is also the triumph of the reactive forces that find their corresponding principle in the will to nothingness. *Ressentiment* needs negative premises, two negations, in order to produce a phantom of affirmation; the ascetic ideal needs *ressentiment* itself and bad conscience, like the conjuror needs his marked cards. Everywhere there are sad passions; the unhappy consciousness is the subject of the whole dialectic. The dialectic is, first of all, the thought of the theoretical man, reacting against life, claiming to judge life, to limit and measure it. In the second place, it is the thought of the priest who subjects life to the labour of the negative: he needs negation to establish his power, he represents the strange will which leads reactive forces to triumph. Dialectic in this sense is the authentically Christian ideology. Finally, it is the thought of the slave, expressing reactive life in itself and the becoming-reactive of the universe. Even the atheism that it offers us is a clerical atheism, even its image of the master is a slavish one. – It is not surprising that the dialectic only produces a phantom of affirmation. Whether as overcome opposition or as resolved contradiction, the image of positivity is radically falsified. Dialectical positivity, the real in the dialectic, is the yes of the ass. The ass knows how to affirm because it takes things upon itself, but it only takes on the products of the negative. For the demon, Zarathustra's ape, it is sufficient to jump on our shoulders; those who carry are always tempted to think that by carrying they affirm and that the positive is assessed by weight. The ass in a lion's skin – this is what Nietzsche calls the "man of the present".

Nietzsche's greatness was to know how to separate these two plants, *ressentiment* and bad conscience. If this were its only aspect Nietzsche's philosophy would be of the greatest importance. But in his work polemic is only the aggression which derives from a deeper, active and affirmative instance. Dialectic emerged from Kantian critique, from false critique. Carrying out a true critique implies a philosophy which develops itself for itself and only retains the negative as a mode of being. Nietzsche reproaches the dialecticians for going no further than an abstract conception of universal and particular; they were prisoners of symptoms and did not reach the forces or the will which give to these sense and value. They moved within the limits of the question "What is … ?", the contradictory question *par excellence*. Nietzsche creates his own method: dramatic, typological and differential. He turns philosophy into an art, the art of interpreting and evaluating. In every case he asks the question "Which one?" The one that … is Dionysus. That which … is the will to power as plastic and genealogical principle. The will to power is not force but the differential element which simultaneously determines the relation of forces (quantity) and the respective qualities of related forces. It is in this element of difference that affirmation manifests itself and develops itself as creative. The will to power is the principle of multiple affirmation, the donor principle or the bestowing virtue.

The sense of Nietzsche's philosophy is that multiplicity, becoming and chance are objects of pure affirmation. The affirmation of multiplicity is the speculative proposition, just as the joy of diversity is the practical proposition. The player only loses because he does not affirm strongly enough, because he introduces the negative into chance and opposition into becoming and multiplicity. The true dicethrow necessarily produces the winning number, which *re*-produces the dicethrow. We affirm chance and the necessity of chance; becoming and the being of becoming; multiplicity and the unity of multiplicity. Affirmation turns back on itself, then returns once more, carried to its highest power. Difference reflects itself and repeats or reproduces itself. The eternal return is this highest power, the synthesis of affirmation which finds its principle in the will. The lightness of that which affirms against the weight of the negative; the games of the will to power against the labour of the dialectic; the affirmation of affirmation against that famous negation of the negation.

Negation, it is true, appears primarily as a quality of the will to power. But in the sense that reaction is a quality of force. More profoundly, negation is only one face of the will to power, the face by which it is known to us, insofar as knowledge itself is the expression of reactive forces. Man inhabits only the dark side of the Earth, of which he only understands the becoming-reactive which permeates and constitutes it. Which is why the history of man is that of nihilism, negation and reaction. But the long story of nihilism has a conclusion: the full stop where negation turns back on reactive forces themselves. This is the point of transmutation or transvaluation; negation loses its own power, it becomes active, it is now only the mode of being of the powers of affirming. The negative changes quality, passes into the service of affirmation; it is now only valid as a preliminary offensive or a subsequent aggression. Negativity as negativity *of the positive* is one of Nietzsche's anti-dialectic discoveries. This is the same as saying that transmutation is a condition of the eternal return, or rather, that it depends on the eternal return from the standpoint of a deeper principle. Because the will to power only makes what is affirmed return: it is the will to power which both transforms the negative and reproduces affirmation. That the one is *for* the other, that the one is *in* the other, means that eternal return is being but being is selection. Affirmation remains as the sole quality of the will to power, action as the sole quality of force, becoming-active as the creative identity of power and willing.

PART TWO

The postmodern condition
A concept in emergence

THE SELECTIONS ASSEMBLED IN PART TWO encompass the elements central to a prescriptive postmodernism. The themes of direct and unmediated experience, event, incommensurability, difference and authenticity are all stressed in these extracts.

The previous Part concluded with Gilles Deleuze's critique of the Hegelian dialectic as an inverted image of difference and therefore not true difference at all. Jean-François Lyotard pursues and expands quite considerably upon this theme in his classic *The Postmodern Condition*, a work that brought together many of his diverse and disparate interests. Whereas Deleuze's analysis of Nietzsche had implications that went beyond its narrow philosophical focus, the object of Lyotard's own enquiry was very large indeed. It was an examination of the state of knowledge in the twentieth century. Lyotard's principal contention was that the scientific discourse offered a model of legitimation for other discreet discourses such as, for example, politics and ethics. While the origins of this condition lay in the Socratic philosophy of the ancient Greeks, Lyotard was keen to show, like Heidegger before him, that the scientific discourse was, through its own principles of legitimation, close to dominating all other discourses. But curiously the more this scientific discourse served as a model of legitimation for other discourses the less this model became credible. This is what Lyotard stressed as the 'process of delegitimation fueled by the demand for legitimation itself'. The result was a 'crisis' of scientific knowledge which extended to science's own reliance on a higher-level narrative, meta-narrative, of legitimation.

According to Lyotard the clearest sign of this crisis lay in individuals' growing incredulity toward the 'meta-narratives' of human emancipation or human progress that underpinned scientific knowledge itself. The result had important implications for how knowledge was accumulated, organised and classified, foremost of which was a 'loosening ... of the encyclopedic net in which each science was to find its place'. This erosion of the boundaries between disciplines was the beginnings of a process in which knowledge was to be set free of all constraint. The result would be knowledge splintered into a plethora of incommensurate discourses. And this, according to Lyotard, is the chief characteristic of postmodern condition.

The liberation of knowledge from all restrictions results in a new postmodern knowledge defined in terms of 'difference understood as paralogy'. This new postmodern knowledge defines our very existence today – a theme which is later pursued by Fredric Jameson in his discussion on schizophrenia as symptomatic of the experience of contemporary reality. But as Lyotard is well aware this new postmodern knowledge is far from fully accepted. Traditional forms of knowledge continue to define and constrain the human sciences and people's outlooks. What is necessary is the shattering of this 'terroristic totality', as he polemically calls it. The various ways this can be achieved are explored in the remaining selections to this Part.

Jacques Derrida's 'Hors Livre: Outwork, Hors d'oeuvre, extratext, foreplay, bookend, facing * prefacing' pursues Deleuze's and Lyotard's critique of the Western philosophical tradition. This short excerpt to the much longer 'preface' to three essays presents in a concentrated form the core elements of Derrida's thought: 'differance', trace and dissemination. Derrida mobilises these concepts in his 'preface' in order to deconstruct the very concept of the preface itself; and the irony of this is fully intended. Yet the deconstruction of the preface is but a prelude to a larger and more ambitious undertaking which is to deconstruct the Western philosophical tradition itself. Derrida's purpose here is to show that the very idea of the preface is the embodiment of what cannot be adequately assimilated into a philosophical discourse which purports to be totalising. This point he illustrates by deconstructing G.W.F. Hegel's preface to the *Phenomenology of Spirit*, a work considered by many to be the greatest achievement of the Western philosophical tradition. Derrida shows how Hegel in his own denunciation of the concept of preface as 'not only superfluous but, in view of the nature of the subject-matter [philosophy], even inappropriate and misleading' cannot escape from the fact that that which is supposed to be effaced in the wider body of text is not. The result is that, as Derrida contends, there is 'a certain spacing between concept and being-there, between concept and existence, between thought and time', and that this constitutues 'the rather unqualifiable lodging of the preface'. This 'lodging of the preface' is the embodiment of difference because it can never be entirely assimilated; of trace because its effacement by the main body of text is never total; and of deferral because its position in relation to the main body of work never arrives at an adequate resolution.

The theme of difference is pursued in Gilles Deleuze's *Difference and Repetition* and 'Immanence: A Life'. Both of these excerpts emphasise the importance of difference as incommensurability. In his endeavour to theorise this in *Difference and Repetition* Deleuze distinguishes between two types of repetition. The first is what he terms 'external to the concept'. It involves 'a difference between objects represented by the same concept'. This form of repetition 'is repetition of the Same' and the difference it spawns fails to engender incommensurability. It is therefore not creative. The other type of repetition includes difference. This difference 'is internal to the Idea'. It embodies incommensurability, and is therefore 'creative' and 'dynamic'.

Deleuze's emphasis on the creative and dynamic is central to his 'Immanence: A Life'. This essay was representative of Deleuze's mature metaphysical (almost spiritual) reflections. Its emphasis on life as pure and unmediated through restrictive and restraining concepts and categories highlighted Deleuze's attempts to reflect upon philosophy as a creative and transforming enterprise. And it was this enterprise which had attracted Michel Foucault. His considered appreciation of this undertaking was given in 'Theatrum Philosophicum', a review of Deleuze's *Difference and Repetition* and *The Logic of Sense*. In this review Foucault was eager to stress both Deleuze's estimation for psychoanalysis and the insights philosophy might derive from it, his understanding of repetition as simulacrum and therefore not creative, and 'the original and the perfect copy' as creative. Both Foucault and Deleuze were attentive to their respective engagements with Lacanian psychoanalysis as a vehicle for evoking the experiences necessary to shattering the constraints on knowledge and action. Deleuze's most serious attempt to use Lacanian psychoanalysis to this end was in his joint work with Félix Guattari, *Anti-Oedipus*. Foucault's essay represents a clear and lucid account of Deleuze's philosophical thinking.

Foucault's honest portrayal is followed by an equally clear self-portrayal by Derrida. 'The Time of a Thesis' was given as Derrida's opening presentation to the defence of his *Doctorat d'État*. This is one of the clearest and fullest accounts of Derrida's philosophical interests, his preoccupations and the individuals and ideas that inspired his particular way of philosophising.

The concluding essays to this Part sketch out, in their distinct ways, the task set before a postmodern politics. Lyotard's 'The Intimacy of Terror' is a powerful attack on logocentrism. Many of the themes of *The Postmodern Condition* are repeated here. But its tone is far more pessimistic. Lyotard's assessment of modernity's terroristic totality is an Orwellian nightmare vision which offers few possibilities of escape. Nonetheless, the utopian impulse that ran through the whole of his work is not lost here. Lyotard saw in art and aesthetic experience an important possibility for liberation. His mature work would explore this possibility.

Lyotard's pessimistic assessment about the possibilities for human liberation is not shared by Fredric Jameson, whose celebrated 'Postmodernism, or, the Cultural Logic of Late Capitalism' concludes this Part. Jameson's essay, which first appeared in *New Left Review*, asserted that postmodernism was the natural outgrowth of an advanced capitalism. Drawing on the analysis of late capitalism set out in the work of the Marxist political economist Ernest Mandel, Jameson argued that capitalism in the late twentieth century not only dominated commodity production but had now penetrated cultural production too. In complementing Mandel's work with a judicious use of ideas on myth and ideology drawn from Ronald Barthes and Louis Althusser, Jameson reveals how the commodification of culture is concomitant with post-modernism. In this highly stimulating and thoughtful essay, Jameson sets out to define postmodernism's chief attributes. Just as Lyotard asserted in *The Postmodern Condition* that knowledge is splintered into a plethora of incommensurate discourses, Jameson argues that the whole of human experience is now reduced to momentary, discreet and incommensurable events that escape ready assimilation. Postmodernism as the cultural logic of late capitalism involves the effacement between high and low culture, resulting in a certain flatness. Concurrent to the erasure of the distinction between high and low culture is a blurring of the boundaries between different disciplines. This liberation of knowledge, as Lyotard also described it, is complemented by a certain intensification of human experience. As knowledge and reality escape organisation and classification they are experienced with a heightened immediacy which Jameson believes is akin to a new form of schizophrenia as described by Deleuze and Guattari. In the complete version of his text, Jameson draws upon various cultural examples such as painting, the visual arts, literature and architecture to illustrate his point. He contends that the postmodern condition has profound implications for individual and class identity with its obvious ramifications for politics. Jameson, like Marshall Berman, seeks a renewal of the politics of emancipation. His ingenious employment of the idea of cognitive mapping, adapted from the work of the geographer Kevin Lynch, is, perhaps, the most significant contribution to emancipatory politics in a postmodern age.

Chapter 7

Jean-François Lyotard

■ from *THE POSTMODERN CONDITION: A REPORT ON KNOWLEDGE*, Geoff Bennington and Brian Massumi trans., Manchester: Manchester University Press, 1984

Introduction

THE OBJECT OF THIS STUDY is the condition of knowledge in the most highly developed societies. I have decided to use the word *postmodern* to describe that condition. The word is in current use on the American continent among sociologists and critics; it designates the state of our culture following the transformations which, since the end of the nineteenth century, have altered the game rules for science, literature, and the arts. The present study will place these transformations in the context of the crisis of narratives.

Science has always been in conflict with narratives. Judged by the yardstick of science, the majority of them prove to be fables. But to the extent that science does not restrict itself to stating useful regularities and seeks the truth, it is obliged to legitimate the rules of its own game. It then produces a discourse of legitimation with respect to its own status, a discourse called philosophy. I will use the term *modern* to designate any science that legitimates itself with reference to a metadiscourse of this kind making an explicit appeal to some grand narrative, such as the dialectics of Spirit, the hermeneutics of meaning, the emancipation of the rational or working subject, or the creation of wealth. For example, the rule of consensus between the sender and addressee of a statement with truth-value is deemed acceptable if it is cast in terms of a possible unanimity between rational minds: this is the Enlightenment narrative, in which the hero of knowledge works toward a good ethico-political end – universal peace. As can be seen from this example, if a metanarrative implying a philosophy of history is used to legitimate knowledge, questions are raised concerning the validity of the institutions governing the social bond: these must be legitimated as well. Thus justice is consigned to the grand narrative in the same way as truth.

Simplifying to the extreme, I define *postmodern* as incredulity toward metanarratives. This incredulity is undoubtedly a product of progress in the sciences: but that progress in turn presupposes it. To the obsolescence of the metanarrative apparatus of legitimation corresponds, most notably, the crisis of metaphysical philosophy and of the university institution which in the past relied on it. The narrative function is losing its functors, its great hero, its great dangers, its great voyages, its great goal. It is being dispersed in clouds of narrative language elements – narrative, but also denotative, prescriptive, descriptive, and so on. Conveyed within each cloud are pragmatic valencies specific to its kind. Each of us lives at the intersection of many of these. However, we do not necessarily establish stable language combinations, and the properties of the ones we do establish are not necessarily communicable.

Thus the society of the future falls less within the province of a Newtonian anthropology (such as structuralism or systems theory) than a pragmatics of language particles. There are many different language games – a heterogeneity of elements. They only give rise to institutions in patches – local determinism.

The decision makers, however, attempt to manage these clouds of sociality according to input/output matrices, following a logic which implies that their elements are commensurable and that the whole is determinable. They allocate our lives for the growth of power. In matters of social justice and of scientific truth alike, the legitimation of that power is based on its optimizing the system's performance – efficiency. The application of this criterion to all of our games necessarily entails a certain level of terror, whether soft or hard: be operational (that is, commensurable) or disappear.

The logic of maximum performance is no doubt inconsistent in many ways, particularly with respect to contradiction in the socioeconomic field: it demands both less work (to lower production costs) and more (to lessen the social burden of the idle population). But our incredulity is now such that we no longer expect salvation to rise from these inconsistencies, as did Marx.

Still, the postmodern condition is as much a stranger to disenchantment as it is to the blind positivity of delegitimation. Where, after the metanarratives, can legitimacy reside? The operativity criterion is technological; it has no relevance for judging what is true or just. Is legitimacy to be found in consensus obtained through discussion, as Jürgen Habermas thinks? Such consensus does violence to the heterogeneity of language games. And invention is always born of dissension. Postmodern knowledge is not simply a tool of the authorities; it refines our sensitivity to differences and reinforces our ability to tolerate the incommensurable. Its principle is not the expert's homology, but the inventor's paralogy.

Here is the question: is a legitimation of the social bond, a just society, feasible in terms of a paradox analogous to that of scientific activity? What would such a paradox be?

1   The field: knowledge in computerized societies

Our working hypothesis is that the status of knowledge is altered as societies enter what is known as the postindustrial age and cultures enter what is known as the postmodern age.[1] This transition has been under way since at least the end of the 1950s, which for Europe marks the completion of reconstruction. The pace is faster or slower depending on the country, and within countries it varies according to the sector of activity: the general situation is one of temporal disjunction which makes sketching an overview difficult. A portion of the description would necessarily be conjectural. At any rate, we know that it is unwise to put too much faith in futurology.

Rather than painting a picture that would inevitably remain incomplete, I will take as my point of departure a single feature, one that immediately defines our object of study. Scientific knowledge is a kind of discourse. And it is fair to say that for the last forty years the "leading" sciences and technologies have had to do with language: phonology and theories of linguistics, problems of communication and cybernetics, modern theories of algebra and informatics, computers and their languages, problems of translation and the search for areas of compatibility among computer languages, problems of information storage and data banks, telematics and the perfection of intelligent terminals, paradoxology. The facts speak for themselves (and this list is not exhaustive).

These technological transformations can be expected to have a considerable impact on knowledge. Its two principal functions – research and the transmission of acquired learning – are already feeling the effect, or will in the future. With respect to the first function, genetics provides an example that is accessible to the layman: it owes its theoretical paradigm to cybernetics. Many other examples could be cited. As for the second function, it is common knowledge that the miniaturization and commercialization of machines is already changing the way in which learning is acquired, classified, made available, and exploited. It is reasonable to suppose that the proliferation of information-processing machines is having, and will continue to have, as much of an effect on the circulation of learning as did advancements in human circulation (transportation systems) and later, in the circulation of sounds and visual images (the media).

The nature of knowledge cannot survive unchanged within this context of general transformation. It can fit into the new channels, and become operational, only if learning is translated into quantities of information. We can predict that anything in the constituted body of knowledge that is not translatable in this way will be abandoned and that the direction of new research will be dictated by the possibility of its eventual results being translatable into computer language. The "producers" and users of knowledge must now, and will have to, possess the means of translating into these languages whatever they want to invent or learn. Research on translating machines is already well advanced. Along with the hegemony of computers comes a certain logic, and therefore a certain set of prescriptions determining which statements are accepted as "knowledge" statements.

We may thus expect a thorough exteriorization of knowledge with respect to the "knower," at whatever point he or she may occupy in the knowledge process. The old principle that the acquisition of knowledge is indissociable from the training (*Bildung*) of minds, or even of individuals, is becoming obsolete and will become ever more so. The relationship of the suppliers and users of knowledge to the knowledge they supply and use is now tending, and will increasingly tend, to assume the form already taken by the relationship of commodity producers and consumers to the commodities they produce and consume – that is, the form of value. Knowledge is and will be produced in order to be sold, it is and will be consumed in order to be valorized in a new production: in both cases, the goal is exchange. Knowledge ceases to be an end in itself, it loses its "use-value."[2]

It is widely accepted that knowledge has become the principal force of production over the last few decades; this has already had a noticeable effect on the composition of the work force of the most highly developed countries and constitutes the major bottleneck for the developing countries. In the postindustrial and postmodern age, science will maintain and no doubt strengthen its preeminence in the arsenal of productive capacities of the nation-states. Indeed, this situation is one of the reasons leading to the conclusion that the gap between developed and developing countries will grow ever wider in the future.

But this aspect of the problem should not be allowed to overshadow the other, which is complementary to it. Knowledge in the form of an informational commodity indispensable to productive power is already, and will continue to be, a major — perhaps *the* major — stake in the worldwide competition for power. It is conceivable that the nation-states will one day fight for control of information, just as they battled in the past for control over territory, and afterwards for control of access to and exploitation of raw materials and cheap labor. A new field is opened for industrial and commercial strategies on the one hand, and political and military strategies on the other.

However, the perspective I have outlined above is not as simple as I have made it appear. For the mercantilization of knowledge is bound to affect the privilege the nation-states have enjoyed, and still enjoy, with respect to the production and distribution of learning. The notion that learning falls within the purview of the State, as the brain or mind of society, will become more and more outdated with the increasing strength of the opposing principle, according to which society exists and progresses only if the messages circulating within it are rich in information and easy to decode. The ideology of communicational "transparency," which goes hand in hand with the commercialization of knowledge, will begin to perceive the State as a factor of opacity and "noise." It is from this point of view that the problem of the relationship between economic and State powers threatens to arise with a new urgency.

Already in the last few decades, economic powers have reached the point of imperiling the stability of the State through new forms of the circulation of capital that go by the generic name of *multinational corporations*. These new forms of circulation imply that investment decisions have, at least in part, passed beyond the control of the nation-states. The question threatens to become even more thorny with the development of computer technology and telematics. Suppose, for example, that a firm such as IBM is authorized to occupy a belt in the earth's orbital field and launch communications satellites or satellites housing data banks. Who will have access to them? Who will determine which channels or data are forbidden? The State? Or will the State simply be one user among others? New legal issues will be raised, and with them the question: "who will know?"

Transformation in the nature of knowledge, then, could well have repercussions on the existing public powers, forcing them to reconsider their relations (both de jure and de facto) with the large corporations and, more generally, with civil society. The reopening of the world market, a return to vigorous economic competition, the breakdown of the hegemony of American capitalism, the decline of the socialist alternative, a probable opening of the Chinese market — these and many other factors are already, at the end of the 1970s, preparing States for a serious reappraisal of the role they have been accustomed to playing since the 1930s: that of guiding, or even directing investments. In this light, the new technologies can only increase the urgency of such a reexamination, since they make the information used in decision making (and therefore the means of control) even more mobile and subject to piracy.

It is not hard to visualize learning circulating along the same lines as money, instead of for its "educational" value or political (administrative, diplomatic, military) importance; the pertinent distinction would no longer be between knowledge and ignorance, but rather, as is the case with money, between "payment knowledge" and "investment knowledge" — in other words, between units of knowledge exchanged in a daily maintenance framework (the reconstitution of the work force, "survival") versus funds of knowledge dedicated to optimizing the performance of a project.

If this were the case, communicational transparency would be similar to liberalism. Liberalism does not preclude an organization of the flow of money in which some channels are used in decision making while others are only good for the payment of debts. One could similarly imagine flows of knowledge traveling along identical channels of identical nature, some of which would be reserved for the "decision makers," while the others would be used to repay each person's perpetual debt with respect to the social bond.

2   The problem: legitimation

That is the working hypothesis defining the field within which I intend to consider the question of the status of knowledge. This scenario, akin to the one that goes by the name "the computerization of society" (although ours is advanced in an entirely different spirit), makes no claims of being original, or even true. What is required of a working hypothesis is a fine capacity for discrimination. The scenario of the computerization of the most highly developed societies allows us to spotlight (though with the risk of excessive magnification) certain aspects of the transformation of knowledge and its effects on public power and civil institutions — effects it would be difficult to perceive from other points of view. Our hypothesis, therefore, should not be accorded predictive value in relation to reality, but strategic value in relation to the question raised.

Nevertheless, it has strong credibility, and in that sense our choice of this hypothesis is not arbitrary. It has been described extensively by the experts and is already guiding certain decisions by the governmental agencies and private firms most directly concerned, such as those managing the telecommunications industry. To some extent, then, it is already a part of observable reality. Finally, barring economic stagnation or a general recession (resulting, for example, from a continued failure to solve the world's energy problems), there is a good chance that this scenario will come to pass: it is hard to see what other direction contemporary technology could take as an alternative to the computerization of society.

This is as much as to say that the hypothesis is banal. But only to the extent that it fails to challenge the general paradigm of progress in science and technology, to which economic growth and the expansion of sociopolitical power seem to be natural complements. That scientific and technical knowledge is cumulative is never questioned. At most, what is debated is the form that accumulation takes — some picture it as regular, continuous, and unanimous, others as periodic, discontinuous, and conflictual.

But these truisms are fallacious. In the first place, scientific knowledge does not represent the totality of knowledge; it has always existed in addition to, and in competition and conflict with, another kind of knowledge, which I will call narrative in the interests of simplicity (its characteristics will be described later). I do not mean to say that narrative knowledge can prevail over science, but its model is related to ideas of internal equilibrium and conviviality next to which contemporary scientific knowledge cuts a poor figure, especially if it is to undergo an exteriorization with respect to the "knower" and an alienation from its user even greater than has previously been the case. The resulting demoralization of researchers and teachers is far from negligible; it is well known that during the 1960s, in all of the most highly developed societies, it reached such explosive dimensions among those preparing to practice these professions — the students — that there was noticeable decrease in productivity at laboratories and universities unable to protect themselves from its contamination. Expecting this, with hope or fear, to lead to a revolution (as was then often the case) is out of the question: it will not change the order of things in postindustrial society overnight. But this doubt on the part of scientists must be taken into account as a major factor in evaluating the present and future status of scientific knowledge.

It is all the more necessary to take it into consideration since – and this is the second point – the scientists' demoralization has an impact on the central problem of legitimation. I use the word in a broader sense than do contemporary German theorists in their discussions of the question of authority.[3] Take any civil law as an example: it states that a given category of citizens must perform a specific kind of action. Legitimation is the process by which a legislator is authorized to promulgate such a law as a norm. Now take the example of a scientific statement: it is subject to the rule that a statement must fulfill a given set of conditions in order to be accepted as scientific. In this case, legitimation is the process by which a "legislator" dealing with scientific discourse is authorized to prescribe the stated conditions (in general, conditions of internal consistency and experimental verification) determining whether a statement is to be included in that discourse for consideration by the scientific community.

The parallel may appear forced. But as we will see, it is not. The question of the legitimacy of science has been indissociably linked to that of the legitimation of the legislator since the time of Plato. From this point of view, the right to decide what is true is not independent of the right to decide what is just, even if the statements consigned to these two authorities differ in nature. The point is that there is a strict interlinkage between the kind of language called science and the kind called ethics and politics: they both stem from the same perspective, the same "choice" if you will – the choice called the Occident.

When we examine the current status of scientific knowledge – at a time when science seems more completely subordinated to the prevailing powers than ever before and, along with the new technologies, is in danger of becoming a major stake in their conflicts – the question of double legitimation, far from receding into the background, necessarily comes to the fore. For it appears in its most complete form, that of reversion, revealing that knowledge and power are simply two sides of the same question: who decides what knowledge is, and who knows what needs to be decided? In the computer age, the question of knowledge is now more than ever a question of government.

3   The method: language games

The reader will already have noticed that in analyzing this problem within the framework set forth I have favored a certain procedure: emphasizing facts of language and in particular their pragmatic aspect.[4] To help clarify what follows it would be useful to summarize, however briefly, what is meant here by the term *pragmatic*.

A denotative utterance such as "The university is sick," made in the context of a conversation or an interview, positions its sender (the person who utters the statement), its addressee (the person who receives it), and its referent (what the statement deals with) in a specific way: the utterance places (and exposes) the sender in the position of "knower" (he knows what the situation is with the university), the addressee is put in the position of having to give or refuse his assent, and the referent itself is handled in a way unique to denotatives, as something that demands to be correctly identified and expressed by the statement that refers to it.

If we consider a declaration such as "The university is open," pronounced by a dean or rector at convocation, it is clear that the previous specifications no longer apply. Of course, the meaning of the utterance has to be understood, but that is a general condition of communication and does not aid us in distinguishing the different kinds of utterances or their specific effects. The distinctive feature of this second, "performative," utterance is that its effect upon the referent coincides with its enunciation. The university is open because it has been declared open in the above-mentioned circumstances. That this is so is not subject to discussion or verification on the part of the addressee, who is immediately placed within the new context created by the utterance. As for the sender, he must be invested with the authority to make such a statement. Actually, we could say it the other way around: the sender is dean or rector – that is, he is invested with the authority to make this kind of statement – only insofar as he can directly affect both the referent (the university) and the addressee (the university staff) in the manner I have indicated.

A different case involves utterances of the type, "Give money to the university"; these are prescriptions. They can be modulated as orders, commands, instructions, recommendations, requests, prayers, pleas, etc. Here, the sender is clearly placed in a position of authority, using the term broadly (including the authority of a sinner over a god who claims to be merciful): that is, he expects the addressee to perform the action referred to. The pragmatics of prescription entail concomitant changes in the posts of addressee and referent.

Of a different order again is the efficiency of a question, a promise, a literary description, a narration, etc. I am summarizing. Wittgenstein, taking up the study of language again from scratch, focuses his attention on the effects of different modes of discourse; he calls the various types of utterances he identifies along the way (a few of which I have listed) *language games*.[5] What he means by this term is that each of the various categories of utterance can be defined in terms of rules specifying their properties and the uses to which they can be put – in exactly the same way as the game of chess is defined by a set of rules determining the properties of each of the pieces, in other words, the proper way to move them.

It is useful to make the following three observations about language games. The first is that their rules do not carry within themselves their own legitimation, but are the object of a contract, explicit or not, between players (which is not to say that the players invent the rules). The second is that if there are no rules, there is no game,[6] that even an infinitesimal modification of one rule alters the nature of the game, that a "move" or utterance that does not satisfy the rules does not belong to the game they define. The third remark is suggested by what has just been said: every utterance should be thought of as a "move" in a game.

This last observation brings us to the first principle underlying our method as a whole: to speak is to fight, in the sense of playing, and speech acts[7] fall within the domain of a general agonistics.[8] This does not necessarily mean that one plays in order to win. A move can be made for the sheer pleasure of its invention: what else is involved in that labor of language harassment undertaken by popular speech and by literature? Great joy is had in the endless invention of turns of phrase, of words and meanings, the process behind the evolution of language on the level of *parole*. But undoubtedly even this pleasure depends on a feeling of success won at the expense of an adversary – at least one adversary, and a formidable one: the accepted language, or connotation.[9]

This idea of an agonistics of language should not make us lose sight of the second principle, which stands as a complement to it and governs our analysis: that the observable social bond is composed of language "moves." An elucidation of this proposition will take us to the heart of the matter at hand.

4   The nature of the social bond: the modern alternative

If we wish to discuss knowledge in the most highly developed contemporary society, we must answer the preliminary question of what methodological representation to apply to that society. Simplifying to the extreme, it is fair to say that in principle there have been, at least over the last half-century, two basic representational models for society: either society forms a functional whole, or it is divided in two. An illustration of the first model is suggested by Talcott Parsons (at least the postwar Parsons) and his school, and of the second, by the Marxist current (all of its component schools, whatever differences they may have, accept both the principle of class struggle and dialectics as a duality operating within society).[10]

This methodological split, which defines two major kinds of discourse on society, has been handed down from the nineteenth century. The idea that society forms an organic whole, in the absence of which it ceases to be a society (and sociology ceases to have an object of study), dominated the minds of the founders of the French school. Added detail was supplied by functionalism; it took yet another turn in the 1950s with Parsons' conception of society as a self-regulating system. The theoretical and even material model is no longer the living organism; it is provided by cybernetics, which, during and after the Second World War, expanded the model's applications.

In Parsons' work, the principle behind the system is still, if I may say so, optimistic: it corresponds to the stabilization of the growth economies and societies of abundance under the aegis of a moderate welfare state. In the work of contemporary German theorists, *systemtheorie* is technocratic, even cynical, not to mention despairing: the harmony between the needs and hopes of individuals or groups and the functions guaranteed by the system is now only a secondary component of its functioning. The true goal of the system, the reason it programs itself like a computer, is the optimization of the global relationship between input and output – in other words, performativity. Even when its rules are in the process of changing and innovations are occurring, even when its dysfunctions (such as strikes, crises, unemployment, or political revolutions) inspire hope and lead to belief in an alternative, even then what is actually taking place is only an internal readjustment, and its result can be no more than an increase in the system's "viability." The only alternative to this kind of performance improvement is entropy, or decline.

Here again while avoiding the simplifications inherent in a sociology of social theory, it is difficult to deny at least a parallel between this "hard" technocratic version of society and the ascetic effort that was demanded (the fact that it was done in the name of "advanced liberalism" is beside the point) of the most highly developed industrial societies in order to make them competitive – and thus optimize their "rationality" – within the framework of the resumption of economic world war in the 1960s.

Even taking into account the massive displacement intervening between the thought of a man like Comte and the thought of Luhmann, we can discern a common conception of the social: society is a unified totality, a "unicity." Parsons formulates this clearly: "The most essential condition of successful dynamic analysis is a continual and systematic reference of every problem to the state of the system as a whole ... A process or set of conditions either 'contributes' to the maintenance (or development) of the system or it is 'dysfunctional' in that it detracts from the integration, effectiveness, etc., of the system."[11] The "technocrats"[12] also subscribe to this idea. Whence its credibility: it has the means to become a reality, and that is all the proof it needs. This is what Horkheimer called the "paranoia" of reason.[13]

But this realism of systemic self-regulation, and this perfectly sealed circle of facts and interpretations, can be judged paranoid only if one has, or claims to have, at one's disposal a viewpoint that is in principle immune from their allure. This is the function of the principle of class struggle in theories of society based on the work of Marx.

"Traditional" theory is always in danger of being incorporated into the programming of the social whole as a simple tool for the optimization of its performance; this is because its desire for a unitary and totalizing truth lends itself to the unitary and totalizing practice of the system's managers. "Critical" theory,[14] based on a principle of dualism and wary of syntheses and reconciliations, should be in a position to avoid this fate. What guides Marxism, then, is a different model of society, and a different conception of the function of the knowledge that can be produced by society and acquired from it. This model was born of the struggles accompanying the process of capitalism's encroachment upon traditional civil societies. There is insufficient space here to chart the vicissitudes of these struggles, which fill more than a century of social, political, and ideological history. We will have to content ourselves with a glance at the balance sheet, which is possible for us to tally today now that their fate is known: in countries with liberal or advanced liberal management, the struggles and their instruments have been transformed into regulators of the system; in communist countries, the totalizing model and its totalitarian effect have made a comeback in the name of Marxism itself, and the struggles in question have simply been deprived of the right to exist. Everywhere, the *Critique of Political Economy* (the subtitle of Marx's *Capital*) and its correlate, the critique of alienated society, are used in one way or another as aids in programming the system.

Of course, certain minorities, such as the Frankfurt School or the group *Socialisme ou barbarie*,[15] preserved and refined the critical model in opposition to this process. But the social foundation of the principle of division, or class struggle, was blurred to the point of losing all of its radicality; we cannot conceal the fact that the critical model in the end lost its theoretical standing and was reduced to the status of a "utopia" or "hope,"[16] a token protest raised in the name of man or reason or creativity, or again of some social category – such as the Third World or the students – on which is conferred in extremis the henceforth improbable function of critical subject.

The sole purpose of this schematic (or skeletal) reminder has been to specify the problematic in which I intend to frame the question of knowledge in advanced industrial societies. For it is impossible to know what the state of knowledge is – in other words, the problems its development and distribution are facing today – without knowing something of the society within which it is situated. And today more than ever, knowing about that society involves first of all choosing what approach the inquiry will take, and that necessarily means choosing how society can answer. One can decide that the principal role of knowledge is as an indispensable element in the functioning of society, and act in accordance with that decision, only if one has already decided that society is a giant machine.[17]

Conversely, one can count on its critical function, and orient its development and distribution in that direction, only after it has been decided that society does not form an integrated whole, but remains haunted by a principle of opposition. The alternative seems clear: it is a choice between the homogeneity and the intrinsic duality of the social, between functional and critical knowledge. But the decision seems difficult, or arbitrary.

It is tempting to avoid the decision altogether by distinguishing two kinds of knowledge. One, the positivist kind, would be directly applicable to technologies bearing on men and materials, and would lend itself to operating as an indispensable productive force within the system. The other – the critical, reflexive, or hermeneutic kind – by reflecting directly or indirectly on values or aims, would resist any such "recuperation."[18]

5   The nature of the social bond: the postmodern perspective

I find this partition solution unacceptable. I suggest that the alternative it attempts to resolve, but only reproduces, is no longer relevant for the societies with which we are concerned and that the solution itself is still caught within a type of oppositional thinking that is out of step with the most vital modes of postmodern knowledge. As I have already said, economic "redeployment" in the current phase of capitalism, aided by a shift in techniques and technology, goes hand in hand with a change in the function of the State: the image of society this syndrome suggests necessitates a serious revision of the alternate approaches considered. For brevity's sake, suffice it to say that functions of regulation, and therefore of reproduction, are being and will be further withdrawn from administrators and entrusted to machines. Increasingly, the central question is becoming who will have access to the information these machines must have in storage to guarantee that the right decisions are made. Access to data is, and will continue to be, the prerogative of experts of all stripes. The ruling class is and will continue to be the class of decision makers. Even now it is no longer composed of the traditional political class, but of a composite layer of corporate leaders, high-level administrators, and the heads of the major professional, labor, political, and religious organizations.

What is new in all of this is that the old poles of attraction represented by nation-states, parties, professions, institutions, and historical traditions are losing their attraction. And it does not look as though they will be replaced, at least not on their former scale. The Trilateral Commission is not a popular pole of attraction. "Identifying" with the great names, the heroes of contemporary history, is becoming more and more difficult. [...] Each individual is referred to himself. And each of us knows that our self does not amount to much.

This breaking up of the grand Narratives leads to what some authors analyze in terms of the dissolution of the social bond and the disintegration of social aggregates into a mass of individual atoms thrown into the absurdity of Brownian motion.[19] Nothing of the kind is happening: this point of view, it seems to me, is haunted by the paradisaic representation of a lost "organic" society.

A *self* does not amount to much, but no self is an island; each exists in a fabric of relations that is now more complex and mobile than ever before. Young or old, man or woman, rich or poor, a person is always located at "nodal points" of specific communication circuits, however tiny these may be. Or better: one is always located at a post through which various kinds of messages pass. No one, not even the least privileged among us, is ever entirely powerless over the messages that traverse and position him at the post of sender, addressee, or referent. One's mobility in relation to these language game effects (language games, of course, are what this is all about) is tolerable, at least within certain limits (and the limits are vague); it is even solicited by regulatory mechanisms, and in particular by the self-adjustments the system undertakes in order to improve its performance. It may even be said that the system can and must encourage such movement to the extent that it combats its own entropy; the novelty of an unexpected "move," with its correlative displacement of a partner or group of partners, can supply the system with that increased performativity it forever demands and consumes.

It should now be clear from which perspective I chose language games as my general methodological approach. I am not claiming that the *entirety* of social relations is of this nature – that will remain an open question. But there is no need to resort to some fiction of social origins to establish that language games are the minimum relation required for society to exist: even before he is born, if only by virtue of the name he is given, the human child is already positioned as the referent in the story recounted by those around him, in relation to which he will inevitably chart his course. Or more simply still, the question of the social bond, insofar as it is a question, is itself a language game, the game of inquiry. It immediately positions the person who asks, as well as the addressee and the referent asked about: it is already the social bond.

On the other hand, in a society whose communication component is becoming more prominent day by day, both as a reality and as an issue, it is clear that language assumes a new importance. It would be superficial to reduce its significance to the traditional alternative between manipulatory speech and the unilateral transmission of messages on the one hand, and free expression and dialogue on the other.

A word on this last point. If the problem is described simply in terms of communication theory, two things are overlooked: first, messages have quite different forms and effects depending on whether they are, for example, denotatives, prescriptives, evaluatives, performatives, etc. It is clear that what is important is not simply the fact that they communicate information. Reducing them to this function is to adopt an outlook which unduly privileges the system's own interests and point of view. A cybernetic machine does indeed run on information, but the goals programmed into it, for example, originate in prescriptive and evaluative statements it has no way to correct in the course of its functioning – for example, maximizing its own performance. How can one guarantee that performance maximization is the best goal for the social system in every case? In any case the "atoms" forming its matter are competent to handle statements such as these – and this question in particular.

Second, the trivial cybernetic version of information theory misses something of decisive importance, to which I have already called attention: the agonistic aspect of society. The atoms are placed at the crossroads of pragmatic relationships, but they are also displaced by the messages that traverse them, in perpetual motion. Each language partner, when a "move" pertaining to him is made, undergoes a "displacement," an alteration of some kind that not only affects him in his capacity as addressee and referent, but also as sender. These "moves" necessarily provoke "countermoves" – and everyone knows that a countermove that is merely reactional is not a "good" move. Reactional countermoves are no more than programmed effects in the opponent's strategy; they play into his hands and thus have no effect on the balance of power. That is why it is important to increase displacement in the games, and even to disorient it, in such a way as to make an unexpected "move" (a new statement).

What is needed if we are to understand social relations in this manner, on whatever scale we choose, is not only a theory of communication, but a theory of games which accepts agonistics as a founding principle. In this context, it is easy to see that the essential element of newness is not simply "innovation." Support for this approach can be found in the work of a number of contemporary sociologists,[20] in addition to linguists and philosophers of language.

This "atomization" of the social into flexible networks of language games may seem far removed from the modern reality, which is depicted, on the contrary, as afflicted with bureaucratic paralysis. The objection will be made, at least, that the weight of certain institutions imposes limits on the games, and thus restricts the inventiveness of the players in making their moves. But I think this can be taken into account without causing any particular difficulty.

In the ordinary use of discourse – for example, in a discussion between two friends – the interlocutors use any available ammunition, changing games from one utterance to the next: questions, requests, assertions, and narratives are launched pell-mell into battle. The war is not without rules, but the rules allow and encourage the greatest possible flexibility of utterance.

From this point of view, an institution differs from a conversation in that it always requires supplementary constraints for statements to be declared admissible within its bounds. The constraints function to filter discursive potentials, interrupting possible connections in the communication networks: there are things that should not be said. They also privilege certain classes of statements (sometimes only one) whose predominance characterizes the discourse of the particular institution: there are things that should be said, and there are ways of saying them. Thus: orders in the army, prayer in church, denotation in the schools, narration in families, questions in philosophy, performativity in businesses. Bureaucratization is the outer limit of this tendency.

However, this hypothesis about the institution is still too "unwieldy": its point of departure is an overly "reifying" view of what is institutionalized. We know today that the limits the institution imposes on potential language "moves" are never established once and for all (even if they have been formally defined). Rather, the limits are themselves the stakes and provisional results of language strategies, within the institution and without. Examples: Does the university have a place for language experiments (poetics)? Can you tell stories in a cabinet meeting? Advocate a cause in the barracks? The answers are clear: yes, if the university opens creative workshops; yes, if the cabinet works with prospective scenarios; yes, if the limits of the old institution are displaced. Reciprocally, it can be said that the boundaries only stabilize when they cease to be stakes in the game.

This, I think, is the appropriate approach to contemporary institutions of knowledge.

6   The pragmatics of narrative knowledge

In Section 1, I leveled two objections against the unquestioning acceptance of an instrumental conception of knowledge in the most highly developed societies. Knowledge is not the same as science, especially in its contemporary form; and science, far from successfully obscuring the problem of its legitimacy, cannot avoid raising it with all of its implications, which are no less sociopolitical than epistemological. Let us begin with an analysis of the nature of "narrative" knowledge; by providing a point of comparison, our examination will clarify at least some of the characteristics of the form assumed by scientific knowledge in contemporary society. In addition, it will aid us in understanding how the question of legitimacy is raised or fails to be raised today.

Knowledge [*savoir*] in general cannot be reduced to science, nor even to learning [*connaissance*]. Learning is the set of statements which, to the exclusion of all other statements, denote or describe objects and may be declared true or false. Science is a subset of learning. It is also composed of denotative statements, but imposes two supplementary conditions on their acceptability: the objects to which they refer must be available for repeated access; in other words, they must be accessible in explicit conditions of observation; and it must be possible to decide whether or not a given statement pertains to the language judged relevant by the experts.

But what is meant by the term *knowledge* is not only a set of denotative statements, far from it. It also includes notions of "know-how," "knowing how to live," "how to listen" [*savoir-faire, savoir-vivre, savoir-écouter*], etc. Knowledge, then, is a question of competence that goes beyond the simple determination and application of the criterion of truth, extending to the determination and application of criteria of efficiency (technical qualification), of justice and/or happiness (ethical wisdom), of the beauty of a sound or color (auditory and visual sensibility), etc. Understood in this way, knowledge is what makes someone capable of forming "good" denotative utterances, but also "good" prescriptive and "good" evaluative utterances. ... It is not a competence relative to a particular class of statements (for example, cognitive ones) to the exclusion of all others. On the contrary, it makes "good" performances in relation to a variety of objects of discourse possible: objects to be known, decided on, evaluated, transformed. ... From this derives one of the principal features of knowledge: it coincides with an extensive array of competence-building measures and is the only form embodied in a subject constituted by the various areas of competence composing it. [...]

7   The pragmatics of scientific knowledge

Let us attempt to characterize, if only in summary fashion, the classical conception of the pragmatics of scientific knowledge. In the process, we will distinguish between the research game and the teaching game.

Copernicus states that the path of the planets is circular. Whether this proposition is true or false, it carries within it a set of tensions, all of which affect each of the pragmatic posts it brings into play: sender, addressee, and referent. These "tensions" are classes of prescriptions which regulate the admissibility of the statement as "scientific."

First, the sender should speak the truth about the referent, the path of the planets. What does this mean? That on the one hand he is supposed to be able to provide proof of what he says, and on the other hand he is supposed to be able to refute any opposing or contradictory statements concerning the same referent.

Second, it should be possible for the addressee validly to give (or refuse) his assent to the statement he hears. This implies that he is himself a potential sender, since when he formulates his agreement or disagreement he will be subject to the same double requirement (or proof or refutation) that Copernicus was. He is therefore supposed to have, potentially, the same qualities as Copernicus: he is his equal.

But this will only become known when he speaks and under the above conditions. Before that, it will be impossible to say whether or not he is a scientific scholar.

Third, the referent (the path of the planets) of which Copernicus speaks is supposed to be "expressed" by his statement in conformity with what it actually is. But since what it is can only be known through statements of the same order as that of Copernicus, the rule of adequation becomes problematical. What I say is true because I prove that it is — but what proof is there that my proof is true?

The scientific solution of this difficulty consists in the observance of two rules. The first of these is dialectical or even rhetorical in the forensic sense: a referent is that which is susceptible to proof and can be used as evidence in a debate. Not: I can prove something because reality is the way I say it is. But: as long as I can produce proof, it is permissible to think that reality is the way I say it is. The second rule is metaphysical; the same referent cannot supply a plurality of contradictory or inconsistent proofs. Or stated differently: "God" is not deceptive.[21]

These two rules underlie what nineteenth-century science calls verification and twentieth-century science, falsification. They allow a horizon of consensus to be brought to the debate between partners (the sender and the addressee). Not every consensus is a sign of truth; but it is presumed that the truth of a statement necessarily draws a consensus.

That covers research. It should be evident that research appeals to teaching as its necessary complement: the scientist needs an addressee who can in turn become the sender; he needs a partner. Otherwise, the verification of his statements would be impossible, since the nonrenewal of the requisite skills would eventually bring an end to the necessary, contradictory debate. Not only the truth of a scientist's statement, but also his competence, is at stake in that debate. One's competence is never an accomplished fact. It depends on whether or not the statement proposed is considered by one's peers to be worth discussion in a sequence of argumentation and refutation. The truth of the statement and the competence of its sender are thus subject to the collective approval of a group of persons who are competent on an equal basis. Equals are needed and must be created.

Didactics is what ensures that this reproduction takes place. It is different from the dialectical game of research. Briefly, its first presupposition is that the addressee, the student, does not know what the sender knows: obviously, that is why he has something to learn. Its second presupposition is that the student can learn what the sender knows and become an expert whose competence is equal to that of his master. This double requirement supposes a third: that there are statements for which the exchange of arguments and the production of proof constituting the pragmatics of research are considered to have been sufficient, and which can therefore be transmitted through teaching as they stand, in the guise of indisputable truths.

In other words, you teach what you know: such is the expert. But as the student (the addressee of the didactic process) improves his skills, the expert can confide to him what he does not know but is trying to learn (at least if the expert is also involved in research). In this way, the student is introduced to the dialectics of research, or the game of producing scientific knowledge.

If we compare the pragmatics of science to that of narrative knowledge, we note the following properties:

1   Scientific knowledge requires that one language game, denotation, be retained and all
    others excluded. A statement's truth-value is the criterion determining its acceptability.
    Of course, we find other classes of statements, such as interrogatives ("How can we
    explain that … ?") and prescriptives ("Take a finite series of elements …"). But they
    are only present as turning points in the dialectical argumentation, which must end
    in a denotative statement. In this context, then, one is "learned" if one can produce
    a true statement about a referent, and one is a scientist if one can produce verifiable
    or falsifiable statements about referents accessible to the experts.

2   Scientific knowledge is in this way set apart from the language games that combine to
    form the social bond. Unlike narrative knowledge, it is no longer a direct and shared
    component of the bond. But it is indirectly a component of it, because it develops
    into a profession and gives rise to institutions, and in modern societies language
    games consolidate themselves in the form of institutions run by qualified partners
    (the professional class). The relation between knowledge and society (that is, the sum
    total of partners in the general agonistics, excluding scientists in their professional
    capacity) becomes one of mutual exteriority. A new problem appears – that of the
    relationship between the scientific institution and society. Can this problem be solved
    by didactics, for example, by the premise that any social atom can acquire scientific
    competence?

3   Within the bounds of the game of research, the competence required concerns the
    post of sender alone. There is no particular competence required of the addressee (it
    is required only in didactics – the student must be intelligent). And there is no
    competence required of the referent. Even in the case of the human sciences, where
    it is an aspect of human conduct, the referent is in principle external to the partners
    engaged in scientific dialectics. Here, in contrast to the narrative game, a person does
    not have to know how to be what knowledge says he is.

4   A statement of science gains no validity from the fact of being reported. Even in the
    case of pedagogy, it is taught only if it is still verifiable in the present through
    argumentation and proof. In itself, it is never secure from "falsification." The knowledge
    that has accumulated in the form of already accepted statements can always be
    challenged. But conversely, any new statement that contradicts a previously approved
    statement regarding the same referent can be accepted as valid only if it refutes the
    previous statement by producing arguments and proofs.

5   The game of science thus implies a diachronic temporality, that is, a memory and a
    project. The current sender of a scientific statement is supposed to be acquainted
    with previous statements concerning its referent (bibliography) and only proposes a
    new statement on the subject if it differs from the previous ones. Here, what I have
    called the "accent" of each performance, and by that token the polemical function of
    the game, takes precedence over the "meter." This diachrony, which assumes memory
    and a search for the new, represents in principle a cumulative process. Its "rhythm,"
    or the relationship between accent and meter, is variable.[22]

These properties are well known. But they are worth recalling for two reasons. First,
drawing a parallel between science and nonscientific (narrative) knowledge helps us understand, or at least sense, that the former's existence is no more – and no less – necessary
than the latter's. Both are composed of sets of statements; the statements are "moves"
made by the players within the framework of generally applicable rules; these rules are

specific to each particular kind of knowledge, and the "moves" judged to be "good" in one cannot be of the same type as those judged "good" in another, unless it happens that way by chance.

It is therefore impossible to judge the existence or validity of narrative knowledge on the basis of scientific knowledge and vice versa: the relevant criteria are different. All we can do is gaze in wonderment at the diversity of discursive species, just as we do at the diversity of plant or animal species. Lamenting the "loss of meaning" in postmodernity boils down to mourning the fact that knowledge is no longer principally narrative. Such a reaction does not necessarily follow. Neither does an attempt to derive or engender (using operators like development) scientific knowledge from narrative knowledge, as if the former contained the latter in an embryonic state.

Nevertheless, language species, like living species, are interrelated, and their relations are far from harmonious. The second point justifying this quick reminder on the properties of the language game of science concerns, precisely, its relation to narrative knowledge. I have said that narrative knowledge does not give priority to the question of its own legitimation and that it certifies itself in the pragmatics of its own transmission without having recourse to argumentation and proof. This is why its incomprehension of the problems of scientific discourse is accompanied by a certain tolerance: it approaches such discourse primarily as a variant in the family of narrative cultures.[23] The opposite is not true. The scientist questions the validity of narrative statements and concludes that they are never subject to argumentation or proof. He classifies them as belonging to a different mentality: savage, primitive, underdeveloped, backward, alienated, composed of opinions, customs, authority, prejudice, ignorance, ideology. Narratives are fables, myths, legends, fit only for women and children. At best, attempts are made to throw some rays of light into this obscurantism, to civilize, educate, develop.

This unequal relationship is an intrinsic effect of the rules specific to each game. We all know its symptoms. It is the entire history of cultural imperialism from the dawn of Western civilization. It is important to recognize its special tenor, which sets it apart from all other forms of imperialism: it is governed by the demand for legitimation. [...]

10   Delegitimation

In contemporary society and culture – postindustrial society, postmodern culture[24] – the question of the legitimation of knowledge is formulated in different terms. The grand narrative has lost its credibility, regardless of what mode of unification it uses, regardless of whether it is a speculative narrative or a narrative of emancipation.

The decline of narrative can be seen as an effect of the blossoming of techniques and technologies since the Second World War, which has shifted emphasis from the ends of action to its means; it can also be seen as an effect of the redeployment of advanced liberal capitalism, after its retreat under the protection of Keynesianism during the period 1930–60, a renewal that has eliminated the communist alternative and valorized the individual enjoyment of goods and services.

Anytime we go searching for causes in this way we are bound to be disappointed. Even if we adopted one or the other of these hypotheses, we would still have to detail the correlation between the tendencies mentioned and the decline of the unifying and legitimating power of the grand narratives of speculation and emancipation.

It is, of course, understandable that both capitalist renewal and prosperity and the disorienting upsurge of technology would have an impact on the status of knowledge. But in order to understand how contemporary science could have been susceptible to those effects long before they took place, we must first locate the seeds of "delegitimation" and nihilism that were inherent in the grand narratives of the nineteenth century.

First of all, the speculative apparatus maintains an ambiguous relation to knowledge. It shows that knowledge is only worthy of that name to the extent that it reduplicates itself ("lifts itself up," *hebt sich auf*; is sublated) by citing its own statements in a second-level discourse (autonymy) that functions to legitimate them. This is as much as to say that, in its immediacy, denotative discourse bearing on a certain referent (a living organism, a chemical property, a physical phenomenon, etc.) does not really know what it thinks it knows. Positive science is not a form of knowledge. And speculation feeds on its suppression. The Hegelian speculative narrative thus harbors a certain skepticism toward positive learning, as Hegel himself admits.[25]

A science that has not legitimated itself is not a true science; if the discourse that was meant to legitimate it seems to belong to a prescientific form of knowledge, like a "vulgar" narrative, it is demoted to the lowest rank, that of an ideology or instrument of power. And this always happens if the rules of the science game that discourse denounces as empirical are applied to science itself.

Take, for example, the speculative statement: "A scientific statement is knowledge if and only if it can take its place in a universal process of engendering." The question is: Is this statement knowledge as it itself defines it? Only if it can take its place in a universal process of engendering. Which it can. All it has to do is to presuppose that such a process exists (the Life of spirit) and that it is itself an expression of that process. This presupposition, in fact, is indispensable to the speculative language game. Without it, the language of legitimation would not be legitimate; it would accompany science in a nosedive into nonsense, at least if we take idealism's word for it.

But this presupposition can also be understood in a totally different sense, one which takes us in the direction of postmodern culture: we could say [...] that this presupposition defines the set of rules one must accept in order to play the speculative game. Such an appraisal assumes first that we accept that the "positive" sciences represent the general mode of knowledge and second, that we understand this language to imply certain formal and axiomatic presuppositions that it must always make explicit. This is exactly what Nietzsche is doing, though with a different terminology, when he shows that "European nihilism" resulted from the truth requirement of science being turned back against itself.

There thus arises an idea of perspective that is not far removed, at least in this respect, from the idea of language games. What we have here is a process of delegitimation fueled by the demand for legitimation itself. The "crisis" of scientific knowledge, signs of which have been accumulating since the end of the nineteenth century, is not born of a chance proliferation of sciences, itself an effect of progress in technology and the expansion of capitalism. It represents, rather, an internal erosion of the legitimacy principle of knowledge. There is erosion at work inside the speculative game, and by loosening the weave of the encyclopedic net in which each science was to find its place, it eventually sets them free.

The classical dividing lines between the various fields of science are thus called into question – disciplines disappear, overlappings occur at the borders between sciences, and from these new territories are born. The speculative hierarchy of learning gives way to an immanent and, as it were, "flat" network of areas of inquiry, the respective frontiers of which are in constant flux. The old "faculties" splinter into institutes and foundations of all kinds, and the universities lose their function of speculative legitimation. Stripped of the responsibility for research (which was stifled by the speculative narrative), they limit themselves to the transmission of what is judged to be established knowledge, and through didactics they guarantee the replication of teachers rather than the production of researchers. This is the state in which Nietzsche finds and condemns them.

The potential for erosion intrinsic to the other legitimation procedure, the emancipation apparatus flowing from the *Aufklärung*, is no less extensive than the one at work within speculative discourse. But it touches a different aspect. Its distinguishing characteristic is that it grounds the legitimation of science and truth in the autonomy of interlocutors involved in ethical, social, and political praxis. There are immediate problems with this form of legitimation: the difference between a denotative statement with cognitive value and a prescriptive statement with practical value is one of relevance, therefore of competence. There is nothing to prove that if a statement describing a real situation is true, it follows that a prescriptive statement based upon it (the effect of which will necessarily be a modification of that reality) will be just.

Take, for example, a closed door. Between "The door is closed" and "Open the door" there is no relation of consequence as defined in propositional logic. The two statements belong to two autonomous sets of rules defining different kinds of relevance, and therefore of competence. Here, the effect of dividing reason into cognitive or theoretical reason on the one hand, and practical reason on the other, is to attack the legitimacy of the discourse of science. Not directly, but indirectly, by revealing that it is a language game with its own rules (of which the a priori conditions of knowledge in Kant provide a first glimpse) and that it has no special calling to supervise the game of praxis (nor the game of aesthetics, for that matter). The game of science is thus put on a par with the others.

If this "delegitimation" is pursued in the slightest and if its scope is widened (as Wittgenstein does in his own way, and thinkers such as Martin Buber and Emmanuel Lévinas in theirs)[26] the road is then open for an important current of postmodernity: science plays its own game; it is incapable of legitimating the other language games. The game of prescription, for example, escapes it. But above all, it is incapable of legitimating itself, as speculation assumed it could.

The social subject itself seems to dissolve in this dissemination of language games. The social bond is linguistic, but is not woven with a single thread. It is a fabric formed by the intersection of at least two (and in reality an indeterminate number) of language games, obeying different rules. Wittgenstein writes: "Our language can be seen as an ancient city: a maze of little streets and squares, of old and new houses, and of houses with additions from various periods; and this surrounded by a multitude of new boroughs with straight regular streets and uniform houses."[27] And to drive home that the principle of unitotality – or synthesis under the authority of a metadiscourse of knowledge – is inapplicable, he subjects the "town" of language to the old sorites paradox by asking: "how many houses or streets does it take before a town begins to be a town?"[28]

New languages are added to the old ones, forming suburbs of the old town: "the symbolism of chemistry and the notation of the infinitesimal calculus."[29] Thirty-five years later we can add to the list: machine languages, the matrices of game theory, new systems of musical notation, systems of notation for nondenotative forms of logic (temporal logics, deontic logics, modal logics), the language of the genetic code, graphs of phonological structures, and so on.

We may form a pessimistic impression of this splintering: nobody speaks all of those languages, they have no universal metalanguage, the project of the system-subject is a failure, the goal of emancipation has nothing to do with science, we are all stuck in the positivism of this or that discipline of learning, the learned scholars have turned into scientists, the diminished tasks of research have become compartmentalized and no one can master them all. Speculative or humanistic philosophy is forced to relinquish its legitimation duties, which explains why philosophy is facing a crisis wherever it persists in arrogating such functions and is reduced to the study of systems of logic or the history of ideas where it has been realistic enough to surrender them.

Turn-of-the-century Vienna was weaned on this pessimism: not just artists such as Musil, Kraus, Hofmannsthal, Loos, Schönberg, and Broch, but also the philosophers Mach and Wittgenstein.[30] They carried awareness of and theoretical and artistic responsibility for delegitimation as far as it could be taken. We can say today that the mourning process has been completed. There is no need to start all over again. Wittgenstein's strength is that he did not opt for the positivism that was being developed by the Vienna Circle, but outlined in his investigation of language games a kind of legitimation not based on performativity. That is what the postmodern world is all about. Most people have lost the nostalgia for the lost narrative. It in no way follows that they are reduced to barbarity. What saves them from it is their knowledge that legitimation can only spring from their own linguistic practice and communicational interaction. Science "smiling into its beard" at every other belief has taught them the harsh austerity of realism.[31]

11   Research and its legitimation through performativity

[...] This is where technology comes in. Technical devices originated as prosthetic aids for the human organs or as physiological systems whose function it is to receive data or condition the context. They follow a principle, and it is the principle of optimal performance: maximizing output (the information or modifications obtained) and minimizing input (the energy expended in the process). Technology is therefore a game pertaining not to the true, the just, or the beautiful, etc., but to efficiency: a technical "move" is "good" when it does better and/or expends less energy than another.

This definition of technical competence is a late development. For a long time inventions came in fits and starts, the products of chance research, or research as much or more concerned with the arts (*technai*) than with knowledge: the Greeks of the Classical period, for example, established no close relationship between knowledge and technology. In the sixteenth and seventeenth centuries, the work of "perspectors" was still a matter of curiosity and artistic innovation. This was the case until the end of the eighteenth century. And it can be maintained that even today "wildcat" activities of technical invention, sometimes related to *bricolage*, still go on outside the imperatives of scientific argumentation.

Nonetheless, the need for proof becomes increasingly strong as the pragmatics of scientific knowledge replaces traditional knowledge or knowledge based on revelation. By the end of the *Discourse on Method*, Descartes is already asking for laboratory funds. A new problem appears: devices that optimize the performance of the human body for the purpose of producing proof require additional expenditures. No money, no proof – and that means no verification of statements and no truth. The games of scientific language become the games of the rich, in which whoever is wealthiest has the best chance of being right. An equation between wealth, efficiency, and truth is thus established.

What happened at the end of the eighteenth century, with the first industrial revolution, is that the reciprocal of this equation was discovered: no technology without wealth, but no wealth without technology. A technical apparatus requires an investment; but since it optimizes the efficiency of the task to which it is applied, it also optimizes the surplus-value derived from this improved performance. All that is needed is for the surplus-value to be realized, in other words, for the product of the task performed to be sold. And the system can be sealed in the following way: a portion of the sale is recycled into a research fund dedicated to further performance improvement. It is at this precise moment that science becomes a force of production, in other words, a moment in the circulation of capital.

It was more the desire for wealth than the desire for knowledge that initially forced upon technology the imperative of performance improvement and product realization. The "organic" connection between technology and profit preceded its union with science. Technology became important to contemporary knowledge only through the mediation of a generalized spirit of performativity. Even today, progress in knowledge is not totally subordinated to technological investment.

Capitalism solves the scientific problem of research funding in its own way: directly by financing research departments in private companies, in which demands for performativity and recommercialization orient research first and foremost toward technological "applications"; and indirectly by creating private, state, or mixed-sector research foundations that grant program subsidies to university departments, research laboratories, and independent research groups with no expectation of an immediate return on the results of the work – this is done on the theory that research must be financed at a loss for certain length of time in order to increase the probability of its yielding a decisive, and therefore highly profitable, innovation. Nation-states, especially in their Keynesian period, follow the same rule: applied research on the one hand, basic research on the other. They collaborate with corporations through an array of agencies. The prevailing corporate norms of work management spread to the applied science laboratories: hierarchy, centralized decision making, teamwork, calculation of individual and collective returns, the development of saleable programs, market research, and so on. Centers dedicated to "pure" research suffer from this less, but also receive less funding.

The production of proof, which is in principle only part of an argumentation process designed to win agreement from the addressees of scientific messages, thus falls under the control of another language game, in which the goal is no longer truth, but performativity – that is, the best possible input/output equation. The State and/or company must abandon the idealist and humanist narratives of legitimation in order to justify the new goal: in the discourse of today's financial backers of research, the only credible goal is power. Scientists, technicians, and instruments are purchased not to find truth, but to augment power.

The question is to determine what the discourse of power consists of and if it can constitute a legitimation. At first glance, it is prevented from doing so by the traditional distinction between force and right, between force and wisdom – in other words, between what is strong, what is just, and what is true. I referred to this incommensurability earlier in terms of the theory of language games, when I distinguished the denotative game (in which what is relevant is the true/false distinction) from the prescriptive game (in which the just/unjust distinction pertains) from the technical game (in which the criterion is the efficient/inefficient distinction). "Force" appears to belong exclusively to the last game, the game of technology. I am excluding the case in which force operates by means of terror. This lies outside the realm of language games, because the efficacy of such force is based entirely on the threat to eliminate the opposing player, not on making a better "move" than he. Whenever efficiency (that is, obtaining the desired effect) is derived from a "Say or do this, or else you'll never speak again," then we are in the realm of terror, and the social bond is destroyed.

But the fact remains that since performativity increases the ability to produce proof, it also increases the ability to be right: the technical criterion, introduced on a massive scale into scientific knowledge, cannot fail to influence the truth criterion. The same has been said of the relationship between justice and performance: the probability that an order would be pronounced just was said to increase with its chances of being implemented, which would in turn increase with the performance capability of the prescriber. This led Luhmann to hypothesize that in postindustrial societies the normativity of laws is replaced by the performativity of procedures. "Context control," in other words, performance improvement won at the expense of the partner or partners constituting that context (be they "nature" or men), can pass for a kind of legitimation. De facto legitimation.

This procedure operates within the following framework: since "reality" is what provides the evidence used as proof in scientific argumentation, and also provides prescriptions and promises of a juridical, ethical, and political nature with results, one can master all of these games by mastering "reality." That is precisely what technology can do. By reinforcing technology, one "reinforces" reality, and one's chances of being just and right increase accordingly. Reciprocally, technology is reinforced all the more effectively if one has access to scientific knowledge and decision-making authority.

This is how legitimation by power takes shape. Power is not only good performativity, but also effective verification and good verdicts. It legitimates science and the law on the basis of their efficiency, and legitimates this efficiency on the basis of science and law. It is self-legitimating, in the same way a system organized around performance maximization seems to be. Now it is precisely this kind of context control that a generalized computerization of society may bring. The performativity of an utterance, be it denotative or prescriptive, increases proportionally to the amount of information about its referent one has at one's disposal. Thus the growth of power, and its self-legitimation, are now taking the route of data storage and accessibility, and the operativity of information.

The relationship between science and technology is reversed. The complexity of the argumentation becomes relevant here, especially because it necessitates greater sophistication in the means of obtaining proof, and that in turn benefits performativity. Research funds are allocated by States, corporations, and nationalized companies in accordance with this logic of power growth. Research sectors that are unable to argue that they contribute even indirectly to the optimization of the system's performance are abandoned by the flow of capital and doomed to senescence. The criterion of performance is explicitly invoked by the authorities to justify their refusal to subsidize certain research centers. [...]

13   Postmodern science as the search for instabilities

As previously indicated, the pragmatics of scientific research, especially in its search for new methods of argumentation, emphasizes the invention of new "moves" and even new rules for language games. We must now take a closer look at this aspect of the problem, which is of decisive importance in the present state of scientific knowledge. We could say, tongue in cheek, that scientific knowledge is seeking a "crisis resolution" – a resolution of the crisis of determinism. Determinism is the hypothesis upon which legitimation by performativity is based: since performativity is defined by an input/ output ratio, there is a presupposition that the system into which the input is entered is stable; that system must follow a regular "path" that it is possible to express as a continuous function possessing a derivative, so that an accurate prediction of the output can be made.

Such is the positivist "philosophy" of efficiency. I will cite a number of prominent examples as evidence against it to facilitate the final discussion of legitimation. Briefly, the aim is to demonstrate on the basis of a few exhibits that the pragmatics of postmodern scientific knowledge per se has little affinity with the quest for performativity.

Science does not expand by means of the positivism of efficiency. The opposite is true: working on a proof means searching for and "inventing" counterexamples, in other words, the unintelligible; supporting an argument means looking for a "paradox" and legitimating it with new rules in the games of reasoning. In neither case is efficiency sought for its own sake; it comes, sometimes tardily, as an extra, when the grant givers finally decide to take an interest in the case. But what never fails to come and come again, with every new theory, new hypothesis, new statement, or new observation, is the question of legitimacy. For it is not philosophy that asks this question of science, but science that asks it of itself.

What is outdated is not asking what is true and what is just, but viewing science as positivistic, relegating it to the status of unlegitimited learning, half-knowledge, as did the German idealists. The question, "What is your argument worth, what is your proof worth?" is so much a part of the pragmatics of scientific knowledge that it is what assures the transformation of the addressee of a given argument and proof into the sender of a new argument and proof – thereby assuring the renewal of scientific discourse and the replacement of each generation of scientists. Science develops – and no one will deny that it develops – by developing this question. And this question, as it develops, leads to the following question, that is to say, metaquestion, the question of legitimacy: "What is your 'what is it worth' worth?"

I made the point that the striking feature of postmodern scientific knowledge is that the discourse on the rules that validate it is (explicitly) immanent to it. What was considered at the end of the nineteenth century to be a loss of legitimacy and a fall into philosophical "pragmatism" or logical positivism was only an episode, from which knowledge has recovered by including within scientific discourse the discourse on the validation of statements held to be laws. As we have seen, this inclusion is not a simple operation, but gives rise to "paradoxes" that are taken extremely seriously and to "limitations" on the scope of knowledge that are in fact changes in its nature. [...]

[...] The conclusion we can draw from this research (and much more not mentioned here) is that the continuous differentiable function is losing its preeminence as a paradigm of knowledge and prediction. Postmodern science – by concerning itself with such things as undecidables, the limits of precise control, conflicts characterized by incomplete information, "*fracta*," catastrophes, and pragmatic paradoxes – is theorizing its own evolution as discontinuous, catastrophic, nonrectifiable, and paradoxical. It is changing the meaning of the word *knowledge*, while expressing how such a change can take place. It is producing not the known, but the unknown. And it suggests a model of legitimation that has nothing to do with maximized performance, but has as its basis difference understood as paralogy. [...]

14   Legitimation by paralogy

Let us say at this point that the facts we have presented concerning the problem of the legitimation of knowledge today are sufficient for our purposes. We no longer have recourse to the grand narratives — we can resort neither to the dialectic of Spirit nor even to the emancipation of humanity as a validation for postmodern scientific discourse. But as we have just seen, the little narrative [*petit récit*] remains the quintessential form of imaginative invention, most particularly in science. In addition, the principle of consensus as a criterion of validation seems to be inadequate. It has two formulations. In the first, consensus is an agreement between men, defined as knowing intellects and free wills, and is obtained through dialogue. [It ...] is based on the validity of the narrative of emancipation. In the second, consensus is a component of the system, which manipulates it in order to maintain and improve its performance. It is the object of administrative procedures, [...] its only validity is as an instrument to be used toward achieving the real goal, which is what legitimates the system — power.

The problem is therefore to determine whether it is possible to have a form of legitimation based solely on paralogy. Paralogy must be distinguished from innovation: the latter is under the command of the system, or at least used by it to improve its efficiency; the former is a move (the importance of which is often not recognized until later) played in the pragmatics of knowledge. The fact that it is in reality frequently, but not necessarily, the case that one is transformed into the other presents no difficulties for the hypothesis.

Returning to the description of scientific pragmatics, it is now dissension that must be emphasized. Consensus is a horizon that is never reached. Research that takes place under the aegis of a paradigm tends to stabilize; it is like the exploitation of a technological, economic, or artistic "idea." It cannot be discounted. But what is striking is that someone always comes along to disturb the order of "reason." It is necessary to posit the existence of a power that destabilizes the capacity for explanation, manifested in the promulgation of new norms for understanding or, if one prefers, in a proposal to establish new rules circumscribing a new field of research for the language of science. This, in the context of scientific discussion, is the same process Thom calls morphogenesis. It is not without rules (there are classes of catastrophes), but it is always locally determined. Applied to scientific discussion and placed in a temporal framework, this property implies that "discoveries" are unpredictable. In terms of the idea of transparency, it is a factor that generates blind spots and defers consensus. [...]

Consensus has become an outmoded and suspect value. But justice as a value is neither outmoded nor suspect. We must thus arrive at an idea and practice of justice that is not linked to that of consensus.

A recognition of the heteromorphous nature of language games is a first step in that direction. This obviously implies a renunciation of terror, which assumes that they are isomorphic and tries to make them so. The second step is the principle that any consensus on the rules defining a game and the "moves" playable within it *must* be local, in other words, agreed on by its present players and subject to eventual cancellation. The orientation then favors a multiplicity of finite meta-arguments, by which I mean argumentation that concerns metaprescriptives and is limited in space and time.

This orientation corresponds to the course that the evolution of social interaction is currently taking; the temporary contract is in practice supplanting permanent institutions in the professional, emotional, sexual, cultural, family, and international domains, as well as in political affairs. This evolution is of course ambiguous: the temporary contract is favored by the system due to its greater flexibility, lower cost, and the creative turmoil of its accompanying motivations — all of these factors contribute to increased operativity. In any case, there is no question here of proposing a "pure" alternative to the system: we all now know [...] that an attempt at an alternative of that kind would end up resembling the system it was meant to replace. We should be happy that the tendency toward the temporary contract is ambiguous: it is not totally subordinated to the goal of the system, yet the system tolerates it. This bears witness to the existence of another goal within the system: knowledge of language games as such and the decision to assume responsibility for their rules and effects. Their most significant effect is precisely what validates the adoption of rules — the quest for paralogy.

We are finally in a position to understand how the computerization of society affects this problematic. It could become the "dream" instrument for controlling and regulating the market system, extended to include knowledge itself and governed exclusively by the performativity principle. In that case, it would inevitably involve the use of terror. But it could also aid groups discussing metaprescriptives by supplying them with the information they usually lack for making knowledgeable decisions. The line to follow for computerization to take the second of these two paths is, in principle, quite simple: give the public free access to the memory and data banks. Language games would then be games of perfect information at any given moment. But they would also be nonzero-sum games, and by virtue of that fact discussion would never risk fixating in a position of minimax equilibrium because it had exhausted its stakes. For the stakes would be knowledge (or information, if you will), and the reserve of knowledge — language's reserve of possible utterances — is inexhaustible. This sketches the outline of a politics that would respect both the desire for justice and the desire for the unknown.

Chapter 8

Jacques Derrida

■ from **OUTWORK, PREFACING** in *Dissemination*, Barbara Johnson trans., London: The Athlone Press, 1981

T**HIS (THEREFORE) WILL NOT HAVE BEEN A BOOK.**
Still less, despite appearances, will it have been a collection of *three* "essays" whose itinerary it would be time, after the fact, to recognize; whose continuity and underlying laws could now be pointed out; indeed, whose overall concept or meaning could at last, with all the insistence required on such occasions, be squarely set forth. I will not feign, according to the code, either premeditation or improvisation. These texts are assembled otherwise; it is not my intention here to *present* them.

The question astir here, precisely, is that of presentation.

While the form of the "book" is now going through a period of general upheaval, and while that form now appears less natural, and its history less transparent, than ever, and while one cannot tamper with it without disturbing everything else, the book form alone can no longer settle – here for example – the case of those writing processes which, in *practically* questioning that form, must also dismantle it.

Hence the necessity, today, of working out at every turn, with redoubled effort, the question of the preservation of names: of *paleonymy*. Why should an old name, for a determinate time, be retained? Why should the effects of a new meaning, concept, or object be damped by memory?

Posed in these terms, the question would already be caught up in a whole system of presuppositions that have now been elucidated: for example, here, that of the signifier's *simple* exteriority to "its" concept. One must therefore proceed otherwise.

Let us begin again. To take some examples: why should "literature" still designate that which already breaks away from literature – away from what has always been conceived and signified under that name – or that which not merely escaping literature, implacably destroys it? (Posed in these terms, the question would already be caught in the assurance of a certain fore-knowledge: can "what has always been conceived and signified under that name" be considered fundamentally homogeneous, univocal, or nonconflictual?) To take other examples: what historical and strategic function should henceforth be assigned to the quotation marks, whether visible or invisible, which transform this into a "book," or which still make the deconstruction of philosophy into a "philosophical discourse"?

This structure of the *double mark* (*caught* — both seized and entangled — in a binary opposition, one of the terms retains its old name so as to destroy the opposition to which it no longer quite belongs, to which in *any* event it has *never* quite yielded, the history of this opposition being one of incessant struggles generative of hierarchical configurations) works the entire field within which these texts move. This structure itself is worked in turn: the rule according to which every concept necessarily receives two similar marks — a repetition without identity — one mark inside and the other outside the deconstructed system, should give rise to a double reading and a double writing. And, as will appear in due course: a *double science*.

No concept, no name, no signifier can escape this structure. We will try to determine the law which compels us (by way of example and taking into account a general remodeling of theoretical discourse which has recently been rearticulating the fields of philosophy, science, literature, etc.) to apply the name "writing" to that which critiques, deconstructs, wrenches apart the traditional, hierarchical opposition between writing and speech, between writing and the (idealist, spiritualist, phonocentrist: first and foremost logocentric)[1] system of all of what is customarily opposed to writing; to apply the name "work" or "practice" to that which disorganizes the philosophical opposition *praxis/theoria* and can no longer be sublated[2] according to the process of Hegelian negativity; to apply the name "unconscious" to that which can never have been the symmetrical negative or the potential reservoir of "consciousness"; to apply the name "matter" to that which lies outside all classical oppositions and which, provided one takes into account certain theoretical achievements and a certain philosophical deconstruction belonging to a not so distant time, should no longer be able to assume any reassuring form: neither that of a referent (at least if conceived as a real thing or cause, anterior and exterior to the system of general textuality), nor that of presence in any of its modes (meaning, essence, existence — whether objective or subjective; form, i.e. appearance, substance, etc.; sensible presence or intelligible presence), nor that of a fundamental or totalizing principle, nor even of a last instance: in short, the classical system's "outside" can no longer take the form of the sort of extra-text which would arrest the concatenation of writing (i.e. that movement which situates every signified as a differential trace) and for which I had proposed the concept of "transcendental signified." "Differance"[3] also designated, within the same problematic field, that kind of economy — that war economy — which brings the radical otherness or the absolute exteriority of the outside into relation with the closed, agonistic, hierarchical field of philosophical oppositions, of "differends" or "difference":[4] an economic movement of the trace that implies both its mark and its erasure — the margin of its impossibility — according to a relation that no speculative dialectic of the same and the other can master, for the simple reason that such a dialectic always remains an operation of mastery.[5]

To put the old names to work, or even just to leave them in circulation, will always, of course, involve some risk: the risk of settling down or of regressing into the system that has been, or is in the process of being, deconstructed. To deny this risk would be to confirm it: it would be to see the signifier — in this case the name — as a merely circumstantial, conventional occurrence of the concept or as a concession without any specific effect. It would be an affirmation of the autonomy of meaning, of the ideal purity of an abstract, theoretical history of the concept. Inversely, to claim to do away immediately with previous marks and to cross over, by decree, by a simple leap, into the outside of the classical oppositions is, apart from the risk of engaging in an interminable "negative theology," to forget that these oppositions have never constituted a *given* system, a sort of ahistorical, thoroughly homogeneous table, but rather a dissymmetric, hierarchically ordered space whose closure is constantly being traversed by the forces, and worked by the exteriority, that it represses: that is, expels and, which amounts to the same, internalizes as one of *its* moments. This is why deconstruction involves an indispensable phase of *reversal*. To remain content with reversal is of course to operate within the immanence of the system to be destroyed. But to sit back, in order to go *further*, in order to be more radical or more daring, and take an attitude of neutralizing indifference with respect to the classical oppositions would be to give free rein to the existing forces that effectively and historically dominate the field. It would be, for not having seized the means to *intervene*,[6] to confirm the established equilibrium.

These two operations must be conducted in a kind of disconcerting *simul*, in a movement of the entire field that must be coherent, of course, but at the same time divided, differentiated, and stratified. The gap between the two operations must remain open, must let itself be ceaselessly marked and remarked. This is already a sufficient indication of the necessary heterogeneity of each text participating in this operation and of the impossibility of summing up the gap at a single point or under a single name. Responsibility and individuality are values that can no longer predominate here: that is the first effect of dissemination.

There is no such thing as a "metaphysical-concept." There is no such thing as a "metaphysical-name." The "metaphysical" is a certain determination or direction taken by a sequence or "chain." It cannot as such be opposed by a concept but rather by a process of textual labor and a different sort of articulation. This being the case, the development of this problematic will inevitably involve the movement of differance as it has been discussed elsewhere: a "productive," conflictual[7] movement which cannot be preceded by any identity, any unity, or any original simplicity; which cannot be "relieved" [*relevé*],[8] resolved, or appeased by any philosophical dialectic; and which disorganizes "historically," "practically," textually, the opposition or the difference (the static distinction) between opposing terms.

A *preface* would retrace and presage here a *general* theory and practice of deconstruction, that strategy without which the possibility of a critique could exist only in fragmentary, empiricist surges that amount in effect to a non-equivocal confirmation of metaphysics. The preface would announce in the future tense ("this is what you are going to read") the conceptual content or significance (here, that strange strategy without finality, the debility or failure that organizes the *telos* or the *eschaton*, which reinscribes restricted economy within general economy) of what will *already* have been *written*. And thus sufficiently *read* to be gathered up in its semantic tenor and proposed in advance. From the viewpoint of the fore-word, which recreates an intention-to-say after the fact, the text exists as something written – a past – which, under the false appearance of a present, a hidden omnipotent author (in full mastery of his product) is presenting to the reader as his future. Here is what I wrote, then read, and what I am writing that you are going to read. After which you will again be able to take possession of this preface which in sum you have not yet begun to read, even though, once having read it, you will already have anticipated everything that follows and thus you might just as well dispense with reading the rest. The *pre* of the preface makes the future present, represents it, draws it closer, breathes it in, and in going ahead of it puts it ahead. The *pre* reduces the future to the form of manifest presence.

This is an essential and ludicrous operation: not only because writing as such does not consist in any of these tenses (present, past, or future insofar as they are all modified presents); not only because such an operation would confine itself to the discursive effects of an intention-to-mean, but because, in pointing out a single thematic nucleus or a single guiding thesis, it would cancel out the textual displacement that is at work "here." (Here? Where? The question of the here and now is explicitly enacted in dissemination.) Indeed, if such a thing were justifiable, we would have to assert right now that one of the theses – there is more than one – inscribed within dissemination is precisely the impossibility of reducing a text as such to its effects of meaning, content, thesis, or theme. Not the impossibility, perhaps, since *it is commonly done*, but the resistance – we shall call it the *restance*[9] – of a sort of writing that can neither adapt nor adopt such a reduction.

Hence this is not a preface, at least not if by preface we mean a table, a code, an annotated summary of prominent signifieds, or an index of key words or of proper names.

But what do prefaces actually do? Isn't their logic more surprising than this? Oughtn't we some day to reconstitute their history and their typology? Do they form a genre? Can they be grouped according to the necessity of some common predicate, or are they otherwise and in themselves divided?

These questions will not be answered, at least not finally in the declarative mode. *Along the way*, however, a certain *protocol* will have – destroying this future perfect[10] – taken up the pre-occupying place of the *preface*.[11] If one insists on fixing this protocol in a representation, let us say in advance that, with a few supplementary complications, it has the structure of a *magic slate*.[12]

Prefaces, along with forewords, introductions, preludes, preliminaries, preambles, prologues, and prolegomena, have always been written, it seems, in view of their own self-effacement. Upon reaching the end of the *pre-* (which presents and precedes, or rather forestalls, the presentative production, and, in order to put before the reader's eyes what is not yet visible, is obliged to speak, predict, and predicate), the route which has been covered must cancel itself out. But this subtraction leaves a mark of erasure, a *remainder* which is added to the subsequent text and which cannot be completely summed up within it. Such an operation thus appears contradictory, and the same is true of the interest one takes in it.

But does a preface exist?

On the one hand – this is logic itself – this residue of writing remains anterior and exterior to the development of the content it announces. Preceding what ought to be able to present itself on its own, the preface falls like an empty husk, a piece of formal refuse, a moment of dryness or loquacity, sometimes both at once. From a point of view which can only, ultimately, be that of the science of logic, Hegel thus disqualifies the preface. Philosophical exposition has as its essence the capacity and even the duty to do without a preface. This is what distinguishes it from empirical discourses (essays, conversations, polemics), from particular philosophical sciences, and from exact sciences, whether mathematical or empirical. Hegel keeps coming back to this with unflagging insistence in the "foreword"s which open his treatises (prefaces to each edition, introductions, etc.) Even before the *Introduction* (*Einleitung*) to the *Phenomenology of Spirit* (a circular anticipation of the critique of sensible certainty and of the origin of phenomenality) has announced "the presentation of appearing knowledge" (*die Darstellung des erscheinenden Wissens*), a *Preface* (*Vorrede*) will already have warned us against its own status as a fore-word:

It is customary to preface a work (*Schrift*) with an explanation of the author's aim, why he wrote the book, and the relationship in which he believes it to stand to other earlier or contemporary treatises on the same subject. In the case of a philosophical work, however, such an explanation seems not only superfluous but, in view of the nature of the subject-matter, even inappropriate and misleading (*sondern um der Natur der Sache willen sogar unpassend und zweckwidrig zu sein*). For whatever might appropriately be said about philosophy in a preface — say a historical *statement* of the main drift and the point of view, the general content and results, a string of random assertions and assurances about truth — none of this can be accepted as the way in which to expound philosophical truth. Also, since philosophy moves essentially in the element of universality, which includes within itself the particular, it might seem that here more than in any of the other sciences the subject-matter or thing itself (*die Sache selbst*), even in its complete nature, were expressed in the aim and the final results, the execution (*Ausführung*) being by contrast really the unessential factor (*eigentlich das Unwesentliche sei*).[13]

The preface to a philosophical work thus runs out of breath on the threshold of science. It is the site of a kind of chit-chat external to the very thing it appears to be talking about. This gossipy small talk of history reduces *the thing itself* (here the concept, the meaning of thought in the act of thinking itself and producing itself in the element of universality) to the form of a particular, finite object, the sort of object that determinate modes of knowledge — empirical descriptions or mathematical sciences — are incapable of producing spontaneously through their own workings and must therefore, for their part, *introduce* from the outside and define as a given:

On the other hand, in the ordinary view of anatomy, for instance (say, the knowledge of the parts of the body regarded as inanimate), we are quite sure that we do not as yet possess the thing itself, the content of this science, but must in addition exert ourselves to know the particulars. Further, in the case of such an aggregate of information, which has no right to bear the name of Science, an opening talk (*Konversation*) about aim and other such generalities is usually conducted in the same historical and non-conceptual (*begrifflosen*) way in which the content itself (these nerves, muscles, etc.) is spoken of. In the case of philosophy, on the other hand, this would give rise to the incongruity that along with the employment of such a method its inability to grasp the truth would also be demonstrated.[14]

This preface to a philosophical text thus explains to us that, for a philosophical text as such, a preface is neither useful nor even possible. Does the preface take place, then? Where would it take place? How does this preface (the negative of philosophy) erase itself? In what mode does it come to predicate? A negation of negation? A denial? Is it left high and dry by the philosophical process which acts for itself as its own presentation, as the very domestic retinue of its own exposition (*Darstellung*)? ("The inner necessity that knowing should be science (*das Wissen Wissenschaft sei*) lies in its nature, and only the systematic exposition (*Darstellung*) of philosophy itself provides it."[15] Or is the prologue already carried away, beyond itself, in the movement which is located *in front of* it and which seems to follow it only for having *in truth* preceded it? Isn't the preface both negated and internalized in the presentation of philosophy by itself, in the self production and self-determination of the concept?

But if something were to remain of the prolegomenon once inscribed and interwoven, something that would not allow itself to be sublated [*relevé*] in the course of the philosophical presentation, would that something necessarily take the form of that which *falls away* [*la tombée*]? And what about such a fall? Couldn't it be read otherwise than as the excrement of philosophical essentiality – not in order to sublate it back into the latter, of course, but in order to learn to take it differently into account?

Yes – if – Hegel writes beyond what he wants to say, each page of the preface comes unglued from itself and is forthwith divided: *hybrid* or *bifacial*. (Dissemination generalizes the theory and practice of the *graft* without a body proper, of the *skew* without a straight line, of the *bias* without a front.) The preface that Hegel *must* write, in order to denounce a preface that is both impossible and inescapable, must be assigned two locations and two sorts of scope. It belongs both to the inside and to the outside of the concept. But according to a process of mediation and dialectical reappropriation, the inside of speculative philosophy sublates *its own* outside as a moment of its negativity. The prefatory moment is necessarily opened up by the critical gap between the logical or scientific development of philosophy and its empiricist or formalist lag. This, indeed, is a lesson of Hegel's to be maintained, if possible, beyond Hegelianism: the essential complicity between empiricism and formalism. If the foreword is indispensable, it is because the prevailing culture still imposes both formalism and empiricism; that culture must be fought, or rather "formed" (*gebildet*) better, cultivated more carefully. The necessity of prefaces belongs to the *Bildung*. This struggle appears to be external to philosophy since it takes place rather in a didactic setting than within the self-presentation of a concept. But it is internal to philosophy to the extent that, as the Preface also says, the exteriority of the negative (falsehood, evil, death) still belongs to the process of truth and must leave its trace upon it.[16]

Thus, after defining the *internal necessity* of the self-presentation of the concept, Hegel identifies its *external necessity*, the necessity that takes time into account as the existence (*Dasein*) of the concept. But it is at first only a question of the necessity of time as a *universal* form of sensibility. One must then go on to recognize the gap between this formal notion of time, the general matrix in which the concept is present, and the empirical or historical determination of time, that of *our time*, for example:

> But the *external* necessity, so far as it is grasped in a general way, setting aside accidental matters of person and motivation, is the same as the inner, or in other words it lies in the shape (*Gestalt*) in which time sets forth the sequential existence of its moments (*wie die Zeit das Dasein ihrer Momente vorstellt*). To show that now is the propitious time (*an der Zeit*) for philosophy to be elevated to the status of a Science would therefore be the only true justification of any effort that has this aim, for to do so would demonstrate the necessity of the aim, would indeed at the same time be the accomplishing of it.[17]

But since *our time* is not exactly, not simply propitious for such an elevation (*Erhebung*), since it is not yet quite the right time (*an der Zeit*), since the time, at any rate, is not equal to itself, it is still necessary to prepare it and make it join up with itself by didactic means; and if one judges that the time *has* come, one must make others aware of it and introduce them to what is already *there*; better yet: one must bring the being-there back to the concept of which it is the temporal, historical presence (*Dasein*) or, in a circular fashion, introduce the concept into its own being-there. A certain spacing between concept and being-there, between concept and existence, between thought and time, would thus constitute the rather unqualifiable lodging of the preface.

Time is the time of the preface; space – whose time *will have been* the Truth – is the space of the preface. The preface would thus occupy the entire *location* and *duration* of the book.

When the double necessity, both internal and external, *will have been* fulfilled, the preface, which will in a sense have introduced it as one makes an introduction to the (true) beginning (of the truth), will no doubt have been raised to the status of philosophy, will have been internalized and sublated into it. It will also, simultaneously, have *fallen away* of its own accord and been left "in its appropriate place in ordinary conversation."[18] A double topography, a double face, an overwritten erasure. What is the *status* of a text when it itself carries *itself* away and marks itself down? Is it a dialectical contradiction? A negation of negation? A labor of the negative and a process that works in the service of meaning? Of the being-abreast-of itself of the concept?

Chapter 9

Gilles Deleuze

■ from **INTRODUCTION** in *Difference and Repetition,*
Paul Patton trans., London: The Athlone Press, 1994

OUR PROBLEM CONCERNS the essence of repetition. It is a question of knowing why repetition cannot be explained by the form of identity in concepts or representations; in what sense it demands a superior "positive" principle. This enquiry must embrace all the concepts of nature and freedom. Consider, on the border between these two cases, the repetition of a decorative motif: a figure is reproduced, while the concept remains absolutely identical. ... However, this is not how artists proceed in reality. They do not juxtapose instances of the figure, but rather each time combine an element of one instance with *another* element of a following instance. They introduce a disequilibrium into the dynamic process of construction, an instability, dissymmetry or gap of some kind which disappears only in the overall effect. Commenting on such a case, Lévi-Strauss writes: "These elements interlock with each other through dislocation, and it is only at the end that the pattern achieves a stability which both confirms and belies the dynamic process according to which it has been carried out."[1] These remarks stand for the notion of causality in general. For it is not the elements of symmetry present which matter for artistic or natural causality, but those which are missing and are not in the cause; what matters is the possibility of the cause having less symmetry than the effect. Moreover, causality would remain eternally conjectural, a simple logical category, if that possibility were not at some moment or other effectively fulfilled. For this reason, the logical relation of causality is inseparable from a physical process of signalling, without which it would not be translated into action. By "signal" we mean a system with orders of disparate size, endowed with elements of dissymmetry; by "sign" we mean what happens within such a system, what flashes across the intervals when a communication takes place between disparates. The sign is indeed an effect, but an effect with two aspects: in one of these it expresses, *qua* sign, the productive dissymmetry; in the other it tends to cancel it. The sign is not entirely of the order of the symbol; nevertheless, it makes way for it by implying an internal difference (while leaving the conditions of its reproduction still external).

The negative expression "lack of symmetry" should not mislead us: it indicates the origin and positivity of the causal process. It is positivity itself. For us, as the example of the decorative motif suggests, it is essential to break down the notion of causality in order to distinguish two types of repetition: one which concerns only the overall, abstract effect, and the other which concerns the acting cause. One is a static repetition, the other is dynamic. One results from the work, but the other is like the "evolution" of a bodily movement. One refers back to a single concept, which leaves only an external difference between the ordinary instances of a figure; the other is the repetition of an internal difference which it incorporates in each of its moments, and carries from one distinctive point to another. One could try to assimilate these two repetitions by saying that the difference between the first and the second is only a matter of a change in the content of the concept, or of the figure being articulated differently, but this would be to fail to recognise the respective order of each repetition. For in the dynamic order there is no representative concept, nor any figure represented in a pre-existing space. There is an Idea, and a pure dynamism which creates a corresponding space.

Studies on rhythm or symmetry confirm this duality. A distinction is drawn between arithmetic symmetry, which refers back to a scale of whole or fractional coefficients, and geometric symmetry, based upon proportions or irrational ratios; a static symmetry which is cubic or hexagonal, and a dynamic symmetry which is pentagonal and appears in a spiral line or in a geometrically progressing pulsation – in short, in a living and mortal "evolution". Now, the second of these is at the heart of the first; it is the vital, positive, active procedure. In a network of double squares, we discover radiating lines which have the centre of a pentagon or a pentagram as their asymmetrical pole. The network is like a fabric stretched upon a framework, "but the outline, the principal rhythm of that framework, is almost always a theme independent of the network": such elements of dissymmetry serve as both genetic principle and principle of reflection for symmetrical figures.[2] The static repetition in the network of double squares thus refers back to a dynamic repetition, formed by a pentagon and "the decreasing series of pentagrams which may be naturally inscribed therein". Similarly, the study of rhythm allows us immediately to distinguish two kinds of repetition. Cadence-repetition is a regular division of time, an isochronic recurrence of identical elements. However, a period exists only in so far as it is determined by a tonic accent, commanded by intensities. Yet we would be mistaken about the function of accents if we said that they were reproduced at equal intervals. On the contrary, tonic and intensive values act by creating inequalities or incommensurabilities between metrically equivalent periods or spaces. They create distinctive points, privileged instants which always indicate a poly-rhythm. Here again, the unequal is the most positive element. Cadence is only the envelope of a rhythm, and of a relation between rhythms. The reprise of points of inequality, of inflections or of rhythmic events, is more profound than the reproduction of ordinary homogeneous elements. As a result, we should distinguish cadence-repetition and rhythm-repetition in every case, the first being only the outward appearance or the abstract effect of the second. A bare, material repetition (repetition of the Same) appears only in the sense that another repetition is disguised within it, constituting it and constituting itself in disguising itself. Even in nature, isochronic rotations are only the outward appearance of a more profound movement, the revolving cycles are only abstractions: placed together, they reveal evolutionary cycles or spirals whose principle is a variable curve, and the trajectory of which has two dissymmetrical aspects, as though it had a right and a left. It is always in this gap, which should not be confused with the negative, that creatures weave their repetition and receive at the same time the gift of living and dying.

Finally, to return to nominal concepts: is it the identity of the nominal concept which explains the repetition of a word? Take the example of rhyme: it is indeed verbal repetition, but repetition which includes the difference between two words and inscribes that difference at the heart of a poetic Idea, in a space which it determines. Nor does its meaning lie in marking equal intervals, but rather, as we see in a notion of strong rhyme, in putting tonal values in the service of tonic rhythm, and contributing to the independence of tonic rhythms from arithmetic rhythms. As for the repetition of a single word, we must understand this as a "generalised rhyme", not rhyme as a restricted repetition. This generalisation can proceed in two ways: either a word taken in two senses ensures a resemblance or a paradoxical identity between the two senses; or a word taken in one sense exercises an attractive force on its neighbours, communicating an extraordinary gravity to them until one of the neighbouring words takes up the baton and becomes in turn a centre of repetition. Raymond Roussel and Charles Péguy were the great repeaters of literature, able to lift the pathological power of language to a higher artistic level. Roussel takes ambiguous words or homonyms and fills the entire distance between their meanings with a story presented twice and with objects themselves doubled. He thereby overcomes homonymity on its own ground and inscribes the maximum difference within repetition, where this is the space opened up in the heart of a word. This space is still presented by Roussel as one of masks and death, in which is developed both a repetition which enchains and a repetition which saves – which saves above all from the one which enchains. Roussel creates an after-language where once everything has been said, everything is repeated and recommenced.[3] Péguy's technique is very different: it substitutes repetition not for homonymity but for synonymity; it concerns what linguists call the function of contiguity rather than that of similarity; it forms a before-language, an auroral language in which the step-by-step creation of an internal space within words proceeds by tiny differences. This time, everything leads to the problem of aging and premature deaths, but in relation to this problem also to the extraordinary chance to affirm a repetition which saves against that which enchains. Both Péguy and Roussel take language to one of its limits. In the case of Roussel, that of similarity and selection, the "distinctive feature" between *billard* and *pillard*; in the case of Péguy, that of contiguity or combination, the famous *tapestry points*. Both substitute a vertical repetition of distinctive points, which takes us inside the words, for the horizontal repetition of ordinary words repeated. Both substitute a positive repetition, one which flows from the excess of a linguistic and stylistic Idea, for a repetition by default which results from the inadequacy of nominal concepts or verbal representations. How does death inspire language, given that it is always present when repetition is affirmed?

The reproduction of the Same is not a motor of bodily movements. We know that even the simplest imitation involves a difference between inside and outside. Moreover, imitation plays only a secondary and regulatory role in the acquisition of a behaviour: it permits the correction of movements being made, but not their instigation. Learning takes place not in the relation between a representation and an action (reproduction of the Same) but in the relation between a sign and a response (encounter with the Other). Signs involve heterogeneity in at least three ways: first, in the object which bears or emits them, and is necessarily on a different level, as though there were two orders of size or disparate realities between which the sign flashes; secondly, in themselves, since a sign envelops another "object" within the limits of the object which bears it, and incarnates a natural or spiritual power (an Idea); finally, in the response they elicit, since the movement of the response does not "resemble" that of the sign. The movement of the swimmer does not resemble that of the wave, in particular, the movements of the swimming instructor which we reproduce on the sand bear no relation to the movements of the wave, which we learn to deal with only by grasping the former in practice as signs. That is why it is so difficult to say how someone learns: there is an innate or acquired practical familiarity with signs, which means that there is something amorous – but also something fatal – about all education. We learn nothing from those who say: "Do as I do". Our only teachers are those who tell us to "do with me", and are able to emit signs to be developed in heterogeneity rather than propose gestures for us to reproduce. In other words, there is no ideo-motivity, only sensory-motivity. When a body combines some of its own distinctive points with those of a wave, it espouses the principle of a repetition which is no longer that of the Same, but involves the Other – involves difference, from one wave and one gesture to another, and carries that difference through the repetitive space thereby constituted. To learn is indeed to constitute this space of an encounter with signs, in which the distinctive points renew themselves in each other, and repetition takes shape while disguising itself. Apprenticeship always gives rise to images of death, on the edges of the space it creates and with the help of the heterogeneity it engenders. Signs are deadly when they are lost in the distance, but also when they strike us with full force. Oedipus receives a sign once from too far away, once from too close, and between the two a terrible repetition of the crime is woven. Zarathustra receives his "sign" either from too near or from too far, and only at the end does he foresee the correct distance which will turn that which in eternal return makes him ill into a liberatory and redemptive repetition. Signs are the true elements of theatre. They testify to the spiritual and natural powers which act beneath the words, gestures, characters and objects represented. They signify repetition as real movement, in opposition to representation which is a false movement of the abstract.

We are right to speak of repetition when we find ourselves confronted by identical elements with exactly the same concept. However, we must distinguish between these discrete elements, these repeated objects, and a secret subject, the real subject of repetition, which repeats itself through them. Repetition must be understood in the pronominal; we must find the Self of repetition, the singularity within that which repeats. For there is no repetition without a repeater, nothing repeated without a repetitious soul. As a result, rather than the repeated and the repeater, the object and the subject, we must distinguish two forms of repetition. In every case repetition is difference without a concept. But in one case, the difference is taken to be only external to the concept; it is a difference between objects represented by the same concept, falling into the indifference of space and time. In the other case, the difference is internal to the Idea; it unfolds as pure movement, creative of a dynamic space and time which correspond to the Idea. The first repetition is repetition of the Same, explained by the identity of the concept or representation; the second includes difference, and includes itself in the alterity of the Idea, in the heterogeneity of an "a-presentation". One is negative, occurring by default in the concept; the other affirmative, occurring by excess in the Idea. One is conjectural, the other categorical. One is static, the other dynamic. One is repetition in the effect, the other in the cause. One is extensive, the other intensive. One is ordinary, the other distinctive and singular. One is horizontal, the other vertical. One is developed and explicated, the other enveloped and in need of interpretation. One is revolving, the other evolving. One involves equality, commensurability and symmetry; the other is grounded in inequality, incommensurability and dissymmetry. One is material, the other spiritual, even in nature and in the earth. One is inanimate, the other carries the secret of our deaths and our lives, of our enchainment and our liberations, the demonic and the divine. One is a "bare" repetition, the other a covered repetition, which forms itself in covering itself, in masking and disguising itself. One concerns accuracy, the other has authenticity as its criterion.

The two repetitions are not independent. One is the singular subject, the interiority and the heart of the other, the depths of the other. The other is only the external envelope, the abstract effect. The repetition of dissymmetry is hidden within symmetrical ensembles or effects; a repetition of distinctive points underneath that of ordinary points; and everywhere the Other in the repetition of the Same. This is the secret, the most profound repetition: it alone provides the principle of the other one, the reason for the blockage of concepts. In this domain, as in *Sartor Resartus*,[4] it is the masked, the disguised or the costumed which turns out to be the truth of the uncovered. Necessarily, since this repetition is not hidden by something else but forms itself by disguising itself, it does not pre-exist its own disguises and, in forming itself, constitutes the bare repetition within which it becomes enveloped. Important consequences follow from this. When we are confronted by a repetition which proceeds masked, or comprises displacements, quickenings, slowdowns, variants or differences which are ultimately capable of leading us far away from the point of departure, we tend to see a mixed state in which repetition is not pure but only approximative: the very word repetition seems to be employed symbolically, by analogy or metaphor. It is true that we have strictly defined repetition as difference without concept. However, we would be wrong to reduce it to a difference which falls back into exteriority, because the concept embodies the form of the Same, without seeing that it can be internal to the Idea and possess in itself all the resources of signs, symbols and alterity which go beyond the concept as such. The examples invoked above concern the most diverse kinds of case, from nominal concepts to concepts of nature and freedom, and we could be charged with having mixed up all kinds of physical and psychical repetitions, even with having run together stereotypical repetitions and latent, symbolic repetitions in the psychical domain. However, we wished to show the coexistence of these instances in every repetitive structure, to show how repetition displays identical elements which necessarily refer back to a latent subject which repeats itself through these elements, forming an "other" repetition at the heart of the first. We therefore suggest that this other repetition is in no way approximative or metaphorical. It is, on the contrary, the spirit of every repetition. It is the very letter of every repetition, its watermark or constitutive cipher. It forms the essence of that in which every repetition consists: difference without a concept, non-mediated difference. It is both the literal and spiritual primary sense of repetition. The material sense results from this other, as if secreted by it like a shell.

We began by distinguishing generality and repetition. Then we distinguished two forms of repetition. These two distinctions are linked: the consequences of the first are unfolded only in the second. For if we were content to treat repetition abstractly and as devoid of any interior, we would remain incapable of understanding why and how a concept could be naturally blocked, allowing a repetition which has nothing to do with generality to appear. Conversely, when we discover the literal interior of repetition, we have the means not only to understand the outer repetition as a cover, but also to recapture the order of generality (and, following Kierkegaard's wish, to carry out the reconciliation of the singular with the general). For to the extent that the internal repetition projects itself through a bare repetition which covers it, the differences that it includes appear to be so many factors which oppose repetition, which attenuate it and vary it according to "general" laws. Beneath the general operation of laws, however, there always remains the play of singularities. Cyclical generalities in nature are the masks of a singularity which appears through their interferences; and beneath the generalities of habit in moral life we rediscover singular processes of learning. The domain of laws must be understood, but always on the basis of a Nature and a Spirit superior to their own laws, which weave their repetitions in the depths of the earth and of the heart, where laws do not yet exist. The interior of repetition is always affected by an order of difference: it is only to the extent that something is linked to a repetition of an order other than its own that the repetition appears external and bare, and the thing itself subject to the categories of generality. It is the inadequation between difference and repetition which gives rise to the order of generality. Gabriel Tarde suggested in this sense that resemblance itself was only displaced repetition: real repetition is that which corresponds directly to a difference of the same degree as itself. Better than anyone, Tarde was able to elaborate a new dialectic by discovering in mind and nature the secret effort to establish an ever more perfect correspondence between difference and repetition.[5]

So long as we take difference to be conceptual difference, intrinsically conceptual, and repetition to be an extrinsic difference between objects represented by the same concept, it appears that the problem of their relation may be resolved by the facts. Are there repetitions – yes or no? Or is every difference indeed intrinsic and conceptual in the last instance? Hegel ridiculed Leibniz for having invited the court ladies to undertake experimental metaphysics while walking in the gardens, to see whether two leaves of a tree could not have the same concept. Replace the court ladies by forensic scientists: no two grains of dust are absolutely identical, no two hands have the same distinctive points, no two typewriters have the same strike, no two revolvers score their bullets in the same manner .... . Why, however, do we feel that the problem is not properly defined so long as we look for the criterion of a *principium individuationis* in the facts? It is because a difference can be internal, yet not conceptual (as the paradox of symmetrical objects shows). A dynamic space must be defined from the point of view of an observer tied to that space, not from an external position. There are internal differences which dramatise an Idea before representing an object. Difference here is internal to an Idea, even though it be external to the concept which represents an object. That is why the opposition between Kant and Leibniz seems much less strong to the extent that one takes account of the dynamic factors present in the two doctrines. If, in the forms of intuition, Kant recognised extrinsic differences not reducible to the order of concepts, these are no less "internal" even though they cannot be regarded as "intrinsic" by the understanding, and can be represented only in their external relation to space as a whole.[6] In other words, following certain neo-Kantian interpretations, there is a step-by-step, internal, dynamic construction of space which must precede the "representation" of the whole as a form of exteriority. The element of this internal genesis seems to us to consist of intensive quantity rather than schema, and to be related to Ideas rather than to concepts of the understanding. If the spatial order of extrinsic differences and the conceptual order of intrinsic differences are finally in harmony, as the schema shows they are, this is ultimately due to this intensive differential element, this synthesis of continuity at a given moment which, in the form of a *continua repetitio*, first gives rise internally to the space corresponding to Ideas. With Leibniz, the affinity between extrinsic differences and intrinsic conceptual differences already appealed to the internal process of a *continua repetitio*, grounded upon an intensive differential element which ensures the synthesis of continuity at a point in order to engender space from within.

There are repetitions which are not only extrinsic differences, just as there are internal differences which are neither intrinsic nor conceptual. We are thus in a better position to identify the source of the preceding ambiguities. When we define repetition as difference without concept, we are drawn to conclude that only extrinsic difference is involved in repetition; we consider, therefore, that any internal "novelty" is sufficient to remove us from repetition proper and can be reconciled only with an approximative repetition, so-called by analogy. Nothing of the sort is true. For we do not yet know what is the essence of repetition, what is positively denoted by the expression "difference without concept", or the nature of the interiority it may imply. Conversely, when we define difference as conceptual difference, we believe we have done enough to specify the concept of difference as such. Nevertheless, here again we have no idea of difference, no concept of difference as such. Perhaps the mistake of the philosophy of difference, from Aristotle to Hegel via Leibniz, lay in confusing the concept of difference with a merely conceptual difference, in remaining content to inscribe difference in the concept in general. In reality, so long as we inscribe difference in the concept in general we have no singular Idea of difference, we remain only with a difference already mediated by representation. We therefore find ourselves confronted by two questions: what is the concept of difference – one which is not reducible to simple conceptual difference but demands its own Idea, its own singularity at the level of Ideas? On the other hand, what is the essence of repetition – one which is not reducible to difference without concept, and cannot be confused with the apparent character of objects represented by the same concept, but bears witness to singularity as a power of Ideas? The meeting between these two notions, difference and repetition, can no longer be assumed: it must come about as a result of interferences and intersections between these two lines: one concerning the essence of repetition, the other the idea of difference.

Chapter 10

Michel Foucault

■ from **THEATRUM PHILOSOPHICUM**,[1] in James D. Faubion (ed.), *Essential Works of Michel Foucault, 1954–84. Volume II: Aesthetics, Method, and Epistemology*, Robert Hurley et al. trans., London: Penguin Books, 1998

I **MUST DISCUSS TWO BOOKS** of exceptional merit and importance: *Difference and Repetition* and *The Logic of Sense*.[2] Indeed, these books are so outstanding that they are difficult to discuss; this may explain, as well, why so few have undertaken this task. I believe that these words will continue to revolve about us in enigmatic resonance with those of Klossowski, another major and excessive sign, and perhaps one day, this century will be known as Deleuzian.

One after another, I should like to explore the many paths that lead to the heart of these challenging tests. As Deleuze has said to me, however, this metaphor is misleading: there is no heart, but only a problem – that is, a distribution of notable points; there is no center but always decenterings, series, from one to another, with the limp of a presence and an absence – of an excess, of a deficiency. Abandon the circle, a faulty principle of return; abandon our tendency to organize everything into a sphere. All things return on the straight and narrow, by way of a straight and labyrinthine line. Thus, fibrils and bifurcation (Leiris's marvelous series would be well suited to a Deleuzian analysis).

Overturn Platonism: what philosophy has not tried? If we defined philosophy at the limit as any attempt, regardless of its source, to reverse Platonism, then philosophy begins with Aristotle; or better yet, it begins with Plato himself, with the conclusion of the *Sophist* where it is impossible to distinguish Socrates from the crafty imitator; or it begins with the Sophists who were extremely vocal about the rise of Platonism and who ridiculed its future greatness with their perpetual play on words.

Are all philosophies individual species of the genus "anti-Platonic"? Would each begin with a declaration of this fundamental rejection? Can they be grouped around this desired and detestable center? Should we instead say that the philosophical nature of a discourse is its Platonic differential, an element absent in Platonism but present in the discourse itself? A better formulation would be: It is an element in which the effect of absence is induced in the Platonic series through a new and divergent series (consequently, its function in the Platonic series is that of a signifier both excessive and absent); and it is also an element in which the Platonic series produces a free, floating, and excessive circulation in that other discourse. Plato, then, is the excessive and deficient father. It is useless to define a philosophy by its anti-Platonic character (as a plant is distinguished by its reproductive organs); but a philosophy can be distinguished somewhat in the manner in which a phantasm is defined, by the effect of a lack when it is distributed into its two constituent series – the "archaic" and the "real" – and you will dream of a general history of philosophy, a Platonic phantasmatology, and not an architecture of systems.

In any event, here is Deleuze. His "reversed Platonism" consists of displacing himself within the Platonic series in order to disclose an unexpected facet: division. Plato did not establish a weak separation between the genus "hunter," "cook," or "politician," as the Aristotelians said; neither was he concerned with the particular characteristics of the species "fisherman" or "one who hunts with snares", he wished to discover the identity of the true hunter. *Who is?* and not *What is?* He searched for the authentic, the pure gold. Instead of subdividing, selecting, and pursuing a productive seam, he chose among the pretenders and ignored their fixed cadastral properties, he tested them with the strung bow, which eliminates all but one (the nameless one, the nomad). But how does one distinguish the false (the simulators, the "so-called") from the authentic (the unadulterated and pure)? Certainly not by discovering a law of the true and false (truth is not opposed to error but to false appearances), but by looking above these manifestations to a model, a model so pure that the actual purity of the "pure" resembles it, approximates it, and measures itself against it; a model that exists so forcefully that in its presence the sham vanity of the false copy is immediately reduced to nonexistence. With the abrupt appearance of Ulysses, the eternal husband, the false suitors disappear. *Exeunt* simulacra.

Plato is said to have opposed essence to appearance, a higher world to this world below, the sun of truth to the shadows of the cave (and it becomes our duty to bring essences back into the world, to glorify the world, and to place the sun of truth within man). But Deleuze locates Plato's singularity in the delicate sorting, in this fine operation that precedes the discovery of essence precisely because it calls upon it, and tries to separate malign simulacra from the masses [*peuple*] of appearance. Thus it is useless to attempt the reversal of Platonism by reinstating the rights of appearances, ascribing to them solidity and meaning, and bringing them closer to essential forms by lending them a conceptual backbone: these timid creatures should not be encouraged to stand upright. Neither should we attempt to rediscover the supreme and solemn gesture that established, in a single stroke, the inaccessible Idea. Rather, we should welcome the cunning assembly that simulates and clamors at the door. And what will enter, submerging appearance and breaking its engagement to essence, will be the event; the incorporeal will dissipate the density of matter; a timeless insistence will destroy the circle that imitates eternity; an impenetrable singularity will divest itself of its contamination by purity; the actual semblance of the simulacrum will support the falseness of false appearances. The sophist springs up and challenges Socrates to prove that he is not the illegitimate usurper.

To reverse Platonism with Deleuze is to displace oneself insidiously within it, to descend a notch, to descend to its smallest gestures – discreet, but *moral* – which serve to exclude the simulacrum; it is also to deviate slightly from it, to open the door from either side to the small talk it excluded; it is to initiate another disconnected and divergent series; it is to construct, by way of this small lateral leap, a dethroned para-Platonism. To convert Platonism (a serious task) is to increase its compassion for reality, for the world, and for time. To subvert Platonism is to begin at the top (the vertical distance of irony) and to grasp its origin. To pervert Platonism is to search out the smallest details, to descend (with the natural gravitation of humor) as far as its crop of hair or the dirt under its fingernails – those things that were never hallowed by an idea; it is to discover the decentering it put into effect in order to recenter itself around the Model, the Identical, and the Same; it is the decentering of oneself with respect to Platonism so as to give rise to the play (as with every perversion) of surfaces at its border. Irony rises and subverts; humor falls and perverts.[3] To pervert Plato is to side with the Sophists' spitefulness, the unmannerly gestures of the Cynics, the arguments of the Stoics, and the fluttering chimeras of Epicurus. It is time to read Diogenes Laertius.

We should be alert to the surface effects in which the Epicurians take such pleasure: emissions proceeding from deep within bodies and rising like the wisps of a fog – interior phantoms that are quickly reabsorbed into other depths by the sense of smell, by the mouth, by the appetites, extremely thin membranes that detach themselves from the surfaces of objects and proceed to impose colors and contours deep within our eyes (floating epiderm, visual idols); phantasms of fear or desire (cloud gods, the adorable face of the beloved, "miserable hope transported by the wind"). It is all this swarming of the impalpable that must be integrated into our thought: we must articulate a philosophy of the phantasm construed not through the intermediary of perception of the image, as being of the order of an originary given but, rather, left to come to light among the surfaces to which it is related, in the reversal that causes every interior to pass to the outside and every exterior to the inside, in the temporal oscillation that always makes it precede and follow itself – in short, in what Deleuze would perhaps not allow us to call its "incorporeal materiality."

It is useless, in any case, to seek a more substantial truth behind the phantasm, a truth to which it points as a rather confused sign (thus, the futility of "symptomatologizing"); it is also useless to contain it within stable figures and to construct solid cores of convergence where we might include, on the basis of their identical properties, all its angles, flashes, membranes, and vapors (no possibility of "phenomenalization"). Phantasms must be allowed to function at the limit of bodies; against bodies, because they stick to bodies and protrude from them, but also because they touch them, cut them, break them into sections, regionalize them, and multiply their surfaces; and equally, outside of bodies, because they function between bodies according to laws of proximity, torsion, and variable distance – laws of which they remain ignorant. Phantasms do not extend organisms into the imaginary; they topologize the materiality of the body. They should consequently be freed from the restrictions we impose upon them, freed from the dilemmas of truth and falsehood and of being and nonbeing (the essential difference between simulacrum and copy carried to its logical conclusion); they must be allowed to conduct their dance, to act out their mime, as "extrabeings."

The Logic of Sense can be read as the most alien book imaginable from *The Phenomenology of Perception*.[4] In this latter text, the bodyorganism is linked to the world through a network of primal significations which arise from the perception of things, while, according to Deleuze, phantasms form the impenetrable and incorporeal surface of bodies; and from this process, simultaneously topological and cruel, something is shaped that falsely presents itself as a centered organism and distributes at its periphery the increasing remoteness of things. More essentially, however, *The Logic of Sense* should be read as the boldest and most insolent of metaphysical treatises – on the simple condition that instead of denouncing metaphysics as the neglect of being, we force it to speak of extrabeing. Physics: discourse dealing with the ideal structure of bodies, mixtures, reactions, internal and external mechanisms, metaphysics: discourse dealing with the materiality of incorporeal things – phantasms, idols, and simulacra.

Illusion is certainly the misfortune of metaphysics, but not because metaphysics, by its very nature, is doomed to illusion, but because for too long it has been haunted by illusion and because, in its fear of the simulacrum, it was forced to hunt down the illusory. Metaphysics is not illusory – it is not merely another species of this particular genus – but illusion is a metaphysics. It is the product of a particular metaphysics that designated the separation between the simulacrum on one side and the original and the perfect copy on the other. There was a critique whose task was to unearth metaphysical illusion and to establish its necessity; Deleuze's metaphysics, however, initiates the necessary critique for the disillusioning of phantasms. With this grounding, the way is cleared for the advance of the Epicurean and materialist series, for the pursuit of their singular zigzag. And it does not lead, in spite of itself, to a shameful metaphysics; it leads joyously to metaphysics – a metaphysics freed from its original profundity as well as from a supreme being, but also one that can conceive of the phantasm in its play of surfaces without the aid of models, a metaphysics where it is no longer a question of the One Good but of the absence of God and the epidermic play of perversity. A dead God and sodomy are the thresholds of the new metaphysical ellipse. Where natural theology contained metaphysical illusion in itself and where this illusion was always more or less related to natural theology, the metaphysics of the phantasm revolves around atheism and transgression. Sade and Bataille and somewhat later, the palm upturned in a gesture of defense and invitation, Roberte.[5]

Moreover, this series of liberated simulacrum is activated, or mimes itself, on two privileged sites: that of psychoanalysis, which should eventually be understood as a metaphysical practice since it concerns itself with phantasms; and that of the theater, which is multiplied, polyscenic, simultaneous, broken into separate scenes that refer to each other, and where we encounter, without any trace of representation (copying or imitating), the dance of masks, the cries of bodies, and the gesturing of hands and fingers. And throughout each of these two recent and divergent series (the attempt to "reconcile" these series, to reduce them to either perspective, to produce a ridiculous "psychodrama," has been extremely naive), Freud and Artaud exclude each other and give rise to a mutual resonance. The philosophy of representation – of the original, the first time, resemblance, imitation, faithfulness – is dissolving; and the arrow of the simulacrum released by the Epicureans is headed in our direction. It gives birth – rebirth – to a "phantasmaphysics."

Occupying the other side of Platonism are the Stoics. Observing Deleuze in his discussion of Epicurus and Zeno, of Lucretius and Chrysippus, I was forced to conclude that his procedure was rigorously Freudian. He does not proceed – with a drum roll – toward the great Repression of Western philosophy; he registers, as if in passing, its oversights. He points out its interruption, its gaps, those small things of little value neglected by philosophical discourse. He carefully reintroduces the barely perceptible omissions, knowing full well that they imply an unlimited negligence. Through the insistence of our pedagogical tradition, we are accustomed to reject the Epicurean simulacra as useless and somewhat puerile; and the famous battle of Stoicism, which took place yesterday and will reoccur tomorrow, has become cause for amusement in the schools. Deleuze did well to combine these tenuous threads and to play, in his own fashion, with this network of discourses, arguments, replies, and paradoxes, those elements that circulated for many centuries throughout the Mediterranean. We should not scorn Hellenistic confusion or Roman platitudes but listen to those things said on the great surface of the empire; we should be attentive to those things that happened in a thousand instances, dispersed on every side: fulgurating battles, assassinated generals, burning triremes, queens poisoning themselves, victories that invariably led to further upheavals, the endlessly exemplary Actium, the eternal event.

To consider a pure event, it must first be given a metaphysical basis.[6] But we must be agreed that it cannot be the metaphysics of substances, which can serve as a foundation for accidents; nor can it be a metaphysics of coherence, which situates these accidents in the entangled nexus of causes and effects. The event – a wound, a victory defeat, death – is always an effect produced entirely by bodies colliding, mingling, or separating, but this effect is never of a corporeal nature; it is the intangible, inaccessible battle that turns and repeats itself a thousand times around Fabricius, above the wounded Prince Andrew.[7] The weapons that tear into bodies form an endless incorporeal battle. Physics concerns causes, but events, which arise as its effects, no longer belong to it. Let us imagine a stitched causality: as bodies collide, mingle, and suffer, they create events on their surfaces, events that are without thickness, mixture, or passion; for this reason, they can no longer be causes. They form, among themselves, another kind of succession whose links derive from a quasi-physics of incorporeals – in short, from metaphysics.

Events also require a more complex logic.[8] An event is not a state of things, something that could serve as a referent for a proposition (the fact of death is a state of things in relation to which an assertion can be true or false; dying is a pure event that can never verify anything). For a ternary logic, traditionally centered on the referent, we must substitute an interrelationship based on four terms. "Marc Antony is dead" *designates* a state of things; *expresses* my opinion or belief; *signifies* an affirmation; and, in addition, has a *meaning*: "dying." An intangible meaning with one side turned toward things because "dying" is something that occurs, as an event, to Antony, and the other toward the proposition because "dying" is what is said about Antony in a statement. To die: a dimension of the proposition; an incorporeal effect produced by a sword; a meaning and an event; a point without thickness or substance of which someone speaks, which roams the surface of things. We should not restrict meaning to the cognitive core that lies at the heart of a knowable object; rather, we should allow it to reestablish its flux at the limit of words and things, as what is said of a thing (not its attribute or the thing in itself) and as something that happens (not its process or its state). Death supplies the best example, being both the event of events and meaning in its purest state. Its domain is the anonymous flow of discourse; it is that of which we speak as always past or about to happen, and yet it occurs at the extreme point of singularity. A meaning-event is as neutral as death: "not the end, but the unending; not a particular death, but any death; not true death, but as Kafka said, the snicker of its devastating error."[9]

Finally, this meaning-event requires a grammar with a different form of organization,[10] since it cannot be situated in a proposition as an attribute (to be *dead*, to be *alive*, to be *red*) but is fastened to the verb (to die, to live, to redden). The verb, conceived in this fashion, has two principal forms around which the others are distributed: the present tense, which posits an event, and the infinitive, which introduces meaning into language and allows it to circulate as the neutral element to which we refer in discourse. We should not seek the grammar of events in temporal inflections; nor should we seek the grammar of meaning in fictitious analysis of the type: to live = to be alive. The grammar of the meaning-event revolves around two asymmetrical and hobbling poles: the infinitive mode and the present tense. The meaning-event is always both the displacement of the present and the eternal repetition of the infinitive. To die is never localized in the density of a given moment, but from its flux it infinitely divides the shortest moment. To die is even smaller than the moment it takes to think it, and yet dying is indefinitely repeated on either side of this widthless crack. The eternal present? Only on the condition that we conceive the present as lacking plenitude and the eternal as lacking unity: the (multiple) eternity of the (displaced) present.

To summarize: At the limit of dense bodies, an event is incorporeal (a metaphysical surface); on the surface of words and things, an incorporeal event is the *meaning* of a proposition (its logical dimension); in the thread of discourse, an incorporeal meaning-event is fastened to the verb (the infinitive point of the present).

In the more or less recent past, there have been, I think, three major attempts at conceptualizing the event: neopositivism, phenomenology, and the philosophy of history. Neopositivism failed to grasp the distinctive level of the event; because of its logical error, the confusion of an event with a state of things, it had no choice but to lodge the event within the density of bodies, to treat it as a material process, and to attach itself more or less explicitly to a physicalism ("in a schizoid fashion," it reduced surfaces into depth); as for grammar, it transformed the event into an attribute. Phenomenology, on the other hand, reoriented the event with respect to meaning: either it placed the bare event before or to the side of meaning — the rock of facticity, the mute inertia of occurrences — and then submitted it to the active processes of meaning, to its digging and elaboration; or else it assumed a domain of primal significations which always existed as a disposition of the world around the self, tracing its paths and privileged locations, indicating in advance where the event might occur and its possible form. Either the cat whose good sense precedes the smile or the common sense of the smile that anticipates the cat. Either Sartre or Merleau-Ponty. For them, meaning never coincides with an event; and from this evolves a logic of signification, a grammar of the first person, and a metaphysics of consciousness. As for the philosophy of history, it encloses the event in a cyclical pattern of time. Its error is grammatical; it treats the present as framed by the past and future: the present is a former future where its form was prepared; it is the past to come, which preserves the identity of its content. On the one hand, this sense of the present requires a logic of essences (which establishes the present in memory) and of concepts (where the present is established as a knowledge of the future), and on the other, a metaphysics of a crowned and coherent cosmos, of a hierarchical world.

Thus, three philosophies that fail to grasp the event. The first, on the pretext that nothing can be said about those things which lie "outside" the world, rejects the pure surface of the event and attempts to enclose it forcibly — as a referent — in the spherical plenitude of the world. The second, on the pretext that signification only exists for consciousness, places the event outside and beforehand, or inside and after, and always situates it with respect to the circle of the self. The third, on the pretext that events can only exist in time, defines its identity and submits it to a solidly centered order. The world, the self, and God (a sphere, a circle, and a center): three conditions that make it impossible to think through the event. Deleuze's proposals, I believe, are directed to lifting this triple subjection that, to this day, is imposed on the event: a metaphysics of the incorporeal event (which is consequently irreducible to a physics of the world), a logic of neutral meaning (rather than a phenomenology of signification based on the subject), and a thought of the present infinitive (and not the raising up of the conceptual future in a past essence). [...]

Chapter 11

Jacques Derrida

■ THE TIME OF A THESIS: PUNCTUATIONS,[1] in
Alan Montefiore (ed.), *Philosophy in France Today,* Kathleen
McLaughlin trans., Cambridge: Cambridge University Press,
1998

SHOULD ONE SPEAK OF AN EPOCH of the thesis? Of a thesis which
would require time, sometimes a great deal of time? Or of a thesis whose time would
belong to the past?

In short, is there a time of the thesis? And even, should one speak of an age of the
thesis, of an age for the thesis?

Allow me to begin by whispering a confidence which I shall not abuse: never have I
felt so young and at the same time so old. At the same time, in the same instant ... and it
is one and the same feeling, as if two stories and two times, two rhythms were engaged in
a sort of altercation in one and the same feeling of oneself, in a sort of anachrony of
oneself, anachrony in oneself. It is in this way that I can, to an extent, make sense to
myself of a certain confusion of identity. This confusion is, certainly, not completely foreign
to me and I do not always complain about it; but just now it has suddenly got much worse
and this bout is not far from leaving me bereft of speech.

Between youth and old age, one and the other, neither one nor the other, an
indecisiveness of age, it is like a discomfiture at the moment of installation, an instability,
I will not go so far as to say a disturbance of stability, of posture, of station, of the thesis or
of the pose, but rather of a pause in the more or less well-regulated life of a university
teacher, an end and a beginning which do not coincide and in which there is involved once
again no doubt a certain gap of an alternative between the delight of pleasure and fecundity.

This anachrony (I am, obviously, speaking of my own) has for me a very familiar feel,
as if a rendezvous had forever been set for me with what should above all and with the
utmost punctuality never come at its appointed hour, but always, rather, too early or too
late.

As to this stage on which I here appear for the defence of a thesis, I have been
preparing myself for it for too long, I have doubtless premeditated it, adjourned it and
finally excluded its possibility, excluded it for too long so that when, thanks to you, I at last

find myself engaged upon it, it is impossible for it not to have for me a slight character of phantasy or irreality, an air of improbability, of unpredictability, even an air of improvisation.

It is now almost twenty-five years ago that I committed myself to working on a thesis. Or rather, it was scarcely a decision; I was at that time simply following the course that was taken to be more or less natural and which was at the very least classical, classifiable, typical of those who found themselves in a certain well determined social situation upon leaving the Ecole Normale and after the *agrégation*.[2]

But these twenty-five years have been fairly peculiar. Here I am not referring to my modest personal history or to all those routes that, after starting by leading me away from this initial decision, then brought me deliberately to question it, deliberately and as I honestly thought, definitively, only to end up, just a very short while ago, by deciding in a context which, rightly or wrongly, I believed to be quite new to take the risk of another evaluation, of another analysis.

By saying that these twenty-five years have been peculiar, I am not first thinking, then, of this personal history or even of the paths my own work has taken, even supposing that it could, improbably, be isolated from the environment in which it has moved through a play of exchanges, of resemblances, of affinities, of influences, as people say, but also and especially, more and more indeed, through a play of divergences and of marginalization, in an increasing and at times sheer isolation, whether as regards contents, positions, let us just say "theses", or whether more especially as regards ways of proceeding, socio-institutional practices, a certain style of writing as well as — regardless of the cost, and today this amounts to a great deal — of relations with the university milieu, with cultural, political, editorial, journalistic representations, there where, today, it seems to me, are located some of the most serious, the most pressing, and the most obscure responsibilities facing an intellectual.

No, it is not of myself that I am thinking when I allude to the span of these twenty-five years, but rather of a most remarkable sequence in the history of philosophy and of French philosophical institutions. I should not have the means here and now, and in any case, this is not the place, to analyse this sequence. But as, for reasons that are due not only to the limited amount of time available to me, there can be equally no question of putting together the works that have been submitted to you in something like a presentation in the form of conclusions or of theses; and as, on the other hand, I do not want to limit the discussion that is to follow by making an overly long introduction, I thought that I might perhaps hazard a few fragmentary and preliminary propositions, indicating a few among the most obvious points concerning the intersections between this historical sequence and some of the movements or themes that have attracted me, that have retained or displaced my attention within the limits of my work.

Around 1957, then, I had *registered*, as one says, my first thesis topic. I had entitled it "The ideality of the literary object". Today this title seems strange. To a lesser degree it seemed so even then and I shall discuss this in a moment. It received the approval of Jean Hyppolite who was to direct this thesis, which he did, which he did without doing so, that is as he knew how to do so, as in my opinion he was one of the very few to know how to do so, in a free and liberal spirit, always open, always attentive to what was not, or not yet, intelligible, always careful to exert no pressure, if not no influence, by generously letting me go wherever my path led me. I want to salute his memory here and to recall all that I owe to the trust and encouragement he gave me, even when, as he one day told me, he did not see at all where I was going. This was in 1966 during a colloquium in the United

States in which we were both taking part. After a few friendly remarks on the paper I had just given, Jean Hyppolite added: "That said, I really do not see where you are going." I think that I replied to him more or less as follows: "If I clearly saw ahead of time where I was going, I really don't believe that I should take another step to get there." Perhaps I then thought that knowing where one is going may doubtless help in orientating one's thought, but that it has never made anyone take a single step, quite the opposite in fact. What is the good of going where one knows oneself to be going and where one knows that one is destined to arrive? Recalling this reply today, I am not sure that I really understand it very well, but it surely did not mean that I *never* see or *never* know where I am going and that to this extent, to the extent that I do know, it is not certain that I have ever taken any step or said anything at all. This also means, perhaps, that, concerning this place where I am going, I in fact know enough about it to think, with a certain terror, that things there are not going very well and that, all things considered, it would be better not to go there at all. But there's always Necessity, the figure I wanted recently to call Necessity with the initial capital of a proper noun, and Necessity says that one must always yield, that one has always to go where it calls. At the risk of never arriving. At the risk, it says, of never arriving. Calling it even, prepared for the fact that you won't make it. (*Quitte à ne pas arriver. Quitte, dit-elle, à ne pas arriver. Quitte pour ce que tu n'arrives pas.*)

The ideality of the literary object; this title was somewhat more comprehensible in 1957 in a context that was more marked by the thought of Husserl than is the case today. It was then for me a matter of bending, more or less violently, the techniques of transcendental phenomenology to the needs of elaborating a new theory of literature, of that very peculiar type of ideal object that is the literary object, a bound ideality Husserl would have said, bound to so-called "natural" language, a non-mathematical or non-mathematizable object, and yet one that differs from the objects of plastic or musical art, that is to say from all of the examples privileged by Husserl in his analyses of ideal objectivity. For I have to remind you, somewhat bluntly and simply, that my most constant interest, coming even before my philosophical interest I should say, if this is possible, has been directed towards literature, towards that writing which is called literary.

What is literature? And first of all what is it "to write"? How is it that the fact of writing can disturb the very question "what is?" and even "what does it mean?" To say this in other words — and here is the *saying otherwise* that was of importance to me — when and how does an inscription become literature and what takes place when it does? To what and to whom is this due? What takes place between philosophy and literature, science and literature, politics and literature, theology and literature, psychoanalysis and literature? It was here, in all the abstractness of its title, that lay the most pressing question. This question was doubtless inspired in me by a desire which was related also to a certain uneasiness: why finally does the inscription so fascinate me, preoccupy me, precede me? Why am I so fascinated by the literary ruse of the inscription and the whole ungraspable paradox of a trace which manages only to carry itself away, to erase itself in marking itself out afresh, itself and its own idiom, which in order to take actual form must erase itself and produce itself at the price of this self-erasure.

Curious as it may seem, transcendental phenomenology was able, in the first stages of my work, to help me sharpen some of these questions, which at the time were not as well marked out as they seem to be today. In the fifties, when it was still not well received, was little-known or too indirectly understood in the French universities, Husserlian phenomenology seemed to some young philosophers to be inescapable. I still see it today, if in a different way, as a discipline of incomparable rigour. Not – especially not – in the versions proposed by Sartre or by Merleau-Ponty which were then dominant, but rather in opposition to them, or without them, in particular in those areas which a certain type of French phenomenology appeared at times to avoid, whether in history, in science, in the historicity of science, the history of ideal objects and of truth, and hence in politics as well, and even in ethics. I should like to recall here, as one indication among others, a book which is no longer discussed today, a book whose merits can be very diversely evaluated, but which for a certain number of us pointed to a task, a difficulty and no doubt to an impasse. This is Tran Duc Tao's *Phénoménologie et matérialisme dialectique*.[3] After a commentary which retraced the movement of transcendental phenomenology and in particular the transition from static constitution to genetic constitution, the book attempted, with less obvious success, to open the way for a dialectical materialism that would admit some of the rigorous demands of transcendental phenomenology. One can imagine what the stakes of such an attempt might have been and its outcome was of less importance than the stakes involved. Moreover, some of Cavaillès's dialectical, dialecticist conclusions proved of interest to us for the same reasons. It was in an area marked out and magnetized by these stakes, at once philosophical and political, that I had first begun to read Husserl, starting with a *Mémoire* (Master's thesis) on the problem of genesis in the phenomenology of Husserl. At this early date Maurice de Gandillac was kind enough to watch over this work; twenty-six years ago he alone served as my entire examination committee, and if I recall that he was reduced to one-third of the committee for a *3ᵉ cycle* thesis (*De la grammatologie* in 1967) and that he has been further reduced to one-sixth of the committee today, I do so not only to express my gratitude to him with that feeling of fidelity which is comparable to no other, but to promise him that henceforth this parcelling out, this proliferating division will cease. This will be my last thesis defence.

Following this first work, my Introduction to *The Origin of Geometry*[4] enabled me to approach something like the unthought-out axiomatics of Husserlian phenomenology, its "principle of principles", that is to say, its intuitionism, the absolute privilege of the living present, the lack of attention paid to the problem of its own phenomenological enunciation, to transcendental discourse itself, as Fink used to say, to the necessity of recourse, in eidetic or transcendental description, to a language that could not itself be submitted to the *épochè* – without itself being simply in the world – thus to a language which remained naïve, even though it was by virtue of this very language that all the phenomenological bracketings and parentheses were made possible. This unthought-out axiomatics seemed to me to limit the scope of a consistent problematic of writing and of the trace, even though the necessity of such a problematic had been marked out by *The Origin of Geometry* with a rigour no doubt unprecedented in the history of philosophy. Husserl indeed located the recourse to writing within the very constitution of those ideal objects *par excellence*, mathematical objects, though without considering – and for good reason – the threat that the logic of this inscription represented for the phenomenological project itself. Naturally, all of the problems worked on in the Introduction to *The Origin of Geometry* have continued to organize the work I have subsequently attempted in connection with philosophical, literary and even non-discursive corpora, most notably that of pictorial works: I am thinking, for example, of the historicity of ideal objects, of tradition, of inheritance, of filiation or of wills and testaments, of archives, libraries, books, of writing and living speech, of the relationships between semiotics and linguistics, of the question of truth and of undecidability, of the irreducible otherness that divides the self-identity of the living present, of the necessity for new analyses concerning non-mathematical idealities.

During the years that followed, from about 1963 to 1968, I tried to work out – in particular in the three works published in 1967 – what was in no way meant to be a system but rather a sort of strategic device, opening onto its own abyss, an unclosed, unenclosable, not wholly formalizable ensemble of rules for reading, interpretation and writing. This type of device may have enabled me to detect not only in the history of philosophy and in the related socio-historical totality, but also in what are alleged to be sciences and in so-called post-philosophical discourses that figure among the most modern (in linguistics, in anthropology, in psychoanalysis), to detect in these an evaluation of writing, or, to tell the truth, rather a devaluation of writing whose insistent, repetitive, even obscurely compulsive, character was the sign of a whole set of long-standing constraints. These constraints were practised at the price of contradictions, of denials, of dogmatic decrees; they were not to be localized within a limited domain of culture, of the whole encyclopedia of knowledge or of ontology. I proposed to analyse the non-closed and fissured system of these constraints under the name of logocentrism in the form that it takes in Western philosophy and under that of phonocentrism as it appears in the widest scope of its dominion. Of course, I was able to develop this device and this interpretation only by according a privileged role to the guideline or analyser going under the names of writing, text and trace, and only by proposing a reconstruction and a generalization of these concepts: writing, the text, the trace as the play and work of *différance*, whose role is at one and the same time both of constitution and of deconstitution. This strategy may have appeared to be an abusive deformation – or, as some have cursorily said, a metaphorical usage – of the current notions of writing, text or trace, and have seemed to those who continued to cling to these old self-interested representations to give rise to all sorts of misunderstandings. But I have untiringly striven to justify this unbounded generalization, and I believe that every conceptual breakthrough amounts to transforming, that is to deforming, an accredited, authorized relationship between a word and a concept, between a trope and what one had every interest to consider to be an unshiftable primary sense, a proper, literal or current usage. Moreover, the strategic and rhetorical bearing of these attitudes has never ceased to engage me in numerous subsequent texts. All of this was grouped together under the title of deconstruction, the graphics of *différance*, of the trace, the supplement, etc., and here I can only indicate them in an algebraic manner. What I proposed at that time retained an oblique, deviant, sometimes directly critical, relationship with respect to everything that seemed then to dominate the main, most visible, the most spectacular and sometimes the most fertile outcrop of French theoretical production, a phenomenon which, in its various different forms, was known, no doubt abusively, as "structuralism". Certainly, these forms were very diverse and very remarkable, whether in the domains of anthropology, history, literary criticism, linguistics or psychoanalysis, in the re-readings, as people said, of Freud or of Marx. But regardless of their indisputable interest, in the course of this period which was also in appearance the most static period of the Gaullist republic of 1958–68, what I was attempting or what was tempting me was of an essentially different nature. And so, aware of the cost of these advances in terms of their metaphysical presuppositions, to say nothing of what was, less evidently, their political price, I buried myself from this time on in a sort of retreat, in a solitude which I mention here without pathos, as simply self-evident, and merely as a reminder that increasingly in regard to academic tradition as well as to established modernity – and in this case the two are but one – this solitude has been and often still is considered to be the well-deserved consequence of an hermetic and unjustified reclusiveness. Is it necessary to say that I do not think this is so and that I interpret in an entirely different manner the reasons for this verdict? It is also true that the living thinkers who gave me the most to think about or who most provoked me to reflection, and who continue to do so, are not among those who break through a solitude, not among those to whom one can simply feel oneself close, not among those who form groups or schools, to mention only Heidegger, Levinas, Blanchot among others whom I shall not name. It is thinkers such as these to whom, strangely enough, one may consider oneself most close; and yet they are, more than others, other. And they too are alone.

It was already clear to me that the general turn that my research was taking could no longer conform to the classical norms of the thesis. This "research" called not only for a different mode of writing but also for a work of transformation applied to the rhetoric, the staging and the particular discursive procedures, which, historically determined as they very much are, dominate university discourse, in particular the type of text that is called the "thesis"; and we know how all these scholarly and university models likewise provide the laws regulating so many prestigious discourses, even those of literary works or of eloquent political speeches which shine outside the university. And then, too, the directions I had taken, the nature and the diversity of the corpora, the labyrinthian geography of the itineraries drawing me on towards relatively unacademic areas, all of this persuaded me that the time was now past, that it was, in truth, no longer possible, even if I wanted to, to make what I was writing conform to the size and form then required for a thesis. The very idea of a thetic presentation, of positional or oppositional logic, the idea of position, of *Setzung* or *Stellung*, that which I called at the beginning the epoch of the thesis, was one of the essential parts of the system that was under deconstructive questioning. What was then put forth under the heading – itself lacking any particular status – of dissemination explicitly dealt, in ways that were in effect neither thematic nor thetic, with the value of the thesis, of positional logic and its history, and of the limits of its rights, its authority and its legitimacy. This did not imply on my part, at least at that particular time, any radical institutional critique of the thesis, of the presentation of university work in order to have it legitimized or of the authorization of competence by accredited representatives of the university. If, from this moment on, I was indeed convinced of the necessity for a profound transformation, amounting even to a complete upheaval of university institutions, this was not, of course, in order to substitute for what existed some type of non-thesis, non-legitimacy or incompetence. In this area I believe in transitions and in negotiation – even if it may at times be brutal and speeded up – I believe in the necessity for a certain tradition, in particular for political reasons that are nothing less than traditionalist, and I believe, moreover, in the indestructibility of the ordered procedures of legitimation, of the production of titles and diplomas and of the authorization of competence. I speak here in general and not necessarily of the *universitas*, which is a powerful but very particular, very specific, and indeed very recent, model for this procedure of legitimation. The structure of the *universitas* has an essential tie with the ontological and logocentric ontoencyclopedic system; and for the past several years it has seemed to me that the indissociable link between the modern concept of the university and a certain metaphysics calls for investigations such as I pursued in my teaching or in essays that have been published or are in the course of being published on *The Conflict of the Faculties*[5] by

Kant, and on Hegel, Nietzsche and Heidegger in their political philosophy of the university. If I insist on this theme, it is because, given the circumstances and the impossibility in which I find myself of summing up or presenting thetic conclusions, I feel that I should attend first and foremost to what is happening here and now, and I should wish to assume responsibility as clearly and as honestly as possible from my very limited place and in my own way.

In 1967 I was so little bent on questioning the necessity of an institution such as this, of its general principle in any case, if not its particular university structure and organization, that I thought I could make a sort of compromise and division of labour and time, according its share to the thesis, to the time of the thesis. On the one hand, I would have let the work in which I was engaged develop freely and outside the usual forms and norms, a work which decidedly did not conform to such university requirements and which was even to analyse, contest, displace, deform them in all their rhetorical or political bearing; but at the same time, and on the other hand, the transaction and the time or the epoch of the thesis would have amounted to setting apart one piece of this work, a theoretical sequence playing the role of an organizing element, and treating it in accordance with one of those acceptable forms which are, within the context of the university, so reassuring. This would have involved an interpretation of the Hegelian theory of the sign, of speech and of writing in Hegel's semiology. It seemed indispensable to me, for reasons I have discussed especially in *Marges*,[6] to propose a systematic interpretation of this semiology. Jean Hyppolite gave me his consent yet once again and this second thesis topic was in its turn – registered.

This, then, was in 1967. Things were so intertwined and overdetermined that I cannot even begin to say what was the impact on me, on my work and my teaching, on my relationship to university institutions and to the domain of cultural representation of that event which one still does not know how to name other than by its date, 1968, without ever having any very clear idea of just what it is one is naming in this way. The least that I can say about it is this: something I had been anticipating found its confirmation at that time and this confirmation accelerated my own movement away, as I was then moving away more quickly and more resolutely *on the one hand* from the places where, as early as the autumn of 1968, the old armatures were being hastily recentred, reconstituted, reconcentrated and *on the other hand* from a style of writing guided by the model of the classical thesis, and even directed by a concern for recognition by academic authorities who, at least in those bodies in which were to be found gathered together, officially and in terms of built-in majorities, their most effective powers of evaluation and decision, seemed to me, after '68, to be both overreactive and too effective in their resistance to all that did not conform to the most tranquillizing criteria of acceptability. I had numerous indications of this; certain concerned me personally, and if I say that politics was also involved it is because, in this case, politics does not take only the conventional distribution along an axis running from left to right. The reproductive force of authority can get along more comfortably with declarations or theses whose content presents itself as revolutionary, provided that they respect the rites of legitimation, the rhetoric and the institutional symbolism which defuses and neutralizes whatever comes from outside the system. What is unacceptable is what, underlying positions or theses, upsets this deeply entrenched contract, the order of these norms and which does so in the very *form* of works, of teaching or of writing.

The death of Jean Hyppolite in 1968 was not only for me, as for others, a moment of great sadness. By a strange coincidence, it marked at that date – the autumn of 1968 and it was indeed the autumn – the end of a certain type of membership of the university. Certainly, from the first day of my arrival in France this membership had not been simple, but it was during these years no doubt that I came to understand better to what extent the necessity of deconstruction (I use this word for the sake of rapid convenience, though it is a word I have never liked and one whose fortune has disagreeably surprised me) was not primarily a matter of philosophical contents, themes or theses, philosophemes, poems, theologemes or ideologemes, but especially and inseparably meaningful frames, institutional structures, pedagogical or rhetorical norms, the possibilities of law, of authority, of evaluation, and of representation in terms of its very market. My interest for these more or less visible framework structures, for these limits, these margin effects or these paradoxes of edgings continued to relate to the same question: how is it that philosophy finds itself inscribed, rather than itself inscribing itself, within a space which it seeks but is unable to control, a space which opens out onto another which is no longer even *its* other, as I have tried to make apparent in a *tympanum* as little Hegelian as possible. How is one to name the structure of this space? I do not *know*; nor do I know whether there can even be what may be called *knowledge* of such a space. To call it socio-political is a triviality which does not satisfy me, and even the most indisputable of what are said to be socio-analyses have often enough very little to say on the matter, remaining blind to their own inscription, to the law of their reproduction performances, to the stage of their own heritage and of their self-authorization, in short to what I will call their writing.

I have chosen, as you can see, to confide to you without circumlocution, if not without a certain simplification, all the uncertainties, the hesitations, the oscillations by way of which I sought the most fitting relationship with the institution of the university, on a plane that was not simply political and that concerned not only the thesis. It was at first a somewhat passive reaction: the thing no longer interested me very much. I should have had to come up with a new formulation, come to an understanding with a new supervisor, etc. And as doctorates based on published works, theoretically possible, were evidently not encouraged, to say the very least, I turned away, at first somewhat passively, I repeat, from those places which seemed to me less and less open to what really mattered to me. But I have to admit that in certain situations, most notably those in which I am writing and in which I am writing about writing, my obstinacy is so great as to constitute a compelling constraint upon me, even when it is forced to take the most roundabout paths. And so beyond the three works published in 1972, I kept worrying away at the same problematic, the same open matrix (opening onto the linked series formed by the trace, *différance*, undecidables, dissemination, the supplement, the graft, the hymen, the parergon, etc.), pushing it towards textual configurations that were less and less linear, logical and topical forms, even typographical forms that were more daring, the intersection of corpora, mixtures of genera or of modes, changes of tone (*Wechsel der Töne*), satire, rerouting, grafting, etc., to the extent that even today, although these texts have been published for years, I do not believe them to be simply presentable or acceptable to the university and I have not dared, have not judged it opportune, to include them here among the works to be defended. These texts include *Glas*,[7] despite the continued pursuit there of the project of grammatology, that is the discussion with the arbitrary character of the sign and the thesis of onomatopoeia in Saussure as well as with the Hegelian *Aufhebung*, the relation between the undecidable, the dialectic and the double bind, the concept of generalized fetishism, the pull of the discourse on/of castration towards an affirmative dissemination and towards another rhetoric of the whole and the part, the reelaboration of a problematic dealing with the proper noun and the signature, with the testament and the monument and many other themes besides; all of this indeed was an expansion of earlier attempts. I should say the same thing with respect to the other works that I have deliberately left aside from this submission, works such as *Eperons, les styles de Nietzsche*[8] or *La Carte postale*,[9] which, each in their own way, nevertheless extend a reading (of Freud, of Nietzsche and some others) begun at an earlier stage, the deconstruction of a certain hermeneutics as well as of a certain way of theorizing about the signifier and the letter with its authority and institutional power (I am referring here to the whole psychoanalytic set-up as well as to the university), the analysis of logocentrism as phallogocentrism, a concept by means of which I tried to indicate, in my analysis, the essential indissociability of phallocentrism and logocentrism, and to locate their effects wherever I could spot them – but these effects are everywhere, even where they remain unnoticed.

The expansion of these texts dealing with textuality might seem anamorphic or labyrinthian, or both at once, but what in particular made them just about unsubmittable as a thesis was less the multiplicity of their contents, conclusions and demonstrative positions, than, it seems to me, the acts of writing and the performative stage to which they ought to give rise and from which they remained inseparable and hence not easily capable of being represented, transported and translated into another form; they were inscribed in a space that one could no longer, that I myself could no longer, identify or classify under the heading of philosophy *or* of non-fiction, etc., especially at a time when what others would call the autobiographical involvement of these texts was undermining the very notion of autobiography, giving it over to what the necessity of writing, the trace, the remainder, etc. could offer of all that was most baffling, undecidable, wily or despairing. And since I have just alluded to the performative structure, let me note in passing that, for the same reasons, I have held back from the thesis corpus, along with a good many other essays, a debate that I had in the United States with a speech act theorist, John Searle, in an opuscule that I entitled "Limited Inc".[10]

During an initial period, then, from 1968 to 1974, I simply neglected the thesis. But during the years that followed I deliberately decided – and I sincerely believed that this decision was final – not to submit a thesis at all. For, besides the reasons I have just mentioned and which seemed to me to be more and more solid, I have been engaged since 1974 with friends, colleagues and university and high school students in a work which I should dare to call a long-term struggle which directly concerns the institutions of philosophy as they exist, especially in France. The context of this work is to be found first and foremost in a situation whose nature has been determined by a long history, but which was seriously aggravated in 1975 by a policy which could – or, one may fear, will – lead to the destruction of philosophical teaching and research, with all that this implies by way of consequences for this country. For all the women and men who, like me, worked to organize the Groupe de Recherches sur l'Enseignement Philosophique (GREPH) and who participated in its rough draft, its works and its actions, from 1974 until the meeting of the Estates General of Philosophy in this very place just one year ago, for all of us the task was of the utmost urgency, and the responsibility ineluctable. I must specify: this task was urgent and ineluctable in the places which we occupy – those of teaching or research in philosophy – the places to which we cannot deny that we belong and in which we find ourselves inscribed. But of course, other things are urgent too, this philosophical realm is not the only one available to thought; it is neither the first one in the world, nor is it the one with the greatest determining influence on, for example, politics. We dwell elsewhere as well, and this I have tried never to forget; nor indeed is it something that allows itself to be forgotten. What we in GREPH were questioning with respect to philosophical teaching could not be separated, and we have always been attentive to this point, from all of the other cultural, political and other contending forces in this country and in the world.

In any case, as far as I was concerned, my participation in GREPH's works and struggles had to be as consistent as possible with what I was trying to write elsewhere, even if the middle terms between the two necessities were not always either easy or obvious. I have to say this here: although among the works presented to you I have included neither the texts I have signed or those that I have prepared as a militant of GREPH nor, *a fortiori*, the collective actions in which I have participated or which I have endorsed in that capacity, I consider them to be inseparable, let us say in spirit, from my other public acts – most notably from my other publications. And the gesture I make today, far from signifying that I have abandoned anything in this respect, will, on the contrary I hope, make possible other involvements or other responsibilities in the *same* struggle.

It remains the case that during this second period, beginning around 1974, I thought, rightly or wrongly, that it was neither consistent nor desirable to be a candidate for any new academic title or responsibility. Not consistent given the work of political criticism in which I was participating, not desirable with regard to a little forum that was more internal, more private and upon which, through a whole endless scenography of symbols, representations, phantasies, traps and strategies, a self-image recounts all sorts of interminable and incredible stories to itself. So I thought I had decided that, without further changing anything in my university situation, I would continue for better or for worse doing what I had done up to then, remaining in the place where I had been immobilized, without knowing anything more about where I was going, indeed knowing less no doubt about it than ever. It is not insignificant, I believe, that during this period most of the texts I published placed the greatest, if not the most novel, emphasis on rights and on what is proper, what is one's own, on the rights of property, on copyright, on the signature and the market, on the market for painting or, more generally, for culture and all its representations, on speculation on what is proper, one's own, on the name, on destination and restitution, on all the institutional borders and structures of discourses, on the whole machinery of publishing and on the media. Whether in my analyses of the logic of the parergon or the interlacing stricture of the double bind, or in my discussions of the paintings of Van Gogh, Adami or Titus Carmel, of the meditations on art by Kant, Hegel, Heidegger or Benjamin (in *La Vérité en peinture*),[11] or again in my attempts to explore new questions in conjunction with psychoanalysis (for example, in relating to the works of Nicolas Abraham and Maria Torok, works that are so alive today) – in all of these cases I have been increasingly preoccupied with the necessity of making a fresh start in working on questions said to be classically institutional. I should have liked in this respect to have been able to shape both my discourse and my practice, as one says, to fit the premises of my earlier undertakings. In fact, if not in principle, this was not always easy, not always possible, at times indeed very burdensome in a number of ways.

Of the third and final period, the one in which I find myself here and now, I can say very little. Only a few months ago, and after taking account of a very wide number of different factors which I cannot analyse here, I came to the conclusion, thus putting an abrupt end to a process of deliberation that was threatening to become interminable, that everything that had justified my earlier resolution (concerning the thesis, of course) was no longer likely to be valid for the years to come. In particular, for the very same reasons of institutional politics which had until now held me back, I concluded that it was perhaps better, and I must underline the "perhaps", to prepare myself for some new type of mobility. And as is often, as is always the case, it is the friendly advice of this or that person among those here present, before or behind me, it is other people, always others, who effected in me a decision I could not have come to alone. For not only am I not sure, as I never am, of being right in taking this step, I am not sure that I see in all clarity what led me to do so. Perhaps because I was beginning to know only too well not indeed where I was going, but where I had not so much arrived as simply stopped.

I began by saying that it was as if I was bereft of speech. You recognized, of course, that this was just another manner of speaking; nevertheless it was not false. For the *captatio* in which I have just indulged has been not only excessively coded, excessively narrative – the chronicle of so many anachronies – it has been also as impoverished as a punctuation mark, rather, I should say, an apostrophe in an unfinished text. And above all, above all, it has sounded too much like the totting up of a calculation, a self-justification, a self-submission (as of a thesis), a self-defence (in the United States one speaks of a thesis defence for a *soutenance de thèse*). You have heard too much talk of strategies. Strategy is a word that I have perhaps abused in the past, especially as it has been always only to specify *in the end*, in an apparently self-contradictory manner and at the risk of cutting the ground from under my own feet – something I almost never fail to do – that this strategy is a strategy without any finality; for this is what I hold and what in turn holds me in its grip, the aleatory strategy of someone who admits that he does not know where he is going. This, then, is not after all an undertaking of war or a discourse of belligerence. I should like it to be also like a headlong flight straight towards the end, a joyous self-contradiction, a disarmed desire, that is to say something very old and very cunning, but which also has just been born and which delights in being without defence.

Chapter 12

Gilles Deleuze

■ **IMMANENCE: A LIFE** in *Pure Immanence: Essays on a Life*, Anne Boyman trans., New York: Zone Books, 2001

WHAT IS A TRANSCENDENTAL FIELD? It can be distinguished from experience in that it doesn't refer to an object or belong to a subject (empirical representation). It appears therefore as a pure stream of a-subjective consciousness, a pre-reflexive impersonal consciousness, a qualitative duration of consciousness without a self. It may seem curious that the transcendental be defined by such immediate givens: we will speak of a transcendental empiricism in contrast to everything that makes up the world of the subject and the object. There is something wild and powerful in this transcendental empiricism that is of course not the element of sensation (simple empiricism), for sensation is only a break within the flow of absolute consciousness. It is, rather, however close two sensations may be, the passage from one to the other as becoming, as increase or decrease in power (virtual quantity). Must we then define the transcendental field by a pure immediate consciousness with neither object nor self, as a movement that neither begins nor ends? (Even Spinoza's conception of this passage or quantity of power still appeals to consciousness.)

But the relation of the transcendental field to consciousness is only a conceptual one. Consciousness becomes a fact only when a subject is produced at the same time as its object, both being outside the field and appearing as "transcendents." Conversely, as long as consciousness traverses the transcendental field at an infinite speed everywhere diffused, nothing is able to reveal it.[1] It is expressed, in fact, only when it is reflected on a subject that refers it to objects. That is why the transcendental field cannot be defined by the consciousness that is coextensive with it, but removed from any revelation.

The transcendent is not the transcendental. Were it not for consciousness, the transcendental field would be defined as a pure plane of immanence, because it eludes all transcendence of the subject and of the object.[2] Absolute immanence is in itself: it is not in something, *to* something; it does not depend on an object or belong to a subject. In Spinoza, immanence is not immanence *to* substance; rather, substance and modes are in immanence. When the subject or the object falling outside the plane of immanence is taken as a universal subject or as any object *to which* immanence is attributed, the transcendental is entirely denatured, for it then simply redoubles the empirical (as with Kant), and immanence is distorted, for it then finds itself enclosed in the transcendent. Immanence is not related to Some Thing as a unity superior to all things or to a Subject as an act that brings about a synthesis of things: it is only when immanence is no longer immanence to anything other than itself that we can speak of a plane of immanence. No more than the transcendental field is defined by consciousness can the plane of immanence be defined by a subject or an object that is able to contain it.

We will say of pure immanence that it is A LIFE, and nothing else. It is not immanence to life, but the immanent that is in nothing is itself a life. A life is the immanence of immanence, absolute immanence: it is complete power, complete bliss. It is to the degree that he goes beyond the aporias of the subject and the object that Johann Fichte, in his last philosophy, presents the transcendental field as a *life*, no longer dependent on a Being or submitted to an Act — it is an absolute immediate consciousness whose very activity no longer refers to a being but is ceaselessly posed in a life.[3] The transcendental field then becomes a genuine plane of immanence that reintroduces Spinozism into the heart of the philosophical process. Did Maine de Biran not go through something similar in his "last philosophy" (the one he was too tired to bring to fruition) when he discovered, beneath the transcendence of effort, an absolute immanent life?[4] The transcendental field is defined by a plane of immanence, and the plane of immanence by a life.

What is immanence? A life … No one has described what *a* life is better than Charles Dickens, if we take the indefinite article as an index of the transcendental. A disreputable man, a rogue, held in contempt by everyone, is found as he lies dying. Suddenly, those taking care of him manifest an eagerness, respect, even love, for his slightest sign of life. Everybody bustles about to save him, to the point where, in his deepest coma, this wicked man himself senses something soft and sweet penetrating him. But to the degree that he comes back to life, his saviors turn colder, and he becomes once again mean and crude. Between his life and his death, there is a moment that is only that of *a* life playing with death.[5] The life of the individual gives way to an impersonal and yet singular life that releases a pure event freed from the accidents of internal and external life, that is, from the subjectivity and objectivity of what happens: a "Homo tantum" with whom everyone empathizes and who attains a sort of beatitude. It is a haecceity no longer of individuation but of singularization: a life of pure immanence, neutral, beyond good and evil, for it was only the subject that incarnated it in the midst of things that made it good or bad. The life of such individuality fades away in favor of the singular life immanent to a man who no longer has a name, though he can be mistaken for no other. A singular essence, a life …

But we shouldn't enclose life in the single moment when individual life confronts universal death. *A* life is everywhere, in all the moments that a given living subject goes through and that are measured by given lived objects: an immanent life carrying with it the events or singularities that are merely actualized in subjects and objects. This indefinite life does not itself have moments, close as they may be one to another, but only between-times, between-moments; it doesn't just come about or come after but offers the immensity of an empty time where one sees the event yet to come and already happened, in the absolute of an immediate consciousness. In his novels, Alexander Lernet-Holenia places the event in an in-between time that could engulf entire armies. The singularities and the events that constitute *a* life coexist with the accidents of *the* life that corresponds to it, but they are neither grouped nor divided in the same way. They connect with one another in a manner entirely different from how individuals connect. It even seems that a singular life might do without any individuality, without any other concomitant that individualizes it. For example, very small children all resemble one another and have hardly any individuality, but they have singularities: a smile, a gesture, a funny face – not subjective qualities. Small children, through all their sufferings and weaknesses, are infused with an immanent life that is pure power and even bliss. The indefinite aspects in a life lose all indetermination to the degree that they fill out a plane of immanence or, what amounts to the same thing, to the degree that they constitute the elements of a transcendental field (individual life, on the other hand, remains inseparable from empirical determinations). The indefinite as such is the mark not of an empirical indetermination but of a determination by immanence or a transcendental determinability. The indefinite article is the indetermination of the person only because it is determination of the singular. The One is not the transcendent that might contain immanence but the immanent contained within a transcendental field. One is always the index of a multiplicity: an event, a singularity, a life ... Although it is always possible to invoke a transcendent that falls outside the plane of immanence, or that attributes immanence to itself, all transcendence is constituted solely in the flow of immanent consciousness that belongs to this plane.[6] Transcendence is always a product of immanence.

A life contains only virtuals. It is made up of virtualities, events, singularities. What we call virtual is not something that lacks reality but something that is engaged in a process of actualization following the plane that gives it its particular reality. The immanent event is actualized in a state of things and of the lived that make it happen. The plane of immanence is itself actualized in an object and a subject to which it attributes itself. But however inseparable an object and a subject may be from their actualization, the plane of immanence is itself virtual, so long as the events that populate it are virtualities. Events or singularities give to the plane all their virtuality, just as the plane of immanence gives virtual events their full reality. The event considered as non-actualized (indefinite) is lacking in nothing. It suffices to put it in relation to its concomitants: a transcendental field, a plane of immanence, a life, singularities. A wound is incarnated or actualized in a state of things or of life; but it is itself a pure virtuality on the plane of immanence that leads us into a life. My wound existed before me: not a transcendence of the wound as higher actuality, but its immanence as a virtuality always within a milieu (plane or field).[7] There is a big difference between the virtuals that define the immanence of the transcendental field and the possible forms that actualize them and transform them into something transcendent.

Chapter 13

Jean-François Lyotard

■ THE INTIMACY OF TERROR in *Postmodern Fables*,
Georges van den Abbeele trans., Minneapolis, Minn.: University
of Minnesota Press, 1997

THE CONTEMPORARY WORLD OFFERS a picture of liberal, imperialist capitalism after its triumph over its last two challengers, fascism and communism: so Marxism would say, were it not defunct. A posthumous critique, for which the system has no concern. It is quite simply called the system. It does not permit peace, it guarantees security, by means of competition. It does not promise progress, it guarantees development, by the same means. It has no others. It arouses disparities, it solicits divergences, multiculturalism is agreeable to it but under the condition of an agreement concerning the rules of disagreement. This is what is called consensus. The intrinsic constitution of the system is not subject to radical upheaval, only to revision. Radicalism is becoming rare, as is every search for roots. In politics, alternation is the rule, while the alternative is excluded. Globally, the system functions according to the rules of a game with several players. These rules determine the elements that are allowed and the operations permitted for every domain. The object of the game is always to win. Within the framework of these rules, freedom of strategy is left entirely open. It is forbidden to kill one's adversary.

The system is continually revised by its integration of winning strategies in the various domains: you could say it constructs itself. Its complexification allows it to control and exploit "natural" or "human" energies that were previously dispersed. Health is a silence of the organs, said René Leriche, the surgeon of pain. The system silences noises; in any case, it keeps watch over them.

Two principles of legitimation clashed in the politics and warfare of Modernity: God and the Republic, Race and Universal Humanity, the Proletariat and the Citizen. This conflict for legitimacy, whether national or international, always took the form of civil and total war. Postmodern politics are managerial strategies, its wars, police actions. The latter do not have the aim of delegitimizing the adversary but of constraining it, according to the rules, to negotiate its integration into the system. If it has nothing to add to the game, being too poor, it can at least play out its indebtedness. As for the legitimacy of the system, it consists in its ability to self-construct. Out of this situation where right is based on fact, there result a few difficulties, in the administration of justice, for example, or in the aims of scholarly instruction. Finally, national frontiers are mere abstractions with regard to the needs of development.

In the face of these banal bits of evidence, "geonoetics" appears obsolete. It belongs to a time when thought, *noesis*, believed it could be authorized by a land and its name. German philosophy, the American dream, French thought, "English eyeglasses," as Rosa Luxemburg said. Or rather, it was the reverse: the "spirit" of a people became, for a time, the depository of and witness for a founding Idea: liberty in Athens, Philadelphia, or Paris; imperial peace in Rome, London; the saving race in Berlin or Tokyo. Each of these figures, be it bastardized, a racial Reich, or a republican empire, had a calling for which to fight.

Today, we say that the most appropriate system for development sought itself astride these conflicts between ideals housed under proper names. Each one was measured against its capacity to mobilize and organize the forces available in the demographic area whose name it proudly bore. In 1920, a little after the defeat of the German Empire, Ernst Jünger evaluated the Allied success in these cynically thermodynamic terms: a community of citizens who believe themselves free is better suited for a "total mobilization" than the hierarchical social body of Wilhelm II's subjects. This diagnostic was verified by the outcome of the Second World War and by that of the Cold War. The superiority of capitalist democracy is no longer at issue. Under the perfectly neutral name of system, it in truth emerges triumphant from several millennia passed in trying out all kinds of communitarian organizations. Human history was nothing more than a process of natural selection driven – precisely – by the competition between forms born by chance of the best performing one, the system itself. It's from this henceforth established fact that the world in its present state draws its prestige, or its authority, and it's to that fact that we (including the French …) give our consent: consensus proceeds from this self-evidence.

Need we be more specific? Respect for human rights, the duty of humanitarian aid, the right to intervene (as in Somalia), the status of immigrants and refugees, the protection of minority cultures, the right to work and to lodging, help for the sick and the old, respect for the individual in biological and medical experimentation, the right to schooling, respect for the individual in judicial inquiry and in conditions of incarceration, the right of women over their own bodies, the duty to give financial and technical assistance to the populations left destitute in the wake of the disappearance of the colonial empires and the Soviet Empire: these are, among others, problems to solve, questions to debate, sometimes with urgency. But always playing by the rules of the game, in consensus with the system.

Should this unanimity be called humanist? Yes, of course, if by that we understand that the system must show regard for the human beings of which it is made, but without neglecting, on the other hand, that the system requires the said human beings to bend to the needs of its development. For example, to be precise, they need to admit that, under current conditions, there is certainly no longer enough work for everyone in the production of goods and services. If there is humanism here, it must not, without risking imposture, be taken for the humanism of the Enlightenment. The latter gave itself the ideal aim of a community of equal and enlightened citizens deliberating with utter freedom about decisions to be taken concerning common affairs.

Humanism today is a pragmatism, less contractualist than utilitarian, where utility is calculated according to the supposed needs of individuals as well as those of the system. These needs are supposed, because within the system, games are always played with "partial information," as one said in the time of von Neumann and Rappoport: whatever one expects from opinion polls, statistics, and espionage, for the purposes of better locating one's adversary or partner (who are the same from now on), there remains an invincible margin of chance. (Unless I'm wrong, isn't the "veil of ignorance" John Rawls uses to dramatize his theory of justice simply the old concept of "incomplete information"?) But the system favors this uncertainty since it is not closed.

My point in recalling these banalities is not to signify that the world in which we live has nothing more to offer for thought and intervention. On the contrary, as we've seen, many things must be said and done, and must be proposed, precisely, within that margin of uncertainty that the system leaves to reflection. Who, among us, does not cooperate with this or that local, national, or international association, whose aim is to contribute to the solution of one or more of the – sometimes dramatic – difficulties I've named, or others I haven't named; and who does not publish, in one's own name, the reasons one has for opting toward this solution or that one and for helping to bring it about? We participate in debates, we enlist ourselves in combats no less than our ancestors, the Voltaires, the Deweys, the Zolas, or the Russells have done for two hundred years.

But they did it under wholly different auspices, and for a wholly different price. Their combat invoked some ideal – the Common Folk, Freedom, the Individual, Humanity, in sum – not yet received within the system at that time; or if it was in principle received, it was in point of fact violated. In either case, they exposed themselves to censorship, to juridical proceedings, to prison, exile, to some kind of death finally, not of their body but of their speech. For their speech was insurrectional. As for us, whatever our intervention, we know before speaking or acting that it will be taken into account by the system as a possible contribution to its perfection. It's not that the system is totalitarian, as was long believed, still by Sartre, perhaps by Foucault, to their great disappointment (for no proceedings were ever made against them); on the contrary, its margin of uncertainty is quite open. One can't help but congratulate oneself on this latitude, but one must also measure the price that must be paid by thought and writing, which are our lot, for the attention that surrounds them.

That price was explicitly laid down in the program/article that Pierre Nora, one of the masters of the French school of history, published in the first issue of the journal *Le Débat*, which he had just founded in 1980. The moment had come, he declared in substance, to put an end to the disorder and the terror that reigned in French criticism and philosophy to the point of prohibiting all debate. Posing themselves as the inheritors of the artistic and literary avant-gardes, trying to outdo the incomprehensible poetics of Mallarmé or Artaud, reveling in the sibylline prose of the likes of Heidegger or Lacan, Parisian writers and thinkers were forming groups who waged a war of words with each other, taking no care to make themselves understood by each other or by the public. Every sect pursued in schizo-phrenic fashion the illegible exercise of its talent. These irresponsible ones had ripped the cultural tissue to shreds, as the warfare between clans had in another time torn Gaul apart. It was time that some "Roman legion" brought order out of this anarchy and reconstituted, through debate, the order of the mind.

May Pierre Nora pardon me, I am too far from my hometown to cite the exact words of his text. I'm relying here on the impression of stupor that struck me in reading his text. We had an enemy, who showed himself, out in the open, in order to impose a *pax romana* on our domestic squabbles. He was advancing with the "heavy step of the Roman legions" – I remember that menacing metaphor. The new order did not take long in coming. The "new philosophers" in the workings of thought, the new subjectivity and trans-avantgardism in the visual arts, a poetics of procedures and genres, a genetics of texts, a sociology of cultural facts (considered to be merely the effects of forces at play in the social field), a history of mentalities, which in particular led to a treatment of the fact of revolution as a symptom: everything that called itself human science and positive reason advanced, with the noted "heavy step," to impose dialogue and argument on the aggressive and confused scriveners that we were. This spirit of seriousness had an assured advantage over us, which is that it had to exert no effort in attracting the favor of public opinion and of the media, which asked above all "to be able to know where they were" within the affairs of thought. The writings of the Roman Party were soon found on every dentist's coffee table, as Picabia used to say.

My stupor was as follows: Could the *Essays* of Montaigne become the object of a debate and would one be able to know where one was in reading them? Augustine's *Confessions*? *A Season in Hell*? But also Hegel's *Phenomenology*? And that of Husserl, or of Merleau-Ponty? Claude Simon's *Georgics*, *Doktor Faustus*, *The Castle*? What was there to debate, and how then to know where you were, in *Les Demoiselles d'Avignon*, in Delaunay's *Eiffel Tour*, Cage's *Mureau*, or Boulez's *Répons*, in Beethoven's thirteenth string quartet? Whether their material was language, timbre, or color, wasn't there some solitude, some retreat, some excess beyond all possible discourse, the silence of some terror, in the works of thought? And not out of capriciousness, fashion, or bravura, but in essence – if it was true, as Apollinaire said, that the work of art requires the artist to become inhuman. Is it possible without terror to bring something you don't understand to "signify" by means you don't control, since those means must be liberated from the ones tradition has controlled?

For works of art to be destined for entry in, or to have already entered, the World Museum, and to be catalogued in the Universal Library, and consequently filed away in the cultural stockpile, in memory, in rhetoric, which the system needs for differentiating itself, changes nothing pertaining to the fact that those works were never "produced" (what a word!) by the system, but only contextualized, being neither with it nor against it. They were born elsewhere, however, far from all communicational transparency: they are cultural objects, of course, and more or less accessible to the community, but irreducible to its usages or mentalities through the stunning power that we call their beauty and that resists the passage of time. This resistance and this opacity must be respected in the reception of works of art, even when one is trying to make commentary on them. Commenting is neither debating nor "finding where you are." It's rather about letting that residue follow itself out and allowing oneself to get lost in it: terror, once again.

I was not giving the works I cited by way of example with the intention of equating our poor essays with their greatness, but rather to recall that, in the face of what's called creation, the spirit of seriousness is not serious, nor are the claims of reason reasonable. True scholars are not unaware that this is how it is with scientific inventions: their appearance is no less wondrous than that of arts and letters; the state of knowledge in their time does not explain why they emerge; often they are resisted by that state of knowledge.

It does not follow that it suffices to be obscure in order to attain the measurelessness I am talking about. Nor to oppose a stony silence to the questions asked of a work of art in order to be its defender. Of those works I've cited, more than one was very civil and lent itself to discussion. That had no great importance, it did not hold the secret of the thing any more than another, but it may have liked to talk about it. Between the artist's studio or writer's desk – desperately lonely or rather deserted for the benefit of something unknown – and the armchair of conversation or roundtables, the gap remained and it remains unbridgeable.

Imagine Flaubert chatting about *Madame Bovary* with Bernard Pivot.[1] He would certainly have been able to do so, with all his knowing how to deal with received ideas. But how could Flaubert succeed in making the project of writing clear to our dear viewers, that overly subtle project that is less the project of writing about the distress of the petite-bourgeoisie than the misery of the model, received from the rhetoric of romanticism, by which it thinks it can express and soothe that distress? (And how, let us add in passing, could he make this clear to theorists of reception? Reception theory is precisely what Flaubert did in *The Dictionary of Received Ideas*, and in *Bouvard and Pécuchet*.)

I mention Flaubert, the Idiot in the family, because he was one of the first, like Baudelaire, to confront the stupidity of the system. Baudelaire writes in his *Notebooks*: "I cultivated my hysteria with joy and terror. Now, I've always got this vertigo, and today January 23, 1862, I felt before me *the breeze of imbecility flapping its wing*" (*Oeuvres complètes*, Pléiade edition, p. 1265). If you have to go to the point of becoming an imbecile, it's because "the world is about to end." We know this text, this "hors-d'oeuvre," as Baudelaire so appropriately calls it, which describes that outside-of-every-work that the world is in the process of becoming under the poet's horrified eyes. It's the stupid world of total exchangeability, under the rule of money, the general equivalent for all commodities: goods, bodies, and souls. Our world (the system) is but the extension to language of the same routine of exchange: interlocution, interactiveness, transparency, and debate, words are exchanged for words as use value is exchanged for use value. Poetic hysteria abruptly cuts off the circuit of repetitions. It confesses that it cultivates its retreat with joy and terror.

Where I hear repetition, Jürgen Habermas and Manfred Frank decipher a promise of liberty and equality. Isn't it true that messages are exchanged on the condition that they are comprehensible? And on the condition that you and I can occupy the positions of locutor and allocutor, one after the other. Richard Rorty goes so far as to maintain that this pragmatic condition is sufficient by itself to guarantee democratic solidarity, regardless of what is said or the manner in which it is said. Language may be "blank," like in Camus's *The Stranger*, but what matters is that it be addressed to someone else.

Human languages structurally confer on the locutor the capacity to speak to others. But capacity is not duty. It has not yet been proved that a willed silence constituted a fault. What is a crime is to impose that silence on another, who is then excluded from the interlocutory community. Moreover, an even greater wrong is added to this injustice, since the one who is banished, being prohibited from speaking, has no means to appeal his/her banishment. Whether political, social, or cultural, the exercise of terror is as follows: to deprive the other of the ability to respond to that deprivation. Whatever else you may think, the death penalty however legalized always evokes this crime. But it could just as well be said that the child whose playmates say they will no longer play with him/her and refuse to talk about it is in truth the victim of a crime against humanity.

It is thus taken for granted that the human community rests upon the capacity for interlocution and upon the right to interlocution and that it's up to the republic to watch over this right and to teach that capacity. This thing – a banality, to speak truthfully – must be clearly stated in order to put an end to the accusations of irrationalism, obscurantism, terrorism, and sometimes fascism that have been leveled, here and there, against so-called French thought. It would be fastidious to refute in detail each one of these counts. The following ought to suffice: just as terror, and the abjection that is its doublet, must be excluded from the regime of the community, so must it be sustained and assumed, singularly, in writing as its condition.

That said, it is not forbidden to feel some unease on the subject of what founded, and perhaps still founds, the republican community itself. I know the system could care less and is trying to forget the Revolutionary Terror in France two centuries ago. Let's say, then, that the following reflections will have no importance.

In December 1792, during the trial of the king, held in his presence at the National Convention, Saint-Just turned to the right, on which side the Gironde was seated, and he declared: "This man must reign or die." The alternative excluded survival. Louis Capet could not enter into the republican community. As king, he held his authority from God. The only law the republic knows is that of liberty. When the head of Louis XVI was cut off in January 1793 in the Place de la Révolution, God was the one whose word was cut off. The republic, and hence interlocution, can only be founded upon a deicide; it begins with the nihilist assertion that there is no Other. Are these the beginnings of an orphaned humanity? That's not what Saint-Just understands. Nothing is more suspicious than an orphan, who incarnates metaphysical melancholia, whose thoughts keep alive the vanished father and mother. It is necessary that the mourning be completed. "Happiness," Saint-Just decides, "is a novel idea in Europe." Happiness, the forgetting of the murder, is a republican duty. Just one more effort. ...

While waiting for this terrible civic paradise, melancholics must be held in suspicion. This man who must either reign or die is the king, but every man must both reign as liberty and die as submission. Every motivation other than the fulfillment of the law of liberty is subject to suspicion: passions, interests, everything that lends itself to tyranny in the soul of the empirical people. Saint-Just's alternative thus draws a line between democracy, which is tyranny, Kant says, and a holy republic.

But where do you draw the edge of this line? Liberty, first of all, is an idea of reason, which is never unequivocally incarnated in experience. There is never any assurance that a given decree, taken in the name of reason, does not conceal unavowable motivations. Can one ever be sufficiently liberated of these, and how could you know it? Everyone, starting with Robespierre, is suspicious to him- or herself. Terror is exerted intimately.

And then, if liberty is what speaks the law, what can the law be, except: be free? Liberty is pure beginning. It is unaware of what was before its action, and thus too of the traces left by its previous actions. What can it institute? It cannot avoid dreading its works, on the same level as everything that precedes its present action, the entire ancien régime of the soul. Intimate Terror exerts itself without respite.

Do we need to recall these well-known things? Obviously, they must be recalled for the benefit of our adversaries. Their interest in consensus is surely not wholly republican in nature; it's also in the interest of the system, as I've said, in the interest of its calculations, which Baudelaire called Prostitution. And even if we give credit to their virtue, we beg them to remember the crime of which she is the child. The horizon of universal intelligibility to which they appeal has been detached by a bloody stroke. The price of the deicide cannot be measured, the debt of reparation will never be acquitted by some reasonable exchange on the subject, because that very exchange, its liberty and its right, are due to the crime.

The Terror is not just the historical event we know. Its gesture of interruption is repeated every time the republic legislates, every time the citizen speaks up. Liberty is supposed to be what pronounces the law, for all and for each, but it can never be sure that it is not corrupted by some utilitarian end. The era of suspicion is not ready to come to a close. Did Saint-Just know that the Terror would be the lot of a world dedicated to liberty? That brother would not cease to contest the authority of brother, that every tribunal could be impugned, that, for two centuries, Europe and the world would make war to decide how the law is incarnated and what it says? Politics became modern tragedy, Napoleon said. That's over now, and in consensus, we celebrate the disappearance of those quarrels of investiture.

That does not change the persistence of the torment, for "sensitive souls," of not being what one is, of being another and of not being that other, of having to answer to that other and for that other, who asks nothing definite. Augustine was the first, along with Paul, to reveal that inner split between the ego and the Other, who within the ego is deeper than the ego. Deeper insofar as the ego cannot comprehend the Other. Yet, Augustine still had faith that this Other, the God of love, wished only the good.

After the deicide, God did not succumb. Baudelaire writes: "God is the only being who does not even need to exist in order to reign." He reigns therefore, but his decrees, if there even are any, are incomprehensible. Even his law is suspect. How can we decide that what the Other inspires in us is not due to Satan? Evil is not the opposite of Good, it is the indecidability between Good and Evil. Just as corruption can pass for a virtue, Satan can pass for God. Bernanos said that faith today is to believe in Satan. But this is still to believe that the scandal will be pardoned. Now, the law of liberty, without permitted faith, has no power to keep this promise. Consensus is not to redeem the crime, it is to forget it. We are asked to help resolve the injustices that abound in the world. We do it. But the anguish of which I speak is of another temper than that of civic concerns. It resists the republic and the system, it is older than them, it protects and flees at the same time the inhuman stranger within us, "joy and terror," says Baudelaire.

If works of art are still possible, if the system is not what alone produces them and addresses them to itself, if therefore literature, art, and thought are not dead, it is because they hysterically cultivate this relation with what is irrelevant. Baudelaire says hysteria because this relation must inscribe itself – this is what writing means – and because it must trace itself in the matter of bodies, colors, sounds, in words too, that overabundant matter. Not in order to have a dialogue with these matters and for them to "speak" clearly (there is no need of writing for that), but to give them back to *their* silence, which makes so much noise in the human body, to expose them to their potentiality and to obtain from them the gesture of a poem.

Jean Paulhan, in *Les Fleurs de Tarbes* (The Flowers of Tarbes), subtitled *La Terreur dans les Lettres* (Terrorism in Literature),[2] expressed his astonishment that the criticism of his time (this was the time of the Occupation, and Paulhan was occupied in working with a network of resistance – a lovely expression) kept on deploring the place given to the matter of language in writings of literature. They are only words, this criticism repeated, believing, along with Bergson, that language is merely the dead discards living thought leaves after itself. And so it is that Pierre Nora and many others enjoin us to be legible and communicable, to be consensual, in a word.

But if it's a question of writing, painting, or composing, what does one encounter right off the bat? Words, sounds, colors, not in a raw state, of course, but already organized by the rhetorics we have inherited, and also predisposed by our temperament in what Barthes after Buffon called a style: a history, a nature. And writing is the labor that aims to silence that learned or spontaneous eloquence. Here, terror exerts itself, to impose silence, and with regard to what is closest to us, to cut off the most familiar repetitions and expressions. By the same stroke, as with the law of liberty, a followup terror is set up, subjugating the previous terror for not knowing what it is that is desired in those mute and noisy matters.

The intellectual, once upon a time, was a happy writer or artist: his/her works, though obtained under the conditions we've described, had in themselves the power to call civil or political society back to its ideal destination. Intellectuals today do not need to be exposed to the trials of writing. They are called upon by the system to make public proclamations, for the sole reason that they know a little better than others how *to make use* of language to restate the urgency of consensus. The terror of which I speak comes down to this, that if one writes, it is forbidden to make use of language, which is the Other. One can, one must, do the intellectual thing on the speaker's platform. But in front of the canvas or the page, consensus is null and void.

Chapter 14

Fredric Jameson

■ from *POSTMODERNISM, OR, THE CULTURAL LOGIC OF LATE CAPITALISM*,[1] London: Verso, 1991

T**HE LAST FEW YEARS HAVE BEEN MARKED** by an inverted millenarianism in which premonitions of the future, catastrophic or redemptive, have been replaced by senses of the end of this or that (the end of ideology, art, or social class; the "crisis" of Leninism, social democracy, or the welfare state, etc., etc.); taken together, all of these perhaps constitute what is increasingly called postmodernism. The case for its existence depends on the hypothesis of some radical break or *coupure*, generally traced back to the end of the 1950s or the early 1960s.

As the word itself suggests, this break is most often related to notions of the waning or extinction of the hundred-year-old modern movement (or to its ideological or aesthetic repudiation). Thus abstract expressionism in painting, existentialism in philosophy, the final forms of representation in the novel, the films of the great *auteurs*, or the modernist school of poetry (as institutionalized and canonized in the works of Wallace Stevens) all are now seen as the final, extraordinary flowering of a high-modernist impulse which is spent and exhausted with them. The enumeration of what follows, then, at once becomes empirical, chaotic, and heterogeneous: Andy Warhol and pop art, but also photorealism, and beyond it, the "new expressionism"; the moment, in music, of John Cage, but also the synthesis of classical and "popular" styles found in composers like Phil Glass and Terry Riley, and also punk and new wave rock (the Beatles and the Stones now standing as the high-modernist moment of that more recent and rapidly evolving tradition); in film, Godard, post-Godard, and experimental cinema and video, but also a whole new type of commercial film (about which more below); Burroughs, Pynchon, or Ishmael Reed, on the one hand, and the French *nouveau roman* and its succession, on the other, along with alarming new kinds of literary criticism based on some new aesthetic of textuality or *écriture* ... The list might be extended indefinitely; but does it imply any more fundamental change or break than the periodic style and fashion changes determined by an older high-modernist imperative of stylistic innovation?

It is in the realm of architecture, however, that modifications in aesthetic production are most dramatically visible, and that their theoretical problems have been most centrally raised and articulated; it was indeed from architectural debates that my own conception of postmodernism – as it will be outlined in the following pages – initially began to emerge. More decisively than in the other arts or media, postmodernist positions in architecture have been inseparable from an implacable critique of architectural high modernism and of Frank Lloyd Wright or the so-called international style (Le Corbusier, Mies, etc.), where formal criticism and analysis (of the high-modernist transformation of the building into a virtual sculpture, or monumental "duck," as Robert Venturi puts it)[2] are at one with reconsiderations on the level of urbanism and of the aesthetic institution. High modernism is thus credited with the destruction of the fabric of the traditional city and its older neighborhood culture (by way of the radical disjunction of the new Utopian high-modernist building from its surrounding context), while the prophetic elitism and authoritarianism of the modern movement are remorselessly identified in the imperious gesture of the charismatic Master.

Postmodernism in architecture will then logically enough stage itself as a kind of aesthetic populism, as the very title of Venturi's influential manifesto, *Learning from Las Vegas*, suggests. However we may ultimately wish to evaluate this populist rhetoric,[3] it has at least the merit of drawing our attention to one fundamental feature of all the postmodernisms enumerated above: namely, the effacement in them of the older (essentially high-modernist) frontier between high culture and so-called mass or commercial culture, and the emergence of new kinds of texts infused with the forms, categories, and contents of that very culture industry so passionately denounced by all the ideologues of the modern, from Leavis and the American New Criticism all the way to Adorno and the Frankfurt School. The postmodernisms have, in fact, been fascinated precisely by this whole "degraded" landscape of schlock and kitsch, of TV series and *Reader's Digest* culture, of advertising and motels, of the late show and the grade-B Hollywood film, of so-called paraliterature, with its airport paperback categories of the gothic and the romance, the popular biography, the murder mystery, and the science fiction or fantasy novel: materials they no longer simply "quote," as a Joyce or a Mahler might have done, but incorporate into their very substance.

Nor should the break in question be thought of as a purely cultural affair: indeed, theories of the postmodern – whether celebratory or couched in the language of moral revulsion and denunciation – bear a strong family resemblance to all those more ambitious sociological generalizations which, at much the same time, bring us the news of the arrival and inauguration of a whole new type of society, most famously baptized "postindustrial society" (Daniel Bell) but often also designated consumer society, media society, information society, electronic society or high tech, and the like. Such theories have the obvious ideological mission of demonstrating, to their own relief, that the new social formation in question no longer obeys the laws of classical capitalism, namely, the primacy of industrial production and the omnipresence of class struggle. The Marxist tradition has therefore resisted them with vehemence, with the signal exception of the economist Ernest Mandel, whose book *Late Capitalism*[4] sets out not merely to anatomize the historic originality of this new society (which he sees as a third stage or moment in the evolution of capital) but also to demonstrate that it is, if anything, a purer stage of capitalism than any of the moments that preceded it. [...]

A last preliminary word on method: what follows is not to be read as stylistic description, as the account of one cultural style or movement among others. I have rather meant to offer a periodizing hypothesis, and that at a moment in which the very conception of historical periodization has come to seem most problematical indeed. I have argued elsewhere that all isolated or discrete cultural analysis always involves a buried or repressed theory of historical periodization; in any case, the conception of the "genealogy" largely lays to rest traditional theoretical worries about so-called linear history, theories of "stages," and teleological historiography. In the present context, however, lengthier theoretical discussion of such (very real) issues can perhaps be replaced by a few substantive remarks.

One of the concerns frequently aroused by periodizing hypotheses is that these tend to obliterate difference and to project an idea of the historical period as massive homogeneity (bounded on either side by inexplicable chronological metamorphoses and punctuation marks). This is, however, precisely why it seems to me essential to grasp postmodernism not as a style but rather as a cultural dominant [...].

What has happened is that aesthetic production today has become integrated into commodity production generally: the frantic economic urgency of producing fresh waves of ever more novel-seeming goods (from clothing to airplanes), at ever greater rates of turnover, now assigns an increasingly essential structural function and position to aesthetic innovation and experimentation. Such economic necessities then find recognition in the varied kinds of institutional support available for the newer art, from foundations and grants to museums and other forms of patronage. [...] Yet this is the point at which I must remind the reader of the obvious; namely, that this whole global, yet American, postmodern culture is the internal and superstructural expression of a whole new wave of American military and economic domination throughout the world: in this sense, as throughout class history, the underside of culture is blood, torture, death, and terror.

The first point to be made about the conception of periodization in dominance, therefore, is that even if all the constitutive features of postmodernism were identical with and coterminous to those of an older modernism [...] the two phenomena would still remain utterly distinct in their meaning and social function, owing to the very different positioning of postmodernism in the economic system of late capital and, beyond that, to the transformation of the very sphere of culture in contemporary society. [...]

I have felt, however, that it was only in the light of some conception of a dominant cultural logic or hegemonic norm that genuine difference could be measured and assessed. I am very far from feeling that all cultural production today is "postmodern" in the broad sense I will be conferring on this term. The postmodern is, however, the force field in which very different kinds of cultural impulses – what Raymond Williams has usefully termed "residual" and "emergent" – forms of cultural production – must make their way. If we do not achieve some general sense of a cultural dominant, then we fall back into a view of present history as sheer heterogeneity, random difference, a coexistence of a host of distinct forces whose effectivity is undecidable. At any rate, this has been the political spirit in which the following analysis was devised: to project some conception of a new systematic cultural norm and its reproduction in order to reflect more adequately on the most effective forms of any radical cultural politics today.

The exposition will take up in turn the following constitutive features of the post-modern: a new depthlessness, which finds its prolongation both in contemporary "theory" and in a whole new culture of the image or the simulacrum; a consequent weakening of historicity, both in our relationship to public History and in the new forms of our private temporality, whose "schizophrenic" structure (following Lacan) will determine new types of syntax or syntagmatic relationships in the more temporal arts; a whole new type of emotional ground tone – what I will call "intensities" – which can best be grasped by a return to older theories of the sublime; the deep constitutive relationships of all this to a whole new technology, which is itself a figure for a whole new economic world system. [...]

This is perhaps the moment to say something about contemporary theory, which has, among other things, been committed to the mission of criticizing and discrediting this very hermeneutic model of the inside and the outside and of stigmatizing such models as ideological and metaphysical. But what is today called contemporary theory – or better still, theoretical discourse – is also, I want to argue, itself very precisely a postmodernist phenomenon. It would therefore be inconsistent to defend the truth of its theoretical insights in a situation in which the very concept of "truth" itself is part of the metaphysical baggage which poststructuralism seeks to abandon. What we can at least suggest is that the poststructuralist critique of the hermeneutic, of what I will shortly call the depth model, is useful for us as a very significant symptom of the very postmodernist culture which is our subject here.

Overhastily, we can say that besides the hermeneutic model of inside and outside [...], at least four other fundamental depth models have generally been repudiated in contemporary theory:

1   the dialectical one of essence and appearance (along with a whole range of concepts of ideology or false consciousness which tend to accompany it);
2   the Freudian model of latent and manifest, or of repression (which is, of course, the target of Michel Foucault's programmatic and symptomatic pamphlet *La Volonté de savoir* [*The History of Sexuality*]);
3   the existential model of authenticity and inauthenticity whose heroic or tragic thematics are closely related to that other great opposition between alienation and disalienation, itself equally a casualty of the poststructural or postmodern period; and
4   most recently, the great semiotic opposition between signifier and signified, which was itself rapidly unraveled and deconstructed during its brief heyday in the 1960s and 1970s. What replaces these various depth models is for the most part a conception of practices, discourses, and textual play [...]; let it suffice now to observe that here too depth is replaced by surface, or by multiple surfaces (what is often called inter-textuality is in that sense no longer a matter of depth).

[...] All of which suggests some more general historical hypothesis: namely, that concepts such as anxiety and alienation [...] are no longer appropriate in the world of the postmodern. The great Warhol figures – Marilyn herself or Edie Sedgewick – the notorious cases of burnout and self-destruction of the ending 1960s, and the great dominant experiences of drugs and schizophrenia, would seem to have little enough in common any more either with the hysterics and neurotics of Freud's own day or with those canonical experiences of radical isolation and solitude, anomie, private revolt, Van Gogh-type madness, which dominated the period of high modernism. This shift in the dynamics of cultural pathology can be characterized as one in which the alienation of the subject is displaced by the latter's fragmentation.

Such terms inevitably recall one of the more fashionable themes in contemporary theory, that of the "death" of the subject itself – the end of the autonomous bourgeois monad or ego or individual – and the accompanying stress, whether as some new moral ideal or as empirical description, on the *decentering* of that formerly centered subject or psyche. (Of the two possible formulations of this notion – the historicist one, that a once-existing centered subject, in the period of classical capitalism and the nuclear family, has today in the world of organizational bureaucracy dissolved; and the more radical post-structuralist position, for which such a subject never existed in the first place but constituted something like an ideological mirage [. . .]).

[. . .] Postmodernism presumably signals the end of this dilemma, which it replaces with a new one. The end of the bourgeois ego, or monad, no doubt brings with it the end of the psychopathologies of that ego – what I have been calling the waning of affect. But it means the end of much more – the end, for example, of style, in the sense of the unique and the personal, the end of the distinctive individual brush stroke (as symbolized by the emergent primacy of mechanical reproduction). As for expression and feelings or emotions, the liberation, in contemporary society, from the older *anomie* of the centered subject may also mean not merely a liberation from anxiety but a liberation from every other kind of feeling as well, since there is no longer a self present to do the feeling. This is not to say that the cultural products of the postmodern era are utterly devoid of feeling, but rather that such feelings – which it may be better and more accurate, following J.-F. Lyotard, to call "intensities" – are now free-floating and impersonal and tend to be dominated by a peculiar kind of euphoria [. . .].

[. . .] Cultural production [in the postmodern age] is thereby driven back inside a mental space which is no longer that of the old monadic subject but rather that of some degraded collective "objective spirit": it can no longer gaze directly on some putative real world, at some reconstruction of a past history which was once itself a present; rather, as in Plato's cave, it must trace our mental images of that past upon its confining walls. If there is any realism left here, it is a "realism" that is meant to derive from the shock of grasping that confinement and of slowly becoming aware of a new and original historical situation in which we are condemned to seek History by way of our own pop images and simulacra of that history, which itself remains forever out of reach.

The crisis in historicity now dictates a return, in a new way, to the question of temporal organization in general in the postmodern force field, and indeed, to the problem of the form that time, temporality, and the syntagmatic will be able to take in a culture increasingly dominated by space and spatial logic. If, indeed, the subject has lost its capacity actively to extend its pro-tensions and re-tensions across the temporal manifold and to organize its past and future into coherent experience, it becomes difficult enough to see how the cultural productions of such a subject could result in anything but "heaps of fragments" and in a practice of the randomly heterogeneous and fragmentary and the aleatory. These are, however, very precisely some of the privileged terms in which postmodernist cultural production has been analyzed (and even defended, by its own apologists). They are, however, still privative features; the more substantive formulations bear such names as textuality, *écriture*, or schizophrenic writing, and it is to these that we must now briefly turn.

I have found Lacan's account of schizophrenia useful here not because I have any way of knowing whether it has clinical accuracy but chiefly because – as description rather than diagnosis – it seems to me to offer a suggestive aesthetic model.[5] [. . .]

Very briefly, Lacan describes schizophrenia as a breakdown in the signifying chain, that is, the interlocking syntagmatic series of signifiers which constitutes an utterance or a meaning. I must omit the familial or more orthodox psychoanalytic background to this situation, which Lacan transcodes into language by describing the Oedipal rivalry in terms not so much of the biological individual who is your rival for the mother's attention but rather of what he calls the Name-of-the-Father, paternal authority now considered as a linguistic function.[6] His conception of the signifying chain essentially presupposes one of the basic principles (and one of the great discoveries) of Saussurean structuralism, namely, the proposition that meaning is not a one-to-one relationship between signifier and signified, between the materiality of language, between a word or a name, and its referent or concept. Meaning on the new view is generated by the movement from signifier to signifier. What we generally call the signified – the meaning or conceptual content of an utterance – is now rather to be seen as a meaning-effect, as that objective mirage of signification generated and projected by the relationship of signifiers among themselves. When that relationship breaks down, when the links of the signifying chain snap, then we have schizophrenia in the form of a rubble of distinct and unrelated signifiers. The connection between this kind of linguistic malfunction and the psyche of the schizophrenic may then be grasped by way of a twofold proposition: first, that personal identity is itself the effect of a certain temporal unification of past and future with one's present; and, second, that such active temporal unification is itself a function of language, or better still of the sentence, as it moves along its hermeneutic circle through time. If we are similarly unable to unify the past, present, and future of the sentence, then we are unable to unify the past, present, and future of our own biographical experience or psychic life. With the breakdown of the signifying chain, therefore, the schizophrenic is reduced to an experience of pure material signifiers, or, in other words, a series of pure and unrelated presents in time. [...]

In our present context, this experience suggests the following: first, the breakdown of temporality suddenly releases this present of time from all the activities and intentionalities that might focus it and make it a space of praxis; thereby isolated, that present suddenly engulfs the subject with undescribable vividness, a materiality of perception properly overwhelming, which effectively dramatizes the power of the material – or better still, the literal – signifier in isolation. This present of the world or material signifier comes before the subject with heightened intensity, bearing a mysterious charge of affect, here described in the negative terms of anxiety and loss of reality, but which one could just as well imagine in the positive terms of euphoria, a high, an intoxicatory or hallucinogenic intensity.

[...] This account of schizophrenia and temporal organization might, however, have been formulated in a different way, which brings us back to Heidegger's notion of a gap or rift between Earth and World, albeit in a fashion that is sharply incompatible with the tone and high seriousness of his own philosophy. I would like to characterize the postmodernist experience of form with what will seem, I hope, a paradoxical slogan: namely, the proposition that "difference relates." [...]

[...] It has proved fruitful to think of [the experiences of postmodern culture] in terms of what Susan Sontag, in an influential statement, isolated as "camp." I propose a somewhat different cross-light on it, drawing on the equally fashionable current theme of the "sublime," as it has been rediscovered in the works of Edmund Burke and Kant: or perhaps one might want to yoke the two notions together in the form of something like a camp or "hysterical" sublime. The sublime was for Burke an experience bordering on terror, the fitful glimpse, in astonishment, stupor, and awe, of what was so enormous as to crush human life altogether: a description then refined by Kant to include the question of representation itself, so that the object of the sublime becomes not only a matter of sheer power and of the physical incommensurability of the human organism with Nature but also of the limits of figuration and the incapacity of the human mind to give representation to such enormous forces. Such forces Burke, in his historical moment at the dawn of the modern bourgeois state, was only able to conceptualize in terms of the divine, while even Heidegger continues to entertain a phantasmatic relationship with some organic precapitalist peasant landscape and village society, which is the final form of the image of Nature in our own time.

Today, however, it may be possible to think all this in a different way, at the moment of a radical eclipse of Nature itself: Heidegger's "field path" is, after all, irredeemably and irrevocably destroyed by late capital, by the green revolution, by neocolonialism and the megalopolis, which runs its superhighways over the older fields and vacant lots and turns Heidegger's "house of being" into condominiums, if not the most miserable unheated, rat-infested tenement buildings. The *other* of our society is in that sense no longer Nature at all, as it was in precapitalist societies, but something else which we must now identify.

I am anxious that this other thing not overhastily be grasped as technology per se, since I will want to show that technology is here itself a figure for something else. Yet technology may well serve as adequate shorthand to designate that enormous properly human and anti-natural power of dead human labor stored up in our machinery – an alienated power, what Sartre calls the counterfinality of the practico-inert, which turns back on and against us in unrecognizable forms and seems to constitute the massive dystopian horizon of our collective as well as our individual praxis.

Technological development is however on the Marxist view the result of the development of capital rather than some ultimately determining instance in its own right. It will therefore be appropriate to distinguish several generations of machine power, several stages of technological revolution within capital itself. I here follow Ernest Mandel, who outlines three such fundamental breaks or quantum leaps in the evolution of machinery under capital. [. . .]

[Mandel's] periodization underscores the general thesis of [his] book *Late Capitalism*; namely, that there have been three fundamental moments in capitalism, each one marking a dialectical expansion over the previous stage. These are market capitalism, the monopoly stage or the stage of imperialism, and our own, wrongly called postindustrial, but what might better be termed multinational, capital. I have already pointed out that Mandel's intervention in the postindustrial debate involves the proposition that late or multinational or consumer capitalism, far from being inconsistent with Marx's great nineteenth-century analysis, constitutes, on the contrary, the purest form of capital yet to have emerged, a prodigious expansion of capital into hitherto uncommodified areas. This purer capitalism of our own time thus eliminates the enclaves of precapitalist organization it had hitherto tolerated and exploited in a tributary way. One is tempted to speak in this connection of a new and historically original penetration and colonization of Nature and the Unconscious: that is, the destruction of precapitalist Third World agriculture by the Green Revolution, and the rise of the media and the advertising industry. At any rate, it will also have been clear that my own cultural periodization of the stages of realism, modernism, and postmodernism is both inspired and confirmed by Mandel's tripartite scheme.

We may therefore speak of our own period as the Third Machine Age; and it is at this point that we must reintroduce the problem of aesthetic representation already explicitly developed in Kant's earlier analysis of the sublime, since it would seem only logical that the relationship to and the representation of the machine could be expected to shift dialectically with each of these qualitatively different stages of technological development.

It is appropriate to recall the excitement of machinery in the moment of capital preceding our own, the exhilaration of futurism, most notably, and of Marinetti's celebration of the machine gun and the motorcar. These are still visible emblems, sculptural nodes of energy which give tangibility and figuration to the motive energies of that earlier moment of modernization. The prestige of these great streamlined shapes can be measured by their metaphorical presence in Le Corbusier's buildings, vast Utopian structures which ride like so many gigantic steamship liners upon the urban scenery of an older fallen earth.[7] […]

It is immediately obvious that the technology of our own moment no longer possesses this same capacity for representation: not the turbine, nor even Sheeler's grain elevators or smokestacks, not the baroque elaboration of pipes and conveyor belts, nor even the streamlined profile of the railroad train — all vehicles of speed still concentrated at rest — but rather the computer, whose outer shell has no emblematic or visual power, or even the casings of the various media themselves, as with that home appliance called television which articulates nothing but rather implodes, carrying its flattened image surface within itself.

Such machines are indeed machines of reproduction rather than of production, and they make very different demands on our capacity for aesthetic representation than did the relatively mimetic idolatry of the older machinery of the futurist moment, of some older speed-and-energy sculpture. Here we have less to do with kinetic energy than with all kinds of new reproductive processes; and in the weaker productions of postmodernism the aesthetic embodiment of such processes often tends to slip back more comfortably into a mere thematic representation of content — into narratives which are *about* the processes of reproduction and include movie cameras, video, tape recorders, the whole technology of the production and reproduction of the simulacrum. […]

Yet something else does tend to emerge in the most energetic postmodernist texts, and this is the sense that beyond all thematics or content the work seems somehow to tap the networks of the reproductive process and thereby to afford us some glimpse into a postmodern or technological sublime, whose power or authenticity is documented by the success of such works in evoking a whole new postmodern space in emergence around us. Architecture therefore remains in this sense the privileged aesthetic language; and the distorting and fragmenting reflections of one enormous glass surface to the other can be taken as paradigmatic of the central role of process and reproduction in postmodernist culture.

As I have said, however, I want to avoid the implication that technology is in any way the "ultimately determining instance" either of our present-day social life or of our cultural production: such a thesis is, of course, ultimately at one with the post-Marxist notion of a postindustrial society. Rather, I want to suggest that our faulty representations of some immense communicational and computer network are themselves but a distorted figuration of something even deeper, namely, the whole world system of a present-day multinational capitalism. The technology of contemporary society is therefore mesmerizing and fascinating not so much in its own right but because it seems to offer some privileged representational shorthand for grasping a network of power and control even more difficult for our minds and imaginations to grasp: the whole new decentered global network of the third stage of capital itself. This is a figural process presently best observed in a whole mode of contemporary entertainment literature — one is tempted to characterize it as "high-tech paranoia" — in which the circuits and networks of some putative global computer hookup are narratively mobilized by labyrinthine conspiracies of autonomous but deadly interlocking and competing information agencies in a complexity often beyond the capacity of the normal reading mind. Yet conspiracy theory (and its garish narrative manifestations) must be seen as a degraded attempt — through the figuration of advanced technology — to think the impossible totality of the contemporary world system. It is in terms of that enormous and threatening, yet only dimly perceivable, other reality of economic and social institutions that, in my opinion, the postmodern sublime can alone be adequately theorized. [...]

The conception of postmodernism outlined here is a historical rather than a merely stylistic one. I cannot stress too greatly the radical distinction between a view for which the postmodern is one (optional) style among many others available and one which seeks to grasp it as the cultural dominant of the logic of late capitalism: the two approaches in fact generate two very different ways of conceptualizing the phenomenon as a whole: on the one hand, moral judgments (about which it is indifferent whether they are positive or negative), and, on the other, a genuinely dialectical attempt to think our present of time in History.

Of some positive moral evaluation of postmodernism little needs to be said: the complacent (yet delirious) camp-following celebration of this aesthetic new world (including its social and economic dimension, greeted with equal enthusiasm under the slogan of "postindustrial society") is surely unacceptable, although it may be somewhat less obvious that current fantasies about the salvational nature of high technology, from chips to robots — fantasies entertained not only by both left and right governments in distress but also by many intellectuals — are also essentially of a piece with more vulgar apologias for post-modernism.

But in that case it is only consequent to reject moralizing condemnations of the postmodern and of its essential triviality when juxtaposed against the Utopian "high seriousness" of the great modernisms: judgments one finds both on the Left and on the radical Right. And no doubt the logic of the simulacrum, with its transformation of older realities into television images, does more than merely replicate the logic of late capitalism; it reinforces and intensifies it. Meanwhile, for political groups which seek actively to intervene in history and to modify its otherwise passive momentum (whether with a view toward channeling it into a socialist transformation of society or diverting it into the regressive reestablishment of some simpler fantasy past), there cannot but be much that is deplorable and reprehensible in a cultural form of image addiction which, by transforming the past into visual mirages, stereotypes, or texts, effectively abolishes any practical sense of the future and of the collective project, thereby abandoning the thinking of future change to fantasies of sheer catastrophe and inexplicable cataclysm, from visions of "terrorism" on the social level to those of cancer on the personal. Yet if postmodernism is a historical phenomenon, then the attempt to conceptualize it in terms of moral or moralizing judgments must finally be identified as a category mistake. All of which becomes more obvious when we interrogate the position of the cultural critic and moralist; the latter, along with all the rest of us, is now so deeply immersed in postmodernist space, so deeply suffused and infected by its new cultural categories, that the luxury of the old-fashioned ideological critique, the indignant moral denunciation of the other, becomes unavailable.

The distinction I am proposing here knows one canonical form in Hegel's differentiation of the thinking of individual morality or moralizing (*Moralität*) from that whole very different realm of collective social values and practices (*Sittlichkeit*).[8] But it finds its definitive form in Marx's demonstration of the materialist dialectic, most notably in those classic pages of the *Manifesto*[9] which teach the hard lesson of some more genuinely dialectical way to think historical development and change. The topic of the lesson is, of course, the historical development of capitalism itself and the deployment of a specific bourgeois culture. In a well-known passage Marx powerfully urges us to do the impossible, namely, to think this development positively *and* negatively all at once; to achieve, in other words, a type of thinking that would be capable of grasping the demonstrably baleful features of capitalism along with its extraordinary and liberating dynamism simultaneously within a single thought, and without attenuating any of the force of either judgment. We are somehow to lift our minds to a point at which it is possible to understand that capitalism is at one and the same time the best thing that has ever happened to the human race, and the worst. The lapse from this austere dialectical imperative into the more comfortable stance of the taking of moral positions is inveterate and all too human: still, the urgency of the subject demands that we make at least some effort to think the cultural evolution of late capitalism dialectically, as catastrophe and progress all together.

Such an effort suggests two immediate questions, with which we will conclude these reflections. Can we in fact identify some "moment of truth" within the more evident "moments of falsehood" of postmodern culture? And, even if we can do so, is there not something ultimately paralyzing in the dialectical view of historical development proposed above; does it not tend to demobilize us and to surrender us to passivity and helplessness by systematically obliterating possibilities of action under the impenetrable fog of historical inevitability? It is appropriate to discuss these two (related) issues in terms of current possibilities for some effective contemporary cultural politics and for the construction of a genuine political culture.

To focus the problem in this way is, of course, immediately to raise the more genuine issue of the fate of culture generally, and of the function of culture specifically, as one social level or instance, in the postmodern era. Everything in the previous discussion suggests that what we have been calling postmodernism is inseparable from, and unthinkable without the hypothesis of, some fundamental mutation of the sphere of culture in the world of late capitalism, which includes a momentous modification of its social function. Older discussions of the space, function, or sphere of culture (mostly notably Herbert Marcuse's classic essay "The Affirmative Character of Culture")[10] have insisted on what a different language would call the "semiautonomy" of the cultural realm: its ghostly, yet Utopian, existence, for good or ill, above the practical world of the existent, whose mirror image it throws back in forms which vary from the legitimations of flattering resemblance to the contestatory indictments of critical satire or Utopian pain.

What we must now ask ourselves is whether it is not precisely this semiautonomy of the cultural sphere which has been destroyed by the logic of late capitalism. Yet to argue that culture is today no longer endowed with the relative autonomy it once enjoyed at one level among others in earlier moments of capitalism (let alone in precapitalist societies) is not necessarily to imply its disappearance or extinction. Quite the contrary; we must go on to affirm that the dissolution of an autonomous sphere of culture is rather to be imagined in terms of an explosion: a prodigious expansion of culture throughout the social realm, to the point at which everything in our social life – from economic value and state power to practices and to the very structure of the psyche itself – can be said to have become "cultural" in some original and yet untheorized sense. This proposition is, however, substantively quite consistent with the previous diagnosis of a society of the image or the simulacrum and a transformation of the "real" into so many pseudoevents.

It also suggests that some of our most cherished and time-honored radical conceptions about the nature of cultural politics may thereby find themselves outmoded. However distinct those conceptions – which range from slogans of negativity, opposition, and subversion to critique and reflexivity – may have been, they all shared a single, fundamentally spatial, presupposition, which may be resumed in the equally time-honored formula of "critical distance." No theory of cultural politics current on the Left today has been able to do without one notion or another of a certain minimal aesthetic distance, of the possibility of the positioning of the cultural act outside the massive Being of capital, from which to assault this last. What the burden of our preceding demonstration suggests, however, is that distance in general (including "critical distance" in particular) has very precisely been abolished in the new space of postmodernism. We are submerged in its henceforth filled and suffused volumes to the point where our now postmodern bodies are bereft of spatial coordinates and practically (let alone theoretically) incapable of distantiation; meanwhile, it has already been observed how the prodigious new expansion of multinational capital ends up penetrating and colonizing those very precapitalist enclaves (Nature and the Unconscious) which offered extraterritorial and Archimedean footholds for critical effectivity. [...]

What we must now affirm is that it is precisely this whole extraordinarily demoralizing and depressing original new global space which is the "moment of truth" of postmodernism. What has been called the postmodernist "sublime" is only the moment in which this content has become most explicit, has moved the closest to the surface of consciousness as a coherent new type of space in its own right – even though a certain figural concealment or disguise is still at work here, most notably in the high-tech thematics in which the new spatial content is still dramatized and articulated. Yet the earlier features of the postmodern which were enumerated above can all now be seen as themselves partial (yet constitutive) aspects of the same general spatial object.

The argument for a certain authenticity in these otherwise patently ideological productions depends on the prior proposition that what we have been calling postmodern (or multinational) space is not merely a cultural ideology or fantasy but has genuine historical (and socioeconomic) reality as a third great original expansion of capitalism around the globe (after the earlier expansions of the national market and the older imperialist system, which each had their own cultural specificity and generated new types of space appropriate to their dynamics). The distorted and unreflexive attempts of newer cultural production to explore and to express this new space must then also, in their own fashion, be considered as so many approaches to the representation of (a new) reality (to use a more antiquated language). As paradoxical as the terms may seem, they may thus, following a classic interpretive option, be read as peculiar new forms of realism (or at least of the mimesis of reality), while at the same time they can equally well be analyzed as so many attempts to distract and divert us from that reality or to disguise its contradictions and resolve them in the guise of various formal mystifications.

As for that reality itself, however – the as yet untheorized original space of some new "world system" of multinational or late capitalism, a space whose negative or baleful aspects are only too obvious – the dialectic requires us to hold equally to a positive or "progressive" evaluation of its emergence, as Marx did for the world market as the horizon of national economies, or as Lenin did for the older imperialist global network. For neither Marx nor Lenin was socialism a matter of returning to smaller (and thereby less repressive and comprehensive) systems of social organization; rather, the dimensions attained by capital in their own times were grasped as the promise, the framework, and the precondition for the achievement of some new and more comprehensive socialism. Is this not the case with the yet more global and totalizing space of the new world system, which demands the intervention and elaboration of an internationalism of a radically new type? The disastrous realignment of socialist revolution with the older nationalisms (not only in Southeast Asia), whose results have necessarily aroused much serious recent left reflection, can be adduced in support of this position.

But if all this is so, then at least one possible form of a new radical cultural politics becomes evident, with a final aesthetic proviso that must quickly be noted. Left cultural producers and theorists – particularly those formed by bourgeois cultural traditions issuing from romanticism and valorizing spontaneous, instinctive, or unconscious forms of "genius," but also for very obvious historical reasons such as Zhdanovism and the sorry consequences of political and party interventions in the arts – have often by reaction allowed themselves to be unduly intimidated by the repudiation, in bourgeois aesthetics and most notably in high modernism, of one of the age-old functions of art – the pedagogical and the didactic. The teaching function of art was, however, always stressed in classical times (even though it there mainly took the form of moral lessons), while the prodigious and still imperfectly understood work of Brecht reaffirms, in a new and formally innovative and original way, for the moment of modernism proper, a complex new conception of the relationship between culture and pedagogy. The cultural model I will propose similarly foregrounds the cognitive and pedagogical dimensions of political art and culture, dimensions stressed in very different ways by both Lukács and Brecht (for the distinct moments of realism and modernism, respectively).

We cannot, however, return to aesthetic practices elaborated on the basis of historical situations and dilemmas which are no longer ours. Meanwhile, the conception of space that has been developed here suggests that a model of political culture appropriate to our own situation will necessarily have to raise spatial issues as its fundamental organizing concern. I will therefore provisionally define the aesthetic of this new (and hypothetical) cultural form as an aesthetic of *cognitive mapping*.

In a classic work, *The Image of the City*,[11] Kevin Lynch taught us that the alienated city is above all a space in which people are unable to map (in their minds) either their own positions or the urban totality in which they find themselves: grids such as those of Jersey City, in which none of the traditional markers (monuments, nodes, natural boundaries, built perspectives) obtain, are the most obvious examples. Disalienation in the traditional city, then, involves the practical reconquest of a sense of place and the construction or reconstruction of an articulated ensemble which can be retained in memory and which the individual subject can map and remap along the moments of mobile, alternative trajectories. Lynch's own work is limited by the deliberate restriction of his topic to the problems of city form as such; yet it becomes extraordinarily suggestive when projected outward onto some of the larger national and global spaces we have touched on here. Nor should it be too hastily assumed that his model — while it clearly raises very central issues of representation as such — is in any way easily vitiated by the conventional poststructural critiques of the "ideology of representation" or mimesis. The cognitive map is not exactly mimetic in that older sense; indeed, the theoretical issues it poses allow us to renew the analysis of representation on a higher and much more complex level.

There is, for one thing, a most interesting convergence between the empirical problems studied by Lynch in terms of city space and the great Althusserian (and Lacanian) redefinition of ideology as "the representation of the subject's *Imaginary* relationship to his or her *Real* conditions of existence."[12] Surely this is exactly what the cognitive map is called upon to do in the narrower framework of daily life in the physical city: to enable a situational representation on the part of the individual subject to that vaster and properly unrepresentable totality which is the ensemble of society's structures as a whole.

Yet Lynch's work also suggests a further line of development insofar as cartography itself constitutes its key mediatory instance. A return to the history of this science (which is also an art) shows us that Lynch's model does not yet, in fact, really correspond to what will become map-making. Lynch's subjects are rather clearly involved in precartographic operations whose results traditionally are described as itineraries rather than as maps: diagrams organized around the still subject-centered or existential journey of the traveler, along which various significant key features are marked — oases, mountain ranges, rivers, monuments, and the like. The most highly developed form of such diagrams is the nautical itinerary, the sea chart, or *portulans*, where coastal features are noted for the use of Mediterranean navigators who rarely venture out into the open sea. [...]

Transcoding all this now into the very different problematic of the Althusserian definition of ideology one would want to make two points. The first is that the Althusserian concept now allows us to rethink these specialized geographical and cartographic issues in terms of social space — in terms, for example, of social class and national or international context, in terms of the ways in which we all necessarily *also* cognitively map our individual social relationship to local, national, and international class realities. Yet to reformulate the problem in this way is also to come starkly up against those very difficulties in mapping which are posed in heightened and original ways by that very global space of the postmodernist or multinational moment which has been under discussion here. These are not merely theoretical issues; they have urgent practical political consequences, as is evident from the conventional feelings of First World subjects that existentially (or "empirically") they really do inhabit a "postindustrial society" from which traditional production has disappeared and in which social classes of the classical type no longer exist — a conviction which has immediate effects on political praxis.

The second point is that a return to the Lacanian underpinnings of Althusser's theory can afford some useful and suggestive methodological enrichments. Althusser's formulation remobilizes an older and henceforth classical Marxian distinction between science and ideology that is not without value for us even today. The existential — the positioning of the individual subject, the experience of daily life, the monadic "point of view" on the world to which we are necessarily, as biological subjects, restricted — is in Althusser's formula implicitly opposed to the realm of abstract knowledge, a realm which, as Lacan reminds us, is never positioned in or actualized by any concrete subject but rather, by that structural void called *le sujet supposé savoir* (the subject supposed to know), a subject-place of knowledge. What is affirmed is not that we cannot know the world and its totality in some abstract or "scientific" way. Marxian "science" provides just such a way of knowing and conceptualizing the world abstractly, in the sense in which, for example, Mandel's great book offers a rich and elaborated *knowledge* of that global world system, of which it has never been said here that it was unknowable but merely that it was unrepresentable, which is a very different matter. The Althusserian formula, in other words, designates a gap, a rift, between existential experience and scientific knowledge. Ideology has then the function of somehow inventing a way of articulating those two distinct dimensions with each other. What a historicist view of this definition would want to add is that such coordination, the production of functioning and living ideologies, is distinct in different historical situations, and, above all, that there may be historical situations in which it is not possible at all – and this would seem to be our situation in the current crisis.

But the Lacanian system is threefold, and not dualistic. To the Marxian-Althusserian opposition of ideology and science correspond only two of Lacan's tripartite functions: the Imaginary and the Real, respectively.

Our digression on cartography, however, with its final revelation of a properly representational dialectic of the codes and capacities of individual languages or media, reminds us that what has until now been omitted was the dimension of the Lacanian Symbolic itself.

An aesthetic of cognitive mapping – a pedagogical political culture which seeks to endow the individual subject with some new heightened sense of its place in the global system – will necessarily have to respect this now enormously complex representational dialectic and invent radically new forms in order to do it justice. This is not then, clearly, a call for a return to some older kind of machinery, some older and more transparent national space, or some more traditional and reassuring perspectival or mimetic enclave: the new political art (if it is possible at all) will have to hold to the truth of postmodernism, that is to say, to its fundamental object – the world space of multinational capital – at the same time at which it achieves a breakthrough to some as yet unimaginable new mode of representing this last, in which we may again begin to grasp our positioning as individual and collective subjects and regain a capacity to act and struggle which is at present neutralized by our spatial as well as our social confusion. The political form of postmodernism, if there ever is any, will have as its vocation the invention and projection of a global cognitive mapping, on a social as well as a spatial scale.

PART THREE

Difference, aesthetics, politics and history
Postmodern reflections

T HE EXTRACTS INCLUDED IN THIS PART exemplify the serious ethical, aesthetical, political and historical engagements of postmodern authors. The opening texts, those of Lyotard, Irigaray and Bauman, are important reflections on ways a politics of difference might be theorised. The concluding texts, Baudrillard's and Derrida's, are direct political challenges to liberal and conservative thinkers who endorsed Francis Fukuyama's thesis from *The End of History and the Last Man*[1] that, with the fall of communism and the victory of free market capitalism, the great ideological struggle that was the driving force of history – that defined it and gave it meaning – had ended. The end of this dialectic resulted in the end of history itself. This particular understanding of history presumed that history embodied some deep meaning that could be discovered. But as we have seen postmodernist and poststructuralist thinkers believe history is not governed by hidden rules. According to them history is random and cannot reveal some deep meaning. When meaning is supposedly discovered it is in fact arbitrarily imposed.

The arbitrary imposition of meaning and understanding is a central consideration of Jean-François Lyotard's *The Differend: Phrases in Dispute* (Chapter 15). This work, strongly political in character, is a critical analysis of justice. Organised as a series of different yet related propositions, which reflect the book's theme, it explores Lyotard's own conception of differend and the incommensurability of different discourses. Lyotard begins his considerations by reflecting on the important controversy over the truth of the Holocaust between the French historian Pierre Vidal-Naquet and the revisionist historian Robert Faurisson. In focusing on this debate Lyotard is able to direct our attention to the differend which he characterises as a dispute that arises when individuals or groups employ discourses that are incommensurable with each other.

His contention is that differends can never be justly resolved, and any attempt at their resolution always involves an injustice because the discourse of the weaker party to the dispute is inevitably suppressed. The theme and argument of this text unveil the deep and hidden power relations that govern our traditional conceptions of justice.

The themes of power and injustice run through the work of Luce Irigaray. From the time of her first major feminist work, *Speculum of the Other Woman*[2] in 1974, Irigaray has been preoccupied with achieving a voice for women. She has sought to accomplish this first through a deconstruction of Western philosophy and then by exploring the themes of linguistic and sexual difference. It is this latter theme that is the object of the 1992 public lecture given at the University of Rotterdam included here (Chapter 16). Irigaray's principal thesis is that 'the role historically alloted to woman ... has been determined by the necessities of a traditional sociocultural organization'. This 'organization', which excludes the feminine, is fundamentally determined through language and thought. Irigaray explores the various instances in language, philosophy and the sciences in which this has occurred, and she proposes ways in which a feminine identity may emerge through the rethinking of these domains.

The problem of difference is the focus of the first essay in Lyotard's *The Postmodern Explained to Children* (Chapter 17). As in *The Differend: Phrases in Dispute* Lyotard focuses on the differend. But in this essay he takes his own work as an expression of differend and, in his opening polemical remarks, asserts that the defenders of modern philosophy such as Jürgen Habermas continue to adhere to a discourse which does not permit difference and endeavours to eradicate it. Lyotard's essay, in discussing the avant-garde, explores aesthetic experience as a way of creating difference. The focus on aesthetics, particularly the aesthetic experience of the sublime, dominated much of Lyotard's later work. But it represented a return to his preoccupations with the avant-garde before the 1979 publication of *The Postmodern Condition*.[3] And it allowed him to unite his considerations on art with his thoughts on subconscious creative drives which were also at the forefront of his early writings. These reflections were integral to the differend, which Lyotard evokes in his definition of the postmodern that concludes this essay.

Zygmunt Bauman's 'A Sociological Theory of Postmodernity' (Chapter 18) is a considered attempt to formulate a postmodern politics and ethics which are integral to a more comprehensive sociology of postmodernity. Bauman's sociology is a clear challenge to the functionalist analyses inspired by the work of Talcott Parsons and systemist studies modelled on the work of David Easton. Its principal characteristic, underpinned by a powerful utopian impulse, is to 'conceive of itself as a participant within' and to devise a strategy toward a 'never-ending, self-reflexive process of reinterpretation' which defines the postmodern condition. In order to achieve this Bauman focuses on the issue of individual and group identity and explores in a masterful analysis the 'most conspicuous features of the postmodern condition'. His account, which shares a number of similiarities with Jameson's and Lyotard's reflections on the postmodern condition, is both lucid and thoroughly stimulating.

In 1987 Jean-François Lyotard participated in an interview conducted in Paris and Utrecht by Willem van Reijen and Dick Veerman. The interview, reproduced here in full (Chapter 19), offers one of the clearest and most thorough accounts of Lyotard's principal political, psychoanalytic, philosophical and artistic interests and therefore is one of the most useful guides to his thoughts on postmodernism. The text explores the links and differences between Lyotard's various writings, and examines his reflections on the crisis of the human and natural sciences along with his considerations on art and aesthetics and Lacanian psychoanalysis. It situates Lyotard's work in relation to that of his contemporaries, particularly Derrida and the American philosopher Richard Rorty and it highlights Lyotard's engagement with the idea of justice as central to postmodern politics.

This Part concludes with two classic examples of the postmodern rejection of history as having meaning. Baudrillard's *The Illusion of the End* (Chapter 20) and Derrida's *Specters of Marx* (Chapter 21) are very different engagements with the idea that history can discern a pattern to past events and that in so doing it can uncover some deep meaning about humanity and its destiny. Derrida's approach to this issue is highly characteristic of his form of deconstruction. Yet it is also overtly more political than many of his previous works and indicates a shift toward overtly political themes culminating in the 2003 publication of *Voyous: Deux essais sur la raison* (*Rogues: Two Essays on Reason*).[4]

Baudrillard's *The Illusion of the End* is also highly characteristic of his style of writing with bold, dramatic and uncompromising statements. His principal assertion is that within a postmodern age it is absurd to speak about history as either being progressive or having meaning. He argues that 'our non-Euclidean *fin de siècle*' is characterised by 'the end of linearity' and that this means there is no future, and therefore that the past cannot be projected into the future. Baudrillard contends that the search for meaning in history in order to render the present intelligible is no longer possible within the postmodern world because the changes economy, culture and society have undergone in the last 40 years means that 'the more we seek to rediscover the real and the referential, the more we sink into simulation'. Finding inspiration in Barthes, Lacan, Althusser and others, Baudrillard asserts that the quest for meaning in history, and reality itself, is totally illusory. This is an audacious and, if taken seriously, thoroughly unsettling proposition.

'Injunction of Marx', the excerpt from Derrida's *Specters of Marx: The State of the Debt, the Work of Mourning, and the New International*, begins with Derrida's belief that there is 'a certain haunting obsession that seems ... to organize the *dominant* influence on discourse today'. This haunting, similar to the concept of trace, is always present even 'at a time when a new world disorder is attempting to install its neo-capitalism and neo-liberalism'. The theme of specter is, given the current international situation post-September 11, 2001, highly topical and one Derrida has revisited in his latest work *Rogues: Two Essays on Reason*. Yet this theme applies not only to the 'new world disorder' but to Marx's analysis of capitalism and alienation themselves: 'The whole movement of idealization that Marx then describes, whether it is a question of money or of ideologems, is a production of ghosts, illusions, simulacra, appearances, or apparitions'. But like his liberal adversaries Marx harbours a violent 'hostility toward ghosts'. He tries to 'conjure (away)' these ghosts. And this 'conjuration' or exorcism 'pretends to declare the death only in order to put to death'.

This excerpt from *Specters*, Derrida's deconstruction of Marx, is a prelude to the deconstruction of a contemporary adversary: Francis Fukayama and the end-of-history ideologists. Derrida attacks the 'remarkable consensus' about the justice of liberal democracy which Fukayama and his followers eagerly believe dominates world opinion. He points to liberal democracy's failings and calls for establishing a 'New International' of left-wing interests that, like Marx in the nineteenth century, will fight against injustice. This remarkable work may well represent Derrida's own recognition of a certain justice in Foucault's response to his 'Cogito and the History of Madness', for in *Specters* we have deconstruction deployed to an unambiguous political end: the quest for justice and the desire to give the oppressed a voice. These concerns unite *Specters* with Foucault's 'What is Enlightenment?' For both work toward liberating individuals from the intellectual dogmatism that lies at the heart of oppression and the current crisis of the human sciences. This noble ambition defines postmodernism.

Chapter 15

Jean-François Lyotard

■ from *THE DIFFEREND: PHRASES IN DISPUTE*,
Georges van de Abbeele trans., Minneapolis, Minn.: University
of Minnesota Press, 1988

THE DIFFEREND

1. You are informed that human beings endowed with language were placed in a situation such that none of them is now able to tell about it. Most of them disappeared then, and the survivors rarely speak about it. When they do speak about it, their testimony bears only upon a minute part of this situation. How can you know that the situation itself existed? That it is not the fruit of your informant's imagination? Either the situation did not exist as such. Or else it did exist, in which case your informant's testimony is false, either because he or she should have disappeared, or else because he or she should remain silent, or else because, if he or she does speak, he or she can bear witness only to the particular experience he had, it remaining to be established whether this experience was a component of the situation in question.

2. "I have analyzed thousands of documents. I have tirelessly pursued specialists and historians with my questions. I have tried in vain to find a single former deportee capable of proving to me that he had really seen, with his own eyes, a gas chamber."[1] To have "really seen with his own eyes" a gas chamber would be the condition which gives one the authority to say that it exists and to persuade the unbeliever. Yet it is still necessary to prove that the gas chamber was used to kill at the time it was seen. The only acceptable proof that it was used to kill is that one died from it. But if one is dead, one cannot testify that it is on account of the gas chamber. – The plaintiff complains that he has been fooled about the existence of gas chambers, fooled that is, about the so-called Final Solution. His argument is: in order for a place to be identified as a gas chamber, the only eyewitness I will accept would be a victim of this gas chamber; now, according to my opponent, there is no victim that is not dead; otherwise, this gas chamber would not be what he or she claims it to be. There is, therefore, no gas chamber.

3. Can you give me, says an editor defending his or her profession, the title of a work of major importance which would have been rejected by every editor and which would

therefore remain unknown? Most likely, you do not know any masterpiece of this kind because, if it does exist, it remains unknown. And if you think you know one, since it has not been made public, you cannot say that it is of major importance, except in your eyes. You do not know of any, therefore, and the editor is right. – This argument takes the same form as those in the preceding numbers. Reality is not what is "given" to this or that "subject," it is a state of the referent (that about which one speaks) which results from the effectuation of establishment procedures defined by a unanimously agreed-upon protocol, and from the possibility offered to anyone to recommence this effectuation as often as he or she wants. The publishing industry would be one of these protocols, historical inquiry another.

4. Either the Ibanskian[2] witness is not a communist, or else he is. If he is, he has no need to testify that Ibanskian society is communist, since he admits that the communist authorities are the only ones competent to effectuate the establishment procedures for the reality of the communist character of that society. He defers to them then just as the layperson defers to the biologist or to the astronomer for the affirmation of the existence of a virus or a nebula. If he ceases to give his agreement to these authorities, he ceases to be a communist. We come back then to the first case: he is not a communist. This means that he ignores or wishes to ignore the establishment procedures for the reality of the communist character of Ibanskian society. There is, in this case, no more credit to be accorded his testimony than to that of a human being who says he has communicated with Martians. "There is therefore nothing surprising in the fact that the [Ibanskian] State regards opposition activity in general as a criminal activity on the same level as robbery, gangsterism, speculation and so on … It is a nonpolitical society."[3] More exactly, it is a learned State,[4] it knows no reality other than the established one, and it holds the monopoly on procedures for the establishment of reality.

5. The difference, though, between communism, on the one hand, and a virus or a nebula, on the other hand, is that there are means to observe the latter – they are objects of cognition – while the former is the object of an idea of historical-political reason, and this object is not observable […]. There are no procedures, defined by a protocol unanimously approved and renewable on demand, for establishing in general the reality of the object of an idea. For example, even in physics, there exists no such protocol for establishing the reality of the universe, because the universe is the object of an idea. As a general rule, an object which is thought under the category of the whole (or of the absolute) is not an object of cognition (whose reality could be subjected to a protocol, etc.). The principle affirming the contrary could be called totalitarianism. If the requirement of establishing the reality of a phrase's referent according to the protocol of cognition is extended to any given phrase, especially to those phrases that refer to a whole, then this requirement is totalitarian in its principle. That's why it is important to distinguish between phrase regimens, and this comes down to limiting the competence of a given tribunal to a given kind of phrase.

6. The plaintiff's conclusion (No. 2) should have been that since the only witnesses are the victims, and since there are no victims but dead ones, no place can be identified as a gas chamber. He should not have said that there are none, but rather that his opponent cannot prove that there are any, and that should have been sufficient to confound the tribunal. It is up to the opponent (the victim) to adduce the proof of the wrong done to him or her!

7. This is what a wrong [*tort*] would be: a damage [*dommage*] accompanied by the loss of the means to prove the damage. This is the case if the victim is deprived of life, or of all his or her liberties, or of the freedom to make his or her ideas or opinions public, or simply of the right to testify to the damage, or even more simply if the testifying phrase is itself deprived of authority [...]. In all of these cases, to the privation constituted by the damage there is added the impossibility of bringing it to the knowledge of others, and in particular to the knowledge of a tribunal. Should the victim seek to bypass this impossibility and testify anyway to the wrong done to him or to her, he or she comes up against the following argumentation: either the damages you complain about never took place, and your testimony is false; or else they took place, and since you are able to testify to them, it is not a wrong that has been done to you, but merely a damage, and your testimony is still false.

8. Either you are the victim of a wrong, or you are not. If you are not, you are deceived (or lying) in testifying that you are. If you are, since you can bear witness to this wrong, it is not a wrong, and you are deceived (or lying) in testifying that you are the victim of a wrong. Let p be: you are the victim of a wrong; *not p*: you are not; *Tp*: phrase p is true; *Fp*: it is false. The argument is: either p or *not p*; if *not-p*, then *Fp*; if p, then *not-p*, then *Fp*. The ancients called this argument a dilemma. It contains the mechanism of the *double bind* as studied by the Palo Alto School,[5] it is a linchpin of Hegelian dialectical logic. This mechanism consists in applying to two contradictory propositions, p and *not-p*, two logical operators: exclusion (*either ... or*) and implication (*if ... then*). So, at once [(*either p or not-p*) and (*if p, then not-p*)]. It's as if you said both, *either it is white*, or *it is not white*; and *if it is white, it is not white*. [...]

9. It is in the nature of a victim not to be able to prove that one has been done a wrong. A plaintiff is someone who has incurred damages and who disposes of the means to prove it. One becomes a victim if one loses these means. One loses them, for example, if the author of the damages turns out directly or indirectly to be one's judge. The latter has the authority to reject one's testimoney as false or to impede its publication. But this is only a particular case. In general, the plaintiff becomes a victim when no presentation is possible of the wrong he or she says he or she has suffered. Reciprocally, the "perfect crime" does not consist in killing the victim or the witnesses (that adds new crimes to the first one and aggravates the difficulty of effacing everything), but rather in obtaining the silence of the witnesses, the deafness of the judges, and the inconsistency (insanity) of the testimony. You neutralize the addressor, the addressee, and the sense of the testimony; then everything is as if there were no referent (no damages). If there is nobody to adduce the proof, nobody to admit it, and/or if the argument which upholds it is judged to be absurd, then the plaintif is dismissed, the wrong he or she complains of cannot be attested. He or she becomes a victim. If he or she persists in invoking this wrong as if it existed, the others (addressor, addressee, expert commentator or the testimony) will easily be able to make him or her pass for mad. Doesn't paranoia confuse the *As if it were the case* with the *it is the case*?

10. But aren't the others acting for their part as if this were not the case, when it is perhaps the case? Why should there be less paranoia in denying the existence of gas chambers than in affirming it? Because, writes Leibniz, "nothing is simpler and easier than something".[6] The one who says there is something is the plaintiff, it is up to him or her to bring forth a demonstration, by means of well-formed phrases and of procedures for establishing the existence of their referent. Reality is always the plaintiff's responsibility. For the defense, it is sufficient to refute the argumentation and to impugn the proof by a counter-example.

This is the defense's advantage, as recognized by Aristotle and by strategists.[7] Likewise, it cannot be said that a hypothesis is verified, but only that until further notice it has not yet been falsified. The defense is nihilistic, the prosecution pleads for existents [*l'étant*]. That is why it is up to the victims of extermination camps to prove the extermination. This is our way of thinking that reality is not a given, but an occasion to require that establishment procedures be effectuated in regard to it.

11.   The death penalty is supposed out of nihilism, out of a cognitive consideration for the referent, out of a prejudice in favor of the defense. The odds that it is not the case are greater than the odds that it is. This statistical estimation belongs to the family of cognitive phrases. The presumed innocence of the accused, which obligates the prosecution with adducing the proof of the offense, is the "humanist" version of the same playing rule of cognition. – If the rules of the game are inverted, if everyone accused is presumed guilty, then the defense has the task of establishing innocence while the prosecution has only to refute the argumentation and to impugn the proofs advanced by the defense. Now, it may be impossible to establish that the referent of a phrase does not have a given property, unless we have the right to resort to a refutation of the phrase in which the referent does have that property. How can I prove that I am not a drug dealer without asking my accuser to bring forth some proof of it and without refuting that proof? How can it be established that labor power is not a commodity without refuting the hypothesis that it is? How can you establish what is not without criticizing what is? The undetermined cannot be established. It is necessary that negation be the negation of a determination. – This inversion of the tasks expected on one side and on the other may suffice to transform the accused into a victim, if he or she does not have the right to criticize the prosecution, as we see in political trials. Kafka warned us about this. It is impossible to establish one's innocence, in and of itself. It is a nothingness.

12.   The plaintiff lodges his or her complaint before the tribunal, the accused argues in such a way as to show the inanity of the accusation. Litigation takes place. I would like to call a *differend* [*différend*] the case where the plaintiff is divested of the means to argue and becomes for that reason a victim. If the addressor, the addressee, and the sense of the testimony are neutralized, everything takes place as if there were no damages (No. 9). A case of differend between two parties takes place when the "regulation" of the conflict that opposes them is done in the idiom of one of the parties while the wrong suffered by the other is not signified in that idiom. For example, contracts and agreements between economic partners do not prevent – on the contrary, they presuppose – that the laborer or his or her representative has had to and will have to speak of his or her work as though it were the temporary cession of a commodity, the "service," which he or she putatively owns. This "abstraction," as Marx calls it (but the term is bad, what concreteness does it allege?), is required by the idiom in which the litigation is regulated ("bourgeois" social and economic law). In failing to have recourse to this idiom, the laborer would not exist within this field of reference, he or she would be a slave. In using it, he or she becomes a plaintiff. Does he or she also cease for that matter to be a victim?

13.   One remains a victim at the same time that one becomes a plaintiff. Does one have the means to establish that one is a victim? No. How can you know then that one is a victim? What tribunal can pass judgment in this matter? In effect, the differend is not a matter for litigation; economic and social law can regulate the litigation between economic and social partners but not the differend between labor-power and capital. By what well-formed phrase and by means of what establishment procedure can the worker affirm before

the labor arbitrator that what one yields to one's boss for so many hours per week in exchange for a salary is *not* a commodity? One is presumed to be the owner of something. One is in the case of the accused who has to establish a non-existent or at least a non-attribute. It is easy to refute him or her. It all happens as if what one is could only be expressed in an idiom other than that of social and economic law. In the latter, one can only express what one has, and if one has nothing, what one does not have either will not be expressed or will be expressed in a certifiable manner as if one had it. If the laborer evokes his or her essence (labor-power), he or she cannot be heard by this tribunal, which is not competent. The differend is signaled by this inability to prove. The one who lodges a complaint is heard, but the one who is a victim, and who is perhaps the same one, is reduced to silence.

14. "The survivors rarely speak." But isn't there an entire literature of testimonies ...? – That's not it, though. Not to speak is part of the ability to speak, since ability is a possibility and a possibility implies something and its opposite. *Possible that p* and *Possible that not-p* are equally true. It is in the very definition of the possible to imply opposites at the same time. That the opposite of speaking is possible does not entail the necessity of keeping quiet. To be able not to speak is not the same as not to be able to speak. The latter is a deprivation, the former a negation.[8] If the survivors do not speak, is it because they cannot speak, or because they avail themselves of the possibility of not speaking that is given them by the ability to speak? Do they keep quiet out of necessity, or freely, as it is said? Or is the question poorly stated?

15. It would be absurd to suppose that human beings "endowed with language" cannot speak in the strict sense, as is the case for stones. Necessity would signify here: they do not speak because they are threatened with the worst in the case that they would speak, or when in general a direct or indirect attempt is made against their ability to speak. Let's suppose that they keep quiet under threat. A contrary ability needs to be presupposed if the threat is to have an effect, since this threat bears upon the hypothesis of the opposite case, the one in which the survivors would speak. But how could a threat work when it is exerted upon something (here, the eventuality that the survivors will speak) which does not currently exist? What is threatened? This is said to be the life, or happiness, etc., of the one who would speak. But the one who *would* speak (an unreal, conditional state) has no life, no happiness, etc., which can be threatened, since one is oneself unreal or conditional as long as one has not spoken, – if indeed it is that I am never but the addressor of a current phrase.

16. What is subject to threats is not an identifiable individual, but the ability to speak or to keep quiet. This ability is threatened with destruction. There are two means to achieve this: making it impossible to speak, making it impossible to keep quiet. These two means are compatible: it is made impossible for *x* to speak about this (through incarceration, for example); it is made impossible for him or her to keep quiet about that (through torture, for example). The ability is destroyed as an ability: *x* may speak about this *and* keep quiet about that, but he or she ceases to be able *either* to speak *or* not to speak about this or about that. The threat ("If you were to tell (signify) this, it would be your last phrase" or, "If you were to keep quiet about that, it would be your last silence") is only a threat because the ability to speak or not to speak is identified with *x*'s existence.

17. The paradox of the last phrase (or of the last silence), which is also the paradox of the series, should give *x* not the vertigo of what cannot be phrased (which is also called the fear of death), but rather the irrefutable conviction that phrasing is endless. For a phrase to

be the last one, another one is needed to declare it, and it is then not the last one. At the least, the paradox should give *x* both this vertigo and this conviction. – Never mind that the last phrase is the last one that *x* says! – No, it is the last one that has *x* as its direct or "current" addressor.

18. It should be said that addressor and addressee are instances, either marked or unmarked, presented by a phrase. The latter is not a message passing from an addressor to an addressee both of whom are independent of it.[9] They are situated in the universe the phrase presents, as are its referent and its sense. "*X*'s phrase, *my* phrase, *your* silence": do *we*, identifiable individuals, *x, y*, speak phrases or make silences, in the sense that we would be their authors? Or is it that phrases or silences take place (happen, come to pass), presenting universes in which individuals *x, y*, you, me are situated as the addressors of these phrases or silences? And if this is so, at the price of what misunderstanding can a threat exerted against *x* threaten "his" or "her" phrase?

19. To say that *x* can be threatened for what he or she might say or keep quiet is to presuppose that one is free to use language or not and therefore that this freedom to use can be revoked by a threat. This is not false, it is a way of talking about language, humanity, and their interrelations which obeys the rules of the family of certain cognitive phrases (the human sciences). The phrase, "Under threat, under torture, in conditions of incarceration, in conditions of 'sensory deprivation,' etc., the linguistic behavior of a human being can be dictated to him or to her," is a well-formed phrase, and examples can, alas, be presented for which the scientist can say: here are some cases of it. But the human and linguistic sciences are like the juries of labor arbitration boards.

20. Just as these juries presuppose that the opponents they are supposed to judge are in possession of something they exchange, so do the human and linguistic sciences pre-suppose that the human beings they are supposed to know are in possession of something they communicate. And the powers that be (ideological, political, religious, police, etc.) presuppose that the human beings they are supposed to guide, or at least control, are in possession of something they communicate. Communication is the exchange of messages, exchange the communication of goods. The instances of communication like those of exchange are definable only in terms of property or propriety [*propriété*]: the propriety of information, analogous to the propriety of uses. And just as the flow of uses can be controlled, so can the flow of information. As a perverse use is repressed, a dangerous bit of information is banned. As a need is diverted and a motivation created, an addressor is led to say something other that what he or she was going to say. The problem of language, thus posited in terms of communication, leads to that of the needs and beliefs of interlocutors. The linguist becomes an expert before the communication arbitration board. The essential problem he or she has to regulate is that of sense as a unit of exchange independent of the needs and beliefs of interlocutors. Similarly, for the economist, the problem is that of the value of goods and services as units independent of the demands and offers of economic partners.

21. Would you say that interlocutors are victims of the science and politics of language understood as communication to the same extent that the worker is transformed into a victim through the assimilation of his or her labor-power to a commodity? Must it be imagined that there exists a "phrase-power," analogous to labor-power, and which cannot find a way to express itself in the idiom of this science and this politics? – Whatever this power might be, the parallel must be broken right away. It can be conceived that work is something other than the exchange of a commodity, and an idiom other than that of the labor arbitrator must be found in order to express it. It can be conceived that language is

something other than the communication of a bit of information, and an idiom other than that of the human and linguistic sciences is needed in order to express it. This is where the parallel ends: in the case of language, recourse is made to another family of phrases; but in the case of work, recourse is not made to another family of work, recourse is still made to another family of phrases. The same goes for every differend buried in litigation, no matter what the subject matter. To give the differend its due is to institute new addressees, new addressors, new significations, and new referents in order for the wrong to find an expression and for the plaintiff to cease being a victim. This requires new rules for the formation and linking of phrases. No one doubts that language is capable of admitting these new phrase families or new genres of discourse. Every wrong ought to be able to be put into phrases. A new competence (or "prudence") must be found.

22. The differend is the unstable state and instant of language wherein something which must be able to be put into phrases cannot yet be. This state includes silence, which is a negative phrase, but it also calls upon phrases which are in principle possible. This state is signaled by what one ordinarily calls a feeling: "One cannot find the words," etc. A lot of searching must be done to find new rules for forming and linking phrases that are able to express the differend disclosed by the feeling, unless one wants this differend to be smothered right away in a litigation and for the alarm sounded by the feeling to have been useless. What is at stake in a literature, in a philosophy, in a politics perhaps, is to bear witness to differends by finding idioms for them.

23. In the differend, something "asks" to be put into phrases, and suffers from the wrong of not being able to be put into phrases right away. This is when the human beings who thought they could use language as an instrument of communication learn through the feeling of pain which accompanies silence (and of pleasure which accompanies the invention of a new idiom), that they are summoned by language, not to augment to their profit the quantity of information communicable through existing idioms, but to recognize that what remains to be phrased exceeds what they can presently phrase, and that they must be allowed to institute idioms which do not yet exist.

24. It is possible then that the survivors do not speak even though they are not threatened in their ability to speak should they speak later. The socio-linguist, the psycho-linguist, the bio-linguist seek the reasons, the passions, the interests, the context for these silences. Let us first seek their logic. We find that they are substitutes for phrases. They come in the place of phrases during a conversation, during an interrogation, during a debate, during the *talking* of a psychoanalytic session, during a confession, during a critical review, during a metaphysical exposition. The phrase replaced by silence would be a negative one. Negated by it is at least one of the four instances that constitute a phrase universe: the addressee, the referent, the sense, the addressor. The negative phrase that the silence implies could be formulated respectively: *This case does not fall within your competence*, *This case does not exist*, *It cannot be signified*, *It does not fall within my competence*. A single silence could be formulated by several of these phrases. — Moreover, these negative formulations, which deny the ability of the referent, the addressor, the addressee and the sense to be presented in the current idiom, do not point to the other idiom in which these instances could be presented.

25. It should be said by way of simplification that a phrase presents what it is about, the case, *ta pragmata*, which is its referent; what is signified about the case, the sense, *der Sinn*; that to which or addressed to which this is signified about the case, the addressee; that "through" which or in the name of which this is signified about the case, the addressor.

The disposition of a phrase universe consists in the situating of these instances in relation to each other. A phrase may entail several referents, several senses, several addressees, several addressors. Each of these four instances may be marked in the phrase or not.[10]

26.   Silence does not indicate which instance is denied, it signals the denial of one or more of the instances. The survivors remain silent, and it can be understood 1) that the situation in question (the case) is not the addressee's business (he or she lacks the competence, or he or she is not worthy of being spoken to about it, etc.); or 2) that it never took place (this is what Faurisson understands); or 3) that there is nothing to say about it (the situation is senseless, inexpressible); or 4) that it is not the survivors' business to be talking about it (they are not worthy, etc.). Or, several of these negations together.

27.   The silence of the survivors does not necessarily testify in favor of the nonexistence of gas chambers, as Faurisson believes or pretends to believe. It can just as well testify against the addressee's authority (we are not answerable to Faurisson), against the authority of the witness him- or herself (we, the rescued, do not have the authority to speak about it), finally against language's ability to signify gas chambers (an inexpressible absurdity). If one wishes to establish the existence of gas chambers, the four silent negations must be withdrawn: There were no gas chambers, were there? Yes, there were. – But even if there were, that cannot be formulated, can it? Yes, it can. – But even if it can be formulated, there is no one, at least, who has the authority to formulate it, and no one with the authority to hear it (it is not communicable), is there? Yes, there is.
[...]

28.   To establish the reality of a referent, the four silences must be refuted, though in reverse order: there is someone to signify the referent and someone to understand the phrase that signifies it; the referent can be signified; it exists. The proof for the reality of gas chambers cannot be adduced if the rules adducing the proof are not respected. These rules determine the universes of cognitive phrases, that is, they assign certain functions to the instances of referent, addressor, addressee, and sense. Thus: the addressor presumably seeks to obtain the addressee's agreement concerning the referent's sense: the witness must explain to the addressee the signification of the expression, *gas chamber*. When he or she has nothing to object to the explicative phrase, the addressee presumably gives his or her agreement to the addressor: one either accepts or does not accept the signification, that is, the explanation given by the addressor. If one does not accept it, one presumably proposes another explanation for the expression. When agreement is achieved, a well-formed expression becomes available. Each one can say: we agree that a gas chamber is this or that. Only then, can the existence of a reality which might suit as a referent for that expression be "shown" by means of a phrase in the form: *This or that is a case of a gas chamber.* This phrase fills an ostensive function, which is also required by the rules of the cognitive genre.

29.   But is this really so in the sciences? It seems doubtful.[11] – The question does not even need to be answered unless this is not so, for then the game played with regard to the phrase in question is not scientific. This is what Latour[12] affirms when he says that the game is rhetorical. But to what game does this last phrase, in its turn, belong? This, rather, is what should be answered: it's up to you to supply the proof that it is not so, but that it is otherwise. And this will be done according to the minimal rules for adducing a proof [...], or it will not be done at all. To say that it is not really so in the sciences is to set about establishing what really happens, and that can be done only according to the rules of

scientific cognitives, which allow for the reality of a referent to be established. If the phrase affirming that science is really a rhetoric is scientific, we have one of two things: either this phrase is itself rhetorical because it is scientific, and it can bring forth the proof neither for the reality of its referent nor for the truth of its sense. Or else, it is declared scientific because it is not rhetorical. It is an exception then to what it nonetheless affirms to be universal, and it should not be said that science is rhetoric, but that some science is rhetoric.

30. Why say a "well-formed expression" rather than a "meaningful phrase"? The former is subject to rules for forming cognitive phrases, in which truth and falsehood are at stake. In turn, these rules are the object of studies in formal logic, and, insofar as the phrases bear upon domains of reference, they are the object of axiomatic studies. With respect to their good formation, it is not pertinent whether the phrases obeying these rules are meaningful or not, in the sense of their meaning in ordinary language. Transcribed into ordinary language, they may appear absurd. Conversely, phrases from ordinary language may appear "meaningful" in that language and be poorly formed or at least equivocal with respect to the rules for cognitive phrases. X calls up his friend Y whom he hasn't seen for a long time and says to him: *I can come by your place* [...]. In a critical situation, a highly placed bureaucrat orders his subordinates to *Disobey*. The first phrase is equivocal, the second poorly formed, but both are accepted as meaningful by their addressees. Similarly, the phrase *The garbage pail is full* does not induce for the logician or the scholar the nonetheless common response: *Okay, I'll be right there*.[13] The "restrictions" placed on phrases acceptable in the sciences are necessary in order for the verification or falsification of these phrases to be effective: they determine effectible procedures whose reiterable effectuation authorizes the consensus between addressor and addressee.

31. These are not really "restrictions." On the contrary, the more you specify rules for the validation of phrases, the more you can distinguish different ones, and conceive other idioms. The ballgame is not the same if the rule states that the ball must never touch the ground, or that it may touch the ground once only per return for each player, or only once per team for a serve, or once per team for a return, etc. It is as if the conditions of sense were changing. Vidal-Naquet quotes Lucien Febvre quoting Cyrano de Bergerac: "We must not believe everything about a man, because a man can say everything. We must believe only what is human about him."[14] The historian asks: "What is human? What impossible? The question we must answer is: Do these words still have a meaning?" Shouldn't we believe the inhumanity reported by the testimonies of Auschwitz? — *Inhuman* means incompatible with an Idea of humanity. This sense is pertinent for the ethical, the juridical, the political, and the historical families of phrases, where this Idea is necessarily at stake. In cognitive phrases, *human* predicates an event which relates to the human species, and for which cases can be shown. The victims, the executioners, and the witnesses at Auschwitz enter into the class of human beings; the messages we receive from them are meaningful and offer material for verification, even if they are incompatible with any Idea of humanity. Voyager II's messages about Saturn can almost be said to be inhuman in the second sense, because most humans understand nothing in them and could not vouch for them, but they are human at least in the first sense to the extent that they would not take place were they not required by the Idea of a humanity progressing in its knowledge.

32. Even if the verification procedures are specified as they should be, how does the addressor know that the addressee correctly understands what he or she wants to say, and that, like the addressor, the addressee desires that the truth about which they speak be established? — The addressor presupposes it. He or she believes that it is so. He or she also

believes that the addressee believes the same thing about the addressor. Etc. – Here you are in the act of doing "human sciences," of probing the meanings (*vouloir-dire*), the desires, the beliefs that you presuppose to be the property of these entities, human beings. You presuppose by the same token that they use language for certain ends. Psychology, sociology, pragmatics, and a certain philosophy of language have in common this presupposition of an instrumental relation between thoughts and language. This relation follows a technological model: thought has ends, language offers means to thought. How can the addressee discern the addressor's ends from the means of language put to work in the message? For questions of language, the pertinence of the ideas of Homo, of Homo faber, of will, and of good will, which belong to other realms, appears not to raise any doubts!

33. It remains that, if Faurisson is "in bad faith," Vidal-Naquet cannot convince him that the phrase *There were gas-chambers* is true. The historian bitterly notes that, in an analogous fashion, "There are still anti-Dreyfusards."[15] Consensus may be missing even in a case, such as that of the falsehoods fabricated by Colonel Henry,[16] whose reality has been established as much as the procedures for establishing reality will permit. Thus bad will, or bad faith, or a blind belief (the ideology of the League for the French Fatherland[17]) can prevent truth from manifesting itself and justice from being done. – No. What you are calling bad will, etc., is the name that you give to the fact that the opponent does not have a stake in establishing reality, that he does not accept the rules for forming and validating cognitives, that his goal is not to convince. The historian need not strive to convince Faurisson if Faurisson is "playing" another genre of discourse, one in which conviction, or, the obtainment of a consensus over a defined reality, is not at stake. Should the historian persist along this path, he will end up in the position of victim.

34. But how can you know that the opponent is in bad faith as long as you haven't tried to convince him or her and as long as he or she has not shown through his or her conduct a scorn for scientific, cognitive rules? – One "plays the game" permitted by these rules; and the addressee's rejoinder shows that he or she does not observe them. – But, what if the opponent strives to hide that he or she does not observe the rules of cognition, and acts as if he or she were observing them? I would need to know his or her intentions. … – Either way, it comes down to the same thing: the phrases, whose addressor he or she is, satisfy or do not satisfy the rules. They cannot be equivocal on this score, since equivocalness is what the rules exclude. – But you can simulate that they satisfy the rules, that they are univocal; you can invent convicting evidence. In the Dreyfus case, the French high command did not hesitate. – Of course, but it is up to the defense to refute the argument, to object to the witness, to reject the proof, as much as needed and up until the accusation is withdrawn. Then you'll see that the accuser was playing another game. – Undoubtedly, but is it not possible to evade the differend by anticipating it? – This seems to be impossible. What would distinguish such an anticipation from a prejudice, whether favorable or unfavorable, bearing upon the person of your opponent, or upon his or her way of phrasing? Now, prejudging is excluded by the rules of scientific cognitives. – But what about those who establish these rules, aren't they prejudging their competence to establish them? How, indeed, could they not prejudge it as long as the rules have not been established and as long as they therefore lack the criteria by which to distinguish competence? […]

221. What would be modern would be to raise the question of politics, the question of linkings, on the scale of the human, without recourse (in principle) to legitimation by

names and narratives? — By narratives, at least in the sense of myths, tales, and rumors. The narrative form persists, however; and it undergoes the same sublimation as the story's hero. As he is no longer a Cashinahua,[18] but man, so the narrative form no longer recounts "little stories" [*petites histoires*] but the story of History [*l'Histoire*]. The little stories received and bestowed names. The great story of history has its end in the extinction of names (particularisms). At the end of the great story, there will simply be humanity. The names humanity has taken will turn out to be superfluous, at best they will have designated certain stations along the way of the cross [...]. This universalism and this pure teleology is not classical in the sense of Antiquity, but modern in the sense of Christianity. "Philosophies of history" are forged around a redemptive future. (Even capitalism, which has no philosophy of history, disguises its 'realism' under the Idea of an emancipation from poverty.)

222. A non-cosmopolitical (or "savage") narrative proceeds by phrases like *On that date*, *in that place*, *it happened that x*, etc. The question raised by cosmopolitical narrative would be the following: since this *x*, this date, and this place are proper names and since proper names belong by definition to worlds of names and to specific "savage" narratives, how can these narratives give rise to a single world of names and to a universal narrative? The question may seem absurd: aren't these communities human ones? — No, they are "Cashinahua" and they call themselves the community of "true men," if not in exception to others, then at least in distinction from them.[19] The bond woven around "Cashinahua" names by these narratives procures an identity that is solely "Cashinahua." Were this identity already human in the cosmopolitical sense, it would not entail the excepting of other communities, or even the difference between them, and the universal history of humanity would consist in the simple extension of particular narratives to the entire set of human communities.

223. The objection may be made that narratives which result in a "savage" community, "despite everything," "already" have a cosmopolitical "import." It is sufficient to admit an equivocation in them: they present what they present (the "Cashinahua" world), but they also present what they don't present (the "human" world). — There is no objection in admitting this. The question is that of linkage: what genre of discourse governs the linking onto the "Cashinahua" narrative of a phrase discerning a "human" world therein which would stem from a universal history? What is not in doubt is that this genre, whichever one it is, "already" has universal human history for its referent, in order for it to be able to link onto "savage" narratives by placing them into that history. This linkage may be characterized as "projection." I would prefer to call it a begging of the question. If the "Cashinahua" story co-presents the universal history of humanity, it is because it is presented within a genre that presupposes a universal history of humanity. This genre allows for certain variants. The most explicit and most "impoverished" one consists in placing the Cashinahua story on the referent instance of phrases of historical (or anthropological) cognition. — This is always possible (any "object," if it satisfies the cognitive genre, can be situated on the referent instance in the universe of a phrase of cognition), but no proof results from this that the historical (or anthropological) cognition of the narrative of the community has been engendered, throughout the continuous trajectory of a universal history of humanity, from this narrative taken as origin. Yet this "engenderment" is what the concept of a universal history requires.

224. In the "impoverished" variant, the anthropologist-historian's relation to the Cashinahua (the West's relation to "savages") is solely "epistemological." The "archaic" narrative becomes the object of a genre of discourse, that of cognition, which obeys certain

rules and which summons the "savage" narrative genre to appear only when these rules require that proofs (cases, that is to say, examples) be brought to bear upon an assertion relating to the "savage." The heterogeneity between the cognitive genre and its referent, the "savage" narrative genre, is not to be doubted (and in no way does it prohibit cognition). There is an abyss between them. The savage thus suffers a wrong on account of the fact that he or she is "cognized" in this manner, that is, judged, both he or she and his or her norms, according to criteria and in an idiom which are neither those which he or she obeys nor their "result" [...]. What is at stake in savage narratives is not what is at stake in the descriptions of those narratives.

225.   The historian of humanity will object that the epistemological linkage is not the one made by the genre of universal history. He or she invokes a "richer" variant of this linkage [...]. The equivocation that was supposed in the world presented by the "Cashinahua" narrative is, so it is said, intrinsic to that narrative. It becomes cognizable only when it has been deployed. It is then that the concept it contained, now fully disengaged, allows that equivocation to be retroactively cognized. The historian adds that this concept, though, was implied in it "as the form of the oak tree is contained in an acorn." The symbol is not the concept, but it "gives something to think." — We recognize the speculative genre or one of its variations (hermeneutics, in particular). It requires that a self be supposed, which is neither the Cashinahua nor the historian, but the movement of an entity whose figures they are. They cannot be isolated. Man is this entity who only identifies himself in the referral of these moments to his end (as the sense of a movie shot depends upon its insertion into a sequence of shots, and the sense of the sequence upon the arrangement of the shots). — The rules for this "rich" linkage are those of the speculative genre as applied to historical-political realities.

226.   The universal history of humanity should be told in the narrative genre. Like all narratives, it would proceed by means of phrases like *On that date*, *in that place*, *it happened that x*, etc. But, as opposed to the savage narrative, it would be necessary that the onomastics of persons, places, and times, as well as the sense given the reported event, be accepted by all the addressees of the universal narrative (and even that these addressees be able to become in turn its addressors, if the stakes pursued by the narrative genre are indeed those of the narrative's recurrence), and that this community be the one to which those addressees belong. There would then need to be addressees who were themselves "universal." If one wants to escape the preceding question begging (No. 223), renewed here in this form, then in order for the history of humanity to be recounted, a universal, "human" narrator and corresponding narratee would have to be able to be engendered from "savage" ("national") narrators and narratees in their particularity and multiplicity.

227.   The universalization of narrative instances cannot be done without conflict. Traditions are mutually opaque. Contact between two communities is immediately a conflict, since the names and narratives of one community are exclusive of the names and narratives of the other (principle of exception, vainglory and jealousy of names) [...]. The conflict does not result from a problem of language, every language is translatable (this does not prevent linguistic differences from contributing on occasion to the exacerbation of a conflict). Nor is it a differend, since we have the same genre of discourse on each side: narration. It is thus a litigation over the names of times, places, and persons, over the senses and referents attached to those names (*This place*, *this woman*, *this child*, *is not yours*). This litigation, though, has no tribunal before which it can be presented, argued, and decided. For this tribunal would already have to be 'universal,' human, having an (international) law at its disposal,

etc. (And nothing is said by saying at that moment that this tribunal is universal history unless it is to say that judgment is the very "course" of reality; for, if the end of time is awaited, there will no longer be enough time for a judgment) [...]. It is said that force is what decides. What is force, though, when it is a question of deciding between phrases? Are some phrases and genres strong, and others weak (No. 231)?

228.   You assert (No. 227) that between two particular narratives there is no differend, but only litigation, because they both belong to the same genre of discourse and are ruled by the same set of stakes. In order to judge in this way, you have therefore neglected the particular stories (diegeses) told by these narratives and singled out the form of narrative, which you declare to be identical in each. This distinction is the work of a genre of discourse, "critical" examination, which is not narrative. In declaring that there is a litigation, you have already passed judgment from a "universal" point of view, that of the analysis of genres of discourse. The interests put into play through this point of view are not those of the narrations. You too do them a wrong. What is at stake in them is not, as it is for you, that "language" knows itself, but rather that the occurrence be linked onto [...]. – As a matter of fact, the examination of phrases is but a genre, it cannot take the place of politics. For the philosopher to be at the governorship of phrases would be as unjust as it would be were it the jurist, the priest, the orator, the storyteller (the epic poet), or the technician. There is no genre whose hegemony over the others would be just. The philosophical genre, which looks like a metalanguage, is not itself (a genre in quest of its rules) unless it knows that there is no metalanguage. It thereby remains popular, humorous [...].

229.   Certainly, what is just is that "the people" be at the governorship of phrases, if it is true that "the people" is the totality of addressors, addressees, and referents of prose, which is not a genre, nor even a species of language, but the ungraded supply of phrases from all regimens and of linkages from all genres (including poetry). – Nevertheless, this mode of government is called demagogy. It is observed that the people contradicts itself, tears itself asunder, and annihilates itself, that it is trifling and enslaved to opinions. – It is not the people that is fickle, but "language." At each occurrence, the continuity between the phrase that happens and those that precede it is threatened, and the war between the genres is opened in order to assure its succession. Maybe prose is impossible. It is tempted on one side by despotism and on the other by anarchy. It succumbs to the seduction of the former by turning itself into the genre of all genres (the prose of popular Empire) and to the seduction of the latter by trying to be no more than an unregulated assemblage of all phrases (the vagabond's prose, Gertrude Stein?). But the unity of genres is impossible, as is their zero degree. Prose can only be their multitude and the multitude of their differends.

230.   The multitude of phrase regimens and of genres of discourse finds a way to embody itself, to neutralize differends, in narratives [...]. There is a privileging of narrative in the assemblage of the diverse. It is a genre that seems able to admit all others (according to Marx, there is a history of everything). There is an affinity between narrative and the people. "Language's" popular mode of being is the deritualized short story. Short because it is faithful to phrase regimens and to differends, which popular narratives do not seek to dissipate but only to neutralize. They contradict each other. They are resumed in maxims, proverbs, and morals that contradict each other. The wisdom of nations is not only their scepticism, but also the "free life" of phrases and genres. That is what the (clerical, political, military, economic, or informational) oppressor comes up against in the long run. Prose is the people of anecdotes.

231. Which has more "force" (No. 227), a narrative phrase or a critical phrase? Aryan myth or Kantian philosophy? A direct answer would presuppose that "language" is a unity, that it has only one interest, and that the force of a genre is measured by the closeness of its stakes to the interests of language. But genres are incommensurable, each has its own "interests." The "force" of a phrase is judged by the standard of a genre's rules, the same phrase is weak or strong depending upon what is at stake. That is why it is legitimate for the weaker argument to be the stronger one: the rules of the genre in which it is placed have been changed, the stakes are no longer the same. Aristophanes does not see that what is at stake for the sophists and for Socrates is not what is at stake in the popular tradition. The "ironic" phrase is a weak one in the tradition, and vice versa [...]. Language does not have a single finality, or, if it has one, it is not known. Everything is as if "language" were not.

232. At least, between two narratives belonging to the same genre, one can be judged stronger than the other if it comes nearer the goal of narratives: to link onto the occurrence as such by signifying it and by referring to it. The Christian narrative vanquished the other narratives in Rome because by introducing the love of occurrence into narratives and narrations of narratives, it designated what is at stake in the genre itself. To love what happens as if it were a gift, to love even the *Is it happening?* as the promise of good news, allows for linking onto whatever happens, including other narratives (and, subsequently, even other genres). Love as the principal operator of exemplary narrations and diegeses is the antidote to the principle of exception that limits traditional narratives. The authorization to tell, to listen, and to be told about does not result from a common affiliation with a world of names which are themselves descended from primordial narratives, it results from a commandment of universal attraction, *Love one another*, addressed to all heroes, all narrators, and all narratees. This commandment is authorized by the revelation (itself loving) of a primordial story in which we learn that the god of love was not very well loved by his children and about the misfortunes that ensued. This authorization remains in the circular form common to narratives, but it is extended to all narratives. The obligation to love is decreed by the divine Absolute, it is addressed to all creatures (who are none other than His addressees), and it becomes transitive (in an interested sense, because it is conditional): if you are loved, you ought to love; and you shall be loved only if you love.

233. Thanks to the precept of love, all of the events already told in the narratives of infidels and unbelievers can be re-told as so many signs portentous of the new commandment (the synoptic tables of the two Testaments). Not only are the narrative instances universalized, but occurrence is problematized. Christian narration not only tells what has happened, thereby fixing a tradition, but it also prescribes the *caritas* for what can happen, whatever it might be. This commandment orders the narrators and narratees to go to the forefront of the event and to make and carry out its narrative as if it told the story of a loving gift. Any referent can be signified as the sign of the good news announcing that "we" creatures are loved.

234. Inasmuch as it is a matter of ethics, obligation has, nonetheless, no need of an addressor, it is even in need of the contrary. At stake in it is: ought I to do this? The answer given the obligated one is that God wants it. S/he asks: is it really His will? The answer is that He declared His will at the beginning. The obligated one: but I don't feel it now, I don't understand what is prescribed by the authorized interpreters of the Scriptures, I feel the obligation for some other action (Joan of Arc's trial). The holding in suspicion of idiolects not only motivates witchcraft trials, but it already motivates the reception given

the prophets, and still motivates the resistance to the Reformation. For his or her sake, though, the suspect holds the authority of tradition in suspicion. To believe in the narratives of love, he or she opposes faith in the signs of obligation. The latter is only actualized as the obligated one's feeling (the voice of conscience, respect for the moral law). The authority of the commandment to love is not necessarily called back into question, but the repetitive, narrative mode of its legitimation certainly is. To judge that one ought to do *this* thing because *that* thing has already been prescribed is to defy the occurrence and the addressee's responsibility before it. The time invoked by the free examination of one's conscience is no longer the before/after but the now. Narrative politics is shaken, including its way of receiving and neutralizing events, the commutability of addressors, addressees, and heroes (referents) that is constitutive of community, etc. The deliberative concatenation, which welcomes the competition between multiple genres of discourse to signify the event, and which favors judgment over tradition, has more affinity with obligation than with narrative (which passes to the rank of fictive scenario) [...].

235. Obligation cannot engender a universal history, nor even a particular community. Love supplied with its narrative of authorization can engender a universal history as progress toward the redemption of creatures. Relieved of the notion of revelation (the narrative of authorization in its beginnings, which determines its end), love persists in secular, universal history in the form of republican brotherhood, of communist solidarity. Humanity is not made of creatures in the process of redeeming themselves, but of wills in the process of emancipating themselves. Authorization does not reside in a myth of beginnings, but in an Idea which exerts its finality upon phrases and which ought to allow for a way to regulate the differends between genres. The obstacle, though, to this finalization by the Idea of freedom persists in the form of "national" names and traditions, which are woven into popular prose. Peoples do not form into one people, whether it be the people of God or the sovereign people of world citizens. There is not yet one world, but some worlds (with various names and narratives). Internationalism cannot overcome national worlds because it cannot channel short, popular narratives into epics, it remains "abstract": it must efface proper names (Marx trying to rid the name of Alsace-Lorraine from the litigation between French and German socialists in 1870). Even the communist epic of workers' liberation splits off into national-communist epics. There is no differend between national narratives (unless one of them conceals the hegemony of another genre of discourse: the first French Republic up against the Austrian Empire); but the differend between the Idea of freedom and narratives of legitimation is inevitable.

Chapter 16

Luce Irigaray

■ from *AN ETHICS OF SEXUAL DIFFERENCE*,[1]
Carolyn Burke and Gillian C. Gill trans., Ithaca, New York:
Cornell University Press, 1993

COMING TO ROTTERDAM TO TEACH PHILOSOPHY represents something rather special. An adventure of thought, an adventure of discovery, or rediscovery, in a country that has offered a haven to several philosophers. Offered them tolerance and encouragement in their work. Outside of any dogmatic passion. In most cases.

Astonishingly, yet correlatively, these philosophers were often interested in passion. And it is almost a tradition that Holland should be the territory where the issue of the passions is raised.

I shall not fail that history. Or rather, that history, knowingly or not, consciously or not, has chosen me, this year, to speak, in Rotterdam, in a course titled "The Ethics of the Passions." It is as if a certain necessity has led me to this part of the Netherlands to speak on this topic.

To each period corresponds a certain way of thinking. And even though the issues relating to passion and its ethics which need careful consideration today are still clearly linked to Descartes's *wonder* and Spinoza's *joy*, the perspective is no longer the same. This change in perspective is, precisely, a matter of ethics. We are no longer in an era where the subject reconstitutes the world in solitude on the basis of one fixed point: Descartes's certainty that he is a man. This is no longer the era of Spinoza, who wrote: "It is easy to see that if men and women together assumed political authority, peace would suffer great harm from the permanent probability of conflict."

Perhaps we need to reconsider Hegel's analysis of the ethical world and the interpretation of sexual difference he founds on the brother-sister couple he borrows from ancient tragedy: a couple in which sexual difference seems to find harmony through the neutering of the passion "of the blood," through suspension of the carnal act. A couple whose fecundity, while loving, leads to real death. A couple forming the substrate for both the conceptualization and realization of the family and of the state which still hold sway today.

But, in this couple, whereas the brother is still able to see himself in his sister as if she were a living mirror, she finds in him no image of herself that would allow her to leave the family and have a right to the "for-itself" of the spirit "of daylight." It is understood that she accedes to generality through her husband and her child but only at the price of her singularity. She would have to give up her sensibility, the singularity of her desire, in order to enter into the immediately universal of her family duty. Woman would be wife and mother without desire. Pure obligation dissociates her from her affect.

This duty, abstract and empty of all feeling, is supposedly at the root of woman's identity, once the sister is dead and the chorus of women has been buried under the town so that the order of the city-state may be founded.

An ethical imperative would seem to require a practical and theoretical revision of the role historically allotted to woman. Whereas this role was still interpreted by Freud as anatomic destiny, we need to understand that it has been determined by the necessities of a traditional sociocultural organization – one admittedly in the process of evolving today.

Philosophy, thought, and discourse do not evolve swiftly enough in response to "popular" movements. One of the places in our time where we can locate a people is the "world of women." Nonetheless, if there is to be neither repression of this "people" nor ethical error on its part, an access to sexual difference becomes essential, and society must abandon the murderous hierarchy as well as the division of labor which bars woman from accomplishing the task reserved for her by Hegel – the task of going from the deepest depths to the highest heavens. In other words, of being faithful to a process of the divine which passes through her, whose course she must sustain, without regressing or yielding up her singular desire or falling prisoner to some fetish or idol of the question of "God." Could it be that one of the qualities of this divine process is to leave woman open, her threshold free, with no closure, no dogmatism? Could this be one of its ethical deeds, in sexual exchange as well?

This opportunity to question the ethical status of sexual difference is the result of an invitation to give the lecture series established in honor of Jan Tinbergen – a man who set himself the task, among others, of trying to solve certain socioeconomic problems of the third world. If I take this occasion to broach the problem of the sociocultural situation of women (sometimes referred to as the fourth world), at the request of women, and thanks to them, it will, I hope, be seen as a gesture of respect toward a vocation of generosity that is the motivation for this lectureship dedicated to theoretical research and social practice.

So let me return to the character of Antigone, though I shall not identify with it. Antigone, the antiwoman, is still a production of a culture that has been written by men alone. But this figure, who, according to Hegel, stands for ethics, has to be brought out of the night, out of the shadow, out of the rock, out of the total paralysis experienced by a social order that condemns itself even as it condemns her. Creon, who has forbidden burial for Polynices, who has suggested that Antigone keep quiet from now on about her relations with the gods, Creon who has ordered Antigone to be closed up in a hole in the rock, leaving just a little food so that he cannot be guilty of her death – this Creon has condemned society to a split in the order of reason that leaves nature without gods, without grace. Leaves the family with no future other than work for the state, procreation without joy, love without ethics.

Creon, the king, will, in the end, endure a fate as cruel as Antigone's. But he will be master of that destiny.

Antigone is silenced in her action. Locked up – paralyzed, on the edge of the city. Because she is neither master nor slave. And this upsets the order of the dialectic.

She is not a master, that much is clear.

She is not a slave. Especially because she does nothing by halves. Except for her suicide, perhaps? Suicide, the only act left to her. Given that society passes – as Hegel would say – onto the side of darkness when it is a question of the right of the female to act.

But who would dare condemn Antigone?

Not those who denied her air, love, the gods, and even the preparation of food.

Antigone has nothing to lose. She makes no attempt on another's life. Hence the fear she arouses in Creon, who, for his part, has much at risk. I am no longer a man, he says: she is the man if I let her live. These words reveal the nature or the very essence of his crime. For him, the king, the only values are masculine, virile ones. Creon takes a risk when he wounds the other, the female, in the worship of her gods, in her right to love, to conscience, to speech. This wound will come back to haunt him as that abyss, that chasm, that night inscribed in the very heart of the dialectic, of reason, of society. Chasm or night that demands attention, like a "calvary" or a "chalice," writes Hegel.

If society today is afraid of certain men or certain women, we might ask ourselves what "crime" against them that fear might connote. And wonder if it is impossible to "imprison" or silence more than half of the world's population, for example.

This is all the more true when sensitivity becomes specularization, speculation, discourses that enter a loop of mutual interaction or lose their substance by depriving themselves of what once fed them, or fed them anew. Man is forced to search far and wide, within his memory, for the source of meaning. But by moving back into the past one risks losing the future. Discourse is a tight fabric that turns back upon the subject and wraps around and imprisons him in return. It is as if Agamemnon no longer needed Clytemnestra to catch him in her toils: discourse is net enough for him.

In the end, every "war" machine turns against the one who made it. At least according to Hegel? At least according to a certain logic of conscience? Unless we can pass into another?

Unless, at every opportunity, we ourselves take the negative upon ourselves. Which would amount to allowing the other his/her liberty, and sex. Which would assume that we accept losing ourselves by giving ourselves. Which would leave the decision about time to us. By giving us control over the debts we lay *on the future.*

Do we still have the time to face those debts?

Ethically, we have to give ourselves the time. Without forgetting to plan. Giving ourselves time is to plan on abjuring our deadly polemics so that we have time for living, and living together.

This ethical question can be approached from different perspectives, if I give myself, give us, time to think it through.

Given that *science* is one of the last figures, if not the last figure, used to represent absolute knowledge, it is – ethically – essential that we ask science to reconsider the nonneutrality of the supposedly universal subject that constitutes its scientific theory and practice.

In actual fact, the self-proclaimed universal is the equivalent of an idiolect of men, a masculine imaginary, a sexed world. With no neuter. This will come as a surprise only to an out-and-out defender of idealism. It has always been men who spoke and, above all, wrote: in science, philosophy, religion, politics.

But, nothing is said about scientific intuition (except by a few rare scientists, notably physicists). Intuition would apparently arise ex nihilo, aseptic as by right. And yet a few modalities or qualities of that intuition can be sorted out. It is always a matter of:

- Positing *a* world in front of the self, constituting a world *in front of the self*.
- Imposing *a model* on the universe so as to take possession of it, an abstract, invisible, intangible model that is *thrown over* the universe like an encasing garment. Which amounts to clothing the universe in one's own identity. One's own blindness, perhaps?
- Claiming that, as a subject, one is rigorously alien to the model, i.e., to prove that the model is purely and simply *objective*.
- Demonstrating that the model is "insensible" when in fact it has virtually been pre-scribed at least by the privilege accorded to the *visual* (i.e., by the absence, the distancing, of a subject that is yet surreptitiously there).
- A move out of the world of the senses made possible by the *mediation of the instrument*, the intervention of a technique that separates the subject from the object under investigation. A process of moving away and delegating power to something that intervenes between the universe observed and the observing subject.
- Constructing an *ideal* or *idea-generated* model, independent of the physical and mental makeup of its producer. With games of induction, as well as deduction, passing through an ideal elaboration.
- Proving the *universality* of the model, at least within a given time. And its absolute power (independent of its producer), its constitution of a unique and total world.
- Buttressing that *universality* by protocols of experiments which at least two (identical?) subjects must agree on.
- Proving that the discovery is *efficient, productive, profitable, exploitable* (or is it rather *exploitative* of a natural world increasingly drained of life?). Which is assumed to mean *progress*.

These characteristics reveal an "isomorphism with man's sexual imaginary." Which has to be kept strictly under wraps. "Our subjective experiences or our personal opinions can never be used to justify any statement," claims the epistemologist of science.

But it is apparent in many ways that the subject in science is not neuter or neutral. Particularly in the way certain things are not discovered at a given period as well as in the research goals that science sets, or fails to set, for itself. Thus, in a more or less random list that refuses to respect the hierarchy of the sciences:

- *The physical sciences* constitute research targets in regard to a nature which they measure in an ever more formal, abstract, and modeled fashion. Their techniques, based on more and more sophisticated axiom-building, concern a matter which certainly still exists but cannot be perceived by the subject operating the experiment. At least in most sectors of these sciences. And "nature," the stake of the physical sciences, risks being exploited and torn apart at the hands of the physicist, even without his knowing. Given that the Newtonian dividing line has led scientific inquiry into a "universe" in which perception by the senses has almost no validity and which may even entail annulling precisely the thing that is at stake in the object of physics: the matter (whatever the predicates of matter may be) of the universe and of the bodies constituting it.

Within this very theory, in fact, there are deep divisions: theory of quanta/theory of fields, solid mechanics/ fluid dynamics, for example. But the fact that the matter under study is inaccessible to the senses often involves the paradoxal privilege accorded to "solidity" in the discoveries, and science has been slow, or has even given up, trying to analyze the infinite of force fields. Could this be interpreted as a refusal to take into account the dynamics of the subject researching himself?

- *The mathematical sciences*, in set theory, take an interest in closed and open spaces, in the infinitely large and infinitely small. They are less concerned with the question of the half-open, of fluid sets, of anything that analyzes the problem of edges, of the passage between things, of the fluctuations taking place from one threshold to the other of defined sets. (Even if topology raises such issues, does it not place far more emphasis on that which closes up than on that which remains without possible circularity?)
- *The biological sciences* have been very slow to take on certain problems. The constitution of the placental tissue, the permeability of membranes, for example. Are these not questions directly correlated to the female and the maternal sexual imaginary?
- *The logical sciences* are more concerned with bivalent theories than with trivalent or polyvalent ones. Is that because the latter still appear marginal? Because they upset the discursive economy?
- *The linguistic sciences* have concerned themselves with models for utterances, with synchronic structures of speech, with language models "known intuitively to any normally constituted subject." They have not faced, and at times even refuse to face, the question of the sexuation of discourse. They accept, perforce, that certain items of vocabulary may be added to the established lexicon, that new stylistic figures may potentially become acceptable, but they refuse to consider that syntax and the syntactic – semantic – operation might be sexually determined, might not be neuter, universal, unchanging.
- *Economics* and perhaps even the social sciences have preferred to emphasize the phenomenon of scarcity and the question of survival rather than that of abundance and life.
- *Psychoanalytic science* is based on the two first principles of thermodynamics that underlie Freud's model of the libido. However, these two principles seem more isomorphic to male sexuality than to female. Given that female sexuality is less subject to alternations of tension-discharge, to conservation of required energy, to maintaining states of equilibrium, to functioning as a closed circuit that opens up through saturation, to the reversibility of time, etc.

If a scientific model is needed, female sexuality would perhaps fit better with what Prigogine calls "dissipatory" structures, which function through exchanges with the exterior world, which proceed in steps from one energy level to another, and which are not organized to search for equilibrium but rather to cross thresholds, a procedure that corresponds to going beyond disorder or entropy without discharge.

As we face these claims, these questions, this issue arises: *either* to do science *or* to become "militant." Or is it rather: to continue to do science *and* to divide oneself into several functions, several persons or characters? Should the "truth" of science and that of life remain separate, at least for the majority of researchers? What science or what life is at issue here, then? Particularly since life in our era is largely dominated by science and its techniques.

What is the origin of this split imposed and suffered by scientists? Is it a model of the subject that has not been analyzed? A "subjective" revolution that has not taken place? Given that the disintegration of the subject is programmed by the *episteme* and the power structures it has set up. Must we assume that the Copernican revolution has occurred but that the epistemological subject has yet to act on it and move beyond it? The discourse of the subject has been altered but finds itself even more disturbed by this revolution than the language of the world which preceded it. Given that the scientist, now, wants to be *in front of* the world: naming the world, making its laws, its axioms. Manipulating nature, exploiting it, but forgetting that he too is *in* nature. That he is still *physical*, and not only when faced with phenomena whose *physical* nature he tends to ignore. As he progresses according to an objective method designed to shelter him from any instability, any "mood," any feelings and affective fluctuations, from any intuition that has not been programmed in the name of science, from any influence of his desire, particularly his *sexual* desires, over his discoveries. Perhaps by installing himself within a system, within something that can be assimilated to what is already dead? Fearing, sterilizing the losses of equilibrium even though these are necessary to achieve a new horizon of discovery.

One of the ways most likely to occasion an interrogation of the scientific horizon is to question discourse about the subject of science, and the psychic and sexuate involvement of that subject in scientific discoveries and their formulation.

Such questions clamor to be answered, or at least raised, from somewhere outside, from a place in which the subject has not or has scarcely begun to be spoken. An outside placed on the other slope of sexual difference, the one which, while useful for reproducing the infrastructure of social order, has been condemned to imprisonment and silence within and by society. It remains true that the feminine, in and through her language, can, today, raise questions of untold richness. Still she must be allowed to speak; she must be heeded. This may lead to the avoidance of two ethical mistakes, if I may return again to Hegel:

- Subordinating women to destiny without allowing them any access to mind, or consciousness of self and for self, offering them only death and violence as their part.
- Closing man away in a consciousness of self and for self that leaves no space for the gods and whose discourse, even today and for that same reason, goes in search of its meaning.

In other words, in this division between the two sides of sexual difference, one part of the world would be searching for a way to find and speak its meaning, its side of signification, while the other would be questioning whether meaning is still to be found in language, values, and life.

This desperately important question of our time is linked to an injustice, an ethical mistake, a debt still owing to "natural law" and to its gods.

If this question is apparent in the dereliction of the feminine, it is also raised on the male side, in quest for its meaning. Humanity and humanism have proved that their ethos is difficult to apply outside certain limits of tolerance. Given that the world is not undifferentiated, not neuter, particularly insofar as the sexes are concerned.

The meaning that can be found on the male side is perhaps that of a debt contracted toward the one who gave and still gives man life, in language as well.

Language, however formal it may be, feeds on blood, on flesh, on material elements. Who and what has nourished language? How is this debt to be repaid? Must we produce more and more formal mechanisms and techniques which redound on man, like the inverted outcome of that mother who gave him a living body? And whom he fears in direct ratio to the unpaid debt that lies between them.

To remember that we must go on living and creating worlds is our task. But it can be accomplished only through the combined efforts of the two halves of the world: the masculine and the feminine.

And I shall end with an example of something that can constitute or entail an unpaid debt to the maternal, the natural, the matrical, the nourishing.

As we move farther away from our condition as living beings, we tend to forget the most indispensable element in life: *air*. The air we breathe, in which we live, speak, appear; the air in which everything "enters into presence" and can come into being.

This air that we never think of has been borrowed from a birth, a growth, a *phusis* and a *phuein* that the philosopher forgets.

To forget being is to forget the air, this first fluid given us gratis and free of interest in the mother's blood, given us again when we are born, like a natural profusion that raises a cry of pain: the pain of a being who comes into the world and is abandoned, forced henceforth to live without the immediate assistance of another body. Unmitigated mourning for the intrauterine nest, elemental homesickness that man will seek to assuage through his work as builder of worlds, and notably of the dwelling which seems to form the essence of his maleness: language.

In all his creations, all his works, man always seems to neglect thinking of himself as flesh, as one who has received his body as that primary home (that *Gestell*, as Heidegger would say, when, in "Logos," the seminar on Heraclitus, he recognizes that what metaphysics has not begun to address is the issue of the body) which determines the possibility of his coming into the world and the potential opening of a horizon of thought, of poetry, of celebration, that also includes the god or gods.

The fundamental dereliction in our time may be interpreted as our failure to remember or prize the element that is indispensable to life in all its manifestations: from the lowliest plant and animal forms to the highest. Science and technology are reminding men of their careless neglect by forcing them to consider the most frightening question possible, the question of a radical polemic: the destruction of the universe and of the human race through the splitting of the atom and its exploitation to achieve goals that are beyond our capacities as mortals.

"Only a god can save us now," said Heidegger, who was also remembering the words of Hölderlin, the poet with whom his thought was indissolubly linked. Hölderlin says that the god comes to us on a certain *wind* that blows from the icy cold of the North to the place where every sun rises: the East. The god arrives on the arms of a wind that sweeps aside everything that blocks the light, everything that separates fire and air and covers all with imperceptible ice and shadow. The god would refer back to a time before our space-time was formed into a closed world by an economy of natural elements forced to bow to man's affect and will. Demiurge that could have closed up the universe into a circle, or an egg, according to Empedocles.

Man's technical prowess today allows him to blow up the world just as, at the dawn of our culture, he was able to establish a finite horizon to it.

Is a god what we need, then? A god who can upset the limits of the possible, melt the ancient glaciers, a god who can make a future for us. A god carried on the breath of the *cosmos*, the song of the poets, the respiration of lovers.

We still have to await the god, remain ready and open to prepare a way for his coming. And, with him, for ourselves, to prepare, not an implacable decline, but a new birth, a new era in history.

Beyond the circularity of discourse, of the nothing that is in and of being. When the copula no longer veils the abyssal burial of the other in a gift of language which is neuter only in that it forgets the difference from which it draws its strength and energy. With a neuter, abstract *there is* giving way to or making space for a "we are" or "we become," "we live here" together.

This creation would be our opportunity, from the humblest detail of everyday life to the "grandest" by means of the opening of a *sensible transcendental* that comes into being through us, of which *we would be* the mediators and bridges. Not only in mourning for the dead God of Nietzsche, not waiting passively for the god to come, but by conjuring him up among us, within us, as resurrection and transfiguration of blood, of flesh, through a language and an ethics that is ours.

Chapter 17

Jean-François Lyotard

■ from ANSWER TO THE QUESTION: WHAT IS THE POSTMODERN? in *The Postmodern Explained to Children: Correspondence 1982–1985*, Don Barry et al. trans., London: Power Institute of Fine Arts, 1992

To Thomas E. Carroll
Milan, May 15, 1982

A DEMAND

WE ARE IN A MOMENT OF RELAXATION – I am speaking of the tenor of the times. Everywhere we are being urged to give up experimentation, in the arts and elsewhere. I have read an art historian who preaches realism and agitates for the advent of a new subjectivity. I have read an art critic who broadcasts and sells "Transavantgardism" in the marketplace of art. I have read that in the name of postmodernism architects are ridding themselves of the Bauhaus project, throwing out the baby – which is still experimentation – with the bath water of functionalism. I have read that a new philosopher has invented something he quaintly calls Judeo-Christianism, with which he intends to put an end to the current impiety for which we are supposedly responsible. I have read in a French weekly that people are unhappy with *Mille Plateaux* because, especially in a book of philosophy, they expect to be rewarded with a bit of sense. I have read from the pen of an eminent historian that avant-garde writers and thinkers of the sixties and seventies introduced a reign of terror into the use of language, and that the imposition of a common mode of speech on intellectuals (that of historians) is necessary to reestablish the conditions for fruitful debate. I have read a young Belgian philosopher of language complaining that continental thought, when faced with the challenge of talking machines, left them to look after reality; that it replaced the paradigm of referentiality with one of adlinguisticity (speaking about speech, writing about writing, intertextuality); he thinks it is time that language recovered a firm anchorage in the referent. I have read a talented theatrologist who says that the tricks and caprices of postmodernism count for little next to authority, especially when a mood of anxiety encourages that authority to adopt a politics of totalitarian vigilance in the face of the threat of nuclear war.

I have read a reputable thinker who defends modernity against those he calls neo-conservatives. Under the banner of postmodernism they would like, he believes, to extricate themselves from the still incomplete project of modernity, the project of Enlightenment. By his account, even the last partisans of the *Aufklärung*, like Popper or Adorno, were able to defend that project only in particular spheres of life – politics for the author of *The Open Society*, art for the author of *Aesthetic Theory*. Jürgen Habermas (you will have recognised him) thinks that if modernity has foundered, it is because the totality of life has been left to fragment into independent specialties given over to the narrow competence of experts, while the concrete individual experiences "desublimated meaning" and "destructured form", not as a liberation, but in the manner of that immense ennui Baudelaire described over a century ago.

Following Albrecht Wellmer's lead, the philosopher believes that the remedy for this parcelling of culture and its separation from life will only come from a "change in the status of aesthetic experience when it is no longer primarily expressed in judgments of taste", when instead "it is used to illuminate a life-historical situation" that is to say, when "it is related to the problems of existence". For this experience "then enters into a language game which is no longer just that of the aesthetic critic"; it intervenes "in cognitive procedures and normative expectations"; it "changes the way these different moments *refer* to one another". In short, the demand Habermas makes of the arts and the experience they provide is that they should form a bridge over the gap separating the discourses of knowledge, ethics, and politics, thus opening the way for a unity of experience.

My problem is knowing what sort of unity Habermas has in mind. What is the end envisaged by the project of modernity? Is it the constitution of a sociocultural unity at the heart of which all elements of daily life and thought would have a place, as though within an organic whole? Or is the path to be cut between heterogeneous language games – knowledge, ethics, and politics – of a different order to them? And if so, how would it be capable of realising their effective synthesis?

The first hypothesis, Hegelian in inspiration, does not call into question the notion of a dialectically totalising *experience*. The second is closer in spirit to the *Critique of Judgment*; but, like the *Critique*, it must be submitted to the severe reexamination postmodernity addresses to the thought of the Enlightenment, to the idea of a uniform end of history and the idea of the subject. This critique was started not only by Wittgenstein and Adorno but also by other thinkers, French or otherwise, who have not had the honour of being read by Professor Habermas – at least this spares them getting bad marks for neoconservatism.

Realism

The demands I cited to you at the beginning are not all equivalent. They may even be contradictory. Some are made in the name of postmodernism, some in opposition to it. It is not necessarily the same thing to demand the provision of a referent (and objective reality), or a meaning (and credible transcendence), or an addressee (and a public), or an addressor (and expressive subjectivity), or a communicative consensus (and a general code of exchange, the genre of historical discourse, for example). But in these various invitations to suspend artistic experimentation, there is the same call to order, a desire for unity, identity, security, and popularity (in the sense of *Öffentlichkeit*, "finding a public"). Artists and writers must be made to return to the fold of the community; or at least, if the community is deemed to be ailing, they must be given the responsibility of healing it.

There exists an irrefutable sign of this common disposition: for all these authors, nothing is as urgent as liquidating the legacy of the avant-gardes. The impatience of so-called transavantgardism is a case in point. The replies an Italian critic recently gave to French critics leave no doubt on the matter. The procedure of mixing avant-gardes together means that artists and critics can feel more confident of suppressing them than if they were to attack them head on. They can then pass off the most cynical eclecticism as an advance on the no doubt partial nature of earlier explorations. If they turned their backs on such explorations overtly, they would expose themselves to ridicule for neoacademicism. At the time the bourgeoisie was establishing itself in history, the Salons and Academies assumed a purgative function – awarding prizes for good conduct in the plastic and literary arts under the guise of realism. But capitalism in itself has such a capacity to derealise familiar objects, social roles and institutions that so called "realist" representations can no longer evoke reality except through nostalgia or derision – as an occasion for suffering rather than satisfaction. Classicism seems out of the question in a world where reality is so destabilised that it has no material to offer to experience, but only for analysis and experimentation.

This theme is familiar to readers of Walter Benjamin. Still, its precise implications need to be grasped. Photography did not pose an external challenge to painting any more than did industrial cinema to narrative literature. The former refined certain aspects of the program of ordering the visible elaborated by the Quattrocento, and the latter was able to perfect the containment of diachronies within organic totalities – the ideal of exemplary educative novels since the eighteenth century. The substitution of mechanical and industrial production for manual and craft production was not a catastrophe in itself, unless the essence of art is thought to be the expression of individual genius aided by the skills of an artisanal élite.

The greatest challenge lay in the fact that photographic and cinematic processes could accomplish better and faster – and with a diffusion a hundred thousand times greater than was possible for pictorial and narrative realism – the task that academicism had assigned to realism: protecting consciousness from doubt. Industrial photography and cinema always have the edge over painting and the novel when it is a matter of stabilising the referent, of ordering it from a point of view that would give it recognisable meaning, of repeating a syntax and lexicon that would allow addressees to decode images and sequences rapidly, and make it easy for them to become conscious both of their own identities and of the approval they thereby receive from others – since the structures in these images and sequences form a code of communication between them all. So effects of reality – or the fantasms of realism, if you prefer – are multiplied.

If the painter and novelist do not want to be, in their turn, apologists of what exists (and minor ones at that), they have to renounce such therapeutic occupations. They must question the rules of the art of painting and narration as learnt and received from their predecessors. They soon find that such rules are so many methods of deception, seduction and reassurance which make it impossible to be "truthful". An unprecedented split occurs in both painting and literature. Those who refuse to reexamine the rules of art will make careers in mass conformism, using "correct rules" to bring the endemic desire for reality into communication with objects and situations capable of satisfying it. Pornography is the use of photographs and film to this end. It becomes a general model for those pictorial and narrative arts which have not risen to the challenge of the mass media.

As for artists and writers who agree to question the rules of the plastic and narrative arts and perhaps share their suspicions by distributing their work – they are destined to lack credibility in the eyes of the devoted adherents of reality and identity, to find themselves without a guaranteed audience. In this sense, we can impute the dialectic of the avant-gardes to the challenge posed by the realisms of industry and the mass media to the arts of painting and literature. The Duchampian readymade does no more than signify, actively and parodically, this continual process of the dispossession of the painter's craft, and even the artist's. As Thierry de Duve astutely observes, the question of modern aesthetics is not "What is beautiful?" but "What is art to be (and what is literature to be)?"

Realism – which can be defined only by its intention of avoiding the question of reality implied in the question of art – always finds itself somewhere between academicism and kitsch. When authority takes the name of the party, realism and its complement, neoclassicism, triumph over the experimental avant-garde by slandering and censoring it. Even then, "correct" images, "correct" narratives – the correct forms that the party solicits, selects and distributes – must procure a public which will desire them as the appropriate medicine for the depression and anxiety it feels. The demand for reality, that is, for unity, simplicity, communicability, etc., did not have the same intensity or continuity for the German public between the wars as it had for the Russian public after the revolution: here one can draw a distinction between Nazi and Stalinist realism.

All the same, any attack on artistic experimentation mounted by political authority is inherently reactionary: aesthetic judgment would only have to reach a verdict on whether a particular work conforms to the established rules of the beautiful. Instead of the work having to bother with what makes it an art object and whether it will find an appreciative audience, political academicism understands and imposes a priori criteria of the "beautiful", criteria which can, in one move and once and for all, select works and their public. So the use of categories in an aesthetic judgment would be similar to their use in a cognitive judgment. In Kant's terms, both would be determinant judgments: an expression is first "well formed" in the understanding, then only those "cases" which can be subsumed within this expression are retained in experience.

When authority does not take the name of the party but that of capital, the "trans-avantgardist" solution (postmodernist in Jencks' sense) turns out to be more appropriate than the anti-modern one. Eclecticism is the degree zero of contemporary general culture: you listen to reggae, you watch a western, you eat McDonald's at midday and local cuisine at night, you wear Paris perfume in Tokyo and dress retro in Hong Kong, knowledge is the stuff of TV game shows. It is easy to find a public for eclectic works. When art makes itself kitsch, it panders to the disorder which reigns in the "taste" of the patron. Together, artist, gallery owner, critic and public indulge one another in the Anything Goes – it's time to relax. But this realism of Anything Goes is the realism of money: in the absence of aesthetic criteria it is still possible and useful to measure the value of works of art by the profits they realise. This realism accommodates every tendency just as capitalism accommodates every "need" – so long as these tendencies and needs have buying power. As for taste, there is no need to be choosy when you are speculating or amusing yourself. Artistic and literary investigation is doubly threatened: by "cultural politics" on one side, by the art and book market on the other. The advice it receives, from one or other of these channels, is to provide works of art which, first, relate to subjects already existing in the eyes of the public to which they are addressed and which, second, are made ("well formed") in such a way that this public will recognise what they are about, understand what they mean, and then be able to grant or withhold its approval with confidence, possibly even drawing some solace from those it accepts.

The sublime and the avant-garde

This interpretation of the contact of the mechanical and industrial arts with the fine arts and literature is acceptable as an outline, but you would have to agree it is narrowly sociologistic and historicising, in other words, one-sided. Notwithstanding the reservations of Benjamin and Adorno, it should be remembered that science and industry are just as open to suspicion with regard to reality as art and writing. To think otherwise would be to subscribe to an excessively humanist idea of the Mephistophelian functionalism of science and technology. One cannot deny the predominance of technoscience as it exists today, that is, the massive subordination of cognitive statements to the finality of the best possible performance – which is a technical criterion. Yet the mechanical and the industrial, particularly when they enter fields traditionally reserved for the artist, are bearers of something more than effects of power. The objects and thoughts issuing from scientific knowledge and the capitalist economy bring with them one of the rules underwriting their possibility: the rule that there is no reality unless it is confirmed by a consensus between partners on questions of knowledge and commitment.

This rule is of no small consequence. It is the stamp left on the politics of both the scientist and the manager of capital by a sort of flight of reality from the metaphysical, religious and political assurances which the mind once believed it possessed. This retreat is indispensable to the birth of science and capitalism. There would be no physics had doubt not been cast on the Aristotelian theory of movement. No industry without the refutation of corporatism, mercantilism and physiocracy. Modernity, whenever it appears, does not occur without a shattering of belief, without a discovery of the *lack of reality* in reality – a discovery linked to the invention of other realities.

What would this "lack of reality" mean if we were to free it from a purely historicising interpretation? The phrase is clearly related to what Nietzsche calls nihilism. Yet I see a modulation of it well before Nietzschean perspectivism, in the Kantian theme of the sublime. In particular, I think the aesthetic of the sublime is where modern art (including literature) finds its impetus and where the logic of the avant-garde finds its axioms.

The sublime feeling, which is also the feeling of the sublime, is, according to Kant, a powerful and equivocal emotion: it brings both pleasure and pain. Or rather, in it pleasure proceeds from pain. In the tradition of the philosophy of the subject coming from Augustine and Descartes – which Kant does not radically question – this contradiction (which others might call neurosis or masochism) develops as a conflict between all of the faculties of the subject, between the faculty to conceive of something and the faculty to "present" something. There is knowledge first if a statement is intelligible, and then if "cases" which "correspond" to it can be drawn from experience. There is beauty if a particular "case" (a work of art), given first by the sensibility and with no conceptual determination, arouses a feeling of pleasure that is independent of any interest and appeals to a principle of universal consensus (which may never be realised).

Taste in this way demonstrates that an accord between the capacity to conceive and the capacity to present an object corresponding to the concept – an accord that is undetermined, without rule, giving rise to what Kant calls a reflective judgment – may be felt in the form of pleasure. The sublime is a different feeling. It occurs when the imagination in fact fails to present any object which could accord with a concept, even if only in principle. We have the Idea of the world (the totality of what is) but not the capacity to show an example of it. We have the Idea of the simple (the non-decomposable), but we cannot illustrate it by a sensible object which would be a case of it. We can conceive of the absolutely great, the absolutely powerful; but any presentation of an object – which would be intended to "display" that absolute greatness or absolute power – appears sadly lacking to us. These Ideas, for which there is no possible presentation and which therefore provide no knowledge of reality (experience), also prohibit the free accord of the faculties that produces the feeling of the beautiful. They obstruct the formation and stabilisation of taste. One could call them unpresentable.

I shall call modern the art which devotes its "trivial technique", as Diderot called it, to presenting the existence of something unpresentable. Showing that there is something we can conceive of which we can neither see nor show: this is the stake of modern painting. But how do we show something that cannot be seen? Kant himself suggests the direction to follow when he calls *formlessness*, the *absence of form*, a possible index to the unpresentable. And, speaking of the empty *abstraction* felt by the imagination as it searches for a presentation of the infinite (another unpresentable), he says that it is itself like a presentation of the infinite, its *negative presentation.* He cites the passage "Thou shalt not make unto Thee any graven image, etc." (*Exodus 2, 4*) as the most sublime in the Bible, in that it forbids any presentation of the absolute. For an outline of an aesthetic of sublime painting, there is little we need to add to these remarks: as painting, it will evidently "present" something, but negatively: it will therefore avoid figuration or representation; it will be "blank" [*blanche*] like one of Malevich's squares; it will make one see only by prohibiting one from seeing; it will give pleasure only by giving pain. In these formulations we can recognise the axioms of the avant-gardes in painting to the extent that they dedicate themselves to allusions to the unpresentable through visible presentations. The systems of reasoning in whose name or with which this task could support and justify itself warrant a good deal of attention; but such systems cannot take shape except by setting out from the vocation of the sublime with the aim of legitimating this vocation, in other words, of disguising it. They remain inexplicable without the incommensurability between reality and concept implied by the Kantian philosophy of the sublime.

I do not intend to analyse in detail here the way the various avant-gardes have, as it were, humiliated and disqualified reality by their scrutiny of the pictorial techniques used to instil a belief in it. Local tone, drawing, the blending of colours, linear perspective, the nature of the support and of tools, "execution", the hanging of the work, the museum: the avant-gardes continually expose the artifices of presentation that allow thought to be enslaved by the gaze and diverted from the unpresentable. If Habermas, like Marcuse, takes this work of derealisation as an aspect of the (repressive) "desublimation" characterising the avant-garde, it is because he confuses the Kantian sublime with Freudian sublimation, and because for him aesthetics is still an aesthetics of the beautiful.

The postmodern

What then is the postmodern? What place, if any, does it occupy in that vertiginous work of questioning the rules that govern images and narratives? It is undoubtedly part of the modern. Everything that is received must be suspected, even if it is only a day old (*modo*, *modo*, wrote Petronius). What space does Cézanne challenge? The Impressionists'. What object do Picasso and Braque challenge? Cézanne's. What presupposition does Duchamp break with in 1912? The idea that one has to make a painting – even a cubist painting. And Buren examines another presupposition that he believes emerged intact from Duchamp's work: the place of the word's presentation. The "generations" flash by at an astonishing rate. A work can become modern only if it is first postmodern. Thus understood, postmodernism is not modernism at its end, but in a nascent state, and this state is recurrent.

But I would not wish to be held to this somewhat mechanistic use of the word. If it is true that modernity unfolds in the retreat of the real and according to the sublime relationship of the presentable with the conceivable, we can (to use a musical idiom) distinguish two essential modes in this relationship. The accent can fall on the inadequacy of the faculty of presentation, on the nostalgia for presence experienced by the human subject and the obscure and futile will which animates it in spite of everything. Or else the accent can fall on the power of the faculty to conceive, on what one might call its "inhumanity" (a quality Apollinaire insists upon in modern artists) – since it is of no concern to the understanding whether or not the human sensibility or imagination accords with what it conceives – and on the extension of being and jubilation which come from inventing new rules of the game, whether pictorial, artistic, or something else. A caricatured arrangement of several names on the chessboard of avantgardist history will show you what I mean: on the side of *melancholy,* the German Expressionists, on the side of *novatio*, Braque and Picasso; on the one hand, Malevich, on the other, El Lissitsky; on one side, de Chirico, on the other, Duchamp. What distinguishes these two modes may only be the merest nuance: they often coexist almost indiscernibly in the same piece, and yet they attest to a *différend* [an incommensurable difference of opinion] within which the fate of thought has, for a long time, been played out and will continue to be played out – a differend between regret and experimentation.

The works of Proust and Joyce both allude to something that does not let itself be made present. Allusion (to which Paulo Fabbri has recently drawn my attention) is, perhaps, an indispensable mode of expression for works which belong to the aesthetic of the sublime. In Proust the thing that is eluded as the price of this allusion is the identity of consciousness, falling prey to an excess of time. But in Joyce it is the identity of writing which falls prey to an excess of the book or literature. Proust invokes the unpresentable by means of a language which keeps its syntax and lexicon intact, and a writing which, in terms of most of its operators, is still part of the genre of the narrative novel. The literary institution as Proust inherits it from Balzac or Flaubert is undoubtedly subverted since the hero is not a character but the inner consciousness of time, and also because the diachrony of the diegesis, already shaken by Flaubert, is further challenged by the choice of narrative voice. But the unity of the book as the odyssey of this consciousness is not disturbed, even if it is put off from chapter to chapter: the identity of the writing with itself within the labyrinth of its interminable narration is enough to connote this unity, which some have compared to that of the *Phenomenology of Spirit*. Joyce makes us discern the unpresentable in the writing itself, in the signifier. A whole range of accepted narrative and even stylistic operators is brought into play with no concern for the unity of the whole, and experiments are conducted with new operators. The grammar and vocabulary of literary language are no longer taken for granted; instead they appear as academicisms, rituals born of a piety (as Nietzsche might call it) that do not allow the invocation of the unpresentable.

So this is the differend: the modern aesthetic is an aesthetic of the sublime, but it is nostalgic; it allows the unpresentable to be invoked only as absent content, while form, thanks to its recognisable consistency, continues to offer the reader or spectator material for consolation and pleasure. But such feelings do not amount to the true sublime feeling, which is intrinsically a combination of pleasure and pain: pleasure in reason exceeding all presentation, pain in the imagination or sensibility proving inadequate to the concept.

The postmodern would be that which in the modern invokes the unpresentable in presentation itself, which refuses the consolation of correct forms, refuses the consensus of taste permitting a common experience of nostalgia for the impossible, and inquires into new presentations — not to take pleasure in them but to better produce the feeling that there is something unpresentable. The postmodern artist or writer is in the position of a philosopher: the text he writes or the work he creates is not in principle governed by pre-established rules and cannot be judged according to a determinant judgment, by the application of given categories to this text or work. Such rules and categories are what the work or text is investigating. The artist and the writer therefore work without rules, and in order to establish the rules for what *will have been made.* This is why the work and the text can take on the properties of an event; it is also why they would arrive too late for their author or, in what amounts to the same thing, why their creation would always begin too soon. *Postmodern* would be understanding according to the paradox of the future (*post*) anterior (*modo*).

It seems to me that the essay (Montaigne) is postmodern, and the fragment (the *Athenaeum*) is modern.

Finally, it should be made clear that it is not up to us to *provide reality* but to invent allusions to what is conceivable but not presentable. And this task should not lead us to expect the slightest reconciliation between "language games" — Kant, naming them the faculties, knew that they are separated by an abyss and that only a transcendental illusion (Hegel's) can hope to totalise them into a real unity. But he also knew that the price of this illusion is terror. The 19th and 20th centuries have given us our fill of terror. We have paid dearly for our nostalgia for the all and the one, for a reconciliation of the concept and the sensible, for a transparent and communicable experience. Beneath the general demand for relaxation and appeasement, we hear murmurings of the desire to reinstitute terror and fulfil the fantasm of taking possession of reality. The answer is: war on totality. Let us attest to the unpresentable, let us activate the differends and save the honour of the name.

Chapter 18

Zygmunt Bauman

■ A SOCIOLOGICAL THEORY OF POSTMODERNITY
in *Intimations of Postmodernity*, London: Routledge, 1992

I PROPOSE THAT:

1. The term *postmodernity* renders accurately the defining traits of the social condition that emerged throughout the affluent countries of Europe and of European descent in the course of the twentieth century, and took its present shape in the second half of that century. The term is accurate as it draws attention to the continuity and discontinuity as two faces of the intricate relationship between the present social condition and the formation that preceded and gestated it. It brings into relief the intimate, genetic bond that ties the new, postmodern social condition to *modernity* – the social formation that emerged in the same part of the world in the course of the seventeenth century, and took its final shape, later to be sedimented in the sociological models of modern society (or models of society created by modern sociology), during the nineteenth century; while at the same time indicating the passing of certain crucial characteristics in whose absence one can no longer adequately describe the social condition as modern in the sense given to the concept by orthodox (modern) social theory.

2. Postmodernity may be interpreted as fully developed modernity taking a full measure of the anticipated consequences of its historical work; as modernity that acknowledged the effects it was producing throughout its history, yet producing inadvertently, rarely conscious of its own responsibility, by default rather than design, as by-products often perceived as waste. Postmodernity may be conceived of as modernity conscious of its true nature – *modernity for itself*. The most conspicuous features of the postmodern condition: institutionalized pluralism, variety, contingency and ambivalence – have been all turned out by modern society in ever increasing volumes; yet they were seen as signs of failure rather than success, as evidence of the insufficiency of efforts so far, at a time when the institutions of modernity, faithfully replicated by the modern mentality, struggled for *universality*, *homogeneity*, *monotony* and *clarity*. The postmodern condition can be therefore described, on the one hand, as modernity emancipated from false consciousness; on the other, as a new type of social condition marked by the overt

institutionalization of the characteristics which modernity – in its designs and managerial practices – set about to eliminate and, failing that, tried to conceal.

3. The twin differences that set the postmodern condition apart from modern society are profound and seminal enough to justify (indeed, to call for) a separate sociological theory of postmodernity that would break decisively with the concepts and metaphors of the models of modernity and lift itself out of the mental frame in which they had been conceived. This need arises from the fact that (their notorious disagreements notwithstanding), the extant models of modernity articulated a shared vision of modern history as *a movement with a direction* – and differed solely in the selection of the ultimate destination or the organizing principle of the process, be it universalization, rationalization or systemization. None of those principles can be upheld (at least not in the radical form typical of the orthodox social theory) in the light of postmodern experience. Neither can the very master-metaphor that underlies them be sustained: that of the process with a pointer.

4. Postmodernity is not a transitory departure from the "normal state" of modernity; neither is it a diseased state of modernity, an ailment likely to be rectified, a case of "modernity in crisis". It is, instead, a self-reproducing, pragmatically self-sustainable and logically self-contained social condition defined by *distinctive features of its own*. A theory of postmodernity therefore cannot be a modified theory of modernity, a theory of modernity with a set of negative markers. An adequate theory of postmodernity may be only constructed in a cognitive space organized by a different set of assumptions; it needs its own vocabulary. The degree of emancipation from the concepts and issues spawned by the discourse of modernity ought to serve as a measure of the adequacy of such a theory.

Conditions of theoretical emancipation

What the theory of postmodernity must discard in the first place is the assumption of an "*organismic*", equilibrated social totality it purports to model in Parsons-like style: the vision of a "principally coordinated" and enclosed totality (a) with a degree of cohesiveness, (b) equilibrated or marked by an overwhelming tendency to equilibration, (c) unified by an internally coherent value syndrome and a core authority able to promote and enforce it and (d) defining its elements in terms of the function they perform in that process of equilibration or the reproduction of the equilibrated state. The sought theory must assume instead that the social condition it intends to model is essentially and perpetually *unequilibrated*: composed of elements with a degree of autonomy large enough to justify the view of totality as a kaleidoscopic – momentary and contingent – outcome of interaction. The orderly, structured nature of totality cannot be taken for granted; nor can its pseudorepresentational construction be seen as the purpose of theoretical activity. The randomness of the global outcome of uncoordinated activities cannot be treated as a departure from the pattern which the totality strives to maintain; any pattern that may temporarily emerge out of the random movements of autonomous agents is as haphazard and unmotivated as the one that could emerge in its place or the one bound to replace it, if also for a time only. All order that can be found is a local, emergent and transitory phenomenon; its nature can be best grasped by a metaphor of a whirlpool appearing in the flow of a river, retaining its shape only for a relatively brief period and only at the expense of incessant metabolism and constant renewal of content.

The theory of postmodernity must be free of the metaphor of progress that informed all competing theories of modern society. With the totality dissipated into a series of randomly emerging, shifting and evanescent islands of order, its temporal record cannot be linearly represented. Perpetual local transformations do not add up so as to prompt (much less to assure) in effect an increased homogeneity, rationality or organic systemness of the whole. The postmodern condition is a site of constant mobility and change, but no clear direction of development. The image of Brownian movement offers an apt metaphor for this aspect of postmodernity: each momentary state is neither a necessary effect of the preceding state nor the sufficient cause of the next one. The postmodern condition is both *undetermined* and *undetermining*. It "unbinds" time; weakens the constraining impact of the past and effectively prevents colonization of the future.

Similarly, the theory of postmodernity would do well if it disposed of concepts like *system* in its orthodox, organismic sense (or, for that matter, *society*), suggestive of a sovereign totality logically prior to its parts, a totality bestowing meaning on its parts, a totality whose welfare or perpetuation all smaller (and, by definition, subordinate) units serve; in short, a totality assumed to define, and be practically capable of defining, the meanings of individual actions and agencies that compose it. A sociology geared to the conditions of postmodernity ought to replace the category of *society* with that of *sociality*; a category that tries to convey the processual modality of social reality, the dialectical play of randomness and pattern (or, from the agent's point of view, of freedom and dependence); and a category that refuses to take the structured character of the process for granted – which treats instead all found structures as emergent accomplishments.

With their field of vision organized around the focal point of system-like, resourceful and meaning-bestowing totality, sociological theories of modernity (which conceived of themselves as sociological theories *tout court*) concentrated on the vehicles of homogenization and conflict-resolution in a relentless search for a solution to the "Hobbesian problem". This cognitive perspective (shared with the one realistic referent of the concept of "society" – the national state, the only totality in history able seriously to entertain the ambition of contrived, artificially sustained and managed monotony and homogeneity) a priori disqualified any "uncertified" agency; unpatterned and unregulated spontaneity of the autonomous agent was predefined as a destabilizing and, indeed, antisocial factor marked for taming and extinction in the continuous struggle for societal survival. By the same token, prime importance was assigned to the mechanisms and weapons of order promotion and pattern-maintenance: the state and the legitimation of its authority, power, socialization, culture, ideology, etc. – all selected for the role they played in the promotion of pattern, monotony, predictability and thus also manageability of conduct.

A sociological theory of postmodernity is bound to reverse the structure of the cognitive field. The focus must be now on agency; more correctly, on the *habitat* in which agency operates and which it produces in the course of operation. As it offers the agency the sum total of resources for all possible action as well as the field inside which the action-orienting and action-oriented relevancies may be plotted, the habitat is the territory inside which both freedom and dependency of the agency are constituted (and, indeed, perceived as such). Unlike the system-like totalities of modern social theory, habitat neither determines the conduct of the agents nor defines its meaning; it is no more (but no less either) than the setting in which both action and meaning-assignment are *possible*. Its own identity is as under-determined and motile, as emergent and transitory, as those of the actions and their meanings that form it.

There is one crucial area, though, in which the habitat performs a determining (systematizing, patterning) role: it sets the agenda for the "business of life" through supplying the inventory of ends and the pool of means. The way in which the ends and means are supplied also determines the meaning of the "business of life": the nature of the tasks all agencies confront and have to take up in one form or another. In so far as the ends are offered as potentially alluring rather than obligatory, and rely for their choice on their own seductiveness rather than the supporting power of coercion, the "business of life" splits into a series of choices. The series is not pre-structured, or is pre-structured only feebly and above all inconclusively. For this reason the choices through which the life of the agent is construed and sustained is best seen (as it tends to be seen by the agents themselves) as adding up to the process of *self-constitution*. To underline the graduated and ultimately inconclusive nature of the process, self-constitution is best viewed as *self-assembly*.

I propose that sociality, habitat, self-constitution and self-assembly should occupy in the sociological theory of postmodernity the central place that the orthodoxy of modern social theory had reserved for the categories of society, normative group (like class or community), socialization and control.

Main tenets of the theory of postmodernity

1. Under the postmodern condition, habitat is a *complex system*. According to contemporary mathematics, complex systems differ from mechanical systems (those assumed by the orthodox, modern theory of society) in two crucial respects. First, they are unpredictable; second, they are not controlled by statistically significant factors (the circumstance demonstrated by the mathematical proof of the famous "butterfly effect"). The consequences of these two distinctive features of complex systems are truly revolutionary in relation to the received wisdom of sociology. The "systemness" of the postmodern habitat no longer lends itself to the organismic metaphor, which means that agencies active within the habitat cannot be assessed in terms of functionality or dysfunctionality. The successive states of the habitat appear to be unmotivated and free from constraints of deterministic logic. And the most formidable research strategy modern sociology had developed – statistical analysis – is of no use in exploring the dynamics of social phenomena and evaluating the probabilities of their future development. Significance and numbers have parted ways. Statistically insignificant phenomena may prove to be decisive, and their decisive role cannot be grasped in advance.

2. The postmodern habitat is a complex (non-mechanical) system for two closely related reasons. First, there is no "goal setting" agency with overall managing and co-ordinating capacities or ambitions – one whose presence would provide a vantage point from which the aggregate of effective agents appears as a "totality" with a determined structure of relevances; a totality which one can think of as an *organization*. Second, the habitat is populated by a great number of agencies, most of them single-purpose, some of them small, some big, but none large enough to subsume or otherwise determine the behaviour of the others. Focusing on a single purpose considerably enhances the effectiveness of each agency in the field of its own operation, but prevents each area of the habitat from being controlled from a single source, as the field of operation of any agency never exhausts the whole area the action is affecting. Operating in different fields yet zeroing in on shared areas, agencies are *partly* dependent on each other, but the lines of dependence

cannot be fixed and thus their actions (and consequences) remain staunchly under-determined, that is autonomous.

3.   Autonomy means that agents are only partly, if at all, constrained in their pursuit of whatever they have institutionalized as their purpose. To a large extent, they are free to pursue the purpose to the best of their mastery over resources and managerial capacity. They are free (and tend) to view the rest of the habitat shared with other agents as a collection of opportunities and "problems" to be resolved or removed. Opportunity is what increases output in the pursuit of purpose, problems are what threatens the decrease or a halt of production. In ideal circumstances (maximization of opportunities and minimization of problems) each agent would tend to go in the pursuit of their purpose as far as resources would allow; the availability of resources is the only reason for action they need and thus the sufficient guarantee of the action's reasonability. The possible impact on other agents' opportunities is not automatically reforged into the limitation of the agent's own output. The many products of purpose-pursuing activities of numerous partly interdependent but relatively autonomous agents must yet find, *ex post facto*, their relevance, utility and demand-securing attractiveness. The products are bound to be created in volumes exceeding the pre-existing demand motivated by already articulated problems. They are still to seek their place and meaning as well as the problems that they may claim to be able to resolve.

4.   For every agency, the habitat in which its action is inscribed appears therefore strikingly different from the confined space of its own autonomic, purpose-subordinated pursuits. It appears as a space of chaos and chronic *indeterminacy*, a territory subjected to rival and contradictory meaning-bestowing claims and hence perpetually *ambivalent*. All states the habitat may assume appear equally *contingent* (that is, they have no overwhelming reasons for being what they are, and they could be different if any of the participating agencies behaved differently). The heuristics of pragmatically useful "next moves" displaces, therefore, the search for algorithmic, certain knowledge of deterministic chains. The succession of states assumed by the relevant areas of the habitat no agency can interpret without including its own actions in the explanation; agencies cannot meaningfully scan the situation "objectively", that is in such ways as allow them to eliminate, or bracket away, their own activity.

5.   The existential modality of the agents is therefore one of insufficient determination, inconclusiveness, motility and rootlessness. The identity of the agent is neither given nor authoritatively confirmed. It has to be construed, yet no design for the construction can be taken as prescribed or foolproof. The construction of identity consists of successive trials and errors. It lacks a benchmark against which its progress could be measured, and so it cannot be meaningfully described as "progressing". It is now the incessant (and non-linear) *activity* of self-constitution that makes the identity of the agent. In other words, the self-organization of the agents in terms of a *life-project* (a concept that assumes a long-term stability; a lasting identity of the habitat, in its duration transcending, or at least commen-surate with, the longevity of human life) is displaced by the *process of self-constitution*. Unlike the life-project self-constitution has no destination point in reference to which it could be evaluated and monitored. It has no visible end; not even a stable direction. It is conducted inside a shifting (and, as we have seen before, unpredictable) constellation of mutually autonomous points of reference, and thus purposes guiding the self-constitution at one stage may soon lose their current authoritatively confirmed validity. Hence the self-assembly of the agency is not a cumulative process; self-constitution entails disassembling alongside

the assembling, adoption of new elements as much as shedding of others, learning together with forgetting. The identity of the agency, much as it remains in a state of permanent change, cannot be therefore described as "developing". In the self-constitution of agencies, the "Brownian movement"-type spatial nature of the habitat is projected onto the time axis.

6. The only visible aspect of continuity and of the cumulative effects of self-constitutive efforts is offered by the human body – seen as the sole constant factor among the protean and fickle identities: the material, tangible substratum, container, carrier and executor of all past, present and future identities. The self-constitutive efforts focus on keeping alive (and preferably enhancing) the *capacity* of the body for absorbing the input of sensuous impressions and producing a constant supply of publicly legible self-definitions. Hence the centrality of *body-cultivation* among the self-assembly concerns, and the acute attention devoted to everything "taken internally" (food, air, drugs, etc.) and to everything coming in touch with the skin – that interface between the agent and the rest of the habitat and the hotly contested frontier of the autonomously managed identity. In the postmodern habitat, DIY operations (jogging, dieting, slimming, etc.) replace and to a large extent displace the panoptical drill of modern factory, school or the barracks; unlike their predecessors, however, they are not perceived as externally imposed, cumbersome and resented necessities, but as manifestos of the agent's freedom. Their heteronomy, once blatant through coercion, now hides behind seduction.

7. As the process of self-constitution is not guided or monitored by a sovereign life-project designed in advance (such a life-project can only be imputed in retrospect, reconstructed out of a series of emergent episodes), it generates an acute demand for a substitute: a constant supply of orientation points that may guide successive moves. It is the other agencies (real or imagined) of the habitat who serve as such orientation points. Their impact on the process of self-constitution differs from that exercised by normative groups in that they neither monitor nor knowingly administer the acts of allegiance and the actions that follow it. From the vantage point of self-constituting agents, other agents can be metaphorically visualized as a randomly scattered set of free-standing and unguarded totemic poles which one can approach or abandon without applying for permission to enter or leave. The self-proclaimed allegiance to the selected agent (the act of selection itself) is accomplished through the adoption of *symbolic tokens* of belonging, and freedom of choice is limited solely by the availability and accessibility of such tokens.

8. *Availability* of tokens for potential self-assembly depends on their visibility, much as it does on their material presence. Visibility in its turn depends on the perceived *utility* of symbolic tokens for the satisfactory outcome of self-construction; that is, on their ability to reassure the agent that the current results of self-assembly are indeed satisfactory. This reassurance is the substitute for the absent certainty, much as the orientation points with the attached symbolic tokens are collectively a substitute for predetermined patterns for life-projects. The reassuring capacity of symbolic tokens rests on borrowed (ceded) authority; of *expertise*, or of *mass following*. Symbolic tokens are actively sought and adopted if their relevance is vouched for by the trusted authority of the expert, or by their previous or concurrent appropriation by a great number of other agents. These two variants of authority are in their turn fed by the insatiable thirst of the self-constituting agents for reassurance. Thus *freedom* of choice and *dependence* on external agents reinforce each other, and arise and grow together as products of the same process of self-assembly and of the constant demand for reliable orientation points which it cannot but generate.

9. *Accessibility* of tokens for self-assembly varies from agent to agent, depending mostly on the resources that a given agent commands. Increasingly, the most strategic role among the resources is played by knowledge; the growth of individually appropriated knowledge widens the range of assembly patterns which can be realistically chosen. Freedom of the agent, measured by the range of realistic choices, turns under the postmodern condition into the main dimension of inequality and thus becomes the main stake of the *redistributional* type of conflict that tends to arise from the dichotomy of privilege and deprivation; by the same token, access to knowledge – being the key to an extended freedom – turns into the major index of social standing. This circumstance increases the attractiveness of *information* among the symbolic tokens sought after for their reassuring potential. It also further enhances the authority of experts, trusted to be the repositories and sources of valid knowledge. Information becomes a major resource, and experts the crucial brokers of all self-assembly.

Postmodern politics

Modern social theory could afford to separate theory from policy. Indeed, it made a virtue out of that historically circumscribed plausibility, and actively fought for the separation under the banner of value-free science. Keeping the separation watertight has turned into a most distinctive mark of modern theory of society. A theory of postmodernity cannot follow that pattern. Once the essential contingency and the absence of supra- or pre-agentic foundations of sociality and of the structured forms it sediments has been acknowledged, it becomes clear that the politics of agents lies at the core of the habitat's existence; indeed, it can be said to be its existential modality. All description of the postmodern habitat must include politics from the beginning. Politics cannot be kept outside the basic theoretical model as an epiphenomenon, a superstructural reflection or belatedly formed, intellectually processed derivative.

It could be argued (though the argument cannot be spelled out here) that the separation of theory and policy in modern *theory* could be sustained as long as there was, unchallenged or effectively immunized against challenge, a *practical* division between theoretical and political practice. The latter separation had its foundation in the activity of the modern national state, arguably the only social formation in history with pretensions to and ambitions of administering a global order, and of maintaining a total monopoly over rule-setting and rule-execution. Equally policy was to be the state's monopoly, and the procedure for its formulation had to be made separate and independent from the procedure legitimizing an acceptable theory and, more generally, intellectual work modelled after the latter procedure. The gradual, yet relentless erosion of the national state's monopoly (undermined simultaneously from above and from below, by transnational and subnational agencies, and weakened by the fissures in the historical marriage between nationalism and the state, none needing the other very strongly in their mature form) ended the plausibility of theoretical segregation.

With state resourcefulness and ambitions shrinking, responsibility (real or just claimed) for policy shifts away from the state or is actively shed on the state's own initiative. It is not taken over by another agent, though. It dissipates; it splits into a plethora of localized or partial policies pursued by localized or partial (mostly one issue) agencies. With that, vanishes the modern state's tendency to condense and draw upon itself almost all social protest arising from unsatisfied redistributional demands and expectations – a quality that further enhanced the inclusive role of the state among societal agencies, at the same time rendering it vulnerable and exposed to frequent political crises (as conflicts fast turned into political protests). Under the postmodern condition grievances which in the past would cumulate into a collective political process and address themselves to the state, stay diffuse and translate into self-reflexivity of the agents, stimulating further dissipation of policies and autonomy of postmodern agencies (if they do cumulate for a time in the form of a one-issue pressure group, they bring together agents too heterogeneous in other respects to prevent the dissolution of the formation once the desired progress on the issue in question has been achieved; and even before that final outcome, the formation is unable to override the diversity of its supporters' interests and thus claim and secure their *total* allegiance and identification). One can speak, allegorically, of the "functionality of dissatisfaction" in a postmodern habitat.

Not all politics in postmodernity is unambiguously postmodern. Throughout the modern era, politics of *inequality* and hence of *redistribution* was by far the most dominant type of political conflict and conflict-management. With the advent of postmodernity it has been displaced from its dominant role, but remains (and in all probability will remain) a constant feature of the postmodern habitat. Indeed, there are no signs that the postmodern condition promises to alleviate the inequalities (and hence the redistributional conflicts) proliferating in modern society. Even such an eminently modern type of politics acquires in many cases a postmodern tinge, though. Redistributional vindications of our time are focused more often than not on the winning of *human rights* (a code name for the agent's autonomy, for that freedom of choice that constitutes the agency in the postmodern habitat) by categories of population heretofore denied them (this is the case of the emancipatory movements of oppressed ethnic minorities, of the black movement, of one important aspect of the feminist movement, much as of the recent rebellion against the "dictatorship over needs" practiced by the communist regimes), rather than at the express redistribution of wealth, income and other consumable values by society at large. The most conspicuous social division under postmodern conditions is one between *seduction* and *repression*: between the choice and the lack of choice, between the capacity for self-constitution and the denial of such capacity, between autonomously conceived self-definitions and imposed categorizations experienced as constraining and incapacitating. The redistributional aims (or, more precisely, consequences) of the resulting struggle are mediated by the resistance against repression of human agency. One may as well reverse the above statement and propose that in its postmodern rendition conflicts bared their true nature, that of the drive toward freeing of human agency, which in modern times tended to be hidden behind ostensibly redistributional battles.

Alongside the survivals of the modern form of politics, however, specifically postmodern forms appear and gradually colonize the centre-field of the postmodern political process. Some of them are new; some others owe their new, distinctly postmodern quality to their recent expansion and greatly increased impact. The following are the most prominent among them (the named forms are not necessarily mutually exclusive; and some act at cross-purposes):

1. *Tribal politics*. This is a generic name for practices aimed at collectivization (supra-agentic confirmation) of the agents' self-constructing efforts. Tribal politics entails the creation of tribes as *imagined communities*. Unlike the premodern communities the modern powers set about uprooting, postmodern tribes exist in no other form but the symbolically

manifested commitment of their members. They can rely on neither executive powers able to coerce their constituency into submission to the tribal rules (seldom do they have clearly codified rules to which submission could be demanded), nor on the strength of neighbourly bonds or intensity of reciprocal exchange (most tribes are de-territorialized, and communication between their members is hardly at any time more intense than the intercourse between members and non-members of the tribe). Postmodern tribes, are, therefore, constantly in *statu nascendi* rather than *essendi*, brought over again into being by repetitive symbolic rituals of the members but persisting no longer than these rituals' power of attraction (in which sense they are akin to Kant's *aesthetic communities* or Schmalenbach's *communions*). Allegiance is composed of the ritually manifested support for positive tribal tokens or equally symbolically demonstrated animosity to negative (antitribal) tokens. As the persistence of tribes relies solely on the deployment of the affective allegiance, one would expect an unprecedented condensation and intensity of emotive behaviour and a tendency to render the rituals as spectacular as possible – mainly through inflating their power to shock. Tribal rituals, as it were, compete for the scarce resource of public attention as the major (perhaps sole) resource of survival.

2. *Politics of desire.* This entails actions aimed at establishing the relevance of certain types of conduct (tribal tokens) for the self-constitution of the agents. If the relevance is established, the promoted conduct grows in attractiveness, its declared purposes acquire *seductive* power, and the probability of their choice and active pursuit increases: promoted purposes turn into agents' needs. In the field of the politics of desire, agencies vie with each other for the scarce resource of individual and collective dreams of the good life. The overall effect of the politics of desire is heteronomy of choice supported by, and in its turn sustaining, the autonomy of the choosing agents.

3. *Politics of fear.* This is, in a sense, a supplement (simultaneously a complement and a counterweight) of the politics of desire, aimed at drawing boundaries to heteronomy and staving off its potentially harmful effects. If the typical modern fears were related to the threat of totalitarianism perpetually ensconced in the project of rationalized and state-managed society (Orwell's "boot eternally trampling a human face", Weber's "cog in the machine" and "iron cage", etc.), postmodern fears arise from uncertainty as to the soundness and reliability of advice offered through the politics of desire. More often than not, diffuse fears crystallize in the form of a suspicion that the agencies promoting desire are (for the sake of self-interest) oblivious or negligent of the damaging effects of their proposals. In view of the centrality of body-cultivation in the activity of self-constitution, the damage most feared is one that can result in poisoning or maiming the body through penetration or contact with the skin (the most massive panics have focused recently on incidents like mad cow disease, listeria in eggs, shrimps fed on poisonous algae, dumping of toxic waste – with the intensity of fear correlated to the importance of the body among the self-constituting concerns, rather than to the statistical significance of the event and extent of the damage).

The politics of fear strengthens the position of experts in the processes of self-constitution, while ostensibly questioning their competence. Each successive instance of the suspension of trust articulates a new area of the habitat as problematic and thus leads to a call for more experts and more expertise.

4. *Politics of certainty.* This entails the vehement search for social confirmation of choice, in the face of the irredeemable pluralism of the patterns on offer and acute awareness that

each formula of self-constitution, however carefully selected and tightly embraced, is ultimately one of the many, and always "until further notice". Production and distribution of certainty is the defining function and the source of power of the experts. As the pronouncements of the experts can be seldom put to the test by the recipients of their services, for most agents certainty about the soundness of their choices can be plausibly entertained only in the form of *trust*. The politics of certainty consists therefore mainly in the production and manipulation of trust; conversely, "lying", "letting down", "going back on one's words", "covering up" the unseemly deeds or just withholding information, betrayal of trust, abuse of privileged access to the facts of the case – all emerge as major threats to the already precarious and vulnerable self-identity of postmodern agents. Trustworthiness, credibility and perceived sincerity become major criteria by which merchants of certainty – experts, politicians, sellers of self-assembly identity kits – are judged, approved or rejected.

On all four stages on which the postmodern political game is played, the agent's initiative meets socially produced and sustained offers. Offers potentially available exceed as a rule the absorbing capacity of the agent. On the other hand, the reassuring potential of such offers as are in the end chosen rests almost fully on the *perceived* superiority of such offers over their competitors. This is, emphatically, a perceived superiority. Its attractiveness relies on a greater volume of allocated trust. What is perceived as superiority (in the case of marketed utilities, life-styles or political teams alike) is the visible amount of *public attention* the offer in question seems to enjoy. Postmodern politics is mostly about the reallocation of attention. Public attention is the most important – coveted and struggled for – among the scarce commodities in the focus of political struggle.

Postmodern ethics

Like politics, ethics is an indispensable part of a sociological theory of postmodernity pretending to any degree of completeness. The description of modern society could leave ethical problems aside or ascribe to them but a marginal place, in view of the fact that the moral regulation of conduct was to a large extent subsumed under the legislative and law-enforcing activity of global societal institutions, while whatever remained unregulated in such a way was "privatized" or perceived (and treated) as residual and marked for extinction in the course of full modernization. This condition does not hold anymore; ethical discourse is not institutionally pre-empted and hence its conduct and resolution (or irresolution) must be an organic part of any theoretical model of postmodernity.

Again, not all ethical issues found in a postmodern habitat are new. Most importantly, the possibly extemporal issues of the orthodox ethics – the rules binding short-distance, face-to-face intercourse between moral agents under conditions of physical and moral proximity – remain presently as much alive and poignant as ever before. In no way are they postmodern; as a matter of fact, they are not modern either. (On the whole, modernity contributed little, if anything, to the enrichment of moral problematics. Its role boiled down to the substitution of legal for moral regulation and the exemption of a wide and growing sector of human actions from moral evaluation.)

The distinctly postmodern ethical problematic arises primarily from two crucial features of the postmodern condition: *pluralism* of authority, and the centrality of *choice* in the self-constitution of postmodern agents.

1. Pluralism of authority, or rather the absence of an authority with globalizing ambitions, has a twofold effect. First, it rules out the setting of binding norms each agency must (or could be reasonably expected to) obey. Agencies may be guided by their own purposes, paying in principle as little attention to other factors (also to the interests of other agencies) as they can afford, given their resources and degree of independence. "Non-contractual bases of contract", devoid of institutional power support, are thereby considerably weakened. If unmotivated by the limits of the agency's own resources, any constraint upon the agency's action has to be negotiated afresh. Rules emerge mostly as reactions to strife and consequences of ensuing negotiations; still, the already negotiated rules remain by and large precarious and under-determined, while the needs of new rules – to regulate previously unanticipated contentious issues – keep proliferating. This is why the *problem* of rules stays in the focus of public agenda and is unlikely to be conclusively resolved. In the absence of "principal coordination" the negotiation of rules assumes a distinctly *ethical* character: at stake are the principles of non-utilitarian self-constraint of autonomous agencies – and both non-utility and autonomy define *moral* action as distinct from either self-interested or legally prescribed conduct. Second, pluralism of authorities is conducive to the resumption by the agents of moral responsibility that tended to be neutralized, rescinded or ceded away as long as the agencies remained subordinated to a unified, quasi-monopolistic legislating authority. On the one hand, the agents face now point-blank the consequences of their actions. On the other, they face the evident ambiguity and controversiality of the purposes which actions were to serve, and thus the need to justify argumentatively the values that inform their activity. Purposes can no longer be substantiated *monologically*; having become perforce subjects of a *dialogue,* they must now refer to principles wide enough to command authority of the sort that belongs solely to ethical values.

2. The enhanced autonomy of the agent has similarly a twofold ethical consequence. First – in as far as the centre of gravity shifts decisively from heteronomous control to self-determination, and autonomy turns into the defining trait of postmodern agents – self-monitoring, self-reflection and self-evaluation become principal activities of the agents, indeed the mechanisms synonymical with their self-constitution. In the absence of a universal model for self-improvement, or of a clear-cut hierarchy of models, the most excruciating choices agents face are between life-purposes and values, not between the means serving the already set, uncontroversial ends. Supra-individual criteria of propriety in the form of technical precepts of instrumental rationality do not suffice. This circumstance, again, is potentially propitious to the sharpening up of moral self-awareness: only ethical principles may offer such criteria of value-assessment and value-choice as are at the same time supra-individual (carrying an authority admittedly superior to that of individual self-preservation), and fit to be used without surrendering the agent's autonomy. Hence the typically postmodern heightened interest in ethical debate and increased attractiveness of the agencies claiming expertise in moral values (e.g., the revival of religious and quasi-religious movements). Second, with the autonomy of all and any agents accepted as a principle and institutionalized in the life-process composed of an unending series of choices, the limits of the agent whose autonomy is to be observed and preserved turn into a most closely guarded and hotly contested frontier. Along this borderline new issues arise which can be settled only through an ethical debate. Is the flow and the outcome of self-constitution to be tested before the agent's right to autonomy is confirmed? If so, what are the standards by which success or failure are to be judged (what about the autonomy

of young and still younger children, of the indigent, of parents raising their children in unusual ways, of people choosing bizarre lifestyles, of people indulging in abnormal means of intoxication, people engaging in idiosyncratic sexual activities, individuals pronounced mentally handicapped)? And, how far are the autonomous powers of the agent to extend and at what point is their limit to be drawn (remember the notoriously inconclusive contest between "life" and "choice" principles of the abortion debate)?

All in all, in the postmodern context agents are constantly faced with moral issues and obliged to choose between equally well founded (or equally unfounded) ethical precepts. The choice always means the assumption of responsibility, and for this reason bears the character of a moral act. Under the postmodern condition, the agent is perforce not just an actor and decision-maker, but a *moral subject*. The performance of life-functions demands also that the agent be a morally *competent* subject.

Sociology in the postmodern context

The strategies of any systematic study are bound to be resonant with the conception of its object. Orthodox sociology was resonant with the theoretical model of the modern society. It was for that reason that the proper accounting for the self-reflexive propensities of human actors proved to be so spectacularly difficult. Deliberately or against its declared wishes, sociology tended to marginalize or explain away self-reflexivity as rule-following, function performing or at best sedimentation of institutionalized learning; in each case, as an epiphenomenon of social totality, understood ultimately as "legitimate authority" capable of "principally coordinating" social space. As long as the self-reflexivity of actors remained reduced to the subjective perception of obedience to impersonal rules, it did not need to be treated seriously; it rarely came under scrutiny as an independent variable, much less as a principal condition of all sociality and its institutionalized sedimentations.

Never flawless, this strategy becomes singularly inadequate under the postmodern condition. The postmodern habitat is indeed an incessant flow of reflexivity; the sociality responsible for all its structured yet fugitive forms, their interaction and their succession, is a discursive activity, an activity of interpretation and reinterpretation, of interpretation fed back into the interpreted condition only to trigger off further interpretive efforts. To be effectively and consequentially present in a postmodern habitat sociology must conceive of itself as a participant (perhaps better informed, more systematic, more rule-conscious, yet nevertheless a participant) of this never ending, self-reflexive process of reinterpretation and devise its strategy accordingly. In practice, this will mean in all probability, replacing the ambitions of the judge of "common beliefs", healer of prejudices and umpire of truth with those of a clarifier of interpretative rules and facilitator of communication; this will amount to the replacement of the dream of the legislator with the practice of an interpreter.

Chapter 19

Jean-François Lyotard

■ PSYCHOANALYSIS, AESTHETICS AND THE POLITICS OF DIFFERENCE, An interview with Jean-François Lyotard,[1] by W. van Reijen and D. Veerman, Roy Boyne trans., in *Theory, Culture and Society*, 5, 1988, 277–309

Q1: Monsieur Lyotard, as you have said several times[2] you now think that you have moved beyond the language-game approach of The Postmodern Condition *(1979); speaking of* Le Différend *(1984), you have said that this is "your book of philosophy".[3] Do you think that the polemic stirred up by your association with* The Postmodern Condition *has distracted attention from your other writings, and in particular from* Le Différend?

A1: Has *The Postmodern Condition* effaced or occluded *Le Différend*? The answer is yes. The former book effectively provoked a number of polemics. I did not expect that; nor was it what I was looking for. But, on reflection, it is understandable. I mean that, having been presented with the usage of this term, borrowed, as I explained, from American literary criticism and the crisis of modernism in the arts, especially architecture and painting, one might have expected that on that side at least there might be some reaction. The reason for this is that I take the term in a sense which is completely different from that which is generally accepted in these matters, from its designation as the end of modernism. I have said and will say again that "postmodern" signifies not the end of modernism, but another relation to modernism. On the other hand, if we turn to the philosophers, *The Postmodern Condition* was received by them rather as a book which sought to put an end to philosophical reflection as it had been established by Enlightenment rationalism. But what is certain is that *The Postmodern Condition* is not a book of philosophy. It is rather a book which is very strongly marked by sociology, by a certain historicism, and by epistemology. These were the subjects which were imposed on me by the task of providing a report on the actual state of the sciences in the advanced countries. The philosophical basis of the report could not be elaborated there; and, besides, I explained that in my small introduction to the book. I think that the philosophical basis of *The Postmodern Condition* will be found, directly or indirectly, in *Le Différend*. As to the latter book, I developed it at length, very slowly, starting on it immediately after the publication of *Economie libidinale* (so it took me ten years), and resuming there the philosophical readings of the great tradition because these readings appeared to me to be indispensable. These readings only appear to a very limited extent in *The Postmodern Condition*.

Q2: *You ascribe to certain American and, especially, German philosophers a rationalist or consensualist terror.*[4] *These philosophers, in their turn, reproach you for being irrationalist and for betraying the positive side – this hard-won baby did not have to be thrown out with the dirty bath-water – of the Enlightenment and the 1789 revolution. What do you think about these allegations of irrationalism, and of the stigmatization that accompanies them?*

A2: I think that, in effect, a part of the attack against the position developed in *The Postmodern Condition* – my critics generally not having read the other works – bears the marks of a summary and totalizing idea of reason. I would oppose them simply with the following principle (which seems to me much more rationalist than they think): there is no reason, only reasons. And here I can draw support from the example, from the model, if I may put it that way, of Kant. I can follow the line of Kantian thought, and also, to a very large extent, that of Wittgensteinian thought. Finding or trying to elaborate the rules which make the discourse of knowledge, for example, possible – rules which we know to be under a general regime where truth or falsehood is at stake – is not the same thing as trying to elaborate the rules of a discourse, for example ethics, whose regime is one where good or evil, justice or injustice are at stake; nor is it the same thing for the discourse of aesthetics whose field of play is defined by the question of beauty or ugliness (or, at least, lack of beauty).

These rules are quite different. By "quite different" I mean that the presuppositions which are necessary, which are accepted as prerequisites for successful participation in one field or another, their *a priori* conditions – by this I mean the *a priori* conditions of, let us call them in a very wide sense, phrases (we could also call them acts of language, although this seems to me even more confusing than "phrase") – are not the same. This is what Kant shows when he passes from the first to the second *Critique*.[5] It is clear that reason in its, as Kant puts it, theoretic or theoretical usage is quite different from reason in its practical usage. It is not the same thing, on the one hand, conceptually to subsume the sensible given which is already preformed, or if you prefer, preschematized by the sensibility, which is to say by the imagination, as it is; and on the other hand, to hold oneself accountable to the demands of the moral law, that is to say, to be obliged, without interest, to allow this law to prescribe, in principle, those objects of interest which are defined as good, whether as phrases or acts – at the same time as, in actual fact, the definition of those acts or phrases as good remains, as you know, dependent on the reflexive judgment. And if one takes the example of aesthetics, one would have no difficulty in showing that the regime of phrases concerning beauty and non-beauty is again quite different for Kant, since it is here a question of, as he puts it, a state of mind, which is to say of a sentiment, an elementary form, one might say, of the reflexive judgment.

As we think through this side of Kant's thought (and it is also possible to find an analogue in the late work of Wittgenstein), it is easy to show that it is never a question of *one* massive and unique reason – that is nothing but an ideology. On the contrary, it is a question of *plural* rationalities, which are, at the least, respectively, theoretical, practical, aesthetic. They are profoundly heterogeneous, "autonomous" as Kant says. The inability to think this is the hallmark of the great idealist rationalism of nineteenth-century German thought, which presupposes without any explication that reason is the same in all cases. It is a sort of identitarianism which forms a pair with a total-itarianism of reason, and which, I think, is simultaneously erroneous and dangerous.

Let me add two further things to this first reply. The first is that the rationalism of the Enlightenment and of the 1789 revolution was infinitely more subtle than my critics recognize. If I examine, for example, the thought of someone like Diderot, who in my view is probably the most eminent of French Enlightenment thinkers, perhaps more so than Rousseau, it is extremely evident that his "rationalism" is infinitely complex. I cannot enlarge upon this here and now – it is one of the projects that I have always had in mind and I do not know if the gods will grant me the time to pursue it properly. But my intention would be to show both the complexity of this rationalism and how it incorporates elements – that is to say those elements of rationality which do not subordinate their arguments to the end of *consensus* – which are totally excluded from the current American-German version.

The other thing that I would wish to add, and we remain here on the same territory, is that today there is a generally recognized "crisis" of what is called reason in the sciences. I am speaking of the hard sciences. The names of Kuhn and Feyerabend come to mind in connection with this crisis. I am probably not in agreement with the whole scheme of thought of these celebrated epistemologists; but, since the middle of the nineteenth century, the question of what is rational in mathematics and the sciences of animate and inanimate nature is an open one. This question has such force that it even affects the nature, whether rational or non-rational, of space and time. What has been called "the crisis of the foundations" is not something that can be neglected today to the pretended advantage of a consensus of arguments, when this consensus is precisely what is missing from the interior of the, let us say physical, sciences. And far from suppressing the possibility, contrary to what might be thought, this absence of consensus has, on the contrary, only worked to allow a more rapid and more impressive development of the sciences. I am thinking, for example, of the discussion between Einstein, who was in a certain way a classical rationalist, a Leibnizian we might say, and the Danes, who showed themselves to be very adventurous in these matters, or, again, with Louis de Broglie.

What conclusions can we draw, bearing in mind that I am not competent to go any further in this direction? I would say one thing, which is that the crisis of reason has been precisely the bath in which scientific reason has been immersed for a century, and this crisis, this continual interrogation of reason, is certainly the most rational thing around. In the deepest sense, it is there, in this "critical" – in the two senses of the term – movement that I would like to situate my thought.

(Coup didactique, I)

VAN REIJEN AND VEERMAN: *In your 1985 interview with Bernard Blistène, you accept the qualification that he makes of you as a philosopher who shows something.*[6] *Since* Discours, figure *(1971) and the essays which surround that intricate book,*[7] *you seem to appear as an aesthetician rather than a philosopher; you present something to the senses instead of trying to recover and articulate that which isn't said in what you say. Three years ago, you yourself remarked on the continuity which exists from your first to your most recent writing,*[8] *notably between the* *figural of* Discours, figure *and the has-it-happened-yet which is introduced in* Le Différend. *Your writings could be summed up by saying that they all bear witness to the monster of truth and of good which exists outside of discourse and its oppositional values, outside of our languages, whether denotative or axiological, and the criteria which define them, but that a refusal of articulation is achieved by a discursive skewing. This monstrosity – which is nothing other than being – has access to the discourse at the critical moment, which is to say at the moment that the discourse cannot manage to sustain and continue itself out of its own resources. Thus we have the "line", the figure of* Discours, figure: *is it a place of intensity (a notion fundamental to* Economie libidinale *[1974])*[9] *or a place within the discourse of ontico-ontological being (completely destroying it, which is to say crushing it under its enormous weight); thus we have the has-it-happened-yet: isn't this the uncertain but inescapable moment which precedes the chaining (up) of one phrase to another, and which is characterized by the anguishing embarrassment of choice with regard to the kind of discourse which will fix the regime of the phrase with which I am now confronted, and to which I must fasten myself?*

It is here that the possibility of articulating being is arrested, at the point which precedes its articulation and which is never itself articulated. And it is here that we discover that, at the most, we can bear witness for being, and for the revolution that it implies; to articulate it is to have lost it. Now, with his notion of the sublime, Kant tried to think within the world, as it were, what could not be presented there, in other words, what could not be recovered and therefore articulated and demonstrated. Kant's mode of thought here is symbolic; it is a question of alluding to something impresentable. In the text which clearly parodies the title of Kant's piece on the Enlightenment – "Answering the question: what is postmodernism"[10] *– you indicate that from the time of the Enlightenment two paths are open. The symbolic stress may be placed on the powerlessness of the faculty or presentation, and therefore on nostalgia for what is absent. It may, on the other hand, be placed on the power of the faculty of imaginative understanding, which results in a "growth of being" accompanied by "jubilation" – which is simultaneously an expression of delight and anguish – at the creative achievement of the imagination, at its invention of new ideas and symbolic presentations, which is to speak of, in your Kantian-Wittgensteinian idiom, "new rules of the game, pictural, artistic, or whatever". These remarks betray the interest which you have maintained since the late seventies in the aesthetic reflections of the* Critique of Judgement.

If we restrict ourselves to the Kantian vocabulary – to which, in part, a brief remark in 1977[11] *and the dialogues of* Au juste[12] *mark your manifest passage for the first time – you must opt for the second path, and bear witness for the unthought, for the difference from what has been thought, for the other (should we write Other?) of thought. It will not be a question of dealing with what comes along in so far as it is articulable, but of giving sensible form to what is there before discursive thought. It will be as a witness for the ineffable (in a sense which may be neither nostalgic nor melancholic) nature of the ontological and essential ground of discourse.*

The writings of your "first period" which run from Discours, figure *to* Economie libidinale *inclusively provide parallel evidence. The "line" in the former book and the "tensor" in the latter relate to a point of arrival, an event (in the sense of* ereignen[13]*), without which that which has arrived can never be presented, receding before its moment of demonstration. As in* Le Différend, *you are not looking to recover this ontological thing, whatever it may be. In* Discours, figure, *you write with a feeling of regret which is different to the melancholia and nostalgia which defines the first Kantian path: "This book is not an honest book, it remains within the field of signification; deconstruction [which assumes the burden of ontological difference – D.V.] does not take place here directly, it is signified."*[14] *In* Economie libidinale, *in a more radical, even ecstatic vein, it* is said, straight away: "No need to criticise metaphysics ... since such criticism presupposes and continually recreates that very theatricality [of the representation which tries to recover the 'thing' – D.V.], better to be inside and forget it."[15]

We would like to cite several passages from Le Différend, which is at the centre of your "second period", in order to show the analogy – non-melancholic but sensitive – between your first and most recent writings, in respect of which the common aim is defined as, following your formulation in "Sensus communis",[16] the undoing of the mind.

As to what remains unarticulated:

113 Can we specify the presentation comprised in the phrase being? But this is a presentation, or: what in the case of a phrase is the case ... Not being, but a being, once only.

114 ... The phrase which ... presents [being] itself comprises a presentation that it does not present. Can it even be said that it escapes, or differs from itself? That would presuppose that it is the same over several phrases. ...

126 ... In ... addressing [the absolute presentation comprised by a phrase] you present it. That is why the absolute is not presentable. With the sublime ... Kant was always right over Hegel. The sublime persists, not beyond, but in the heart of the Aufgehobenen.

As to the confusing force of the ontological difference which results from this:

136 To link or chain together is necessary, a series is not ...

147 From one phrase regime (descriptive, cognitive, prescriptive, evaluative, interrogative ...) to another, a connection may not always be relevant. It is not appropriate to connect Open the door with You have laid down a prescription or What a beautiful door! ... The type of discourse fixes the rule for the linking of phrases ... This may provide the opportunity for irrelevant connections so as to produce such and such an effect. Teleology begins with the genres of discourse ...

150 The error implied in the last judgment: After this I will say, there is nothing more to say – But you say it! –

151 ... We can never know about the Ereignis. What idiom does this phrase come from, from what regime? The mistake is always to anticipate, that is to say, to forbid.

JEAN-FRANÇOIS LYOTARD: I would like to make some observations on this *coup didactique* before passing to the next question. I admire its precision, and, if I may say, the svelteness of your argument. Overall, I find myself in agreement with what you say. I would simply like to make some points more precise.

I really do not use, in the way you suggest, the word "revolution" in the phrase "*it is here that we discover that, at the most, we can bear witness for being, and for the revolution that it implies*". I do not see exactly what you understand by this word, but I will not discuss it now.

A second observation is inspired by the following phrase: "*Kant's mode of thought here is symbolic; it is a question of alluding to something unpresentable.*" I know that I have often used this term; it appears in the title of a text to which I have signed my name. But the title: "Presenting the Impresentable"[17] was made up by the American revue, *Artforum*, it was not my title, and I could never have written it. "Unpresentable" is a Kantian term, but I should like to make a comment, itself Kantian, about it.

In the third *Critique*, Kant observed that it is always necessary to distinguish between two sorts of presentation, or exposition, as he put it. It is not only necessary to differentiate between two forms of exposition, but also between two forms of absence.[18]

Firstly, with regard to exposition, Kant says that it is important to see that there are two styles of exposition. One of them is argumentation, and he calls this the *modus logicus*, or simply the mode (or method), and this is, in the final analysis, a procedure of connection which employs the operations of rational logic. But there is, he says, another form of exposition, which he calls the *modus estheticus* or the "manner".[19] Kant says that presentation can proceed by focusing on manner, through an exposition centred on the form and not on the concept to be displayed. In this case, he explains, the unity to be exposed finds itself in the spatiotemporal organization of the exposition itself. This is the open gateway into the arts, whose modes of exposition, seen in this way, and while without doubt not at the same level as the philosophico-logical method, must in every case be taken into account when addressing the unpresentable.

Turning now to the second distinction, which is also Kantian, but which does not seem to be properly attended to in your commentary. It is a question of the distinction between ideas of the imagination and ideas of reason. For example, when you speak of "*the creative achievement of the imagination, of its invention of new ideas and symbolic presentations*", I think you cover over too quickly the distinction that I have in mind. The ideas of reason are truly indemonstrable – I use the Kantian term – in the sense that one cannot show the intuitions corresponding to them. We agree about this. But the ideas of the imagination are, on the contrary, inscribed in the presentation. They are suggested by the presentation itself, or they are immanent to it and are there for all that, and such is their mode of absence, inexplicable as Kant writes: they cannot be articulated logically (thus it is that we must return to the *modus estheticus* or "manner").

I think that this distinction is important because it makes us reconsider with more precision the very notion of the unpresentable. The way in which an idea of reason, say liberty or the absolute, is unpresentable is not the same as the "manner" of an idea of the imagination, which is a sort of type or monogramme (these terms are equally Kantian), which, if it can be put this way, expresses itself in the arrangement of sensible materials through creative forms – it is not the same therefore as the "manner" in which this idea is suggested in the work of art or in the natural landscape. You see that the unpresentable there is not to be taken in the sense of the "indemonstrable", which is to say unshowable by reason, or at least unshowable by the intuition in accordance with reason, but that it is a question of the unpresentable as inexplicable in at least the sense that it cannot be rationally articulated.

My third remark concerns the use you make of the notion of an "*ontological and essential ground of discourse*". I should tie this to the critique of the usage of the term *Grund* in the very citations from *Le Différend* that you have happily provided. Numbers 113 and 114, with some others, precisely distance themselves from the notion of a ground which would be ineffably the same, the unthought as a unity which thought could never attain. I think that it is important to keep one's distance from such a notion of the unthought, whose being would be singular. We have no means of sustaining the thesis that its being is singular. Except that in naming being as such, we already, so to speak, employ the singular; and we forget that singularity denotes plurality, as I have explained in *Le Différend*.[20]

I think that it is important, at least to distinguish between the usage which would precisely universalize the singular (or its definite article), *the being*, and a usage which is on the contrary singularizing: *this being, this time*. But I think that, above all, it would be preferable not to use the term being very much at all. In consequence, with regard to your "*ontological and essential ground of discourse*", I would object at once that "ontological" and "essential" are not appropriate to qualify the term. The situation may be entirely contrary. Above all it is a question of withdrawing from the very possibility of an ontology.

Q3: How do you establish today the relationship which exists between the positive sensibility of the authentic ontological force, at the heart of which you used to appeal to the "line", and that which you call, in "Judicieux dans le différend",[21] the ontological well-being of the second path of the sublime, which, to read you, is the properly Kantian result of the "critique of critique"? This question contains another, which, if you will permit us, we will add straight away.

We refer here to your evidence for the other of discourse. This other is present but ineffable, absenting itself from the product of the discursive process. In an interview in 1970,[22] entirely in the style of Discours, figure*, you criticize the Derridean notions of "trace" and "archi-writing" for being unable to take any account of the positive presence of the other in relation to discourse. It seems to us that, for example, your comment on Kant's critical aesthetic: "... the critical aesthetic, at the same time as it is wound up with the decline of metaphysics, opens and reopens the way to ontology"[23] makes the same point. Of course, we do not forget that the point of departure of* Discours, figure *was linguistic (on page 11 of that book, we read, "We must start from where we are: in the heart of words"); but given that the approach of your recent work puts the emphasis on "phrases" rather than on ontology, and that because of this it has become more rigorously "discursive", isn't there a danger of your arriving at an ontology of absence such as you found in Derrida?*

A3: I do not really understand the first part of this question, but would repeat the reservations which I have with regard to the usage of the term "ontological", and would also refer to the two paths of the sublime with which I have been concerned for some years now, and, as you remind me, appear to me to stand in need of re-examination today. Let me pass rather to the last part of your question; it is a very good question, and raises difficult matters. To get straight to the point, the question concerns my relation to Derrida's thought. You ask whether I run the risk of committing myself to the kind of ontology of absence that is found in Derrida. Obviously I must begin by explaining my reservations with regard to this ontology.

I think that the notion of absence is itself deconstructed in and by Derrida's thought; it is rendered undecidable there. That any being whatever may be absent, and this applies all the more strongly to being itself, is in my view an idea that is much too simple, for at least the absence of being is present, being presents itself *in absentia*, and if it is absent, this is *in presentia* (to the extent that these terms still retain some meaning in Derridean thought). If there is a variation between my thought and Derrida's, it is expressed in the extension given to the idea of difference.

It seems to me that Derrida brings difference into play over all genres, all phrases, all linkages, as I would put it – excuse me for employing a vocabulary which is mine rather than his; I do this to make myself understood to my questioners. To make difference cover everything, to show or exhibit the difference in all kinds of linkages, in all kinds of phrases, there is a risk (I speak of *risk*, which is also a courting of difference) of being accused of scepticism. In any event, I do not regard such accusations as well founded. It is not that it would be wrong, *a priori*, to be sceptical; there is no need to tremble before such an accusation. Rather it is necessary to examine if it is right to make that accusation: how well has it been argued? Here I will open a parenthesis which will recall an intervention which Derrida made – in an open letter, for he was absent – at the International College of Philosophy on the occasion of a paper given by Karl-Otto Apel. Derrida was indignant, in any event he jibbed, against the lack of care in reading which characterized most of our critiques. Against this eagerness to locate us among such cases, to label us, to fix our place among those families of thought which are openly and mutually hostile, and which will therefore at once go on to the attack, all the evidence, once it is surveyed, shows that what is said is not at issue. It is fantasies which are attacked, not the *texts themselves* which ought to have been read. I close the parenthesis.

To return to the question of my relationship to Derrida's thought, I would say that the notion of difference mainly rests upon, it seems to me, an idea of time which comes from the transcendental deduction of the first *Critique* as it was deployed by Heidegger from his book on Kant to his essay on Husserl's "Internal Time-consciousness". This notion of time – which can be shown, following Heidegger, to come down to the place of the subject, a subject which, as Derrida has never failed to stress, is evidently never given in itself, but perpetually lacks and differs from itself – is assuredly the schema of all schemas, that is to say the form of all internal syntheses of the given. Now this form of the synthesis of the given is elaborated in the *Critique of Theoretical Reason;* it is subordinated to a language-game, let us say, in which truth and falsehood are at stake. If we examine the question of temporality in the second *Critique,* for example, that is to say ethical temporality, difficulties of quite another kind are immediately encountered; they concern the time of obligation.

But in the third *Critique*,[24] it is very clear that the minute examination of the syntheses at play in the aesthetic sensibility, in taste, without speaking of the Analytic of the sublime, bring us to the conclusion that temporality there is completely different again from the first *Critique.* Here it is not at all a matter of a self which is perpetually different from itself. Rather it is a question of something like a suspension of the kinds of temporal syntheses examined in the first *Critique* – I refer to three kinds of synthesis, those of apprehension, reproduction and recognition – owing to the fact that in the aesthetic judgment it can be a question neither of recognition nor even of reproduction. I would add that apprehension itself is understood in a most rudimentary and minimal way, at least in the Analytic of the sublime, where the comprehension of the given seems like a request which is beyond the synthetic capacities of the imagination. And so one is led to "conceive", for the beautiful as well as for the sublime (even though totally different in the two cases), an aesthetic temporality which would not at all be of the order of difference, which would defer not to the *durchlaufen* of the first *Critique,* but to a state of time which, in comparison with that of difference, would appear as a suspension or an "interdiction", which would be in sum a sort of "interruption" of difference itself.

I would say one thing more, to try and make myself understood quickly (and badly as a result). This refers to what I have been able to write in recent works concerning the visual arts, especially painting (but sketched out earlier in regard to the cinema[25]). It seems to me that precisely what is important in aesthetic time is what can be called "presence". Not in the sense of the present, nor in the sense of what is there, but in that sense in which, on the contrary, the activity of the very minimal synthesis of the given into the very forms which are free (forms properly speaking, not merely schemas) is suspended. It would be a question of a kind of, let us say, spasm or stasis (it does not matter which word of that genre) which has a relation, I think, with a "direct" access not to the meaning of the situation (which is the case with the forms), but to the material. One would be on this side of the synthetic activity by means of forms, in a relation with the great X, to use the Kantian term, with that enigmatic *Mannigfaltigkeit*, that diversity, that *poikilon*. — I have wondered for a long time why the material is always presented as a diversity, a mixture, but it is obviously on account of the obsession to safeguard the unifying activity of mind. In the "strongly" aesthetic moments (but what does that mean? They are at the same time the weakest moments for mind seen as a power of synthesis), it would perhaps be a matter of a non-mediated relationship with the material, without even the most elementary synthetic activity.

This is not so enigmatic. It is very clear that the usage made of colour, by someone like Barnett Newman, the great postwar American painter (labelled an expressionist although one wonders why), or someone like [...] Karel Appel (also a very great painter, although very different), shows that what is important to both is not the form within which colour is held captive, like a material which depended on its form to be made presentable, but very much to the contrary it is a question of material-colour having in itself a power to suspend the formative activity of mind. This sort of painting calls to mind what musicians call *timbre*. You know that when they speak of timbre, musicians happily use metaphors borrowed from the visual arts. We can speak of the colour or the chromatism of a sound — independent of the note or the duration or intensity of the sound — as it is produced by this or that instrument, even, I would say in general, by this or that impact, or percussion in the wide sense.

One of the current aims of my work is to show that there is, I would not say an ontology, but a mode of relation to something which is very certain within the given, but which also transcends those very empty forms within which the given is habitually synthesized. It is there that I would find presence, in short, a kind of stupefaction or stupidity suspending the activity of mind. This "stupefaction" should be understood in relation to what I have called elsewhere "obedience" or "soul" (the latter term being employed by Kant). Nevertheless, it remains the case that this presence, which cannot be a presence since truly the mind is absent from it, is not a theme which is compatible with Kant, except perhaps in certain passages of the text on the sublime. At least, the time of the sublime, of its presence, is neither accountable nor appreciable in terms of the apperceptive synthesis; the latter's deferrals are not to be found there.

(Coup didactique, II)

VAN REIJEN AND VEERMAN: In Le Différend, *No. 126, you criticize Kant's melancholic presentation of totality. The force of his critique would result only in failure, as you say in arguing against Gérard Raulet. The critique would consist in the oscillation of judgments "on the line of division between genres".*[26] *Your "reply" explains that there is a difference between the aesthetic of the sublime, in the sense of the first path – which according to Kant is a mode of presentation of the existent, or in the case of the absolute totality, of being – and a postmodern sublime which allows being outside of being presented and unpresentable, indeed this is a being which never ceases producing more. Thus we find you often producing variations on the theme of the work of anamnesis in the modern plastic and visual arts. This process is taken, as you have explained,*[27] *in the sense of psychoanalytic therapy. The work of Cézanne, Picasso, Delaunay, Kandinsky, Klee, Mondrian, Malévitch and "finally Duchamp" would be like a gliding through*[28] *which elaborated an initial moment of forgetfulness. The phrase "and finally" indicates a displacement. The movement of return, anagogic and anamorphic, the process of "ana-", would pass; this seems to us to be your thesis, which concerns the work of a forgetfulness and of a destruction of the – let us say, naïve – sensible, which operates to develop the forgotten presupposition in the naïve work of forgetfulness. And, in fact, there will always be presuppositions, the least reflection will be a moving on and a moving from. This last point suggests that the work of reflection will never be finished; it is without doubt to say that the aesthetic withdraws from the sensible but always remains there. So Duchamp, on account of his reflexive work, would be closer to postmodern than to modern. This complex of ideas evokes a complex of questions.*

Firstly:

Q4: What is the relation between the two sublimes, that of the first path, which is modern and which moves naïvely to and from a sensible loss, and that of the second, postmodern, path which perlaborates the very work of perlaboration? And, since you suggest that there is a transition from one to the other, where is this located?

A4: First let me make a comment on your second *coup didactique*. The least that I can say is that what you make me think appears acceptable to me, and I am grateful for the numerous things that I have learnt from what is a beautiful and useful piece of elaboration. But your question troubles me. You tell me that there are two sorts of sublime, that of the first path which is a sublime in some way nostalgic about the impossibility of presentation, and that of the second path, a postmodern sublime, which consists simply in putting back into an endless play the presuppositions which are at work in all work. And next you tell me that the first path perlaborates naïvely a loss of the sensible. I would not say that the loss is one of sensibility, unless we give that phrase an almost British meaning; what is in question is perhaps a loss of meaning. It is above all the understanding that something gives us the material-sensible, and this something can never be reached.

I am reminded here of what Bettina von Arnim wrote, in regard to Hölderlin, in a "letter" in the *Günderrode*: "And we, we who have not been put to the test, will we ever see the day?" "To see the day" that would be precisely to have access to that "thing" (a term that I prefer to "being"), that resonous, visual, timbrous, chromatic, nuanced, etc., matter. I use the phrase as a kind of inscription, although it is not my normal practice, in my *Que peindre?*.[29]

When you ask me where the transition from one sublime to the other takes place, I wonder if I understand this "where" properly, because it seems very clear to me (but perhaps I am mistaken) that what you are asking for is a sort of periodization of the passage from an aesthetic of the nostalgic sublime to an aesthetic of a joyful sublime. This is a direction I pointed toward in, for example, "The Sublime and the Avant-Garde" or "Answering the Question: What is Postmodernism?"[30] However, I believe that I am always cautious as far as periodizing this passage is concerned. Rather I have shown, in several examples, even if I have never truly analysed any one of them, that examples of both forms of sublime can be found — in the *writing* (in the widest possible sense of the term), that is to say in the mode of inscription which, whatever its historical conditions and surface form, will always dictate what cannot be expressed — let us leave it at that — in no matter what epoch of the history of literature, or of art, or of ideas. Thus I do not think that, correctly speaking, periodization is possible.

I would take for today, if you would like, not a transition but a sort of opposition between something like the Suprematism of Malévich and the "expressionism" of Karel Appel. The former's work would be seen in the sense of a rarefaction of presentation aimed at giving expression to the thing which cannot present itself; the latter's on the contrary would be taken in a completely opposite sense of chromatic superabundance, and of a heedlessness, both voluntary and involuntary, of the form in which the colours are put together. In doing this, Appel tries to show moreover, but in a style which is, if I may say, rich (in reality this richness is also a poverty as the examination of both his works and their accompanying texts shows), the operation of a "thing" which is completely different from Malévich's "thing".

Secondly:

Q5: *The sophisticated development of the artistic conditions which characterize the postmodern arts (as you define them) functions to explode established discursive and conceptual truths. In the rather more political context of "Judicieux dans le différend" you say: "The clear task of the critical observer is continually to dissipate illusion, the situation is made obscure, however, because this dissipation may itself be illusory".*[31] *The Kantian idiom is here used, so to speak, against itself, against the* a priori, *and the rules that it seeks to establish. The facility, if such it is, which enables you to draw your disunifying and shattering conclusions is the faculty (a notion whose illusory unity you have criticized)*[32] *of judgment. The question, then, is this: given that it is learnt in the preface to the* Critique of Judgement *that the faculty of judgment makes possible the way toward agreement, which, at bottom, is the unifying concordance between the first two* Critiques *and not the bursting apart of the well-defined fruits of critical thought, does not your readiness to fragment these products of critical thought constitute a betrayal of the faculty of judgment?*

A5: I would like to make two observations. The first is a sort of parenthesis, although essential, which bears on Kant's particular usage of the term faculty in the expression, "faculty of judgement", but also certainly in that of "faculty of presentation" and so on. You tell me that I have written in *L'Enthousiasme* that the very notion of a faculty introduces the illusion of a unity. You ask me if in engineering the fragmentation of thought I am not betraying the "faculty of judgement" itself. My first observation bears on the notion of faculty, and my second on this question of fragmentation.

I must unhappily be brief as far as the notion of faculty is concerned. It is a very large problem that I have tackled in a recent text entitled *L'Intérêt du sublime*. The notion of faculty is that of the Aristotelian *dynamis*. It is a 'power of mind' as Kant puts it, especially in the second *Critique*. The mind has several powers which, as I have just said, respond to practical conditions, to the different functions according to which it is a question of judgments of truth or justice or beauty. What is awkward in the notion of faculty is that it is often taken as a metaphysics of power and action as may be found in Aristotle, or else in a weaker hypothesis, largely of Platonic origin, as part of a sort of metapsychology. The former connotation is often to be found in Kant's work. It is on that that I have worked, with respect to the notion of interest, in the third *Critique*. There must be an interest for the faculty to actualize itself, and there must be an interest which the empirical mind has in actualizing the power of the said faculty. There is therefore a double interest which operates in one sense as in the other, and this does not go without saying. A form of economy is necessarily introduced with these notions of faculty and act. For "interest" is an economic term, whether libidinal or not. This economy, for Kant, is ultimately a practical economy. And I think that the privilege that Kant accords to the practical resides just there. For to have some interest in an object is always to want it. A faculty "wants" its own actualization. Each faculty is under the regime of a "metawill", of a "drive" towards actualization. This metaphysic of power and action is the direction taken by the third *Critique*. Prudently, this direction is only made subject to a hypothetical idea, for which, according to Kant, there is no demonstrable proof available within the sensible world. This hypothetical idea is the idea of nature. It is an extremely important idea. It is not a simple question of a nature outside the subject, but of a nature "within" the subject. The third *Critique* cannot be understood unless one develops fully this hypothesis which belongs, I repeat, to a metaphysics of power and of the act, and to an economy of faculties.

If, so far as the usage of the term "faculty" is concerned, one wants to avoid the hypothesis of a metaphysic of nature which derives from Aristotle, a weaker hypothesis is taken. It is then a question of a sort of metaphysical psychology which will evidently have the merit of drawing nearer to what interests us under the name, for instance, of "language game". But here still the question which arises is how, according to Plato (rather than Aristotle this time), the three instances of the Platonic mind or the three faculties of the Kantian mind can co-exist. You can see that this is very much a question of the unity of the subject rather than of the metaphysic of nature. In fact these two hypotheses, the natural metaphysic and the subjective metaphysic, are tightly interwoven in Kant, even though Aristotle and Plato are in profound divergence on the matter.

Let me pass to the question of fragmentation. Does my work betray the faculty of judgment in advocating fragmentation? I am not the one who advocates this. It is the critical method itself which insists upon the differentiation between the regimes of judgment according to which it is a question of truth, or of beauty, or of the good. It is from this point that Kant finds himself confronted with the problem of reconstructing the subject as if the regimes of judgment were perfectly autonomous. What he finds, at the end of his diverse "deductions", that is to say these legitimations of the demand that judgment be considered valid for the beautiful, for the good, or for the true, are principles which are heterogeneous with respect to each other. This is the whole of the problem of the constitution of the unity of the subject which is posed after that, and which Kant poses, in effect, in the preface to the third *Critique*. Kant tries to resolve this problem *by* the third *Critique* itself, by opening a possible passage between reason in its theoretical usage and reason in its practical usage. As you know, he has the greatest difficulty in succeeding in this. For finally the passage itself cannot be traced, it is open only by virtue of a general hypothesis of a natural finality, of nature as pursuing, both within human beings and outside of them, the supreme end of the development of its powers of liberty which have a "primacy" over that of the power of knowledge. All this amounts to the fact that the question which you ask me is much more embarrassing for Kant than it is for me. For, as far as I am concerned, I am in the situation of thought today, and this is marked, shall we say, by the critique of the subject. This critique does not mean that we can dispense with the subject. It does mean that in every way that we relate to the notion of the subject, we carry the Kantian and Wittgensteinian heritage with us, and that we cannot continue to think under the general regime of the *cogito*. The evidence for the "I think" is for us as scarce as it could possibly be. This is a point of severe disagreement with Karl-Otto Apel, and perhaps with the whole of phenomenology.

I would add that Heidegger's conclusions in the *Kantbuch* do not allow us to think ourselves free of the crisis of the critique of the subject in contemporary thought. For, once again, these considerations only relate to the evanescence, if I may put it like this, of the knowing subject in the time of knowing. We have to deal with a crisis of the subject which is much more serious. It concerns the unification of the heterogeneous or autonomous regimes of judgment, that is to say the regimes of different phrases. Can we think without the subject? There again it is necessary to add something, which is that even the considerable contribution that psychoanalysis, especially in its Lacanian form, has been able to contribute to the elaboration of this question does not seem to us philosophers to be sufficient (I say "us" because I believe that I am far from alone in thinking this). This also arises in so far as, in one way or another, but principally in (re)introducing the capitalized Other, Lacanian thought reconnects with a certain idea of the unity of "sense". Obviously, I am well aware that it is a unity of sense of the singular unconscious, and that this sense remains a problem concerning the communicability of the different unconsciences governed by the *grands A* which are in principle heterogeneous each from the others. Nevertheless, the properly theoretical aspect of Lacanian thought (at the beginning, at least) seems to me to resort more to a very profound and very subtle renewal of Platonic thought as a way of taking serious consideration of the crisis of the subject after Kant.

Thirdly, a little more complex:

Q6: It is in answering the question of what is at stake in modern art and the postmodern arts that it seems to you opportune to parody "An Answer to the Question: 'What is Enlightenment?'" We know that the bearing of this famous Kantian text is upon the political; it is counted, and you do not contest this in any way, among Kant's historico-political texts. It does not treat aesthetic or artistic issues. It could be said that he speaks about religion when speaking of the political class,[33] but that would make the general view mistaken. The actual choice of subject matter is arbitrary in comparison with the essentially political nature of Kant's concerns. He writes: "I have portrayed matters of religion as the focal point of enlightenment, i.e. of man's emergence from his self-incurred immaturity. This is firstly because our rulers have no interest in assuming the role of guardians over their subjects so far as the arts and sciences are concerned, and secondly, because religious immaturity is the most pernicious and dishonourable variety of all."[34] The religious issue only obscures the fact that the text is essentially political. Therefore, since you parody the title of

Kant's text, and since your own text aims at providing a critique of the political thought of Habermas, that defender of the Enlightenment tradition, what is it that makes your aesthetic reflections political? It seems to us that there are two sub-questions here.

First, in what way is the aesthetic political?

Second, does the transformation of the aesthetic, about which you have spoken, have implications with respect to the form of politics that we could tentatively call "postmodern", or has a kind of reversal taken place whereby the "political" has become "aesthetic"? It will be useful to cast our minds back in this connection. You have said about politics, understood here as that consideration of creativity which has been at the core of modern philosophical reflection: "What is striking is that I have been required to abandon [the task of constructing a theory of history] and have made an enormous detour [the reference here is to the aesthetics of Discours, figure *– D.V.] which has displaced the initial object." And it is certainly in reasserting the bond with your active political past that you follow on to say: "Basically, what interests me is, in effect, to return to practical critique and to the theory of practical critique: to see what politics can be."*[35] *In the 1985 interview with Blistène, you evince the same objective throughout. How do we make a politics when we are confronted with politics which manifestly (Stalin, the Prague Spring, Solidarity)*[36] *do not work? – There are your reasons for leaving the critical Marxism of* Socialisme ou barbarie, *first of all, and then leaving* Pouvoir ouvrier, *and, at the same time, always the same question: "What is to be done when there is no horizon of emancipation; where do we resist?."*[37] *Aesthetics or politics, that is to say: does philosophy bring something into view, or is it reflection? Or, perhaps, this dichotomy is obsolete?*

A6:   If you will allow me, I will take these questions together. I will reply as to how the aesthetic is political. Aesthetics in the Western tradition has always been political in the sense that politics has always been aesthetic. I would refer you to an unpublished thesis by Philippe Lacoue-Labarthe, titled *La Fiction du politique*, which is a totally remarkable consideration of aesthetics and politics in the work of Heidegger. To speed things up, and I make my apologies to Philippe Lacoue-Labarthe for this, the essential point can be put very briefly (not that briefly, for I do not wish what I say to falsify what I mean); what he shows very clearly is that at least since Plato, all politics has obeyed a politics of fashioning. You know that the Greeks called that *to plattein*, and that the Sophists made a word-play on *Platon* and *plattein*. It is a question of fashioning and refashioning the city of fashion to make it appropriate to a metaphysical paradigm which would be precisely that of the good arrangement of the three instances, the *logos*, the *thumos*, and the *eputhimetikon*, so that they will be accurately mirrored in the copy constituted by the well-fashioned city. This idea of having to fashion the human community is fundamentally an aesthetic idea. It is a question of making a work. And this is clearly what Jean-Luc Nancy presupposes when he writes of an idle community.[38] What he seeks to show is that we are kept in check by this traditional connotation of the political to the aesthetics of the work.

I am well aware that Plato has not reigned supreme right up to the present day without opposition. But I think it can be shown that even after or during the Enlightenment, where however great a rupture with Platonism Kant shows to have occurred, it is possible to continue to think of fashioning as being the secret of politics. I mean that while it is certainly not a question of fashioning with eyes fixed on a metaphysical paradigm already constituted in the heaven of ideas, it is a question of fashioning in accordance with what Kant calls an idea of reason, that is to say a concept, but one which is not presented in the intuition. One finds oneself therefore in the familiar paradox of modern societies (more than one, with Leo Strauss, has exposed and denounced the rest), which is that a community moulded on an idea which has no reference mark in the sensible world (the idea of liberty is such an idea), that is to say an idea which cannot be demonstrated (in the sense used just now), an ideal of political design, whether it is the work of the left or of the right, will always remain contestable with regard to its legitimacy. To the extent that, in the case of Platonism, the model is in principle present in everyone's mind, and therefore all can judge whether the political organization of the city conforms to it or not, and to the extent that, after the Enlightenment [if one does not take account of the re-establishment of a certain Platonism which is clearly inscribed in Hegel, and even in Nietzsche], the idea of liberty is *ex hypothesi* singularly unavailable to any possible sensible intuition, then, to that extent, political fashioning will always be suspect.

It is as a result of this that modern politics constructs itself as suspicion and conflict interior to the community. This conflict may assume exorbitant proportions, even to the point of civil war. It is too easy to show that all modern wars differ from classical wars in that the former are always civil wars, whether internal or external, that is to say that they are wars over the legitimacy of one form or another of the political modelling of human communities. You see that we come back here to the problem of nature, which can clearly be found in what are called natural rights, in the fundamental freedoms which prescribe the limits of social fabrication. It can be seen that ultimately the legitimacy of the resistance to Nazism was located just there, to the extent that the "natural order" invoked by Nazism did not seem to respect (this is the least that can be said) these rights. But these rights are only the minima whose violation takes us into the very heart of suspicion. I mean that if one abandons the observation of these rights, one is in a certain way absolutely condemnable, obviously evil, but on the other hand respect for rights does not guarantee that the political fabrication will properly correspond to it. It is not enough then to observe these rights in order to say that a good political order has been constructed.

We have to deal here with an entire problematic which, in a certain sense, remains "aesthetic". This no longer refers to the aesthetic of the beautiful as defined by Plato, but rather to an aesthetic of the sublime, rational in the sense that it is a question of shaping human communities according to an idea of reason, which is however not presentable. Does it follow that there is a reversal of the relation between politics and aesthetics? I do not think so. I would simply say this (with respect to the last part of your question): that it is necessary to distinguish between what is aesthetical and what is political, and what would be interesting is not pursuing the idea of fabrication with an obsessive regard for developing the aesthetic aspect under the heading of the political work, but developing the dissociation between what is at stake in the aesthetic and the political, in the way that I have already indicated but also (please excuse the comparison) as already indicated by Kant and Wittgenstein. This is a work of critique and of critique alone. For why must the social or human (an unimportant distinction for the moment) community not only be good but beautiful? And how would the fact that it was beautiful guarantee that it was good?

I am well aware that Greek tradition had it that the *kalos kagathos* was at once beautiful and good, and that Kant admitted an analogy between the beautiful, as a symbol, and the good. But Kant explained also that, even though the analogy is possible, nevertheless nothing authorizes the conclusion that the analogy is a substitute for a rational deduction. "If beautiful, then good" cannot be said. There is a sort of privilege of the aesthetic over the political in the tradition which has in effect come down to us from Greece. This primacy seems to me to stand in need of being broken, and I think that this is the moment. Briefly, I would say that politics in itself is not a rule-bound enterprise, that it is much more complex than a *genre*. It is that, as I tried to show at the end of *Le Différend*, politics combines discursive genres (but also phrase-regimes) which are totally heterogeneous. Within the political there are interrogative genres and affirmative or assertive genres; there are questions which imply descriptions and questions which imply prescriptions; there is the aesthetic and poetic use of discourse in parliamentary rhetoric, or in the equivalent politics of publicity like propaganda. And certainly the use of reflective judgment must be added to this, when people ask themselves how they should vote, or what should be done in a particular situation, when the question cannot be disposed of under the rule of a single judgment.

Politics is not a free-standing genre of discourse; it is a profoundly unstable combination (although it may be relatively stabilized in the countries we call democratic) because it is subject to the instability of the "polygon of forces" in which different discursive genres are combined. It can be said that the situation today is characterized by the fact that these genres concern areas, "objects", which are more and more numerous. In a certain sense, everything has become political, as we used to say although it is a bad expression. Rather it is politics which has become invested in territories and in relation to objects which formerly were held to be outside of it. I am thinking here particularly about problems like those of health or those of destruction, although the latter may be more classically associated with the political; but they are assuming such proportions in contemporary physics and chemistry, that it is evidently science itself which has become a political affair. All we refer to as the "cultural" has acquired a hegemony in the combination of different genres which constitutes politics; and the "cultural" is not the aesthetic.

To get right to the heart of it, what I want to point to again is that, having admitted this plurality of genres articulated together in politics today, an essential philosophical task will be to refuse the aesthetic its two thousand year-old privilege, which in one sense was given its "final" particularly disquieting expression by Nazism. This is nothing other than the complete aestheticization of the political. It would be desirable to rethink the political rather than set out from the disquieting appeal to "doing good", in other words, we should rather begin from the Kant of the second *Critique* or from the thought of Levinas. That would allow at least — I do not say that this hypothesis can take us very far, I am not qualified to see so far — the avoidance of the understanding of politics in terms of fabrication and fashioning.

Q7: *In* Au juste *you say that the problem of injustice has caused you to reconsider the libidinal-figural philosophy of* Discours, figure *and, more especially, the theorizing of intensities of* Economie libidinale.[39] Le Différend *is the most wide-sweeping result of this reconsideration. What exactly is the problem and how does* Le Différend *remedy it?*

A7: This is a simple enough question. In *Economie libidinale*, the aim was the elimination of the game of good/evil in favour of that of intensities. The only criterion taken into account was the event itself. Now the event cannot be a criterion because it never stops retreating, because it is never there. Expressed in the terms of the philosophy of desire or of energy (I would rather say energetics) the event is construed as intensity. The few readers of *Economie libidinale* (you know that the book was very badly received) were shocked by this position, and this is not the worst that was said about the book. I think these readers did not appreciate the aspect of despair in the book, a desperation which appeared clear to me when I reread it (I do not usually reread my books, but I am obliged to when precise questions are put to me about them, as was the case recently with David Carroll in the United States). It is a book of desperation. It cannot be understood, or supported, except from the basis of the crisis I was going through at the time, and I was not alone (otherwise the book would have had no public interest at all). The crisis pertains to the ending of all the attempts to moralize politics which were incarnated in Marxism. The source of *The Postmodern Condition,* of the theme that is referred to as the crisis or the end of the great metanarratives, is found in *Discours, figure* (you have been perceptive in speaking of the nostalgic tone of that book). It is a theme which seeks to find affirmative expression in *Economie libidinale* (under the obvious influence of Nietzsche, and of a certain Freud). This position has since led me towards, *mutatis mutandis,* Diderot's *Rameau's Nephew.* It is certain that there is no rationalism, understood in Habermas's sense, which does not pass through that terrible moment of nihilism or complete scepticism. *Economie libidinale* represented for me that moment, or rather the return of that moment for I believed I had already passed through it and rid myself of it. It was, on the historico-social scale, perhaps even ontological.

Le Différend remedies the shortcomings of *Economie libidinale;* it is an attempt to try and say the same things, but without unloading problems so important as justice. On the one hand in *Le Différend*, what is specifically at stake is the re-establishment of justice under the form of the ethical (in the part which is entitled "Obligation"), on the other hand, in the total scheme of the book, *Le Différend* re-establishes what is at stake in justice as *Au juste* had summarily but not – even though I now see that the arguments were full of doubts and objections – falsely indicated. In *Le Différend*, it is said that there is an inevitable difficulty with respect to the possibilities of enchaining arising out of each phrase, out of each event by means of other phrases, because only a single phrase is possible at any one time (and therefore the others are for the moment different and not "actualized"). In spite of the ineluctable nature of this problem, the demand remains. Properly speaking, the demand is not moral – I think that I examined moral exigency in the section entitled "obligation" – when I now speak of an exigency which hangs over the whole of the book, it is to respect as much as possible the has-it-happened-yet. It is that *thing* that the event is even before signification, before connotation, its *quiddity* whether determined or determinable. This determination is precisely the enchainment which will be made out of it, which will say it and, therefore, make it.

As to a politics of justice, you tell me that this interest in the event reduces political philosophy to almost nothing, to an ontological attitude, and that this is because of respecting or listening for the has-it-happened-yet. My response is that it is not so simple. I want to say at least two things. First, it is probable that now and for the foreseeable future we, as philosophers, as much as we may be concerned by politics (and inevitably we are so concerned), are no longer in a position to say publicly: "Here is what you must do." I developed this theme particularly in the *Tombeau de l'intellectuel* which, all the same, did not mean following Maurice Blanchot's idea that the intellectual is dead and must be buried. You know that "*tombeau*" is also a term which, in French, designates a literary or musical genre, a sort of memorial movement.

The "*tombeau*" of the intellectual is also the memorial of the intellectual. So we are *in memoriam*. This is not to say that there are no longer any intellectuals, but that today's intellectuals, philosophers in so far as they are concerned by politics and by questions of community, are no longer able to take up obvious and pellucid positions; they cannot speak in the name of an "unquestionable" universality as, for example, Zola or Sartre were able to. Sartre was the limit of this because he is clearly mistaken in the positions he defends. But why has this period ended? It is because the modern intellectual was an Enlightenment figure, and all intellectuals, no matter what side they were on (except, of course, the Nazis) found their legitimacy, the legitimacy of the public speech through which they designated the just cause and made themselves its spokespersons, in the grand metanarrative of emancipation. It was possible to disagree about how to proceed, about how to work toward emancipation. But always the intellectuals had the authority of this kind of speaking in common, and it was founded on the general idea of a history developing toward its "natural" end, which was the emancipation of humanity from poverty, ignorance, prejudice and the absence of enjoyment.

Now we do not have the resource of the emancipatory metanarrative(s). What we have left is the minimum required for, what I call, a politics of resistance. What does resistance mean? What are the points of resistance? They are, on the other hand, the points about which I just spoke with regard to the respect for natural rights, in other words those liberties which are said to be elementary (and our clear duty there is to intervene when they are at stake), but on the other hand there is a resistance that is perhaps more secret and more specific, at the same time moreover as being more pertinent to the contemporary political condition which, as we have just been saying, is invested in the field of culture as well. I am talking about resistance in and through writing as, in the sense just outlined, inscription which attends to the uninscribable. The real political task today, at least in so far as it is also concerned with the cultural (and we should surely not forget, even though we may maintain a prudent silence on the subject which is nevertheless very important, at least in so far as it is also "just simply" capital), is to carry forward the resistance that writing offers to established thought, to what has already been done, to what everyone thinks, to what is well-known, to what is widely recognized, to what is "readable", to everything which can change its form and make itself acceptable to opinion in general. The latter, you understand, always works with what is taken for granted and with what is forgotten as such – for it grants no place to anamnesis. It is prejudiced. "Culture" consists, as "activity" and "animation", in introducing all that into the order of writing, in the wide sense, into literature, painting, architecture and so on. The name most often given to this is "postmodernism".

I think that we have to resist. In the section of *Le Postmoderne expliqué aux enfants*, entitled "Gloss on resistance", I cited the very important example – Claude Lefort has also developed this – of Winston in Orwell's *Nineteen Eighty Four*.[40] The line of resistance there is traced by the writing of the journal, and by the anamnesis that this writing demands of Winston in those circumstances. This example is a kind of model. I can take as well the artists and writers whom I hold to be (and you understand why I value them so much), in their various ways, models of resistance (they may hate to be so described but that is quite another problem). Perhaps they lock themselves away, apart from everyone, unknown to the general public; I would say that in one sense that does not matter, for they do not owe this resistance to the community directly but to thought. Whether it is in a century or in six months that the community realizes the necessity of what they have done is another question. Their essential task is above all to write, to paint, and so on, and to do this here and now in response (and responsibility) to that question: what is writing, painting?

Q8: *The special issue of* Critique, *entitled "La traversée de l'Atlantique" (1985) contains texts from yourself and Richard Rorty, and amounts to a "discussion" between you. In spite of the profound differences that you note between you, you do not appear to disapprove too much of what he has to say since you describe his exposition as "excellent". However, it seems to us that there is a radical difference between your conclusions and those which Rorty draws in "The End of Philosophy". He thinks that we can and must abandon philosophy, and that amounts to turning away from that source of philosophy to which you have always remained faithful, that source being the question, the questioning of everything, even the question itself. It seems to us that you continue to do philosophy, but radically. A quick indication of this would be your conversation with Derrida on "France-Culture" printed in* Le Monde *under the title of "Plaidoyer pour la métaphysique".*[41] *From this perspective, is your description of Rorty's thought as "excellent" an acceptance of his ultimately non-philosophical point of view, with all the machinery of "enlightened" bourgeois North American values which are uncritically accepted there, realizing that it is precisely in this latter respect that Rorty's thought looks ill when faced with your continually questioning and honestly philosophical refusal of emancipatory thought?*

A8: You are referring to the discussion which we had at Johns Hopkins some two and a half years ago. You suggest that I was very generous in describing Rorty's presentation as excellent, and you have the feeling that there is, on the contrary, a radical divergence between his thought and mine. If I described his discourse in this way, it is because it was an excellent exposition of his thesis. It is a homage that should be paid to an interlocutor, whether an adversary or not, in recognition that everything has been made understandable. Now, such was the case with Richard Rorty (without taking any account of my sympathy for the man himself). As to the divergence between our tendencies, I agree with you that this is radical. In support of your interpretation, you cite the publication in *Le Monde* of a radio interview between Derrida and myself. The title – "Metaphysics: The Case for the Defence" – was given to it by the newspaper. I would not have chosen it. I certainly do not think that it might be time for a return to metaphysics as has been suggested by some of my young French colleagues. I would have preferred that the title referred to the defence of *philosophy*, because no one knows exactly what that marvellous term means (if it is only a discursive genre in pursuit of its own rule, there can be no certainty in regard to its pronouncements; it does not have the dominion over itself to be assured that what is said provides an effective plea for its own defence).

Let us go back to my relation with Rorty. There is something very powerful, but sophisticated, in his rhetoric. He says, "we should drop all foundationalism, as it is put in the United States; it is without interest since it is indecidable. Only one thing is decidable, that is whether we do or do not speak together". Conversation becomes the absolute safeguard of the rationalist heritage. It is absolute because it is so minimal that it is totally incontestable. It is not even a question of "opening a dialogue", taking that term in its highest sense, of pursuing a hermeneutic of the kind elaborated by Ricoeur, Gadamer or Buber. No, it is simple conversation, the fact that we talk to each other. This is a pragmatist minimalism which can distinguish itself by recovering the essential heritage of the Enlightenment in so far as it truly concerns the "practice" of democracy. It demands that instead of killing, or putting in prison, or effacing, or eliminating in whatever way, or using those critical methods which rely on exclusion, one listens to the other and constitutes the other through speech as an interlocutor. Rorty's thesis of generalized interlocution can avail itself of a rationalism, which I would say is neither bourgeois North American, as you suggest, nor anaemic, but of a rationalism conscious of that which comprises what is absolutely discussable, which rationalism is not itself discussable, since it is both it and what makes it possible. This is the clear opposition between Rorty and Karl-Otto Apel or even with Habermas. The only true problem is whether discussion can take place. It is not a question of looking for the foundation behind, at the source, underneath or at the root of what is said; but it is a matter of what lies ahead of conversation, in a future which can only be that of interlocution. All conversation, even if it results in the greatest dissension (which was the case at the time of my public discussion with Rorty at Baltimore), nevertheless attests to the work of interlocution. This is where Rorty's sophistication lies: even if we do not agree, this disagreement implies that there is still an accord over the necessity of talking to each other. There is, if you will, a pragmatic *Mitsein* which in Rorty's view is the only essential thing to preserve, all the attempts to arrive at a semantic *consensus* being doomed to failure or at least always subordinated to this pragmatic *Mitsein*. It is what Rorty calls "solidarity".[42] This is a powerful thesis.

That said, it is also an 'imperialist' thesis, as I objected to him. The notion of an interlocution, as a passage or circulation of speech in the first person – from *I* to *you*, and from *you* to *I* – firstly does not guarantee that the *I* and *you* must make a *We* (and moreover Rorty comes up against a difficult problem with the enigma of the *We*). Secondly, and above all, it is not certain and it seems to me even very improbable that this pragmatic relationship of interlocution may be constitutive of our relations with language. I am prepared to argue the thesis that, in the case of ethical obligation for example, there is no interlocution. If I follow the way in which Kant or Levinas have analysed obligation, what strikes me is that being obliged is a relation with the law, a law which does not above all focus on the *I*, but rather on the *you*: "You will do this", "You must act in such and such a way", "You will listen to me", "You must listen" (I revive these terms which are those of Kant, of Levinas, of the Jewish tradition). Are others implicated by conversational address through my relation to the law? Neither for Kant, nor for Levinas. According to Levinas, this is because the relationship is one of hostage-taking and not at all one of interchange. The Other takes me hostage, and hostage-taking, as I understand it, is neither exactly conversational nor a matter of interlocution. It is violence. There is violence exercised by the law over its subject. In Kant's case, it is said that the maxim of my action must be able to be extended to the entire human (reasonable-practical) community. And it is the case that this is what Kant tells us that the law demands. "Act in such a way that" or "Act as if the maxim of your will could be established as the principle of a universal law", as a law valid for the totality of reasonable, practical, finite beings that we are. But it is up to me to judge, in the solitude of my seizure by the law, that my intention of doing or that my judgment (which comes to the same thing) is in effect universalizable. If we now take the case of the critique of aesthetic judgment, it can be seen that the aesthetic judgment, "This is beautiful", is singular, and, even if it contains a pretension to universality, i.e. to communicability (and it is in order to found this that Kant elaborates the notion of a *sensus communis*, and for no other reason), it still is the case that aesthetic judgment is equally exempt from the dominion of conversation. Even if my taste for a work or for a landscape leads me to discuss it with others (taking that last term in the sense, this time, of an empirical group), it is no less true that any assent that I can obtain from them has nothing to do with the validity of my aesthetic judgment. For the conditions of validity of this judgment are transcendental, and are clearly not subject to the opinions of any others whatsoever. The communicability, and even, to speak rigorously, the communion of aesthetic sentiments, cannot be obtained *de facto*, empirically, and much less by means of conversation. At this point conversation encounters the antinomy of *La Faculté de juger*, which is that there must certainly be some promise of universality, which creates the need for argumentation, but, at the same time, aesthetic judgment does not proceed through concepts, it cannot be validated by argumentative consensus. That does not mean that we do not talk to each other; we certainly do. But the question is about knowing if such conversation is constitutive of aesthetic judgment, of taste.

In putting forward the principle of interlocution, Rorty carries – and this is neither a shortcoming nor an error, I would say rather "illusion", and not only his today – the pragmatic relation to a transcendental level. It is as if the *I/you* relationship marked by the exchangeability of letters between persons or empirical individuals were a transcendental condition of philosophy, of history, of progress, of Enlightenment, in short of those things that he is concerned with (and I am certainly not scornful of them). But to accord oneself the privilege of the pragmatic, even under the most minimal form given by interlocution, even under the cloak of the greatest modesty (simple "solidarity"), is finally to get the essential on the cheap. Although it might seem otherwise, his position does not really pose the question of the other as such. It is as if the thought about constitution (let us say, so as not to go too far, in the sense of it elaborated by Husserl in his *Cartesian Meditations*) had not run aground on the problem of the constitution of others. Now, it is clear that it did come to grief, and we know very well why. It is because the other in its empiricity, in its pretended "presence" as the interlocutor with whom I can exchange speech, does not constitute a transcendental figure in the strict sense of the term. The transcendental figures are the "either/ors", either the true or the false, either the just or the unjust, either the beautiful or the not-beautiful, but not either the other or the not other. Let me note besides something which seems to me quite fascinating, which is that Kant always refers to others, in a more or less explicit way (less so in the first *Critique*, more so in the second and third), in the constitution of universality. Thus while it arises in a response to the question of the what-is-otherwise, it is not an answer, only a reference to them. The empirical other(s) is not a transcendental figure. Now Rorty treats other(s) as not only the single transcendental figure, since either solidarity or the invalidity of philosophy, and since if solidarity then the other(s) as interlocutor, but also takes it to be the case that the question thereby posed is already resolved: "we" talk to each other. I think that on this point the divergence between our positions is profound. I think moreover that it would be interesting to see if a *Critique of Altruistic Reason* could be written. This would be essential because what we would confront at this point, whether under the form of Apel's foundationalism, or of Habermas's communicationalism, or of Rorty's non-foundationalist and strictly interlocutory pragmatics, is finally the acceptance without examination (I would rather say, if you will allow it, without anamnesis) of the idea of others as the principal figure of contemporary thought. Now, whether others can be properly spoken of as a figure is problematic, as would be its "constitution"; and whether it might be the principal figure, I very much doubt.

Chapter 20

Jean Baudrillard

■ from *THE ILLUSION OF THE END*, Chris Turner trans., Cambridge: Polity Press, 1994

The reversal of history

AT SOME POINT IN THE 1980S, history took a turn in the opposite direction. Once the apogee of time, the summit of the curve of evolution, the solstice of history had been passed, the downward slope of events began and things began to run in reverse. It seems that, like cosmic space, historical space-time is also curved. By the same chaotic effect in time as in space, things go quicker and quicker as they approach their term, just as water mysteriously accelerates as it approaches a waterfall.

In the Euclidean space of history, the shortest path between two points is the straight line, the line of Progress and Democracy. But this is only true of the linear space of the Enlightenment. In our non-Euclidean *fin de siècle* space, a baleful curvature unfailingly deflects all trajectories. This is doubtless linked to the sphericity of time (visible on the horizon of the end of the century, just as the earth's sphericity is visible on the horizon at the end of the day) or the subtle distortion of the gravitational field.

Ségalen says that once the Earth has become a sphere, every movement distancing us from a point by the same token also begins to bring us closer to that point. This is true of time as well. Each apparent movement of history brings us imperceptibly closer to its antipodal point, if not indeed to its starting point. This is the end of linearity. In this perspective, the future no longer exists. But if there is no longer a future, there is no longer an end either. *So this is not even the end of history*. We are faced with a paradoxical process of reversal, a reversive effect of modernity which, having reached its speculative limit and extrapolated all its virtual developments, is disintegrating into its simple elements in a catastrophic process of recurrence and turbulence.

By this retroversion of history to infinity, this hyperbolic curvature, the century itself is escaping its end. By this retroaction of events, we are eluding our own deaths. Metaphorically, then, we shall not even reach the symbolic term of the end, the symbolic term of the year 2000.

Can one escape this curving back of history which causes it to retrace its own steps and obliterate its own tracks, escape this fatal asymptote which causes us, as it were, to rewind modernity like a tape? We are so used to playing back every film – the fictional ones and the films of our lives – so contaminated by the technology of retrospection, that we are quite capable, in our present dizzy spin, of running history over again like a film played backwards.

Are we condemned, in the vain hope of not abiding in our present destruction, as Canetti has it, to the retrospective melancholia of living everything through again in order to correct it all, in order to elucidate it all (it is almost as though psychoanalysis were spreading its shadow over the whole of our history: when the same events, the same conjunctures are reproduced in almost the same terms, when the same wars break out between the same peoples, and all that had passed and gone re-emerges as though driven by an irrepressible phantasm, one might almost see this as the work of a form of primary process or unconscious), do we have to summon all past events to appear before us, to reinvestigate it all as though we were conducting a trial? A mania for trials has taken hold of us in recent times, together with a mania for responsibility, precisely at the point when this latter is becoming increasingly hard to pin down. We are looking to remake a clean history, to whitewash all the abominations: the obscure (resentful) feeling behind the proliferation of scandals is that history itself is a scandal. A retroprocess which may drag us into a mania for origins, going back even beyond history, back to the conviviality of animal existence, to the primitive biotope, as can already be seen in the ecologists' flirtation with an impossible origin.

The only way of escaping this, of breaking with this recession and obsession, would seem to be to set ourselves, from the outset, on a different temporal orbit, to leapfrog our shadows, leapfrog the shadow of the century, to take an elliptical short-cut and pass beyond the end, not allowing it time to take place. The advantage is that we would at least preserve what remains of history, instead of subjecting it to an agonizing revision, and deliver it up to those who will carry out the post-mortem on its corpse, as one carries out a post-mortem on one's childhood in an interminable analysis. This would at least mean conserving its memory and its glory, whereas currently, in the guise of revision and rehabilitation, we are cancelling out one by one all the events which have preceded us by obliging them to repent.

If we could escape this end-of-century moratorium, with its deferred day of reckoning, which looks curiously like a work of mourning – a *failed* one – and which consists in reviewing everything, rewriting everything, restoring everything, face-lifting everything, to produce, as it seems, in a burst of paranoia a perfect set of accounts at the end of the century, a universally positive balance sheet (the reign of human rights over the whole planet, democracy everywhere, the definitive obliteration of all conflict and, if possible, the obliteration of all "negative" events from our memories), if we could escape this international cleaning and polishing effort in which all the nations of the world can be seen vying today, if we could spare ourselves this democratic extreme unction by which the New World Order is heralded, we would at least allow the events which have preceded us to retain their glory, character, meaning and singularity. Whereas we seem in such a hurry to cover up the worst before the bankruptcy proceedings start (everyone is secretly afraid of the terrifying balance sheet we are going to present in the year 2000) that there will be nothing left of our history at the end of the millennium, nothing of its illumination, of the violence of its events. If there is something distinctive about an event – about what constitutes an event and thus has historical value – it is the fact that it is irreversible, that there is always something in it which exceeds meaning and interpretation. But it is precisely the opposite we are seeing today: all that has happened this century in terms of progress, liberation, revolution and violence is about to be revised for the better.

This is the problem: is the course of modernity reversible, and is that reversal itself irreversible? How far can this retrospective form go, this end-of-millennium dream? Is there not a "history barrier", analogous to the sound or speed barrier, beyond which, in its palinodical movement, it could not pass?

Hysteresis of the millennium

We are, self-evidently, entering upon a retroactive form of history, and all our ideas, philosophies and mental techniques are progressively adapting to that model. We may perhaps even see this as an adventure, since the disappearance of the end is in itself an original situation. It seems to be characteristic of our culture and our history, which cannot even manage to come to an end, and are, as a result, assured of an indefinite recurrence, a backhanded immortality. Up to now, immortality has been mainly that of the beyond, an immortality yet to come, but we are today inventing another kind in the here and now, an immortality of endings receding to infinity.

The situation is, perhaps, an original one, but clearly, so far as the final result is concerned, the game is already lost. We shall never experience the original chaos, the Big Bang: the file is closed on that; we weren't there. But, where the final moment is concerned – the Big Crumb – we might have some hope of seeing that. Some hope of enjoying the end, to make up for not being able to enjoy the origin. These are the only two interesting moments and, since we have been denied the first, we might as well put all our energies into accelerating the end, into hastening things to their definitive doom, which we could at least consume as spectacle. Just imagine the extraordinary good luck of the generation which would have the end of the world to itself. It is every bit as marvellous as being present at the beginning. But we came too late for the beginning. Only the end seemed to be within our means.

We had come close to this possibility with the atomic age. Alas, the balance of terror suspended the ultimate event, then postponed it for ever(?) and, now deterrence has succeeded, we have to get used to the idea that *there is no end any longer, there will no longer be any end,* that history itself has become interminable. Thus, when we speak of the "end of history", the "end of the political", the "end of the social", the "end of ideologies", none of this is true. The worst of it all is precisely that there will be no end to anything, and all these things will continue to unfold slowly, tediously, recurrently, in that hysteresis of everything which, like nails and hair, continues to grow after death. Because, at bottom, all these things are already dead and, rather than have a happy or tragic resolution, a destiny, we shall have a thwarted end, a homeopathic end, an end distilled into all the various metastases of the refusal of death. The metastases of all that resurfaces as history goes back over its own tracks in a compulsive desire for rehabilitation, as though with regard to some crime or other (a crime committed by us, but in spite of ourselves, a crime of the species against itself, by a process which is quickening with contemporary history, a crime of which universal waste, universal repentance and universal *ressentiment* are, today, the surest signs), a crime on which the file has to be reopened, which necessarily involves going back into the past, right back to origins if necessary, where, for want of being able to find a resolution of our destiny in the future, we seek a retrospective absolution. We absolutely have to know what went wrong at a certain point and, hence, explore all the vestiges of the path we have travelled, root through the dustbins of history, revive both the best and the worst in the vain hope of separating good from evil. To return to Canetti's hypothesis: we have to get back beyond a fateful demarcation line which, in history too, might separate the human from the inhuman, a line which we might be said to have thoughtlessly crossed, in the dizzying whirl of some liberation of the species or other. It seems as though, caught up in a collective panic over this blind spot at which we passed out of history and its ends (but what were those ends? all we know is that we passed beyond them without noticing), we are hurriedly trying to get into reverse, in order to escape this state of empty simulation. Trying to relocate the zone of reference, the earlier scene, the Euclidean space of history. Thus the events in Eastern Europe claimed to set in train the onward march of peoples once more and the democratic process. And the Gulf War sought to reopen the space of war, the space of a violence that could establish a new world order.

This is, in every case, a failure. This revival of vanished – or vanishing – forms, this attempt to escape the apocalypse of the virtual, is a utopian desire, the last of our utopian desires. The more we seek to rediscover the real and the referential, the more we sink into simulation, in this case a shameful and, at any event, hopeless simulation.

By analogy with illnesses, which are perhaps merely the reactivation of previous states (cancer, for example, reproducing the undifferentiated proliferation of the first living cells, or viral pathology, which causes the earlier states of the biogenetic substance to resurface in moments when the body is weak and its immune defences low), can we not imagine that, in history itself, previous states have never disappeared, but present themselves again in succession, as it were, taking advantage of the weakness or excessive complexity of the present structures?

However, these earlier forms never resurface as they were; they never escape the destiny of extreme modernity. Their resurrection is itself hyper-real. The resuscitated values are themselves fluid, unstable, subject to the same fluctuations as fashion or stock-exchange capital. The rehabilitation of the old frontiers, the old structures, the old elites will therefore never have the same meaning. If, one day, the aristocracy or royalty recover their old position, they will, nonetheless, be "post-modern". None of the "retro" scenarios that are being got up has any historical significance: they are occurring wholly on the surface of *our* age, as though all images were being superimposed one upon another, but with no change to the actual course of the film. Relapsed events: defrosted democracy, *trompe-l'oeil* freedoms, the New World Order cellophane-wrapped and ecology in mothballs, with its immune-deficient human rights. None of these will make any difference to the *present* melancholy of the century, which we shall never get right through, since it will, in the meantime, have swung around and headed off in the opposite direction.

This is all, at bottom, a triumph for Walt Disney, that inspired precursor of a universe where all past or present forms meet in a playful promiscuity, where all cultures recur in a mosaic (including the cultures of the future, which are themselves already recurrent). For a long time we thought this was all imaginary, that is, derivative and decorative, puerile and marginal. But we are going to see that it was something like a prefiguration of the real trend of things – Disneyworld opening up for us the bewildering perspective of passing through all the earlier stages, as in a film, with those stages hypostasized in a definitive juvenility, frozen like Disney himself in liquid nitrogen: Magic Country, Future World, Gothic, Hollywood itself reconstituted fifty years on in Florida, the whole of the past and the future revisited as living simulation. Walt Disney is the true hero of deep-freezing, with his utopian hope of awakening one day in the future, in a better world. But that is where the irony bites: he had not foreseen that reality and history would turn right around. And he, who expected to wake up in the year 2100, might well, following out his own fairytale scenario, awaken in 1730 or the world of the Pharaohs or any one of his many primal scenes.

We wondered what the point of this coming *fin de siècle* might be. Here we have it: the sale of the century. History is being sold off, as is the end of history. Communism is being sold off, as is the end of communism. Communism will have had no historical end; it will have been sold off, knocked down like useless stock. Just like the Russian army, sold off at the four corners of the earth – an unprecedented event relegated to the status of a banal market operation. All Western ideologies are knocked down too; they can be had at bargain prices in all latitudes.

   The sales used to come after the feast days but now they precede them. It's the same with our century: we are anticipating the end – everything must go, everything has to be sold off. We learn, for example, that, alongside the great Red Army stock clearance, the industrial laboratories are currently "selling off" the human genome, which they are copyrighting and commercialising sequence by sequence. Here again, everything must go, even if we don't know what these genes are for. Things must not be allowed to reach their natural term. They have first to be cryogenized, in order to ensure them a virtual, derisory immortality.

Messianic hope was based on the *reality* of the Apocalypse. But this latter has no more reality than the original Big Bang. We shall never be allowed this dramatic illumination. Even the idea of putting an end to our planet by an atomic clash is futile and superfluous. If it has no meaning for anyone, God or man, then what is the point? Our Apocalypse is not real, it is *virtual*. And it is not in the future, it is *here and now*. Our orbital bombs, even if they did not mean a natural end, were at least manufactured by us, designed, as it seems, the better to end it all. But, in actual fact, that is not how it was: they were made *the better to be rid of the end*. We have now put that end into satellite form, like all those finalities which, once transcendent, have now become purely and simply orbital.

   It circles around us, and will continue to do so tirelessly. We are encircled by our own end and incapable of getting it to land, of bringing it back to earth. This is like the parable of the Russian cosmonaut forgotten in space, with no one to welcome him, no one to bring him back – the sole particle of Soviet territory ironically overflying a deterritorialized Russia. Whereas on earth everything has changed, he becomes practically immortal and continues to circle like the gods, like the stars, like nuclear waste. Like so many events, of which he is the perfect illustration, which continue to circle in the empty space of news [*l'information*], without anyone being able or willing to bring them back into historical space. A perfect image of all those things which continue their uncompromising performance in orbit, but have lost their identity along the way. Our history, for example, has also got lost along the way and revolves around us like an artificial satellite.

Nostalgia for the lost object? Not even that. Nostalgia had beauty because it retained within it the presentiment of what has taken place and could take place again. It was as beautiful as utopia, of which it is the inverted mirror. It was beautiful for never being satisfied, as was utopia for never being achieved. The sublime reference to the origin in nostalgia is as beautiful as the reference to the end in utopia. It is something else again to be confronted with *the literal manifestness of the end* (of which we can no longer dream as end), and the literal manifestness of the origin (of which we can no longer dream as origin). Now, we have the means today to put into play both our origins and our end. We exhume our origins in archaeology, reshape our original capital through genetics, and operationalize our dreams and the wildest utopias by means of science and technology. We appease our nostalgia and our utopian desires *in situ* and *in vitro.*

We are, then, unable to dream of a past or future state of things. Things are in a state which is literally definitive – neither finished, nor infinite, nor definite, but de-finitive that is, deprived of its end. Now, the feeling which goes with a definitive state, even a paradisiac one – is melancholic. Whereas, with mourning, things come to an end and therefore enjoy a possibility of returning, with melancholia we are not even left with the presentiment of an end or of a return, but only with *ressentiment* at their disappearance. The crepuscular profile of the *fin de siècle* is more or less of this order, combining the features of a linear order of progress and a regression, itself also linear, of ends and values.

Against this general movement, there remains the completely improbable and, no doubt, unverifiable hypothesis of a *poetic reversibility of events,* more or less the only evidence for which is the existence of the same possibility in language.

The poetic form is not far removed from the chaotic form. Both flout the law of cause and effect. If, in Chaos Theory, for sensitivity to initial conditions we substitute sensitivity to final conditions, we are in the form of predestination, which is the form of fate [*le destin*]. Poetic language also lives with predestination, with the immanence of its own ending and of reversibility between the ending and the beginning. It is predestined in this sense – it is an unconditional event, without meaning and consequence, which draws its whole being from the dizzying whirl of final resolution.

It is certainly not the form of our present history and yet there is an affinity between the immanence of poetic development and the immanence of the chaotic development which is ours today, the unfolding of events which are themselves also without meaning and consequence and in which – with effects substituting themselves for causes – there are no longer any causes, *but only effects.* The world is there, *effectively.* There is no reason for this, and God is dead.

If nothing exists now but effects, we are in a state of total illusion (which is also that of poetic language). If the effect is in the cause or the beginning in the end, then the catastrophe is behind us. This reversing of the sign of catastrophe is the exceptional privilege of our age. It liberates us from any future catastrophe and any responsibility in that regard. The end of all anticipatory psychoses, all panic, all remorse! The lost object is behind us. We are free of the Last Judgement.

What this brings us to, more or less, is a poetic, ironic analysis of events. Against the simulation of a linear history "in progress", we have to accord a privileged status to these backfires, these malign deviations, these lightweight catastrophes which cripple an empire much more effectively than any great upheavals. We have to accord a privileged status to all that has to do with nonlinearity, reversibility, all that is of the order not of an unfolding or an evolution, but of a winding back, a reversion in time. Anastrophe versus catastrophe. Perhaps, deep down, history has never unfolded in a linear fashion; perhaps language has never unfolded in a linear fashion. Everything moves in loops, tropes, inversions of meaning, except in numerical and artificial languages which, for that very reason, *no longer are* languages. Everything occurs through effects which short-circuit their (metaleptic) causes, through the *Witze* [jokes] of events, perverse events, ironic turnabouts, except within a rectified history, which, for just that reason, is *not* a history.

Might we not transpose language games on to social and historical phenomena: anagrams, acrostics, spoonerisms, rhyme, strophe and catastrophe? Not just the major figures of metaphor and metonymy, but the instant, puerile, formalistic games, the heteroclite tropes which are the delight of a vulgar imagination? Are there social spoonerisms, or an anagrammatic history (where meaning is dismembered and scattered to the winds, like the name of God in the anagram), rhyming forms of political action or events which can be read in either direction? In these times of a retroversion of history, the palindrome, that poetic, rigorous form of palinode, could serve as a *grille de lecture* (might it not perhaps be necessary to replace Paul Virilios dromology with a palindromology?). And the anagram, that detailed process of unravelling, that sort of poetic and non-linear convulsion of language – is there a chance that history lends itself to such a poetic convulsion, to such a subtle form of return and anaphora which, like the anagram, would – beyond meaning – allow the pure materiality of language to show through, and – beyond historical meaning – allow the pure materiality of time to show through?

Such would be the enchanted alternative to the linearity of history, the poetic alternative to the disenchanted confusion, the chaotic profusion of present events.

In this very way, we enter, beyond history, upon pure fiction, upon the illusion of the world. The illusion of our history opens on to *the greatly more radical illusion of the world*. Now we have closed the eyelids of the Revolution, closed our eyes on the Revolution, now we have broken down the Wall of Shame, now that the lips of protest are closed (with the sugar of history which melts on the tongue), now Europe – and memories – are no longer haunted by the spectre of communism, nor even by that of power, now the aristocratic illusion of the origin and the democratic illusion of the end are increasingly receding, we no longer have the choice of advancing, of persevering in the present destruction, or of retreating – but only of facing up to this radical illusion.

Chapter 21

Jacques Derrida

■ from **INJUNCTIONS OF MARX** in *Specters of Marx: The State of the Debt, the Work of Mourning and the New International*, Peggy Kamuf trans., London: Routledge, 1994

IN PROPOSING THIS TITLE, *SPECTERS OF MARX*, I was initially thinking of all the forms of a certain haunting obsession that seems to me to organize the *dominant* influence on discourse today. At a time when a new world disorder is attempting to install its neo-capitalism and neo-liberalism, no disavowal has managed to rid itself of all of Marx's ghosts. Hegemony still organizes the repression and thus the confirmation of a haunting. Haunting belongs to the structure of every hegemony.[1] But I did not have in mind first of all the exordium of the *Manifesto*.[2] In an apparently different sense, Marx-Engels spoke there already, in 1847–8, of a specter and more precisely of the "specter of communism" (*das Gespenst des Kommunismus*). A terrifying specter for all the powers of old Europe (*alle Mächte des alten Europa*), but specter of a communism then *to come*. Of a communism, to be sure, already namable (and well before the League of the Just or the Communist League), but still to come beyond its name. Already promised but only promised. A specter all the more terrifying, some will say. Yes, on the condition that one can never distinguish between the future-to-come and the coming-back of a specter. Let us not forget that, around 1848, the First International had to remain quasi-secret. The specter was there (but what is the *being-there* of a specter? what is the mode of presence of a specter? that is the only question we would like to pose here). But that of which it was the specter, communism (*das Gespenst der Kommunismus*), was itself not there, by definition. It was dreaded as communism to come. It had already been announced, with this name, some time ago, but it was not yet *there*. It is only a specter, seemed to say these allies of old Europe so as to reassure themselves; let's hope that in the future it does not become an actual, effectively present, manifest, non-secret reality. The question old Europe was asking itself was already the question of the future, the question "whither?": "whither communism?" if not "whither Marxism?" Whether one takes it as asking about the future of communism or about communism in the future, this anguished question did not just seek to know how, in the future, communism would affect European history, but also, in a more muffled way, already whether there would still be any future and any history at all for Europe. In 1848, the Hegelian discourse on the end of history in absolute knowledge had already resounded throughout Europe and had rung a consonant note with many other knells [*glas*]. And communism was essentially distinguished from other labor movements by its *international* character. No organized political movement in the history of humanity had ever yet presented itself as *geo-political*, thereby inaugurating the space that is now ours and that today is reaching its limits, the limits of the earth and the limits of the political.

The representative of these forces or all these powers (*alle Mächte*), namely the States, wanted to *reassure* themselves. They wanted to be sure. So they were sure, for there is no difference between "being sure" and "wanting to be sure." They were sure and certain that between a specter and an actually present reality, between a spirit and a *Wirklichkeit*, the dividing line was assured. It *had* to be safely drawn. It *ought* to be assured. No, it *ought to have been* assured. The sureness of this certainty is something they shared, moreover, with *Marx himself*. (This is the whole story, and we are coming to it: Marx thought, to be sure, on his side, from the other side, that the dividing line between the ghost and actuality ought to be crossed, like utopia itself, by a realization, that is, by a revolution; but *he too* will have continued to believe, to try to believe in the existence of this dividing line as real limit and conceptual distinction. He too? No, someone in him. Who? The "Marxist" who will engender what for a long time is going to prevail under the name of "Marxism." And which was also haunted by what it attempted to foreclose.)

Today, almost a century and a half later, there are many who, throughout the world, seem just as worried by the specter of communism, just as convinced that what one is dealing with there is only a specter without body, without present reality, without actuality or effectivity, but this time it is supposed to be a past specter. It was only a specter, an illusion, a phantasm, or a ghost: that is what one hears everywhere today ("Horatio saies, 'tis but our Fantasie,/ And will not let beleefe take hold of him"). A still worried sigh of relief: *let* us make sure that in the future it does not come back! At bottom, the specter is the future, it is always to come, it presents itself only as that which could come or come back; in the future, said the powers of old Europe in the last century, it must not incarnate itself, either publicly or in secret. In the future, we hear everywhere today, it must not re-incarnate itself; it must not be allowed to come back since it is past.

What exactly is the difference from one century to the next? Is it the difference between a past world – for which the specter represented a coming threat – and a present world, today, where the specter would represent a threat that some would like to believe is past and whose return it would be necessary again, once again in the future, to conjure away?

Why in both cases is the specter felt to be a threat? What is the time and what is the history of a specter? Is there a present of the specter? Are its comings and goings ordered according to the linear succession of a before and an after, between a present-past, a present-present, and a present-future, between a "real time" and a "deferred time"?

If there is something like spectrality, there are reasons to doubt this reassuring order of presents and, especially, the border between the present, the actual or present reality of the present, and everything that can be opposed to it: absence, non-presence, non-effectivity, inactuality, virtuality, or even the simulacrum in general, and so forth. There is first of all the doubtful contemporaneity of the present to itself. Before knowing whether one can differentiate between the specter of the past and the specter of the future, of the past present and the future present, one must perhaps ask oneself whether the *spectrality effect* does not consist in undoing this opposition, or even this dialectic, between actual, effective presence and its other. One must perhaps ask oneself whether this opposition, be it a dialectical opposition, has not always been a closed field and a common axiomatic for the antagonism between Marxism and the cohort or the alliance of its adversaries.

Pardon me for beginning with such an abstract formulation.

In the middle of the last century, an alliance was constituted against this specter, to drive off the evil. Marx did not call this coalition a Holy Alliance, an expression he plays with elsewhere. In the *Manifesto*, the alliance of the worried conspirators assembles, more or less secretly, a nobility and a clergy — in the old castle of Europe, for an unbelievable expedition against what will have been haunting the night of these masters. At twilight, before or after a night of bad dreams, at the presumed end of history, it is a "holy hunt against this specter": "All the powers of old Europe have joined [*verbündet*] into a holy hunt against this specter [*zu einer heiligen Hetzjagd gegen dies Gespenst*]."

It would thus be possible to form a secret alliance against the specter. If Marx had written his *Manifesto* in my language, and if he had had some help with it, as a Frenchman can always dream of doing, I am sure he would have played on the word *conjuration*. Then he would have diagnosed today the same *conjuration*, this time not only in old Europe but in the new Europe, the New World, which already interested him very much a century and a half ago, and throughout the world, in the new world order where the hegemony of this new world, I mean the United States, would still exercise a more or less critical hegemony, more and less assured than ever.

The word *conjuration* has the good fortune to put to work and to produce, without any possible reappropriation, a forever errant surplus value. It capitalizes first of all two orders of semantic value. What is a "conjuration"?

The French noun "conjuration" gathers up and articulates the meanings of two English words — and also two German words.

1   *Conjuration* signifies, *on the one hand*, "conjuration" (its English homonym) which itself designates two things at once:

    a   *On the one hand*, the conspiracy (*Verschwörung* in German) of those who promise solemnly, sometimes secretly, by swearing together an oath (*Schwur*) to struggle against a superior power. It is to this conspiracy that Hamlet appeals, evoking the "Vision" they have just seen and the "honest ghost," when he asks Horatio and Marcellus to swear ("swear't," "Consent to swear"). To swear upon his sword, but to swear or to swear together *on the subject of the spectral apparition itself*, and to promise secrecy on the subject of the apparition of an honest ghost that, from beneath the stage, conspires with Hamlet to ask the same thing from the sworn: ("*The Ghost cries from under the stage:* Sweare"). It is the apparition that enjoins them to conspire to *silence the apparition*, and to promise secrecy on the subject of the one who demands such an oath from them: one must not know whence comes the injunction, the conspiracy, the promised secret. A son and the "honest ghost" of the father, the supposedly honest ghost, the spirit of the father, conspire together to bring about such an event.

    b   "Conjuration" signifies, *on the other hand*, the magical incantation destined to *evoke*, to bring forth with the voice, to *convoke* a charm or a spirit. Conjuration says in sum the appeal that causes to come forth *with the voice* and thus it makes come, by, definition, what *is not there* at the present moment of the appeal. This voice does not describe, what it says certifies nothing; its words cause something to happen. This is the usage encountered again in the words of the Poet at the opening of *Timon of Athens*. After having asked "How goes the world?" and after the Painter has told him "It wears, sir, as it grows," the Poet exclaims:

Ay, that's well known;
But what particular rarity, what strange,
Which manifold record not matches? — See,
Magic of bounty, all these spirits thy power
Hath *conjur'd* to attend. I know the merchant.
                                        (I, i)

Marx evokes more than once *Timon of Athens*, as well as *The Merchant of Venice*, in particular in *The German Ideology*. The chapter on "The Leipzig Council – Saint Max," also supplies, and we will say more about this later, a short treatise on the spirit or an interminable theatricalization of ghosts. A certain "Communist Conclusion" appeals to *Timon of Athens*.[3] The same quotation will reappear in the first version of *A Contribution to the Critique of Political Economy*. In question is a spectralizing disincarnation. Apparition of the bodiless body, of money: not the lifeless body or the cadaver, but a life without personal life or individual property. Not without identity (the ghost is a "who," it is not of the simulacrum in general, it has a kind of body, but without property, without "real" or "personal" right of property). One must analyze the proper of property and how the general property (*Eigentum*) of money neutralizes, disincarnates, deprives of its difference all personal property (*Eigentümlichkeit*). The genius of Shakespeare will have understood this phantomalization of property centuries ago and said it better than anyone. The *ingenium* of his paternal geniality serves as reference, guarantee, or confirmation in the polemic, that is, in the ongoing war – on the subject, precisely, of the monetary specter, value, money or its fiduciary sign, gold: "It was known to Shakespeare better than to our theorizing petty bourgeois [*unser theoretisierender Kleinbürger*] ... how little connection there is between money, the most general form of property [*die allgemeinste Form des Eigentums*], and personal peculiarity [*mit der persönlichen*; *Eigentümlichkeit*] ..."[4]

The quotation will also make apparent (as a supplementary benefit but in fact it is altogether necessary) a theologizing fetishization, the one that always links ideology irreducibly to religion (to the idol or the fetish) as its principal figure, a species of "invisible god" to which adoration, prayer, and invocation are addressed ("Thou visible god"). Religion [...] was never one ideology among others for Marx. What, Marx seems to say, the genius of a great poet – and the spirit of a great father – will have uttered in a poetic flash, with one blow going faster and farther than our little bourgeois colleagues in economic theory, is the becoming-god of gold, which is at once ghost and idol, a god apprehended by the senses. After having marked the heterogeneity between the property of money and personal property (there is "little connection" between them), Marx adds, and it is not a negligible clarification it seems to me, that in truth they are not only different but opposed (*entgegensetzt*). And it is then that, cutting into the body of the text and making choices that should be analyzed closely, he wrests a long passage from that prodigious scene in *Timon of Athens* (IV, iii). Marx loves the words of this imprecation. One must never keep silent about the imprecation of the just. One must never silence it in the most analytic text of Marx. An imprecation does not theorize, it is not content to say how things are, it cries out the truth, it promises, it provokes. As its name indicates, it is nothing other than a prayer. Marx appropriates the words of this imprecation with a kind of delight whose signs are unmistakable. Declaring his hatred of the human race ("I am Misanthropos and hate mankind"), with the anger of a Jewish prophet and sometimes the very words of Ezechiel, Timon curses corruption, he casts down anathema, he swears against prostitution – prostitution in the face of gold and the prostitution of gold itself. But he takes the time to analyze, nevertheless, the transfiguring alchemy, he denounces the reversal of values, the falsification and especially the perjury of which it is the law. One imagines the impatient patience of Marx (rather than Engels) as he transcribes in his own hand, at length, in German, the rage of a prophetic imprecation:

> ... Thus much of this will make
> Black white, foul fair, wrong right,
> Base noble, old young, coward valiant.
>
> This yellow slave
> Will ...
> Make the hoar leprosy adored ...
>
> This is it
> That makes the wappen'd widow wed again.
> She whom the spittle house and ulcerous sores
> Would cast the gorge at, this embalms and spices
> To th'April day again ...
>
> Thou visible god,
> That sold'rest closest impossibilities
> And mak'st them kiss ...
>
> *sichtbare Gottheit,*
> *Die du Unmöglichkeiten eng verbrüderst*
> *Zum Kusz sie zwingst!*
>
> (IV, iii)

Among all the traits of this immense malediction of malediction, Marx will have had to efface, in the economy of a long citation, those that are most important for us here, for example, the aporias and the double bind that carry the act of swearing and conjuring off into the history of venality itself. At the moment he goes to bury the gold, a shovel in his hand, the prophet-gravedigger, anything but a humanist, is not content to evoke the breaking of vows, the birth and death of religions ("This yellow slave/ Will knit and break religions; bless the accurs'd"); Timon also begs [*conjure*] the other, he pleads with him to promise, but he conjures thus by perjuring and by confessing his perjury in a same and single bifid gesture. In truth, he conjures *by feigning the truth*, by feigning at least to make the other promise. But if he feigns to make the other promise, it is in truth to make the other promise not to keep his promise, that is, not to promise, even as he pretends to promise: to perjure or to abjure in the very moment of the oath; then following from this same logic, he begs him to spare all oaths. As if he were saying in effect: I beg you [*je vous en conjure*], do not swear, abjure your right to swear, renounce your capacity to swear, moreover no one is asking you to swear, you are asked to be the non-oathables that you are ("you are not oathable"), you, the whores, you who are prostitution itself, you who give yourselves to gold, you who give yourselves for gold, you who are destined to general indifference, you who confuse in equivalency the proper and the improper, credit and discredit, faith and lie, the "true and the false," oath, perjury, and abjuration, and so forth. You the whores of money, you would go so far as to abjure ("forswear") your trade or your vocation (of perjured whore) for money. Like a madam who would give up even her whores for money.

The very essence of humanity is at stake. Absolute double bind on the subject of the *bind* or the *bond* themselves. Infinite misfortune and incalculable chance of the performative – here named literally ("perform" "perform none" are Timon's words when he asks [*conjure*] the other *to promise not to keep a promise*, calling therefore for perjury or abjuration). Force, as weakness, of an ahuman discourse on man. Timon to Alcibiades: "Promise me friendship, but perform none. If thou wilt promise, the gods plague thee, for thou art a man. If thou dost not perform, confound thee, for thou art a man" (IV, iii). Then to Phyrnia and Timandra who ask for gold – and whether Timon has any more:

> Enough to make a whore forswear her trade,
> And to make wholesomeness a bawd. Hold up, you sluts,
> Your aprons mountant. You are not oathable,
> Although I know you'll swear, terribly swear,
> Into strong shudders and to heavenly agues
> Th'immortal gods that hear you. Spare your oaths;
> I'll trust to your conditions. Be whores still ...
>
> (IV, iii)

Addressing himself to prostitution or to the cult of money, to fetishism or to idolatry itself, Timon trusts. He gives faith, he believes, he indeed wants to *credit* ("I'll trust") but only in the imprecation of a paradoxical hyperbole: he himself pretends to trust in that which, from the depths of abjuration, from the depths of that which is not even capable or worthy of an oath ("you are not oathable"), remains nevertheless faithful to a natural instinct, as if there were a pledge of instinct, a fidelity to itself of instinctual nature, an oath of living nature before the oath of convention, society, or law. And it is the fidelity to infidelity, the constancy in perjury. This life enslaves itself regularly, one can trust it to do so, it never fails to kneel to indifferent power, to that power of mortal indifference that is money. Diabolical, radically bad in that way, nature is prostitution, it enslaves itself faithfully, one can have confidence here in it, it enslaves itself to what is betrayal itself, perjury, abjuration, lie, and simulacrum.

Which are never very far from the specter. As is well known, Marx always described money, and more precisely the monetary sign, in the figure of appearance or simulacrum, more exactly of the ghost. He not only described them, he also defined them, but the figural presentation of the concept seemed to describe some spectral "thing," which is to say, "someone." What is the necessity of this figural presentation? What is its relation to the concept? Is it contingent? That is the classic form of our question. As we do not believe in any contingency here, we will even begin to worry about the classical (basically Kantian) form of this question which seems to marginalize or keep at a distance the figural schema even as it takes it seriously. *The Critique of Political Economy* explains to us how the existence (*Dasein*) of money, metallic *Dasein*, gold or silver, produces a remainder.[5] This remainder is – it remains, precisely – but the shadow of a great name: "*Was übrigbleibt ist magni nominis umbra.*" "The body of money is but a shadow [*nur noch ein Schatten*]."[6] The whole movement of idealization (*Idealisierung*) that Marx then describes, whether it is a question of money or of ideologems, is a production of ghosts, illusions, simulacra, appearances, or apparitions (*Scheindasein* of the *Schein-Sovereign* and of the *Schein-gold*). Later he will compare this spectral virtue of money with that which, in the desire to hoard, speculates on the use of money *after death*, in the other world (*nach dem Tode in der andern Welt*).[7] *Geld*, *Geist*, *Geiz*: as if money (*Geld*) were the origin both of spirit (*Geist*) and of avarice (*Geiz*). "*Im Geld liegt der Ursprung des Geizes*," says Pliny as quoted by Marx right after this. Elsewhere, the equation between *Gaz* and *Geist* will be joined to the chain.[8] The metamorphosis of commodities (*die Metamorphose der Waren*) was already a process of transfiguring idealization that one may legitimately call spectropoetic. When the State emits paper money at a fixed rate, its intervention is compared to "magic" (*Magie*) that transmutes paper into gold. The State appears then, for it is an appearance, indeed an apparition; it "seems now to transform paper into gold by the magic of its imprint [*scheint jetzt durch die Magie seines Stempels Papier in Gold zu verwandeln*; Marx is referring to the imprint that stamps gold and prints paper money]."[9] This magic always busies itself with ghosts, it does business with them, it manipulates or busies *itself*, it becomes a business, the business it does in the very element of haunting. And this business attracts the undertakers, those who deal with cadavers but so as to steal them, to make the departed disappear, which remains the condition of their "apparition." Commerce and theater of gravediggers. In periods of social crisis, when the social "*nervus rerum*" is, says Marx, "buried [*bestattet*] along side the body whose sinew it is", the speculative burying of the treasure inters only a useless metal, deprived of its monetary soul (*Geldseele*). This burial scene recalls not only the great scene of the cemetery and gravediggers in *Hamlet*, when one of them suggests that the work of the "grave-maker" lasts longer than any other: until Judgment Day. This scene of burying gold also evokes more than once, and still more exactly, *Timon of Athens*. In Marx's funerary rhetoric, the "useless metal" of the treasure once buried becomes like the burnt-out ashes (*ausgebrannte Asche*) of circulation, like its *caput mortuum*, its chemical residue. In his wild imaginings, in his nocturnal delirium (*Hirngespinst*), the miser, the hoarder, the speculator becomes a martyr to exchange-value. He now refrains from exchange because he dreams of a pure exchange. (And we will see later how the apparition of exchange-value, in *Capital*, is precisely an apparition, one might say a vision, a hallucination, a *properly* spectral apparition if this figure did not prevent us from speaking here properly of the proper.) The hoarder behaves then like an alchemist (*alchimistisch*), speculating on ghosts, the "elixir of life," the "philosophers' stone." Speculation is always fascinated, bewitched by the specter. That this alchemy remains devoted to the apparition of the specter, to the haunting or the return of *revenants* is brought out in the literality of a text that translations sometimes overlook. When, in this same passage, Marx describes the transmutation, there is haunting at stake. What operates in all alchemical fashion are the exchanges and mixtures of *revenants*, the *madly spectral* compositions or conversions. The lexicon of haunting and ghosts (*Spuk*, *spuken*) takes center stage. Whereas the English translation speaks of the "alchemist's apparitions" ("The liquid form of wealth and its petrification, the elixir of life and the philosophers' stone are wildly mixed together like an alchemist's apparitions"), the French translation drops the reference to ghosts (*spuken alchemistisch toll durcheinander*) with the phrase "*fantasmagorie d'une folle achimie.*"[10]

In short, and we will return to this repeatedly, Marx does not like ghosts any more than his adversaries do. He does not want to believe in them. But he thinks of nothing else. He believes rather in what is supposed to distinguish them from actual reality, living effectivity. He believes he can oppose them, like life to death, like vain appearances of the simulacrum to real presence. He believes enough in the dividing line of this opposition to want to denounce, chase away, or exorcise the specters but by means of critical analysis and not by some counter-magic. But how to distinguish between the analysis that denounces magic and the counter-magic that it still risks being? We will ask ourselves this question again, for example, as regards *The German Ideology*. "The Leipzig Council – Saint Max" (Stirner) also organizes, let us recall once more before coming back to it later, an *irresistible* but *interminable* hunt for ghosts (*Gespenst*) and for *revenants* or spooks (*Spuk*). *Irresistible* like an effective critique, but also like a compulsion; *interminable* as one says of an analysis, and the comparison would not be at all fortuitous.

This hostility toward ghosts, a terrified hostility that sometimes fends off terror with a burst of laughter, is perhaps what Marx will always have had in common with his adversaries. He too will have tried to *conjure* (away) the ghosts, and everything that was neither life nor death, namely, the re-apparition of an apparition that will never be either the appearing or the disappeared, the phenomenon or its contrary. He will have tried to conjure (away) the ghosts *like* the conspirators [*conjurés*] of old Europe on whom the *Manifesto* declares war. However inexpiable this war remains, and however necessary this revolution, it conspires [*conjure*] *with them* in order to *exorc-analyze* the spectrality of the specter. And this is today, as perhaps it will be tomorrow, our problem.

2 For "conjuration" means, on the other hand, "conjurement" (*Beschwörung*), namely, the magical exorcism that, on the contrary, tends to expulse the evil spirit which would have been called up or convoked (OED: "the exorcising of spirits by invocation," "the exercise of magical or occult influence").

A conjuration, then, is first of all alliance, to be sure, sometimes a political alliance, more or less secret, if not tacit, a plot or a conspiracy. It is a matter of neutralizing a hegemony or overturning some power. (During the Middle Ages, *conjuratio* also designated the sworn faith by means of which the bourgeois joined together, sometimes against a prince, in order to establish free towns.) In the occult society of those who have sworn together [*des conjurés*], certain subjects, either individual or collective, represent forces and ally themselves together in the name of common interests to combat a dreaded political adversary, that is, also to conjure it away. For to conjure means *also* to exorcise: to attempt both to destroy and to disavow a malignant, demonized, diabolized force, most often an evil-doing spirit, a specter, a kind of ghost who comes back or who still risks coming back *post mortem*. Exorcism conjures away the evil in ways that are also irrational, using magical, mysterious, even mystifying practices. Without excluding, quite to the contrary, analytic procedure and argumentative ratiocination, exorcism consists in repeating in the mode of an incantation that the dead man is really dead. It proceeds by *formulae*, and sometimes theoretical formulae play this role with an efficacy that is all the greater because they mislead as to their magical nature, their authoritarian dogmatism, the occult power they share with what they claim to combat.

But effective exorcism pretends to declare the death only in order to put to death. As a coroner might do, it certifies the death but here it is in order to inflict it. This is a familiar tactic. The constative form tends to reassure. The certification is effective. It wants to be and it must be *in effect*. It is *effectively* a performative. But here effectivity phantomalizes itself. It is in fact [*en effet*] a matter of a performative that seeks to reassure but first of all to reassure itself by assuring itself, for nothing is less sure, that what one would like to see dead is indeed dead. It speaks in the name of life, it claims to know what that is. Who knows better than someone who is alive? it seems to say with a straight face. It seeks to convince (itself) there where it makes (itself) afraid:[11] now, it says (to itself), what used to be living is no longer alive, it does not remain effective in death itself, don't worry. (What is going on here is a way of not wanting to know what everyone alive knows without learning and without knowing, namely, that the dead can often be more powerful than the living; and that is why to interpret a philosophy as philosophy or ontology of life is never a simple matter, which means that it is always too simple, incontestable, like what goes without saying, but finally so unconvincing, as unconvincing as a tautology, a rather heterological tauto-ontology, that of Marx or whomever, which relates everything back to life only on the condition of including there death and the alterity of its other without which it would not be what it is.) In short, it is often a matter of pretending to certify death there where the death certificate is still the performative of an act of war or the impotent gesticulation, the restless dream, of an execution.

Notes

Introduction

1   See, for instance, Luc Ferry and Alain Renaut in *La pensée 68, essai sur l'anti-humanisme contemporain* (Paris: Gallimard, 1988). Ferry and Renaut's reaction is shared by many leading Anglo-American thinkers. A recent example of this is the polemical launched against Michel Foucault and Jacques Derrida in the pages of Mark Lilla's *The Reckless Mind: Intellectuals in Politics* (New York: NYRB, 2001). The hostility to postmodern thought harboured by many Anglo-American philosophers reached an impressive peak when Jacques Derrida was awarded an honourary doctorate by Cambridge University in 1992. Many of the Cambridge dons who considered Derrida to be an obscurantist charlatan were outraged and boycotted the degree ceremony. Another example of the kind of hostile reaction postmodern thought has produced was occasioned by the publication of Alan Sokal and Jean Bricmont's *Impostures intellectuelles* (*Intellectual Impostures: Postmodern Philosophers' Abuse of Science*) (Alan Sokal and Jean Bricmont, trans.) (London: Profile Books, 1998) in 1997. Bricmont and Sokal's text prompted a deluge of articles in the English language press which highlighted how postmodernist writings were 'deliberately obscure, excessively convoluted, pseudo-scientific claptrap'. For one such example see 'Think again, French philosophers', *The Guardian*, 1 October 1997.

2   Daniel Bell, *The Coming of Post-Industrial Society: A Venture in Social Forecasting* (Harmondsworth: Penguin Books, 1976), p. 478. Originally published as *The Coming of Post-Industrial Society: A Venture in Social Forecasting* (New York: Basic Books, 1973).

3   Daniel Bell, *The Cultural Contradictions of Capitalism* (London: Heinemann, 1976), p. 29.

4   Ibid.

5   Bernard Iddings Bell, *Postmodernism and Other Essays* (Milwaukee: Morehouse Publishing Company, 1926). Many of the essays in this book are reprinted in *Religion for Living: A Book for Postmodernists* (London: John Gifford, 1939).

6   Bernard Iddings Bell, *Religion for Living*, pp. xii–xiv.

7   Federico de Onis, *Antología de la Poesía Española e Hispanoamericana (1882–1932)* (Madrid: Centro de Estudios Historicos, 1934).

8   Arnold Toynbee, *A Study of History*, vol. 8 (London: Oxford University Press, 1954), p. 338.

9   Ibid., vol. 9, p. 421.

10   Ibid., vol. 9, pp. 468–9.

11   See, for instance, the first of Olson's Beloit Lectures. Charles Olson, *Poetry and Truth: The Beloit Lectures and Poems* (San Fransisco, Calif.: Four Seasons Foundation, 1971), p. 12.

12   Charles Olson, *Human Universe and Other Essays* (Donald Allen, ed.) (San Franscisco, Calif.: The Auerhahn Society, 1965), p. 3.

13   Charles Olson, *Human Universe and Other Essays*, p. 5.

14   Charles Olson, *Projective Verse, Poetry New York*, 3, 1950, 12–22. Reprinted *Projective Verse* (New York: Totem, 1959), p. 10.

15   Charles Olson, *Poetry and Truth*, p. 46.

16   Robert B. Pippin, *Modernism as a Philosophical Problem: On the Dissatisfactions of European High Culture* (Oxford: Blackwell, 1991), p. 122.

17   William V. Spanos, 'The Detective and the Boundary: Some Notes on the Postmodern Literary Imagination', *boundary 2*, 1, 1, p. 156.

18   Joseph Hudnut, 'The Postmodern House', *Architectural Record,* 97, May 1945, pp. 70–5.

19   First published in the UK as Jane Jacobs, *The Death and Life of Great American Cities* (London: Jonathan Cape, 1962).

20   Robert Venturi, *Complexity and Contradiction in Architecture* (New York: The Museum of Modern Art, 1966), p. 22. Venturi never uses the term 'postmodern' in either the first or second editions (1966 and 1976) of this work. The term will only later become associated with complexity and contradiction.

21   Ibid., pp. 89–90 and pp. 101–3.

22   Robert Venturi, Denise Scott Brown, Steven Izenour, *Learning from Las Vegas* (Cambridge, Mass.: MIT Press, 1977), p. 85. Originally published as *Learning from Las Vegas* (Cambridge, Mass.: MIT Press, 1972).

23   Ada Louis Huxtable, 'The Troubled State of Modern Architecture', *Architectural Design*, 51, 1–2, p. 10.

24   Charles Jencks, 'The Rise of Post-Modern Architecture', *Architectural Association Quarterly*, 7, 4, October/December 1975, pp. 3–14.

25   Charles Jencks, *The Language of Post-Modern Architecture* (2nd edn) (London: Academy Press, 1978), p. 8

26   Jencks, *The Language of Post-Modern Architecture* (2nd edn), p. 6.

27   Jencks, *The Language of Post-Modern Architecture* (3rd edn) (London: Academy Press, 1981), p. 133.

28   'Interview with Charles Jencks', *Art and Design*, 3, 7–8, 1987, pp. 45–7.

29   Hans Bertens, *The Idea of the Postmodern: A History* (London: Routledge, 1995), p. 66.

30   Jürgen Habermas, 'Modern and Postmodern Architecture', *The New Conservatism: Cultural Criticism and the Historians' Debate* (Shierry Weber Nicholson, ed. and trans.) (Cambridge, Mass.: MIT Press, 1990), p. 19.

31   Isaiah Berlin, *The Magus of the North* (London: Fontana Press, 1993), p. 53.

32   Johann Georg Hamann, *Briefwechsel*, VI (W. Ziesemer and A. Henkel, eds) (Frankfurt: Insel, 1955–79) p. 108, cited in Berlin, *The Magus of the North*, p. 83.

33   Johann Georg Hamann, *Briefwechsel*, V, p. 264, cited in Berlin, *The Magus of the North*, p. 40.

34   Berlin, *The Magus of the North*, p. 90.

35   Ibid.

36   Arthur Schopenhauer, *The World as Will and Idea* (trans. from the German by R.B. Haldane and J. Kemp) (London: Tröbner and Co., 1883).

37   This same idea was advanced, almost a century later, by the father of psychoanalysis Sigmund Freud, though Freud only came upon Schopenhauer's work after his own thoughts on psychoanalysis were well established. The final chapter of Freud's *Die Traumdeutung* (Leipzig:

F. Deuticke, 1900) (The Interpretation of Dreams, James Strachey, trans.) (Harmondsworth: Penguin Books, 1976) gives the first full account of his dynamic view of mental processes and of the unconscious.

38 Schopenhauer, *Essays and Aphorisms* (R.J. Hollingdale, trans.) (Harmondsworth: Penguin, 1976), p. 174.

39 Ibid., p. 127.

40 Ibid., p. 129.

41 Immanuel Kant, 'An Answer to the Question: "What is Enlightenment?"', *Political Writings* (H.B. Nisbet, trans.) (Hans Reiss, ed.) (Cambridge: Cambridge University Press, 1991), p. 54.

42 Ibid., p. 54.

43 Friedrich Nietzsche, *The Will to Power* (Walter Kaufmann, trans.) (New York: Vintage Books, 1967), p. 7.

44 Friedrich Nietzsche, *The Birth of Tragedy* (Walter Kaufmann, trans.) (New York: Vintage Books, 1967), §1, p. 33.

45 Nietzsche, *The Birth of Tragedy*, §7, p. 59.

46 J.W. Burrow, *The Crisis of Reason: European Thought, 1848–1914* (New Haven: Yale University Press, 2000), pp. 174–5.

47 Nietzsche, *The Birth of Tragedy*, §7, p. 59.

48 Nietzsche, *The Birth of Tragedy*, §1, p. 34.

49 Nietzsche, *The Birth of Tragedy*, §14, p. 91.

50 Nietzsche, *The Birth of Tragedy*, §14, pp. 88–9.

51 These experiences are discussed in James Miller, *The Passion of Michel Foucault* (London: Harper Collins, 1993).

52 Friedrich Nietzsche, *An Attempt at a Self-Criticism* in 1886 edition of *The Birth of Tragedy*. Reprinted and translated in Friedrich Nietzsche, *The Birth of Tragedy* (Walter Kaufmann, trans.) (New York: Vintage Books, 1967), pp.17–27. *Twilight of the Idols* (R.J. Hollingdale, trans.) (Harmondsworth: Penguin Books, 1990).

53 Friedrich Nietzsche, *Thus Spoke Zarathustra* (R.J. Hollingdale, trans.) (Harmondsworth: Penguin Books, 1969).

54 Charles Taylor, *Sources of the Self: The Making of the Modern Identity* (Cambridge, Mass.: Harvard University Press, 1989), p. 454.

55 Martin Heidegger, *Nietzsche, III. The Will to Power as Knowledge and Metaphysics* (David Krell, trans.) (San Francisco: Harper Row, 1987), p. 178, cited in Pippin, *Modernism as a Philosophical Problem*, p. 122.

56 Pippin, *Modernism as a Philosophical Problem*, p. 124.

57 For more on this see Gary Gutting, *French Philsophy in the Twentieth Century* (Cambridge: Cambridge University Press, 2001), Chapters 8 and 9.

58 Ibid., p. 250.

59 Michel Foucault, *The Order of Things: An Archaeology of the Human Sciences* (Alan Sheridan-Smith, trans.) (New York: Random House, 1970), p. xxii. Originally published as *Les mots et les choses: une archéologie des sciences humaines* (Paris: Gallimard, 1966). Foucault's definition of *epistémè* shared characteristics with Cangulheim's understanding of the history of concepts and bore a striking affinity to the notion of ideology formulated by Althusser, under whom Foucault had studied.

60 J.G. Merquior, *Foucault* (London: Fontana, 1985), p. 36.

61 Michel Foucault, *Folie et déraison: histoire de la folie à l'âge classique* (Paris: Plon, 1961) (*Madness and Civilization*, Richard Howard, trans.) (New York: Pantheon, 1965). *Naissance de la clinique* (Paris: Presses Universitaires de France, 1963) (*The Birth of the Clinic*, A. Sheridan Smith, trans.) (New York: Pantheon, 1973).

62   Michel Foucault, *The Archaeology of Knowledge* (Alan Sheridan, trans.) (New York: Pantheon, 1972).

63   Michel Foucault, 'Sur l'archéologie des sciences. Réponse au Cercle d'épistémologie', *Dits et écrits*, I (Paris: Gallimard, 1994), pp. 705–8. See too Mark Philp, 'Foucault', *The Return of Grand Theory in the Human Sciences* (Quentin Skinner, ed.) (Cambridge: Cambridge University Press, 2000), p. 71 and Barry Smart, *Michel Foucault* (London: Routledge, 1988), p. 41.

64   Michel Foucault, *L'archéologie du savoir* (Paris: Gallimard, 1969), pp. 170–1. See too Michel Foucault, 'Sur l'archéologie des sciences. Réponse au Cercle d'épistémologie', p. 708.

65   See Foucault's introductory remarks to *The Archaeology of Knowledge*.

66   The lecture was given 2 December 1970. Michel Foucault, *L'Ordre du discours* (Paris: Gallimard, 1971); ('Orders of Discourse', Rupert Swyers, trans.) (*Social Sciences Information*, April 1971).

67   Friedrich Nietzsche, *On The Genealogy of Morals* (Walter Kaufmann and R.J. Hollingdale, trans.) (New York: Vintage, 1969).

68   Foucault summarised his account of genealogy in lectures he gave in Turin in January 1976. See Michel Foucault, *Power/Knowledge: Selected interviews and Other Writings, 1972–1977* (Colin Gordon, ed.) (New York: Pantheon, 1980), esp. pp. 80–5.

69   Michel Foucault, *Surveiller et punir, naissance de la prison* (Paris: Gallimard, 1975); *Discipline and Punish: The Birth of the Prison* (Alan Sheridan, trans.) (Harmondsworth: Penguin Books, 1991); *The History of Sexuality*, 3 vols: *Introduction, The Uses of Pleasure, Care of the Self* (Robert Hurley, trans.) (New York: Vintage, 1988–90); *Madness and Civilization*, (Richard Howard, trans.) (New York: Pantheon, 1965) *The Birth of the Clinic* (A. Sheridan Smith, trans.) (New York: Pantheon, 1973).

70   Foucault, *Power/Knowledge*, p. 85.

71   Philp, 'Foucault' p. 78.

72   For more on this see my 'The Wild and the Sublime: Lyotard's Post-Modern Politics', *Political Studies*, 42, 2, 1994, pp. 259–73.

73   Marcel Gauchet and Gladys Swain, *La pratique de l'esprit humain: l'institution asilaire et la révolution démocratique* (Paris: Gallimard, 1980); *Madness and Democracy, the Modern Psychiatric Universe* (Catherine Porter, trans.) (Princeton: Princeton University Press, 1999).

74   Jacques Derrida, *Positions* (Paris: Minuit, 1972), p. 71.

75   Edmund Husserl, *L'Origine de la géométrie* ('Introduction', Jacques Derrida, trans.) (Paris: Presses Universitaires de France, 1962). Jacques Derrida, *Edmund Husserl's Origin of Geometry: An Introduction* (John P. Leavey, Jr., trans.) (New York and Sussex: Nicolas Hays Ltd and Harvester Press, 1978).

76   Derrida now teaches both at the prestigious Ecole des Hautes Etudes en Sciences Sociales, Paris and in America.

77   Jacques Derrida, *Of Grammatology* (Gayatri Spivak, trans.) (Baltimore: Johns Hopkins University Press, 1998).

78   Eric Matthews, *Twentieth-Century French Philosophy* (Oxford: Oxford University Press, 1996), p. 168. See too Gary Gutting, *French Philosophy*, p. 298.

79   David Hoy, 'Jacques Derrida', *The Return of Grand Theory in the Human Sciences* (Quentin Skinner, ed.) (Cambridge: Cambridge University Press, 1985), p. 44.

80   Ibid., pp. 50–4.

81   Ibid., p. 52. There are important affinities here between Derrida's method of deconstruction and Barthes' semiotics. Barthes argued that a text does not have a single overall structure, but rather an irreducible complex of alternative, sometimes conflicting, sometimes intermeshing, structures. Barthes set out to explode text rather than unifying it. Gutting, *French Philosophy*, p. 248.

82   Matthews, *Twentieth-Century French Philosophy*, p. 172.

83   Jean-François Lyotard, *Discours, figure* (Paris: Klincksieck, 1971); *Dérive à partir de Marx et Freud* (Paris: 10/18, 1970); *Libidinal Economy* (Iain Hamilton Grant, trans.) (Bloomington, Ind.: Indiana University Press, 1993).

84   Jean-François Lyotard, *The Postmodern Condition: A Report on Knowledge* (Geoff Bennington and Brian Massumi, trans.) (Manchester: Manchester University Press, 1984), p. xxiv.

85   Ludwig Wittgenstein, *The Blue and Brown Books: Preliminary Studies for the 'Philosophical Investigations'* (Oxford: Blackwell, 1987), p. 18.

86   Ibid., p. 108.

87   Lyotard, *The Postmodern Condition*, p. 10.

88   Ibid., p. 29.

89   Ibid., pp. 34–5.

90   Ibid., p. 37.

91   Ibid., p. 39.

92   Ibid., p. 60.

93   Lyotard, *Dérive à partir de Marx et Freud* (Paris: Union générale d'éditions, 1973); partial translation in *Driftworks* (R. McKeon, trans.) (New York: Semiotext(e), 1984); *Libidinal Economy*, (Iain Hamilton Grant, trans.) (Bloomington, Ind.: Indiana University Press, 1993); *Leçons sur l'analytique du sublime* (Paris: Galilée, 1991); *Lessons on the Analytic of the Sublime* (Elizabeth Rottenberg, trans.) (Stanford: Stanford University Press, 1994).

94   Alan Sokal and Jean Bricmont, *Impostures intellectuelles* (Paris: Odile Jacob, 1997); *Intellectual Impostures, Postmodern Philosophers' Abuse of Science* (Alan Sokal and Jean Bricmont, trans.) (London: Profile Books, 1999). See too Yves Jeanneret, *L'affaire Sokal ou la querelle des impostures* (Paris: Presses Universitaires de France, 1998).

95   Jacques Lacan, 'Subversion du sujet et dialectique du désir dans l'inconscient freudien', *Ecrits* (Paris: Seuil, 1966), p. 822. Throughout this article Lacan refers to a bewildering array of symbols, 'algorithims', 'algebras' and graphs which have no scientific meaning.

96   Gutting, *French Philosophy*, p. 331.

97   For more on Lyotard's postmodern politics see: Bill Readings, *Introducing Lyotard: Art and Politics* (London: Routledge, 1991); Geoff Bennington, *Lyotard: Writing the Event* (Manchester: Manchester University Press, 1988) and my 'The Wild and the Sublime: Lyotard's Post-Modern Politics', *Political Studies*, 42, 2, 1994, pp. 259–73.

98   Gilles Deleuze and Felix Guattari, *What is Philosophy?* (H. Tomlinson and G. Burchell, trans.) (London: Verso, 1994), p. 140.

99   Ibid., p. 139.

100 Gutting, *French Philosophy*, pp. 333–4.

101 Gilles Deleuze, *Logique du sens* (Paris: Minuit, 1969); *The Logic of Sense* (M. Lester with C. Stivale, trans.) (New York: Columbia University Press, 1990).

102 Gutting, *French Philosophy*, p. 335.

103 Gilles Deleuze and Félix Guattari, *Capitalisme et schizophrénie: L'anti-oedipe* (Paris: Minuit, 1972); *Anti-Oedipus* (R. Hurley, M. Seem and H. Lane, trans.) (Minneapolis: University of Minnesota Press, 1983). Gilles Deleuze and Félix Guattari, *Capitalisme et schizophrénie: Mille plateaux* (Paris: Minuit, 1980); *A Thousand Plateaus* (Brian Massumi, trans.) (Minneapolis, Minn.: University of Minnesota Press, 1987).

104 Manfred Frank, *What is Neostructuralism?*, p. 316. Cited in Gutting, *French Philosophy*, p. 339.

105 For more on these works see the two interviews given by Deleuze and Guattari in Gilles Deleuze, *Pourparlers* (Paris: Minuit, 1990), Chapters 2 and 3.

106 For a more detailed discussion see Pauline Marie Rosenau, *Post-Modernism and the Social Sciences: Insights, Inroads, and Intrusions* (Princeton: Princeton University Press, 1992), pp. 70–5.

107 Luce Irigaray, *Éthique de la différence sexuelle* (Paris: Minuit, 1984), p. 13.

108 Luce Irigaray, *Ce sexe qui n'en est pas un* (Paris: Minuit, 1977), p. 72.

109   Luce Irigaray, *Speculum of the Other Woman* (Gillian Gill, trans.) (Ithaca: Cornell University Press, 1985).

110   Irigaray, *Ce sexe qui n'en est pas un*, pp. 75–6.

111   Matthews, *Twentieth Century French Philosophy*, p. 193.

112   Irigaray, *Éthique de la différence sexuelle*, p. 15.

113   Jean Baudrillard, *Le système des objets* (Paris: Gallimard, 1968); *The System of Objects* (James Benedict, trans.) (London: Verso, 1996).

114   Mark Poster, 'Introduction', Jean Baudrillard, *Selected Writings* (Stanford: Stanford University Press, 1988), p. 2.

115   Bertens, *The Idea of the Postmodern*, p. 146.

116   See Naomi Klein, *No Logo* (London: Flamingo, 2000).

117   Jean Baudrillard, *La société de consommation* (Paris: Denoël, 1970); *The Consumer Society: Myths and Structures* (Chris Turner, trans.) (London: Sage, 1998).

118   Jean Baudrillard, *Pour une critique de l'économie politique du signe* (Paris: Gallimard, 1972); *For a Critique of the Political Economy of Sign* (Charles Levin, trans.) (St Louis: Telos Press, 1981).

119   Ibid., p. 196

120   Jean Baudrillard, *De la Séduction* (Paris: Galilée, 1979); *Simulacra and Simulation* (Sheil Glaser, trans.) (Ann Arbor: University of Michigan Press, 1994); *Les stratégies fatales* (Paris: Grasset, 1983).

121   Douglas Kellner, *Jean Baudrillard: From Marxism to Postmodernism and Beyond* (Cambridge: Polity Press, 1989), p. 50.

122   Bertens, *The Idea of the Postmodern*, p. 156.

123   Christopher Norris, *What's Wrong With Postmodernism: Critical Theory and the Ends of Philosophy* (Baltimore: Johns Hopkins University Press, 1990), p. 182. See too Norris's polemic in *Uncritical Theory: Postmodernism, Intellectuals and the Gulf War* (London: Lawrence and Wishart, 1992).

124   Jean Baudrillard, *La guerre du golfe n'a pas eu lieu* (Paris: Galilée, 1991); *The Gulf War Did Not Take Place* (Paul Patton, trans.) (Bloomington, Ind.: Indiana University Press, 1995).

125   Jean Baudrillard, 'The End of the Millenium or the Countdown', *Theory, Culture and Society*, 1, February 1998; *The Spirit of Terrorism and a Requiem for the Twin Towers* (London: Verso, 2002).

126   Jean Baudrillard, *The System of Objects* (James Benedict, trans.) (London: Verso, 1996); *Pour une critique de l'économie politique du signe* (Paris: Gallimard, 1972); *For a Critique of the Political Economy of Sign* (Charles Levin, trans.) (St Louis: Telos Press, 1981).

127   See, for instance: Scott Lash, *Sociology of Postmodernism* (London: Routledge, 1990); Mike Featherstone, *Consumer Culture and Postmodernism* (London: Sage, 1991); David Harvey, *The Condition of Postmodernity: An Enquiry into the Origins of Cultural Change* (Oxford: Blackwell, 1989). A good introduction to these works can be found in Bertens, *The Idea of the Postmodern*, esp. Chapter 10.

128   Fredric Jameson, *Marxism and Form: Twientieth-Century Dialectical Theories of Literature* (Princeton: Princeton University Press, 1971). Fredric Jameson, *The Prison-House of Language: A Critical Account of Structuralism and Russian Formalism* (Princeton: Princeton University Press, 1972). Fredric Jameson, *The Political Unconscious: Narrative as a Socially Symbolic Act* (London: Metheun, 1981).

129   Fredric Jameson, 'Postmodernism, or, the Cultural Logic of Late Capitalism', *New Left Review*, 146, 1984, pp. 53–92.

130   Fredric Jameson, *Postmodernism, or, the Cultural Logic of Late Capitalism* (London: Verso, 1992), p. 45.

131   Ibid., p. 4.

132   Ibid., pp. 4–5.

133   Ibid., p. 5.

134   Ibid., p. 44.

135   Ibid., p. 18.

136 Ibid., p. 19.

137 Ibid.

138 Ibid., p. 18.

139 Jameson, 'Postmodernism and Consumer Society', *The Anti-Aesthetic: Essays in Postmodern Culture* (Hal Foster, ed.) (Port Towsend, Wash.: Bay Press, 1983), p. 119. Cited in Bertens, *The Idea of the Postmodern*, p. 163.

140 Kevin Lynch, *The Image of the City* (Cambridge, Mass.: Technology Press and Harvard University Press, 1960).

141 Jameson, *Postmodernism,* p. 51.

142 Ibid., p. 51.

143 Ibid.

144 Ibid., p. 54.

145 See Edward W. Soja, *Postmodern Geographies: The Reassertion of Space in Critical Social Theory* (London: Verso, 1989).

146 Sokal and Bricmont, *Impostures intellectuelles.*

147 Alan Sokal, 'Transgressing the Boundaries: Toward a Transformative Hermeneutics of Quantum Gravity', *Social Text*, 46/47, 1996, pp. 217–52. John R. Wright, 'Double Death, Double Ethics: On Language and the Community of Finitude', paper title for progamme of The International Association for Philosophy and Literature 21st Annual Conference, University of South Alabama, Mobile, Ala., USA, 1997, p.18. C. Colwell, 'Counter-Actualization and Body Memories', paper title for progamme of The International Association for Philosophy and Literature 21st Annual Conference, University of South Alabama, Mobile, Ala., USA, 1997, p.24.

Part one   The crisis of modernity and the birth of the concept of postmodernism

1 The quote is originally from Horace's *Epistles*, I, 2. 40. It literally means, 'Dare to be wise'. Foucault has inverted Kant's word order.

2 Michel Foucault, *The Order of Things: An Archaeology of the Human Sciences* (Alan Sheridan-Smith, trans.) (New York, Random House, 1970); *Madness and Civilization: A History of Insanity in the Age of Reason* (Richard Howard, trans.) (New York, Pantheon, 1965); *Birth of the Clinic: An Archaeology of Medical Perception* (Alan Sheridan Smith, trans.) (New York: Pantheon, 1973).

3 Michel Foucault, *Histoire de la folie à l'âge classique* (Paris: Gallimard, 1972), pp. 583–603.

4 Christopher Norris, *Derrida* (London: Fontana Press, 1987), p. 215.

5 Michel Foucault, *Histoire de la folie*, p. 603.

1   Michel Foucault, 'What is Enlightenment?'

1 Giambattista Vico, *The New Science of Gambattista Vico* (abridged trans. T.G. Bergin and M.H. Fisch) (Ithaca: Cornell University Press, 1970, 3rd edn; 1st edn1744), p. 370, p. 372.

2 Kant in fact writes: '*Sapare aude!* Have courage to use your *own* understanding!', in Immanuel Kant, *Political Writings* (Hans Reiss, ed.) (H.B. Nisbet, trans.) (Cambridge: Cambridge University Press, 1991), p. 54. [ed.]

3 Charles Baudelaire, *The Painter of Modern Life and Other Essays* (Jonathan Mayne, trans.) (London: Phaidon, 1964), p. 13.

4 Charles Baudelaire, "On the Heroism of Modern Life," in The Mirror of Art: Critical Studies by Charles Baudelaire, trans. Jonathan Mayne (London: Phaidon, 1955), p. 127.

5   Baudelaire, *The Painter*, pp. 12, 11.

6   Ibid., p. 12.

2   Marshall Berman, *All That is Solid Melts Into Air*

1   J.-J. Rousseau, *Emile, ou De l'Education*, 1762, *Oeuvres complètes*, IV (Paris: Gallimard (Bibliothèque de la Pléiade), 1959), p. 551. On the volatile character of European society, and the revolutionary upheavals to come, *Emile*, I, p. 252; III, p. 468; IV, pp. 507–8.

2   J.-J. Rousseau, *Julie, ou la Nouvelle Héloïse*, 1761, Part II, Letters 14 and 17. In *Oeuvres complètes*, II, pp. 231–6, pp. 255–6. I have discussed these Rousseauan scenes and themes from a slightly different perspective in *The Politics of Authenticity* (New York: Atheneum, 1970), esp. pp. 113–19, pp. 163–77.

3   Karl Marx, 'Speech at the Anniversary of the *People's Paper*', in Robert C. Tucker, ed. *The Marx–Engels Reader* (New York: Norton, 1978, 2nd edn), pp. 577–8.

4   Marx, *MER*, pp. 475–6. I have slightly altered the standard translation, which was made by Samuel Moore in 1888.

5   The passages quoted are from Sections 262, 223 and 224 of Nietzsche's *Beyond Good and Evil*. Translations are by Marianne Cowan (South Bend, Ind.: Gateway, 1967), pp. 210–11, pp. 146–50.

6   Umberto Boccioni et al., 'Manifesto of the Futurist Painters, 1910' (Robert Brain, trans.) in Umbro Appollonio, ed., *Futurist Manifestos* (New York: Viking, 1973), p. 25.

7   F.T. Marinetti, 'The Founding and Manifesto of Futurism, 1909' in R.W. Flint, ed., *Marinetti: Selected Writings* (R.W. Flint, trans.) (New York: Farrar, Straus and Giroux, 1972), p. 22.

8   Marinetti, 'Multiplied Man and the Reign of the Machine', from *War, the World's Only Hygiene, 1911–15*, in Flint, *Marinetti*, pp. 90–1.

9   Marshall McLuhan, *Understanding Media: The Extensions of Man* (New York: McGraw-Hill, paperback, 1965), p. 80.

10   Alex Inkeles, 'The Modernization of Man', in Myron Weiner, ed., *Modernization: The Dynamics of Growth* (New York: Basic Books, 1966), p. 149. This collection gives a good picture of the mainstream American paradigm of modernisation in its heyday.

11   Max Weber, *The Protestant Ethic and the Spirit of Capitalism* (Talcott Parsons, trans.) (New York: Scribner, 1930), pp. 181–3. I have slightly altered the translation, in accord with Peter Gay's far more vivid version, in Columbia College, *Man in Contemporary Society* (New York: Columbia University Press, 1953, II, pp. 96–7. Gay, however, substitutes 'strait jacket' for 'iron cage'.

12   Herbert Marcuse, *One-Dimensional Man: Studies in the Ideology of Advanced Industrial Society* (Boston: Beacon Press, 1964), p. 9.

13   Ibid., pp. 256–7. See my critique of this book in the *Partisan Review*, Fall 1964, and the exchange between Marcuse and me in the following number, Winter 1965.

14   Clement Greenberg, 'Modernist Painting', in Gregory Battcock, ed., *The New Art* [1961] (New York: Dutton, 1966), pp. 100–10.

15   Roland Barthes, *Writing Degree Zero* [1953] (Annette Lavers and Colin Smith, trans.) (London: Jonathan Cape, 1967), p. 58. I associate this book with the 1960s because that is when its impact came to be felt on a large scale, in France as well as in England and the USA.

16   Harold Rosenberg, *The Tradition of the New* (New York: Horizon, 1959), p. 81.

17   Lionel Trilling, *Beyond Culture*, Preface (New York: Viking, 1965). This idea is elaborated most vividly in Trilling's 1961 *Partisan Review* piece, 'The Modern Element in Modern Literature', reprinted in *Beyond Culture*, pp. 3–30, but retitled 'On the Teaching of Modern Literature'.

18   Renato Poggioli, *The Theory of the Avant-Garde* [1962] (Gerald Fitzgerald, trans.) (Cambridge, Mass.: Harvard, 1968), p. 111.

19   'Contemporary Art and the Plight of Its Public', a lecture given at the Museum of Modern Art in 1960, printed in *Harper's*, 1962, reprinted in Battcock, *The New Art*, pp. 27–47, and in Leo Stienberg's *Other Criteria: Confrontations with Twentieth Century Art* (New York: Oxford University Press, 1972), p. 15.

20   Irving Howe discusses critically the off-and-on, phony-and-genuine 'war between modernist culture and bourgeois society', in 'The Culture of Modernism', *Commentary*, November 1967; reprinted, under the title of 'The Idea of the Modern', as the Introduction to Howe's anthology, *Literary Modernism* (Greenwich, Conn.: Fawcett Premier, 1967).

21   See the perceptive discussion in Morris Dickstein, *Gates of Eden: American Culture in the Sixties* (New York: Basic Books, 1977), pp. 266–7.

22   Daniel Bell, *Cultural Contradictions of Capitalism* (New York: Basic Books, 1975), p. 19; 'Modernism and Capitalism', *Partisan Review*, 45 (1978), p. 214. This latter essay became the Preface to the paperback edition of *Cultural Contradictions* (1978).

23   John Cage, 'Experimental Music', in *Silence*, 1957 (Middletown, Conn.: Wesleyan, 1961), p. 122. 'Cross the Border, Close the Gap', in Leslie Fiedler's *Collected Essays*, II, 1970 (New York: Stein and Day, 1971). Also in this volume, 'The Death of Avant-Garde Literature', 1964, and 'The New Mutants', 1965.

24   The most energetic early exponents of postmodernism were Leslie Fiedler and Ihab Hassan: Fiedler, 'The Death of Avant-Garde Literature', 1964, and 'The New Mutants', 1965, both in *Collected Essays*, II; Hassan, *The Dismemberment of Orpheus: Toward a Postmodern Literature* (New York: Oxford University Press, 1971), and 'POSTmodernISM: a Paracritical Bibliography', in *Paracriticisms: Seven Speculations of the Times* (Urbana, Ill.: University of Illinois Press, 1975).

25   The mainstream justification for abandoning the concept of modernization is given most clearly in Samuel Huntington, 'The Chance to Change: Modernization, Development and Politics', in *Comparative Politics*, 3 (1970–1), pp. 286–322. See also S.N. Eisenstadt, 'The Disintegration of the Initial Paradigm', in *Tradition, Change and Modernity* (New York: Wiley, 1973), pp. 98–115.

26   Michel Foucault, *The History of Sexuality*, I: An Introduction, 1976 (Michael Hurley, trans.) (New York: Pantheon, 1978), p. 144, p. 155, and the whole of this final chapter.

27   Michel Foucault, *Discipline and Punish: The Birth of the Prison* [1975] (Alan Sheridan, trans.) (New York: Pantheon, 1977), p. 217, pp. 226–8.

28   Octavio Paz, *Alternating Current* [1967] (Helen Lane, trans.) (New York: Viking, 1973), pp. 161–2.

3   Michel Foucault, 'The Order of Things'

1   This is a transcript of an interview conducted by Raymond Bellours which first appeared in *Les Lettres françaises*, 1125 (31 March–6 April 1966), pp. 3–4.

2   Michel Foucault, *The Order of Things: An Archaeology of the Human Sciences* (Alan Sheridan-Smith, trans.) (New York: Random House, 1970); *Madness and Civilization: A History of Insanity in the Age of Reason* (Richard Howard, trans.) (New York: Pantheon, 1965).

3   Michel Foucault, *Birth of the Clinic: An Archaeology of Medical Perception* (Alan Sheridan Smith, trans.) (New York: Pantheon, 1973).

4   The practico-inert is a historical category developed by Jean-Paul Sartre in *The Critique of Dialectical Reason* (Atlantic Highlands, N.J.: Humanities Press, 1976). The practico-inert field is a structure that unifies individuals from without (for example, by common interest).

4   Michel Foucault, 'Nietzsche, Genealogy, History'

1   This essay originally appeared in *Hommage à Jean Hyppolite* (Paris: Presses Universitaires de France, 1971), pp. 145–72. The translation, by Donald F. Brouchard and Sherry Simon, has been slightly amended.

2   Friedrich Nietzsche, *The Gay Science* [1882] (Walter Kaufmann, trans.) (New York: Random House, 1974), no. 7.

3   Friedrich Nietzsche, *Human, All Too Human* [1878] in *Complete Works* (New York: Gordon, 1974), no. 3.

4   Friedrich Nietzsche, *On the Genealogy of Morals* [1887] in (Walter Kaufmann, ed.) *Basic Writings of Nietzsche* (Walter Kaufmann, trans.) (New York: Modern Library, 1968), pt. 2, secs. 6, 8.

5   Nietzsche, *Gay Science*, nos. 110, 111, 300.

6   Nietzsche, *The Dawn of Day* [1881], in *Complete Works*, no. 102. *Pudenda origo* is 'shameful origin'.

7   Nietzsche, *Gay Science*, nos. 151, 353; also *Dawn*, no. 62; *Genealogy*, pt. 1, sec. 14; Nietzsche, 'The Four Great Errors', in (Walter Kaufmann, ed.) *Twilight of the Idols* [1888] in *The Portable Nietzsche* (Walter Kaufmann, trans.) (New York: Viking, 1954), sec. 7. *Schwarzkünstler* is a black magician.

8   Paul Ree's text was entitled *Der Ursprung der moralischen Empfindungen* (Chemnitz: E. Schmeitzner, 1877).

9   In Nietzsche, *Human, All Too Human*, aphorism 92 was entitled *Ursprung der Gerechtigkeit*.

10   In the main body of *The Genealogy*, *Ursprung* and *Herkunft* are used interchangeably in numerous instances (pt. 1, sec. 2; pt. 2, secs. 8, 11, 12, 16, 17).

11   Nietzsche, *Dawn*, no. 123.

12   Nietzsche, *Human, All Too Human*, no. 34.

13   Nietzsche, *The Wanderer and His Shadow* [1880] in *Complete Works*, no. 9.

14   Nietzsche, *The Wanderer*, no. 3.

15   Nietzsche, *Dawn*, no. 49.

16   Nietzsche, *Nietzsche Contra Wagner* [1888] in *Portable Nietzsche*, pp. 661–8.

17   Nietzsche, *Gay Science*, nos. 110, 265.

18   Nietzsche, 'How the True World Finally Became a Fable', *Twilight of Idols*, pp. 485–6.

19   For example, on race, see Nietzsche's *Gay Science*, no. 135; *Beyond Good and Evil* [1886] in *Basic Writings*, nos. 200, 242, 244; Genealogy, pt. 1, sec. 5; on social type see *Gay Science*, nos. 348–9; *Beyond Good and Evil*, no. 260.

20   Nietzsche, *Beyond Good and Evil*, no. 244.

21   Nietzsche, *Genealogy*, pt. 3, sec. 17. The *Abkunft* of feelings of depression.

22   Nietzsche, '"Reason" in Philosophy', *Twilight of Idols*, pp. 479–84.

23   Nietzsche, *Dawn*, no. 247.

24   Nietzsche, *Gay Science*, nos. 348–9.

25   Nietzsche, *Gay Science*, nos. 348–9.

26   Nietzsche, *Dawn*, no. 42.

27   Nietzsche, *Beyond Good and Evil*, no. 262.

28   Nietzsche, *Genealogy*, pt. 3, no. 13.

29   Nietzsche, *Gay Science*, no. 148. It is also to an anemia of the will that one must attribute the *Entstehung* of Buddhism and Christianity.

30   Nietzsche, *Genealogy*, pt.1, sec. 2.

31   Nietzsche, *Beyond Good and Evil*, no. 260; see also Nietzsche, *Genealogy*, pt. 2, sec. 12.

32   Nietzsche, *Wanderer*, no. 9.

33   Nietzsche, *Gay Science*, no. 111.

34   Nietzsche, *Genealogy*, pt. 2, no. 6.

35   Nietzsche, *Genealogy*, preface, sec. 7, and pt. 1, sec. 2; Nietzsche, *Beyond Good and Evil*, no. 224.

36   Nietzsche, *Gay Science*, no. 7.

37   Nietzsche, *Gay Science*, no. 7.

38   Nietzsche, *Genealogy*, pt. 2, sec. 12.

39   Nietzsche, *Dawn*, no. 130.

40   Nietzsche, *Genealogy*, pt. 2, sec. 12.

41   Nietzsche, *Human, All Too Human*, no. 16.

42   Nietzsche, *Twilight of Idol*, no. 44.

43   Nietzsche, '"Reason" in Philosophy', *Twilight of Idol*, nos. 1, 4.

44   Nietzsche, *Wanderer*, no. 188.

45   Nietzsche, *Gay Science*, no. 337.

46   Nietzsche, *Genealogy*, pt. 3. sec. 25.

47   Nietzsche, *Beyond Good and Evil*, no. 223.

48   Nietzsche, *Wanderer*, 'Opinions and Mixed Statements', *Wanderer*, no. 17.

49   Nietzsche, *Human, All Too Human*, no. 274.

50   Nietzsche, *Nietzsche: Untimely Meditations* [1873–4] in *Complete Works*, pt. 2, no. 3.

51   See Nietzsche, *Dawn*, nos. 429, 432; Nietzsche, *Gay Science*, no. 333; Nietzsche, *Beyond Good and Evil*, nos. 229–30.

52   The French phrase *vouloir-savoir* means both the will to knowledge and knowledge as revenge.

53   Nietzsche, *Dawn*, no. 501.

54   Nietzsche, *Dawn*, no. 429.

55   Nietzsche, *Beyond Good and Evil*, no. 39.

56   Nietzsche, *Dawn*, no. 45.

5   Jacques Derrida, 'Cogito and the history of madness'

1   With the exception of several notes and a short passage (in brackets), this paper is the reproduction of a lecture given 4 March 1963 at the Collège Philosophique. In proposing that this text be published in the *Revue de métaphysique et de morale*, M. Jean Wahl agreed that it should retain its first form, that of the spoken word, with all its requirements and, especially, its particular weaknesses: if in general, according to the remark in the *Phaedrus*, the written word is deprived of "the assistance of its father," if it is a fragile "idol" fallen from "living and animated discourse" unable to "help itself," then is it not more exposed and disarmed than ever when, miming the improvisation of the voice, it must give up even the resources and lies of style?

2   Michel Foucault, *Folie et déraison: Histoire de la folie à l'âge classique* (Paris: Plon, 1961); trans. Richard Howard, *Madness and Civilization: A History of Insanity in the Age of Reason* (New York: Pantheon, 1965). [Howard has translated the abridged version of Foucault's book. Whenever possible Alan Bass has used Howard's translations of passages cited by Derrida; all non-footnoted translations of Foucault are Bass's own.]

3   In *The Interpretation of Dreams* (trans. and ed. James Strachey in The Standard Edition of the *Complete Psychological Works of Sigmund Freud*, Vol. 4, London: Hogarth Press, 1955, p. 99, n. 1), speaking of the link between dreams and verbal expression, Freud recalls Ferenczi's remark that every language has its own dream language. The latent content of a dream (and of any behaviour or consciousness in general) communicates with the manifest content only through the unity of a language – a language that the analyst must thus speak as well as possible. (On this subject cf. Daniel Lagache, 'Sur le polyglottisme dans l'analyse', in *La psychanalyse*, vol. 1 [Paris: 1956] 1, pp. 167–78.) As well as possible: progress in the knowledge

and practice of a language being by nature infinitely open (*first* by virtue of the original and essential equivocality of the signifier, at least in the language of 'everyday life', its indeterminateness and playing-space being precisely that which liberates the difference between hidden and stated meaning; then, by virtue of the original and essential communication between different languages throughout history; finally, by virtue of the play, the relation to itself, or 'sedimentation', of every language), are not the insecurities and insufficiencies of analysis axiomatic or irreducible? And does not the historian of philosophy, whatever his method or project, abandon himself to the same dangers? Especially if one takes into account a certain embedding of philosophical language in non-philosophical language.

4   That all history can only be, in the last analysis, the history of meaning, that is, of Reason in general, is what Foucault could not fail to experience – we shall come to this in a moment. What he could not fail to experience is that the general meaning of a difficulty he attributes to the 'classical experience' is valid well beyond the 'classical age'. Cf., for example: 'And when it was a question, in seeking it in its most withdrawn essence, of peeling it away to its last structure, we would discover, in order to formulate it, only the *very language of reason* employed in the impeccable logic of delirium; precisely that which made it accessible counterfeited it as madness.' The very language of reason … but what is a language that would not be one of reason *in general*? And if there is no history, except of rationality and meaning in general, this means that philosophical language, as soon as it speaks, reappropriates negativity – or forgets it, which is the same thing – even when it allegedly affirms or recognizes negativity. More surely then, perhaps. The history of truth is therefore the history of this *economy* of the negative. It is necessary, and it is perhaps time to come back to the ahistorical in a sense radically opposed to that of classical philosophy: not to misconstrue negativity, but this time to affirm it – silently. It is negativity and not positive truth that is the nonhistorical capital of history. In question then would be a negativity so negative that it could not even be called such any longer. Negativity has always been determined by dialectics – that is to say, by metaphysics – as *work* in the service of the constitution of meaning. To affirm negativity in silence is to gain access to a nonclassical type of dissociation between thought and language. And perhaps to a dissociation of thought and philosophy as discourse, if we are conscious of the fact that this schism cannot be enunciated, thereby erasing itself, except within philosophy.

5   Foucault, *Folie et déraison*, pp. x–xi. [Bass has modified Howard's translation of this sentence to include the 'on' whose double sense was played upon above, p. 88.

6   I have consistently translated œuvre as 'work' throughout this essay to avoid confusions that could be caused by translating it as 'work of art', as Howard does. To translate Foucault's definition of madness, commented upon by Derrida, as 'the absence of the work of art' (*l'absence d'œuvre*) does not convey Foucault's sense of the absence of a work governed by institutionalised rationalism. [Trans.]

7   Derrida is making use of the fact that the word *éloge* (praise) is derived from the same word as 'logos'. [Trans.]

8   Foucault, *Folie et déraison*, p. xi.

9   Cf. also, for example, *Symposium* 217e/218b; *Phaedrus* 244b–c/245a/249/265a ff.; *Theatetus* 257e; *Sophist* 228d/229a; *Timeus* 86b; *Republic* 382c; *Laws* X 888a.

10   Cf. note 7 above. [Trans.]

11   René Descartes *The Philosophical Works of Descartes* (Elizabeth S. Haldane and G.R.T. Ross, trans.) (Cambridge: Cambridge University Press, 1970), p. 146. [Trans.]

12   Ibid., p. 146. [Trans.]

13   Ibid., pp. 146–7. [Trans.]

14   Ibid., p. 145. [Trans.]

15   *Madness, theme* or *index*: what is significant is that Descartes, at bottom, never speaks of madness itself in this text. Madness is not his theme. He treats it as the index of a question

of principle, that is, of epistemological value. It will be said, perhaps, that this is the sign of a profound exclusion. But this silence on madness itself simultaneously signifies the opposite of an exclusion, since *it is not a question of madness* in this text, if only to exclude it. It is not in the *Meditations* that Descartes speaks of madness itself.

16   To underline this vulnerability and touch on the greatest difficulty, we would have to specify that the expressions 'sensory or corporeal fault' or 'corporeal error' could have no meaning for Descartes. There is no corporeal error, particularly in illness: jaundice or melancholy are only the *occasions* of an error that itself is born only with the consent or affirmation of the will in judgment, when 'one who is ill with jaundice judges everything to be yellow because his eye is tinged with yellow. So finally, too, when the imagination is diseased, as in cases of melancholia, and a man thinks that his own disorderly fancies represent real things' (*Rule XII*. Descartes emphasizes this point: the most abnormal sensory or imaginative experience, considered in and of itself, at its own level and at its proper moment, never deceives us; or never deceives understanding, 'if it restrict its attention accurately to the object presented to it, just as it is given to it either firsthand or by means of an image; and if it moreover refrain from judging that the imagination faithfully reports the objects of the senses, or that the senses take on the true forms of things, or finally that external things always are as they appear to be' [Haldane and Ross, *The Philosophical Works of Descartes*, p. 44].)

17   The paragraph organization of Haldane and Ross does not correspond to the paragraph organization of the edition of Descartes cited by Derrida. [Trans.]

18   Haldane and Ross, *Philosophical Works of Descartes,* p. 147.

19   Ibid., p. 148.

20   Ibid. It is a question here of the order of reasons, as it is followed in the *Meditations*. It is well known that in the *Discourse* (part 4) doubt very promptly attacks the 'simplest geometrical questions' in which men sometimes 'commit paralogisms'.

21   Like Leibniz, Descartes has confidence in 'scientific' or 'philosophical' language, which is not necessarily the language taught in the Schools (*Rule III*) and which must also be carefully distinguished from the 'terms of ordinary language' which alone can 'deceive us' (*Meditations* II).

22   That is to say, as soon as, more or less implicitly, *Being is called upon* (even before its determination as essence and existence) – which can only mean, *to be called upon by Being*. Being would not be what it is if speech *simply* preceded or invoked it. Language's final protective barrier against madness is the meaning of Being.

23   Haldane and Ross, *Philosophical Works of Descartes*, p. 101.

24   It is a question less of a *point* than of a temporal originality in general.

25   The reference is to Plato's *Republic* 509b–c. [Trans.]

26   It risks erasing the excess by which every philosophy (of meaning) is related, in some region of its discourse, to the nonfoundation of unmeaning.

27   In the next to last paragraph of the sixth *Meditation*, the theme of normality communicates with the theme of memory, at the moment when the latter, moreover, is confirmed by absolute Reason as 'divine veracity', etc.

Generally speaking, does not God's confirmation of the remembrance of obvious truths signify that only the positive infinity of divine reason can absolutely reconcile temporality and truth? In the infinite alone, beyond all determinations, negations, 'exclusions' and 'internments', is produced the reconciliation of time and thought (truth) which Hegel claimed was the task of nineteenth-century philosophy, while the reconciliation of thought and space was to have been the aim of the so-called 'Cartesian' rationalisms. That this divine infinity is the proper location, condition, name, or horizon of these two reconciliations is what has never been contested by any *metaphysician*, neither by Hegel, nor by the majority of those, such as Husserl, who have attempted to think and to name the essential temporality or historicity of truth and meaning. For Descartes, the crisis of which we are speaking would finally have its intrinsic (that is, *intellectual*) origin in time itself, as the absence of a necessary link between its parts, as the contingency and discontinuity of the transition from instant to instant; which supposes that here we follow all the interpretations opposed to Laporte's on the question of the role of the instant in Descartes's philosophy. In the last retort, only continuous creation, uniting conservation and creation, which 'differ only as concerns our way of thinking', reconciles temporality and truth. It is God who excludes madness and crisis, that is to say, embraces them in the presence that encompasses all traces and differences. Which amounts to saying that crisis, anomaly, negativity, etc. are irreducible within the experience of finitude, or of a finite moment, a *determination* of absolute reason, or of reason in general. To attempt to deny this, and allegedly to affirm positivity (the positivity of truth, meaning, norms, etc.) outside the horizon of this infinite reason (reason in general, beyond all its specific determinations), is to attempt to erase negativity, and is to forget finitude at the very moment when one allegedly denounces as mystification the theologism of the great classical rationalisms.

28   But God is the other name of the absolute of reason *itself*, of reason and meaning in general. And what could exclude, reduce, or – amounting to the same thing – *absolutely embrace* madness, if not reason in general, absolute and undetermined reason, whose other name is God, for the classical rationalists? One cannot accuse those, individuals or societies, who use God as a recourse against madness of seeking to *shelter themselves*, to be sure of having protections against madness – the safe boundaries of asylums – except by construing this shelter as a *finite* one, within the world, by making God a third party or finite power, that is, except by deceiving oneself; by deceiving oneself not concerning the content and effective finality of this gesture in history, but concerning the philosophical specificity of the idea and name of God. If philosophy has taken place – which can always be contested – it is only in the extent to which it has formulated the aim of thinking beyond the finite shelter. By describing the historical constitution of these finite protective barriers against madness within the movement of individuals, societies and all finite totalities in general – a legitimate, immense, and necessary task – one can finally describe everything except the philosophical project itself. And except the project of this description itself. One cannot allege that the philosophical project of the 'infinitivist' rationalisms served as an instrument or as an alibi for a finite historico-politico-social violence (which is doubtless the case) without *first* having to acknowledge and respect the intentional meaning of this project itself. Now, within its own intentional meaning, this project presents itself as the conceptualization of the infinite, that is, of that which cannot be exhausted by any finite totality, by any function or by any instrumental, technical, or political determination. It will be said that this presentation of the philosophical project by itself as such is its greatest lie, its violence and its mystification – or, further, its bad faith. And, certainly, the structure which links this intention to exceed the world to the totality of history must be described rigorously, and its economy must be determined. But like all ruses, these economic ones are possible only for finite words and finite intentions, substituting one finitude for another. One cannot lie when one says *nothing* (that is finite or determined), or when one says God, Being, or Nothingness, or when one does not modify the finite by the declared meaning of one's words, or when one says the infinite, that is, when one lets the infinite (God, Being, or Nothingness, for part of the meaning of the infinite is its inability to be an ontic determination among others) be said and conceived. The theme of divine veracity and the difference between God and the evil genius are thus illuminated by a light which is only apparently indirect.

    In short, Descartes knew that, without God, finite thought never had the *right* to exclude madness, etc. Which amounts to saying that madness is never excluded, except *in fact*, violently, in history; or rather that this exclusion, this *difference* between the fact and the principle is historicity, the possibility of history itself. Does Foucault say otherwise? '*The necessity of* madness ... is linked to the *possibility of history*' [M.F.'s italics].

29 Haldane and Ross, *Philosophical Works of Descartes*, p. 171.

30 Foucault, *Folie et déraison*, p. 199.

6 Gilles Deleuze, *Nietzsche and Philosophy*

1 On the first aspect of the demon cf. the theory of the ass and the camel. But also, Z III 'Of the Vision and the Riddle' where the demon (the spirit of gravity) is sitting on the shoulders of Zarathustra himself. And IV 'Of the Higher Man', 10, p. 301: 'If you want to rise high, use your own legs! Do not let yourselves be carried up, do not sit on the backs and heads of strangers!' On the second aspect of the demon, cf. the famous scene of the Prologue where the buffoon catches up with the tightrope walker and jumps over him. This scene is explained in III 'Of Old and New Law Tables', 4, p. 216: 'There are diverse paths and ways to over-coming: just look to it! But only a buffoon thinks: Man can also be jumped over'. Friedrich Nietzsche, *Thus Spoke Zarathustra* (1883–85) (R.J. Hollingdale, trans.) (Harmondsworth: Penguin Books, 1961).

2 Z II 'The Stillest Hour', p. 169. '"O Zarathustra, your fruits are ripe but you are not ripe for your fruits."' On Zarathustra's hesitations and evasions about the eternal return cf. II 'Of Great Events' and above all 'The Stillest Hour' ('It is beyond my strength'); III 'The Convalescent'. Nietzsche, *Thus Spoke Zarathustra*.

7 Jean-François Lyotard, *The Postmodern Condition*

1 Alain Touraine, *La société postindustrielle* (Paris: Denoël, 1969); *The Post-Industrial Society* (Leonard Mayhew, trans.) (London: Wildwood House, 1974); Daniel Bell, *The Coming of the Post-Industrial Society* (New York: Basic Books, 1973); Ihab Hassan, *The Dismemberment of Orpheus: Toward a Post Modern Literature* (New York: Oxford University Press, 1971); Michel Benamou and Charles Caramello, eds, *Performance in Postmodern Culture* (Wisconsin: Center for Twentieth Century Studies and Coda Press, 1977); M. Köhler, 'Postmodernismus: ein begriffgeschichtlicher Überblick', *Amerikastudien*, 22, 1 (1977).

2 Jürgen Habermas, *Knowledge and Human Interest* (Jeremy Shapiro, trans.) (Boston: Beacon Press, 1971).

3 Jürgen Habermas, *Legitimation Crisis* (Thomas McCarthy, trans.) (Boston: Beacon Press, 1975).

4 Lyotard refers especially to: Ludwig Wittgenstein, *Philosophical Investigations* (G.E.M. Anscombe, trans.) (New York: Macmillan, 1953); J.L. Austin, *How to do Things with Words*, (Oxford: Oxford University Press, 1962); J.R. Searle, *Speech Acts* (Cambridge: Cambridge University Press, 1969).

5 Wittgenstein *Philosophical Investigations*, sec. 23.

6 John von Neumann and Oskar Morgenstern, *Theory of Games and Economic Behavior* (Princeton: Princeton University Press, 1944), p. 49.

7 The term comes from Searle: 'Speech acts ... are the basic minimal units of linguistic communication' [*Speech Acts*, p. 16]. I [J.-F. L.] place them within the domain of *agon* (the joust) rather than that of communication. [J.-F. L.]

8 Agonistics is the basis of Heraclitus's ontology and of the Sophists' dialectic, not to mention the early tragedians. A good part of Aristotle's reflections in the *Topics* and the *Sophistici*

Elenchi is devoted to it. See F. Nietzsche, 'Homer's Contest' *Complete Works*, II (Maximilian A. Mügge, trans.) (New York: Gordon Press, 1974).

9   In the sense established by Louis Hjelmslev, in *Prolegomena to a Theory of Language* (Madison: University of Wisconsin Press, 1963) and taken up by Roland Barthes, *Eléments de sémiologie* (Paris: Seuil, 1966), 4:1.

10   Talcott Parsons, *The Social System* (Glencoe, Ill.: Free Press, 1967) and *Sociological Theory of Modern Society* (New York: Basic Books, 1970); Pierre Souyri, *Le Marxisme après Marx* (Paris: Flammarion, 1970).

11   Talcott Parsons, *Essays in Sociological Theory Pure and Applied*, rev. edn (Glencoe, Ill.: Free Press, 1954), pp. 216–18.

12   I [J.-F. L.] am using this word in the sense of John Kenneth Galbraith's term *technosctructure* as presented in *The New Industrial State* (Boston: Houghton Mifflin, 1967), or Raymond Aaron's term *technico-buereaucratic structure*, in *Eighteeen Lectures on Industrial Society* (M.K. Bottomore, trans.) (London: Weidenfeld and Nicholson, 1967). [J.-F. L.]

13   Max Horkheimer, *Eclipse of Reason* (New York: Oxford University Press, 1947), p. 176.

14   Max Horkheimer, *Critical Theory: Selected Essays* (J. O'Connell *et al.*, trans.) (New York: Herder and Herder, 1972).

15   This was the title of the 'organ of critique and revolutionary orientation' published between 1949 and 1965 by a group whose principal editors were C. de Beaumont, D. Blanchard, C. Castoriadis, S. de Diesbach, C. Lefort, J.-F. Lyotard, A. Maso, D. Mothé, P. Simon, P. Souyri.

16   Ernest Bloch, *Das Prinzip Hoffnung* (Frankfurt: Suhrkamp Verlag, 1959).

17   Lewis Mumford, *The Myth of the Machine: Technics and Human Development* (New York: Harcourt Brace, 1967).

18   The origin of the theoretical opposition between natural sciences [*Naturwissenschaft*] and human sciences [*Geisteswissenschaft*] is to be found in the work of Wilhelm Dilthey (1863–1911).

19   Jean Baudrillard, *In the Shadow of the Silent Majority* (New York: Semiotexte, 1983).

20   For example, Erving Goffman, *The Presentation of Self in Everyday Life* (Garden City, NY: Doubleday, 1959); Alain Touraine et al., *Lutte étudiante* (Paris: Seuil, 1978).

21   René Descartes, *Metaphysical Meditations* (Harmondsworth: Penguin, 1998), Meditation 4.

22   Thomas Kuhn, *The Structure of Scientific Revolutions* (Chicago: University of Chicago Press, 1962).

23   Cf. children's attitude toward their first science lessons, or the way natives interpret the ethnologist's explanations; see Lévi-Strauss, *The Savage Mind* (John Weightman and Doreen Weightman, trans.) (Chicago: University Of Chicago Press, 1966).

24   Certain scientific aspects of postmodernism are inventoried by Ihab Hassan in 'Culture, Indeterminancy, and Immanence: Margins of the (Postmodern) Age', *Humanities in Society*, 1, 1978, pp. 51–85.

25   'Road of doubt … road of despair … skepticism', writes G.W.F. Hegel in the preface to the *Phenomenology of Spirit* (A.V. Miller, trans.) (New York: Oxford University Press, 1977) to describe the effect of the speculative drive on natural knowledge.

26   Martin Buber, *I and Thou* (Ronald G. Smith, trans.) (New York: Charles Scribner's Sons, 1937) and Emmanuel Lévinas, *Totality and Infinity: An Essay on Exteriority* (Alphonso Lingis, trans.) (Pittsburgh: Duquesne University Press, 1969).

27   Wittgenstein, *Philosophical Investigations*, sec. 18, p. 8.

28   Ibid.

29   Ibid.

30   See Allan Janik and Stephan Toulmin, *Wittgenstein's Vienna* (New York: Simon and Schuster, 1973)

31   'Science Smiling into its Beard' is the title of ch. 72, vol. 1 of Robert Musil's *The Man without Qualities* (Sophie Wilkins, trans.) (London: Picador, 1997).

8 Jacques Derrida, *Dissemination*

1 'Logocentric' – that which is 'centered' on the 'Logos' (= speech, logic, reason, the Word of God) – is the term used by Derrida to characterize any signifying system governed by the notion of the self-presence of meaning; i.e. any system structured by a valorization of speech over writing, immediacy over distance, identity over difference, and (self-)presence overall forms of absence, ambiguity, simulation, substitution, or negativity. [Trans.]

2 'Sublation' is the traditional English translation of the German *Aufhebung*, which is Hegel's term for the simultaneous negation and retention of what is being surpassed by the progress of dialectical thought. [Trans.]

3 *Differance* is a Derridean neologism combining the two senses of the French verb *différer* – 'to differ' and 'to defer or postpone' – into a noun designating active non-self, presence both in space and time. [Trans.]

4 Cf. 'La différance', in *Théorie d'ensemble*, coll. Tel Quel (Paris: Le Seuil, 1968), pp. 58ff. Reprinted in *Marges* (Paris: Editions de Minuit, 1972). Translated as 'Differance' by David Allison in *Speech and Phenomena* (Evanston: Northwestern University Press, 1973).

5 Cf. 'De l'économie restreinte à l'économie générale', in *L'Ecriture et la différence*, coll. 'Tel Quel (Paris: Le Seuil, 1967). Translated as 'From Restricted to General Economy', in *Writing and Difference* (Alan Bass, trans.) (Chicago: Chicago University Press, 1978).

6 On the concepts of *intervention* and *paleonymy*, and on the conceptual operation of reversal/displacement (the withdrawal of a predicate, the adherence of a name, the processes of grafting, extending, and reorganizing), cf. 'Positions', in *Promesse*, nos. 30–1, p. 37. Reprinted in *Positions* (Paris: Editions de Minuit, 1972). Translated as *Positions* by Alan Bass (Chicago: Chicago University Press, 1981).

7 Derrida, 'La différance', pp. 46 ff.

8 *Aufgehoben* (concerning this translation of '*aufheben*' [to sublatel by '*relever*' (to relieve), cf. 'Le puits et la pyramide', in *Hegel et la pensée moderne* (Paris: Presses Universitaires de France, 1971). The movement by which Hegel determines difference as contradiction ('Der Unterschied überhaupt ist schon der Widerspruch *an sich*', *The Science of Logic* II, I, Chapter 2, C) is designed precisely to make possible the ultimate (onto-theo-teleo-logical) sublation [la relève] of difference. *Differance* – which is thus by no means dialectical contradiction in this Hegelian sense – marks the critical limit of the idealizing powers of relief [*la relève*] wherever they are able, directly or indirectly, to operate. Differance *inscribes* contradiction, or rather, since it remains irreducibly differentiating and disseminating, contradiction*s*. In marking the 'productive' (in the sense of general economy and in accordance with the loss of presence) and differentiating movement, the *economic* 'concept' of differance does not reduce all contradictions to the homogeneity of a single model. It is the opposite that is likely to happen when Hegel makes difference into a moment within general contradiction. The latter is always ontotheological in its foundation. As is the reduction of the complex general economy of differance to difference. (Belated residual note for a postface.)

9 The word *restance*, coined from the verb *rester* (to remain), means 'the fact or act of remaining or of being left over'. [Trans.]

10 The French designation of the future perfect tense, *le futur antérieur*, literally means 'the prior future'. Derrida here both plays upon the simultaneous pastness and futureness of a book with respect to its preface and employs the future perfect tense in the very sentence in which he speaks about it. In French, the future perfect is often used to express hypothesis or opinion. Although this usage is not common in English, I have retained the future perfect in such cases whenever its temporal paradoxes are relevant to the context (cf. the first sentence of the book). [Trans.]

11 The preface does not expose the frontal, preambulary façade of a certain space. It does not exhibit the first face or the sur-face of a development that can thus be fore-seen and presented.

It is what comes in advance of a speech (*praefatio, prae-fari*). In place of this discursive anticipation, the notion of 'protocol' substitutes a textual monument: the *first* (*proto-*) page *glued* (*kollon*) over the opening – the first page of a register or set of records. In all contexts in which it intervenes, the protocol comprises the meanings of priority, formula (form, pharmacopoeia), and writing: pre-scription. And through its 'collage', the *protokollon* divides and undoes the inaugural pretention of the first page, as of any *incipit*. Everything, then, begins – this is a law of dissemination – doubled by a 'facing'. Of course, if the protocol itself amounted to the gluing in of a simple sheet (for example the recto/verso of the sign), it would become a preface again, in accordance with an order in which one can recognize the features of the Greater Logic. It avoids this only insofar as it forms a block, magically slated according to the 'graphics' of a completely different structure: neither depth nor surface, neither substance nor phenomenon, neither in itself nor for itself.

(This outwork would then constitute – for example – the sketch, according to protocol, of an oblique introduction to two treatises (treatments, rather, and so strangely contemporaneous: to their own practice), the two most remarkable treatises, indefinitely re-markable, on the *pre written* [*le pré écrit*: can also mean 'the written meadow']: these two musical machines, as different as they can be – Francis Ponge's *le Pré* [*The Meadow*] in Francis Ponge, *Oeuvres complètes* (Paris: Gallimard, 1999); or *la Fabrique du pré* [*Meadow Making*] and Roger Laporte's *Fugue* (Paris: Gallimard, 1970).)

12   *Un bloc magique*. This is a reference to Freud's comparison of the psychic apparatus to a 'mystic writing-pad', [*Wunderblock*] ('Note on the Mystic Writing-Pad', 1925). The 'mystic writing-pad', which I am here calling a 'magic slate', is a child's writing toy composed of a stiff dark waxed surface covered by a thin opaque sheet protected by a transparent piece of cellophane. Marks are made when pressure is exerted through all three layers, making the opaque layer take on the dark color of the waxed surface. When the top two layers are detached from the wax, the mark disappears, but the wax surface retains a furrow. The 'magic slate', like the psychic apparatus, thus exhibits the capacity both to retain an imprint (memory) and to clear itself for the receipt of new marks (perception). Derrida has discussed this comparison of the psyche to a writing device in 'Freud and the Scene of Writing' (in *Writing and Difference*, pp. 196–231).

13   Hegel's *Phenomenology of Spirit* (A.V. Miller, trans.) (New York: Oxford University Press, 1977), p. 1. The translation has occasionally been modified (e.g. the translation of *der Begriff* has been changed from 'the Notion' to 'the concept', and that of *die Sache selbst* has been changed from 'the subject matter' or 'the real issue' to 'the thing itself') to bring it closer to the French translation Derrida is using. Derrida's interpolations from the German have been added. [Trans.]

14   Hegel, *Phenomenology*, p. 1.

15   Ibid., p. 3.

16   'Against this view it must be maintained that truth is not a minted coin that can be given and pocketed ready-made'. 'Out of this distinguishing, of course, comes identity, and this resultant identity is the truth. But it is not truth as if the disparity had been thrown away, like dross from pure metal, not even like the tool which remains separate from the finished vessel; disparity, rather, as the negative, the self (*Selbst*), is itself still directly present (*vorhanden*) in the True as such' (Ibid., pp. 22–3).

17   Ibid., p. 3–4.

18   'From its very beginning, culture (*Bildung*) must leave room for the earnestness of life in its concrete richness; this leads the way to an experience of the thing itself (*in die Erfahrung der Sache selbst hineinführt*). And even when the thing itself has been penetrated to its depths by serious speculative effort, this kind of knowing and judging (*Beurteilung*) will still retain its appropriate place in ordinary conversation (*Konversation*)', Ibid., p. 3.

9 Gilles Deleuze, *Difference and Repetition*

1   Claude Lévi-Strauss, *Tristes tropiques* (Paris: Plon, 1955), pp. 197–9.

2   Matila Ghyka, *Le nombre d'or*, I (Paris: Gallimard, 1931), p. 65.

3   See Michel Foucault, *Raymond Roussel* (Paris: Gallimard, 1963).

4   By Thomas Carlyle. *Sartor Resartus* means literally 'The Tailor Re-Patched'. The text was written in 1830–1.

5   Gabriel Tarde, *Lois de l'imitation* (Paris: Alcan, 1890).

6   Immanuel Kant, *Prolegomena to any Future Metaphysics* (Gary Hatfield, trans.) (Cambridge: Cambridge University Press, 1997), sec. 13.

10 Michel Foucault, 'Theatrum philosophicum'

1   This review essay originally appeared in *Critique* 282 (1970), pp. 885–908. The translation, by Donald F. Brouchard and Sherry Simon, has been slightly amended.

2   Gilles Deleuze, *Différence et Répétition* (Paris: Presses Universitaires de France, 1969); *Difference and Repetition* (Paul Patton, trans.) (New York: Columbia University Press, 1994). Deleuze, *Logique du sens* (Paris: Minuit, 1969); *The Logic of Sense* (Mark Lester with Charles Stivale, trans.) (New York: Columbia University Press, 1990).

3   On the rise of irony and the fall of humour see Deleuze, *Différence et Répétition*, p. 5, and *The Logic of Sense*, pp. 134–41.

4   Maurice Merleau-Ponty, *La Phénémenólgie de la perception* (Paris: Gallimard, 1945); *The Phenomenology of Perception* (Colin Smith, trans.) (London: Routledge and Kegan Paul, 1962).

5   A character in Klossowski's *Les Lois de l'hospitalité* (Paris: Gallimard, 1965).

6   Deleuze, *The Logic of Sense*, pp. 6–11.

7   Fabricius was a Roman general and statesman (d. 250 BC); Prince Andrew is a main character in Tolstoi's *War and Peace*.

8   Deleuze, *The Logic of Sense*, pp. 12–22.

9   M. Blanchot, *L'Espace littéraire*, cited in Deleuze, *Différence et Répétition*, p.112; see also Deleuze, *The Logic of Sense*, pp. 148–53.

10   Deleuze, *The Logic of Sense*, pp. 148–53.

11 Jacques Derrida, 'The Time of a Thesis'

1   This is the text of a presentation which was given, according to custom, at the opening of a thesis defence (based on published works), 2 June 1980 at the Sorbonne. The jury consisted of M.M. Aubenque, De Gandillac, Desanti, Joly, Lascault, Levinas.

2   The qualification necessary to teach at secondary school and university in France.

3   Tran Duc Tao, *Phénoménologie et matérialisme dialectique* (Paris: Minh-Tân, 1951).

4   Edmund Husserl, *L'Origine de la géométrie* ('Introduction', Jacques Derrida, trans.) (Paris: Presses Universitaires de France, 1962). Jacques Derrida, *Edmund Husserl's* Origin of Geometry: *An Introduction* (John P. Leavey, Jr., trans.) (New York and Sussex: Nicolas Hays Ltd and Harvester Press, 1978).

5   Immanuel Kant, *The Conflict of the Faculties* (Mary J. Gregor, trans.) (Lincoln, Nebr.: University of Nebraska Press, 1992).

6   Jacques Derrida, *Marges de la philosophie* (Paris: Minuit, 1972). *Margins of Philosophy* (Alan Bass, trans.) (Chicago: University of Chicago Press, 1982).

7   Jacques Derrida, *Glas* (Paris: Galilée, 1974). *Glas* (John P. Leavey, Jr. and Richard Rand, trans.) (Lincoln, Nebr.: University of Nebraska Press, 1986).

8   Jacques Derrida, *Éperons: les styles de Nietzsche* (Paris: Flammarion, 1978). *Spurs: Nietzsche's styles* (Barbara Harlow, trans.) (Chicago: University of Chicago Press, 1979).

9   Jacques Derrida, *La carte postale. De Socrate à Freud et au delà* (Paris: Flammarion, 1980). *The Post Card: From Socrates to Freud and Beyond* (Alan Bass, trans.) (Chicago: University of Chicago Press, 1987).

10 Jacques Derrida, 'Limited Inc abc (response to John Searle)', *Glyph*, vol. II (Baltimore: Johns Hopkins University Press, 1977), pp.162–254. *Limited Inc* (Paris: Galilée, 1990).

11 Jacques Derrida, *La verité en peinture* (Paris: Flammarion, 1978). *The Truth in Painting* (Geoffrey Bennington and Ian McLeod, trans.) (Chicago: University of Chicago Press, 1987).

12   Gilles Deleuze, *Pure Immanence*

1   'As though we reflected back to surfaces the light which emanates from them, the light which, had it passed unopposed, would never have been revealed'; Henri Bergson, *Matter and Memory* (New York: Zone Books, 1988), p. 36.

2   Cf. Jean-Paul Sartre, who posits a transcendental field without a subject that refers to a consciousness that is impersonal, absolute, immanent: with respect to it, the subject and the object are 'transcendents'; *La transcendance de l'Ego* (Paris: Vrin, 1966), pp. 74–87. On William James, see David Lapoujade's analysis, 'Le Flux intensif de la conscience chez William James', *Philosophie*, 46, June 1995.

3   Already in the second introduction to *La Doctrine de la science*: 'The intuition of pure activity which is nothing fixed, but progress, not a being, but a life'; Johann Fichte, *Oeuvres choisies de la philosophie première* (Paris: Vrin, 1964), p. 274. On the concept of life according to Fichte, see *Initiation à la vie bienheureuse* (Paris: Aubier, 1944), and Martial Guéroult's commentary (p. 9).

4   Maine de Biran was considered the most talented philosopher of the first quarter of the nineteenth century. His work was defined by three distinct stages of development. In the final stage he tried to develop a comprehensive spiritualist philosophy. [Ed.]

5   Charles Dickens, *Our Mutual Friend* (New York: Oxford University Press, 1989), p. 443.

6   Even Edmund Husserl admits this: 'The being of the world is necessarily transcendent to consciousness, even within the originary evidence, and remains necessarily transcendent to it. But this doesn't change the fact that all transcendence is constituted solely in the *life of consciousness*, as inseparably linked to that life …'; *Méditations cartésiennes* (Paris: Vrin, 1947), p. 52. This will be the starting point of Sartre's text.

7   Cf. Joë Bousquet, *Les Capitales* (Paris: Le Cercle du Livre, 1955).

13   Jean-François Lyotard, *Postmodern Fables*

1   The host of a long-standing French television program, *Apostrophe*, in which writers were invited to discuss their works. [Trans.]

2   Jean Paulhan, *Les Fleurs de Tarbes ou la terreur dans les lettres* (Paris: Gallimard, 1941).

14 Fredric Jameson, *Postmodernism, or, the Cultural Logic of Late Capitalism*

1 The following first appeared as 'Postmodernism, Or, The Cultural Logic of Late Capitalism', *New Left Review*, 146, July–August, pp. 59–92. [Ed.]

2 Robert Venturi and Denise Scott-Brown, *Learning from Las Vegas*, (Cambridge, Mass.: MIT Press, 1972).

3 The originality of Charles Jencks's pathbreaking *Language of Post-Modern Architecture* (London: Academy Press, 1977) lay in its well-nigh dialectical combination of postmodern architecture and a certain kind of semiotics, each being appealed to to justify the existence of the other. Semiotics becomes appropriate as a mode of analysis of the newer architecture by virtue of the latter's populism, which does emit signs and messages to a spatial 'reading public', unlike the monumentality of the high modern. Meanwhile, the newer architecture is itself thereby validated, insofar as it is accessible to semiotic analysis and thus proves to be an essentially aesthetic object (rather than the transaesthetic constructions of the high modern). Here, then, aesthetics reinforces an ideology of communication, and vice versa. Besides Jencks's many valuable contributions, see also Heinrich Klotz, *History of Postmodern Architecture* (Cambridge, Mass.: MIT Press, 1988); Pier Paolo Portoghesi. *After Modern Architecture* (New York: Rizzoli, 1982).

4 Ernest Mandel, *Late Capitalism* (Joris de Bres, trans.) (London: NLB, 1975).

5 The basic reference, in which Lacan discusses Schreber, is 'D'une question préliminaire à tout traitement possible de la psychose', in *Écrits* (Alan Sheridan, trans.) (New York: W.W. Norton & Co., 1977), pp. 179–225. Most of us have received this classical view of psychosis by way of Deleuze and Guattari's *Anti-Oedipus*; Gilles Deleuze, *Anti-Oedipus* (R. Hurley, M. Seem and H. Lane, trans.) (Minneapolis, Minn.: University of Minnesota Press, 1987).

6 See Fredric Jameson, 'Imaginary and Symbolic in Lacan', in *The Ideologies of Theory*, vol. I (Minneapolis: Minn.: University of Minnesota Press, 1988), pp. 75–115.

7 See, particularly on such motifs in Le Corbusier, Gert Kähler, *Architektur als Symbolverfall: Das Dampfermotiv in der Baukunst* (Brunswick: Vieweg, 1981).

8 See Fredric Jameson, 'Morality and Ethical Substance', in *The Ideologies of Theory*, vol. I.

9 Karl Marx and Friedrich Engels, *The Communist Manifesto* (With introduction and notes by Gareth Stedman Jones) (Harmondsworth: Penguin Books, 2002).

10 Herbert Marcuse, 'The Affirmative Character of Culture', *Negations: Essays in Critical Theory* (Boston: Beacon Press, 1968).

11 Kevin Lynch, *The Image of the City* (Cambridge, Mass.: Technology Press and Harvard University Press, 1960).

12 Louis Althusser, 'Ideological State Apparatuses', in *Lenin and Philosophy* (New York: Monthly Review Press, 1972).

Part three   Difference, aesthetics, politics and history

1 Francis Fukuyama, *The End of History and the Last Man* (London: Hamilton 1992).

2 Luce Irigaray, *Speculum of the Other Woman* (Gillian Gill, trans.) (Ithaca: University of Cornell Press, 1993).

3 Jean-François Lyotard, *The Postmodern Condition: A Report on Knowledge* (Geoff Bennington and Brian Massumi, trans.) (Manchester: Manchester University Press, 1984).

4 Jacques Derrida, *Voyous: deux essais sur la raison* (Paris: Galilée, 2003).

15   Jean-François Lyotard, *The Differend: Phrases in Dispute*

1   Faurisson in Pierre Vidal-Naquet, 'A Paper Eichmann' (M. Jolas, trans.), *Democracy* I, 2, 1981, p. 81

2   The term is from Alexander Zinoviev's satirical novel *The Yawning Heights*, set in a fictitious locale – Ibansk – whose name is a derivative of Ivan, the stereotypical Russian name. [Trans.]

3   Alexander Zinoviev, *The Yawning Heights* (G. Clough, trans.) (New York: Random House, 1978), pp. 600–1.

4   François Châtelet, *L'Etat savant*, unpublished typescript (Paris, 1981).

5   The foremost member of which was Gregory Bateson. [Trans.]

6   Gottried Leibniz, 'The Principle of Nature and of Grace, Based on Reason', in *Philosophical Papers and Letters*, II (L. Loemker, trans. and ed.) (Dordrecht: Reidel, 1969), § 7.

7   Aristotle, *Rhetoric*, in *The Complete Works of Aristotle* (W. Rhys Roberts, trans.) (J. Barnes, ed.) (Oxford: Oxford University Press, 1984), 1402 b, pp. 24–5.

8   Aristotle, *De Interpretatione,* in *The Complete Works of Aristotle*, 21 b, pp. 12–17; *Metaphysics* IV in *The Complete Works of Aristotle*, 1022 b, p. 22ff.

9   John Lawler, 'Quelques problèmes de référence', *Langages*, 48, 1977.

10   Paolo Fabri and Marina Sbisa, 'Models (?) for a Pragmatic Analysis', *Journal of Pragmatics*, 4, 1980.

11   Paul Feyerabend, *Against Method* (London: NLB, 1975).

12   Bruno Latour, *Irréductions. Tractatus scientifico-politicus*, unpublished typescript (Paris, 1981).

13   Paolo Fabri, Private conversations (1980).

14   Vidal-Naquet, 'A Paper Eichmann', ibid., p. 93.

15   Ibid., p. 93.

16   The author of a phony document injurious to Dreyfus's case written after the initial trial and designed as part of a cover-up by the French military to prevent a re-opening of the investigation. Subsequent to the revelation of the document's inauthenticity, Henry committed suicide. [Trans.]

17   An extreme right-wing organization, many of whose members were notorious for their anti-Semitism, egregiously supportive of the verdict against Dreyfus – even after the proof of his innocence had become manifest – in order to protect the 'sanctity' and 'authority' of France's military, judicial and political institutions. [Trans.]

18   The Cashinuahua people, who number between 1,600 and 2,000, inhabit the areas within Peru and Brazil near the Curanja and Perus rivers. [Ed.]

19   André-Marcel d'Ans, *Le dit des Vrais Hommes* (Paris: Gallimard, 1978).

16   Luce Irigaray, *An Ethics of Sexual Difference*

1   This is the text of a public lecture, delivered November 18, 1982 in Rotterdam, The Netherlands. Irigaray gives no references. [Ed.]

19   W. van Reijen and D. Veerman, 'An interview with Jean-François Lyotard'

1   This interview was originally recorded in April 1987 in Paris and Utrecht. The original French text has been published in the Social Philosophy/Philosophical Anthropology Group Reprint Series, No. 1, 1987, Department of Philosophy, University of Utrecht and in *Les Cahiers de philosophie*, 5, 1988.

2   J.-F. Lyotard, 'Judicieux dans le différend', in *La faculté de juger* (Paris: Minuit, 1985), p. 229 and J.-F. Lyotard, *Le postmoderne expliqué aux enfants* (Paris: Galilée, 1986), p. 37 and p. 45.

3   J.-F. Lyotard, *The Postmodern Condition: A Report on Knowledge* (Geoff Bennington and Brian Massumi, trans.) (Manchester: Manchester University Press, 1984); *Le Différend* (Paris: Minuit, 1984).

4   J.-F. Lyotard, 'Appendice svelte à la question postmoderne', in *Tombeau de l'intellectuel* (Paris: Galilée, 1984), p. 81.

5   Kant's first *Critique* was *Critique of Pure Reason* (Norman Kemp Smith, trans.) (London: Macmillan, 1933). His second *Critique* was *Critique of Practical Reason* (T.K. Abbott, trans.) (Amherst, NY: Prometheus Books, 1996). His third critique was *Critique of Judgment* (James Creed Meredith, trans.) (Oxford: Oxford University Press, 1964). [Ed.]

6   J.-F. Lyotard, 'Kunst Heute', in *Immaterialität und Postmoderne* (Berlin: Merve, 1985), p. 62.

7   J.-F. Lyotard, *Discours, figure* (Paris: Klincksieck, 1971).

8   J.-F. Lyotard, *Économie libidinale* (Paris: Minuit, 1974).

9   J.-F. Lyotard, 'Interview with G. van den Abbeele', *Diacritics*, 14, 3, 1984, p. 17.

10   J-.F.Lyotard, *Economie libidinale*.

11   J.-F. Lyotard, 'An Answer to the question "What is Postmodernism?"', appendix to *The Postmodern Condition*.

12   J.-F. Lyotard, *Instructions païennes* (Paris: Galilée, 1977), p. 36.

13   J.-F. Lyotard and J.-L. Thébaud, *Au Juste* (Paris: Christian Bourgeois, 1979).

14   See Martin Heidegger, *On Time and Being* (New York: Harper and Row, 1972), p. 19: 'What determines both, time and Being, in their own, that is, in their belonging together, we shall call: *Ereignis*, the event of appropriation. *Ereignis* will be translated as Appropriation or event of Appropriation. One should bear in mind. however, that "event" is not simply an occurrence, but that which makes any occurrence possible'. [Trans.]

15   J.-F. Lyotard, *Discours, figure*, p. 18.

16   J.-F. Lyotard, *Economie libidinale*, p. 11.

17   J.-F. Lyotard, 'Sensus communis', *Le Cahier*, 3, 1987.

18   J.-F. Lyotard, 'Presenting the Impresentable', *Artforum*, 1982.

19   I. Kant, 'An Answer to the Question "What is Enlightenment?"', in H. Reiss, ed., *Kant's Political Writings* (Cambridge: Cambridge University Press, 1970), p. 19, para 57, note 1.

20   Ibid., para 57.

21   J.-F. Lyotard, *Le Différend* (Paris: Minuit, 1984), p. 9.

22   J.-F. Lyotard, 'Judicieux dans le différend', *La faculté de juger* (Paris: Minuit, 1985), pp. 195–236.

23   J.-F. Lyotard, 'Sur la théorie' (Interview with B. Devismes), in J.-F. Lyotard, *Dérive à partir de Marx et Freud* (Paris: 10/18, 1970), pp. 228–9.

24   J.-F. Lyotard, 'Argumentation and Presentation: the Crisis of Foundations', *Neue Hefte für Philosophie*, 26, 1986, p. 13.

25   Immanuel Kant, *Critique of Judgment* (James Creed Meredith, trans.) (Oxford: Oxford University Press, 1964).

26   J.-F. Lyotard, 'L'Acinéma' in *Cinéma théorie, lectures* (Paris: Klincksieck, 1978) reprinted in *Les Dispositifs pulsionnels* (Paris: 10/18).

27   J.-F. Lyotard, *Le postmoderne expliqué aux enfants* (Paris: Galilée, 1986), p. 110.

28   Ibid., p. 125.

29   The word used here, which I have translated here as *gliding through* is *perlaboration*. This word appears to be a neologism in the French language, and there is no directly comparable word in English (the word 'perlaboration' does not appear in the *Oxford English Dictionary*). The word is derived from the Latin: *perlabor*, an intransitive verb meaning to move on, to glide along, to pass through. Sometimes it has been possible to translate the usage in the text in the way that I have done here; but at other points, its usage is determined not only

by its Latin root, but also by its close relation to the word 'elaboration', and where this has happened, the translator has allowed the term (in both noun and verb form) to stand as an acceptable neologism in English. [Trans.]

30 J.-F. Lyotard, *Que peindre?* (Paris: Editions de la différence, 1987).

31 J.-F. Lyotard, 'The Sublime and the Avant-Garde', *Artforum*, 22, 1984; J.-F. Lyotard, 'An Answer to the Question: "What is Postmodernism"', Appendix to *The Postmodern Condition*.

32 J.-F. Lyotard, 'Judicieux dans le différend', in *La faculté de juger* (Paris: Minuit, 1985), p. 235.

33 J.-F. Lyotard, *L'Enthousiasme – la critique kantienne de l'histoire* (Paris: Galilée, 1986), pp. 112–14.

34 Kant writes, "But should not a society of clergymen, for example an ecclesiastical synod or a venerable presbytery (as the Dutch call it), be entitled to commit itself by oath to a certain unalterable set of doctrines, in order to secure for all time a constant guardianship over each of its members, and through them over the people?" Immanuel Kant, 'An Answer to the Question: "What is Enlightenment?"', in *Kant's Political Writings*, p. 57.

35 Ibid., p. 57.

36 J.-F. Lyotard, 'En finir avec l'illusion de la politique' (interview with Gilbert Lascault) *La Quinzaine littéraire*, 1, 15 May, 1972, p. 19.

37 See J.-F. Lyotard, *Instructions païennes* (Paris: Galilée, 1977), p. 19 and J.-F. Lyotard, *Le Différend*, No. 257.

38 J.-F. Lyotard, 'Kunst Heute', in *Immaterialität und Postmoderne*, p. 69.

39 Jean-Luc Nancy, *La communauté desoeuvrée* (Paris: Christain Bourgeois, 1986).

40 J.-F. Lyotard, *Just Gaming* (Manchester: Manchester University Press, 1985), p. 90.

41 J.-F. Lyotard, *Le Postmoderne expliqué aux enfants*,

42 J.-F. Lyotard, 'Plaidoyer pour la métaphysique' (conversation with Jacques Derrida), *Le Monde*, 28–29 September, 1984.

43 Richard Rorty, 'Solidarity or Objectivity', in J. Rachman and C. West, eds, *Post-Analytic Philosophy* (New York: Columbia University Press, 1985).

21 Jacques Derrida, 'Injunctions of Marx'

1 For a novel elaboration, in a 'deconstructive' style, of the concept of *hegemony*, I refer to Ernesto Laclau and Chantal Mouffe, *Hegemony and Socialist Strategy: Towards Radical Democratic Politics* (London: Verso, 1985).

2 Karl Marx and Friedrich Engels, *The Communist Manifesto* (With introduction and notes by Gareth Stedman Jones) (Harmondsworth: Penguin Books, 2002).

3 Karl Marx and Friedrich Engels, *The German Ideology*, in *Collected Works* (New York: International Publishers, 1976), pp. 230–1.

4 Marx and Engels, *The German Ideology*, p. 230.

5 Karl Marx, *A Contribution to the Critique of Political Economy*, chapter 2, pt. 2 b ('The Circulation of Money') (New York: International Publishers, 1970).

6 Ibid., p. 109.

7 Ibid., p. 132.

8 Ibid., p. 142. This is a semantic chain that we have examined in *Glas* (in Hegel) and in *Of Spirit: Heidegger and the Question*.

9 Ibid., p. 119 and p. 140.

10 Ibid., p. 134.

11 The idiomatic expression here is '(se) fait peur', frightens (itself). Literally, however, it says: to make (itself) fright. Later, the text will exploit this literality when it describes a structure of the self as fear or fright, as that which makes itself into fear. [Trans.]

Glossary of names

Althusser, Louis (1918–90). Born in Algeria, Louis Althusser was educated at Algiers, Marseilles, and the École Normale Supérieure, Paris, where he taught philosophy. In 1948 Althusser joined the French Communist Party, later becoming its leading theoretician. While teaching at the École Normale, where the whole of his academic career was to be based, Althusser developed an enthusiastic following among Marxist students, including Pierre Macherey and Étienne Balibar, who would later co-author his famous analysis of Karl Marx's *Capital, Lire Le Capital* (1968) (*Reading Capital*). As a leading structuralist, Althusser sought to reinterpret Marx in the light of ideas on science developed by Gaston **Bachelard.** Althusser argued that there was a two-fold development in Marx's thought from his early works which were marked by philosophical idealism to his mature writings in which he developed an objective science of society. This controversial thesis of an 'epistemic break' in Marx's work was both widely admired and hotly contested. Althusser's most significant contribution was to retheorise the Marxist concept of ideology. This was to have profound implications for areas of research such as cultural studies and it was to mark the thought of a whole generation of thinkers, including **Foucault** and **Lyotard.** Throughout his life Althusser suffered from debilitating bouts of depression. In 1980 he strangled his wife. He was declared mentally ill and admitted to a psychiatric hospital. The last years of his life are described in his *L'avenir dure longtemps* (1992) (*The Future Lasts a Long Time*, 1993).

Bachelard, Gaston (1884–1962). A self-taught mathematician and philosopher of science, Bachelard worked first for the French postal service and then from 1919 to 1930 taught physics, chemistry and philosophy at the *collège* (secondary school) of Bar-sur-Aude, in the south-west of France. After receiving his *licence* in mathematics in 1912, Bachelard went on to obtain his *agrégation* in philosophy in 1922 at the age of 38. In 1927 he was awarded a doctorate in philosophy and the following year published his doctoral thesis under the title *Essai sur la connaissance approchée* (*Essay on Approximate Knowledge*). In 1930 he became professor of philosophy of science at Dijon and ten years later was awarded a chair at the Sorbonne where he taught until 1955. Bachelard's understanding of philosophy and scientific enquiry was heavily influenced by his doctoral supervisor Léon Brunschvicg (1869–1944). Like Brunschvicg he believed that philosophy could only arrive at a clear understanding of reason by considering the historical development of science. Bachelard believed that the development of science was not a linear process but was marked by clear epistemological breaks. His understanding of scientific development was to have a profound impact on **Foucault's** thought, particularly through the advent of Foucault's concept of *épistémè*. The idea of epistemological break became central to **Althusser's** reworking of Marxism.

Barthes, Roland (1915–80). First influenced by Marxism and existentialism in the 1940s, Barthes became one of the leading structuralist thinkers of the twentieth century. His approach to literary criticism and the study of culture was to revolutionise these disciplines. Born at Cherbourg, Barthes taught both in Romania and Egypt and later held a post at the École des Hautes Études en Sciences Sociales in Paris. In 1977 he was made professor at the prestigious Collège de France. He died three years later after having been hit by a van. Barthes most influential early work was a series of reflections on the state of contemporary French culture. Published in the journal *Les lettres nouvelles* these essays later made up a collection entitled *Mythologies* (1957) (*Mythologies*, 1972). This was a significant contribution to semiology or the 'science of signs' which had been initiated by the Swiss linguist Ferdinand de **Saussure**. In the 1960s Barthes refined his approach to semiology, publishing in 1967 his seminal *Système de la mode* (*The Fashion System*, 1983) a structuralist and semiotic analysis of the social phenomenon of fashion. Yet by the time this work appeared many of its ideas had been superseded by the new and poststructuralist writings of Jacques **Derrida** and Julia **Kristeva**. Barthes learned much from these new approaches and sought to revise his own methodology. The result was his remarkable *S/Z* (1970) (*S/Z*, 1974), an analysis of Balzac's short story *Sarrasine*. *S/Z* was an attempt to unearth the narrative codes that were at work in a work of classic realism. Barthes' writings were critical to social theorists like Jean **Baudrillard**.

Baudrillard, Jean (b. 1929). Born in Reims into a lower middle-class family, Baudrillard began his academic career as a student of **Althusser's** arch-rival, the anti-structuralist Marxist Henri Lefebvre. Having completed a thesis in sociology, Baudrillard soon fell under the influence of **Barthes** and wrote a number of important works on object and sign-function. His early publications – *Le système des objets* (1968) (*System of Objects*, 1996), *La société de consommation* (1970) (*The Consumer Society: Myths and Structures* ,1998) and *Pour une critique de l'économie politique du signe* (1972) (*For a Critique of the Political Economy of Sign*, 1981) – examine aspects of mass consumer society through a judicious and innovative combination of semiotics with Marxist political economy. But with the publication of his 1973 *Le miroir de la production* (*Mirror of Production*, 1975) Baudrillard distanced himself from Marxism, breaking from it definitively with *L'échange symbolique de la mort* (1976) (*Symbolic Exchange and Death*, 1993).Throughout the 1970s and 1980s Baudrillard explored the theme of postmodern society where simulation and simulacra – the reproduction of objects and events – dominate the human condition and where ideas of authentic meaning and awareness of origin are lost in a world of infinitely replicating sign systems. His 1986 *Amérique* (*America*, 1988) is a classic example of this kind of judgement on a world where reality has been replaced by image.

Bataille, Georges (1897–1962). Educated at Reims, Epernay, Paris and Madrid, Bataille studied to be a Mediaevalist but quickly became fascinated with the works of Nietzsche and Freud. After becoming a librarian at the Bibliothèque Nationale in Paris in 1924 he began to write erotic novels and radical philosophical essays. Bataille was initially associated with the surrealists but soon broke from them. He became interested in anthropological studies of primitive societies and joined forces with the classicist and the surrealist writer Roger Callois. From 1937 to 1939 they ran a discussion group devoted to the study of sacred experiences. During this period Bataille also attended Alexandre Kojève's celebrated lectures on G.W.F. Hegel's *Phenomenology of Spirit* (1807), and was fascinated with the role Hegel assigned to violence and destruction, through the concept of negation, in the progress of history. Yet Bataille would return to his initial philosophical inspiration in Nietzsche with *Sur Nietzsche* (1945) (*On Nietzsche*, 1992). His fascination with violence, transgressive action and radical irrationalism alienated many of his generation, particularly Jean-Paul Sartre. But his thoughts on these phenomena inspired thinkers such as **Foucault**.

Bauman, Zygmunt (b. 1925). Born and educated in Poland, Bauman was expelled from that country after the 1968 invasion of Czechoslovakia. After emigrating to the United Kingdom, Bauman began teaching sociology at the University of Leeds in 1971. As one of the clearest and most theoretically sophisticated writers on modernity and postmodernity, Bauman has grappled with themes of individual and social identity in a series of important works such as *Legislators and Interpreters: On Modernity, Postmodernity and Intellectuals* (1987). His concern with ethics and morality are at the forefront of such works as *Modernity and the Holocaust* (1989), *Modernity and Ambivalence* (1991), *Postmodern Ethics* (1993) and *Postmodernity and its Discontents* (1997).

Blanchot, Maurice (1907–2003). Born in Quain in Saône et Loire, Blanchot's writings defy classification. Neither a surrealist nor a dadaist, Blanchot's literary output draws inspiration principally from Nietzsche's and Hegel's philosophies and the writings of Kafka and Mallarmé. There is a powerful modernist impulse that runs through the whole of his work, and a genuine attempt, in response to the Holocaust, to express a vision of community open to radical difference. Blanchot's central preoccupations were with being, death and language. His writings engage with these concerns through the evocation of concepts such as forgetting, waiting and effacement and by provoking the indeterminate. His ideas inspired **Foucault's** pronouncement in *The Order of Things* on the death of the subject.

Canguilhem, Georges (1904–95). Born at Castelnaudary in south-west France, Georges Canguilhem is best known outside of France as Michel **Foucault's** doctoral supervisor. Canguilhem studied at the École Normale Supérieure under the philosopher Émile Cartier, called Alain (1886–1951). After obtaining his *agrégation* in 1924 he studied medicine and obtained a doctorate in it in 1943. During the war he taught at the University of Strasbourg. In 1955 Canguilhem succeeded **Bachelard** in the chair of philosophy at the Sorbonne where he was to influence **Althusser** and **Foucault**. Though Canguilhem's approach to the philosophy of science was strongly influenced by Bachelard, his interests in philosophical history and the biological and medical sciences resulted in important innovations on Bachelard's views. The most significant of these involved rethinking the relation between theory and concept with the result that Canguilhem asserted the primacy of concepts over theory. This allowed for an important refinement in the idea of epistemological rupture and led to the introduction of the notion of 'scientific ideology' which later became crucial to Althusser. Canguilhem's treatment of norms – biological and social – and normativity was the foundation to Foucault's discussion in *Discipline and Punish* and *The History of Sexuality* of norms as instruments of social power.

Cixous, Hélène (b. 1937). A leading figure in French feminist thought, Cixous was born in Algeria and is Professor of Literature at the University of Paris VIII (Vincennes). A strong advocate of feminine writing, Cixous' work is often considered, alongside Luce **Irigaray's** and Julia **Kristeva's**, exemplary of difference feminism. Cixous' writings attempt to undermine logocentrism and phallocentrism. To this end she deploys concepts and theoretical models derived from **Lacanian** psychoanalysis and deconstruction. Her writing has a powerful utopian impulse and is visionary.

Deleuze, Gilles (1925–95). After studying at the Lycée Carnot, Paris, Deleuze entered the Sorbonne to study philosophy in 1944 and was a student of Ferdinand Aliquié (an expert on Descartes' philosophy), Georges **Canguilhem** and Jean Hyppolite (France's leading Hegel specialist). In 1948 he obtained his *agrégation* and began teaching philosophy at various secondary schools (*lycées*). From 1957 until 1960 he taught the history of philosophy at the Sorbonne. In 1960 he obtained a research post at the Centre National de Recherche Scientifique (CNRS) and remained there until 1964 when he moved to the University of Lyon, teaching philosophy there until 1969. At the behest of Michel **Foucault**, who was head of the philosophy department at the University of Paris, Vincennes, Deleuze was appointed Professor of Philosophy there in 1969. Between 1953 and 1966 Deleuze wrote a series of important studies on philosophers who, with the exception of one on Nietzsche, were not part of mainstream philosophical debates in France at the time: Hume, Nietzsche, Kant, Bergson and Spinoza. These works served to nourish Deleuze's distinctive and more mature works *Différence et répétition* (*Difference and Repetition*) (1968) and *Logique du sens* (*The Logic of*

Sense) (1969) where he formulated his distinctive metaphysics of difference. In 1972 he published his first collaborative work with Félix **Guattari** *L'anti-oedipe* (Anti-Oedipus) followed by a second book *Mille plateaux* (A Thousand Plateaus) in 1980. These two works were part of a larger project entitled *Capitalisme et schizophrénie* which reflected Deleuze's engagement in radical political activism. Deleuze and Guattari redefined schizophrenia not as an illness to be cured but as a creative power to be nurtured. They attacked established conceptions of Marxism and psychoanalysis as buttressing logocentrism and capitalism and presented their own idea of schizophrenia as both creative and liberating.

Derrida, Jacques (b. 1930). Born into an Algerian Jewish family, Derrida was introduced to the work of the philosophers Rousseau and Nietzsche at the Lycée Ben Aknoun. After intensive studies of Bergson, Sartre, Kierkegaard and Heidegger, Derrida entered the famous Louis-le-Grand school, Paris, in 1949 and attended lectures by the philosopher Simone Weil. His time there was unhappy and was punctuated by periods of poor health. In 1952 he began studying philosophy at the École Normale Supérieure where he was to meet **Althusser**. One year later he began a serious study of the work of Edmund Husserl at the Husserl archives in Louvain. After having obtained his *agrégation* in 1956 he went on to teach classes in philosophy at the Sorbonne between 1960 and 1964. It is during this time that he published his first important articles in the journals *Critiques* and *Tels quels*. In 1966 he gave a paper at a conference at Johns Hopkins University, Baltimore where he would meet the Belgian critic Paul de Man and a number of important French thinkers including Jacques **Lacan** and Roland **Barthes**. The conference was to establish Derrida as a philosophical presence in America, where he now spends part of the year teaching. In 1967 he published his doctoral thesis *De la grammatologie* (Of Grammatology), a work that set out his new approach to philosophy known as deconstruction. Celebrated and reviled for his approach to philosophy, Derrida has been awarded numerous honorary doctorates in America and Europe, but he did not obtain his *doctorat d'État* until 1980. Now one of the directors of the École des Hautes Études en Sciences Sociales, Paris, Derrida has acquired a certain cult status in France and America; a feature film was made of him in 2002 by Kirby Dick and Amy Ziering.

Foucault, Michel (1926–84). Born in Poitiers, Foucault studied under the eminent Hegel scholar Jean Hyppolite at the Lycée Henri IV. In 1946 he entered the École Normale Supérieure. He obtained degrees (*licences*) in philosophy and psychology. During the first half of the 1950s Foucault worked in a psychiatric hospital. This experience marked the composition of his first work *Maladie mentale et personalité* in 1954 (*Mental Illness and Psychology*, 1987). Rather than follow the traditional path to university teaching by teaching at various lycées, Foucault undertook a number of temporary academic posts in Sweden, Poland and Germany between 1955 and 1960. During this time he worked on his doctoral thesis *Folie et Déraison: Histoire de la folie à l'âge classique* (*Madness and Civilization: A History of Insanity in the Age of Reason*) which he successfully defended in 1959 and published in 1961. Two years later he published *Birth of the Clinic: An Archaeology of Medical Perception* where he set out his archaeological approach to the history of ideas and human practices. This approach was refined in his important *The Order of Things* (1966) where he introduced the concept *epistémè* to denote an historical *a priori* which delimits and defines individuals' perceptions and understandings. With the publication of *Archaeology of Knowledge* in 1969 Foucault abandoned the concept of *epistémè* and introduced the more subtle concept of discourse. In 1970 Foucault was elected to a personal chair at the prestigious Collège de France. His inaugural lecture *L'Ordre du discours* set out his interest in the Nietzschean concept of genealogy which he deployed to expose the workings of power and society's repressive and permissive procedures. His 1975 *Discipline and Punish: The Birth of the Prison* and his mammoth and highly ambitious three-volume history of sexuality, begun in 1976 but never completed, were superb examples of this approach.

Guattari, Felix (1930–92). Though a practising psychiatrist, Guattari was best known for his many philosophical writings and his militant political activism. As one of the leading members of the Italian *autonomia* movement, Guattari strove toward a reworking of politics in order to foster self-organising 'minoritarian' groupings. This ambitious enterprise drew on a vast array of different disciplines, including the natural sciences. Guattari's commitment to rethinking politics was a direct challenge to established political practices which, through internalised norms of discipline and self-policing, impose a repressive order. His reflections on the ways individuals might be liberated from the constraints of Western thought and practices include *Anti-oedipe* (Anti-Oedipus)(1972) and *Milles plateaux* (*A Thousand Plateaus*) (1980), jointly written with Gilles **Deleuze**.

Irigaray, Luce (b. 1932). Born in Louvain, Belgium, Irigaray obtained a doctorate in philosophy from the University of Louvain (1955), a degree in psychopathology from the Institut de Psychologie in Paris (1962), a doctorate in linguistics from the University of Paris at Vincennes (1968) and a Doctorat d'État in philosophy in 1974. Though she started out as one of Jacques **Lacan's** disciples, she was soon expelled from Lacan's Department of Psychoanalysis at Vincennes for her feminist critique of psychoanalysis. This was formulated most powerfully in her 1974 critique of Freudian psychoanalysis and Western philosophy from the time of Plato, *Speculum of the Other Woman*. In this work Irigaray argued that the Western philosophical tradition prevented the formulation of a genuine feminine identity because it denied women the status of a subject and only allowed for the subjectivity of the male sex. Irigaray explored this problem by focusing on the questions of language and sexual difference in a number of works such as Ce sexe qui n'est pas un (1977) (*This Sex Which is Not One*, 1985), *Ethique de la différence sexuelle* (1984) (*An Ethics of Sexual Difference*, 1993), *Sexes et parentés* (1987) (*Sexes and Genealogies*, 1993), and *Je, Tu, Nous* (1990) (*Je, Tu, Nous: Towards a Culture of Difference*, 1993). Her incisive and critical reflections on Western philosophy and psychoanalysis are part of an ambitious attempt to empower women through the freeing and reconstruction of a feminine symbolic universe that has been suppressed within the masculine symbolic order.

Jameson, Fredric (b. 1934). A former student of the German philologist, critic and literary historian Erich Auerbach, and currently William Lane Professor of Comparative Literature at Duke University, North Carolina, Fredric Jameson is one of the best known Marxist literary and cultural critics writing in English. Jameson's early work was devoted to an analysis of Hegelian and existentialist Marxism. His 1961 *Sartre: The Origins of a Style* focused on the question of narrative. This was followed by *Marxism and Form* (1971) and his serious engagement with French thought in *The Prison-House of Language* (1972). Developments in structuralist thought and linguistics proved crucial to one of his most ambitious works, *The Political Unconscious: Narrative as Socially Symbolic Act* (1981). This bold work of criticism sought to enrich and refine the Marxist political and historical framework of analysis with elements from structuralism and linguistics. This attempt at a renewal of Marxism by improving on its analytic foundations was brilliantly achieved in 1984 with a long article on contemporary cultural phenomena for the *New Left Review*, 'Postmodernism, or, the Cultural Logic of Late Capitalism'.

Jencks, Charles (b. 1939). Educated at Harvard and the University of London where he obtained a PhD in Architectural History (1971), Jencks is a prolific author best known for his *The Language of Post-Modern Architecture* (1971). Though he began as an historian of architectural modernism he soon became one of its leading critics. His *The Language of Post-Modern Architecture* was one of the first works to introduce semiotic analysis into architecture. His use of the term 'double-coding' to denote postmodern architecture's ability to communicate with 'the public and a concerned minority', has also been used by him in *What is Post-Modernism?* (1986) to describe postmodern literature and other forms of postmodern art.

Kristeva, Julia (b. 1941). Born in Bulgaria, Kristeva came to Paris as a student in 1966. She studied linguistics in Roland **Barthes'** seminar at the École des Hautes Études en Sciences Sociales and later trained as a **Lacanian** psychoanalyst. Almost immediately upon her arrival in Paris, Kristeva immersed herself in Parisian intellectual life and was soon associated with the structuralist and avant-garde writers of the radical journal *Tel quel* edited by Philippe Sollers, whom she would later marry. Her doctoral thesis *La révolution du langage poétique* (1974) (*Revolution in Poetic Language*, 1984) set out her basic theories on language and its role in consti-tuting individual identity. In this work she introduced the important concepts of *semiotic* and *symbolic*. For Kristeva the symbolic referred to our standard conception of language as a rule-governed system employed by a given community. Semiotic, however, referred to pre-Oedipal articulations of unconscious drives and bodily functions. The distinction between symbolic and semiotic rested on Kristeva's belief that language originated in the pre-Oedipal phase. In psychoanalytic terms the semiotic was the state from which the self is generated. At the same time, however, the semiotic – because it is an articulation of unconscious drives – also threatened the stability of the self. Kristeva applied this psychoanalytic and linguistic theory to literature, con-tending that it is dominated by the semiotic. It is because of this that literature has the power to unsettle, even shatter, the stability of the symbolic order. Kristeva would use these ideas to theorise a new form of feminism.

Lacan, Jacques (1901–81). Born into a strict Catholic family, Jacques Lacan was to become one of the most brilliant and provocative psychoanalysts of the twentieth century. After being educated at the famous Jesuit Collège Stanislas, Lacan began his medical and clinical training in 1927. In 1932 he was awarded a doctorate for *De la psychose paranoïque dans les rapports avec la personalité* (*Of Paranoid Psychosis in its Relation With the Personality*). In 1933 Lacan joined with other Parisian intellectuals and attended Alexandre Kojève's famous lectures on Hegel. Like **Bataille**, Lacan was fascinated with the role Hegel assigned to violence and destruction, through the concept of negation, in the progress of history. His interest in Hegel reflected a deep fascination with the role other disciplines could play in nourishing and refining psychiatry. This later characterised Lacan's re-reading of Freud in the light of developments in contemporary philosophy, linguistics, anthropology and biology. His reinterpretation of Freud, given as a series of seminars, occasioned a split within the French psychoanalytic community in 1953. Lacan's unorthodox therapeutic practices and his use of structuralist linguistics and structuro-anthropology widened the divide between him and traditional Freudians. In 1964 he was expelled from the International Psychoanalytic Association but formed his own school, École freudienne de Paris. Lacan reacted against the biological and reductionist reading of Freud which was dominant in the Anglo-American world. His particular interest was in Freud's earlier works, *The Interpretation of Dreams* and *Psychopathology of Everyday Life* (1901), where the role of social and cultural elements in marking emotions and behaviour was stressed at the expense of biological factors. Like other structuralist thinkers, Lacan emphasised the importance of language to the operation of both the conscious and unconscious mind, and he considered the unconscious mind to be structured like language itself. Arguing that the orthodox Freudian view of the ego was incorrect, Lacan explained mental illness in terms of an imbalance between three connected psychic orders: the imaginary, the symbolic and the real. His understanding of structural anthropology and linguistics was crucial to this formulation and proved inspirational to, among others, thinkers like **Kristeva**, **Irigaray**, **Deleuze** and **Guattari**.

Lyotard, Jean-François (1924–98). Born in Versailles, Lyotard began studying philosophy first at the École Normale Supérieure and then at the Sorbonne where he developed a keen interested in the writings of Hegel, Husserl and Heidegger. After considering becoming a Dominican priest, Lyotard chose to teach philosophy at secondary school instead. His first teaching appointment was in 1952 at a *lycée* in Constantine, Algeria. Four years later he returned to France and joined the editorial board of the Marxist journal *Socialisme ou Barbarie*. He became disenchanted with the journal's work and joined the more radical *Pouvoir ouvrier* in 1963. In May 1968, Lyotard, by now a university lecturer at the University of Paris, Nanterre, joined the radical and quasi-anarchist group *Le Mouvement du 22 mars*. His participation in the events of May 1968 were to have a profound impact on his thought. Lyotard's early works explored those experiences which could not be expressed through language. His doctoral thesis, *Discours, figure* (1971) introduced the notion of figural which represented that aspect of a work whose meaning or effect could not be expressed linguistically. Two years later he published a collection of essays, *Des dispositifs* *pulsionnels* (*Mechanisms of the Drives*) and in 1974 *Économie libidinale*. These works all endeavoured to explore deep psychic drives. They were motivated by a desire on Lyotard's part to achieve a synthesis of Freud and Marx. The exploration of the inexpressible became central to Lyotard's concept of the differend which he theorised in *The Differend* (1984). But Lyotard is best known for his famous pronouncement on the state of knowledge in advanced Western societies, *The Postmodern Condition*. Though this work is not entirely representative of his oeuvre, it does bring together many of his central concerns. Lyotard's later writings on art and aesthetic experience engage with his earlier preoccupation with the figural and are all motivated by his deep-seated commitment to lend a voice to the marginalised and the oppressed.

Saussure, Ferdinand de (1857–1913). Born in Geneva, Saussure began his university studies in 1875, first in Geneva studying physics and chemistry and then in Leipzig studying languages. After 18 months studying Sanskrit and at the age of 21, Saussure published a celebrated thesis *Mémoire sur le système primitif des voyelles dans les langues indo-européennes* (1879) (*Memoir on the Primitive System of Vowels in Indo-European Languages*). Two years later he completed his doctorate on aspects of Sanskrit. In 1881 he moved to Paris where he was appointed a lecturer at the École Pratique des Hautes Études. He remained in this post for ten years and then returned to Geneva to become Professor of Sanskrit and Indo-European Languages. From 1907 to 1911 Saussure offered a course on general linguistics. It served as the basis for his famous *Cours de linguistique général* (*Course in General Linguistics*) (1915), which was compiled from notes taken by students (Saussure made very few notes himself). This revolutionary work advanced the fundamental concepts of structuralism which were to mark linguistics and the social sciences. The *Cours* set out Saussure's principal concern which was to offer a clear and systematic account of the nature of linguistics. To this end he worked with a set of conceptual distinctions. The first was between *parole* (actual utterances or speech acts) and *langue* (the totality of rules governing speech acts). The second was between synchronic (the structure of a language at a given time) and diachronic (the development of language over time). Saussure's principal thesis was that language is a system of signs and that each sign is made up of two elements: signifier (a word) and a signified (a concept). The distinction, which harboured Saussure's structuralist assumptions about language, revealed the relative autonomy of language in relation to reality. At the same time it showed that the relation between signifier and signified was entirely arbitrary and simply a matter of social practice. These ideas proved fundamental to many, like the anthropologist Claude Lévi-Strauss, the psychoanalyst Jacques **Lacan**, the political theorist Louis **Althusser**, and the cultural theorist Roland **Barthes**, who sought to develop a rigorous and systematic approach to the human sciences.

Select bibliography

Althusser, Louis. *For Marx* (Ben Brewster, trans.). Harmondsworth: Penguin, 1972.

Althusser, Louis. *Reading Capital* (Ben Brewster, trans.). London: New Left Books, 1975.

Althusser, Louis. *The Future Lasts a Long Time* (Richard Veasey, trans.). London: Chatto and Windus, 1993.

Anderson, Perry. *The Origins of Postmodernity*. London: Verso, 1998.

Ankersmit, F.R. 'Historiography and Postmodernism', *History and Theory*, 28, 1989, 137–53.

Ankersmit, F.R. 'Reply to Professor Zagorin', *History and Theory*, 29, 1990, 275–96.

Aronowitz, Stanley. 'Postmodernism and Politics', *Social Text*, 18, 1987, 99–115.

Bachelard, Gaston. *The New Scientific Spirit* (Arthur Goldhammer, trans.). Boston: Beacon, 1984.

Barthes, Roland. *Mythologies* (Annette Lavers, trans.). London: Jonathan Cape, 1972.

Barthes, Roland. *S/Z* (Richard Miller, trans.). New York: Hill and Wang, 1974.

Barthes, Roland. *The Fashion System* (Matthew Ward and Richard Howard, trans.). New York: Hill and Wang, 1984.

Baudrillard, Jean. *For a Critique of the Political Economy of Sign* (Charles Levin, trans.). St Louis: Telos Press, 1981.

Baudrillard, Jean. *America* (Chris Turner, trans.). London: Verso, 1988.

Baudrillard, Jean. *Revenge of the Crystal: A Baudrillard Reader*. London: Pluto Press, 1990.

Baudrillard, Jean. *The Illusion of the End* (Chris Turner, trans.). Cambridge: Polity Press, 1994.

Baudrillard, Jean. *Simulacra and Simulation* (Sheila Faria Glaser, trans.). Ann Arbor, Mich.: University of Michigan Press, 1994.

Bauman, Zygmunt. *Legislators and Interpreters: On Modernity, Postmodernity, and Intellectuals*. Cambridge: Polity Press, 1987.

Bauman, Zygmunt. *Intimations of Postmodernity*. London: Routledge, 1992.

Deilharz, Peter. *The Bauman Reader.* Oxford: Blackwell, 2001.

Bell, Daniel. *The Coming of Post-Industrial Society.* New York: Basic Books, 1973.

Bell, Daniel. *The Cultural Contradictions of Capitalism.* London: Heinemann, 1976.

Bennington, Geoffrey. *Lyotard: Writing the Event.* Manchester: Manchester University Press, 1988.

Berman, Marshall. *All That is Solid Melts into Air: The Experience of Modernity.* London: Verso, 1991.

Bernstein, Richard J., ed. *Habermas and Modernity.* Cambridge: Polity Press, 1985.

Bertens, Hans. *The Idea of the Postmodern: A History.* London: Routledge, 1995.

Callinicos, Alex. *Against Postmodernism: A Marxist Critique.* Cambridge: Polity Press, 1989.

Connor, Steven. *Postmodernist Culture: An Introduction to Theories of the Contemporary.* Oxford: Blackwell, 1989.

Creed, Barbara. 'From Here to Modernity: Feminism and Postmodernism', *Screen*, 28, 1987, 47–68.

Delaporte, François, ed. *A Vital Rationalist: Selected Writings from Georges Canguilhem* (Arthur Goldhammer, trans.). New York: Zone Books, 1994.

Deleuze, Gilles. *Nietzsche and Philosophy.* London: Continuum, 1986.

Deleuze, Gilles. *What is Philosophy?* (H. Tomlinson and G. Burchell, trans.). New York: Columbia University Press, 1987.

Deleuze, Gilles. *Difference and Repetition.* London: The Athlone Press, 1994.

Deleuze, Gilles. *Pure Immanence: Essays on a Life* (Anne Boyman, trans.). New York: Zone Books, 2001.

Deleuze, Gilles and Guattari, Félix. *Anti-Oedipus* (R. Hurley, M. Seem and H. Lane, trans.). Manchester: University of Manchester Press, 1983.

Deleuze, Gilles and Guattari, Félix. *A Thousand Plateaus* (Brian Massumi, trans.). Manchester: University of Manchester Press, 1987.

Derrida, Jacques. *Dissemination* (Barbara Johnson, trans.). Chicago, Ill.: University of Chicago Press, 1981.

Derrida, Jacques. *Limited Inc* (Elizabeth Weber, trans.). Evanston, Ill.: Northwestern University Press, 1988.

Derrida, Jacques. *Specters of Marx* (Peggy Kamuf, trans.). London: Routledge, 1994.

Derrida, Jacques. *Politics of Friendship* (George Collins, trans.). London: Verso, 1997.

Derrida, Jacques. *Of Grammatology* (Gayatri Spivak, trans.). Baltimore: Johns Hopkins University Press, 1998.

Derrida, Jacques. *Writing and Difference* (Alan Bass, trans.). London: Routledge, 2002.

Derrida, Jacques and Geoffrey Bennington. *Jacques Derrida.* Chicago, Ill.: University of Chicago Press, 1993.

Descombes, Vincent. *Modern French Philosophy.* Cambridge: Cambridge University Press, 1980.

Dews, Peter. *Logics of Disintegration: Post-Structuralist Thought and the Claims of Critical Theory.* London: Verso, 1987.

Easthope, Anthony. *British Post-Structuralism Since 1968.* London: Routledge, 1988.

Eribon, Didier. *Michel Foucault* (Betsy Wing, trans.). Cambridge, Mass.: Harvard University Press, 1991.

Featherstone, Mike. *Consumer Culture and Postmodernism.* London: Sage, 1991.

Ferry, Luc and Renaut, Alain. *French Philosophy of the Sixties* (Mary Cattaini, trans.). Amherst, Mass.: University of Massachusetts Press, 1990.

Flax, Jane. *Thinking Fragments: Psychoanalysis, Feminism, and Postmodernism in the Contemporary West*. Berkeley, Calif.: University of California Press, 1990.

Foster, Hal. *The Anti-Aesthetic: Essays in Postmodern Culture*. Port Towsend, Wash.: Bay Press, 1983.

Foucault, Michel. *Madness and Civilization* (Richard Howard, trans.). New York: Pantheon, 1965.

Foucault, Michel. *The Archaeology of Knowledge* (Alan Sheridan, trans.). New York: Pantheon, 1972.

Foucault, Michel. *The Order of Things* (Alan Sheridan, trans.). New York: Vintage, 1973.

Foucault, Michel. *History of Sexuality*, 3 vols.: *Introduction, The Uses of Pleasure*, and *Care of the Self* (Robert Hurley, trans.). New York: Vintage, 1988–1990.

Gane, Mike. *Baudrillard: Critical and Fatal Theory*. London: Routledge, 1991.

Gane, Mike. *Baudrillard Live. Selected Interviews*. London: Routledge, 1993.

Gill, Carolyn, ed. *Georges Bataille: Writing and Sacred*. London: Routledge, 1994.

Grosz, Elizabeth. *Sexual Subversions. Three French Feminists: Julia Kristeva, Luce Irigaray, Michèle Le Doeuff*. London: Allen and Unwin, 1989.

Gutting, Gary. *Michel Foucault's Archaeology of Scientific Reason*. Cambridge: Cambridge University Press, 1989.

Gutting, Gary. ed. *The Cambridge Companion to Foucault*. Cambridge: Cambridge University Press, 1994.

Gutting, Gary. *French Philosophy in the Twentieth Century*. Cambridge: Cambridge University Press, 2001.

Habermas, Jürgen. 'Modernity versus Postmodernity', *New German Critique*, 22, 1981, 3–14.

Habermas, Jürgen. *The New Conservatism: Cultural Criticism and the Historians' Debate* (Shierry Weber Nicholsen, trans.). Cambridge, Mass.: MIT Press, 1989.

Hardt, Michael. *Gilles Deleuze: An Apprenticeship in Philosophy*. Minneapolis, Minn.: University of Minnesota Press, 1993.

Harvey, David. *The Condition of Postmodernity: An Enquiry into the Origins of Cultural Change*. Oxford: Blackwell, 1989.

Hassan, Ihab. 'POSTmodernISM: a Paracritical Bibliography', *New Literary History*, 3, 1971, 5–30.

Hassan, Ihab. *The Dismemberment of Orpheus: Toward a Postmodern Literature*. Madison, Wis.: University of Wisconsin Press, 1982.

Hassan, Ihab. *The Postmodern Turn: Essays in Postmodern Theory and Culture*. Columbus, Ohio: Ohio State University Press, 1987.

Heller, Agnes and Feher, Férenc. *The Postmodern Political Condition*. Oxford: Blackwell, 1988.

Horrocks, Christopher. *Baudrillard and the Millennium*. Cambridge: Icon Books, 1999.

Hoy, David. 'Jacques Derrida', *The Return of Grand Theory in the Human Sciences* (Quentin Skinner, ed.). Cambridge: Cambridge University Press, 1985.

Hutcheon. Linda. *A Poetics of Postmodernism: History, Theory, Fiction*. London: Routledge, 1988.

Hutcheon. Linda. *The Politics of Postmodernism*. London: Routledge, 1989.

Huyssen, Andreas. 'Mapping the postmodern', *New German Critique*, 33, 1984, 5–52.

Irigaray, Luce. *This Sex Which Is Not One* (C. Porter with C. Burke, trans.). Ithaca: Cornell University Press, 1985.

Irigaray, Luce. *Speculum of the Other Woman* (Gillian Gill, trans.). Ithaca: Cornell University Press, 1985.

Irigaray, Luce. *An Ethics of Sexual Difference* (C. Burke and G. Gill, trans.). Ithaca: Cornell University Press, 1993.

Irigaray, Luce. *Sexes and Genealogies* (G. Gill, trans.). New York: Columbia University Press, 1993.

Jameson, Fredric. *Postmodernism, or, the Cultural Logic of Late Capitalism.* London: Verso, 1991.

Jencks, Charles. *The Language of Post-Modern Architecture.* London: Academy Press, 1981.

Jencks, Charles. *What is Post-Modernism?* London: Academy Press, 1986.

Judt, Tony. *Past Imperfect: French Intellectuals, 1944–1956.* Berkeley, Calif.: University of California Press, 1992.

Kaplan, E. Ann *Postmodernism and its Discontents: Theories, Practices.* London: Verso, 1988.

Kellner, Douglas. *Jean Baudrillard: From Marxism to Postmodernism and Beyond.* Cambridge: Polity Press, 1989.

Kolb, David. *Postmodern Sophistications: Philosophy, Architecture, and Tradition.* Chicago, Ill.: University of Chicago Press, 1990.

Lacan, Jacques. *Ecrits: A Selection* (Alan Sheridan, trans.). New York: Norton, 1977.

Lash, Scott. *Sociology of Postmodernism.* London: Routledge, 1990.

Lechte, John. *Julia Kristeva.* London: Routledge, 1990.

Lechte, John. *Fifty Key Contemporary Thinkers: From Structuralism to Postmodernity.* London: Routledge, 1994.

Lyotard, Jean-François. *Discours, figure.* Paris: Klincksieck, 1971.

Lyotard, Jean-François. *The Postmodern Condition* (G. Bennington and B. Massumi, trans.). Manchester: Manchester University Press, 1984.

Lyotard, Jean-François. *The Differend* (Georges van den Abbeele, trans.). Manchester: Manchester University Press, 1988.

Lyotard, Jean-François. *Peregrinations: Law, Form, Event.* New York: Columbia University Press, 1988.

Lyotard, Jean-François. *The Postmodern Explained to Children: Correspondence 1982–1985* (Don Barry et al., trans). London: Turnaround, 1992.

Lyotard, Jean-François. *Libidinal Economy* (Iain Hamilton Grant, trans.). Bloomington, Ind.: Indiana University Press, 1993.

Matthews, Eric. *Twentieth-Century French Philosophy.* Oxford: Oxford University Press, 1996.

McGowan, John. *Postmodernism and its Critics.* Ithaca: Cornell University Press, 1991.

Merquior, J.G. *Foucault.* London: Fontana, 1985.

Miller, James. *The Passion of Michel Foucault.* London: Harper Collins, 1993.

Moi, Toril (ed.). *The Kristeva Reader.* Oxford: Blackwell, 1986.

Munslow, Alan. *Deconstructing History.* London: Routledge, 1997.

Norris, Christopher. *Derrida.* London: Fontana, 1987.

Norris, Christopher. *What's Wrong with Postmodernism?* Baltimore: Johns Hopkins University Press, 1990.

Norris, Christopher. *Uncritical Theory: Postmodernism, Intellectuals and the Gulf War.* London: Lawrence and Wishart, 1992.

Olson, Charles. 'Projective Verse', *Poetry New York*, 3, 1950, 13–22. Reprinted *Projective Verse*. New York: Totem, 1959.

Philp, Mark. 'Michel Foucault', *The Return of the Grand Theory in the Human Sciences* (Quentin Skinner, ed.). Cambridge: Cambridge University Press, 1985.

Poster, Mark. *Critical Theory and Poststructuralism: In Search of a Context*. Ithaca: Cornell University Press, 1989.

Rabinow, Paul, ed. *The Foucault Reader: An Introduction to Foucault's Thought*. Harmondsworth: Penguin, 1991.

Rabinow, Paul, ed. *Essential Works of Foucault, 1954–1984*, 3 vols. London: Allen Lane, 1997–9.

Readings, Bill. *Introducing Lyotard: Art and Politics*. London: Routledge, 1991.

Rorty, Richard. *Contingency, Irony, and Solidarity*. Cambridge: Cambridge University Press, 1989.

Rose, Margaret. *The Post-Modern and the Post-Industrial: A Critical Analysis*. Cambridge: Cambridge University Press, 1991.

Rosenau, Pauline Marie. *Post-Modernism and the Social Sciences: Insights, Inroads, and Intrusions*. Princeton: Princeton University Press, 1992.

Sarup, Madan. *An Introductory Guide to Post-Structuralism and Postmodernism*. London: Harvester Wheatsheaf, 1993.

Saussure, Ferdinand de. *Course in General Linguistics* (Wade Baskin, trans.). London: Duckworth, 1983.

Sheridan, Alan. *Michel Foucault: The Will to Truth*. London: Tavistock, 1980.

Sim, Stuart. *Beyond Aesthetics: Confrontations with Poststructualism and Postmodernism*. London: Harvester Wheatsheaf, 1992.

Sim, Stuart. *Derrida and the End of History*. Cambridge: Icon Books, 1999.

Sim, Stuart. *Post-Marxism: An Intellectual History*. London: Routledge, 2000.

Sim, Stuart. *The Routledge Companion to Postmodernism*. London: Routledge, 2001.

Smart, Barry. *Postmodernity*. London: Routledge, 1993.

Soja, Edward W. *Postmodern Geographies: The Reassertion of Space in Critical Social Theory*. London: Verso, 1989.

Sokal, Alan and Bricmont, Jean. *Intellectual Impostures: Postmodern Philosophers' Abuse of Science* (Alan Sokal and Jean Bricmont, trans.). London: Profile, 1998.

Stoekl, Allan, ed. *Georges Bataille: Visions of Excess: Selected Writings, 1927–1939* (Allan Stoekl with Carl R. Lovitt and Donald M. Leslie, Jr., trans.). Minneapolis, Minn.: University of Minnesota Press, 1985.

Turner, Bryan S. *Theories of Modernity and Postmodernity*. London: Sage, 1990.

Vattimo, Gianni. *The End of Modernity: Nihilism and Hermeneutics in Post-Modern Culture*. Baltimore: Johns Hopkins University Press, 1988.

White, Hayden. *Tropics of Discourse: Essays in Cultural Criticism*. Baltimore: Johns Hopkins University Press, 1978.

Zagorin, Perez. 'Historiography and Postmodernism: Reconsideration', *History and Theory*, 29, 1990, 263–75.

Index

1960s 62–4

absence 256
'act of force' 96–7
aesthetic experience 204, 231, 233, 258
aesthetics 15–16, 233–7, 263–5, 269–70
affirmation 114–15, 116–17
Althusser, Louis 18, 201, 312, 313, 315
Americanization 191
Ankersmit, Frank 20
Anselm, Saint 108
anthropomorphism 39
Antigone 223–4
'Apollonian and Dionysian' duality 15–16
Appel, Karel 260
archaeological method 19–20, 39, 49–50, 67–8, 317
architecture 2–3, 10–12, 190, 196
archive 20
Ariadne 114
Arnim, Bettina von 259
art: aesthetic time 258; difference and repetition in 154; modern 62–3, 235, 236; pedagogical function of 200; postmodern 260
artists: and the mass media 232–3; modernist 59–60, 62–3, 64; and postmodernism 267–8

Augustine, Saint 5, 187
authenticity 39, 158, 162, 192, 199
authority 244–9
autonomia movement 317
autonomy 242, 245
avant-garde/avant-gardism 204, 234–5; "transavantgardism" 232, 233

Bachelard, Gaston, 312–13
Balzac, Honoré de, *Sarrasine* 313
Barthes, Roland 3, 63, 313
Bataille, Georges 23, 314
Baudelaire, Charles 45–7, 185, 186
Baudrillard, Jean 3, 30–1, 205, 272–8, 313–14
Bauman, Zygmunt 4, 204, 238–49, 314
Being 14, 17, 22, 23, 228; language and death 314
Bell, Bernard Iddings 4–5
Bell, Daniel 3, 63–4
Berman, Marshall 38–9, 53–66
Biran, Maine de 179
Black Mountain College 8
Blanchot, Maurice 23, 314–15
the body 76, 228, 243
boundary 2 8, 9
bourgeoisie 7, 57
Burke, Edmund 195

Cage, John 8, 64

Callois, Roger 314

Canguilhem, Georges 315

capitalism 31–2, 121, 142, 181, 195–6, 198–200; and mass culture 233

Cashinahua narrative 217–18

causality 154–5

certainty, politics of 246–7

change: and modernity 53–4; and postmodernity 239–41; technological change 7, 53–4, 60

choice 245, 248–9

Christianity: and modernity 57; and narrative 220–1

city 33

civilization 6–7, 6–8, 82

Cixous, Hélène 315

classical age 69, 92–3, 94–5, 107, 161–2

classicism 111

Cogito 87–8, 103, 105–6, 107–9

cognitive mapping 33–4, 122, 200–1

Cold War 6, 182

Collège de France 18

commodification 31–2, 62; of culture 121, 191; of knowledge 126–7

communication, and information 212

communication theory 133, 134

communism 276, 279–80

Communist Manifesto (Marx) 28, 57, 198, 279, 286

computerization 124–7, 132, 143, 146, 196–7

conjuration 281–2, 286

connaissance 67, 74, 84, 85, 135

conscious selfhood 9

consciousness 178

consensus 181; and dissension 145

consumer society 6, 233, 314

consumerization, and knowledge 125–6

contemporary theory (theoretical discourse) 192–3

conversation 268–9

Creon 223–4

critical theory 131

culture: commodification of 121, 191, 233; high and mass culture 190; and the political 266–8; postmodernism as a cultural dominant 197, 198–9

Cunningham, Merce 8

dandysme 47

death: of God 113; language and being 314; of the subject 193

'de-composition' 8, 9

deconstruction 120, 149–53, 171, 174, 316

delegitimation 138–41

Deleuze, Gilles 27–8, 40, 119, 120–1, 315–16; on difference and repetition 154–60, 316; Foucault on 121, 161–6; on Nietzsche 112–17; on pure immanence 178–80

Derrida, Jacques 21–4, 40, 120, 121, 167–77, 205–6; biographical note 316; Lyotard on 27, 256–7; on madness and Cogito 86–111; on Marx 279–87; on the preface 147–53

Descartes, René 3; Foucault on 98–101, 102–3; and madness 87, 88, 96–106, 107–10

descent 75–6, 81

desire 246

diachronic development (of language) 137, 320

dialectic: Hegelian 115–16; Marxist 198; on sexual difference 222, 223, 227

Dickens, Charles 179

didactics 136, 137

différance 14, 22–3, 148

'differance' 120

difference 115–16, 257; and event 28; and repetition 120, 159–60, 316; sexual difference 29, 222–9

the differend 27, 203–4, 207–21, 237, 320

Dionysius 15–16, 114, 115

discourse, 69, 219; Foucault on 20, 39, 317; Irigary on 29; Lyotard, *Discours* 252–3, 319

Disney, Walt 275–6

dissemination 147–53

dissension 92

domination 77–8

double bind 209

double mark 148

double-coding 12, 318

dreams 98–9, 100, 102

duality 15–16

Duve, Thierry de 233

efficiency 124, 141, 144

elitism 11–12
emergence 77
Enlightenment 2, 13, 37–8, 48–9; Foucault
  on 41–52; Lyotard on 252
Entstehung 75, 76–8, 82
Epicurians 163
epistémè 18–19, 313, 317
'epistemic break' 312
ethics 220–1, 222–9, 247–9, 314, *see also*
  morality
the event 165–6, 265–6
evil genius 103–4
existence *see* Being
existentialism 192, 201–2
experts 246, 247

faculty, notion of 260–1
falsification 136, 137
Faurisson, Robert 203, 214, 216
fear 246
feminism 28–9, 204, 315; feminist
  psychoanalysis 317, *see also* women
Fichte, Johann 179
flâneur 46
Flaubert, Gustave 70, 185, 236
Foucault, Michel 2, 18–21, 37–8, 39, 65;
  biographical note 316–17; on Deleuze
  121, 161–6; Derrida's critique of 40, 86,
  88–93, 94, 96, 98–101, 102–3, 110,
  111; on Descartes 98–101, 102–3; on
  the Enlightenment 41–52; influences on
  312, 313, 315; on Nietzsche 70, 72–85;
  The Order of Things 67–71
fragmentation 261
French Revolution 38, 54, 186–7, 251
Freud, Sigmund 29, 319
Freudian psychoanalysis 317
Fukuyama, Francis 203, 206
futurists 59–60, 196

gas chambers 207, 208, 209–10, 214
Gauchet, Marcel 21
genealogy 20–1, 38, 39, 49–50, 191; and
  history 72–85
global network 197
global space 201
God 103, 107–8, 108–9, 187; death of
  113
Greenberg, Clement 62–3

Groupe de Recherches sur l'Enseignement
  Philosophique (GREPH) 175–6
Guattari, Felix 27, 316, 317
Guéroult, M. 102
Gutting, Gary 18
Guys, Constantin 46–7

Habermas, Jürgen 12–13, 231, 235
habitat 240–1, 242
Hamann, Johann Georg 13
Hegel, G.W.F. 115, 120, 139, 314; concept
  of negation in history 314, 319; on the
  preface 150–2
Heidegger, Martin 7–8, 9, 10–11, 17, 195;
  influence on Derrida 22
Herder, Gottfried 13, 97
Herkunft 73, 75–6, 81
hermeneutics 23, 192, 194
historicity 95, 110
history 39, 216; the end of history 203,
  205, 206, 272–8, 279–80; and genealogy
  72–85; madness and reason 90, 95, 110;
  as narrative 217–19, 221; and origins of
  postmodernism 6, 7, 21; philosophy of
  166; postmodernism as a historical
  concept 197, *see also* time
Hölderlin, Friedrich 228
Holocaust 203, 207, 208, 209–10, 214
Hudnut, Joseph 10
humanism 17–18, 48–9, 182–3
humanity 215, 217–18, *see also* mankind
Husserl, Edmund 109, 170, 316
hybris 93, 94
hyperbole 107, 109
Hyppolite, Jean 168–9, 173, 174, 315,
  316

iconology 11
identity 39–40; female 223–4; and the
  genealogy of history 83–4; the individual
  and society 314; and language 29, 318;
  and language 29; postmodern 242–4
ideology 201–2, *see also* liberalism; Marxism;
  totalitarianism
image 196, 197
'imaginary' 29
imagination 255
immanence 178–80

immaturity 42–3
inequality 245
information 125, 126, 132, 133–4; and
    communication 212
Inkeles, Alex 60–1
insanity 101–2, *see also* madness
intellectuals 230–1, 266–7
International Style 10, 190
Irigary, Luce 3, 28–9, 204, 222–9, 317
'the iron cage' 61, 65

Jacobs, Jane 10
Jameson, Fredric 4, 31–4, 120, 121,
    189–202; biographical note 318
Jencks, Charles 2, 11–12, 318
judgement 260–2; aesthetic 269–70
Jünger, Ernst 182
justice 145, 206, 266–8

Kant, Immanuel 14–15, 37–8; difference
    and repetition 159; Foucault on 41–4,
    52; Lyotard on 251–2, 260–2, 264–5,
    269; on the sublime 195, 234–5, 259
Kellner, Hans 20
Kierkegaard, Søren 8–9, *see also* authenticity
knowledge: history as 84; postmodern
    119–20, 121–2, 123–46, *see also*
    narrative knowledge; scientific knowledge
Kojève, Alexandre 314, 319
Kristeva, Julia 313, 318

Lacan, Jacques 319; ideology and the
    Symbolic 202; Lacanian psychoanalysis
    121, 262, 315, 317; on schizophrenia
    193–4
Lacoue-Labarthe, Philippe 263
language: being and death 314; and the
    differend 211–14; and the end of history
    277–8; and hermeneutics 23; and
    identity 29, 318; knowledge and
    information 133–4; and logocentrism
    185–6, 187–8; and meaning 215; and
    the meaning-event 165–6; reason and
    madness 89–90, 104–5; repetition in
    156; science and technology 125; and
    sexual difference 227–8, 317, *see also*
    conversation; linguistics; speaking; speech
language games 25, 128–30, 133, 140–1,
    145, 146

langue 320
law 78, 128, 269
learning 125, 135
legitimation: by parology 145–6; and
    delegitimation 138–41; of knowledge
    124, 127–8, 138, 139–40, 141–3,
    145–6; political 181
Lernet-Holenia, Alexander 179–80
Lévi-Strauss, Claude 3, 154, 320
Levinas, Emmanuel 269
liberalism 4–5
liberty 74
life 179–80
'limit attitude' 49–50
linguistics 2–3, 226, 318, 320, *see also*
    language
literary criticism 5–6, 9, 189, 318
literature 169, 232–3, 236
litigation 210–11
logocentrism 181–8
logos 92–3, 95
Lucretius 112
Luhmann, H. 143
Lynch, Kevin 200–1
Lyotard, Jean-François 24–7, 119, 121,
    204–5, 250–71; biographical note
    319–20; on the differend 203–4,
    207–21, 237; influences on 312; on
    knowledge 24, 25, 123–46; on
    logocentrism 181–8; on the postmodern
    230–7, *see also* narrative knowledge;
    scientific knowledge

McLuhan, Marshall 3, 60
madness 68, 86–111
Malévich, Kazimir 260
Mandel, Ernest 121, 190, 195, 202
mankind: and modernity 56–8, 61, 62; signs
    and discourse 69–70
Marcuse, Herbert 62
Marx, Karl 55–7, 198, 200; Althusser on
    312; Derrida's *Specters of Marx* 205–6,
    279–87
Marxism 33, 131; Marxist literary criticism
    318
masculinity 224, 227
mass culture 190, 233
mass media 232–3
Matthews, Eric 29

meaning: in history 203, 205; and language 215; and names 147, 148–9; and sign 69–70, 71, 87

meaning-event 165–6

Mendelssohn, Moses 41–2

mental illness *see* madness

meta-narrative (grand narrative) 24, 119, 123–4, 138–9, 267

metaphysics 163–4

millennium 273, 274–8

modern: architecture 10; art 62–3, 235, 236

modernisation and modernism 38, 54, 189, 190

modernity: Berman on 53–66; crisis of 34, 37–40; defence of 231; Foucault on 45–7; and the postmodern 236, 238–9, 250

modus logicus and *modus estheticus* 255

morality: and postmodernism 197–8, 247, 248–9, 266–7, 314, *see also* ethics

multinational corporations 126

names (*paleonymy*) 147, 148–9

narrative 24, 123–4, 217–21, 318, *see also* meta-narrative

narrative knowledge 24, 25, 134–5, 137–8

nature 195, 261–2, 264

the negative 112–13, 117; concept of negation in history 314, 319

neopositivism 166

Nietzsche, Friedrich 15–17, 40, 57–8; Bataille on 314; Deleuze on 112–17, 315; Foucault on 70, 72–85; on scientific knowledge 139

nihilism 15, 113

Nora, Pierre 183–4, 187

norms/normativity 315

Norris, Christopher 40

nostalgia 277

obligation 220–1

Olson, Charles 2, 7–8, 10–11

Onis, Federico de 5–6

origin 73, 74, 75

Other 187, 195, 270–1

Overman (*Übermensch*) 113–14

painting: and modernity 46–7, 59, 62–3,

235; and photography 232; and 'presence' 258; and the sublime 260

parody 83

Parsons, Talcott 130–1

Paulhan, Jean 187

Paz, Octavio 65

Péguy, Charles 156

performativity 130, 141–3, 144

phantasms 163

phenomenology 14, 166, 169–70

philosophy 111, 268; and historical development of science 313; prefaces 149–52; teaching of 175–6

photography 232

Plato/Platonism 16, 42, 161–3, 261, 263–4

poetic form 277–8

political economy 282–6

political theory 262–3

politics: and the aesthetic 263–5; and justice 266–8; postmodern 121, 181–2, 244–7

Pollock, Jackson 59

pop modernism 64

post-structuralism 18

Poster, Mark 30

postindustrial society 124, 143, 190, 201

postmodern condition 239–41

postmodernism 189–202; architectural 10–12, 190, 318; definitions and concepts of 2–4, 123, 141, 235–7, 238–49, 267; and modernity 236, 238–9, 250; negative reactions to 230–1; origins of concept 4–9; philosophical origins 13–17; the social bond 132–4

power 20–1, 124; and communication 212–13; and information 126, 132, 142–3; and the State 51; will to power 16, 113–14, 116–17

preface 149–53

presence 258

presentation 254–5

psychiatry 88, 89

psychoanalysis 29, 121, 164, 226; feminist 317; and linguistic theory 318

rationalism: anti-rationalism and romanticism 13–14; and reason 251–2

Rauschenberg, Robert 2, 8

realism/reality 199–200, 231–4, 276; and image 314

reason: history of 73; and imagination 255; and madness 88, 90, 95, 111; and obedience 43–5; and origins of postmodernism 4, 5; and rationality 251–2

Ree, Paul 72

reflexivity 249

repetition 154–60

representation 196, 200–1

research 141–3

research game 135, 136, 137

ressentiment 112, 116

rhyme 156

rhythm 155

rights, natural 264

romanticism 2, 13–14

Rorty, Richard 268–70

Rousseau, Jean-Jacques 54–5

Roussel, Raymond 156

Same 156, 157

Saussure, Ferdinand de 2–3, 313, 320

savoir (knowledge) 67, 74, 84, 135

schizophrenia 28, 193–4

Schopenhauer, Arthur 14–15, 115

science: and the crisis of reason 252; and the differend 214–15; historical development of, and philosophy 313; and ideology 201–2; and language 125; modern and postmodern 26–7, 143–4; and narrative 123; and the origins of postmodernism 5, 20–1; and reality 234; and sexual difference 224–7

scientific discourse 119

'scientific ideology' 315

scientific knowledge 24, 25, 119, 125, 127–8, 135–8, 139–40

self 132–3; the Me 75

self-assembly 241, 243–4

self-constitution 241, 242–3, 245

semiotics 30, 192; and architecture 318; and language 318, *see also* sign

senses/sensory knowledge 97–8, 100–1, 102

sexism 28–9

sexual difference 222–9, 317

Shakespeare, William 281–2, 283, 284

sign: difference and repetition 154–5, 156–7; and language 320; and meaning 69–70, 71, 87; and structure 99–100; and the symbolic 30–1, *see also* semiotics

signal 154

signifier/signified 87, 99, 148, 192, 194, 320

signifying chain 194

silence 89–90, 91–2, 95–6, 104–5, 213–14

simulacrum 196, 197, 314

social bond 130–4, 140

social condition 238, 239, 240–1

social interaction 145–6

sociality 241

Société française de philosophie 2

society: concepts of 130–1, 190, 200–1, 238–9; knowledge in 124–7, 131–2; modern and postmodern 245–6, 247

sociology 49, 240–1

Socratic dialogue 93–4, 95

Soja, Edward 35

Sontag, Susan 194

space/spaciality 193, 201

Spanos, William 8, 9, 24

speaking 211–12, 213

speculation 139

speech 110, 268–9

Spinoza, Benedict de 112, 178–9

the State 126, 132, 244–5, 280

structuralism 3, 18, 318, 319, 320

subject, death of 193

sublime 194–5, 199, 234–5, 259–60

Swain, Gladys 21

the symbolic: and ideology 202; semiotics and language 318; and the sign 30–1

symmetry 154–5

synchronic structure (of language) 226, 320

Tarde, Gabriel 159

teaching game 135, 136

technical knowledge 127

technology: and knowledge 141–3; and language 125; and modernity 60, 61; and postmodernism 195–7; and reality 234; technological change 7, 53–4, 60

temporality *see* time

theatre 164

theology 220–1; and origins of postmodernism 5

thesis 166–77
time 152–3, 193, 194, 257–8, 272; the
    present 280–1, *see also* history
Timon of Athens (Shakespeare) 282–4
tokens (symbolic) 243–4
totalitarianism 4–5, 107, 208
Toynbee, Arnold 6–7
trace 68, 148
tragedy 15–16
Tran Duc Tao 170
transcendental empiricism 178
transmutation 113–14, 115
tribal politics 245–6
trust 247
truth 20, 74, 142–3

university 172–3, 174
Ursprung 73

value 248–9
Venturi, Robert 2, 10, 190

victims 208–11, 215
Vidal-Naquet, Pierre 203, 215, 216
virtuality 180

wealth 141–2
Weber, Max 61
White, Hayden 21
will 14, 81–2, 103; to knowledge 84, 85; to
    nothingness 113, 116; to power 16,
    113–14, 116–17; to truth 20, 57, 84
Williams, Raymond 191
Wittgenstein, Ludwig 25, 140, 141
women 223–4, 227–9, 317, *see also*
    feminism
writers: and the mass media 232–3;
    modernist 61, 63, 64, 236;
    postmodernist 267–8
writing 67–8, 169, 171, 174; and
    logocentrism 187–8

Zarathustra 113–15, 157